The Baltic Revolution

Estonia, Latvia, Lithuania and the Path to Independence

Anatol Lieven

Yale University Press
New Haven and London

Set in Baskerville by SX Composing Ltd, Essex
Printed and bound in Great Britain by Biddles Ltd, King's Lynn, Norfolk

Library of Congress Cataloging-in-Publication Data

Lieven, Anatol,
   The Baltic Revolution: Estonia, Latvia, Lithuania, and the path to
independence/by Anatol Lieven.
   p. cm.
   Includes index.
   ISBN 0-300-05552-8 (hbk.)
   ISBN 0-300-06078-5 (pbk.)
   1. Baltic States – History. I. Title.
DK502.7.L54 1993   92-47282
947¹.4 – dc20   CIP

A catalogue record for this book is available from the British Library.

To the memory of my parents:

Prince Alexander Lieven,
Princess Veronica Lieven, *née* Monahan.

Requiem aeternam dona eis, Domine,
Et lux perpetua luceat eis.

Contents

List of Illustrations

Acknowledgements

My thanks are due first to Edita Urmonaitė, my assistant and translator in Lithuania. Her work contributed greatly to this book and her good sense corrected the curious impression sometimes made by her country's leaders. Her family showed me great kindness during my visits to them. Sandra Apsane, my assistant in Latvia, helped considerably with my researches there. Albertas Šešplaukis drove me uncomplainingly over some of the worse roads I have encountered. Edward Lucas of the *Baltic Independent*, and Claudia Sinnig were an indispensable source of help and advice. They and Lars Freden, of the Royal Swedish Foreign Service, gave the benefit of their deep knowledge of the Baltic States and fished up my numerous red herrings. I slipped some of them back later, but that was not their fault. Lars also suggested the shape of this book, though it goes without saying that the opinions expressed in it, except where otherwise indicated, are entirely my own. Pauls Raudseps, who has made *Diena* one of the finest papers in the former Soviet Union, took time off to guide me through the thickets of Latvian politics.

Mihkel and Eva Tarm, of the *Estonia Magazine* (Tallinn City Paper) helped generously with acute criticism of my first draft, as well as insights into Estonian life, which I have frequently used. Eugenie Loov showed me great hospitality in Tallinn, Lisa Trei groaned in chorus about darker sides of the Baltic experience, but modified some of my harsher comments.

In Vilnius, Anders Kroeger was a sharp critic, and Jolanta Jacovskienė represented the beauties of French culture in adversity. Irena Veisaitė fed me many dinners and provided valuable views of the Jewish experience and dilemma in Lithuania, and Alex Štromas gave an example of heroic objectivity in this most painful of all fields of study. Edward Tuskenis gave the benefit of his vast if disillusioned knowledge of the Lithuanian scene. Dr Vytautas Kavolis provided fascinating insights, and Professor Romuald Misiunas very kindly commented on part of the text. Saulius Girnius, of Radio Free Europe, was also extremely helpful.

In Riga, the Rubinchik family welcomed and housed me at moments of great strain, and my thanks are due to Tatiana Zhdanok and Višvaldis Brinkmanis for their hospitality, and for civilised expositions of their respective points of view. Professor Pyotr Krupnikov taught me much about my own Baltic German tradition.

Sergei Berezinsky, in St Petersburg, represented for me the best and most generous side of liberal Russia, and Stuart Swanson of the US Foreign Service was a kind host and a most interesting sparring-partner in arguments. Dr David Kirby and Dr Jonathan Steinberg read and commented on the manuscript and helped valuably with academic research.

My colleagues on *The Times*, and especially Martin Ivens, Richard Owen and Anne McElvoy, showed generous understanding of my prolonged absences in the company of Lāčplēsis and Kalevipoeg, characters of little intrinsic interest to *The Times* foreign pages, being both 800 years dead and largely imaginary. John Wilkins of the *Tablet* was most supportive, as was Anthony Hartley of the tragically defunct *Encounter*.

Peter Robinson was a splendid agent and Robert Baldock a most sensitive editor who kindly put up with repeated delays caused by the demands of journalism. Through hard work, intelligence and courtesy, Darius Šilas and Daiva Venckus transformed the Information Office of the Lithuanian Parliament and made the lives of Western journalists in Lithuania a great deal happier.

I thank all the people of the Baltic States, as well as those of St Petersburg and Kaliningrad, who helped me during my stay, spoke with me in interviews, or simply tolerated what was often a hornet's presence in their midst. My brother, Dr D. C. B. Lieven, of the London School of Economics, helped give an All-Union perspective (as we used to say) to this book, and my sister, Dr Elena Lieven, first pushed me to begin writing it.

Finally, my thanks and love go to Kamini, who too endured the rivalry of Lāčplēsis, but won in the end.

Foreword to the Second Edition

On 31 January 1994, I caught a flight to Latvia from Moscow's Sheremetyovo 1 airport, my first return to the Baltic States for almost six months. It provided a not untypical Soviet experience, two-and-a-half years after the Soviet Union formally ceased to exist. Sheremetyovo 1 is clean by the standards of Russian airports, but facilities are minimal and the staff are as vile-tempered, lazy and incompetent as those elsewhere. The flight was delayed by almost three hours, principally because, promptly at noon, the entire airport staff – air-traffic controllers, customs officials, the lot – stopped work for a two-hour lunch-break. Arriving at Riga, in contrast, was almost like landing at a Scandinavian provincial airport. It was spotlessly clean, the English-speaking staff polite and helpful. All the basic facilities of a Western airport were present. Payment for the taxi into town was by flat rate to a taxi office, not via the old exhausting haggle with a mafia-controlled taxi-ring. The Russian friend with whom I was travelling was visibly impressed.

This first appearance of landing in the West is, as I shall show, partly illusory. The Baltic States continue to wrestle with problems and dangers on a scale unknown to any Western government. Moreover, in Latvia especially, there are strong political forces whose ideas are dangerously alien to contemporary Western democratic values, and which are dangerously hostile to Western influence. Nonetheless, a year after I completed the first edition of this book, the ways in which the Balts are the exceptions to the Soviet rule have become ever more apparent. As the rest of the former Soviet Union slides into economic collapse and ever higher inflation, the Balts have established successful currencies and advanced far down the path of economic reform. The appearance of central Tallinn in particular is already close to that of a Western city. As sketched in this book, the Estonians can be an intensely irritating people, but their achievements in recent years have been truly remarkable.

Baltic exceptionalism is equally noticeable in terms of relations with Moscow. At the time of writing, all the other former Soviet republics are members of the Commonwealth of Independent States. Those which left or refused to join, such as Georgia, have been forced back following covert or even overt military and economic pressure from Moscow. In most cases, Russia maintains troops on the soil of these republics, and Russian hegemony in all fields is increasingly apparent.

The three Baltic States by contrast have all successfully refused to join the CIS. The last Russian troops were withdrawn from Lithuania at the end of August 1993, and are due to leave Latvia and Estonia by 31 August 1994. The speed at which withdrawal is occurring makes it seem likely the deadline will be met. By February 1994 Baltic officials estimated the number of Russian troops in Latvia at around 12,000, while in Estonia at a mere 1,900 – a small fraction of those present three years earlier. Estonia, and to a lesser extent Latvia and Lithuania, have vastly reduced their trade dependence on Russia and correspondingly increased their economic links with the West. The Balts are also bound to the West through a growing number of political, social, cultural and criminal ties, of which other former Soviet republics can only dream.

All three Baltic States have held parliamentary elections and established democratic constitutions. Unlike the other former Soviet republics, Latvia and Estonia excluded from automatic citizenship those (mainly Russians) who settled during the period of Soviet rule. However ethnic tensions in the Baltic – also unlike those of other areas – have remained non-violent. There have been no local mass protests, neither open nor covert military intervention from Moscow.

These features of the Baltic States were already apparent when the first edition of this book was written, and the internal and historical reasons for it are among my main themes. However, the policy of the West and of Russia itself have also been of critical importance. The West has effectively turned a blind eye to the extension of Russian influence throughout the rest of the former Soviet Union. In the Baltic, the West has insisted on the withdrawal of Russian troops, and demanded that Moscow treat the three states as fully independent, sovereign countries. For a variety of reasons, discussed below, the main trend of Russian policy has acknowledged this demand.

In view of developments since the first edition of this book, do any of my analyses or conclusions need to be modified? The Baltic currencies have performed better than I expected, owing to Western aid, Baltic gold reserves, and sound and intelligent fiscal policies. John Hansen of the (initially highly sceptical) World Bank described the Kroon as 'an amazing success story ... I've never seen anything like it'. The Balts pursuit of fiscal austerity has been partly at the expense of the local Russian minorities, concentrated in heavy industry; but all three governments (even the LDDP in Lithuania) have also shown considerable courage in sticking to IMF rules even at the price of a steep decline in their own popularity, especially among farmers and the elderly. This commitment has made the Baltic States an oasis of economic stability, and drawn in money from the former Soviet Union as well as the West. Even as trade links with Russia have declined, private financial links have increased.

The old Soviet industries in the Baltic continue to decline, and their privatisation is proceeding very slowly; but at least in Estonia and Latvia, in sharp contrast to the rest of the former Soviet Union, the stability of the currencies makes it worthwhile to invest in new manufacturing industry. This, coupled with proximity to the West, high levels of education and the extreme cheapness of Baltic labour, resulted in a 3 per cent growth in the Estonian economy during 1993, while the decline of Latvia and Lithuania showed signs of bottoming out. Estonia at least looks to be emerging from the post-Communist economic malaise. If it can achieve the government's predicted growth rate of 4 per cent in 1994, it will have overtaken Poland as the fastest growing economy in Europe.

The negative aspects of economic change, (discussed in Chapter 9) however remain evident. In February 1994 an Estonian official told me that the biggest problem in Estonia was organised crime, the next, poverty. This tiny country saw more than 300 murders and attempted murders in 1993, an increase of 40 per cent on the previous year. Some attacks were of exceptional savagery, and in only a handful of cases were the perpetrators brought to trial. Most killings resulted from rivalry between groups involved in organised prostitution, protection rackets, and the vast smuggling trade with Russia.

The integration of the Baltic into world criminal networks is indeed proceeding apace. The region has become one of the biggest markets for cars stolen within Germany. The directors of the Latvian state chemical firm, Latbiopharm, went on trial in December 1993 for involvement in the production and smuggling of synthetic hallucinogenic drugs. In January 1994, a plane which crashed into Lake Constance in Switzerland was revealed to have been carrying radioactive material smuggled from Riga. A very considerable contribution to the wealth of Estonia has in recent years been made by the smuggling of non-ferrous metals from Russia, but there have also been severe side effects. Police judge that around forty Estonian murders in 1993 were associated with the metals trade.

In 1993 too, there were more than fifty bombings by criminal groups groups in Estonia. One was directed against a police station, an attack taken by the (then) Interior Minister, Lagle Parek, as a sign that the police were getting close enough to the gangs to become their target. In all three Baltic States, but especially in Latvia, the control of business and banks by organised criminals, and their penetration of the official and political worlds, threatens to discredit both capitalism and democracy in the eyes of ordinary people. Many of these, meanwhile, are materially much worse off than they were ten years ago. The new, expensive Western shops in Tallinn and Riga offer the young the hope that they will, sooner or later, achieve Western lifestyles; they offer little hope however to pensioners facing bitter poverty during their final years, or to unskilled workers and farmers. Social differentiation is growing fast: by mid-1993 the top 10 per cent of Estonians earned one third of the total income, while the bottom 10 per cent earned no more than 2.1 per cent, or an average of $11 a month. For these, the increasing signs of Western-style affluence are no more than a cruel insult. Such resentment is politically dangerous because in Latvia at least it could take an ethnic form.

Governments and political systems in the Baltic have developed more or less as expected (see Chapter 8). In Lithuania, the former pro-independence communists, now the Lithuanian Democratic Labour Party of Algirdas Brazauskas, have pursued a policy of cautious economic reform and of good relations with Moscow. The relaxation in tension with Moscow paid off in August 1993 when the last Russian troops left the country. At the same time, Brazauskas has been careful to bow to nationalist sentiment by making a dramatic but wholly unreal bid to join NATO and by moving slowly on the issue of normalising relations with Poland. Economic policy has been tailored in part to protect the interests of state managers who, in general, strongly supported the LDDP. However, fears that the government would run up huge budget deficits in order to subsidise agriculture and industry have not proved justified. In February 1994 many farmers, angered by what they saw as broken promises by the Brazauskas government, launched a major strike, refusing to supply food until pricing policy was changed. The absence of encouragement for foreign investment in Lithuania has been strongly criticised by Western observers. However, this is only partly due to the policies of the Brazauskas administration. Western complaints about the obstructionism, arrogance and gut anti-capitalism of Lithuanian officials and politicians were not much different under the regime of Professor Vytautas Landsbergis.*

* As a parody in the *Baltic Outlook* of November 1993 had it, a request to a Lithuanian official to be told why there was hot water in summer, and none in winter, is likely to be met with a reply beginning, 'You know, we were occupied for 50 years . . .', and ending, 'We are Lithuanians, and we do things differently'. It is amusing to

When the Lithuanian government is finally replaced by one from the nationalist opposition, it will not in my view make very much difference to Lithuanian policies. As this book argues, the Lithuanian 'Right' itself has an ambiguous attitude to the free market. Concerning nationalist policies, the small size of the Russian minority in Lithuania (compared to Estonia and Latvia) means that ethnic relations are far calmer, and the ability of radical nationalists to make mischief much less. In respect of relations with Russia, there has been talk among nationalists of the need to stop Russian military trains crossing Lithuanian territory en route to Kaliningrad, and even of annexing Kaliningrad; but Lithuanian pragmatism will probably prevent even radical nationalists from adopting so provocative a stance.

In Estonia, the amazingly youthful government of Mart Laar (by February 1994, as well as a 33-year-old Prime Minister, the cabinet also included 28-year-old Foreign and Defence Ministers and a 27-year-old Interior Minister) has, as expected, pressed ahead with free-market reform. Foreign Minister Trivimi Velliste even remarked with a sort of masochistic relish that 'Estonia is the only country in the world whose economic policies have been even tougher than the IMF has demanded'. In the matter of the privatisation of industry, this has, however, been qualified both by the parlous state of most Estonian industries and by the desire to prevent 'spontaneous privatisation' by managements and takeovers by organised crime. Laar has explained his government's mixture of radicalism and moderation in terms of its youth:

> Our youth has helped us, though it may not help us to stay in power. We are not so expert at political games; but when it comes to changing the country, young people are better, because they have less to lose. Our youth is not a problem for the young, and not a problem for the old people who remember independent Estonia. It is only a problem for the middle generations, brought up under Soviet rule. It is not a question of age as such, but of traditions and experiences. In Estonia, everyone who is achieving anything in any field of life is young – in politics, business, the

note the other ways in which classic patterns of Lithuanian behaviour have continued under Brazauskas. Thus Brazauskas's application to join NATO in December 1993 was exactly what Landsbergis would have done under similar circumstances: made a grand theatrical gesture with no basis in reality. Similarly, theatrically staged state parades and ceremonies have if anything increased. This was especially true during the visit of Pope John Paul II to Lithuania in August–September 1993. The Pope's visit emphasised the conservatism of the Lithuanian Church. Ironically enough, the Pope, regarded in the West as an arch-conservative, appeared in Lithuania in the guise of a Church reformer, forcing the local clergy to take account of changes introduced in the West by Vatican II. An even more positive result of the Pope's visit was the boost it gave to friendlier relations between Lithuania and Poland.

arts. This is because the young are not influenced by Soviet society. We know who we are, and that makes us more free and more calm. It is not as important for us as for some older people to be so nationalist or anti-communist. We don't have to demonstrate this every day.

In one case, the government's ideological commitment to the free market even succeeded in alarming the Scandinavian countries, Estonia's closest friends in the West. A proposed law legalising prostitution was dropped after protests from Sweden and warnings that Tallinn might become 'the Bangkok of the Baltic'. (Prostitution does in fact already play a significant part in the Estonian 'informal economy', but it is relatively veiled and has not yet affected the public face of Tallinn.)

The Laar government's policies of fiscal austerity are in the end likely to make it so many enemies as to bring it down. By early 1994 it had already lost its absolute majority in parliament. The farmers who make up a large proportion of the ethnic Estonian population have in particular been infuriated by the government's failure to increase subsidies or raise tariff barriers against the importation of Western food. The government justifies this refusal by arguing that it is close to reaching a free-trade agreement with the European Union, but (as outlined in Chapter 9) the cost to agriculture has been huge. Even in the traditional Estonian field of dairy products, Western foodstuffs can be seen undercutting Estonian equivalents in every food shop in Tallinn.

The youthfulness of the Laar government has indeed brought it unpopularity. The high proportion of the elderly within the Estonian population, favours the kind of Soviet-style politicians to which it is accustomed, and there is continuing resentment that the popular choice for President in September 1992, former Communist leader Arnold Rüütel, was not elected by the Right-wing dominated parliament. In October 1993, voters demonstrated their dissatisfaction with Laar by giving a huge majority to opposition candidates in local government elections. The Russians exercised their right to vote locally by heavily supporting Russian and former Communist candidates. The coalition government has suffered from internal splits and the occasional hostility of President Lennart Meri who, as I predicted, has proved completely incapable of remaining within the limited presidential role laid down by the constitution. Dr Laar has also been accused of improper links with the Taxpayers' Association, representing the new Estonian business class. These links are very close, but almost unavoidable in a country as small as Estonia, where the elite knows one another and several nights a week half the cabinet may be found in a single pub in Tallinn. In keeping with the public mood, the government which succeeds that of Laar, at or before the next election, is most likely to come from parties based on nationalist sections of the former Communist establishment: the Popular

Front of Edgar Savisaar and the 'Secure Home' of Tiit Vahi. These will probably emphasise their commitment to a more 'humane' and social democratic economic policy, though it is difficult to describe the 'Secure Home' as Left-wing in any meaningful way. If anything, privatisation is likely to proceed faster under such a regime, since it will do little to prevent the existing former Communist managements (most of them Secure Home supporters) from becoming owners of their enterprises via 'spontaneous privatisation', something the present government has resisted. In Laar's own words,

> If we go, we go with the feeling that we have created an irreversible basis for reform. The old nomenklatura won't come back. If there is a new government, it will be a moderate Left-wing alternative.

In respect of policy towards the local Russian population, a government along these lines would be likely to continue the strategy of the Laar government, of steady pressure but along legal lines, and without steps that might forfeit Western support or drive the local Russian population to desperation. With the Russians effectively excluded from parliament, Estonian politics looks like being dominated by a relatively narrow spectrum of democratic, moderately nationalist parties without much to separate them, and all to a greater or lesser degree looking to the West for inspiration. There is one dangerously radical nationalist party in Estonia, the Estonian Citizen ('Eest Kodanik') led by Colonel Juri Toomepuu, but its popularity appears to be declining rapidly, partly as a result of the extreme strangeness of its leader.*

This encouraging picture is not, unfortunately, true of Latvia. There the political landscape is much more reminiscent of that of the 1920s, which helped bring about the collapse of democracy in the Baltic States as sketched in Chapter 3. The Russian immigration into Latvia under Soviet rule was even greater than that into Estonia, and the reaction of Latvian nationalists against the Russians has been correspondingly more intense. Latvia also has a much stronger pre-1940 tradition of romantic, anti-Western chauvinist nationalism, which has been partly revived in the attitudes of the present nationalist parties.

---

* Even Estonian sanity is not to be relied upon unconditionally. The talk in Tallinn is that if Mr Vahi does become Prime Minister, the Foreign Minister is likely to be Professor Endel Lippmaa, described further in this book. Professor Lippmaa has been responsible for a variety of curious national-scientific theories, the latest, reported in the *Tallinn City Paper* of January 1994, being that deep holes dug in Estonia by the Soviets, were part of a plan to destroy Tallinn by means of an artificially induced earthquake. The likely effect of Lipmaa on Estonia's international reputation should be considered by every Estonian patriot.

Moreover, Latvia, unlike Estonia, possessed a large Russian minority before 1940; these Russians have automatically received citizenship together with the other pre-1940 citizens and their descendants. Non-Latvians make up 21.2 per cent of the electorate, and most have voted either for the former Soviet loyalist bloc, 'Equal Rights', which won 7 seats in the 100-seat parliament, or the 'Harmony for Latvia' bloc, with 13 seats. 'Harmony', dominated by former pro-independence Communists and moderate Popular Front leaders, is the only Latvian-led party which attempts to represent the interests of the Russian-speaking minority. There is a third party which calls itself 'Left-wing', the Democratic centre (5 seats); but while on economic policy its attitudes are social democratic, on national questions its deputies have frequently sided with the radical nationalist opposition.

The present government in Latvia, elected in June 1993, is made up of the 'centrist' Latvia's Way (see Chapter 8) and the Farmers Union (12 seats in parliament). Latvia's Way, which won 36 seats, is a highly fissile mixture of former Communists, Latvian emigrés and Popular Frontists, some of them strongly nationalist. The governing coalition has only 48 seats, but has won most parliamentary votes with the tacit support of the Democratic Centre and the Christian Democrats (6), a 'Rightist' group. On national issues, if Latvia's Way could bring itself to make an alliance with 'Harmony', it could win a majority, face down the radical nationalist opposition and guarantee its own survival in office. But any alliance with the Russians, or the 'Latvian traitors' who represent them, is anathema to most of Latvia's Way. A move towards compromise on national questions would probably therefore destroy the governing coalition.

The result is twofold (as described in Chapter 8): the radical nationalists have in effect been able to set the agenda on national questions; and have emerged as the only real opposition. From the days of the independence struggle they retain a strong organisational network across Latvia, while the Popular Front network has collapsed and Latvia's Way is virtually without grassroots organisation.

The rural areas and small towns, where ethnic Latvians are concentrated, are suffering very badly from the impact of economic change, with agriculture, as in Estonia, especially hard hit. The result will almost certainly be a swing against the governing parties at the next election, due in October 1995. The radical nationalists of the National Independence Movement (LNNK) and the Fatherland and Freedom bloc, with 15 and 6 parliamentary seats respectively, appear at present to stand the best chance to benefit and form the next government. These parties' pathological hatred of the Russians and dubious commitment to democratic rules makes this prospect a worrying one.

As regards future Baltic relations with Russia, this foreword is being written in the shadow of the success of Vladimir Zhirinovsky in the

Russian parliamentary elections of December 1993. Like many Russian nationalist extremists, Zhirinovsky has a particular hatred for the Balts, whom he has on occasions threatened to reconquer and even exterminate. He has sent representatives to agitate among the Russian populations of the Baltic States, and one of them, Pyotr Rozhok, is now under arrest in Estonia.

Those members of the Baltic Russian population (a very small minority, numbering 42,000 in Estonia and 23,000 in Latvia) who had by December 1993 taken Russian citizenship, tended to use it to support the Communists or Zhirinovsky. In Latvia, only 3,750 Russian citizens voted; their vote, moreover, was not an index of the mood of the Baltic Russians as a whole, because those that took Russian citizenship first were obviously those that were most dissatisfied with life in the Baltic States. All the same, it is a worrying sign. Many Balts, including as intelligent a statesman as Mart Laar, profess to see no difference between the attitudes of Boris Yeltsin and of Zhirinovsky towards the Baltic States. Baltic newspapers have written of a 'Kozyrev-Zhirinovsky strategy'. After a year in Moscow, this seems to me foolish almost to the point of lunacy, and explicable only in terms of the Baltic neuroses created by the sufferings of the past 55 years. If, which God forbid, Zhirinovsky were actually to come to power in Moscow, the Balts would perceive the differences between him and Yeltsin with extreme speed.

The danger of a fascistic reaction in Russia (outlined in Chapter 7) is now clearly present. The success of Zhirinovsky's electoral propaganda, with its obsessive stress on the position of Russians outside Russia, suggests that, as I argue, the treatment of the Russians living in the Baltic States, and general Baltic behaviour towards Russia, has also had an appreciable and negative effect on domestic politics in Russia and on the politics of the Yeltsin administration. Baltic policies may not have been the last humiliating straw for many Russians, but they certainly numbered among the straws. Nonetheless, under Yeltsin's regime, military withdrawal from the Baltic has continued, and this in itself makes it absurd to equate Russia's Baltic policy of 1991–93 with fascistic imperialism. The principal reason for the withdrawal seems to be the same legal one that has motivated Western 'exceptionalism': that the Baltic states were fully independent countries between 1920 and 1940, and were recognised as such by the Soviet Union as well as the West. In January 1991, the Russian Federation signed treaties with the Baltic States recognising this fact. As Russian Deputy Foreign Minister Vitaly Churkin stated on 27 January 1994 (at a moment of considerable tension between Russia and the Balts):

We have not been putting our relations with CIS member states and the Baltic States on an equal footing . . . . Since the very formation of the

Russian Foreign Ministry, the Baltic States were ascribed to the European Territorial Department, together with Scandinavia.

Underlying this official stance is a general Russian acceptance (analysed in Chapter 7) that culturally speaking the Balts are in a different, 'Western' category, distinct from the other former Soviet peoples. This recognition is coupled with a reluctant admiration, which has survived the growth of anti-Baltic feelings over recent years. On several occasions over the past year, the Russian Foreign Ministry has appeared to be changing its stance on the Baltic States, either claiming them as a Russian sphere of influence, suggesting that military withdrawal would be linked to concessions on rights for local Russians, or warning that current Baltic policies could lead to armed conflict. The strongest remarks were delivered by Foreign Minister Andrei Kozyrev during the winter of 1993–94. For example, in an interview in the magazine *Newsweek* of 14 February 1994 he said that Russia has 'vital interests' in the Baltic States, accused the Latvians of trying to deport thousands of people to Russia, and said there was a danger of conflict in the Baltic States into which Russia would inevitably be drawn. Such statements have provoked furious reactions from the Balts and their lobbies in the West. The curious thing is, however, that Russian military withdrawal on the ground has continued whatever the official Russian line happened to be at the time. On 15 March 1994, the Latvian and Russian Governments formally agreed to the withdrawal of Russian troops by 31 August. In return Latvia had to concede the American proposal whereby Russia would retain the space-radar station at Skrunda for four years, with an additional year-and-a-half for dismantling. This, and other concessions, are bitterly unpopular among the radicals. During the negotiations there were two bomb attacks on power lines leading to Skrunda, probably the work of Latvian radicals, but conceivably also KGB 'provocations'. The odds are the agreement will proceed.

There would seem to be several reasons for the Russian withdrawal. One is Western diplomatic pressure: it was clear to Moscow that it would pay a vastly greater diplomatic price for retaining troops in the Baltic States than, for example, for restoring Russian hegemony over the Transcaucasus. This was all the more evident because the Balts had demonstrated in 1992 that to maintain a military presence against the will of the Baltic governments and peoples would generate an endless series of clashes and incidents, with large-scale violence an increasing possibility. The Baltic threat to blockade Russian bases ultimately left Moscow with the option of either withdrawing them or of invading the Baltic States.

A further reason (mentioned in Chapter 7) is financial. With the establishment of the Baltic currencies, paying for Russian troops became extremely expensive. Moreover, the troops themselves were deteriorating fast, as morale disintegrated. A final reason was suggested to me by Scandinavian diplomats. In their analysis, the Russian Defence Ministry, faced with a radical shrinking of its forces, had decided for its own strategic reasons to withdraw troops from the Baltic, and redeploy them on Russia's southern flank, facing the Ukraine, Turkey, and the conflict zones of the Caucasus.

By 1992 Russian officers were admitting that there was no real strategic threat from NATO, and therefore no real justification for keeping a major strategic force in the Baltic. By contrast, in the course of 1993, Russian newspapers contained numerous articles, in some cases obviously military-inspired, emphasising the geopolitical threat to Russia posed by alleged Turkish ambitions in the Caucasus and Central Asia. Russian forces in the North Caucasus have been greatly strengthened, and at the time of writing, Georgia has just been forced to accept new Russian military bases. At a base in Sukhumi, Abkhazia, in October 1993, I met Russian paratroopers from the division formerly stationed in Lithuania.

Such a decision by the Defence Ministry, to wind down the Baltic Military Region in favour of other areas, would explain the curious phenomenon that military withdrawal continued just as, for diplomatic reasons, it would have made sense to suspend it. In its diplomatic card-game of 1992–93, the Russian Foreign Ministry was playing with a steadily shrinking hand: the soldiers were giving away card after card. This looks like a classic example of two Russian ministries working at cross-purposes. The withdrawal has continued even in the face of what Moscow has seen as gross provocation on the part of the Latvians and Estonians. Kozyrev amongst others has accused the Balts of 'human rights abuses' and 'deportations'. This crude approach has done Moscow no good. As this book argues, there have been no human rights abuses in the Baltic States. It remains true today, and has been certified by several international bodies, including the CSCE and the UN.

What these bodies have also certified, however, is that there has been a drastic curtailment of Russians' civic rights, especially in Latvia, and that considerable administrative harassment has also taken place. In view of the attitudes of the Latvian radical nationalists, there is a real danger of severe economic and social discrimination on the part of the state. The ethnic unrest I feared in Estonia and Latvia has not yet occurred, and at present there is almost no sign of it. In Estonia, there probably never will be serious trouble, unless fascists come to power in Moscow or, as is unlikely, the Estonian line itself hardens severely. In my view, however, the policies of the radical nationalists in Latvia still pose a threat to the peace of Europe.

A central reason for the difference in Estonian and Latvian behaviour lies in their differing attitude to Europe. The Latvians, like the Lithuanians, have a chronic tendency to relapse into romantic isolationism, declaring that they are different from and much better than the West, and will fight against the whole world if necessary; although in both cases, their deep underlying pragmatism means that, in a real crisis, they generally come to their senses. The Estonians by contrast are deeply and permanently committed to Europe, as well as having a cooler and more realistic view of their own position. In an implicit criticism of the Latvians and some Estonian radicals, President Meri told me that he had been reading *Gulliver's Travels*: 'I found an island with no contact with the realities of this world. I wouldn't like to imagine Estonia or Latvia in the same position'.*

In Estonia, the most dangerous recent moment came in June 1993 with the passage of the so-called 'Aliens' Law', which defined the conditions for gaining legal residency in Estonia. It followed a law which adapted earlier Estonian policy by barring non-citizens from standing in local elections, although they were still allowed to vote. The CSCE Commissioner for Ethnic Minorities, Max van der Stoel, made several criticisms of the law, and in private messages several Western governments also expressed their unease. Criticism centred on several points, notably the lack of recognition for Soviet residence permits (forcing everyone to apply anew), the lack of an appeal procedure against arbitrary refusal by officials doing the registering, the complete exclusion of Soviet military pensioners, and a provision that anyone who 'damaged the international reputation of Estonia' was liable to be refused a residence permit, and expelled.

Following this international criticism, President Meri announced that he was withholding his signature pending amendments to the law. Parliament duly stated that anyone who had settled in Estonia before 1990 would be eligible for a residence permit; it established provisions for appeal, and altered the 'slander' clause to one referring only to using 'unconstitutional means' to oppose Estonian independence. The President then signed the amended law. Estonian ministers had to perform a rather two-faced balancing act, insisting to the West that the changes were substantive, while assuring their own people that they were cosmetic. By their 'own people' of course, only the ethnic Estonians are to be understood.

---

* Even the Estonians are not above occasionally reverting to Soviet patterns of behaviour. In response to Western criticism of Estonian policy towards the Russian minority, President Meri in December 1993 set up an official Estonian 'Human Rights Institute' to assure the world that such an institute in Estonia was unnecessary, because there were no human rights abuses; an utterly Soviet thing to do.

The Estonian government also promised to set up with all due speed an office to distribute residence permits and aliens' passports, enabling local Russians to travel to the West. Seven months later it had still not been done, and this failure began to draw strong criticism from the CSCE and local Russians. The fear is that the Estonians may draw out the registration procedure and in the meantime resort to administrative harassment, as in Latvia. The CSCE has warned that if registration were to be made impossible by the lack of the necessary administrative machinery, this would constitute a denial of rights. Concern is increased by the appointment as head of the planned new department of a radical nationalist, who may follow the behaviour of the equivalent office in Latvia.

Other than this, the main Russian concern in Estonia relates to a new education law which proposes to abolish teaching in Russian at state secondary schools by the year 2000 (although the law is unlikely to be implemented in North-East Estonia, and the Laar government and Education Ministry both oppose it on practical grounds). Russian-language teaching can continue in municipal and private schools, and these will be eligible for unspecified amounts of state aid. Russian representatives however, with good reason, accuse the Estonian parliament of breaking the spirit, if not the letter, of past promises to guarantee full schooling in their own tongue. In the words of Hanon Barabaner, a Russian-Jewish leader of the moderate-led Representative Assembly of Russian Speakers,

> The Estonian leaders have always stressed that Russians living here should integrate into the Estonian state, and we in the assembly agree with this. But what we now see, in the education law for example, is that the demand for integration is being mixed up with a demand for assimilation, for sacrifice of cultural and linguistic identity. This is a very different thing, and we protest against it. In the end, it will only hinder integration by creating confrontation.

Despite these concerns, however, the mass political response of the Russians in Estonia has been very slight. In response to the Aliens Law, the local councils in north-east Estonia held a referendum in June 1993 on the issue of autonomy for the region, so often proposed by the local Communist leadership. The referendum was probably a success (though this was disputed by the Estonian authorities who claimed that less than 50 per cent of the population voted). The vast majority of those who did vote, favoured autonomy within Estonia, but it can hardly be called a great victory. The Estonian Supreme Court declared the vote illegal and the government ignored it. The results became academic, for the present at least, when the former Communist town council was removed from office at the local government elections and replaced with a coalition of moderate Russians so none of them could stand. Vladimir Chuikin and his colleagues, however, have now gone into business, and seem happy enough.

In Latvia, at the time of writing, attention is concentrated on the naturalisation law which was finally put forward in November 1993 and which passed its first parliamentary reading the same month. The law lays down a ten-year residence requirement, 'proficiency in the Latvian language to conversational level', and 'knowledge of the fundamental principles of the constitution'. However its ninth article also declares that,

> Naturalisation quotas for each forthcoming year shall be determined by the Cabinet of Ministers and approved by the Saeima, taking into consideration the demographic and economic situation in the country, in order to ensure the development of Latvia as a single-nation state.

This provision, and the entire direction of Latvian policy so far, have borne out the pessimistic predictions of Janis Jurkans (see Chapter 8). It has been strongly criticised by van der Stoel, who wrote to the Latvian government in February 1994 that quotas could mean naturalisation would be eliminated or reduced to a bare minimum for years to come, and that if the great majority of non-Latvians are denied citizenship, then 'the democratic character of the state may be called into question'.

The Council of Europe response has also been negative, and diplomats are of the opinion that if the law passes in its present form, Latvia may be barred from joining the Council. This has caused some concern in Estonia and Lithuania, because membership of the Council is an essential stepping-stone to eventual membership of the European Union. They fear that if Latvia's progress is held up, it will affect them as well. One senior Estonian leader told me that he had privately urged the Latvians to adopt a law closer to that of Estonia. As a result of this pressure, the Latvian government seems currently to be modifying its stand and moving towards a law which would introduce quotas to regulate but not to limit naturalisation, giving priority to younger age-groups, or drop quotas altogether. If so this would represent a success for the quiet, private pressure favoured by Western diplomacy, of which I have been critical. Douglas Hurd, the British Foreign secretary, pressed strongly for moderation during his brief visit to Riga in February 1994.

It will not be easy for the Latvian government to compromise, and any quota system will also be vulnerable to amendment by some future, more hardline government. At the time of writing the 'national bloc' of LNNK and Fatherland and Freedom has proposed a naturalisation bill which is much harsher than that tabled by the government. It would delay naturalisation until after the total withdrawal of Russian troops, presumably until the closure of Skrunda, five-and-a-half years ahead. It would then establish a naturalisation quota of no more than 0.1 per cent of the total number of citizens in the previous year, and within that would give precedence to spouses of Latvian citizens and to ethnic Latvians living outside the country.

The result of this of course would be to bar all but a tiny handful of Russian non-citizens from any hope of gaining citizenship. Moreover, an ambiguity in the language of the draft suggests that those who entered Latvia under Soviet rule are not eligible to apply at all. Leaders of both LNNK and Fatherland and Freedom have repeatedly gone on record as saying that the 'colonists' who entered Latvia under 'Soviet military occupation' are legally liable to deportation under the Geneva Convention, which forbids the settling of colonists on occupied territory. They have declared that no-one will be deported by force, but have spoken openly of Latvia's right to use social and economic pressure. Their desired policy on residence and work permits would in fact amount to mass deportation by softer and slower means, and this policy could be implemented not by the Latvian government, but by local authorities which the radicals already control.

It should be stated that both the government's proposal to establish quotas for naturalisation and the radicals' proposal to bar them altogether are in clear violation of previous statements made by the leadership not only of the Latvian Popular Front and government but of the LNNK itself, which promised clear naturalisation rules and said nothing about quotas. The LNNK proposal illustrates the contempt of the Latvian radical nationalists for the West as well as for Russia, since its adoption would certainly provoke major Western protests, and, most probably, an end to any further progress towards joining Western organisations. Both naturalisation drafts, as well as the entire trend of Latvian policy, have completely ignored the various public recommendations of van der Stoel as well as the report of December 1992 by Ibrahima Fall, Director of the United Nations Centre for Human Rights. The Latvian government has done its utmost to avoid these reports being published inside the country. International criticism has also been focused on Latvian administrative practice. Thus the Latvian Department of Citizenship and Immigration (responsible for issuing residence permits) was heavily criticised by Helsinki Watch in a report of October 1993 (a report which fully bears out the fears about the Department's behaviour expressed in Chapter 8). The report accuses the Department, under Maris Plavnieks and Viesturs Karnups, of systematically breaking the law by denying legal residency to people entitled to it, and of refusing to implement court judgements.

This, together with CSCE criticism, led to the appointment of a more moderate figure as department chief, and Latvian law seems now at least to be being observed. In the meantime, however, a whole set of laws and by-laws have sprung up which discriminate against non-citizens. They are barred from most official jobs, from the police and even from serving with Latvian Airlines. In the case of the police, this ban was introduced in July 1993, in an amendment to the police law of 1991. Only citizens can purchase state housing, and several local authorities also ban non-citizens from buying privatised 'co-operative' apartments. By a law of 13 January 1994, in complete violation of past public promises, non-citizens were barred from voting even in local elections, which means that in many areas they have no protection at all from local legislation. In March 1994 however, the appointment of a new official responsible for human rights gave hope that the Government would modify its attitude. Olafs Bruberis, a former dissident and exile in the US, is highly regarded in the West.

So far, my fears of ethnic unrest in the Baltic States have not been borne out, and in Estonia and Lithuania there is good reason to hope that they never will be. I do not think, however, it was unreasonable to fear this, and to go on fearing it in the case of Latvia: if, four years ago, one had told any outside observer that the Latvians could do all they have done and still not provoke a local Russian revolt, backed by Moscow, he or she would have told you that you were as crazy as a hoot owl. The reasons why the Russians have remained so quiet are rehearsed in Chapter 7. One was suggested to me very forcibly in June 1993 at the Press Ball in Riga, the high point of the Latvian social year. It would be hard to call this a pretty sight. To the strains of a pompous polonaise, independent Latvia's new elites paraded around the former Communist Party's congress hall, shiny new suits on their backs and in many cases, almost equally shiny new wives and girlfriends on their arms. Almost without exception the politicians were Latvians, and the leading intellectuals and cultural figures likewise; but the businessmen, many looking as if they had just climbed out of their tracksuits and knuckledusters, were overwhelmingly Russian and Russian-Jewish. For the moment, they are doing very well in Latvia, and more and more intelligent and determined young local Russians are rising to join their ranks. So far, they have faced no serious obstacles in the economic sphere; and for that matter, for around $500 it is not difficult to buy Latvian citizenship from a corrupt official (a sum which is however far beyond the means of most local Russians).

But as Plato could tell us, such a division between the political and economic elites is inherently unstable. There is strong Latvian feeling against Russian businessmen and *mafiosi* (often regarded, and often rightly, as one and the same). There have been repeated articles in the Latvian press drawing attention to the domination of the economy by non-Latvians, in terms very reminiscent of similar articles written in the

1920s and 1930s. There is, therefore, a strong danger that a future radical nationalist government would move to penalise the non-Latvian business classes, at the same time as ordinary Russians came under heavy pressure over jobs and housing. This could provoke a dangerous reaction and, given the subterranean channels by which these businessmen work, blow up quickly and without warning.

One thing worth stressing is that we do not really know what is going on within these immigrant communities. Neither Western observers, nor the Baltic governments, nor even the new moderate local Russian leaders know fully what Russian workers in the Baltic are thinking. I myself have witnessed two massive failures of political prediction in recent months: the successes of Brazauskas in Lithuania in October 1992 and of Zhirinovsky in Russia in December 1993; and it has made me cautious. In the words of the Latvian-American scholar Dr Nils Muiznieks, the most acute observer of ethnic issues in Latvia,

> Western political scientists and sociologists have concluded that immigrants consider political rights of nominal importance if socio-economic opportunities have been guaranteed. Thus, if Latvia's legislators continue to restrict the socio-economic opportunities of non-citizens, social tension will erupt. Given the ethnic make-up of the non-citizens, this tension could assume an ethnic hue.

I endorse this warning wholeheartedly. As I have written in this book, the real danger of the lack of Russian political rights is not so much those rights themselves, but that Baltic radicals will exploit powerlessness of the Russians to attack their social and economic position, causing a real danger of upheaval. If it can be guaranteed – as may be becoming the case in Estonia – that such an attack will not take place, then there are certainly strong moral and practical arguments for the Balts to establish strict terms for naturalisation, as long as these terms are consistent and not qualified by some arbitrary factor like quotas. The option of simply giving citizenship to all non-citizens, as urged by Moscow, is no longer an option, if it ever was one. Apart from the question of integration, it is also entirely true, as Baltic governments have argued, that the radical economic policies of the past two years could not have taken place if there had been a large bloc of Russian deputies opposing them.

In Estonia, the situation is calmer on both sides than in Latvia. In the words of an Estonian-American journalist,

> Estonians feel much better, much safer now that they have excluded Russians from the political decision-making process, and this has already made emotional hostility to Russians among Estonians less than it was before. Estonians feel that they are masters again in their own country. Apart from that, it's not that most Estonians dislike the Russians they

work with or know personally. They get on with them well enough – but they certainly don't trust them to help decide the future of Estonia.

In Latvia, the number of Russians, and of Russian citizens, and the relative accessibility of the Latvian language, means that the Russians will always have a more visible role, and the Latvians feel correspondingly more threatened. As far as the position of the radical nationalists are concerned, there is no prospect that anti-Russian attitudes will be significantly diminished by the withdrawal of Russian troops. In their propaganda, they have already made the transition to describing the Russian civilian population as an occupying garrison, and their racist language against the Russians has got worse, not better. The Latvian emigré journalist Juris Kaza wrote in the *Baltic Observer* of 6 January 1994 that,

> Estonia and Latvia have an incorrigible, genocide barbarian society [sic] as their eastern neighbour. Russia is a savage, technologically advanced robber tribe with an almost pathological immunity to democracy or any other form of enlightenment.

If this sort of talk becomes a permanent feature of Latvian public life, as seems likely, then if a Russian army should march into Latvia there will not be a single local Russian, however liberal, who will not feel some measure of malignant satisfaction. The stage will then be set for another of the East European ethnic tragedies described in Chapter 6.

The apocalyptic fears of Latvian radicals, too often swallowed by Western observers, concerning the threat of national extinction, are by now wholly unreal – always assuming of course that no new Russian conquest and annexation takes place. This is because of the sizeable and continuing out-migration of non-Latvians which has taken place in recent years. According to figures compiled from official sources by Dr Muiznieks, a net outflow of around 100,000 people has taken place in the past three years, of whom it is safe to assume that the vast majority are Russian-speakers.

According to information supplied by the Citizenship and Immigration Department, Latvians constitute 57.7 per cent of the total registered population of the country (excluding Russian military and their families) rather than the often-quoted 52 per cent. A further 4.5 per cent or so is made up of thoroughly integrated peoples such as the Poles, the Lithuanians and the Estonians. The Russians represent 29.7 per cent of the population, and the mainly Russified Ukrainians, Byelorussians and others another 7 per cent. At October 1993, 78.8 per cent of all citizens were Latvian, with Russians, Byelorussians and Ukrainians together making up 17.6 per cent. Citizens constituted 71.8 per cent of registered residents, with non-citizens numbering 673,398 people or 28.18

per cent. Of the resident non-citizen population, by contrast, Russians made up 64.2 per cent, Byelorussians 12.1 per cent and Ukrainians 8.6 per cent. Dr Muiznieks quotes an official of the Latvian State Statistical Committee as declaring in October 1993 that 'worries about threats to the survival of the Latvian nation now and in future are considerably exaggerated'.

In these circumstances, what should be Western policy? Especially in view of the latest developments in Russia, I feel no need to modify the arguments put forward in the Conclusion. In Estonia especially, Western pressure has brought some significant changes (on paper at least) in policy, but in Latvia it has so far been of limited effectiveness. The CSCE mission to Latvia was set up only in November 1993, ten months after that to Estonia and too late to affect the formulation of the naturalisation law, or the passage of several pieces of discriminatory legislation – reinforcing my accusation of excessive slowness and indifference.

Western governmental pressure on Russia to withdraw its troops has been mainly public, and continuous. Pressure on the Balts to respect Russian rights has been largely private, and intermittent. This has allowed Russians to believe, as one said to me, that 'when you call for Russian withdrawal, you shout, and when you speak on our behalf, you whisper'. This is by no means entirely fair, but it has allowed the Russian opposition to portray Western policy in the Baltic as hostile to Russia's vital interests. For any future Russian government, influence in the Baltic States will be a major interest, and the defence of its Russian population a vital one. In the words of Hanon Barabaner,

> The Russian intelligentsia here agreed with the West in supporting the independence of the Baltic States from the Soviet Union. We look toward the West, and our appeals for support today are directed to the West. If there is no response, then the impression will be created that the West has a dual standard with regard to our rights. In this case, people will begin to look instead to Moscow for support. But we in our organisation don't want to play the Russian card, because it will only play into the hands of Russian and Estonian chauvinists and cause a real confrontation, which hasn't yet occurred.

Western restraint in public has also allowed the Latvian government and much of the press simply to avoid reporting Western and CSCE criticism to their own people, instead simply parroting the line that international bodies had reported 'no human rights abuses'; with the alarming (and from the relatively moderate Latvian government point of view, deeply stupid) result that in February 1994 most Latvians were quite unaware that their naturalisation law might in the long run cost them entry into the European Union. Perhaps ordinary Latvians, even knowing this, would still have pressed for radical anti-Russian measures – but at least they had the right to be told. It is true, as local Western diplomats emphasise, that you have to be careful when dealing with the Latvians. They are liable to flare up and reject not simply Western advice but even the idea of Latvia's belonging to the West. The dangerously irresponsible attitude of the radicals was shown by the incident of 10 January 1994, when a local elected official belonging to Fatherland and Freedom, Andrejs Ručs, ordered the arrest and deportation of two Russian generals in a dispute about the takeover of military property. Russian military intervention was averted only by Latvia's releasing the generals, apologising to Russia and dismissing Mr Ručs. The most worrying aspect of the incident was the fact that for a time at least, Latvian paramilitary units, themselves heavily radical in membership, appeared to be obeying the radical opposition and not the government.*

However, even Latvian radicals listen to Western advice if those giving the advice are sufficiently senior. The way round this problem, therefore, might be serious and consistent interest by senior Western politicians. Thus in February 1994, during the Skrunda negotiations, the effect of the invitation to visit Washington and meet President Clinton and other top officials had a striking effect on Latvian political leaders. Even the most radical opponents of compromise came back visibly softened in their approach. The result was that Latvia accepted the American-sponsored compromise on Skrunda. By contrast, the British Foreign Secretary, on his one-day visit to Riga later that month, had time for precisely forty minutes with each of the Baltic foreign ministers, followed by a working lunch, and no meeting with local Russians. If a journalist spent so little time on a major story, diplomats would sneer at him.

Is it naive to expect Western leaders to pay close attention to the Baltic States? It should not be. Millions of tons of newsprint have been consumed in recent months discussing the new threat of expansionist Russian nationalism, and what the West should do about it. Most of the paper would more fruitfully have remained on the trees. Western analysts have discussed whether or not to extend NATO membership to Poland, Czechia and Hungary – which have no urgent need for such membership because there is no Russian threat to attack them, and never will be, given the state of the Russian armed forces and the lack of an ideological

---

* At the time there was much talk of how this incident represented 'KGB provocation'. The possibility of a KGB role is never wholly to be discounted, but even so the responsibility of the Latvian radicals cannot be removed. The KGB might conceivably have been responsible for the original incident, but they can hardly have been responsible for the subsequent decision of a majority of Mr Ručs' colleagues in the Vidzeme municipality of Riga to reinstate him after he had been removed by the government for exceeding his authority.

or ethnic justification. Even Zhirinovsky has spoken of partitioning Poland only in alliance with Germany.

American analysts have spoken of the need for the West to defend the Ukraine – while the Clinton administration has come up with an aid package for the Ukraine of a princely $300 million, or approximately enough to convert one Ukrainian military-industrial plant. If this is the best the West can do, it would be better to forget the Ukraine ever existed. This it will do sooner or later in any case, because Western governments have already demonstrated that they feel no responsibility whatsoever to defend Ukrainian interests. As for a NATO security guarantee for the Ukraine within its present borders, this is pure fantasy. Given the West's disgusting, pusillanimous failure to defend the Bosnian Muslims, can anyone believe that NATO soldiers would ever be asked to die in the Ukraine? In 1939, the cry of Frenchmen unwilling to fight to defend Poland was the ironical, 'Mourir pour Danzig?'. Today the cry would be 'Mourir pour Donetsk?', and it would be even more effective.

The one area which combines the moral commitment the West feels to Poland with the danger of Russian attack suffered by the Ukraine is the Baltic States. As such, they pose by far the greatest danger of a really serious confrontation between Russia and the West. To avert this danger, the West ought to offer the Balts more carrot, and more stick, and tie the two much more closely together. Carrot, in the form of real help in building up the armed forces and economies, and a real timetable for progress towards membership of both the European Union and NATO, rather than the vague and largely meaningless offer of the 'Partnership for Peace'. Stick, in the sense that this progress should be conditional on acceptance of Western advice concerning the treatment of local Russians.

But, it may be argued, if Zhirinovsky, or whomsoever, wishes to invade the Baltic States, he will do so irrespective of the treatment of the local Russian populations. This seems to me questionable. The slogans 'Munich' and 'appeasement' have now been bandied around so long that people have forgotten the cover that Hitler gave to his first moves, into the Saar, the Rhineland, Austria and the Sudetenland. In each case, this was provided by the enthusiastic support of local German civilians. It was only with the occupation of the whole of Bohemia and Moravia, in March 1939, that Hitler dispensed with any pretence of local democratic support. For the ruling classes and intelligentsia of the West, desperate to find any excuse not to fight another war, this 'democratic' cover was enough, especially given the way that all the East European states, including even Czechoslovakia, had gained a reputation for narrow and stupid linguistic chauvinism.

In 1934–38, the West was still reeling from the losses at Ypres and Verdun. Today we are merely stupefied by forty years of fatty living coupled with neurotic self-analysis. But the effect will be the same. At the slightest hint of the danger of a major war with Russia over the Baltic States, Western publicists and politicians, intellectuals and journalists will be tripping over each other to find any and every possible reason why a defence of the Baltic States by the West would be rationally and above all morally quite unnecessary, why Mr Zhirinovsky (or another) would really have excellent arguments on his side. 'Mourir pour Daugavpils?' A radical nationalist government in Latvia would provide such excuses in bucketfuls.* It would be the craven-hearted Westerner's dream; it would also be the Russian fascist's dream. If, three years hence, a fascistic government in Russia were facing a radical nationalist government in Latvia, then God help Latvia.

Moscow, March 1994

---

* The suspicions of many Jewish people in relation to the Balts, rooted in the Second World War (see Chapter 6) means that any anti-Balt propaganda is likely to receive a certain hearing in the West. Far from trying to neutralise this prejudice, radical nationalist Latvians have sometimes seemed to go out of their way to encourage it. The sheer clumsiness and stupidity of their approach to Western public opinion was exemplified by an advertisement placed by Dr Aivars Slucis, a Latvian emigré, on the op-ed page of the *New York Times* on 26 September 1993, calling for the removal of ethnic Russians from Latvia and Estonia.

Although, under heavy Western pressure, the LNNK formally expelled the extreme Right-wing German politician Joachim Siegerist after the June 1993 elections (see Chapter 8), several of its leaders and those of Fatherland and Freedom have continued a public flirtation with him. The effect of Siegerist on most Western observers can be imagined. The language and attitudes of the Fatherland and Freedom newspaper, *Pavalstnieks*, are reminiscent of the authoritarian nationalism of Latvia in the 1930s. In a column entitled 'enemies of the people', the paper has listed the names, addresses and telephone numbers of people it considers enemies of Latvian independence: at the very least, an ugly incitement to harassment.

Immediately after the founding declaration of the Latvian Union of Non-Citizens on 15 December 1993, a LNNK leader, Aleksanders Kirsteins, wrote that since the Latvian constitution forbids the formation of political parties and organisations by non-citizens, the Union should be banned and its leaders deported from Latvia. This is despite the fact that most of these leaders, like Alexei Grigoriev and Boris Tsilevich, had been activists of the Latvian Popular Front in the struggle for independence.

Introduction

The gentleman is Lithuanian, but speaks Polish? I don't understand at all.
I thought that in Lithuania there were only Muscovites.
I know even less about Lithuania than about China.
I once saw an article about Lithuania in 'The Constitutional'.
But the other papers don't talk about it at all.
    From Adam Mickiewicz, *Dziady* ('Forefathers' Eve'), Part III

There exists in Estonian folklore a monster called 'The Northern Frog'. It has the head of a giant frog, the body of an ox and the tail of a snake; an awkward sort of beast altogether. Possibly for that reason it also has an extremely bad temper.[1] This book is something of the same kind. It attempts to combine elements of a portrait of the contemporary Baltic States and their peoples, a sketch and interpretation of their history and culture, a personal report from the struggle, and elements of oral history from people whom I interviewed. It also contains a polemical argument concerning the position of the Baltic Russians, which I think involves dangers greater than the West has realised.

If the resulting work appears to fall between two or more stools, I hope at least that it does so with a satisfying thump. The attempt to combine these different elements seemed justified in the first place because the Baltic States are so little known in the West. Writing on other areas of Eastern Europe, some cultural and historical background can be taken for granted; not so here. In particular, people in the West, and indeed Western diplomacy, have a tendency to lump the Baltic States together and regard them as identical. As should become apparent, they are in fact very different, and may experience very different fates in the years to come. In this sense at least, there is no 'Baltic Region'. I also shelter behind the words of the great Polish-Lithuanian writer, Czeslaw Milosz:

> When the description of countries and civilisations had not yet been inhibited by a multitude of taboos arising from the compartmentalised division of knowledge, authors, who were usually travellers, did not

disdain continuity as it is written in the slope of a roof, the curve of a plough handle, in gestures or proverbs. A reporter, a sociologist and a historian used to co-exist within one man. To the mutual detriment of all, they parted ways.[2]

It is especially necessary, when analysing the contemporary Baltic scene, to pay great attention to questions of history and culture, because the Balts do this so much themselves. The Baltic independence movements of our own time can be seen as part of a continuous, closely-linked struggle for national self-determination and cultural identity which began under Russian imperial rule in the nineteenth century, and within which the independent states of 1920–40 were only an interlude, albeit an immensely important one. For most of the period, the lack of any possibility of real political action meant that the creation of the nation, and its subsequent defence, was articulated above all in terms of culture. Today, for many on the Right in the Baltic, the defence of national culture takes precedence beyond most questions of economic and social policy.

The Baltic national movements and the reborn Baltic States of today repeatedly look back to the models and traditions of the first period of independence. Although entirely natural this has, as I argue, dangerous aspects since for much of the interwar period, all three states were ruled by authoritarian regimes with intensely nationalist ideologies. While these were not very extreme by the standards of the time, their ideology tends to shock most West Europeans of today: because of their subsequent isolation under Soviet rule, many Balts simply do not realise how far some of these reborn traditions could isolate them from Europe. Until very recently they themselves, of course, never had the chance to discuss or analyse them publicly.[3]

One of the themes of this book therefore suggests itself to me as the story of Sleeping Beauty, as re-written by the Wicked Witch. Certain aspects of the Baltic national cultures, frozen by Soviet rule in the form they held in 1940, have, so to speak, been kissed by the breeze of freedom, and have re-awakened – as frogs. From their very beginning in the nineteenth century, the Baltic national and national-cultural movements have had a relationship to history and time which is alien to most West European experience. This is because, lacking an identity as states or even organised national societies, and lacking also a written literature, the pioneers of nineteenth-century national culture were forced to create an imaginative literary and historical link to pagan Baltic prehistory, predating conquest by the crusaders (or in the case of Lithuania, conversion and assimilation by the Poles) from the thirteenth to the fifteenth centuries.

The past in the Baltic has, as a result, a way of walking around in the present, behaving as if it were alive. This is finely summed up in the *Ballads of Kukutis*, by Marcelus Martinaitis. Rimvydas Šilbajoris writes how the narrator of the poem 'sits at table with his host, the half-blind, half-dead Kukutis, and watches how time is transforming itself into eternity as it passes through the cabin':

> 'While the owl was hooting,
> and the black beetle chewed at the log-house
> and until the graves sank in,
> and the oxen took a deep breath,
> the first news of Troy was rounding the world,
> and the radio said:
> the old Prussians have vanished from the earth.'[4]

This is especially true in Lithuania, where some politicians behave as if they were only half present, the other half of their attention being permanently fixed in a timeless dream of Lithuanian glory. It may be argued, following Fukuyama, that there is little point studying these archaic aspects of the Baltic nationalisms because they are in any case bound to be subsumed by the great wave of Western mass culture and Western ideas which is beginning to break over the region. And it may well be so. The electoral defeat of Dr Vytautas Landsbergis and his rump Sajūdis movement in the Lithuanian elections of October 1992 already showed the lack of resonance of neo-traditionalist ideologies even for the supposedly 'romantic' Lithuanians. In a generation or so, the culture of the region will probably have been transformed, as more and more younger people adopt Western attitudes. Despite this it is still worthwhile to provide a snapshot of a vitally important time in Baltic history (1987–92) when these traditional aspects of the Baltic nationalisms were very important. Moreover it is by no means clear that, even among the younger generation, adoption of a Western outlook will necessarily lead to a stable hegemony of Western liberal democratic values in politics; there could well be hiccups and throwbacks. There are enough examples from the Third World to show that people who adopt Western attitudes and behaviour in their private lives may, out of guilt, cling all the tighter to neo-traditionalist attitudes in politics.

This is even more true in times of massive socio-economic disruption, and when (as in Latvia and Estonia) the nation and its culture appears threatened by huge numbers of internal aliens (the Baltic Russians). Finally, even if, as fortunately seems unlikely, some of my more pessimistic worries about the future of the Baltic States prove ungrounded, I hope that they may provide suggestions for the analysis of events where – as elsewhere in the former Soviet Union – the Western impact is weaker.

It is of course rather early to be analysing a historical process the outcome of which is not yet clear – in Hegel's phrase, the owl of Minerva has not yet taken wing. Moreover there is as yet no real conceptual framework for the analysis of post-communist societies, especially multinational ones. It is however precisely the inchoate nature of so many questions (for example the Russian national identity), and their vast potential for good or evil, which makes the whole process so fascinating.

As a journalist reporting from the Baltic States since 1989, the book emerges to a significant extent from my own notes and interviews. As the Estonian proverb has it, 'One's own eye is King': I did actually witness several of the most important events of the period. For this reason I do not attempt to give a detailed picture of the Baltic role in politics in Moscow (for example in the Supreme Soviet), or to analyse the precise contribution of the Balts to the disintegration of the Soviet Union. Colleagues based in Moscow are better placed to do this.

It will be apparent that I have a fairly critical attitude towards several aspects of the contemporary Baltic nationalisms. This may offend a number of Balts, but in my view they are better off getting criticism which is basically sympathetic rather than the odious mixture of ignorant goodwill, hypocritical rhetoric and indifference which has characterised so much of the West's approach to the region. I believe that the best security for the Balts and for their individual national cultures lies not in the attempt to recreate closed national states, but in finding a place within a stable 'concert of Europe'. This in turn depends not only on international developments, which the Baltic leaders cannot control, but also on internal ethnic peace, for which they bear the chief responsibility.

Given that much of this book is about inherited attitudes, it seems only fair to give the reader some information about my own Baltic background before some critic does so in an attempt to explain my attitudes! The Lieven family were by origin chieftains of the Livonians, a Finno-Ugric people living in what is now Latvia. During the German crusader invasion of the thirteenth century, the family sided with the German crusading knights, and in consequence joined the German élite and became culturally Germanised.

After the fall of the Teutonic Knights' Livonian state in the sixteenth century the Lievens, in common with the rest of the Baltic German nobility, served a succession of different masters, including the Poles, the Swedes and finally the Russian Tsars, but retained throughout a mainly German-Lutheran identity. My immediate branch of the family emigrated from the region to Western Europe during the Russian Civil War. During the Second World War, my father volunteered for the British army. My mother was a native Irish Catholic, and I was brought up in London.

A number of Latvians and Estonians have accused me of having ancestral German noble prejudices against the Balts. Others have accused me of being pro-Russian, while Lithuanian nationalist deputies reportedly believe that I am Jewish, (as an American-Lithuanian friend working in the parliament said, 'Well, you have dark hair and eyes and you criticise Lithuania. For them, there's no question about it – you must be Jewish'), but have also accused me of being pro-Polish. This would make me a Polish-Jewish German-Irish Russian imperialist, which would be nice if true, a creature unique even in the annals of national paranoia, truly a kind of Northern Frog.

I have omitted any reference to my family background in the body of the text, because it is of no relevance to the contemporary Baltic or the development of modern Baltic nationalism. However, this background has certainly given me both an extra sympathy for the Balts and a sense of the complexity and tragedy of Baltic history. This was especially so during a visit to the former estate of my family at Mežotne (Mesoten) in Courland, Southern Latvia.

Through Mežotne, between water-meadows and patches of thick woodland, flows a shallow, reed-choked river, the Lielupa. Following its course, you can trace some of the main events of Latvian history. Before the coming of the German Knights, an earthen fortress of the Semgalan people stood on its banks, which the Crusaders turned into an outpost to defend their new territory from the attacks of the Lithuanians to the South. Thirteen kilometres upriver, the ruined castle of Bauska (Bauske) was once one of the most important fortresses of the Knights.

Viewed from the low hills across the river, the classical profile of the house at Mežotne and its estate buildings is much the same as it appears in an 1850s print in the possession of my uncle in London. The monuments on the bank of the river and in the park have received a historical reshuffle. The neo-classical gazebo in the foreground – presumably for picnics and musical performances – has not survived the twentieth century. Instead, just beyond the house, stands a Soviet monument, in local granite, to the men of the 37th Pontoon Battalion, 9th Brigade, 43rd Army, 'who on this spot, on September 14th 1944, under enemy fire, constructed a pontoon bridge and forced the crossing of the Lielupe River'. Nearby is a recently created monument to eleven pupils of the local highschool, deported to Siberia in 1940 when a portrait of Stalin, placed in the school after Latvia's annexation, was found floating in the Lielupe. Only two returned.

A little way beyond is a Grecian urn in marble, the monument of a nineteenth-century Lieven to his dead wife. It is pitted with bullet holes, though from which war it is impossible to say, for the river Lielupa was the front line in several of them. In the park which stretches along the river bank, the site of one of the battles, stands a late testament to chivalry in war. A granite Orthodox Cross bears an inscription in German: 'Here Lie Seven Brave Russian Soldiers; August 1915'. It was erected by German soldiers to honour the men of the enemy rearguard who gave their lives in battle at Mežotne during the Russian retreat into Riga. Hundreds more are buried in woods to the North. The river itself bears a strange reminder both of 1944 and of our nineteenth-century print, for it is still crossed by a ramshackle pontoon bridge, as it has probably been for many centuries; this spot, where the river slows and becomes shallow, must always have been a natural crossing point and therefore a natural focus for both commerce and war. Since the time of the print, however, the reed beds seem greatly to have spread, another sign perhaps of the return of the countryside to wilderness, so often to be seen in the former Soviet Empire.

The pontoon is supported now by rusty oil-drums, and is decidedly shaky. If you risk it, fending off (in summer) the clouds of mosquitoes emerging from the reed beds, you arrive at a path which winds through undergrowth, between tall oaks and lindens, and around curious mounds, not yet investigated, but perhaps prehistoric defences or the tombs of pre-Christian chieftains. On the edge of the woods are the remains of the church and cemetery of Mežotne.

At first, it looked to me as if the people who destroyed the cemetery had used explosives to blow the tombs apart, possibly under the impression that the Baltic German nobility were buried along with their gold and jewellery. Local Latvians however say that the ordinary instruments of vandalism were, over a number of years, enough to do the trick. Russians were responsible, they say, often veterans, settled in the area after the Soviet reconquest in 1944.

Standing in the litter of the cemetery, beside the ruined church, I well understood the fury Balts feel when confronted by the damage to their culture and traditions inflicted under Soviet rule. Indeed I think that the welcome given to me at Mežotne and our other former estates had less to do with any past affection for my family – or even with the hope of hard currency – than with delight at finding any symbol or relic of a non-Soviet past, a sort of human mnemonic for the revival of memories buried by history.

In the first years of Soviet rule, Mežotne suffered through having some of the richest land in Latvia, and therefore the richest peasants. Many were deported to Siberia, their places taken by Russians. In this area, one of the elements of the attempt to reclaim land owned before 1940 is the desire to evict some of the Russians. This would appear to be a motive for the suggestion that Lievens should reclaim the steward's house where my great uncle lived after the main property was confiscated by the Latvians in 1920, and which is now occupied by Russian veterans and their families. The house and farm are solidly built, but today their walls are crumbling and peeling, the yards surrounded by rickety chicken-wire and piled with rubbish. But although some of those who live there now must have been responsible for destroying our cemetery, I find it difficult to feel hatred for them. These ill-dressed, depressed-looking people, the older ones bent by work and bloated by poor food, the children filthy and often seemingly diseased, do not have the air of victors. They evoke contempt but also a measure of pity.

Apart from sheer joy in vandalism, one motive for the destruction of the cemetery might have been that German soldiers are also buried there, both from the First World War and from the German campaign against the Bolsheviks and Latvians in 1919. A few names can still be read: Theodor Wagner, 3rd Jaegers, 30th August 1915 (the action in which the Russians commemorated in the park lost their lives); a certain Potzsch, 7th Grenadiers, no Christian name, 28th April 1919. In 1944, the next generation of German soldiers used the eighteenth-century Church tower as an artillery-spotting position, and it was shelled and largely destroyed by the Soviet army. The walls of the Church are pocked and pitted from what was obviously a very fierce fight. Oddly enough, a Major Sukhenko, who fought in that battle and captured the palace, was later responsible for its restoration, first as an agricultural research institute, now as a museum.

In view of the blood-soaked history of the locality, a war museum might have been appropriate, but there are already too many of these in Latvia. Instead an effort is being made to recreate the luxurious furnishings of the interior – luxury which in the past, of course, aroused only justifiable fury and envy in the local Latvian peasantry. To them the thought of Latvia making a museum out of the house of their German masters would have seemed the height of absurdity.

In addition to my own connections and resulting prejudices, there is the question of the balance of attention paid by this book to the different nationalities of the region. Several Balts to whom I showed the manuscript felt that I had paid an inordinate amount of attention to the Lithuanian Poles and Jews, now few in number. A core argument of this book, however, is that the Baltic is an area of mixed cultures in which historically a number of different peoples have had a place. Neither in the Baltic nor indeed anywhere else should a history of the dominant (or aboriginal) nationality be allowed to masquerade as a history of the area and all the peoples within it. A history of the Poles is different from a history of Poland, or ought to be, and the same is true for Lithuania. Furthermore, the Poles and Jews of Lithuania, and their descendants, have made contributions to world culture which at least equal those of the indigenous Baltic peoples. These contributions must also be explained not in national isolation (as is usually the case with Jewish approaches to the Litvak tradition) but in the context of the other peoples living in the area.

I concede, however, some disproportion in the discussion of the three Baltic republics. Latvians and Estonians may well feel that too much space is given to Lithuania, and that judgements which should properly be made only about Lithuania have been extended to the region as a whole. There may be some truth in this. The Lithuanians, with their emotional rhetoric and grand gestures, their greater extremism but also their greater readiness to make sacrifices, have indeed tended to elbow their more stolid neighbours out of the limelight. But what to do? This is the way it has been in the history of the Baltic over the past few years. Many people, East and West, have tried to subdue the Lithuanians. No-one has succeeded.*

---

* Concerning my descriptions of national character, some Estonians may feel that my portrait of their nation is frivolous and biased. All the Estonians whom I have consulted however have agreed that my portrait of the Lithuanians is entirely accurate; the Lithuanians feel the same way in reverse. It would appear, then, that I can at least be sure of pleasing all of my Baltic audience some of the time.

A Note on Names and Spellings

Names and the spelling of names are often the single most bitterly controversial part of works on ethnically diverse areas, because they are used as badges of national, political and cultural allegiance and control. Therefore a note on how I have used names is necessary. If my approach seems confusing, this is quite intentional. I wanted to bring home the complications of this area, not to confirm people in simplifications.

I have used personal names in their Baltic nominative grammatical case. In Latvian names, this means that I have retained the final 's' which the Balts, often to the intense irritation of foreigners, add to every male personal name (see Chapter 5, n. 16), and the 'a' in the feminine ending. In one case, that of Soviet Interior Minister Boris Pugo (Boriss Pugos), I have omitted the 's', because his main activity in the period in question was outside the Baltic, and it is by the Russian form that he was best known in the West.

Things become complicated in the case of the local minorities, and of Baltic emigrés. In the case of the minorities, I have used their national form, except where, as with Mavriks Vulfsons (Wulfsohn) or Irena Veisaité (Weiss) or Andrejs Pantelējevs (Panteleyev), they themselves use the Baltic form. In the case of Baltic emigrés, I have used the form they themselves use when writing in English.

Concerning towns: in the main body of the book, I have used the present standard form in the official national language, even when the town concerned has in the past been known in English by a different name: thus Vilnius and Klaipeda, not Vilna and Memel.

The only exception is in the sections on the Poles and the Jews. Here, it seemed only fair and correct to use their forms of the names concerned: thus in the Polish section I have spoken of Wilno, and in the Jewish section Vilna. In the case of the Jews, it is the Vilna and Kovno Ghettoes, not those of Vilnius and Kaunas, which have acquired a tragic meaning in the English language. Some Lithuanians might wish that no-one but Lithuanians had ever lived in these towns, and that no-one had ever called these cities by anything but their Lithuanian names, and would like their other names to be forgotten – but I do not feel inclined to fall in with their wishes.

An exception to the exception is, however, the section on my own ancestral community, the Baltic Germans. Here, as a matter of courtesy, I have used the current local form, not the traditional German one. Thus Tallinn and Tartu, not Reval and Dorpat. Oddly enough, in the Baltic Russian section it is not necessary to change the names, because under Soviet rule, the old Russian imperial forms were abandoned and the names were given in their local form in the cyrillic alphabet. Thus Vilnius is now called in Russian Vilnius, not Vilna.

A curious example is a town in eastern Latvia, Daugavpils, a name meaning the 'town on the river Daugava'. In the Middle Ages, it briefly received the name of Borisoglebsk (after the two Orthodox saints) when it fell under Slavonic rule. The Germans called it Dünaburg, 'Düna' being their name for the Daugava. Under Polish rule, it was renamed Dvinsk, since Dvina is the Slavonic form of the Daugava, and the Russians used it when they annexed the town in the late 18th century. So the Latvian, German, Polish and Russian forms all meant the same thing. However when the town, along with the rest of Latvia, was annexed by the Soviet Union in 1940 and 1944, Moscow went on calling it in Russian by its Latvian form of 'Daugavpils', even while at the same time conducting an immigration policy which eventually resulted in an 87 per cent Russian-speaking population.

This appears to have been part of a general policy of flattering Baltic sensibilities in certain symbolic areas, while undermining their position in important ones (see also Chapter 7, n. 14). This, together with a complete ignorance of local history on the part of the Russian immigrants, led to their still calling it Daugavpils in 1990, though they insisted that it was a Russian town. Some did not know that it had ever been called Dvinsk. It is unlikely that this would still be the case today, thanks to historical propaganda by local Russian nationalists in the local press.

In the case of towns it is difficult, but not impossible, to achieve a satisfactory system of names, because (except in brief periods like 1914–21 or 1939–45) they do not change their character too quickly. In the case of political groups, finding a satisfactory system is at present almost impossible, because the collapse of Communism is producing ever new political organisms. Politicians align and re-align themselves month by month, and words like 'Communist' and 'Nationalist' fly about, confusing not just Western policy-makers but the local participants, who are equally at sea about what sort of political creatures they themselves really are and what they should be called.

The development of half-way satisfactory naming systems will have to wait for the owl of Minerva. When the Soviet Revolution is finished, and stretched out on a table for the historians to work on, it will be possible to start imposing systems of classification. They will be artificial, but useful. For the moment, any names given will have to be provisional. In the course of writing this book, I have developed my own system, so there may well be inconsistencies. For these I apologise.

One example of the power of names is the word 'nationalist'. At the third Lithuanian Sajūdis Congress in November 1991, I was bitterly criticised by parliamentary Deputy Chairman Bronius Kuzmickas for translating the 'Tautininkai' party (then closely allied to the Sajudis) into English as 'Nationalists'. He was both wrong and right. Wrong, because there is no other appropriate translation of the word into English, because it is so translated by all reputable Lithuanian emigré historians and because, in any case, these are nationalists, by all the common definitions of this name. And he was right because the word 'nationalist', now more than ever, has come to have an overwhelmingly negative connotation in the English language and most of the Western world. In English a distinction is drawn between good 'patriots' and bad 'nationalists'. This distinction is to some extent a legitimate one, though not for the reasons usually given.

In Britain, America and France, for historical reasons, national loyalty has to a greater or lesser degree detached itself from the concept of ethnic 'nation' and attached itself instead to certain national institutions and traditions. In the Baltic states, however, there has simply not been the time or the historic opportunity for national institutions and loyalties to develop separately from the concept of the ethnic nation. The nations concerned were created in ethnic struggles, their whole *raison d'être* is an ethnic one. In these circumstances, 'patriotism' in a non-ethnic sense can hardly exist.

Again, because of the small size and resonance of the Baltic linguistic nations, they do not attract that version of non-ethnic attachment to the national language and culture from people of different nationality and outside its borders that has been enjoyed at different times by Britain, France, Russia, the German-speaking empires, Iran and China (for the case of the Jews and the Russian language, see Chapter 6). The only reflection of this in the Baltic is the admiration that many local Russians feel for higher Baltic standards of 'civic culture' and general behaviour, because these are held to be more Western.

In recent years therefore, local people of other nationalities who have supported the national independence struggles have done so either out of a sense of historical justice, or from political opportunism, or out of an aspiration towards general Western standards of democracy, civility, and prosperity. In only a tiny number of cases have they done so out of loyalty to the local majority nation – and in most of these the attachment is one of blood or marriage.

The Baltic national independence movements have therefore also been nationalist movements, and must be described as such. Any negative feelings this may awake should be qualified by an awareness of how, in a post-communist context, nationalism alone can awaken cynical and disillusioned peoples to a spirit of sacrifice and common purpose. It is perhaps also the only force which can return a sense of tradition and roots and local culture to people who have lived under a materialist 'internationalism' of the most grey, shoddy, soulless and banal kind.

Within the former national movement, how should one name the various political forces now making up the Baltic political scene? The question refers particularly to the 'Right', which often bears little resemblance to Right-wing parties as understood in the West. The word 'conservative' has been applied, not unreasonably, to those communist and military figures who wanted to preserve the old communist system and Soviet state more or less unchanged. One could also call some of them 'reactionaries', since they simply reacted against the reformists and nationalists without coming up with any new ideas of their own. They were not however homogenous, and their divisions have now become apparent in Russian politics both in the Baltic and in Moscow itself.

Even in the Baltic the pro-Soviet forces have included convinced Marxist-Leninists, non-Russian Soviet imperialists, Russian nationalist imperialists and members of local minorities who were not especially attached to any of these positions but simply feared Baltic and other majority nationalisms. Some 'Right-wing' Balts would also now call themselves 'conservatives', although (with exceptions like the Fatherland alliance in Estonia) their economic ideology is rarely purely free-market. In the past Moscow referred to them as 'radical nationalists', and this term has also been used by Western commentators, including some very sympathetic to the Baltic national movements.*

What characterises all such people is not so much radicalism as

---

* e.g. Marianna Butenschön *Estland, Lettland, Litauen: Das Baltikum auf dem langen Weg in die Freiheit* (Munich, 1992).

'restorationism'. They are committed to restoring as far as possible the forms of the Baltic States as they existed prior to Soviet annexation in 1940, including a return to their former ethnic balances and social structures. This, however, makes them radicals as far as existing Soviet and post-Soviet conditions are concerned; and it would not be the first time that a revolution had been carried out in the name of a restoration. Therefore I have stuck with the term 'radical', albeit with reservations.

In relation to Latvia and Estonia, I have called groups or individuals 'radical nationalists' if they rejected the existing legislative bodies and constitutions, derived from those of the Soviet Union. This means, in Estonia, that after the adoption of the new constitution in June 1992, the term 'radical' has not been used for Right-wing nationalists, but reserved for the small group which continues to regard the constitution of 1938 as legitimate. Within Latvia, by contrast, during the period studied and described in this book, large nationalist groups rejected the existing, provisional constitution, and may reject any future one which involves the enfranchisement of large numbers of local Russian 'immigrants'; so I have described those as 'radicals'. For Lithuania, I have adopted an even simpler test, though not a very scientific one: anyone more nationalist than Vyautas Landsbergis qualifies as a 'radical' in my book.

1

The Shape of The Land

'Winds whip. Winds beat.
Riga is silent.
Indifference? Obtuseness? Cowardice?
Do not ask. You'll get no answer.
Only the transitory has to shout;
Has to justify itself; to prove.
The eternal can keep silent.'

> Vizma Belševica,
> Latvian poetess under Soviet rule

Marsh and Forest

Travellers from the West should approach Latvia and Estonia by sea, and watch as the spires of Riga and Tallinn rise out of the Daugava (Dvina) River and the Gulf of Finland. Approaching the Lithuanian capital, Vilnius, the traveller also has the impression of being carried on vast dark green waves, but the sea is one of trees, forests mounted on rolling hills. By making this approach, modern visitors follow the routes taken by medieval traders and conquerors who brought the Baltic states into the orbit of the Latin West. Like them, the visitors of today may find the sea approach to Latvia and Estonia easier, for reasons more to do with culture.

For good and evil, the sea, and the great rivers, opened the Latvians and Estonians to the West, to conquest and plunder but also to more direct cultural influence. Lithuania, with little coastline or access to the sea, was protected but also isolated by its forests and marshes. Many of the profound differences between the three states stem from this difference in geographical position. The Baltic was once, and may again be, one of the great waterways of civilisation, but the landscapes which border its Eastern shore are surprisingly wild, even today. The glaciers of the last ice age left behind a huge number of lakes and swamps. The first chapter of the first volume of *Truth and Justice*, the monumental series of novels by Estonia's most famous novelist, A. H. Tammsaare, begins with the unsticking of a bogged cow from a marsh.[1] The swampiness of the country led to a feature of past warfare in the Baltic, recorded by

1

medieval chroniclers. In Western Europe the campaigning season ran from late spring to early autumn, after which the armies went into 'winter quarters'. The German crusaders who invaded the area of the present Baltic States in the thirteenth century were however forced to adapt to local conditions, and fight in summer, when some of the marshes were dry, and in winter, when they were frozen over and could be crossed by the heavily armoured German knights.[2]

The lakes and marshes are the result of large quantities of rain. Even the Germans thought Baltic weather notoriously foul, and 'Courland weather' used to be a byword for wind and rain. For farmers, the rain provides excellent grazing for cattle – the Baltic States produced a large part of the cattle produce of both the Russian Empire and the former Soviet Union – and then washes away the earth roads which take the milk and meat to town. Frequently the dampness gathers itself into mists and fogs, producing an extremely high incidence of tuberculosis and rheumatic diseases, but also giving birth to legends and curious visual effects. When it is not raining, the light of the Baltic States is changeable, sometimes offering a sober clarity, sometimes a freshly washed limpidity which brings out the delicate colours of the countryside and of the painted houses in the old cities of the region.

The Baltic light has been a source of inspiration in Baltic folklore as well as for modern writers. I have occasionally caught glimpses of this myself, as when one time, driving from Riga to Vilnius, I stopped at first light in a forest. The hidden sun turned the mist into an extraordinary blue haze, like the deep sea in a fable, out of which the trees emerged as ghosts or placid sea-monsters. On another occasion, in the lovely forests on the northern coast of Estonia, I found myself walking behind a wagon piled with green hay. Horse and driver were both half-asleep, and as the green mound moved slowly through patches of light green sunlight and deep green shade, I found myself reminded of those migratory hills and other natural features which play so large a part in Estonian folklore. Their movements are often explained by the action of the giant 'Son of Kalev' (see Chapter 5). Baltic summers are not often very hot, but the dampness of the climate can make them unpleasantly humid. The summer of 1992 was the hottest since records began. The winters too are milder than they used to be, a development attributed by some to the 'Greenhouse Effect'. It is several years now since the Daugava River at Riga froze over, and this used to be a regular occurrence.

October 1992 however also saw the heaviest late autumn blizzards in living memory: for brief spells, winter can be very severe. Every year brings its crop of drunks frozen to death by the roadside. In the winter of 1991, the bitter cold gave an extra aspect of courage and determination to the masses of people standing outside the Baltic parliaments, ready to block with their lives an attack by Soviet troops. For me, the sight of those unarmed civilians, of all ages and conditions, huddled round their watch-fires in the snow remains the most heroic image of the Baltic struggle for independence. Baltic rain and snow also feed the forests, an extension of those of the Great Russian Plain, and which used to stretch from there to the Atlantic. Walking among the trees, it is possible to imagine oneself in one endless wood, through which a squirrel could go from tree to tree all the way from the Baltic to the Urals. A Latvian poet writes of

> the hissing desolation of the pine and birch forests through whose paths magicians and witches crept, and where the sons of kings, turned into stags, broke the branches on their way . . . These tales told of hills, the only places where the soil survived the floods. Around them, the forest snored, drowned in the swamps, a forest which had sunk into the souls of the people with its devils and superstitions.[3]

Most forests are mixed, with every variety of northern tree. Some species, like the oak, are traditionally sacred. All have their own legend attached: thus the aspen is a lake-princess shaking permanently with fear as a punishment for having betrayed her father. As you proceed northwards through Latvia into Estonia, the rural population gets even thinner as the soil gets poorer, and these mixed forests give way to pine. A quarter of Lithuania, and more than forty per cent of Latvia and Estonia are covered with forest. The woodlands have in fact grown considerably under Soviet rule, almost doubling in Estonia, as farms abandoned or destroyed under collectivisation have returned to the wilderness – a curious, and almost eerie thing to observe in a part of Europe.

Forestry plays a key part in the rural economies of all three states, and carpentry is the most striking of all the Baltic folk-arts. Wooden furniture is one of the few manufactured products that the Balts have so far succeeded in selling to the West. In Lithuania, love of woodworking is especially apparent, and has helped to protect local traditions – and the very appearance of the Baltic States – from the grey, dead hand of Soviet mass-produced culture.

Love of nature, and most especially of forests and trees, is the key to much of Baltic culture, both traditional and modern. The first major nineteenth-century work of Lithuanian poetry, the *Grove of Anykščiai* by Antanas Baranauskas,[4] described a forest, used it as a symbol of the Lithuanian nation, and lamented the inroads of woodcutters in the pay of foreign landlords. Sometimes this goes rather far; the Latvian exile poet Gunārs Saliņš wrote to a fellow Latvian poet:

> And when you arrive in bare New York
> You will be of one mind with us:
> It has to be forested[5]

Baltic soft-core pornographers also seem affected by this general spirit, and like to place their women in forests. The more artistic ones sometimes give them trees for heads, or bushes for legs. In the animist religions of the Baltic that preceded the Crusades, trees, as living things, were considered to have their own spirits and to share in divinity. Medieval writers, harking back naturally to classical models, described Baltic tree-spirits as dryads. Most of the specific beliefs connected with the trees have now vanished, or are only vaguely echoed in folk-songs. Still in the countryside, you can often see how an oak has been left untouched in the middle of a field cleared for crops; sometimes at its foot will be a bunch of flowers. Lithuanian peasants believe that to stand at the foot of an oak will cure headaches and depression, with other trees providing remedies for their own specific diseases.

The creation of the modern Baltic national cultures by the national intelligentsias of the nineteenth century was marked by a clear return to this tradition of pagan nature-worship, especially in Lithuania and Latvia; it survives today, together with holistic philosophies derived from it. During the unusually early blizzards of October 1992, when the weight of snow on the leaves brought down many trees, my assistant heard one old Lithuanian woman say to another;

> You know, on All Souls Day we go to the cemeteries to light candles for those buried there; but what about all those who were killed in the fields and forests? [a reference to the dead of the partisan wars] We ought to pray to them as well. Because they can't rest, it is their spirits which are causing the snow and breaking the trees.

One of the most common Estonian sayings goes, 'Shit quickly, the bear is coming!', often shortened to simply 'the bear is coming!'. This emphasises the traditional importance of the animal in popular imagination, and indeed there is archaeological evidence of ancient bear-worship. Today, however, bears are very rare. Wolves are more common, and once a year or so, if too many sheep have been attacked, farmers in parts of northern Lithuania make a sweep through the woods to catch the predators. Deer are plentiful, elk and moose rather less so, and very occasionally in Lithuania it is possible to catch sight of a wild bison.

Apart from the omnipresent crows, wildfowl are abundant – especially herons and other waders, not surprisingly in view of all the water. Noblest of the Baltic birds are the storks, surprisingly large and exotic-looking creatures for such a landscape. The loud clacking of their beaks, often done by two storks in a kind of duet, is a frequent surprise. These birds seem to have had some totemic significance for the ancient Balts, and today it is believed that they bring good luck and their faithfulness to their partners is generally admired. Farmers like to have a nest of storks near their houses, and will hang a cartwheel in a tree to encourage them to build on it.

Even without bears and wolves, the forests themselves can be frightening, if only for their size. Today, most of the Lithuanian frontier with Byelorussia still runs through great forests. In August 1991 I drove past the Lithuanian border post at Lavoriškės, on the edge of the forest, and on into Byelorussia, looking for the first Byelorussian police post. Neither set of guards had any intention of living alone in the forest, and it was almost thirty kilometres before we came to the Byelorussian post – surely the widest no-man's-land in Europe.

The woods have always been a refuge for fugitives and rebels of every kind. During the Second World War, they sheltered in turn Poles fighting the Germans, Balts escaping arrest and deportation by Stalin's authorities, Jews and Communists fleeing from the Germans and Balts, and Baltic partisans – the 'Forest Brothers' – fighting their stubborn, ten-year war against renewed Soviet rule after 1945. Especially in the gloomy pine-forests around Vilnius, where so many of all the different sides are buried, their ghosts still seem present. In a field near Šiauliai, in northern Lithuania, a former Forest Brother, Mr Viktoras Snuolis, pointed along the forest verge:

> We spent a long time hiding in that forest. Over there, that is where my family's house used to stand before it was abandoned during collectivisation. We would come back there from the forest to eat, every now and again. And over there, that is where my father was shot, at the edge of the forest, at the foot of a tall birch. He had heard that they were going to sweep the forest for us, and had come to warn us, but the Strybai [Soviet auxiliary troops] were already cordoning off the forest. Later, we were on our way home to ask what had happened. We saw a man lying there, and it was my father.

A sign of the wildness of this country is that even after the few surviving partisan units gave up after Stalin's death, a few determined or desperate souls went on living in the forests, fed by local people, and intermittently hunted by the security forces. This is also of course a supreme testimony to Baltic stubborness and endurance, one of the guiding themes of this book.

The behaviour of the Forest Brothers resembled the heroic determination of the hold-outs from the Japanese Army, hiding in the jungles for decades after the Emperor's surrender – with the difference that, as I shall point out later, there were substantial patriotic, as well as emotional, reasons for the Balts to hold out. The very last of the Forest Brothers, the Estonian August Sabe, was finally cornered by the KGB in a forest in South Estonia only in 1978. By then seventy years old, he refused to surrender, and drowned in a lake while trying to swim to freedom.[6]

The Man-Made Landscape

The smallness of the population of the Baltic States has meant that their natural landscape has not suffered too badly from Soviet rule, or indeed industrialisation in general. There are of course exceptions, such as the oil-shale mining area of North East Estonia, and Saldus, a really appalling aluminium-producing town in Latvia, but they are relatively few. The forests appear in generally good shape, although the threat of acid rain, especially in Estonia (because of the oil-shale-fired power stations) is a concern. Much more serious is the pollution of the rivers, and especially the great Daugava (Dvina or Duna), which flows through Riga carrying a great load of pollutants and untreated sewage. For years now, this has made bathing unsafe at the lovely resort of Jūrmala. Scandinavian efforts are underway to clean up the Daugava as part of a general ecological programme in the Baltic. This could succeed, even though much of the pollution originates not in Latvia but upstream in Byelorussia and Russia. The situation on much of the coast was summed up with brutal clarity by a Lithuanian newspaper report:

> Swedish ecologists on board the ship *Sunbeam* . . . have explored Malku Bay near the naval dockyards of Klaipeda. They have announced that the bottom of the bay is covered by several metres of mud made up of polluting matter, in which there is no sign of life.[7]

If on land, the natural landscape appears at least superficially intact, this can hardly be said of the man-made landscape, even or perhaps especially in the countryside. Collectivisation and almost half a century of Soviet rule did its work all too well. One of the signs are the low mounds, surrounded by small clumps of trees and bushes, that one can often see in the fields. They are the sites of farmhouses belonging to refugees and deportees, or simply abandoned as farmers moved to the cities rather than lose their independence and work on the collective farms. During the great wave of deportations in March 1949, it is estimated that the number of inhabited farms in Estonia dropped by 19,000 in a few weeks, from a total of only about 140,000 farms before 1940.

. Today, as in Russia, farmers' houses over wide areas of Latvia and Lithuania (much less so in Estonia) huddle together in villages, much more than in the past, a visible contrast which symbolises a deep and destructive social and economic change. The villages themselves are clean and well-kept by Soviet standards, but have little that would tempt one to live there. The fields around the villages are often huge, and in winter give the impression almost of deserts. Crawling across them are lumbering pieces of collective farm machinery, too big for the small private farms which need to be restored. Other pieces of machinery lie about, rusting in the rain, beside empty barns.

In Lithuania, unlike the other two states, much of the farmwork, and even the ploughing, is still done by sturdy Baltic ponies – indeed their use seems to be increasing, as petrol shortages get worse and the new private farmers find themselves unable to use tractors. Baltic horses are usually well-kept, well-fed animals, much more encouraging than the wretched nags often seen in Russia, but the Lithuanian carts they pull are among the simplest vehicles known to man, like horse-troughs on wheels with a plank for the driver to sit on. Social life is limited, especially in winter, when driving on the icy tracks to the nearest town can be a real hazard. As everywhere in the former Union as in the West, much of life centres around the television. Here Estonia and southern Lithuania are at an advantage, since they can receive Finnish and Polish television stations respectively. Television also continues to be a source of Russian cultural and linguistic influence, because it is generally more interesting than the Baltic channels themselves.

The monotony of village life has driven many young people to the towns, resulting in a rural population which is in general too old for the new demands which privatisation and commercial farming place on it. But since life in the new suburbs can also be tedious – and television is the same everywhere – the Baltic governments are hoping that unemployed urban youth will return to farm the countryside. The hope is powered in part by a sentimental-nationalist association of Baltic culture with the land, but is helped by the fact that very many urban Balts come from farming families and have a close connection with the countryside. Moreover, as food shortages in the towns intensify, there are signs that people are indeed moving back to the land, although whether they will do more than simply support themselves and their immediate families is not yet clear.

Some elements of traditional rural culture survived collectivisation and Soviet rule. On days of religious festivals, throughout the period of Soviet rule, people would celebrate and visit each other; as far as ordinary farmers were concerned, the Communists made little attempt to stop them. Instances of older traditions of ritual hospitality also survive, especially in Lithuania, although their original religious or mythological significance is lost. Particularly interesting in Lithuania are the practices connected with bees and the sharing of honey, which have been analysed by the great Lithuanian-French semiologist Algirdas Julien Greimas. Greimas has suggested that 'bee-friendships', or brotherhoods, may have been the origin of the Lithuanian military formations which conquered what is now Byelorussia and the Ukraine in the middle ages. He writes that, until the twentieth century, honey was not part of the money economy but was given to friends and neighbours only, or for special purposes, such as to beggars at Christmas or women after giving birth.[8] For Lithuanians bees are associated not simply with fertility and hard work but also with loyalty and decency. The sharing of honey was an act of great ritual significance. A grandmother in the village of Rimšoniai, Eugenija Urmonaitiene, used, before she got too old, to keep a different hive of bees for each of her children; she would host meals at which the honey would be shared between them and with close family friends. *Bičiuliai*, or 'bee-friends', is still a word for especially close friends, though no longer often used.

Traditions such as these form the rich cultural substrata underlying the greater part of the modern Baltic cultures and national identities. Even when not immediately apparent, they are what gives these cultures their uniqueness and charm. They are not, however, the first thing that strikes one on seeing most Baltic villages today. Indeed Baltic emigrés who fled before the Soviet advance in 1944 and return to their old villages from America or other places of exile are often appalled by the changes; even if their confiscated property is returned (a burning question, in the villages and in national politics) very few are likely to come back to the countryside to live, except for brief holidays. This already causes considerable tension since local farmers risk becoming the tenants of virtual absentee landlords.

The golden glow of nostalgia plays a role in this comparison with the past, which in rural Lithuania between the wars was often grim enough. But reading Western accounts of Latvian and Estonian agriculture in the independence period, with their solid commercial farmers, flourishing co-operatives, and thousands of well-built, prosperous new farmsteads on the former noble estates, the changes for the worse are all too clear. In general, the damage done to the Baltic independent farmer may prove one of the longest-lasting and most difficult to repair of all the legacies of Communism. All the same, in the countryside as in the towns, the Balts pay much more attention to appearances than do Russians. The houses and kitchen-gardens are better maintained and not surrounded by rubbish, the interiors are clean, though there are of course major variations within the Baltic, with the Estonians regarding the Latvians and Lithuanians as squalid and the others regarding the Estonians as obsessively house-proud.

Architecture in the countryside is usually simple, whether it is the attractively painted traditional wooden houses, the new collective-farm housing estates in brick, or the ugly, functional office buildings. With few exceptions the only architecture of any distinction consists of the churches, and the surviving manor houses of the former nobility. In

Lithuania the remaining churches stand proudly in the centre of villages, symbolising the continued and now renewed centrality of the Catholic Church in national life. In Latvia and Estonia, they are more often set apart, often on what used to be the estates of the former German nobility. This symbolises the fact that in these countries, Protestant Christianity was a foreign graft which, although it had a tremendous influence, never took hold of national culture in the way of the Catholic Church in Lithuania. The churches and manors often have to be sought out in patches of woodland, where only the unusual height and splendour of the trees tells you that they were once parks.

On the outskirts of many villages in Lithuania stand the traditional high wooden crosses, more and more of which are being erected each year. Whether these should be called Christian is doubtful; they are clearly descended from some sort of pagan totem pole, and are elaborately festooned with carved suns, moons and a variety of pre-Christian symbols and figures, a great opportunity for local craftsmen to show their skill. This integration of the pagan and the Catholic tradition helps explain the greater hold of the Church on the national imagination.

The Baltic Cities

Throughout the last century and into this one, most towns in the Baltic were rooted economically in the surrounding countryside, trading posts where grain and animals were brought to be sold, and people would come to buy basic goods. In Lithuania, from the late middle ages to 1941, they were inhabited largely by Jews, the legal restrictions on whom meant that before the present century, there was little growth of civic government or tradition. Few towns had much wealth, though some are ancient, and a few cities of genuine European stature. Greatest of all was Riga, the Hanseatic city which has traditionally been the entrepôt not only for what are now the Baltic States but for much of Russia and Poland as well. As the Latvian folk-song had it,

> Brothers, we will go to Riga,
> In Riga life is good.
> In Riga golden dogs bark,
> And silver cocks crow.*

The universities of Tartu (Dorpat, Yuryev), founded by the Swedes in 1632, and of Vilnius (Wilno, Vilna), founded by the Polish-dominated

---

* In Lithuanian, however, according to Dr Kavolis, 'to drive to Riga' used to be colloquial for 'to vomit'.

Catholic Church in 1579, also had an important place in European thought, and attracted scholars from all over Europe. The philosophies of Tartu and Vilnius universities were however, until a few decades ago, not formulated in the Estonian and Lithuanian languages. Both began in Latin; Tartu continued in German, the language of the dominant community, until partial Russification was imposed at the end of the nineteenth century. Vilnius University became one of the greatest centres of Polish thought and letters. This reflects the fact that none of the old cities on the eastern shore of the Baltic were founded or built by the Balts, with the partial exception of Vilnius – founded by Grand Duke Gediminas – but largely constructed by Poles and Jews. Riga and Tallinn, although on the sites of previous Baltic settlements, took their historic shape under German rule, after the conquest of the region by the Crusaders in the thirteenth century.

Until the expansion of the economy in the nineteenth century brought tens of thousands of peasants to the towns, the majority of the population of Tallinn and Riga was also German. Latvians became the largest community in Riga in the late nineteenth century, outnumbering the Germans, Jews and Russians. By the 1960s, they had lost their superiority in the face of the massive Russian-speaking immigration which took place under Soviet rule.[9] In terms of population, Vilnius was a Polish-Jewish city until the Second World War, with Lithuanians a small minority. Tallinn acquired an Estonian majority over the Germans and Russians in the nineteenth century. Its Jewish population was less than five thousand. Today, it is evenly balanced between Estonians and Russian-speakers.

A traveller with a sense of history may well therefore in the Baltic cities be haunted by ghosts, not of individuals but of whole communities. Balts, and especially returning Baltic emigrés who fled before the Soviet onslaught of 1944, often remember those tens of thousands of Balts deported from the cities under Stalin, their houses and flats promptly taken over by Russians, and occupied by them today. Behind these images however are others, flickering as if on a super-imposed film: the Poles, who fled Vilnius after 1945; the Baltic Germans, evacuated on Hitler's orders after his pact with Stalin allowed Soviet Russia to swallow the region; and, above all, the annihilated Jews. It is easy to forget the Jews because their monuments were destroyed by the Germans, covered over by the Soviets, and deliberately forgotten by many Balts. The Poles and Baltic Germans are not so easy to forget, because they live on in the stones themselves. Old Tallinn, for example, is a jewel of North German and Scandinavian Gothic architecture, one of the finest in Europe. Under the name of Reval, it was founded by the Danish monarchy in 1219. Its Estonian name, Tallinn, comes from the words for 'Danish Fortress'.

The famous skyline of Tallinn is now marred by two discordant

Intourist hotels, but in the old city one can forget their presence. Still surrounded by walls and towers, its medieval architecture is austere, even grim. Old Tallinn, like so many medieval cities, was divided into two; the Domberg (Toompea), or citadel, housed the local headquarters of the crusading Order, the Livonian Knights (or the Royal Governor, in the periods during which the region was ruled by one or other of the Scandinavian monarchies), the cathedral and its bishop, and their retinues. Today, it contains the Estonian parliament and seat of government, an eighteenth-century pink palace around a medieval core. It is faced, and Toompea partly spoiled, by an enormous nineteenth-century Russian Orthodox Cathedral, a symbol of Russian Imperial rule. Its lurid green and ochre colouring clashes with the colour of the parliament building, and its knobbly, over-ornate design grates against the Domberg's simplicity. Tallinn is already on the route of many of the Baltic tour ships, and its Town Hall Square boasts an Indian restaurant and horse-drawn carriages. For the moment, however, the quiet cobbled streets of the Domberg, with their peeling walls and scaffolding, have a melancholy charm, appropriate for the citadel of a vanished order.

Not all ugliness is Soviet: in the centre but outside the main streets and squares, roads are lined with official or commercial buildings of the 1920s and 1930s, neo-brutalist in shades of black, grey and dark brown, depressing enough in themselves but worse in the long, dark winters, when few days escape from twilight before sinking back into night. It is astonishing that architects could have been so insensitive in an area where the delicate colours of the older houses surely indicate a desire of the inhabitants to do something to offset the Cimmerian greyness of the winters.

Tallinn was bombed by the Soviet airforce during the war, though only one section of the old city was destroyed. To see what the city escaped, one has to go to Narva, on the Russian border. Despite its precarious geopolitical location, this was once a larger port than Tallinn, with a large merchant community that included many Scots. Advancing from the opposite side of the Narva River, a Scottish artillery general in the Russian service captured it for Peter the Great, but it avoided serious damage. Narva was not so fortunate in 1944, when it was flattened during the Soviet advance from Leningrad. Of all its lovely gothic and baroque buildings, recalled in paintings and photographs, only the peach-coloured town-hall is still standing, its interior sadly battered by the Pioneers (the Soviet youth organisation) to whom it was given as a headquarters. The rest of Narva, apart from the fine medieval fortress, is the usual Soviet concrete desert, floating for much of the year on a sea of mud. It is now overwhelmingly inhabited by Russians.

The great surviving centre of the Baroque in this part of Europe is Vilnius, the Easternmost stronghold of the Catholic Church. The

11

rhetorically gesturing saints in its churches seem to be making statements of faith and defiance in the direction of the East. Vilnius has always been on a frontier of one sort or another. It is now in the extreme South East of the Lithuanian Republic, and for a while Soviet leaders hinted at the possibility of transferring it to Byelorussia to punish the Lithuanians for their attempts to leave the Union. Vilnius' geographical position and history produced a very mixed population, including Catholic Poles, Byelorussian Orthodox, and Jews (including a now tiny heretical sect called the Karaites) and Tartars, descended from the Grand Duke's Tartar bodyguard. Today the chief monuments to the Jews in the city once called the 'Jerusalem of Lithuania' are two large clear spaces in the middle of the huddled buildings of the Old Town: there stood the greater part of the Jewish Ghetto, dynamited by the Nazis. There are plaques on the walls of two streets down which the Jewish population was taken to be killed.

In contrast to the Estonians in Tallinn and the Latvians in Riga, Lithuanians in old Vilnius are usually ignorant of the history and legends attached to the streets where they live. The great majority of the Lithuanian population of Vilnius, like the Russians in Riga and Tallinn, moved to the city under Soviet rule. People from Kaunas, Lithuania's second city and its capital from 1918 to 1940, sometimes say dismissively of Vilnius that it is only 'Kaunas plus villages', because that is where its Lithuanian population originated. Around the remains of the Ghetto stretch the streets of the old city, a delightful maze of old houses and courtyards, mostly quite poor and plain but painted in lovely, faded colours of yellow, blue and light green. An English visitor compared one of them to a painting by de Chirico. Among them are the more ornate palaces of the old nobility, with Atlases and Caryatids propping up their gates. The fine architecture of much of Vilnius is not merely an asset for tourism, but can provide some fine offices for business. The new Stock Exchange is in a restored convent, the main computer shop in an eighteenth-century palace, and the Vilnius Youth Theatre in Count Tyszkiewicz's stables.

Vilnius and Tallinn, though very large for the size of their countries, still have some of the atmosphere of small towns. Riga, by contrast, is a major city, and once had almost the pretensions of a world city. Before 1914, Riga had by far the largest Russian population in the Baltic, as well as large numbers of Germans, Jews and western merchants, some of them from families established in the city for several generations. George Armitstead, the last Mayor of Riga before the First World War, came from an English merchant family, and by the river in the heart of the old city is a small Anglican Church, now a students' club.[10] Pre-1914 buildings stretch for miles from the city centre, a tribute to Riga's wealth under the Russian Empire, of which it was at times the biggest port. It

1   Riga, Latvia: characteristically ornate architectural decoration.

gives the present poverty of Riga, and the shabby condition of these huge, ornate apartment blocks, a sadder feel than does the state of the other Baltic capitals. Medieval Tallinn is so old that it has the right to be somewhat decayed; Vilnius, at least since the eighteenth century, was the centre of an impoverished and undeveloped region of Europe, and poverty there seems a natural condition, hallowed in literature (especially Yiddish and Polish) and by tradition. But the architecture of much of Riga has the depressing quality of a *grande bourgeoise* lady fallen upon evil days. With almost a million inhabitants, Riga also has many of the inconveniences of a big city, with very few of the advantages. In Tallinn and Vilnius, the decay of the public transport system and the lack of taxis is not so critical: at a pinch you can walk almost everywhere; not so in Riga.

But though Riga may lack the charm of the other capitals, it remains a fine city. Part of the old town is medieval, and contains some noble churches. The most famous of its medieval buildings, that of the 'Blackheads' Guild' (after their patron saint, the African warrior Saint Maurice), with its row of Gothic statues, was badly damaged during the last war. The Soviet regime demolished it, and on the site built an unattractive ensemble of buildings, including a blank-faced museum and brutalist monument to the Latvian Red Riflemen who played a key part in the Bolshevik victory in the Russian Civil War.*

The most distinctive architecture in Riga is however Art Nouveau, or rather Jugendstil, for its roots lie very clearly in Germany. If nothing else, Riga's Jugendstil architecture is wonderfully funny, full of fantastically shaped houses out of the brothers Grimm – like half-melted chocolate cakes – an astonishing variety of roofs set at increasingly impossible angles, large numbers of assorted animals and strikingly voluptuous female forms, mermaids and others; not your usual emaciated mermaids, but solid beer-drinking German ones, first cousins to the whale.

There is a famously strange example of Jugendstil eclecticism at number eight Elizabetes Street ('Kirov' under Soviet rule), which at roof level is neo-classical but by the time it reaches the street has become Aztec, though retaining the basically classical symbolism: the result is a pair of thoroughly confused-looking aztecised owls.

Riga's nickname was once 'The Paris of the Baltic' – though today Latvians admit this with only a wry smile or a curse at the results of

---

* There is talk now of demolishing this museum and rebuilding the Blackheads' House; but the official line on the Red Riflemen is still uncertain. On one hand they were Communists, but on the other they had a glorious military record, of which Latvia does not have an excess. So there is now a certain historiographic tendency to reclassify them as misguided patriots. One can go into the museum and check the labels on the exhibits, just to see which way the wind is blowing.

Soviet rule. It was always an exaggeration of course, but something of this atmosphere was certainly present when Graham Greene visited the city in the 1920s, and George Kennan a few years later. Then it was a leading Western listening post for Stalin's Soviet Union, and major centre of the Russian emigration, so with ruined artistic Russians to provide the entertainment, and Western – and Baltic – diplomats, businessmen and journalists to do the paying, life went on merrily, the city being known for its night-clubs and restaurants, as well as for its flourishing intellectual life.

Something of the intellectual life remains today, but little of the rest, though new Western hotels are hopefully blazing some sort of trail. None the less the memory of Riga as a cosmopolitan centre remains, and Katya Borschova, a Russian intellectual friend born and brought up in the city, declared that,

> I find it difficult to identify with Russia, because I have never lived there, and anyway I hate Russian chauvinist nationalism; but as a Russian, it would be difficult to identify wholly with Latvia even if the Latvians would allow me to do so. But I do love and identify with Riga, because even under Soviet rule, it has remained a cosmopolitan city, a city of many nationalities, but with its own old and unique character.[11]

Borschova's remark was of course directed partly against Latvian nationalism, which has never been altogether happy with the cosmopolitan flavour of the Latvian state capital, although many Latvian intellectuals also glory in its diversity and love it passionately. In the words of George Kennan:

> In addition to its more serious cultural amenities, Riga had a vigorous night-life, much in the Petersburg tradition . . . Riga was in many ways a minor edition of St Petersburg. The old Petersburg was of course now dead . . . but Riga was still alive.[12]

During my stay between 1990 and 1992, the only night-life was of the sort provided by the sleazy – and sometimes unintentionally amusing – cabaret in the Hotel Latvia, such as the adapted folk dance with the topless national costumes. Economic hardship also means that the dancers in such cabarets are sometimes trained ballet dancers and acrobats, who give superb performances. There were also of course some discos, the best in Riga being, supposedly, 'Robinsons' – so called because it sits on an island in the Daugava. The music and the company were cheerful enough, but to drink there was only coca-cola and vodka. Because Robinsons is heavily patronised by various kinds of criminal – 'the mafia', as they like to call themselves – trouble frequently flares.

As in so many areas, clubs and discos in Estonia have a much more modern feel. The 'Eeslitaal' basement in Tallinn even invited an African band to play on Midsummer Eve, 1992, and provided African, or Soviet-African food. The discrepancy will no doubt alter, as the new economic classes demand their entertainment. Stemming largely from the black market, and from the children of the Communist establishment, these are already to be seen all over the hotels and restaurants. Their strange costumes, both male and female, are always besprinkled with gold: gold watches, bracelets, sometimes gold-sequinned clothes – literally a *jeunesse dorée*.

In Estonia, national tendencies to restraint and lack of ostentation keep such display somewhat in check, and in Lithuania a tradition of national populism may do the same; but in the big port city of Riga, with its commercial traditions, bigger entrepreneurial class, and more chaotic politics, they have free rein. The consequences can be sharply divisive: in Riga, in January 1992, I saw a child beggar outside the door of a hard-currency restaurant, a phenomenon likely to increase, and more so than in either of the other Baltic capitals.

Kennan continues that:

> Riga had the advantages of a variegated and highly cosmopolitan cultural life: newspapers and theatres in the Lettish, German, Russian and Yiddish tongues and vigorous Lutheran, Roman Catholic, Russian Orthodox and Jewish religious communities. Throughout that region religion was still the common hallmark of nationality, so that if you asked a person who he was, he was apt to reply by telling you his religion rather than naming an affinity to any particular country. The politically dominant Letts, becoming increasingly chauvinistic as the years of their independence transpired, were concerned to put an end as soon as possible to all this cosmopolitanism, and eventually did succeed, by 1939, in depriving the city of much of its charm. Their efforts in this direction were of course completed in 1940, when the country was occupied by the Russians . . . and national chauvinism was punished in a way beyond its greatest deserts.

Today, the tension between the Russians and Russian-Jews who make up the majority of Riga's businessmen on one hand, and Latvian nationalist politicians on the other, is once again a major factor in Latvian politics. Much more dangerous however are the huge numbers of Russian and Russian-speaking proletarians brought in to staff the new Soviet factories. Out in the concrete dormitories where they live, life in general leaves much to be desired. Even without the ethnic factor the problem of what to do with the urban unemployed would be bad enough. The Baltic industrial capitals were built up as part of an integrated Soviet economy, and its collapse has left them economically stranded, and, to an extent, ethnically isolated from the republics in which they find themselves. The three capitals are also simply disproportionately large for the Baltic states. Vilnius, with 592,000 people, fits well enough into Lithuania, which has a population of some 3.7 million; but Tallinn with almost half a million inhabitants makes up almost a third of Estonia's population, and Latvia, where the Riga area holds a million people out of a total 2.7 million, is like a deep-sea creature with a monstrous head and an atrophied body. Riga's size made sense only when it was one of the greatest ports of a great empire. Today Riga, like all post-Soviet industrial cities, forms part of an endangered species, and no-one can say what it will look like ten years from now.

Peasant Peoples

It is difficult to avoid discussing questions of national character and identity in the Baltic States, because the Balts do it so often themselves. People construct stereotypes not simply when looking at other nations, but also in thinking about their own and, like self-fulfilling prophesies, self-images play an active role in shaping national behaviour.[13]

During the struggle for independence from Moscow, the obvious point that a peaceful approach was expected by the West, and that violence would play into Moscow's hands, was greatly strengthened by a feeling that 'Balts are not the same as other Soviet peoples; we do not resort to violence'. Balts themselves also used national character and tradition to explain the different approach to the independence struggle among the Baltic nations.

As self-aware nations, the Baltic States are barely a hundred years old and, as elsewhere, the growth of the political nation was inextricably linked to the creation of a national culture by the new national intelligentsia. Part of the process involved a ceaseless repetition of the features making up 'national character' and distinguishing it from that of neighbours and rulers.* Under Soviet rule, the effort to retain a separate national identity became even more difficult and acute. Today, the social pressure to conform to the national stereotype, to uphold the

---

* In the usual nineteenth-century fashion, this extended to a definition of what the nation concerned ought to look like, and the stress on conforming to the national norm of appearance lingers to this day. It is especially noticeable at the great festivals of folk-song and dance, regarded as tremendously important national symbols.

  In Lithuania and Estonia (the Latvians are such a mixture that there is less tendency in this direction), a clear effort is made to select blonde girls for the dance groups. A Lithuanian friend who had performed in one of these groups confirmed that this is so, and said that a dark-haired girl might be given blonde tresses. 'You know our Lithuanian ideal of beauty: blonde, blue-eyed, and, how do you say? Stout? Well-built?'

national image is pervasive and can be acute. The question 'is he Estonian enough?' has influenced a number of Estonian emigrés attempting to integrate into their parents' homeland. The outsider can have a thin time of it in Baltic societies.

The concern to preserve their separate characters at all costs is of course connected to the Balts' acute awareness of themselves as small nations ('Mini-nations', as they have been called) in a world dominated by large and powerful ones. The anxieties this produces were of course greatly increased by the Baltic experience between 1939 and 1944, the Soviet conquest, and mass Russian immigration. In the words of the Estonian translator Enn Soosaar (by no means a narrow or chauvinist figure),

> For centuries, Balts have had only two choices: to survive as nations or to merge into larger nations. You could say that we decided, subconsciously but collectively, to survive. So for us, nationalism is a mode of existence. In our position, you can't have the broad perspective of the English or the French; this would threaten your very existence. To survive, you must be nationalist.[14]

This acute sense of vulnerability appears in the first paragraph of the Latvian language law of 31 March 1992, where it is written that:

> Latvia is the only ethnic territory in the world which is inhabited by the Latvian nation. One of the main prerequisites for the existence of the Latvian nation and for the preservation and development of its culture is the Latvian language. During the last decades there has been a marked decrease in the use of Latvian in state affairs and social life. . . .

If there is one word that encapsulates the three Baltic national characters, it is phlegmatic; Balts themselves often trace this back to their climate. An Estonian emigré writer, Alexis Rannit, has summed up its effects on his people's character:

> The sudden laughter of Mediterranean man is seldom heard there, and all occurrences seem to be part of a slow, predestined ritual born of the measured movements of the fields and forests and of the rather calm, dispassionate sea. Grotesque imagery, maniacal ticks, jocularity, mannered caprice and other such species of humour are barely known in Estonian letters . . . There is a certain lightness in the [Estonian] humour of the absurd [but] here, of course, I am using the word 'lightness' in the Estonian sense. . . . Although it contains real tenderness, the Estonian 'lightness' is clearly of a heavier kind. . . .[15]

Rannit derives this aspect of Estonian 'humour' from the landscape, 'impassive, serene and sad'. The lack of indigenous jokes and anecdotes extends to the other Baltic States as well. Repeated requests to be told local jokes usually result only in hoary recycled Russian and Jewish ones, or curious antique riddles about farmers and geese.

This phlegmatic quality is also reflected in Baltic stoicism, a capacity for enduring oppression without completely surrendering to it, and for stubborn resistance. Very important is the fact that due to the destruction or assimilation of the Baltic élites by foreign rulers, until a hundred years or so ago virtually all Balts were peasants. Two generations before that, most had been serfs. The culture of the Balts was a peasant culture, and the new national intelligentsia was made up of peasants' sons and grandsons. This has led to the growth of a quite different culture, including a political culture, from that of the Poles or Georgians for example, whose national identity was defined above all by their petty nobility. One aspect of the difference is demonstrated in the attitude to hospitality: for the more noble, it is a matter of personal, familial and national honour, but also an expression of grandeur, one form of conspicuous consumption. Interestingly, this view persists in Lithuania, which is the only Baltic State with its own indigenous nobility, parts of which rediscovered their Lithuanian identity during the nineteenth century. Many other Balts by contrast retain something of the old peasant belief that a guest is someone who has to be watched closely lest he rape your daughter or steal your cow. A Lithuanian Jewish writer, Mark Zingeris, described this as 'the suspiciousness of a farmer, with his dog and his hunting rifle, in his farmhouse two miles from the nearest neighbour'. He added that due to the Soviet impact, this suspiciousness has spread everywhere, both with regard to people's politics and concerning anyone's relative economic success. As an old Lithuanian saying has it, 'every Lithuanian hopes that his neighbour's horse dies'.

In all three republics, peasant tradition has also led to an instinctive suspicion of capitalism, which of course has only been strengthened by the decades of Communist rule. In a sense the suspicion is not of capitalism, which everyone now accepts in principle, but of actual, physical, flesh-and-blood *Capitalists*. This is above all true in Lithuania, where until the Second World War, the overwhelming majority of capitalists were non-Lithuanian, and predominantly Jewish. Even in the emigration, according to a Lithuanian-American professor, a Lithuanian who opened a store was regarded as having done something rather dirty, un-Lithuanian and un-Christian.

Enemies of the Balts have always used their peasant past to mock them: in the words of a Jewish friend, speaking of the Estonians, 'centuries of bowing to every lord who came along, and accepting his whippings, does not make for a nation of heroes'. The unarmed crowds defending the Baltic parliaments against attack in January 1991 however showed no lack of courage, and what was most striking, and constituted a great glory of the Baltic independence struggle, was the fact that not even the younger and wilder elements resorted to violence against those local Russians who supported the Soviet military intervention. The reaction of other, 'nobler' societies in the face not simply of this provocation but of the decades of mass immigration which preceded it, would have been very different, and very dangerous.

In the early 1980s, street fights were apparently common between gangs of Estonian and Russian youths. But as the struggle for independence became a reality, young Estonians appeared to realise the seriousness of what was happening, and curb their natural instincts.[16] The leaders of the national movements stressed the need for restraint, and the people listened. This fundamental quality of restraint, pragmatism, and indeed decency in the Estonian character, conditions the policies of even some extreme-sounding politicians. It is extremely difficult to imagine the Estonians ever participating in pogroms.

The Estonian character as a nation seems to me to be summed up in their national anthem, a beautiful but grim and implacable-sounding Protestant hymn which they share with the Finns. Their spirit is also reflected in the ascetic beauty of the blue, black and white Estonian national flag. Cool, rational, organised, hard-working, and careful with money, they are a people who tend to command respect rather than love. The writer Jaan Kross has attributed their national survival to their 'cheerful scepticism'. They 'always doubt' he claims, 'the values being offered to them without becoming too dramatic about it'.[17]

Estonian political culture also contains a strong streak of legalism, and Estonians tend to justify their national positions in legal terms, whereas the Lithuanians are more inclined to emotional arguments. Estonian legalism has been strengthened by the years of internal opposition to Soviet rule when an obstinate (if only internal) insistence on the legal continuity of Estonian independence was one of the few things giving Estonian patriots hope and strength in a seemingly hopeless situation. Paradoxically, however, legalism has also been strengthened by Soviet culture, with its insistence on universally, absolutely, valid rules to the exclusion of considerations of humanity or indeed reality. In Soviet parlance, 'life' was something which had to be beaten over the head until it agreed to conform with the ideological norm. This legacy can be seen in the attitude of many Estonian intellectuals to the Russian 'immigrants' in the republic. Though personally humane, some Estonians are capable of speaking with considerable ruthlessness of the means needed to drive this population out of Estonia. Whether they would really act with such ruthlessness is much more questionable.

Of the Baltic peoples the Estonians are, however, the ones whose present attitudes and culture are closest to those of Western Europe. There are historical reasons, but in recent decades the crucial factor has been Estonia's closeness to Finland, and the fact that Estonians can easily understand the Finnish language. While the Latvians, Lithuanians and other Soviet peoples depended for their impression of the outside world on a handful of Western radio-stations, frequently jammed, and listened to only by a small minority, most Estonians already had access to Finnish television. Visiting Tallinn from other parts of the Soviet region in recent years, I was always struck by two main impressions: intellectually, it is like finding oneself in the cold, clear, bracing air of the Scandinavian mountains. For a while it is a great relief. Later, however, you begin to notice a certain chill in the emotions; they turn blue, go numb, and one begins to fear they will die off altogether, and you plunge with equal relief back into the emotional stews of Russian or Jewish life. Central Tallinn has for a long time now looked more Western than the other Baltic cities, with more Western-style shops and visitors, and far more Estonians in Western dress. Tallinn old town is fast coming to resemble a tourist area somewhere in Central Europe, and is totally unlike anywhere else in the former Soviet Union. Not merely is there a Western style open-air café in the town square, but there are also sometimes Western and even Japanese pop bands, the increasing presence of which should gradually moderate the instinctive racism of Estonians towards non-Europeans.

This has its own dangers however: above all a certain smugness, a conviction that the Estonians are better and more Western than the other Soviet peoples and therefore do not need to try or to change. This is, however, to some extent an illusion. A visit to the city's industrial suburbs, and a talk with some of their Russian inhabitants, will soon remind the visitor that he is still in the Soviet region. Estonians too have been more affected by the Soviet mentality than they like to admit. Service is often poor, and the salespeople usually corrupt. So too is the bureaucracy, although probably to a lesser extent than elsewhere in the former Union.

The knowledge that Westerners regard them as a post-Soviet people is a blow to that Estonian pride, individual as well as national, which has underpinned so many of the nation's great achievements. The reverse side of this pride and individualism is a tendency to chilly egoism. One of the sharpest observers of the contemporary Estonian scene, the Estonian-American editor Mihkel Tarm, pointed out that this too has played its part in keeping the Estonians from political extremism:

> Can you imagine Estonians standing together in a rally, saluting a Leader? They can't even bear to stand next to each other on buses! Besides, they'd rather stay home and salute themselves in the mirror.[18]

Tarm has also compared much of Estonian democratic politics – even in the first completely free elections in 50 years – favourably with those of the United States:

> [By contrast with the Americans] I suspected that the Estonians would prove more sincere, serious and businesslike – that is to say, very boring.

Boring or not, Estonian internal politics, compared to those of the great majority of former Communist states, have been a shining example of calm, rationality and moderation. Unfortunately but not unnaturally, the only partial exception concerns attitudes to the local Russian population. Many Estonians claim to be able to tell Estonians from Russians in the street, not by looks or even by dress, but by body-language. This game of 'Spot-the-Russian' is a staple among Estonians, and marks the racial tension lying just beneath the surface in Estonia, where 39 per cent of the population are now Russian-speakers. An unhappy omen for future relations lies in the sheer difference in character between Russians and Balts, and especially between Russians and Estonians. The Estonian poet, Jaan Kaplinksi, summed this up in an interview:

> Estonians are afraid of intimacy, want to cut it off. Latvians have far less problem with this. It is a problem for poets in Estonia – you feel cut off from your emotional sphere. In Estonian, the word 'poet' – *luuletaja* – also means 'liar'! Even journalists are more popular than poets in Estonia, because they are at least seen as rational. But for this reason, perhaps, Estonia has a more open and free culture than that of Latvia, where poets are national heroes.[19]

Concerning relations with the Russians, he continued that:

> Estonians have difficulty communicating emotionally, and that's how the Russians always want to communicate. I know several Estonian men who had psychological problems with communication. They married Russian women, and everything went much better. Estonian men are particularly oppressed psychologically. They need support, but can't ask for it, because Estonian women consider Estonian men to be rational beings who must fulfil their role. I have read an anthropological study of an Andalusian village – very like a Russian one. All doors are expected to be open; there is no privacy. Anyone who drew apart was automatically suspect. The social control of the community is total. Estonians are far more inner-directed. Even Estonian villages are not really villages; the houses are separate and inner-directed. In mixed communities, sometimes a poor Russian will come and want to talk about his or her family, their problems, and the Estonian neighbour will sit there stony faced. The Russians think the Estonians are icy and hostile, and the Estonians think that the Russians are childish and hysterical.

There is even an Estonian film, *For Crazies Only*, in which a Russian nurse cures an extremely neurotic Estonian by sleeping with him – and is then murdered by the Estonian's even more neurotic father-in-law![20] Among the Estonians' southern neighbours, a higher level of inter-marriage between Latvians and Russians may possibly have resulted in Latvians having a more carefree attitude than other Balts, though only an intolerable provocateur would say so.

Arvo Valton has written a short story, *Love in Mustamae*, in which two Estonians fall in love and, it appears, succeeds in producing a baby without either touching or even speaking to each other! Estonian women were popularly reputed in the Soviet Union to head in droves for Georgia during their holidays to have affairs with the hotter-blooded Georgian men.

For all the chilliness of their approach to life, children and each other, however, the Estonians have a franker attitude to sex than prevails in Lithuania, where considerable hypocrisy results from the mixture of Catholic and Soviet public traditions. Dr Vytautas Kavolis has written of the 'habitual prudery and banality' of Lithuanian prose, 'when matters bearing on the erotic are touched upon'. He has quoted the views of Dr Audrone Žentelytė, contrasting this aspect of Lithuanian literature with the 'more sensuous and decadent' Latvian prose tradition, but arguing that Lithuanian literature has a deeper use of symbolism. Lithuanian young people are in fact quite free in their sexual behaviour, and indeed were so even in the 1920s and 1930s – public prudery notwithstanding. A Latvian friend was once almost physically assaulted by a bunch of outraged Lithuanian Catholic students for providing a simultaneous interpretation during a showing of the film, *Empire of the Senses*.

In all three Baltic states women – and to a lesser extent men – tend to marry very young. Often girls become pregnant (there is a shortage of contraceptives), or simply hope that marriage will aid their escape from home and passage up the housing list. Often it is simply the only way to permit love-making near censorious parents (and grandparents) in over-crowded homes. Young Balts, unlike their American equivalents, do not generally have access to cars. Of course there is always the forest, but then there is also the winter. Finding a dry spot to lie down in the Baltic countryside is not easy in any season of the year.

The result, of course, is to place all the stresses of life upon marriages which, as a result, are breaking up at an even faster rate than in the West. It is commonplace to find, in the Baltic, a woman in her late twenties with a failed marriage, a child, and nowhere to live except with her parents – or worse, with the husband whom she has come to loathe – and a fixed determination not to have any more children, however many abortions it may take.

Between the wars, and for a long time before that, Lithuania was a good deal poorer than Estonia or Latvia – more or less on a level with Poland, though without that country's extremes of wealth and poverty. Lithuanian suggestions that their future lies with Scandinavia are met by representatives of the latter with their customary politeness and total internal rejection. I asked a Scandinavian representative in the Baltic about this:

> 'Do Swedes consider the Estonians to be at least potential Scandinavians?'
> 'In principle, yes'
> 'What about the Latvians?'
> 'Well, it's rather difficult to say, because the Latvians don't really have a national character.'
> 'And the Lithuanians?'
> 'Absolutely not'.

In terms of this distinction between noble and peasant nations, the Lithuanians are in a curious position. A century ago most were peasants, and the Polish stereotype of the Lithuanian is of a rather comically cold and sluggish farmer. Lithuanians however also have a great warrior and royal tradition dating from the Lithuanian Grand Duchy of the Middle Ages; this has been revived – albeit largely artificially – as part of the construction of the modern national culture. Lithuanians see themselves as much more warm-blooded and courageous than the other Balts; their neighbours would throw in 'reckless, romantic, self-intoxicated, mystical and irrational' – in other words, the way the rest of the world often views the Poles.

The Lithuanians' neighbours would in fact be surprised to hear them described as sharing in Baltic dourness and stoicism, particularly in view of the Lithuanian predilection for flowery rhetoric and grand, romantic gestures. A curious feature of Lithuania however is that while this kind of behaviour is very much a feature of the political classes and the intelligentsia, ordinary Lithuanians are not at all given to making grandiloquent gestures or speeches – and, as the failure of Dr Vytautas Landsbergis to gain wide popularity shows, do not like a constant diet of them from their politicians. The aspects of 'baroque theatre' in Lithuanian culture are therefore just that – theatrical performances for special occasions which, though very important in the Lithuanian culture identity, do not necessarily impinge on daily life or practical politics.

For a journalist, the voice of the ordinary Lithuanian is hard to discern, because it is so very difficult to get Lithuanians to show their emotions or say anything worth quoting. Put another way (by an American journalist), 'ordinary people in Lithuania are mostly sane, but their leaders are mostly mad. Now why is this?' In a brilliant article, Dr

Vytautas Kavolis has pointed out how 'heroic' self perceptions in Lithuanian culture are checked by a basic tradition of 'conservative moderation, possibly of peasant origin'.[21] Beneath the romantic rhetoric, Lithuanians tend to be pragmatic people, in private as well as public.

I once wrote that in Lithuania it seemed you had to pass an exam in flowery rhetoric before you could qualify to become a nationalist politician or intellectual. This was a joke, but there may have been some truth in it. In all three Baltic states, the struggle for national independence has always been bound up with a cultural struggle to create and define the nation. Indeed the nationalist intelligentsia, including the grandparents of Dr Landsbergis, can really be said to have created the modern Lithuanian nation. Ever since then, as in some other East European countries but in sharp distinction to Western Europe, it is the intelligentsia which has been at the forefront of nationalist and even chauvinist movements, while ordinary people have often been relatively unmoved. Much of the Lithuanian intelligentsia identifies passionately with a national cultural vision of Lithuania. They love Landsbergis because he is the perfect symbol of that identification.

The idiom of that national-intellectual struggle and that culture was created in the later nineteenth century, on a basis of European neo-romanticism embellished with various local trappings. Of course, due to Lithuania's isolation on the edge of Europe, these trends were in European terms old-fashioned even then. After the achievement of independence in 1918, this became in a sense the official cultural idiom of Lithuania. Subsequent foreign conquests, and decades of Soviet rule, drove Lithuanian culture back on itself, stifled its development, and created a permanent nostalgia for the old models and idioms of the cultural-political struggle.*

Most Lithuanians of course share Catholicism with the Poles, a religion which tolerated the continuation of pagan practices in a way not true of the Lutherans; it contributes strongly to the Lithuanian obsession with symbolism and ceremony. Lithuanians however tend to lack the sometimes agonised Polish concern with details of conscience and creed;

---

* I have sometimes wondered if the relative newness of the Lithuanian literary language is another reason for the exuberance with which Lithuanian writers and also politicians often use it; like a child with a lump of plasticine, twisting it into fantastic shapes and bouncing it off the ceiling. The results are not always comprehensible, but this does not seem to matter very much. My translator and I were once going through an article by the Lithuanian Right-wing deputy and writer, Antanas Patackas, on the mystical and national meaning of Midsummer Day. Even individual sentences appeared bereft of grammatical as well as intellectual logic. 'Edita', I said, 'this doesn't make any sense!' She looked puzzled. 'You're right, it doesn't', she said, 'But you know, it sounds very nice in Lithuanian!'

2   A monument in Antakalnis cemetery, Vilnius, to the Lithuanians killed during the Soviet army's seizure of the television station and tower in January 1991.

3   Rupintojėlis, the 'Man of Sorrows', a traditional Lithuanian figure of pagan origin, but presented as Christ.

for them, Catholicism is above all a semi-pagan matter of outward observance and magical ritual – 'pragmatic religion', in fact. In recent times, this religious ritual and even belief have merged almost inextricably with the national one, contributing to the often observed ritualisation of contemporary Lithuanian nationalist politics. According to Dr Kavolis, this ritualisation is 'much more evident in the second than in the first Lithuanian revival' (of the later nineteenth century).[22] He attributes this to 'a post-Soviet, anti-modern retraditionalisation of life', but it may also derive to some extent from Soviet culture, which was itself in many ways of course highly ritualised (see Chapter 5).

This subsuming of culture and religion into the national ritual has contributed to the Lithuanian difficulty (far greater than in Estonia or even Latvia) in distinguishing individual rights from national ones. The first time I heard the curious phrase 'the human rights of nations' (as deliberately opposed to human rights as such) was from a supporter of President Gamsakhurdia in Georgia; the second was from a Lithuanian radical deputy.

Another borrowing from the Poles is the Lithuanian sense of themselves as a crucified nation, the 'Christ among the Nations', a self-image of Poland coined by the Polish-Lithuanian poet Mickiewicz in the early nineteenth century. This conception of Lithuania is frequently drawn on in art and propaganda, for example in the cross at the graves of those Lithuanians killed by Soviet troops in January 1991, where Christ is shown rising one hand in a 'V for Victory' sign.

A linked image is that of the suffering mother-figure, often explicitly modelled upon the Virgin Mary. Another common Lithuanian image is of Our Lady with her heart pierced by seven swords. Such symbols have clustered thickly around the commemoration of the January killings, and are particularly concentrated on Loreta Asanavičiūtė, the only woman killed. The image connects with the rather mournful, yearning tone of much of Lithuanian culture, which easily spills into self-pity – a tendency very apparent in folksong and hymns. The Lithuanian emigré writer, Algirdas Landsbergis, (a cousin) has written of the 'lyrical acceptance and resignation typical of Lithuanian folksongs.[23] Quite where this aspect of the Lithuanian character comes from is difficult to say, but it would appear to be of great antiquity. It is reflected in many ancient Lithuanian hymns and folk-songs, and archetypically, in the figure of the 'Man of Sorrows' (in Lithuanian, '*Rūpintojėlis*'), a crowned figure sitting with his head against one hand, a carved wooden figure which, before collectivisation, used to stand outside many villages and is now re-appearing. This figure has for centuries been presented as Christ, taking the sorrows of the world on his shoulders, but it is undoubtedly much older.

This dolorous characteristic might also help restrain violence. Given the appalling things politicians in the Baltics say about each other, and the extremist tone of much of the political debate, it would seem reasonable to expect, as in Georgia, regular outbreaks of violence. These are in fact extremely rare. Many Lithuanian deputies detest each other, but unpleasantness in parliamentary debates usually surfaces in sly, indirect remarks rather than shouted insults. Indeed, to a newcomer, parliament might seem a great deal calmer and more harmonious than the British House of Commons. A senior Lithuanian politician once told a Lithuanian-American friend that Lithuanians are not violent, and would not generally attack a rival, 'but they might well denounce you to the secret police'. The element of sly sarcasm in many Lithuanians could also be in part the defensive mechanism of peasants unable to show their feelings about their masters. In a more robust and open form, it is strongly present in Donelaitis's portrait of the German landlords in *The Seasons*, the first major work of Lithuanian literature. It is also strongly marked in the character of Dr Landsbergis. His international image is that of an exceptionally open and forthright critic and enemy of Moscow, and this is entirely true. In internal politics, however, it was only very recently that he began to launch open and savage verbal attacks on his opponents. In the past, his approach was always rather indirect and ironical.

Dr Landsbergis rose to lead Sajūdis largely through his skill in avoiding and preventing open conflict, and in disguising his own position and wishes. Indeed, one of the most irritating things about his public pronouncements, so far as many Lithuanians were concerned, was precisely this avoidance of any direct stand, even when everyone knew he was working behind the scenes. This often left many ordinary Lithuanians feeling bewildered and annoyed. The indirect approach is however useful when it comes to suggesting looming international threats to Lithuania without actually having to name them. Thus for example, 'Somebody is artificially encouraging Polish unrest in Lithuania', or 'It is in Somebody's interest (*kažkam naudinga*) to create opposition to the creation of a Presidency'. If Landsbergis had said 'the Polish government', or 'President Yeltsin', it would be possible to take issue with these claims. As it was, they could not be directly challenged, and go to feed a certain paranoia, a feeling of being surrounded by looming, undefined menaces and conspiracies, which is true of all the post-communist peoples but especially Lithuania. Indeed so widely do Lithuanians use this word 'Somebody' (*Kažkas*) in these contexts of internal and external menace that it seems sometimes that 'Somebody' must be the 'Evil One' in person. No one else could get around so much and back so many different causes simultaneously.

As to the leading Lithuanian patriotic opponent of Satan, the motif of Lithuania as Christ-Redeemer has contributed to an even stronger feeling in Lithuania than in the other Baltic republics that they have

4 A pilgrimage to the Hill of Crosses in Lithuania. The cross-bearer holds a Lithuanian flag in his left hand.

5 A national religious celebration in Kaunas, Lithuania, 1990, marking the re-erection of a traditional cross.

30

sacrificed themselves for the West, are morally better than the West, and therefore have an automatic right to the West's support. It led to the curious belief, apparently sincerely held, on the part of a number of Lithuanian nationalist leaders that the Lithuanian independence movement headed off Soviet aggression against Western Europe in the 1990s.

In this mood Lithuanians tend of course to be particularly impervious to Western advice. The curious thing is that when a Lithuanian rejects Western criticism with the often-used words, 'this is the Lithuanian way of doing things', what he is describing is usually in fact the classically Soviet way of doing things – the government attitude to secrecy being a particularly striking example.

A passionate desire to defend Lithuanian culture and 'the Lithuanian way of doing things' is the heart of Landsbergis's politics. Concrete questions of social and economic policy come very much in second place. Landsbergis is deeply concerned by the damage done to Lithuanian culture by Soviet rule, and by the vulnerability of the Lithuanian cultural identity as that of a small nation in the face of overwhelming pressure from outside cultural forces. His attitude recalls that of a Lithuanian nationalist thinker from the first period of independence, Jonas Aleksa, who wrote of the need to preserve national cultural individuality in the hope that this would produce a culture making Lithuania 'an inimitable phenomenon of the universe' and 'justify the nation's existence'. This too is the root of Landsbergis's attempted alliance with the Catholic Church. He himself comes from a Protestant family and, in an interview in April 1990, remarked he considered himself if anything a 'Čiurlionist', which would make him a sort of holistic mystical freethinker. Catholic clerics however now claim that Landsbergis is a baptised Catholic, and he has gone out of his way to stress his links with the Church.

Quite apart from the political advantages of a clerical alliance, Landsbergis seems to believe that it is only the Church, and Catholic belief, morality and ritual, which can give Lithuanian culture the sort of iron frame it needs to prevent it dissolving into the modern international cultural sea (or, as many Lithuanians see it, an anti-cultural materialist swamp). This is a view shared by many Lithuanian intellectuals (but relatively few ordinary people), who instinctively identify the restoration of national independence with the restoration of a particular vision of its national culture shaped, above all, by the 'first national revival' of the nineteenth century. It points towards some form of officially sponsored, 'official culture'.

Before this is dismissed as a personal or Right-wing aberration, it is worth remembering that a leading Lithuanian liberal philosopher, and bitter opponent of Landsbergis, Dr Arvydas Juozaitis, once told an American interviewer that,

This may not seem serious to you . . . but the Roman Catholic Church will be Lithuania's fortress against the Western invasion, as it has been against the Eastern. Whether the nation can retain its distinctive culture once it has been re-united with Europe depends on how well Lithuanian souls are equipped to resist an unexampled wealth of pleasure. We will all melt away without Christianity.[24]

Carla Gruodis, a Lithuanian-Canadian academic, is preparing a thesis on the way that Lithuanians, in times of political stress, fall back on retrogressive religious female imagery. She has also tried to create some sort of feminist awareness among her students. No doubt such ideas will make progress, but just how far they have to go was shown by a conference on 'Women in Changing World' (sic), organised in Vilnius in May 1992 by Kazimiera Prunskienė. The event's German backers must have had a sense of bewilderment, if not time warp. They may even have felt that the whole affair was some enormous male hoax – which in a sense it was, being entirely dominated by Lithuanian patriotic-patriarchal values. Of the seven summaries of papers presented with the conference programme, five dealt with children and the family, one with the sufferings of mothers whose sons had been killed in the Soviet army, one with Chernobyl, and none with women's rights. Dr Birutė Grinbergienė of the Psychiatric Clinic in Vilnius declared forthrightly that,

Family is the social institution where women may express themselves. For fifty years we lived in opened world and now we have many worries and pain. . . .

Dr Birutė Obelenienė of the 'For Life' (anti-abortion) Association wrote that,

The fact that male and female origin is equal is the greatest miserable [sic] for all community. Woman is always near the nature and she maintains energy of life. . . . (her translation).

A similar gap in comprehension occurred at a conference on 'Women in Economic and Political Life' in Riga on 5–6 September 1992. Scandinavian participants were horrified to hear a Lithuanian woman lawyer declare that women are passive and emotional, while men are rational and dominating, and that, in the words of Andrejs Krastiņš, the Deputy Chairman of the parliament, 'the sharp struggle for power is not for women'. Even Marju Lauristin, the leading woman in Baltic politics today, was criticised by Western participants when she said that women should not complain about their position but work to compete. A request for articles on the question of women's concerns or rights in Baltic newspapers drew an almost complete blank in all three republics, except, revealingly enough, for a few in English-language papers. Mihkel Tarm wrote accurately that:

> Estonian women are, on the whole, more knowledgeable, more creative, more decisive and more capable than most of the men, [but] the tragic, even pathetic side to it is that women continue to play their [male-given] role. . . . Even the few prominent female politicians regularly insist that, no, of course they don't think that women should be in a position of authority. . . .[25]

He suggested that Estonian women are superior to the men because they have not been influenced by the degrading Soviet male culture of institutions like the army and indeed many workplaces.

Women in fact predominate in many of the educated professions, to a greater degree than in the West, but an Estonian academic had a bitter explanation for this:

> Don't you know that in every country, women get the low-paid, low-status jobs? Well in the Soviet Union, these jobs were in the educated professions. Even men from good families in fact often didn't even bother to get an education, because they could make better money working on the black market, or even as factory workers.

In the English language faculty of Tallinn University, there are twenty-seven women and two men – the Director and Deputy Director. One colleague with whom I discussed this book asked why there was so little on the position of women, and so much about Baltic myths. The answer is plain: this is principally a study of politics and political culture, and the four million or so women in the Baltic States play a considerably less important role in current Baltic politics than does the average medieval (male) hero, whether long dead or completely imaginary.

Of seven major Latvian womens' organisations, most are in some way linked to political parties, while two (The Women Scientists' Club and the Latvian Academically Educated Women's Association) act as pressure groups for women in the educated professions. The Latvian Womens' League was founded by the mothers of Latvian youths being persecuted in the Soviet army. It has a generally conservative and traditionalist outlook, and one of its stated aims is to 'organise small businesses that could provide adequate jobs for single mothers or young girls in trouble'.

The Latvian National Women's League, close to the radical National Independence Party (Mr Krastiņš's party), is modelled on an organisation of the same name that existed before 1940, and can hardly be called progressive. The Womens' Association by contrast is more activist, but suffers from being a continuation of a Soviet womens' organisation, and being still largely led by old apparachiks. According to figures compiled by V. Rubina, of the Association, women in Latvia in 1990 made up no less than 63 per cent of people in Latvia with secondary and university education. They also held 80 per cent of teaching posts, but an infinitely lower proportion of senior ones. They formed 82 per cent of people in health care.

Under Soviet rule, women in the Baltic were given quite prominent formal and symbolic roles but largely insignificant real ones. Since the rise of the national movements, their formal role has declined steeply, and their real one has not increased. Thus from 1955 to 1985, between 31 per cent and 35 per cent of deputies in the Latvian Supreme Council were women (just as a disproportionate majority of the deputies to the Latvian and other Supreme Councils were chosen from the indigenous nationality, precisely because these bodies held no real power).

After the elections of 1990 which brought the Popular Front to power, this dropped to only 5.4 per cent (11 out of 201 deputies). In Estonia and Lithuania, Kazimiera Prunskienė and Marju Lauristin have played prominent roles, but they are very untypical, and in general it certainly cannot be said that the public role of women has increased as a result of the national revolutions.

It is also an open question whether the advent of Western attitudes will be good for women, at least in the short term. Soviet rule preserved in aspic traditional male attitudes to women, but also suppressed their treatment as public sex-objects. At the moment, the rise of pornography and blatantly sexist advertising means that as in many parts of the Third World and indeed the West, women risk getting the worst of both worlds.

If the Lithuanians and the Estonians have clearly marked characteristics and self-images, the Latvians are much less easy to define. By language they are close to the Lithuanians, but their religious tradition places them closer to Estonia. In Baltic terms they are an indeterminate nation, neither fish nor fowl, ambling unsteadily between their two more decisive neighbours. Indecision, a certain lack of direction, has been characteristic of Latvian policy in recent years. It recalls a character in a Latvian satirical novel who comes to a crossroads 'and after giving the matter careful consideration, goes in both directions at once'.[26] This cultural confusion is largely due to having come under a greater variety of rulers: in Western Latvia, Lutheran Germans and Swedes, but in the Eastern province of Latgale, Catholic Poles and Orthodox Russians. In the nineteenth century, the Latvians came under greater Russian cultural influence than the other Balts, and the nascent Latvian intelligentsia long tended to identify with Russian culture and to draw on Russian models as part of its rejection of German influence. The Latvians are also less homogeneous, linguistically and ethnically, and the Latgallian dialect remains almost a separate language.

Whereas the other Balts, asked about their own national characters, are usually only too glad to launch into a string of stereotypes, the Latvians find it difficult to define themselves except by contrast with their neighbours: more emotional and mystical than the Estonians, but more cautious than the Lithuanians, and so on. They like to think of themselves as dreamers with a practical streak, or practical people with a capacity to dream. Latvians share, of course, the general Baltic sense of being part of Western Europe and therefore superior to Russia. Latvian literature is far more romantic and mystical than that of Estonia, but remains more firmly planted than that of Lithuania. The Latvian-American journalist Pauls Raudseps has suggested that romanticism in the literature of Latvia, as of some other North European countries, could be in part an artistic reaction against the very unromanticism of the Latvian character.

The Latvians are regarded by the other Balts, and were regarded by the Baltic Germans, as an unreliable people, with a rare capacity to believe two contradictory things at the same time. They are apparently passive and patient but suddenly flare up into gusts of terrible violence: a characteristic not immediately in evidence in recent years, but which may yet be put to the test in the future. Latvia's mixed character is reflected in its language, which to an outsider sounds like Lithuanian spoken with an Estonian accent. This is almost true, for the Latvians are a mixture of Balt and Finno-Ugric peoples, and the grammar and most of the vocabulary of their language is close to Lithuanian, but with lilting inflections which recall those of Estonian.

One feature which distinguishes the Latvians is the importance of Riga, giant among Baltic cities. In the Lithuanian tradition, overwhelmingly peasant, there is a strong undercurrent of dislike for the towns, which as mentioned is connected to a gut distrust of capitalism (see Chapter 5). This nostalgia for the countryside is also present in Latvian culture, but so too is a deep love of Riga. In the words of the Latvian exile poet, Linards Tauns,

> But then I was possessed by desire for the city,
> For once I put my palm against a bare sidewalk.
> It is not cold,
> For with this palm,
> I feel the pulse-beat of my beloved's meandering girlhood steps
> And the stone arteries.
> And I could enjoy the street
> As if I were stroking my beloved's leg.
> I could also be born again;
> In the show-windows, these women's wombs.[27]

35

Alexander Čaks is another fine example of an urban poet, trying to draw beauty from the disillusioned material of the city; there is no-one quite like him in Lithuanian literature. Rarely enough for a Baltic writer, he is also extremely funny. His poem, 'My Ensemble of Cockroaches', in which he attempts to woo a girl with the help of a chorus of these insects, is worthy of any anthology of humorous verse.

It may be that longer experience of life in a big city, among different cultural influences, has also helped to make the Latvians more urbane and easy-going than their Baltic neighbours, without the coarse, insecure arrogance of many Lithuanians or the icy, edgy arrogance of many Estonians. Latvian writers themselves often say that kindness is a leading national characteristic, which, when you think of it, is a humble sort of quality relatively uncelebrated by most national bards – although a popular proverb also says that 'a Latvian's favourite food is another Latvian'.

Latvian Romanticism is considerably different from the Lithuanian variety, precisely because of its more urban, and often self-consciously 'decadent' tone. A classic example is the delicately erotic 1928 Latvian edition of Pierre Louys's *Chansons de Bilitis*, translated by the Latvian expressionist poet Jānis Sudrabkalns and illustrated by Sigismunds Vidbergs.[28] It is difficult to imagine such a work appearing in smaller, dourer Tallinn at that time, and absolutely impossible to imagine in the then Lithuanian capital, Kaunas. At a more popular level, Riga in the 1920s and 30s was home to an erotic magazine, *Mīla un Flirts (Love and Flirtation)* which has now been reprinted as part of the nostalgic craze for the culture of the first Baltic republics.

The romantic and dramatic Lithuanian self-image explains why many Latvians harbour considerable dislike for their neighbours, regarding them as arrogant and violent. However, they have a sneaking admiration for the qualities of the Estonians. The latter repay this with an almost automatic disdain, and talk of a Latvian tendency to collaborate with conquerors, and of Latvian auxiliaries having served the Germans against the Estonians in the thirteenth century. The accusation that the Latvians 'make good servants of other peoples' is sometimes levelled by Latvians themselves, with the Red Riflemen and the Latvian SS units quoted as examples. Kārlis Skalbe wrote during the first Latvian struggle for independence that 'we will win when we conquer the servant's soul within us'. It must be said however that whatever their cruelties, both these formations were at least very good fighters, which disproves the hostile stereotype of the Latvians as cowardly and subservient.

In general, therefore, the most characteristic attitude of all the Baltic peoples to each other remains to a surprising extent one of ignorance (and dislike); when one registers surprise at this their reaction is equally one of surprise. 'But Riga is so far away', a Lithuanian official commented when I asked if he held regular meetings with his Latvian counterparts. Such attitudes are changing as a result of the collapse of the Soviet Union and the opening of all three societies, but not as fast as they should. The rather negative stereotypes the Balts have of each other were strengthened under Soviet rule, when each republic was isolated from the others, and every official cultural exchange had to pass through Moscow. Symbolic of this were the very poor communications between the Baltic States. Under Soviet rule there were only two flights a week between Vilnius, Riga and Tallinn, but several flights each day to Moscow and Leningrad. There is still no direct railway connexion between Riga and Tallinn, but only a long dog-leg via Tartu. Sealed into provincialism as in a pressure-cooker, the Balts boiled and bubbled in their ancestral prejudices. During the first period of independence and equally now, these national feelings have created great obstacles in the path of Baltic co-operation. At least, however, the Balts have not fought a war with each other for seven-hundred years. Even if hopes for a real Baltic common market are likely to prove largely vain, they will doubtless contrive to co-exist somehow.

A far more serious issue of course concerns relations between Balts and local Russians – also, after all, a people with a longstanding stake in the Baltic region. It has been said that those in the Baltic are gradually becoming more like the Balts amongst whom they live, just as the Cossacks took on many features of their adversaries, the Caucasian tribes. The extent to which this happens will be one of the great determining questions in the future of the Baltic states.

2

Surviving the Centuries

'Vercingetorix said: Caesar, you can take
the land where we live away from us,
but you cannot take the land from us where we have died....
My anger will remain alive
to shout like an owl in the hollow years.
Destruction to you and your insatiable city,
Caesar!'
    Jaan Kaplinski, *Vercingetorix Said*, translated from the
        Estonian by Sam Hamill and Jaan Kaplinski

The Ancient Baltic Peoples

Archaeological evidence suggests that Finno-Ugric tribes, the ancestors of the modern Estonians, arrived on the shores of the Baltic some two and a half thousand years before Christ, making the Estonians one of the longest-settled of European peoples. Tacitus speaks of 'Aesti', living on the shores of the northern sea, though these have been claimed as ancestors by all the Baltic peoples.[1]

The Finno-Ugric language group, of which Estonian forms part, extends from Hungary to Siberia. The Estonians and Finns form the westernmost extension of what used to be a vast range of tribal peoples stretching across most of what is now northern Russia. The conquest, conversion to Orthodox Christianity, and assimilation of these forest peoples was one of the main activities of the new Russian princedoms from the ninth century onwards, and much of the North Russian population is by origin Finnic, just as that of Byelorussia is the result of the mixture of East Slavs with the Baltic tribes whose descendants became the Latvians and Lithuanians. The mixture of Russification, Russian colonisation and attempted 'conversion' to a Russia-based ideology in Estonia under Soviet rule can be seen as the latest stage of this longterm transformation of population and culture. It is one of the most significant in European history, though little known outside Russia.

The remaining Finnic tribes in Russia were gradually reduced by the Russians to a scattered and rather sad set of peoples, some of whom were given theoretical 'autonomy' in provinces of the Soviet Russian

Federation. The largest single group – outnumbering the Estonians in fact – are the Udmurts, living in the Urals. The Cheremis, Ostyaks and Mordva are also among the Finno-Ugric peoples. There is considerable ethnographic interest in these peoples in Estonia, and Lennart Meri, Estonian President from October 1992, made his name as a film-maker and anthropologist seeking cousins of the Estonians in Siberia, and looking for clues to the old Estonian religion in their surviving shamanistic practices.[2] After the achievement of Estonian independence in 1991, and as retaliation against Moscow's pressure concerning Russia's rights in Estonia, some Estonian political groups began to encourage these peoples to seek full autonomy or even independence.

The furthest tide of this assimilation of the Finnic peoples by the new power of Kievan Rus during the early middle ages lapped over the borders of present Estonia and Finland. This involved the conversion to Orthodoxy of small Finnic peoples like the Ingri, the Setus and the Karelians, and their intermittent subjugation to Novgorod the Great. This hegemony of Novgorod was continually contested by the German and Swedish Catholics in the Baltic, but these small populations remained Orthodox. Those Karelians who have not moved to Finland retain some sort of national existence in the Karelian Autonomous Republic of Russia (which has a large Russian majority).

The Ingrians were largely deported to Central Asia under Stalin. Some 60,000 now live in Estonia, and depending on where they live, some have become Estonians, others in effect Russians. There have been proposals to establish a small Ingrian national area either in Leningrad province or in the Ivangorod area, if this were returned to Estonia by Russia. Neither of these schemes, however, is plausible, and the Ingrians, like the Livonians, are almost certainly doomed to disappear. The conversion of the Setus to Orthodoxy was sealed in the fifteenth century by the construction of a huge fortified monastery at Pechori (Petseri) just south of Lake Peipus. This also marked the beginning of major Russian settlement in the area.

During the nineteenth century, the Russian state, reviving an old tradition, succeeded in converting a large part of the Estonians themselves to Orthodoxy, playing on hatred of the German landlord and his Lutheran pastor, and on promises of preferential state treatment for the Orthodox. The Estonian President in the first period of independence, Konstantin Päts, was Orthodox – a surprising fact in view of the strongly marked 'Protestant' features in the Estonian character and culture. The very feebleness of the Orthodox cultural impact on the Estonian converts, however, shows the toughness of the Estonian cultural synthesis that was beginning to emerge out of native roots and German and Scandinavian Protestant influence. The Orthodox churches favoured by the few Estonian Orthodox today – like the one in which Päts is buried

– are wholly un-Orthodox, but very Estonian, in their sober lack of decoration. In the nineteenth century therefore, as under Soviet rule, Moscow's attempts failed, and the age-old process of Russification stopped with the Setus and the Ingrians.

In this book the Estonians are described as Balts for the sake of convenience, though strictly speaking the description is false. The 'Baltic' language group refers to a separate group of peoples of whom only the Latvians and Lithuanians now remain. Arriving some six-hundred years before Christ, they inhabited an area which, to judge by place-names, extended as far east as Moscow until the Slavs displaced or assimilated them. This process of assimilation continued into historical times. The Lithuanian language is of great interest to philologists, being an ancient form of Indo-European, and allegedly [though this is disputed] the closest surviving language to Sanskrit.[4]

The elimination of the Old Prussians, one of the Baltic peoples, at the hands of the Germans, also took place in the Middle Ages and early modern period. Their fate has often been cited in Baltic literature as an awful warning, an example of the grim, existential danger facing small nations in the region. Of the other Baltic peoples named by German and other chroniclers in the thirteenth century, over time the Kurs merged into the Letts to become the Latvians, as did the Finno-Ugric Livonians, while the Semgalans and the Samogitians were partly conquered by the German crusaders and ultimately became Latvians, and partly came under the rule of the Lithuanian monarchs and became Lithuanians.

The nature of the pre-Christian Baltic societies is difficult to establish, given the lack of Baltic written sources and the lack of detail in the German ones. Originally they seem to have been relatively egalitarian. According to the English chronicler Wulfstan, until the twelfth century individual wealth among the Lithuanians was not inherited but was competed for in horse-races after the death of its owner. Land was apparently vested in kinship groups, not in lords. The Estonians lived without any centralised authority, and were divided into clans speaking different Finno-Ugric languages, which later merged to make modern Estonian, just as various Balt languages and dialects merged to make up modern standard Latvian and Lithuanian. There were therefore, at this stage, no Baltic nations as such. In the centuries before the German conquest the pre-Christian Estonians did however develop a form of loose polity, divided into 'villages', 'parishes' and 'districts' (the names given by German chroniclers), which united groups of parishes. These groupings were headed by elders or councils of elders, and shared common fortresses into which the population retreated at time of danger, when a common war-leader (like Lembitu, the leader against the German crusaders in 1217) might also be chosen by all the districts. The

Estonians engaged in slave-raiding against their Balt, Slav and Finnic neighbours, and were raided by them.

On the island of Saaremaa, one can visit the earth-form where the Estonian rebels of 1345 made their stand. Its position, in the midst of marshes and deep woods, still evokes the desperation of a people driven into their last fastness. Its best defences indeed are those of nature, for its earthen walls can have been little defence against German siege-engines.

Little is known of prehistoric Estonian religion, beyond what can be gleaned from folklore or from analogy with the pagan religion of Eastern Finland (Karelia) which survived much longer. Lithuanian religion, as that of the longest-surviving pagan kingdom in Europe, was much more intensively described by Medieval and Renaissance chroniclers, allowing us to verify the existence of a group of Indo-European sky-gods. Chief among them was the thunder-god Perkūnas, related to the Slavic thunder-god Perun. It has also been suggested that Lithuania and Latvia possessed a class of hereditary priests and soothsayers, who may have had leadership functions in society. Like the Druids, or the Canaanites of the Old Testament, these priests had their altars in sacred groves. When the Lithuanian Grand Duke Jogaila (Jagiello) finally converted to Christianity in the fourteenth century, his first action was to cut down the sacred trees. The sacred importance of Perkunas was honoured in a back-handed way; the site of his demolished statue was chosen for that of the new church of St Stanislas, patron saint of Poland. The two centuries before the German invasion had already seen certain social developments, probably under influences from Scandinavia and Germany. These included the militarisation of society, the distinction of the warrior class from the rest, the inheritance of property and the establishment of a nobility, at least in Lithuania. On this basis was erected the strikingly successful Lithuanian monarchy of the thirteenth and fourteenth centuries, the only one created by Balts. Other peoples remained at the tribal stage, and proved unable to organise sufficiently to beat off the attacks of the German crusaders. Baltic trade with Western Europe and the Mediterranean long predated Christian attempts at conversion or conquest. Tacitus describes the amber and fur trade from the Baltic, and Roman coins have been found in the region. The great trade routes from Northern Russia also crossed the Baltic region, down the main rivers: the Neva flowing from Lake Ladoga, the Narva from Lake Peipus, and the Dvina (Daugava) flowing south to within portage-distance of the Dnieper and, on it, to the Black Sea.

This trade activity was not however in the hands of the Balts. During the seventh and eighth centuries, it had fallen into the hands of the Vikings, whose descendants, the princes of the House of Rurik, ruled the Russian princedoms. By the time of the arrival of the Crusaders, the Russian city of Novgorod – Lord Novgorod the Great – had already established itself as a major trading power, and was also pushing into the Baltic lands with soldiers and missionaries, as, further south, were the other local Russian centres of Pskov and Polotsk. In the eleventh century, part of what is now Estonia was conquered for a period of a few decades by the Russian prince Yaroslav the Wise.[5]

Russian influence within what are now the Baltic States was centred on Tartu (in German, *Dorpat*, in Russian, *Yuryev*) in Estonia and the forts of Jersika and Koknese on the river Dvina, which the chronicle of Henry of Livonia describes as ruled by Russian Princes. The influence of Russian Orthodoxy on the pagan Letts must have been fairly intensive, because several key religious terms in the Latvian Protestant and Catholic churches are loan-words from Russian, despite the fact that few Latvians today are Orthodox.[6] After the Crusader invasion, according to the German chronicler Henry of Livonia, the Russian Prince of Polotsk, denouncing Crusader claims, declared that 'the Livonians were his subjects and he had the right to baptise them or leave them unbaptised'. The Letts for their part, 'drew lots and asked the opinion of their gods as to whether they should be baptised by the Russians of Pskov or by the Latins'. The gods, for reasons of their own, declared for Rome. Until the mid-eleventh century, Scandinavian and Russian traders competed with the pagan Slavic Wends, from what is now Eastern Germany and northern Poland, for control over the Baltic trade. Thereafter, the Wends were conquered and assimilated by the Germans, and their seapower destroyed and supplanted by the Danes, thereby clearing the road for Germans to move East and invade and forcibly Christianise the area of the present Baltic States.

The Christian Conquest

For a vivid image of how the invasion of the medieval crusaders is remembered in the Baltic States, a Western audience could do worse than to watch the film 'Pathfinder'. As a Lappish film, the anonymous conquerors portrayed are Norwegian, but the principle is the same: an idyllic community of hunters is suddenly attacked by alien warriors in black armour, who outmatch them in weaponry, ferocity and organisation, and slaughter everyone in their path. They are finally overcome not by strength but the cunning of a Lappish boy – an enduring idea in Baltic humour and folklore, as in that of most conquered peoples.[7]

For two hundred years, religious faith as well as lust for conquest drew crusaders from many parts of Europe to fight for a season or so in the Baltic. From England, Chaucer's knight in literature, and King Henry IV (then Earl of Derby) in reality, were among them. They gave the knights the reserves of manpower which enabled them to survive a number of defeats at the hands of the Lithuanians. The monastic discipline of the military orders also made them superior both as fighters and administrators to their main rivals, Christian and pagan. Before the foundation of the Brothers of the Militia of Christ (popularly and aptly known as the Sword-Brothers) in 1202, German attempts to spread the faith in the Baltic region had come to very little. The Scandinavians for their part had launched various raids culminating, in 1219, in a Danish landing in Estonia and the foundation of the town of Tallinn (Reval).

In the 1190s an Augustinian missionary, Bishop Meinhard, attempted to win over the Livonians, north of the Dvina, by building a stone fortress to protect them from the Lithuanians; but 'the Livonians went back on the bargain, and jumped into the Dvina to wash the baptism off again'. (They repeated the same process a few years later, after killing Meinhard's successor in battle, before converting and becoming the first German allies. As such they gave their name to the province of Livonia (German: Livland; Latvian: Vidzeme), which at one stage embraced the whole of what is now Latvia and Estonia. After the achievement of independence in 1918, this province was divided between Estonia and Latvia. The Germans were aided both by technological superiority (crossbows, steel armour, stone castles) and by the traditional hostility between the Baltic peoples themselves. The Livonians, and intermittently other peoples as well, rallied to the Germans for protection against raids by the Estonians and Lithuanians. The German chroniclers – admittedly a biased source – blame much of the savagery of the Baltic crusades on Baltic and Prussian auxiliaries fighting for the Germans.

According to the chronicle, the Estonians called on the neighbouring Russian princes for help, but these were distracted by the Tartar invasion in the East and South and defeated by the Germans. The latter captured the Russian forts on the Dvina, and pushed into Russia before being defeated by Prince Alexander Nevsky in the 'Battle on the Ice' of Lake Peipus in 1242. This Russian assistance to the Balts, against the Germans, has been repeatedly recalled in Soviet propaganda, though it was only part of a long policy on the part of the north-western Russian princes and cities of trying to extend their own control over the Baltic region.

On St George's day 1343, Estonia saw the last great pagan Baltic revolt against foreign control, in which several hundred Germans were killed. Following the suppression of the revolt, the Danes relinquished their hold on Tallinn and Northern Estonia, selling it to the Knights for 10,000 marks. To this day, Estonians remain proud that they resisted the Germans longer than did the ancestors of the Latvians, and blame the Latvians for having fought with the Germans at the battle of Fellinn (*Viljandi*) in 1217. The Lithuanians, for their part, feel superior to everybody else because they were never conquered at all. How real such feelings were among Balts before the early nineteenth century is not clear; they may be the result of efforts of modern nationalist historiographers.

Throughout the Baltic the Military Order was now the Teutonic Knights, who had in the meantime conquered Prussia. The Knights of the Sword had been dissolved in 1237 after defeat by the Lithuanians and repeated feuds with the Archbishop and citizens of Riga.[8] The Teutonic Knights continued these feuds, to the point where the citizens of Riga, at one stage, even allied themselves with the Lithuanians against the German Crusaders. Riga, like Narva, was throughout the Middle Ages a major town of the Hanseatic League, with trading links as far as England and the Mediterranean. Vilnius, though a royal Lithuanian city, adopted German municipal statutes in the fourteenth century.

By the fifteenth century the crusading spirit in the Baltic was already almost dead. The knights found themselves outflanked diplomatically and ideologically when the Lithuanian monarchs converted to Christianity and allied with the Christian Poles. The culmination of this process was the crushing defeat of the Order by the Poles and Lithuanians at the battle of Gruenwald in 1410. In German, this battle is known as Tannenberg, and Marshal Hindenburg also chose to call his victory over the Russians in 1914 by this name.

The intention was to even the historical score, although how a victory over Russians cancels out a victory by Lithuanians and Poles would be difficult to say. The Lithuanians for their part have gone one better. The name of the battle in Lithuanian, Žalgiris, has been given to their most famous football club – 'Agincourt United', as it were. A much more morally impressive borrowing from the world of sport appears in a photograph of a basketball team formed by Lithuanian exiles in Siberia in the early 1950s. Their hollow faces and emaciated limbs make the very idea of sport seem incongruous, but the name 'Žalgiris' is embroidered defiantly on their shirts.

Nothing could demonstrate more vividly the way that history, or something passing for it, lives on in strange but often deeply moving guises in the lives of people in this part of the world today. On 15 July 1990, the celebration of the anniversary of the battle was attended by President Jaruzelski and Professor Landsbergis, and by the ambassadors of Russia and Czechoslovakia. If this was intended to improve contemporary Lithuanian-Polish relations, however, the results were hardly noticeable.

Gruenwald and the wars that followed destroyed crusader and German hopes of further expansion into Poland, Lithuania and Russia. A hundred and twenty years later, the very existence of the Order was threatened by the Reformation, and the existence of the Order's lands in Livonia and Estonia by Russian invasion. The Grand Master in Prussia,

Albrecht of Brandenburg, bowed to the inevitable, converted himself into a secular Protestant prince, and dissolved the Teutonic Knights in his province. He was a prince of the House of Hohenzollern, and his action laid the foundation of the future Prussian monarchy. The Order survived in Livonia for another sixty years until, in 1561, amidst a fresh Russian invasion, the last Master, Gotthard von Kettler, was confirmed as secular Duke of Courland by the Poles.

The rest of Livonia became a disputed territory between them, the Russians and the Swedes. The last knights joined the existing secular German nobility in the Baltic, hitherto their vassals. The Order ended as it had begun, by fire and the sword, with the armies of Ivan the Terrible ravaging the country and committing atrocities which would etch themselves into Baltic memory, to be revived in the twentieth century.

The Crusader State was over, but its effects remain. The leading elements in Baltic tribal society had been destroyed or reduced to the status of peasants. In a few cases, including my own family, they assimilated completely into the German nobility. Initially the Estonians and Latvians remained free peasants, though owing their German masters various services and rents. In the sixteenth and seventeenth centuries, in common with the rest of Eastern Europe, the landlords were able to introduce full serfdom with greatly increased labour dues. The Livonian nobility was notorious throughout the Baltic for the brutality of its treatment of its peasantry, which the Swedish Crown later made attempts to check. This period, which marked a still further decline in the status of the Balts under German rule, also however saw the Reformation, which was to define the Protestant identities of Latvia and Estonia, and the beginnings of the mass education that was to form the basis of future Estonian and Latvian culture and prosperity.

The Reformation broke on a region still only partially converted from heathenism. Innumerable reports by priests and monks throughout the later middle ages speak of the continuation of heathen practices by the peasantry. This was in part because priests were so few on the ground, and those speaking the Baltic languages still fewer, while the Knights, the nobility and the German citizens of the towns resisted the training of native clergy. The persistence of paganism gave additional force to the Churches' hunt for witches and sorcerers in the region during the sixteenth and seventeenth centuries. An Italian traveller in the late sixteenth century declared that Latvian women 'are all soothsayers and very apt magicians'. Christianity was however making progress. Thanks to the eventual Swedish takeover after the collapse of the Teutonic Knights, the Reformation triumphed throughout Livonia, including all Estonian areas except for those already under Russia.

The Eastern part of present-day Latvia, Lettgallia or Latgale, however, was part of Poland, and remained Catholic. In 1772, during the first partition of Poland, Latgale fell to Russia, and was incorporated not into the Baltic provinces but into Russia proper. Latgale remains the poorest part of Latvia, with the heaviest Russian settlement, and somewhat looked down upon by the rest of Latvia, leading in turn to Latgalian expressions of resentment and even occasional demands for autonomy. For the Estonians, Lithuanians and the Latvians-to-be, the greatest gift of the Reformation was their own language, in written form. The first religious works printed in the Baltic languages were destroyed by order of the authorities, but by the seventeenth century there was already an extensive religious literature in early forms of Lithuanian, Latvian and Estonian. With this came more opportunities for native Balts to improve themselves through education. The price, however, was almost always Germanisation. The seventeenth century was long remembered by Balts as 'the good old Swedish time'. Aiming at the complete introduction of Swedish law, the Swedes tried to reduce the nobles' power to flog and imprison their serfs. They also tried to define and guarantee certain peasant rights. The longer Swedish rule may have been partly responsible for the greater class and ethnic harmony in Estonia (compared to Latvia) which endured into this century.

In this connexion it is interesting to compare the situation in the Baltic States with that of Finland. There, the Swedish monarchy did succeed in imposing Swedish laws and institutions, with the result that the position of the peasants, and of the Finns in general, was far better than in the provinces south of the Gulf of Finland. This contributed ultimately to the relative lack of conflict between Finns and the Swedish minority in Finland in this century, in sharp contrast to the situation in most of Eastern Europe. Once, when arguing with a Lithuanian nationalist politician, Rolandas Paulauskas, over the hostile Lithuanian nationalist attitude to the local Polish minority, I drew his attention to the rights given to the Swedish minority in Finland. 'Yes, but this is irrelevant', he said, 'Finland's history is quite different from ours.'[9]

The Lithuanian Empire and the Union with Poland

If the fate of the future Latvian and Estonian peoples in the middle ages was one of straightforward conquest and colonisation, that of the Lithuanians was much more complex: they triumphed, and in doing so lost their souls. They conquered what was for a time the largest European state but, even while this was happening, weaknesses in their own culture and society were opening the Lithuanian rulers themselves to cultural conquest by their Polish neighbours.

The Lithuanian monarchy did not definitively convert to Christianity (as part of a marriage alliance and political union with Poland) until the year 1386, and pockets of explicit pagan worship lingered until the Counter-Reformation. The real founder of this dynasty was Mindaugas, who died in 1263. He converted to Christianity under pressure from the Teutonic Knights, but conversion was largely formal and, in any case, reversed by his successors. The Galician Chronicler accused Mindaugas of having special reverence for the Hare-God, Diveriks: 'When Mindaugas rode into the field and a hare ran across his path, then he would not go into the forest, nor did he dare to break a twig.' On his death (murdered by rivals in his own family) Mindaugas was buried together with his horses, after the fashion of his ancestors.[10]

The failure to develop a written language until the sixteenth century (when, as elsewhere in the Baltic, the impetus was given by the Reformation and Counter-Reformation) was a more important and obvious weakness of the old Lithuanian pagan culture, stemming probably from that culture's very persistence. Everywhere else in Eastern Europe, the designers of alphabets for the different languages were without exception Christian clerics. The Lithuanian rejection of Christianity presumably discouraged such men from offering their services. The consequence was that the language of official documents in the Grand Duchy of Lithuania was not Lithuanian but 'Chancellery Slavonic', a dialect akin to those of present-day Byelorussia. (Later, in the Polish-Lithuanian Commonwealth, all the Slavonic dialects ranging between Russian and Polish and covering present-day Byelorussian and Ukrainian, were collectively described as 'Ruthene'). It seems probable that some form of Slavonic was also the *lingua frança* spoken at the Lithuanian court and in the army since, by the time the Grand Duchy reached its furthest expansion in the fourteenth century, the overwhelming majority of its subjects, and vassal lords, were Orthodox Slavs.

The complexity of the ethnic-religious picture is revealed by the fact that some of the Slavonic princely families later numbered as the greatest in Catholic Poland-Lithuania, like the Czartoryskis, were Orthodox until the late sixteenth century, while some of the descendants of the Lithuanian Grand Dukes, like the Golitsjn, moved to the Eastern marches of Lithuania, converted to Orthodoxy and were later numbered among the great Russian aristocrats. A relic of paganism may have lingered in Lithuania not just in peasant folklore but also in the greater religious tolerance of the nobility and the state, at least until the end of the sixteenth century. Under the pagan Grand Duchy, Catholicism, Orthodoxy, Islam and Judaism had all necessarily been officially recognised by the rulers.

For a time in the mid-sixteenth century, Lithuania under the chancellorship of Prince Nicholas Radžvilas (Radziwill) the Black was one of Europe's main centres of Protestantism and, according to a Venetian envoy, 72 different religions and sects existed in Vilnius. Thereafter, as Polish influence grew and the Polish-Lithuanian state came under increasing outside pressure, a rigid and intolerant Catholicism gained control, and all other religions were persecuted and expelled.[11]

In Byelorussia and Latgale, even into this century, religion defined one's state allegiance; 'nationality' as such was in many cases very vague. Today it is often very difficult to tell a 'Pole' from a 'Byelorussian' in Lithuania, without reference to his family's past religious allegiance. In mixed families, the choice of which nationality to belong to (or to admit to) is often purely arbitrary.

Amazingly enough, by the sixteenth century, there were six officially recognised languages in the Polish-Lithuanian Kingdom, including Polish, Latin, 'Ruthene' (in modern terms, Ukrainian-Byelorussian), German, Armenian and Hebrew – but not Lithuanian.[12] Moreover, the presence of Slavic loan-words for terms like 'lord' and 'town' in Lithuanian itself, and the speed with which the Lithuanian nobility later adopted Polish language and culture, suggests that Lithuanians must have been accustomed to Slavonic influence long before the alliance with Poland was concluded.

Investigation of the relationship between Lithuanians and Orthodox Slavs (Mostly living in what is now the Byelorussian Republic) has been bedevilled by nationalism as well as lack of evidence. Some Byelorussian scholars have claimed that the Lithuanian Grand Duchy was in fact a Byelorussian State – 'Well, they have to get a state tradition from somewhere, not having one of their own', as a Lithuanian friend commented acidly. The Byelorussian state symbol, a knight on horseback, is the same as that of Lithuania.

The situation of the Lithuanian élites in the Middle Ages could perhaps be compared with those of many countries of the present Third World which, while staunchly upholding their national independence and the main symbols of their national culture against foreign attack or criticism, find themselves progressively colonised from within by a Western culture to which they find themselves increasingly drawn.

The culture, the symbolism, and still more the status and power of the Polish aristocracy were to prove irresistibly attractive to their Lithuanian counterparts, even those like the Radziwills (Radvila) who attempted to defend Lithuanian autonomy against the Polish Kingdom.[13] The Catholic Church meanwhile, under completely Polish leadership, was disseminating Polish language and culture ever more deeply. The result in modern times – also common in the Third World – has been a massive Lithuanian inferiority complex and a sense of cultural vulnerability *vis-à-vis* the Poles, which in turn helps explain recent Lithuanian policies towards their Polish minority and towards Warsaw.

Lithuanian and Polish historians have disputed endlessly the meaning and consequences of the marriage of Grand Duke Jogaila (Jagiello) and the Polish princess Jadwige in 1386 (the Union of Kreva or Krewo) which first united the two states, and the Union of Lublin in 1569 which diminished Lithuanian autonomy and bound the Commonwealth in the form it was to hold until its destruction. At the time the obvious reason for both agreements, from the Lithuanian point of view, was to gain extra force to preserve the Lithuanian empire against foreign attack, especially from Moscow. In this the Union was very successful for the first 250 years of its existence, and disastrously unsuccessful after that. Lithuania also shared in the general economic decline of the Polish Commonwealth. By the later nineteenth century Lithuania was markedly poorer than the Latvian or Estonian provinces, lacking both industry and the efficient commercial agriculture introduced by the Baltic German nobility. This was later, however, to prove an advantage for Lithuania under Soviet rule, when those industrial bases of Latvia and Estonia encouraged Moscow to order a huge industrial expansion and an influx of Russian workers.

Politically, by 1772, the date of Poland's first partition, the anarchy of the Polish-Lithuanian nobles had paralysed the state and made it easy prey for its neighbours. In the partitions that followed, Lithuania was to fall to Russia, only to be 'reborn', initially in the minds of nineteenth-century intellectuals, in a new form: a linguistic nation, that could never again live in one state with Poland.

The Baltic Provinces under the Russian Empire

The experiences of the Baltic provinces under the Russian Empire were very different, though this had little to do with the indigenous Baltic peoples themselves. The Lithuanians and Latgalians took part in the risings of their Polish-speaking masters against Russian rule, while the Estonians and most of the Latvians lived in relative peace, thanks to the loyalty of their German masters to the Empire. Finland, which must be viewed historically as another Baltic state, took yet a third path. There Finns and their Swedish masters succeeded in uniting to defend the Grand Duchy's autonomy against Russian encroachment. The administration, initially wholly Swedish, became progressively Finnicised. As so often, the successes of Finland cast a sad light on the difficulties of the other provinces.[14]

The first hundred and fifty years of Russian rule were in many ways the golden age of the Baltic German nobility. Their control over the local administration had been permanently guaranteed by Peter the Great through the Treaty of Nystad (1721). Wars which had previously ravaged the area now took place far away, and service in the imperial army and civil service provided a great array of possible careers for younger sons. The Latvian and Estonian peasantry of course had a different perspective. Russian conquest led initially to the reversal of Swedish attempts to protect the peasants, and the introduction of more brutal Russian attitudes to masters' rights.

In the early nineteenth century the Baltic nobility liberated its serfs, more than forty years before emancipation in Russia, or in Lithuanian and Latgalian areas. Any impression of generosity is however misplaced: unlike the Russian serfs, those in the Baltic were liberated without land. The nineteenth century saw a number of relatively minor peasant disturbances throughout the Baltic, which were suppressed by Russian troops. These were followed by a full-scale peasant revolt in the Latvian and Estonian provinces during the revolution of 1905. Long before, the very peace of the Baltic had worked to undermine the position of the German nobles in the country and the German patriciate in the towns. By the mid-nineteenth century the improved possibilities for commercial agriculture gave new profits to the landlords, but also encouraged the growth of independent peasant farmers and a small native rural professional class.

The spread of education allowed these men to educate their sons, and the general growth in the economy provided jobs in the town for this new intelligentsia. The great majority of the first and indeed the second generation of the Baltic intelligentsias came from this background. So did virtually all the political leaders of the Baltic states in their first period of independence. The absence of famine, war and plague facilitated the growth of the rural population, and in the latter part of the nineteenth century the growth of industry pulled this population to the towns. Cities which, since their foundation six-hundred years before had been overwhelmingly German found themselves within a few decades with Latvian and Estonian majorities or at least pluralities. The immigration of Russians into the Baltic cities outflanked the Germans from the other side. Until the revolution of 1905, the basic tactic of most of the new Baltic nationalists, for obvious enough reasons, was to appeal to the government in St Petersburg for help against the Germans. If the Russian government had been in a position to make this alliance, it could probably have consolidated its political hold on the Baltic for generations.

To have allied with Baltic peasants, workers and petty bourgeois against the Baltic German upper classes would however have contradicted policy everywhere else in the Empire. Moreover, under Alexander III and Nicholas II, the intention of the imperial government was not to strengthen the Russian government's influence on the Baltic provinces but to Russify them completely, by supplanting their autonomous institutions and taking over their school system. The Russian government's education policy up to 1905 brought it into collision with the new Baltic nationalist intelligentsias, who viewed education in the Baltic languages as the single most important factor in the strengthening of their nations and national identity – quite apart from the fact that many were schoolteachers themselves. Indeed the Baltic national movements prior to 1914 were more cultural than they were political, or rather, since the task was actually to create nations where none had existed, politics and culture were indistinguishable. This, and the more immediate threat from the Germans, left room for compromise with Russia; and it is striking that even after the revolutions of 1917, a majority of Latvian and Estonian national spokesmen went on calling not for independence, but for full autonomy within a democratic Russian Federation. By that stage, of course, the Imperial German Army had overrun half of the Baltic States, and was using the Baltic Germans as helpers: the reasons for the Balts to stick to Russia were clear enough.

Up to 1901, Latvians and Russians in the city of Riga allied in opposition to the Germans in municipal elections. The collapse of the alliance that year was partly due to the fact that according to Dr Anders Henriksson, 'the Russian national party had even less respect for the idea of Latvian nationhood than did the Germans', but also a result of the increasing role of class politics, far stronger here than in Estonia and Lithuania. Based on the large Latvian (and Russian) working class in Riga and Liepāja (Libau), the Latvian social democratic movement in 1905 is said to have been bigger than the Russian Menshevik and Bolshevik organisations combined. It drew its inspiration mainly from Germany rather than from Russia. The Latvian poet Jānis Rainis brought Marxist texts from August Bebel to Latvia. In Rainis's case, national allegiance eventually dominated, but his brother-in-law, Pēteris Stučka, became the Bolshevik leader in Latvia during the Civil War. After the defeat of the 1905 revolution, Latvian social democracy grew closer to Bolshevism, but tried to maintain a certain autonomy.

In the course of the 1905 revolution in Latvia, 184 manor houses were burned and 635 Germans (including 82 nobles) and Russians killed by the rebels. In Estonia, perhaps due to a calmer national spirit or a smaller urban proletariat, there was much less violence, although a good deal of arson. The Latvians and to a lesser extent the Estonians showed their resentment of the German-dominated Lutheran church by attacks on its German pastors. The Germans not surprisingly participated enthusiastically in the restoration of order by the Imperial Army, and between 900 and 2,000 Latvians and local Russians were executed or killed, and 2,652 deported to Siberia. Any hope of a long-term compromise between Latvians, Estonians and Baltic Germans vanished, but Imperial Russia was obviously in no position to exploit this.

For much of its period under Russian rule, the Lithuanian provinces of Kovno (Kaunas) and Vilna (Vilnius) behaved as an extension of the Polish lands and rose in revolt in 1830 and 1863. A closeness of outlook between Lithuanian peasant and Polish-speaking lord (whose family was after all usually originally Lithuanian by blood) persisted into the twentieth century, greatly strengthened of course by common religion. The events of 1905 were far less violent in the Lithuanian countryside than in the Latvian and Estonian provinces, and land reforms in Lithuania after 1918 were more generous to the landlords, even though by that stage Lithuania and Poland were at war.

In 1863, the tiny Lithuanian-speaking urban intelligentsia held itself substantially aloof, as did the infinitely larger local Jewish population. Neither was forgiven for this by Polish nationalists, and one of the main Polish charges made against the Lithuanian nationalists up to and after the revolution was that, wittingly or unwittingly, they were playing Russia's game and dividing opposition to the Russian Empire. As in the other provinces, therefore, the first decades of the Lithuanian national movement consisted primarily of a struggle to convince Lithuanians that they were in fact a separate people, and to create a national culture as the essential basis for a future political nation. The struggle was complicated by the role of the Catholic Church, common to both nations. The Church had been one of the main instruments of the Polonisation of Lithuania, a fact that has never been forgotten by more fundamentalist Lithuanian nationalists.* On the other hand, over the centuries, the pagan religious feeling of the Lithuanian peasantry had transferred itself easily enough to Catholicism, and the Church had become part of the national identity to a much greater degree than the German-dominated Lutheran churches in Latvia and Estonia. It played a key part in the development of the new national culture. A Protestant minister in East Prussia, Kristijonas Donelaitis, wrote the first major literary work in the Lithuanian language in the second half of the eighteenth century, and was followed in the nineteenth by several Catholic priests who wrote nationalist poetry. Education in Lithuania developed much more slowly than in Latvia and Estonia, and often the priest was the only literate man in his village. The awakening national consciousness of Lithuanian-speaking priests was therefore of crucial importance. Through them the Church played a vital cultural and political role in developing the national language by smuggling books in the Lithuanian-Latin alphabet across the border

---

* Lithuanian attachment to the Catholic Church was responsible for the country's most bloody incident between 1863 and the First World War, at the village of Kražiai (Kroze). A Russian move to close the village church led to a peasant riot which besieged the Governor of Kovno. He was rescued by Cossacks who proceeded to kill or rape much of the population and plunder the village.

from East Prussia. Between 1863 and 1904 the publication of books in the Latin alphabet, not just in the Polish language but in Lithuanian as well, had been forbidden by Russia.

The Church's national role during these years prefigures that of the Chronicle of the Lithuanian Catholic Church and Catholic resistance to Soviet rule, particularly of course the smuggling of the Chronicle to the West – carrying word of Soviet repression in Lithuania – and the smuggling of religious literature in the reverse direction. The memory of this has always modified anti-clerical feeling among liberals or nationalists in Lithuania.*

A Baltic German newspaper once declared that 'here the family tree has no meaning in determining nationality. This is not inherited, but self-acquired' – on the basis of economic achievement, social rank or marriage.[15] In the German-dominated provinces this was in fact true only to a limited extent because of German resistance to Latvian and Estonian social mobility, but in Lithuania it had been very much the case.

As Lithuanian nationalism grew, the Polish-speaking nobility in the region, who had always considered themselves good Lithuanians as well as good Poles, found themselves faced with an agonising choice of national allegiances, a choice which is as alive and almost as painful today. In this part of Europe fault-lines in the process of self-definition run not just between populations, but right down the middle of families.

---

* In this respect Lithuania may be compared with Ireland where, in the past, the Church has also acted as an agent of Anglicisation but where it too has been forgiven by nationalists because it was both so powerful and so central a part of a national identity in mortal danger.

3

Independence Won and Lost, 1918–40

'O rose, take an axe in your hand,
And smash your way through the dunghill,
Through fate, hardened fate,
Before it is too late.'

Jānis Rokpelnis,
a Latvian poet under Soviet rule

The period of the first Baltic struggles for independence, from 1917 to 1920, has been so intensively mythologised in subsequent Baltic culture that it came as a shock to realise that, as a minor participant in the events of 1990 to 1991, I was myself living through a period to which Balts are already according the same mythology. In the struggle to achieve Baltic independence and Baltic national identities, memory, and memory re-worked as myth, have always been as important as economics or diplomacy, let alone tanks or guns. For Lithuanians in particular, a mythologised history has taken the place of a national myth, encapsulated in Latvia and Estonia within the recreated national poetic epics. Dealing with Lithuanian nationalist politicians during the second independence struggle, I was repeatedly made aware that they were operating only partly in the present; underlying everything that they did was a consideration of how their actions would look before a pageant of Lithuanian history beginning with the Grand Duchy and extending into the history books of the future. The events of 1990 and 1991 were turned into myth even as they occurred, and seized upon by different political forces – above all by Professor Landsbergis and his supporters – as part of their claim to supreme national legitimacy. There have of course been Western examples of this syndrome (Churchill and de Gaulle being the most famous) but they are difficult to find in Western Europe today. This is perhaps another sign of the fact, often repeated by Balts, that for them, the Second World War ended only with the recovery of independence in the early 1990s. Soviet rule in the previous decades, like the partition of

Germany, had been in a sense a continuation of the Second World War and its aftermath.

The history of the first independence struggle and the first period of independence is thus a force in shaping the politics of the present. Not merely are some politicians casting themselves in the role of their childhood heroes, but for lack of any other tradition the new Baltic States are modelling not just their political symbolism, but their political ideologies, parties and state institutions, on those of the period of independence between 1918 and 1940. This alone makes that period an essential object of study for anyone interested in understanding the contemporary Baltic scene. The Europe of the 1920s and 1930s was of course very different; like other European states, the politics of the Baltic in those years incorporated strong anti-democratic trends. Thanks to Soviet rule, the Baltic States have been isolated from subsequent European liberal and democratic influence and there has never been a real debate (except to a limited extend among Baltic emigrés) about the positive and negative aspects of pre-1940 Baltic political traditions.

The effect of too much unanalysed nostalgia has been to distance the Balts from modern Western Europe and to contribute to worrying political tendencies at home. The drawing of lessons from the experience of those years can also lead to serious misjudgements about the international position of the Baltic States today. During the recent independence struggle the recalling of myths of the earlier struggle occasionally led to decisions which at the time looked barely rational – though they may look good in the history books. A historian must therefore be cautious about making too many comparisons between the first struggle for Baltic independence and that of our time. The first was above all an armed struggle; the second, so far at least, has been conducted by peaceful means. In 1917 there had never been Estonian or Latvian states, and the nationalist leaders were aiming at autonomy within a democratic Russian Federation, if only because they regarded such a link as their only protection against conquest by the Germans; they declared full independence only after Russia itself had collapsed into the hands of the Bolsheviks.

It is possible to imagine that a 'bourgeois' government in Russia, had it survived the First World War, could have made sufficient compromises with the Balts to have kept them within such a federation. Despite the Baltic blood shed by the Russian Empire, the last decades of Russian imperial rule had been years of great prosperity and social progress for the Baltic provinces, progress which had indeed spawned the Baltic national intelligentsias. By contrast the nationalist leaders of 1987–91 had always before their eyes an image of the full independence enjoyed by the Baltic States between 1918 and 1940, and the utter failure of Soviet rule to produce stable economic progress. They could not in the long run have

The Baltic Provinces of the Russian Empire in 1914

settled for anything less than full independence, and this in turn would have been bound to undermine Moscow's rule elsewhere in the Soviet Union.

The First Struggle for Independence

As in our own time, the initial chance for Baltic freedom during the First World War was given by events in Russia. The February Revolution of 1917 brought the immediate replacement of imperial governors in Estonia and Livonia by commissioners of the Russian Provisional Government – the Latvian and Estonian Mayors of Riga and Tallinn. Representatives of Latvian organisations met and chose provisional councils to replace the governing institutions of the Baltic German nobility.[2] The Council in Latgale called for union with the other Latvian provinces, but this was opposed by the large local Russian population. Lithuania was not directly affected by the revolution because it was under German occupation, having been overrun in 1915. The position of the Latvians was complicated by the fact that half their area was also under German control. Both Latvians and Estonians were still thinking in terms of autonomy within a Russian federation, and there was general surprise when on 7 September 1917 the Estonian politician, Jaan Tönisson, argued for independence from Russia and the creation of a federation of Scandinavia and the Baltic lands. A majority however continued to advocate union with Russia.

The Bolsheviks meanwhile were strengthening their position on local soldiers' and workers' councils, and in Riga, in municipal elections in August gained 41 per cent of the vote. In Estonia their position was weaker, and based partly on the local Russian working class. After the coup of October 1917, the Bolsheviks took over the administration of much of the Baltic. Bolshevik terror ensued, targeted partly at the politicians and partly at the Baltic German nobility. In both Latvia and Estonia, non-communist leaders were now aiming at complete independence, if only to escape from the Bolsheviks, and were hoping for support from the West.

The Baltic Germans were of course hoping for German conquest, and this came soon enough; by April 1918, the whole area was in German hands. For many Balts it seemed, at the time, a catastrophe as bad or worse than Bolshevik rule.[3] In fact, however, German occupation was to give the Balts a crucial breathing space. Without it there is little reason to doubt that Latvia and Estonia would simply have remained part of Bolshevik Russia.

In November 1918, German defeat in the West led to the armistice with the Western allies and withdrawal from most of the Baltic States. The Soviet commander-in-chief at the time was a Latvian, Jakums Vācietis, a colonel from the Latvian Rifle Regiments. Formed by the Russian Imperial government to fight the Germans, several of these units subsequently joined the Bolsheviks and played a key part in their victory in the Russian Civil War, while others fought for the Latvian national government. The British envoy, Bruce Lockhart, commented on the Riflemen's mixture of dour discipline and savagery. The German ambassador in Moscow described them as 'a corset holding together the friable body of the Red Army'. Latvians also provided some of the most ruthless leaders of the *Cheka*, Lenin's secret police and of Stalin's N.K.V.D. During the struggle for Latvian independence in 1990, a Russian colonel in the republic, protesting his affection for the Latvian people and wanting to pay a national compliment, said that the Latvian 'Chekists' had been his childhood heroes! After the Soviet conquests of 1940 and 1944 these Latvians from Russia were to provide many of the Soviet cadres for the government of Latvia.[4] The tradition continued in our time with men like Colonel Viktors Alksnis, whose grandfather, Jēkabs Alksnis, was one of the founders of the Soviet Air Force before being shot by Stalin in 1937. Whereas in Estonia and Lithuania, the native defenders of Soviet rule between 1988 and 1991 were tiny in number and pathetic in intellect, the Soviet loyalist leadership in Latvia contained a number of significant Latvian figures.

In November 1918 Soviet troops, drawn partly from the Riflemen, marched into the Baltic States immediately behind the retreating Germans, and by 2 January 1919 were within 35 kilometres of Tallinn. Thereafter Estonian troops, superbly led by a former Tsarist colonel, Johannes Laidoner, turned the tide and, within a few weeks, had pushed them back into Russia. Weapons and supplies were provided by a British squadron, which also prevented any landing on the northern coast by the Soviet Baltic fleet, and several hundred volunteers arrived from Finland and Scandinavia.*

Encouraged by the British, the Estonians subsequently gave support to the White Russian forces in their attempt to capture Petrograd; it was however half-hearted support, because of the refusal of the commander, General Yudenich, to guarantee Estonian independence. In support of the Whites, the Estonians advanced into Russia itself, and by the final armistice with Soviet Russia had occupied two strips of territory which, although partly inhabited by Finnic-speaking people, had been a part of

---

* On 18 August 1919, in a striking but strangely uncelebrated victory, British torpedo boats penetrated the heart of the Kronstadt naval base, one of the most heavily defended in the world, and sank two Bolshevik battleships at their moorings.

Russia and had large Russian majorities: the town of Ivangorod opposite Narva and the area of Petseri (Pechori), near Pskov. These areas were then incorporated into independent Estonia by the Treaty of Tartu signed with Soviet Russia on 2 February 1920. In 1945, after the Soviet reconquest, they were returned to Russia by Stalin. Estonia is now asking for their restitution.

Latvia meanwhile had been largely overrun by the Bolsheviks, and the Latvian national government of Kārlis Ulmanis was forced to flee to the port of Liepāja, where it survived under the protection of the German army and the British fleet. A Bolshevik government was instituted in Riga under Pēteris Stučka, and instituted a brutal reign of terror. Famine broke out and thousands starved to death. However, while the invasion of Estonia by the Bolsheviks was a fairly straightforward attempt at conquest, the war in Latvia had far more aspects of a civil war between Latvians themselves.

The anti-Bolshevik forces were deeply divided between the Latvians and the Germans, including the 'Baltische Landeswehr', made up of local Baltic Germans and determined to avoid Latvian rule. On 16 April this force staged a coup against Ulmanis's government and forced it to take refuge on a British warship. Heavy British pressure on Germany compelled the Germans to back down and on 22 May, a combined offensive of German, Latvian and White Russian troops captured Riga from the Bolsheviks, while the Estonians advanced south to liberate northern Latvia. This and the Estonian victories of January were the first military checks to the eastwards advance of Soviet communism into Europe.[5] On 22 June, the Estonians and Latvians also defeated the Baltic German Landeswehr and German 'Freikorps' volunteer units, and avenged themselves for seven-hundred years of rule by the German nobility. The result of the final Latvian-Estonian victory over the Germans in October was a complete German withdrawal from Latvia. In December the Latvians in alliance with Poland, conquered Latgale from the Bolsheviks, and it was incorporated into independent Latvia by the Riga Treaty of 1 August 1920 with Russia.

The Lithuanian national government meanwhile had been facing a double threat from both Soviet Russia and Poland. The Bolsheviks also invaded in November 1918, but by the summer of 1919 had been driven from Lithuanian territory. Vilnius meanwhile had been changing hands (and its official name) with bewildering speed, part 'sacred national symbol', part bargaining-chip.

In January 1919, after a Lithuanian rule of two months following the German collapse, Vilnius fell into the hands of the Bolsheviks. On April 15 it was captured by the Poles, who later made it an autonomous region in the hope of using it to tempt Lithuania to restore the old confederation with Poland. At the time Vilnius was a mainly Polish-Jewish city with a Lithuanian minority variously estimated at between 2 and 20 per cent. A year later, the Poles launched an offensive against Soviet Russia, were initially defeated, and handed Vilnius to the Lithuanians – after they had already lost it to the Bolsheviks. The Bolsheviks themselves gave it to the Lithuanians on 25 August in return for permission to cross Lithuanian territory on their way to attack the Poles. The Poles then counter-attacked and defeated the Bolsheviks. At this time Poles and Lithuanians were also fighting each other, in a desultory way.

On 7 October 1920 a Polish-Lithuanian armistice tacitly left Vilnius in Lithuanian hands but immediately afterwards, the Polish general Lucijan Zeligowski staged a 'revolt' – with the compliance and later open approval of the Polish leader, Marshal Pilsudski – and seized the city. Lithuanians have bemoaned this 'Polish aggression' ever since, and it continues to bedevil Lithuanian-Polish relations and Lithuanian policies towards the Polish minority in Lithuania. For an ironical descant on the competing choirs of Polish and Lithuanian apologists, one can turn to a memoir by a Jewish inhabitant of Vilna, Joseph Buloff, who describes one of the many 'liberations' as follows:

> At the end of the third day, a Polish flag with a white eagle flew from the still-smouldering town hall. A new parade was announced – this time for Poles only. There were no more greens, whites or reds. All and everybody became Poles overnight, except for the Jews. The Jews took it in their stride. They had served, in their life, under many flags. . . .[6]

In January 1923, Lithuania, in order to give itself a port but also to compensate itself for the loss of Vilnius, seized the German town of Memel (now Klaipėda), held since 1919 by the League of Nations, and retained it until Hitler forced its return in 1939. Another effect of the loss of Vilnius was to force the Lithuanians to make their 'provisional' capital in Kaunas (Kovno), a city divided between Lithuanians and Jews, with small Polish and German communities. This move to a smaller and less cosmopolitan city has been responsible for encouraging some of the narrower and more depressing features of subsequent Lithuanian nationalism. During the struggle for independence from Soviet rule, the radical nationalist wing of the Lithuanian national movement was long known simply as 'the Kaunas Faction'. These forces continue to harbour a deep distrust of Vilnius for its 'cosmopolitan' past, still reflected in a more varied and liberal culture. Some would even like to move the capital back to Kaunas, which they term 'the pure home of the race'.

Economic and Social Consolidation

The history of the Baltic States between 1920 and 1940 was characterised by great economic success, internal political failure, and foreign policy frustration followed by catastrophe: in 1940 they were annexed by Stalin's Soviet Union. This catastrophe was however a product of events and forces far beyond the Balt's own control, though controversy rages still as to whether their fate could have been averted or at least altered.

At the end of their wars of independence, the Baltic States were in a state of economic chaos which, on the surface, makes their present situation look almost benign by comparison, although in fact they were better placed than they are today. Latvia had suffered particularly badly because, for most of the war, the front line had run across what was to become Latvian territory. In 1915, much of the population had either fled or been evacuated by the Russian government, along with the major industries, many of which were removed or destroyed.[7] The total population dropped from 2.55 million in 1913 to only 1.84 million in 1925. By 1950, with the effects of the Second World War and Stalinism added, Latvia had become the only European country whose population had declined in absolute terms since 1900, and Estonia was not far behind. The 1915–17 losses, however, helped stabilise independent Latvia, both by sharply reducing the Russian minority and by reducing the number of urban workers, who would otherwise have simply been unemployed. It can be said that, unlike 1991, when the Russian Empire retreated from the Baltic in 1915–17 it took much of the 'imperial' industries (those dependent on the Russian hinterland) and their workforces with it.

During the War and Civil War, all the Baltic provinces suffered from massive requisitions of food, material and animals, and from the transfer of their principal industries to Russia. As today, those industries remaining were severely affected by the loss of their pre-1914 markets and sources of supply in Russia. Monetary confusion was exacerbated by chaos in the banking system, the headquarters of which, in St Petersburg, had been seized by the Bolsheviks. A basic banking infrastructure and personnel however remained in the Baltic states. This was perhaps the greatest advantage of the Baltic States in 1920 as compared with today: then, the Baltic area had long been part of capitalist Europe, and had many people, officials and private businessmen, Balts and members of other communities, with a tradition of experience in the workings of capitalism. Baltic industry was also equipped to Western standards, and the Balts had longstanding markets in the West. Today, these markets have to be created from scratch. Experience of capitalism is present only in the Baltic emigrations in the West, while Balts brought up under Soviet rule have not merely to be trained, but often retrained, and cured of everything they learned under Soviet rule. Moreover, decades of communist influence have strengthened certain traditional peasant suspicions of capitalism, especially in Lithuania.

Lithuania between the Wars was still an overwhelmingly peasant economy, with, in 1920, 79 per cent of the population engaged in agriculture. The Latvian and Estonian economies were more mixed, but in these republics too, 66 and 58 per cent respectively were farmers. This meant that unemployed urban workers could always be absorbed back onto family farms. It also made the land reforms of 1920 of critical importance. These reforms were the rock on which the Baltic republics were founded, and which contributed greatly to their relative social and political stability, until destroyed by outside intervention. The 1920s saw a major swing from radical politics in all three Baltic States, the richer peasants later becoming the mainstay of the nationalist dictatorships. Today this link between the peasantry and the Right has been broken. In Lithuania, most of the peasantry is more strongly attached to the former Communists of Algirdas Brazauskas.

Because in Latvia and Estonia more than half the land had been held by the great landlords, mostly Baltic Germans, the scope of the land reforms of 1920 was enormous. Compensation was minimal, though in conservative Lithuania, landlords succeeded in retaining more than in the other two republics.[8] Before 1914 one third all Russia's European trade had passed through Latvian ports, and Riga, Tallinn and Narva had huge industries (the Kreenholm cotton mill in Narva was the biggest in the Empire) relying on Russian raw materials. Initially both Balts and Western investors assumed, as they do today, that the main economic role of the Baltic States would continue to be that of a bridge to and from Russia. As the 1920s progressed, however, it became clear that Soviet Russia's external trade would never return to its pre-1914 levels, and that opportunities for western investment would remain almost non-existent. 25 per cent of Estonia's trade was still with Russia in 1922, but by 1935 it had fallen to only 3 per cent, and Latvia's was no higher – an extraordinary testimony to the hermetic seal placed by Stalin between the Soviet Union and the rest of the world.[9]

This situation is however very unlikely to replicate itself in the 1990s. Unless Russia were to collapse completely, the Balts, thanks to the way they were integrated into the Soviet economy, will go on trading heavily with Russia, and this is bound to have repercussions on their political situation. Before 1914, Riga and Tallinn were exporting very large quantities of both manufactured and agricultural produce to Western Europe. On the recovery of independence in 1991, due to Soviet rule, their exports to the West were miniscule, although those of Estonia at least have increased greatly since then.

Following the loss of the Russian connection, Baltic trade and industry in the 1920s and 1930s had of necessity to be based chiefly on local

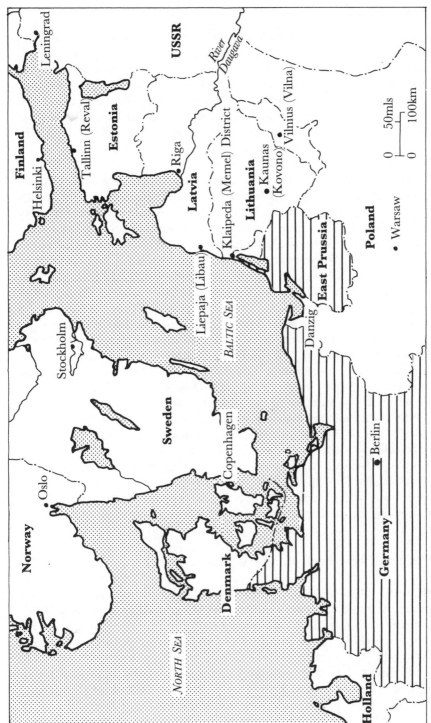

The Baltic Lands between the two World Wars

resources, above all agriculture, while many of the great factories remained idle or were largely dismantled. Agricultural exports however largely compensated for the decline. These rose steadily through the 1920s, before dipping sharply after the Slump of 1929. In the 1930s they recovered, and by 1939 had almost reached their pre-slump level. The Latvian and Estonian economies were in general among the most successful in Europe in their recovery from the depression; this was perhaps the most important achievement of the authoritarian regimes of Kārlis Ulmanis and Konstantin Päts.

The Estonian standard of living in 1939 was roughly equivalent to that of Finland, with Latvia not far behind. Lithuania however was much poorer and more agricultural. Of course even Estonia was considerably poorer than West European countries, but this was not obvious because, like the other Baltic States, Estonia lacked the West's extremes of wealth and poverty. Although in the early 1920s many visitors had commented on the misery left behind by the war and revolution, by the 1930s Western visitors to Latvia and Estonia were greatly impressed by the apparent well-being of ordinary people.[10] The first period of independence saw a great expansion in educational provision within the three republics, and some notable achievements in the field of culture. Lithuania started from a much weaker position, with almost one third of the population illiterate when the republic was established; but by the 1930s it had increased its proportion of pupils almost seven-fold – though its schools remained of a poorer quality than those of the other republics.

When therefore the Balts look back to their first period of independence as an idyllic time, there is a good deal of truth to their view. It makes all the more bitter the contrast between their economic position relative to Scandinavia in those years, and the vast gulf that separates them today. This in itself would have been enough completely to undermine Soviet claims to have brought 'progress' to the Baltic, and to destroy the entire moral basis of Soviet rule.

The Failure of Parliamentary Democracy, 1920–34

After 1918, all three Baltic States adopted democratic constitutions as a matter of course. With the victory of the Western Allies over the Kaiser's Germany, democratic ideals were predominant, strengthened by the almost messianic hopes attached to the League of Nations and to the philosophy of President Woodrow Wilson. By the mid-1930s, all three Baltic democracies had collapsed and been replaced by authoritarian regimes, albeit of a mild kind. One of the problems of all three Baltic constitutions was that they were too democratic for their own good. Parliaments, elected by universal suffrage and full proportional representation, were given almost complete control over the governments. In the words of V. Stanley Vardys, 'the executive branch was completely dependent on unqualified decisions, better described as whims. The Estonian constitution so magnified the powers of the parliament . . . that the institution itself formed the government and accepted its resignation'.[11]

Today the Soviet system and the movements which overthrew it have also, paradoxically, left parliaments in the Baltic with excessive powers. From 1990 to 1992 (and in the case of Latvia, even beyond that), the Baltic States functioned under slightly modified versions of their Soviet constitutions. It made the distribution of power under the constitution extremely unclear, because the real fulcrum, the Communist Party had disappeared. The Supreme Councils or 'parliaments' found themselves issuing administrative decrees and controlling details of government policy. They were able to do this precisely because they and their chairmen had previously been rubber-stamps and their powers had never been defined. This problem of excessive parliamentary powers surfaced all over the former Soviet Union, most dangerously of all in Russia.

The new Estonian and Lithuanian constitutions, adopted in the autumn of 1992, were intended to eliminate these faults (see Chapter 8). However, both undermine collective responsibility and the authority of the prime minister by allowing parliament to dismiss individual ministers, and both allow too many parties into parliament. There is therefore a risk that, as in the 1920s and 1930s, constitutional weaknesses will conspire with political ones – especially the lack of party discipline – to undermine the fledgling parliamentary democracies of the Baltic.

Before democracy was overthrown in Latvia and Estonia in 1934, they experienced sixteen and seventeen governments respectively. In Lithuania, democracy lasted only seven years, but produced eleven governments.* The plethora of governments did not greatly hinder the implementation of major reforms, the stabilisation of the economies, or advances in education and culture – but then these were European bourgeois societies, long accustomed to living in an atmosphere of economic free enterprise, and of considerable freedom of thought.

In recent years too, at least in Lithuania and Estonia, reforms have also proceeded at a fair rate despite frequent parliamentary chaos. However, the underlying cultural situation today is different from that in the first period of independence. After decades of Communist rule, most people instinctively expect the government to provide a lead, and do not

---

* This time, in the 34 months between the Lithuanian declaration of independence on 11 March 1990 and Christmas 1992, Lithuania has had five prime ministers.

take kindly to being led in conflicting directions. Moreover, after 1918, the former republics of Latvia and Estonia possessed at least small but competent civil services, which took over the government after the coups. No such cadres exist today, and their creation is one of the most urgent tasks of Western aid and training in the region.

The coups of Latvia and Estonia came as the result of long political and economic crises resulting in part from the world economic depression. They appear to have been grudgingly accepted by the great majority of the populations. The coup of 1926 in Lithuania, by contrast, appears to have had far more to do with political opportunism and a gut dislike of democracy on the part of Right-wing and military forces in Lithuania. One factor was the way that Antanas Smetona and Augustinas Voldemaras, the main leaders of Lithuania during its struggle for independence between 1918 and 1920, and their party, the Nationalists (*Tautininkai*) had been subsequently excluded from office by other political forces, rooted in Catholicism or socialism (this exclusion from power of the forces which see themselves as the true heroes of the independence struggle could be a major problem in Lithuania today). The Nationalists, with limited public support (except among officers, students and intellectuals), appear to have despaired of ever returning to power by democratic means. By 1926, Mussolini had seised power in Italy and Pilsudski in Poland: the hegemony of democratic ideology in European political thought was already compromised.

In 1926, a Populist-Social Democrat coalition took power, dependent for support on the ethnic minorities, including the Poles. Concessions to the Poles in the field of education, at a time when Poland was closing Lithuanian schools in the Vilnius area, allowed the Right to allege treason. The government was blamed by the public for unpopular economic measures, and by the army for plans to cut costs by reducing the officer corps. In December 1926, therefore, the army, supported by Catholic political forces, overthrew the elected government, imposing Smetona as President and Voldemaras as Prime Minister.[12] Initially Smetona ruled in coalition with the Christian Democrats, but in 1927 dissolved parliament and promulgated a new constitution providing for a strong presidency. Two years later he dismissed Voldemaras, who had turned to fascism, supported by the overtly fascistic 'Iron Wolf' paramilitary organisation (today, once again in the process of revival) which subsequently staged repeated coup attempts to bring Voldemaras to power. The last was in 1934, after which Voldemaras was arrested and imprisoned until 1938. This was one of a series of no fewer than thirteen attempted coups (or movements dubbed as such by the Lithuanian government) by different forces in the first period of Lithuanian independence.

From 1930, Smetona's regime developed certain fascist characteristics.

Smetona was addressed as Leader of the Nation. The Tautininkai Party was reorganised on the 'Leader-Principle' and given extensive state powers, and its linked 'Veterans' Association' expanded to become a state paramilitary volunteer force, on the model of those of Germany or Italy. All other party youth organisations were ultimately incorporated into the Tautininkai's 'Young Lithuania' organisation, with the official motto of 'Lithuania for the Lithuanians'. Both 'Young Lithuania' and the Tautininkai have now been revived, with their pre-1940 ideology and symbolism (which in the case of 'Young Lithuania', initially included the fascist salute).

Under Smetona, a leader of Young Lithuania declared that,

> Young Lithuania operates on an authoritarian basis. It knows only one leader – the Nation's Leader, Antanas Smetona. . . . Young Lithuania steadfastly believes that the nation can only be united when the will of one leader prevails.

Harsh punishments were envisaged for crimes against the state, though the death penalty was rarely imposed. In the opinion of the historian Georg von Rauch, 'as a result of these measures Lithuania had virtually become an authoritarian one-party state', to a much greater extent than in Latvia or Estonia during their period of authoritarian rule in the 1930s. All the elements of Smetona's regime professed a public ideology of intolerant nationalism.

The Lithuanian emigré historian Leonas Sabaliunas quotes Nationalist ideologues of the period on the need for 'total pedagogics in a young nation-state, seeking a monolithic national body and a collective soul', and such regimented aphorisms as 'a national-state, as a matter of course, presupposes a national orientation in art' and 'the nation-state is essentially a totalitarian state'.[13] However Sabaliunas observes correctly that Smetona and his regime were far less radical and above all, less brutal than these ideologues would have wished, and that 'there is reason to assume that Lithuanian politics was modified to a considerable extent by fidelity to ethical norms'. The universities and even the courts retained a real measure of independence.

Although a strong nationalist, Smetona shunned racial ideology. Despite deep conflicts with the Catholic Church over its social and political role, and its relations with Poland, he remained a practising Catholic, unlike Hitler, Mussolini and other fascist leaders. In general, he did not have either the violence or the revolutionary streak of a true fascist. There is about Smetona's regime the air of some Third World countries in recent decades, those which have donned one or other Western ideology and used it for their own ends without participating in it or putting it fully into practice; in Smetona's time, the dominant

European ideology was fascism, and some surprising people in Western Europe were also prepared to admire some of its characteristics.

Although Smetona's regime sometimes used anti-semitic language, this was not its official ideology, and there were no officially sponsored pogroms. Smetona spoke on occasions of the religious tolerance of ancient Lithuania, and the contemporary Jewish-Lithuanian poet, Mark Zingeris, has praised Smetona as a man of the enlightenment who had many Jewish friends and did not share the crude chauvinism of many of his supporters.

There is little doubt that Professor Landsbergis, the Lithuanian leader between 1990 and 1992, regards himself as in some ways the political heir of Smetona. He has referred to him admiringly in speeches, and adopted some of his symbolism, though not the most extreme; Landsbergis also uses more Catholic symbolism, and has a much closer alliance with the Church than did Smetona. Landsbergis certainly has authoritarian tendencies, but he cannot be described as a fascist. His unsuccessful drive to become the 'Father of the Nation' is described in Chapter 8. It has led him into a tactical alliance with some very dubious Right-wing forces, as well as with the Catholic Church, and to demagogic and vicious verbal attacks on his opponents, including old allies. However, Landsbergis sees himself as a force for controlling and moderating the extreme Right; and a number of liberal and objective Lithuanian emigré scholars of my acquaintance were also prepared for a long time to see him in that light. Following the victory of the former Communists in the elections of October 1992, it was widely believed that the extreme Right might be tempted to carry out a coup, but that they would be restrained by Landsbergis, if only for the sake of his reputation in the West. This of course recalls Smetona, for whatever the disquieting sides of his regime, he at least averted a victory by Voldemaras, who it seems safe to say would have introduced fascism in the fullest sense. V. Stanley Vardys's description of Smetona as 'mild-mannered but clever and stubborn' strongly recalls the character of Landsbergis as well; but unfortunately with one difference.[14] Smetona was a fairly able administrator with a long experience of practical affairs. Landsbergis, though a shrewd political tactician, is according to members of his own staff fundamentally uninterested in questions of administration, finance, and legislation, far preferring the worlds of foreign visits, symbolism and rhetoric, and the Lithuanian culture he so deeply loves. This is a common feature among intellectual politicians who have risen to prominence in several former Communist states, for under the Communists they were excluded from any administrative role. These are qualities which would make Landsbergis an excellent symbolic Head of State; unfortunately, the Smetona tradition dictates an executive presidency, which is also possibly what Lithuania needs today. It was Landsbergis's ambition to fill this role – but in February 1993, it was his arch-rival, former Communist leader Algirdas Brazauskas, who was actually to achieve it.

The Roots of Authoritarianism

In Estonia and Latvia, democracy outlived that of Lithuania by seven years, and collapsed only after these societies had suffered several years of economic recession. In both cases, the coups were carried out by men who, like Smetona, had helped to found the new nations, and part of their motivation was to head off a seizure of power by the extreme Right.*

Before 1934, Estonia did not even have a formal head of state, but only a prime minister, wholly dependent upon parliament. The average life of an Estonian government in the 1920s was eight months, and with as many as fourteen parties represented in parliament, forming a government could take weeks. However, the same parties and individuals were represented in many of the governments, so the picture was not much more unstable than that of France at that time. By the world slump of the early 1930s, economic fears, especially on the part of the middle classes, encouraged the growth of a fascistic movement, the League of Veterans (or 'Freedom Fighters') of the War of Independence. The founders of this organisation were in fact veterans, but it expanded to become a general political movement with a uniformed paramilitary wing.

The League's ideology was strongly nationalist, anti-communist, anti-parliamentary, anti-semitic, and opposed to ethnic minorities in general. It was influenced by European fascism, and more immediately by the Lapua movement in neighbouring Finland. In the municipal elections of January 1934 the League won absolute majorities in Estonia's three main cities, and seemed on its way to the presidency. To head off the League's rise, and citing plots for a coup d'état (which has never been proved), the prime minister, Konstantin Päts, on 12 March 1934 proclaimed martial law, banned the League, arrested 400 of its leading members, and banished others from the civil service and army. The action was supported by the Socialists, who saw all too clearly what would happen if the League took power. Later that year, after parliament began to oppose Päts' government, he suspended it and, in March 1935, banned all

---

* Estonia had faced one serious coup attempt on 1 December 1924, but this was the work of a few hundred communists, supported by Moscow. Twenty-one people, including the Communications Minister, were killed during the attempt, and forty or so executed afterwards by the Estonian authorities. There was no general rising of the working class, and thereafter the Communists in Estonia remained largely quiescent until 1939.

political parties. The newly formed 'Fatherland League' was the only permitted political force, though without most of the fascist trimmings of the Tautininkai in Lithuania.

No-one was executed under Päts' rule, though the Veterans' leader, Artur Sirk, may have been murdered by the President's secret service. After the uncovering of a further plot, other leading Veterans were given heavy prison sentences, though almost all, together with the Communists, were released under an amnesty in 1938. The press was strictly controlled, though there was no attempt to restrain intellectual life: the period is known to Estonians as 'the Era of Silence'. Until the end of the republic in 1940, Päts refused to allow the restoration of political parties. In 1937 he called an assembly to rubber-stamp a presidential constitution, with parliament enjoying greatly reduced powers, and appointed local officials to play an important role. Päts' prime minister termed this system 'guided democracy'. It is a matter of debate whether by 1940 Päts was planning a return to the genuine article; in any case, Stalin pre-empted matters.

Events in Latvia followed a similar course, though anti-democratic politics began sooner, under the influence of Germany and neighbouring Lithuania. Latvia had a variety of fascist groups, of which the most notable was the 'Fire Cross', later renamed the 'Thunder Cross'. As in Germany, pagan revivalist thought played a part in the cultural background to fascism (see Chapter 5). All these groups were bitterly hostile to Latvia's Russian, German and Jewish minorities, together making up almost a quarter of the population. The extreme Right also called for the proscription of all Left-wing parties.

Faced with what many saw as impending civil war, the premier, Kārlis Ulmanis (like Päts in Estonia, the chief founder of Latvian independence) declared a state of emergency on the night of 15 March 1934, suspended parliament and banned party activities. He ruled by decree until the end of the republic, but did not introduce a one-party state, although the 'Aizsargi' (Home Guards) functioned in some ways like a nationalist paramilitary force (and have been revived as an unofficial radical nationalist force in the Latvia of today). Ulmanis did not face great opposition to his rule, and was even able to recruit Social Democrats into his government. Although Ulmanis' government was virtually a 'dictatorship of consensus', it made life increasingly uncomfortable for Latvia's minorities, and indeed adopted the Right-wing slogan of 'Latvia for the Latvians' – hardly surprisingly since, in the 1920s, even the 'liberal' Democratic Centre bloc had adopted this phrase. In the 1920s Baltic Germans had played a role in several governments, but in the 1930s they were completely excluded, and the educational autonomy of the minorities was reduced. There was however no severe ethnic persecution in either Estonia or Latvia.

Both Ulmanis and Päts carried out steps to introduce 'corporatist' economic bodies, following a trend present not just in Nazism, but in Christian Democracy and other political forces of the time (and which indeed, in another guise, played a major part in German economic success after 1950). This did not, however, impede a very successful economic recovery in the 1930s, which by the end of the republic had raised the value of Latvian exports to more than five times the level of 1922.

Compared to the first period of independence, democracy in the Baltic States today has certain notable strengths but also certain weaknesses. Imperial Russia before 1917 provided more opportunities for constitutional politics than did the Soviet Union before Gorbachov, and the new national elites had much more experience of constitutionalism and administration. Furthermore, democracy today is strong largely because it is equated with capitalist prosperity (as a placard in East Germany in 1990 had it, 'Helmut [Kohl], Lead Us Into The Land of the Economic Miracle!'). In Russia, for obvious reasons, the 'Far Eastern Model' of authoritarian capitalist development already enjoys great prestige, and such thinking is bound to spread to the Baltic as well, albeit moderated by the history of Baltic emigration to North America, many representatives of which now advise the present Baltic governments. These add to the major strength of present Baltic democracy, which is the hegemony of democratic ideas in contemporary Europe, reinforced by European economic power and the lure of Western lifestyles and culture. This is affected of course by the awareness that the creation of authoritarian regimes would probably, though not necessarily, cost the Balts western aid and support. I have myself spent an inordinate amount of time in the Baltic States arguing with members of the extreme Right-wing parties about some of their ideas, and my knock-out blow (wrapped in less direct language) has always been: 'what you are saying is not European; it will separate you from the modern West'.

There are a good many radical nationalist ideologists in the contemporary Baltic who cordially despise the modern West, a contempt increased by what they see as the West's 'cowardice' and 'treachery' in failing to do more to save the Balts from Soviet conquest in the 1940s, and to support them after 1989, while the Balts were sacrificing themselves to save Europe from a new Soviet attack. In the words of Višvaldis Brinkmanis, a leader of the Latvian Citizens Congress: 'Don't you think that it is just as Oswald Spengler predicted? The Western nations have lost their pride and their morale and are mixing themselves with inferior races. . . .'[15]

At present this is very much a marginal view, compared with the general desire for the Baltic States to forge closer connections with the

West. There remains however another possibility: that Europe itself could swing towards the extreme Right. All the extreme nationalist parties in Latvia and Lithuania have taken great encouragement from the rise of Jean Marie Le Pen and the Front Nationale in France.[16] However, except to an extent in Lithuania, the mainstream Right-wing forces in the Baltic appear at present to be committed to democracy. The leaders of the 'Fatherland' (*Isamaa*) alliance in Estonia are both entirely sincere and very knowledgeable in their attempts to introduce Western conservative democratic ideas into Estonian politics. Even the far Right, the 'Estonian Citizen' group or the Citizens Committees in Latvia, have declared themselves for democracy in principle, even if some of their behaviour appears to belie this.

A further factor today is that this time, the Balts did not have to fight wars of independence. It follows that the various national paramilitary forces, and the new national armies, lack the prestige which comes from being seen as the 'saviours of the nation'. The importance of this is evident both in the history of Central and Eastern Europe in the 1920s, and in developments in the Soviet Caucasus today. Some of today's paramilitary groups would like to portray themselves in this light, but the reality is that it was crowds of ordinary, unarmed Baltic civilians who saved their countries in January 1991 by placing their bodies in the path of the Soviet tanks.

Although in the Baltic states of today there are far fewer people than in the 1920's who reject parliamentary democracy *per se*, there are considerable forces which deny the legitimacy of the existing constitutions. This stems from the rejection, during the struggle for independence, of the legitimacy of the Supreme Councils by former dissidents and more radical nationalist forces in general. This was partly on legalistic grounds, but chiefly because they were elected by all Soviet citizens in the republics, including all those Russian-speakers who moved there under Soviet rule. The radical forces rallied behind the Estonian and Latvian 'Congresses', organised by these forces and elected by pre-1940 citizens and their descendants only.

In Estonia, the problem of constitutional legitimacy appeared to be resolved by the constitutional assembly of 1991–92, which bridged the Congress and the Supreme Council, and adopted a constitution acceptable to both. This in turn was ratified by a referendum on 28 June. Only a small and seemingly insignificant group continued to reject the new order in favour of a return to the 'legitimate' (but authoritarian) constitution of 1938.

Unfortunately, in the elections of September 1992, the 'Estonian Citizen' group, representing this opinion, and led by a retired US colonel of Estonian origin, Juri Toomepuu, won 8 per cent of the parliamentary seats. The group was backed by a small armed volunteer force which rejected the authority of the Estonian government in favour of a self-appointed 'government in exile' of which Toomepuu was the 'Defence Minister'. These elements are also of course bitterly hostile to the Russian minority, much of which they hope to pressure into leaving.

In Lithuania, a referendum accompanying the October 1992 elections ratified the acceptance of the draft parliamentary constitution drawn up by parliament. In Latvia, with the future constitution still wholly unsettled by the end of 1992, much larger forces continued to reject the authority of the Supreme Council, especially when it came to deciding constitutional matters and those of 'national importance' such as the issue of citizenship to the Russian 'immigrant' population. The paper of the Latvian Congress, *Pilsonis*, even on one occasion called for armed revolt against the 'crypto-communist regime', and for this was banned by a Latvian court.

In early 1993 the influence of such rejectionist forces was still limited. The risk for democracy is that the mainstream political forces might find themselves forced to make a compromise with the Russian minorities which would be rejected not only by the radical nationalists but by many ordinary Balts as well. If this came in the context of potential or actual conflict between Balts and local Russians, then the extremist groups could grow rapidly. The prestige of these groups is strengthened by the fact that they are largely led by men and women who resisted Soviet rule, and in some cases paid the price with years of imprisonment. Some of their friends paid with their lives. Even those who find some of their ideas disastrous cannot but respect their personal honour, courage and patriotism. So far, this has not been reflected in strong political support (see Chapter 4), but it remains a reservoir of historical prestige which may be drawn on if the mainstream forces discredit themselves.

By contrast, among the mainstream national leaders, even Landsbergis has no record of anti-Soviet resistance, while several of the leading figures in Latvia and Estonia were communist officials. In the 1920s, the extreme Right regularly raised the cry of 'national treachery' and of 'communist plots', but this cry is far stronger and more effective today. And since – for better or worse – former Communist leaders like Anatolijs Gorbunovs and Arnold Rüütel remain very popular with large sections of the population in their republics (not just local Russians, but Balts as well), the Far Right's denial of their legitimacy extends into a denial of the will of the electorate and anti-democratic feeling in general. To the extreme Right, any senior former Communist is automatically an agent of Moscow (in Lithuania, anyone who opposes the Right is labelled in this way). Since the great majority of the civil services and establishments of the three states are still made up of former Communists, this leads some radicals to a feeling that they have an absolute national duty to watch and control their own governments. In the words of one of the leaders of the *Šauliai*, a Lithuanian nationalist paramilitary force, asked if his force would allow a Left-wing government to take power: 'Of course, if they were properly elected they would be allowed to take power. But we would watch them very carefully; and if we saw that they were betraying Lithuania, we would have to act to save the nation.'[17]

This attitude led to fears – fortunately unfulfilled – that a victory of the former Communists in the 1992 elections would be undermined or even reversed by the paramilitaries, forces strengthened by an element in the dissident tradition which the paramilitary shares with that of the Freikorps. Both have involved small bodies of activists sacrificing themselves on behalf of populations which were basically passive, and which could well be seen as cowardly or lazy. Like the Leninist tradition of a small party of activists acting on behalf of the revolutionary masses, this does not encourage respect for the will of the electorate.

All adult Balts studied Leninism at school, and their model for the role of the activist party is in many ways a Leninist one. Asked about Latvian public support for Gorbunovs, National Independence Party activists in Latvia replied with contempt that this was made up of 'the uneducated, stupid women, ex-Communists and Communist dupes'. After Sajūdis's defeat in 1992, one of its workers snarled that 'the illiterate peasants have been duped by the Communists', and a leader of the radical Liberty League told me that, 'This shows that many Lithuanians want to be slaves. We must teach them to change this mentality' – classically Leninist words, which help explain why such groups are not very good at winning the votes of the 'illiterate peasants' in question.[18]

Another potential problem emerges from the experience of Eastern Europe between the wars. A key weakness of parliamentary government in many states was that it had to be built on coalitions, and the number of 'coalitionable' democratic parties in the centre (parties willing to make coalitions with each other and to support the existing state) was always liable to erosion from Left and Right, until in the end the band of centrist parties was so narrow that it became impossible to govern at all. Moreover, the necessity of repeatedly constructing governments from the same parties was a tremendous spur to political irresponsibility, since none of them could be dispensed with, however disruptive its behaviour.

In independent Latvia and Lithuania, the problem was made worse by the general mood of nationalism which made it impossible to bring the parties representing the minorities into government. In 1926, the Lithuanian government's reliance on the Polish deputies helped provoke the military coup. In contemporary Latvia and Estonia, unless local Russians are to be permanently excluded from citizenship, or even expelled, parliaments will presumably contain a growing number of their representatives.

In Estonia in January 1992, the government of Dr Edgar Savisaar won a parliamentary vote giving it emergency economic powers, but only with the support of Russian deputies, with a majority of Estonian deputies against the move. As the realisation dawned, public outrage was such that Dr Savisaar's own Estonian supporters abandoned him and he was forced to resign.

On the other hand, one reason why in Latvia between the wars the extreme Right could not be brought into government was because its policies towards the minorities, if implemented, would have caused extremely grave problems with Germany. Today the National Independence Movement and Latvian Congress are calling openly for measures against the local Russian population which, if put into effect, could very well provoke revolt and Russian military intervention. But if minorities cannot be brought into government because it would outrage the nationalists, and the extreme Right cannot be brought in because it would drive the minorities to revolt, how long can parliamentary governments survive? It may therefore, at some stage, be replaced by a form of presidential government. The risk is that, as in 1934, this transition would only be possible through a period of authoritarian or at least Gaullist-style rule. This might, as before, take the form of a 'coup from the centre', to prevent the extreme Right, if elected, from taking power.

Such an 'authoritarian transition' would risk severe problems both with the Russian minorities and with Russia. The former are far more numerous than they were before 1940. Moreover, Stalin's Russia was not particularly interested in the internal politics of the Baltic states; due to ferocious Soviet restrictions on contacts with the outside world, economic links between the Soviet Union and the Balts were very limited, and social contacts non-existent. In the 1930s, in any case, the Russian minorities were largely led by White Russian emigrés, hardly likely to appeal to Stalin for protection against the Balts.

The differences today hardly need to be emphasised. They are, however, missed by many Balts, especially returning emigrants. With their eyes firmly fixed on the picture of the independent Baltic states they learned from their emigré history books, and without personal experience of dealing with Russians, they instinctively think in terms of a return to the insulated situation of the first republics.

Orphans of Versailles: Baltic Diplomacy, 1918–40

Between 1918 and 1921 the Balts liberated themselves. Western protection was, however, vital in forcing the German government to withdraw its troops from Latvia, and in stressing to the Soviet government that a renewed offensive against the Balts after 1920 would destroy any possibility of a diplomatic opening to the West. (The contrast with the Caucasus, where the West made clear its lack of interest, was stark). Baltic independence was consolidated under an implicit British and French umbrella. When it was destroyed, the Russian and Germans once again divided the Baltic between them.

In July 1921, following the withdrawal of its Baltic squadron, the British government informed the Baltic States that it could not promise them militarily assistance in the event of a Soviet attack. Between then and 1933, militarily speaking, the Balts were at the mercy of Soviet invasion, and indeed the concensus in British diplomacy for much of the 1920s was that they would in fact return to Russian control. Many Balts continued to believe that in a crisis, the British would save them, but British interest in the region was in fact primarily commercial.

At this stage, however, Stalin's Russia was withdrawing from the cause of world revolution in favour of 'socialism in one country'. Moreover, a disarmed Germany diminished the strategic importance of the Baltic States for Moscow. And finally, it must have been clear to the Soviet government that while an invasion of the Baltic region might not lead to war with Britain and France, it could well lead to conflict with Poland, especially after the Warsaw Accord of 1922 between Poland, Finland, Estonia and Latvia. It would also have completely disrupted the Soviet Union's international policies, made future co-operation with the Western powers extremely difficult, and raised a host of unforeseen dangers.

This last point is also the essential international factor protecting the Baltic States in the 1990s. It is in the highest degree unlikely that if Russia were to invade, NATO troops would come to their aid; but Moscow could certainly face international isolation, probably a United Nations blockade, and a complete cut-off of Western economic co-operation and assistance. Given Russia's economic weakness, a Russian leader would need to be crazy indeed to bring such consequences on his country. The only possible pretext might be a conflict between the Baltic States and their own Russian minorities, and even then, after having seen what an indigestible morsel the Balts can be, it is difficult to see anything but a fascist government in Moscow wishing to annex them outright. The Balts today would probably co-operate more closely in the face of a Russian threat than they did in the 1920s and 1930s. Their failure then has been made a standing reproach by historians, although it is not clear that in 1939 anything they could have done, singly or collectively, could have saved them. As it was, collective action was almost wholly lacking, one reason being the dispute between Poland and Lithuania over Vilnius. Any meaningful Baltic or East European military bloc had to include Poland. Until 1938, however, Poland and Lithuania did not have diplomatic relations and Lithuania resisted any pact that might seem to legitimise Poland's rule over Vilnius, or to bring Lithuania under Polish hegemony. Sweden, the only other significant military power in the region, understandably shunned by military involvement on the Eastern shores of the Baltic, and Jaan Tönisson's dream of a great Northern Union remained stillborn.

Baltic co-operation, however, also suffered from an underlying lack of interest and liking between the three Baltic States themselves. The Estonians regarded the Lithuanians as hopelessly unreliable, and after a single experiment, Estonians and Latvians also ceased to hold joint military exercises or to co-ordinate their military strategy.[19] Between 1919 (when they co-operated closely over the Versailles Peace Conference) and 1934 the Balts did not even try seriously to co-ordinate their approaches to the League of Nations. The Baltic Entente of 1934, created by the three states in response to the rise of Nazi Germany, provided for regular diplomatic consultation. However, it contained no military clauses, and co-operation remained only on paper.

Today the situation seems, on the surface, much better. The three national movements co-operated in their struggle with Moscow, and Baltic deputies tried to work together in the Soviet parliament although, according to the leading Latvian deputy (and later deputy prime minister), Ilmārs Bišers, 'we, the Baltic republics, which seemingly advanced the same proposals, each went on its own road, and that hurt us'.[20]

The Baltic Council, set up on 12 May 1990, revived the tradition of the Baltic Entente of 1934, and led to regular meetings between Baltic leaders and parliamentarians. The 'Baltic Common Market' initiated in April 1990, aimed to co-ordinate economic policy and guarantee free trade between the three states. In fact, it does nothing of the kind. The Balts basically produce the same kind of goods, and none have the raw materials they so desperately need. The opportunities for worthwhile trade between them are therefore limited. After a particularly fruitless meeting of Baltic prime ministers on 11 September 1992 Latvian Prime Minister Ivars Godmanis criticised 'a lack of co-operation' and 'a certain rivalry' on 'the Soviet-imposed parallel economic development' of the three states. In September 1992, Estonian Prime Minister Tiit Vähi said simply, 'there is no Baltic co-operation. We have to start from scratch'.[21]

Economic desperation, in the context of the collapsing Soviet economy, also leads each state to look out for itself. Thus in autumn 1991 the Lithuanians reacted immediately to Russian cuts in oil shipments to their refinery at Mažeikiai by passing on the bulk of the reduction to consumers in Latvia, rather than attempting any equitable distribution. In summer 1992, the Estonians demanded world market prices for electricity supplies to Latvia, and relented only when (as should have been obvious from their own experience) the Latvians proved unable to pay. In the beggar-my-neighbour game of post-Soviet economics, the Balts have been only slightly less ruthless to each other than they have been to Russia, or Russia to them. There has been no real co-ordination of price reforms or moves towards the introduction of independent currencies, with the result that each state tends to be undermined by the other two, as well as by Russia. Lithuania has suggested a much closer common market, but its own policies have been as self-regarding as those of Latvia and Estonia who, for their part, fear that in any really close alliance, the Lithuanians would always insist on taking the lead. The Estonians for their part are opposed to any closer union because of the conviction that, with their links to Scandinavia, they are better off alone. Lithuania's reckless (in the Estonian view) policies during the independence struggle have increased the traditional Estonian distrust of Lithuania, and leading Lithuanians have not improved matters by publicly accusing Estonia of cowardice because of its more cautious approach. On numerous occasions during the independence struggle the governments did not even inform each other what they were doing, even on crucial questions.[22]

A particularly striking piece of opportunism, recalling the failure to co-ordinate security policy in the 1920s and 1930s, was Lithuania's move in September 1992 to seek a separate agreement with Russia on military withdrawal, thereby undermining the united Baltic front. The Latvian and Estonian governments put on a brave face, but the action was severely criticised in the press and by emigré groups (indeed, including Lithuanians) in North America. Another move recalling the 1930s was the Latvian-Polish signature to a military co-operation agreement of 17 September 1992 which worried the more paranoid elements of the Lithuanian Right.

With the rise of Nazi Germany after 1933, Baltic diplomacy became an increasingly desperate balancing act. The three states signed non-aggression pacts with the Soviet Union, but evaded proposals for guarantees of closer protection, fearing this would lead to the stationing of troops and to the events which did indeed occur in 1939–40. Following the restoration of German sea and air power, Britain could no longer intervene militarily in the Baltic even had it wished to. Moscow, for its part, showed increasing sign of strategic interest in the region, issuing stern warnings to the Balts not to draw closer to Germany. The signals were disregarded by the Estonian and Latvian governments, which thought to continue balancing between Germany and the Soviet Union, and did not foresee a pact between them. On 7 June 1939 Estonia and Latvia agreed to non-aggression pacts with Germany, and in the succeeding months, most unwisely, received visits from high-ranking

German officers and the German warship *Hipper*. To the very end of the Estonian republic in July 1940, Konstantin Päts apparently continued to expect the speedy outbreak of a German-Russian war which would deliver the Balts from Soviet hands. He was wrong by only a few months, but those months were crucial. The Molotov-Ribbentrop Pact, signed on 23 August 1939, contained the infamous 'secret protocol', detailing the division of Poland and the Baltic States. Latvia and Estonia were initially to go to the Soviet Union, and Lithuania to Germany, but on 28 September, following the fall of Poland, a second secret protocol allocated Lithuania to the Soviet Union in return for German concessions in Poland and the equivalent of $7.5 million in gold.

Moscow acted swiftly. On 23 September Estonia was confronted with an ultimatum demanding a military alliance and acquiescence in the establishment of Soviet military bases in the republic. The Estonian government consulted the Latvians about the possibility of joint military resistance, but received no encouragement and capitulated on 2 October, Latvia was forced to agree to the same terms.* In Lithuania, Moscow used a mixture of pressure and bribery. In return for an alliance and military bases, it ceded the Vilnius region, seized from Poland under the Molotov-Ribbentrop Pact. This was the basis of later threats from Gorbachov, and from Communist hardliners in neighbouring Byelorussia, to 'take back' Vilnius (and Memel-Klaipeda, ceded to Germany in March 1939) if Lithuania left the Soviet Union. This was a source of some embarrassment in relation to Lithuania's negotiations with Moscow and the creation of a joint Baltic negotiating position since, unlike Latvia and Estonia, Lithuania could not very well ask for a return to the *status quo ante* Molotov-Ribbentrop. It has also of course been a source of lasting anger in Poland, although it was hardly more immoral than Poland's own non-aggression pact with Hitler in 1934 or participation, in November 1938, in Hitler's carve-up of Czechoslovakia. The fact that most of the states in this region have always behaved with sublime egotism adds a certain piquancy to their eternal demands that the West should sacrifice its own interests, and those of Europe as a whole, for the sake of 'justice' and 'morality'.

For several months the situation appeared to stabilise. In December Moscow issued a similar ultimatum to the Finns, provoking the bitterly fought three-month 'winter war' in which the Finns resisted with brilliance and heroism before being forced to yield on terms. From bases

* Today, Russian negotiators seeking to perpetuate or at least regularise the presence of Russian troops in the Baltic occasionally claim that since the independent Baltic governments have been restored, the 1939 'mutual assistance treaties' must still be in force, since they were never abrogated – an argument rejected with scorn by most Balts.

in Estonia, Soviet bombers took part in the campaign. Then, with Hitler's victory over France in May–June 1940, the last possible Western obstacle to Soviet conquest disappeared, while the need to strengthen the Soviet Union's defences against Germany grew even stronger. In mid-June, Moscow issued ultimatums to all three Baltic States requiring full military occupation and the reconstruction of the Baltic governments under Soviet supervision. All three gave in. President Smetona urged resistance, but his government refused. He fled Lithuania, dying in a fire in America four years later.

After the governments of Latvia and Estonia had been taken over, at Moscow's instruction and backed by Soviet troops, by local Communists, elections with a single list of permitted candidates produced parliaments which on 21 and 22 July requested 'admission' to the Soviet Union. Päts, Ulmanis, Voldemaras and a number of other leading figures were arrested and deported to the interior of the Soviet Union, where most of them died.

Should the Balts have resisted? At the time the argument against it looked conclusive. In September 1939, military resistance was already hopeless, and the three states could still hope, by agreeing to the bases, to preserve the remainder of their sovereignty. By June 1940, with tens of thousands of Soviet troops within the Soviet borders, the military situation became even more desperate. The analogy with Finland's long resistance is false, since Finland was helped by the winter as well as the terrain. The argument for resistance, often still heard in the Baltic States, is twofold. In the first place, whatever death, destruction and suffering resulted, it could not easily have exceeded what actually happened to the Baltic States between 1940 and 1954. It is possible that if the Balts had resisted in 1940, especially if they had been united, they might have persuaded Stalin against outright annexation and become Communist satellites, like the later ones of Eastern Europe. The Balts would then have escaped the worst features of Stalinist rule and, most importantly, been spared 'Russification' and the arrival of hundreds of thousands of Russian immigrants.

In Lithuania during the sixteen months following the declaration of independence on 11 March 1990, I often heard people say, 'this time, we must not repeat 1940; we must not give in without a fight', when refusing to bow to Moscow's pressure and seek a compromise with Gorbachov. Humiliation in 1940 contrasted sharply with the rhetoric of national defence and last-ditch resistance used by all three Baltic regimes in the 1930s.

In the course of 1992, Landsbergis tried to use the threat of a 'return to 1940' as a pretext for the creation of a presidential constitution and the exclusion of the former Communist Party and its allies from Lithuanian politics as potential 'Quislings'. The memory of 1940 can thus have very questionable political uses. In terms of more general attitudes, it has led to a strong feeling that even a seemingly hopeless resistance may be the most rational, as well as the most honourable course. In the words of the Latvian poet Augusts Sangs, in an anguished analysis of why he himself did not revolt against Stalinist rule:

> And albeit that it would have been
> a completely hopeless enterprise –
> for senselessness perhaps is sometimes
> the only thing that makes sense.

4

The Troglodyte International:
The Soviet Impact on the Baltic

*'Great advances have been made in teaching cats how to sing, although
mainly in the quantitative sense; nevertheless not to be left
unacknowledged is the unselfish work
of these heroic roof-ploughmen during the night-hours.'*
                    Jānis Rokpelnis (a Soviet-Latvian poet)
                    Annual Report on the Nation's Economy

It is difficult to exaggerate the amount of damage done to the Baltic
States by Soviet rule. Hundreds of thousands of Balts preserve the
memory of Stalinist savagery in the 1940s, which left few families
untouched. Population losses in the Baltic States as a result of execution,
killings in the war, deaths in Siberia and flight to the West, were
enormous.[1] The Estonian population declined by some 25 per cent
between 1939 and 1945. Given the low Estonian birth-rate, it means that
the number of ethnic Estonians alive today is barely higher than it was in
1939.

   An Estonian friend, Eva Tarm, summed up her Soviet experience, and
that of most Estonians, in a memorable interview:

> I was born in 1958, and for most of my life I saw my country being
> degraded before my eyes by Soviet rule. My grandmother showed me
> mementos of the period of independence, and told me how good life had
> been. Meanwhile outside I saw Russians, who had been brought here to
> kill Estonians, being given the flats of their victims, and Estonians living
> in poverty. The country was changing as we looked, and there was
> nothing we could do to stop it. We no longer even felt that it was our
> country. Our district was increasingly inhabited by Russian immigrants.
> Russian was spoken in the trams and shops; the shop windows were
> decorated in a Russian style which was alien to us and which I utterly
> detested. In the shops, if I spoke in my native language, the shop
> assistants yelled at me, and if I sent my son to shop he came back empty-
> handed because he spoke no Russian.

Most terrible was that fear was the central element. Even when it was subdued, it was all-pervading. When I was growing up, it wasn't like Stalin's time – no-one was seized at night, and there were no mass arrests; but this had happened to both my father's and my mother's family, and of course the memory coloured everything . . . my grandfather was arrested one night in 1941 and simply disappeared completely. Nothing was heard from him or about him again, so my grandmother went on hoping that he might turn up. Finally, when she was dying in the 1970s, she said one day, 'Now at last I think my Auguste is not coming back'.

My mother always warned us to be careful, that they [the Soviet secret police] were as powerful and ruthless as ever; and we didn't believe her; but later we found that they really could hurt you, though in a more sophisticated way. . . .

Our generation is permanently depressed, disillusioned with everybody and everything, because under Soviet rule, the only way to improve your life was by compromising yourself completely. Soviet life was like a saw which cut everything down to one level, or a tailor who forced everyone to wear a grey overcoat. If you compromised yourself, you were allowed to wear coloured clothes in private, under the overcoat. It was like being in prison – either people found underhand ways of evading the system, or they developed hobbies which were really just substitutes for real life outside the walls.[2]

Apart from repression, the dreadful effects of Soviet rule on the Baltic economies, Baltic culture and customs confronts anyone who enters a shop or an office, or picks up a telephone in the Baltic States. It strikes Balts especially cruelly when they travel abroad and contrast the living standards they had in 1939 with the ones they possess today.

By the 1980s, the failure of the Soviet economy and the backwardness of Soviet life compared to that of the West was apparent to everyone. A particularly stark example was that of average life expectancy in Estonia which, in 1939, was roughly the same as that of Finland. Today it is several years shorter. A consciousness of the damage done to Baltic culture by Soviet rule, particularly among those intellectuals who came from educated families, has contributed to a desire to restore the forms of the pre-1940 republics as far as possible. The need to defend the Baltic cultures and traditions against Soviet influence prevented Baltic intellectuals, both within and outside the states themselves, from engaging critically with those traditions, as this would have seemed to give help to the enemy. The consequence was a conformism and unreflecting nationalism which characterises so much of Baltic intellectual life today.[3]

Much has been written about former Communist leaders, such as Leonid Kravchuk in the Ukraine and Vladimir Mečiar in Slovakia, who now adopt nationalism in order to remain in power. Arnold Rüütel in Estonia is a further example. These have been contrasted, at least implicitly, with the 'real nationalists' who are seen as 'anti-soviet' but are in fact often all too Soviet in their attitudes and political behaviour. How could they not be, after five decades of Communist rule?

With isolation came tyranny, the loss of large and irreplaceable sections of the national élites and, above all, impoverishment. With the return, under Gorbachov, of press and intellectual freedom, the truth about the annexation of the Baltic States and Stalin's atrocities emerged. Thereafter the chances of the Soviet Union legitimising and stabilising its rule in the region – at least to the degree achieved by Russia before 1914 – vanished. Indeed the survival of Soviet rule in the Baltic after 1987 was always an impossibility and with the Balts demanding independence, could the rest of the Union have been far behind? Given the Soviet legacy of the 1940s, Gorbachov was trying to save the unsaveable.

Conquest and 'Revolution'

Impoverishment came with the very first months of Soviet rule in 1940. The sessions of the 'People's Assemblies' (chosen in elections which were a farce even by Stalinist standards) which 'requested' annexation to the Soviet Union in July 1940 also passed measures nationalising industry and the banks. Many managers were sacked and replaced by local Communists, officials brought in from Russia, or even ordinary workers. The result was a steep fall in productivity. By the time of the German invasion of June 1941, 90 per cent of shops had also been expropriated.

There was neither the time nor the structures to establish full control over local culture. Similarly, full collectivisation of agriculture did not follow annexation. However, all farms over 30 hectares (75 acres) were confiscated and distributed to smaller farmers. This led to a sharp reduction in production. Early in 1941 high requisition quotas were set, partly to compensate for this fall, and partly to put pressure on farmers to join the collectives. The new rulers announced salary increases for poorer workers, but these were soon negated by price rises, and by demands for longer hours and harder work, backed by ferocious sanctions. When, in late 1940, the independent currencies were abolished and replaced by the rouble, the exchange rate was confiscatory and had the effect of destroying Baltic savings.[4]

In forming the new Baltic governments, Stalin and his henchmen adopted a tactic, later to become familiar, of creating 'left fronts' led by leading non-Communist Left-wingers.[5] Some were later dispensed with, others forced to become Communist. A few, like the Lithuanian Prime Minister and left-wing writer, Vincas Kreve-Mickevičius, broke with the regime and survived. Kreve-Mickevičius resigned after failing to persuade Stalin to grant Lithuania a status similar to that of Mongolia, a Communist satellite of the Soviet Union with at least the trappings of independence. This was the hope too of Justas Paleckis, Acting President of Lithuania and Left-wing but non-Communist intellectual. Paleckis's son described his father's initial hope of replacing Smetona with a government led by the socialist-populist President Grinius, overthrown by Smetona's coup in 1926. Eduards Berklavs, a Communist activist in the 1930s, told me that in 1940 he and his comrades wanted to create a Communist state in Latvia, but 'even we didn't think of joining the Soviet Union'.[6]

Justas Paleckis junior evoked for me the hatred of Smetona which existed in Lithuania during the 1930s but which seems inexplicable today when this authoritarian but generally civilised figure is contrasted with Hitler and Stalin. He pointed out that while on the Left people such as his father and Kreve-Mickevičius were intriguing with Moscow against Smetona's regime, on the Right the supporters of Voldemaras were intriguing with Berlin to the same end. He warned that this kind of unpatriotic irresponsibility could recur today if political conflict within Lithuania intensified and a dictatorship were established. Another Lithuanian observer has, however, noticed that in the 1930s, Lithuanians took their independence for granted, and felt safe carrying out these foolish manoeuvres, whereas today everyone is alive to the dangers. The record of Lithuanian politicians in January 1991, however, does not suggest any great improvement.

Real power in 1940–41 was in any case exercised by leaders of the local Communist parties, Stalin's satraps from Moscow close behind them. The existing Communist parties were tiny (fewer than seven hundred identified members in Estonia) but they were rapidly expanded by local recruits, and above all by the transfer of cadres from Russia. These were mainly Russians, but in the case of Estonia and Latvia included large numbers of Latvians and Estonians, the children of Communist parents exiled from the Baltic after 1920, or simply of those who had moved to Russia under Tsarist rule. In many cases they barely spoke the local languages. Those in Estonia were satirised as '*Jeestlased*' (instead of *Eestlased*) for their Russian mispronunciation of the letter 'e'.

Those political and military leaders of the independent states who did not succeed in fleeing during June or July 1940 were, in the main, deported soon after the annexation, along with several thousand others. President Kārlis Ulmanis of Latvia died in prison in Russia two years later. President Konstantin Päts of Estonia lived on until 1956, finally dying in an NKVD 'psychiatric clinic'. Their fates remained unknown to their fellow countrymen until the Gorbachov era. An NKVD photograph of Päts, taken in prison, shows a grim, emaciated, defeated face. This was the end of a man who, whatever the controversy had claims to be regarded as the father of modern Estonia. In 1990 his bones were identified and returned to Tallinn for burial. It was one of the most moving events in recent Baltic history – all the more so for the modest atmosphere of the funeral and the check which as ever the Estonians kept over their emotions. Looking at the photograph of Päts, it was easy to understand the determination of Balts to wipe out every trace of Soviet rule in their countries.

By the end of 1940, arrests and deportations ran at some 200 to 300 per month. The great wave of deportations however came only on 13–14 June, barely a week before the German invasion, when tens of thousands were herded into cattle trucks. A considerable number returned from Siberia after Stalin's death, but many were shot by the NKVD, either immediately after their arrest, or as the secret police 'cleared their stocks' before retreating in the face of the advancing Germans. The discovery of their bodies, often bearing marks of torture, was well publicised by the Germans, and contributed to the level of mass support for them during the first months of their occupation, and to atrocities against the Jews, accused of backing Soviet rule.[7]

The German Occupation

In all three republics, German invasion was accompanied by Baltic revolt. The Lithuanian partisans launched heavy attacks in battles against the retreating Soviet forces which cost thousands of lives. A smaller revolt also took place in Latvia, while in Estonia fighting went on for more than two months, until the capture of Tallinn by the Germans on 28 August. The town of Tartu was held for a week by Estonian rebels.[8]

Provisional governments were set up in all three states, but were soon closed by the Germans; (Landsbergis's father was a minister in the Lithuanian provisional government of 1941). Until German defeat became imminent, in 1944, the Germans played a cat-and-mouse game with the Baltic political leaders, seeking to win their co-operation in the recruiting of soldiers and labourers without sharing real power or making promises on the status of the republics after the war. The real postwar plans of the Nazis were not of course revealed to the Balts. These involved, over a period of several decades, the expansion of the Baltic States eastward into Russia, the bulk of the Baltic populations being deported into the new areas and replaced by German settlers. To these were to be added 'suitably Aryan' elements from among the Balts, and especially the Estonians, while the rest were to be subjected to intense Germanisation.

In Latvia and Estonia the Germans formed SS Legions and police units which subsequently fought bravely in the Russian front line but also carried out numerous atrocities against Jews, Russians, Poles and Byelorussians. In Lithuania the attempt to create Lithuanian military units failed initially in the face of local resistance, but in all three states, thousands were recruited into police battalions. An old Lithuanian priest from the Polish area of Nemencine described an episode in the brutal, many-sided partisan war of 1943; in which Lithuanian forces in the German service fought Polish guerillas:

> A Lithuanian woman came to the priest and told him that [Polish] Home Army men had taken her cow and pig, and the priest wrote down their names . . . the Home Army arrested him after Easter, took him to a nearby village and shot him. . . . Simple Polish people hated the Bolsheviks, like all of us, and were afraid, like all of us . . . Life was complicated. The Home Army fought the Germans, the Lithuanians and the Soviet partisans simultaneously. . . . They burned the houses of German informers and killed their families. Later, in the same villages, Lithuanian partisans did the same to Soviet informers.[9]

In 1944, with the Soviet threat, the Estonian national leadership called for mass mobilisation to defend Estonia. Some 38,000 answered the call, and were joined in the summer by several thousand Estonians who had crossed the Gulf of Finland to join the Finnish army and now returned. Between January and June 1944, Estonian units played a major part in holding the line of the Narva River against the advancing Red Army.* As the German forces retreated in the summer of 1944, the Balts attempted to restore their national governments. By then the Red Army was pouring into the Baltic States, and these provisional governments lasted for only a few days. The Germans held out in the 'Courland Pocket' (western Latvia) to the very end of the war, but resisted until the last the establishment of a Latvian national government.

Resistance: The 'Forest Brothers'

Mr Višvaldis Brinkmanis, now a leader of the radical nationalist Citizens Congress, was a Latvian soldier in the Courland Pocket. As the German surrender approached, he, like many others, left his unit and set out towards the coast, intending to try and find a boat to take him to Sweden to join the tens of thousands of Balts who had already fled. On his way he

---

* A distinction must be drawn between these late recruits and the men of the SS Legions and Police Battalions, although in many cases these too joined to defend their countries from the Soviet army, or were simply conscripted from among Soviet units which surrendered.

passed a German airfield. Soldiers there said they had been listening to the radio, that war was about to break out between the Soviet Union and the Western allies, and that British torpedo boats were already on their way to Courland.[10]

Believing this, Brinkmanis decided not to risk crossing the Baltic, but to stay in Latvia and await its deliverance. Soon afterwards he was arrested by Soviet troops. Though he himself was released after a few months, his father, a Latvian intellectual, committed suicide several years later when threatened with arrest and deportation.

The hope of Western deliverance came through desperation, but also through the memory of what had actually happened in 1919. Its absence is one reason for an enduring suspicion of the West held by some Balts. The hope, and hence the bitterness, was nurtured throughout the eight years of partisan warfare against Soviet rule which followed the Soviet reconquest in 1944. The original resistance movement was made up of soldiers serving in the German forces, others who had collaborated with the Germans and had reason to fear the Soviet authorities, and of course patriotic Balts in general. In Lithuania, priests played a leading part. In due course, and as Soviet deportations gathered pace, the ranks of the resistance were swollen by others who preferred to die fighting than be deported to an unknown fate in Siberia, and by peasants facing collectivisation.[11]

In the countryside, the Soviet authorities did everything in their power to give the conflict the feel of a class war, confiscating the land of suspected partisans and giving it to poorer peasants, many of whom were recruited into Soviet auxiliary battalions. (In Lithuania, these were nicknamed *Stribai*, from *Istrebitelny*, meaning 'Destroyers', the name for the demolition units during the Soviet retreat in 1941.) Memories of this continue to divide many Baltic villages.

The resistance was at its fiercest in Lithuania, where the 'Forest Brothers' had a general staff, printed newspapers, and ran training courses for officers. Surviving photographs show members in the uniforms of the pre-war Lithuanian army, bearing a mixture of Soviet and German weapons. An incongruous touch was that many had very long hair. In a strangely medieval gesture, they had vowed not to cut their hair until Lithuania was free again. More practically, it meant that they were sometimes able to pretend to be women in order to avoid arrest. Something of the tragic spirit of the struggle was expressed by Viktoras Petkus, then an adolescent, later a dissident:

> I was not tempted to join the partisans myself, because a Lithuanian army captain and partisan commander came to my father and advised him not to let his children go to the forest. He said that he knew that the West had betrayed them, and that the movement had no future, but he himself had no choice but to go on to the end.[12]

Rimvydas Šilbajoris, a Lithuanian literary scholar in exile, writes of the partisan war that 'Lithuanians remember it [the war] in every agonising detail, and can no more stop talking and writing about it than can the Russians stop talking about their great struggle against the Nazis. In Lithuanian prose, the guerrilla war is often understood and depicted as a conflict between 'the city' and 'the forest' . . . the partisans were fighting to defend the traditional way of life'.

In Latvia and Estonia, the partisans were no less brave, but a good deal less organised. In all three republics, after the initial battles, the strategy of the partisans was to avoid engagement with the Soviet army. This tactic seems to have been matched by an unwillingness on the Soviet side to use the Red Army in anti-partisan operations, possibly for fear that the mainly peasant troops might find themselves in sympathy with the peasant partisans. Employed instead were the NKVD and *Stribai*. Viktoras Snuolis, a former partisan officer in the Lithuanian district of Šiauliai recalled that 'The Red Army was not generally used. Often, Russian soldiers used to let us past, or simply ignore us. I even talked to one once, and he said that in action against us, he was careful not to take aim'. Mr Snuolis told me of the hunted life of the partisans in the forest, and how his group was once able to evade an NKVD ambush because it heard the sound of the rain pattering on their enemies' capes. He said that the partisans were helped by the fact that the NKVD forces did not know the countryside, while the *Stribai* auxiliaries were 'gutless and undisciplined'.[13]

In the bitter cold of a Lithuanian winter, I once visited the remains of some of the primitive partisan bunkers in the forests of northern Lithuania, and admired the courage and endurance of the men who held out for so long in such dreadful conditions (the wounded often dying for lack of medical care, unless they could be secretly helped by local Lithuanian doctors). One of the bunkers, now a caved-in hollow by a stream of clear water, in the depths of the forest of Mažuolis, held eight men. Thanks to the loyalty of local people, it was never found by the Soviet police, but simply abandoned when the last partisans after Stalin's death in 1953 gave up the struggle, after which the forest gradually reclaimed it.

The partisans concentrated on maintaining their positions, reducing local Communist control in the countryside, and punishing collaborators and informers: in other words, holding out for as long as possible in the hope of outside intervention. It was not an irrational strategy, nor the product of mere obstinacy. If war between the West and the Soviet Union had broken out, the existence of Baltic forces in the field could have been of crucial importance in regaining Baltic independence. The strong partisan resistance in Lithuania also helped discourage Russian settlers from moving to that republic.

The struggle in all three republics was attended by the brutalities common enough in guerrilla wars in our own time. The NKVD and local auxiliaries tortured suspects, executed the families of partisans and burnt their farms, leaving the bodies lying in the streets and fields as a warning. Other skeletons are still sometimes being found where bodies were buried or simply tossed into unused wells. A woman from Utena described how,

> a neighbour of ours was shot, and was dumped in the street; and even his mother did not dare to come and look at him, because if the *Stribai* or NKVD saw people weeping over the dead partisans, they would say, 'So you are crying for the enemies of the Soviet Union?', and sometimes they would simply arrest them on the spot, and they would too disappear.

The partisans themselves carried out atrocities against local communists and auxiliaries and their families. In Joniškis District I was told how in the village of Vainiune, partisans gang-raped the local Komsomol Secretary, a woman called Tūnaitytė. It is difficult however to say with confidence who was responsible for what, because the Soviet side formed *provocateur* units to kill people and then blame the partisans.[14] Caught between the two sides, much of the population of northern Lithuania seems to have ended by regarding both as a plague. This was one factor in the eventual collapse of the partisan movement, though more critical was military attrition by the Soviet security forces: Mr Snuolis reported that a partisan in the late 1940s could realistically expect to live for some two years before being killed or captured. In Lithuania, up to 13,000 collaborators were executed by the partisans, and Soviet sources put the total Soviet losses at 20,000 and the partisans losses at about the same. Lithuanian sources have estimated Soviet casualties at 80,000 and Lithuanian at 50,000, though this is probably too high. Today, all over Lithuanian, and to a lesser extent the other two republics as well, local monuments are springing up to honour the partisans who died. Often these adjoin monuments to local Communist leaders and Soviet security forces, some killed by those same partisans.

Exhaustion and, with the end of the Korean War, abandonment of any hope of Western intervention, helped destroy the movements. The collectivisation of agriculture in 1949, and the mass deportations which accompanied it, produced a new flood of recruits for the partisans but, in the longer run, drained the pool in which they hid (to use Mao's phrase).

Mrs Genovaitė Dubauskienė, a Lithuanian woman deported as the daughter of 'kulaks' in May 1948, described her experience. Although she had a NKVD file of her own for helping the partisans, the NKVD group which finally arrested her in Vilnius did so because they mistook her for her younger sister, who was to be deported together with her parents:

> ˙ They took me to the cellars of the NKVD, and there they beat me with a

whip, telling me to confess and I was my sister. Finally, they accepted that I was telling the truth, and then they didn't know what to do with me. They asked their chief, and he replied, 'Paleckis's signature is on the list, and I have to fulfil it, so I need people'. So I was deported to Krasnoyarsk in Siberia. At that time I didn't know what had happened to my parents. They were also deported to Krasnoyarsk, but I only discovered that months later, when I wrote back to Lithuania. I did not see them again until eight years later. . . . There were about seventy of us in our cattle-truck. We were all students, and were treated a bit better than the people in the other trucks; there were planks to lie on. The other people in the train were mainly farmers from Vilnius region. When we crossed the Urals, we passed seven other trains full of Lithuanian deportees, and we talked to them through the slots in the sides of the truck. One girl even spoke to her parents, but she was not allowed to join them. We thought then that the whole Lithuanian nation had been deported. . . .

After we passed Minsk, we were let out of the trucks once a day to go to the toilet in the fields. Everyone had been allowed to take some food from home, and we shared it. We were fed salt fish and bread, and after we passed Moscow, some watery soup. When we reached Siberia, we could buy milk from Russians who brought it to the train. The guards did not steal from us or maltreat us. Some people got sick – I heard later that my mother on her journey had caught pneumonia – and three old people died on the way. Their companions wanted to keep the bodies to give them a Christian burial, but the guards did not allow it.

When we got to Kamarchaga in Krasnoyarsk province, we had to march for three days through the forest. Then we were pulled on a trailer by a tractor, because it was Spring and the mud was too thick to walk through. We were sent to the village of Khabaidak. It seemed to us that we had reached the end of the world, and would never return. On one side there were huge mountains, on the other, a big, fast river, and everywhere was the forest. We were set to work to cut down trees in the forest, and then they were floated away down the river. There were several accidents at first, because people did not know the work. We got on well with the Finnish exiles there. The Kalmuk exiles were of a lower culture, but they taught us how to survive. . . . On Sundays, the Lithuanians would put on suits and dresses, and meet to sing Lithuanian songs and recite poetry.

After a year, my file caught up with me from Lithuania, and they decided that Khabaidak was too good for me, and I was sent North, to the mining town of Rasdolinsk, where I worked in the hospital. That was where I met may second husband, who had been exiled there after five years in prison. I was divorced from my first husband because he did not want to join me in Siberia . . . my son was born there. Rasdolinsk had every nationality you can imagine, all exiles: among the doctors in my hospital were Russians, Poles, Jews, a Georgian, an Armenian. . . .

In Rasdolinsk, there were many more accidents from the work, but the exiles did not live too badly, because the pay was better and there was more in the shops. The Lithuanians grew potatoes, and bought pigs and chickens, and later cows. In summer, the animals wandered freely, and sometimes the cows would be killed by bears, and we would find their skeletons in the forest. In winter, the temperature would go down sometimes to minus 60 degrees, and we had to bring the chickens and pigs into our houses, even though most had only one room. The animals lived under the bed. That could be a problem, depending on the character of the pig. We had one pig which would not let us sleep. It used to pull the blankets off the bed and try to eat them. . . .

The Lithuanians worked hard, and in the end even the local Russians were buying food from us. I lived there for eleven years, and by the end we were able to live normally. When we were allowed to, a few years after Stalin's death, of course almost all of us went home; but two Lithuanian families are still living there. My parents also came back at that time, but my father had cancer, and died along the way. He is buried in Lithuania. . . .[15]

Stalinism, Normalisation, Stagnation

Soviet pressure on the reconquered Baltic societies grew steadily after 1945. One aspect was the Baltic wing of the 'Zhdanovschina', the campaign directed by Andrei Zhdanov to reassert control over the various cultures of the Soviet Union by terroristic means. Baltic culture had already been harmed by the flight of so many intellectuals to the West. After flight, deportation and murder, it has been estimated for example that, by 1945, no more than 22 per cent of the prewar staff of Tartu University remained in Estonia. The postwar years saw many more writers silenced, killed, deported, or forced into shameful compromise with the system. In the Stalinist jungle, even loyal Communists were not safe – indeed, some of the Baltic Communists from Moscow who had survived Stalin's purges of the 1930s were now eradicated. With the advent of officially sanctioned Russian nationalism, history was rewritten to give the Russian Empire a 'progressive' colouring, and the Russification of language and culture began. A Latvian poet wrote that,

> The Russian language seems to me like a huge bridge of sunbeams
> Over which the Latvian heart will climb to high horizons.[16]

Particularly hard hit were the churches. By 1948, only one bishop was left in Lithuania, all the others having fled, been deported or murdered. Protestant bishops in Latvia and Estonia met a similar fate, while the Estonian Orthodox Church, which in 1920 had declared its independence from the Moscow patriarchate, was forcibly reintegrated into the Russian Orthodox Church. Repression was resumed under Khrushchev, and it was only under Brezhnev that state pressure was somewhat relaxed. Even so, Archbishop Steponavičius of Vilnius remained in internal exile until 1988.

After the death of Stalin, many native Communist officials extended a measure of protection to cultural figures, and indeed justified their own collaboration in terms of preserving the nation's cultural heritage. The writer Arvo Valton (a strong anti-communist) has said of one literary collaborator under Stalin that, 'One cannot condemn him or completely deny his function; it was the means of preserving the national language and identity'. It allowed periodic flourishings of national culture, and the 1960s have even been called a time of 'cultural renaissance' for Estonia.[17]

The smallness of the Baltic populations meant that the educated classes were commensurately tiny. As the process of 'nativisation' of the Baltic Communist Parties proceeded, leading Communists inevitably had close links with the intelligentsias, the majority of whom, even if they did not brave outright dissent, were nationalist in spirit and, above all, committed to preserving their national cultures. An example is Ingrid Rüütel, wife of the Communist Chairman of the Estonian SSR Supreme Council. As the daughter of Neeme Rüüs, Ideology Secretary of the Estonian Communist Party in 1940–41, who was executed by the Nazis, Ingrid Rüütel came from the very heart of the Communist establishment. Yet by profession she was an ethnographer, a branch of academia full, throughout the Soviet years, of crypto-nationalists.

The influence of the intellectuals can hardly have failed to have some effect. In Latvia, Mr Rüütel's equivalent, Anatolijs Gorbunovs, is said to have been persuaded in a patriotic direction by the poet Jānis Peters, whom he met while he was Party Secretary of Central Riga. Such associations helped modify Communist beliefs and loyalty even at the core of the Party. Justas Paleckis junior, born into the very heart of the Lithuanian Communist establishment, commented that for him and for many young Party members, the invasion of Czechoslovakia and the destruction of Dubček's 'socialism with a human face' marked the moment at which the Soviet Communist system forfeited their emotional loyalty. For a number of dissidents, 1968 was the point at which they were forced out of the system and into open opposition. This was true of the future Estonian Congress leader Tunne Kelam who, as a lecturer in International Regulations, had tried to tell the truth within the Soviet academic framework. His support for Dubček led to his dismissal, after which he worked underground within the dissident movement.[18]

Taagepera and Misiunas have suggested that thanks in part to defensive action by local Communist élites, the Soviet period, while it marked a step backwards for the Baltic cultures, left them more secure

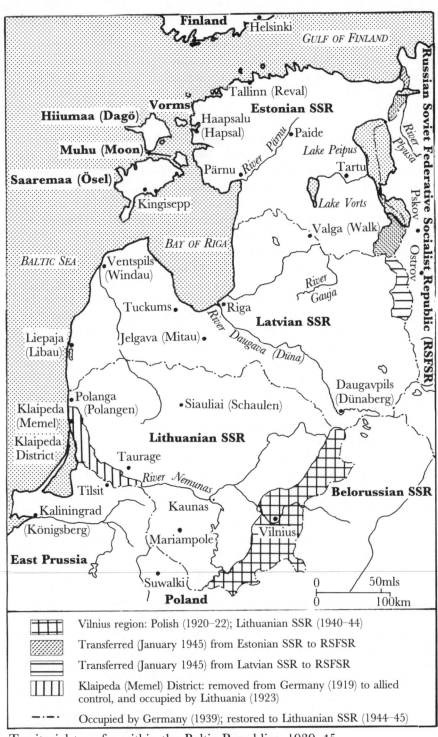

Territorial transfer within the Baltic Republics, 1939–45

than in 1914: that 'in the eighty year perspective, the overall picture was still one of a massive shift from Russian to the national languages', and that even compared to 1940, there had been 'an increase in socio-cultural depth'.[19]

By 1940, use of the Baltic languages in education and higher culture was still new and fragile. Despite Russification, the fact of official status for their languages, and the opportunities afforded by Soviet republican institutions (such as schools and universities in the Baltic languages, Writers' Unions, and so on) put the Balts in a better position to defend their language and identity than several other small linguistic groups in modern Europe: the Gaelic Irish in the last century, or the Basques, Bretons and Welsh in this one, for example.

It is instructive in this context to compare the relative strength of Azeri language and culture in Soviet Azerbaidjan, where they had some defense from Soviet republican institutions, to their almost complete public suppression in neighbouring Iran – where most ethnic Azeris naturally live. Compared to these (or those of the autonomous republics of Russia), the overwhelming majority of Balts used their own languages as their primary tongue, and use of Russian by Estonians actually declined sharply after 1970. This was, however, only because a sufficient number of 'Communist' cultural, academic and even Party figures were prepared to use these institutions discreetly to defend their national cultures; and, of course, because Soviet rule and Russification ended when they did. If it had continued for another generation the Baltic languages and cultures might have been damaged beyond repair.

No equivalent renaissance took place in Baltic agriculture, which never recovered from the devastating blow of collectivisation.* Indus-trialisation, however, proceeded at breakneck speed, accompanied by what most Balts would see as the most malign of all the Soviet legacies – a massive influx of Russian labour. Only Lithuania avoided this fate, thanks to the Forest Brothers and its higher birth rate but also, until his death in 1974, to its Communist ruler Party First Secretary Antanas Sniečkus. Sniečkus, unlike the rulers of Estonia and Latvia, who had been born and brought up in Russian and introduced to their satrapies only in 1940 was a native-born Communist. Through a mixture of

---

* The effects of collectivisation in the Estonian countryside are vividly evoked in Heino Kiik's novel, *Where Hobgoblins Spend the Night*. Amidst a general picture of peasant despair, incompetent leadership by jumped-up Communist flunkeys without farming experience, and crazy orders from above, one famous passage describes how the collective's cows became so weak that they could be blown down by the wind, and a man had to be specially detailed to help them to their feet. These cows were themselves the survivors of repeated slaughterings of animals by the peasants in the face of requisitions and collectivisation.

95

unquestioned loyalty to Moscow and tough, clever manoeuvres and negotiations, Sniečkus succeeded in warding off the worse effects of the rule of Stalin and his successors. Many Lithuanian intellectuals today consider that, in his own brutal and compromised fashion, he did in fact serve his country.

Sniečkus's last successor as First Secretary of the Lithuanian Communist Party, Algirdas Brazauskas, today of course uses such arguments to defend himself against charges of 'collaboration' and treason. In his words, as a Lithuanian State Plan official and a senior Party functionary,

> People don't know what we went through. We had to go twenty times a year to Moscow to beg for extra investment or to try to ward off something that they wanted to impose on Lithuania. I would have to spend the whole summer there, sitting in antechambers. Most of us in our hearts were unhappy about Lithuania's subjugation to the Soviet Union . . . and all of us were angry that they in Moscow were trying to dictate to us exactly how many kindergartens we were supposed to build in every Lithuanian town. We had no choice but to obey, but we did extract advantages. If Lithuania today has a good base of infrastructure, energy and education, and a good prospect for developing a strong economy, it is thanks to us.[20]

Brazauskas stressed that state officials such as himself used to be able to celebrate Christmas and other traditional Christian holidays at home (though not of course in Church) without fear of denunciation by their Lithuanian colleagues, although in the Party structures supervision was tighter.

Despite considerable special pleading, there is a certain amount of truth in this picture. Certainly the Lithuanian Communist élite was not as venal and incompetent as those across most of Russia, let alone in the Muslim republics. If to call them covert patriots is too flattering, at least men like Brazauskas never had any positive enthusiasm for Soviet rule. They were merely a familiar species of collaborator, not particularly brave, not particularly wicked, doing the best for themselves and for their country 'under the circumstances' (see Chapter 8).

In Estonia, the ability of the local party to resist Moscow's policies was largely broken in a purge of 1950–51 which led to the replacement of all native Estonians by Russians or at least Estonians brought up in Russia. The first secretary between 1950 to 1978, Ivan Käbin, also, however, came to be seen as a qualified defender of Estonian interests. Käbin Estonianised his name to Johannes, and sought to improve his knowledge of the Estonian language. In Latvia, a similar purge took place nine years later. The thaw in the first years of Khrushchev's rule allowed a backlash within the Latvian party against Russification and immigration. This is usually taken as having been centred around the figure of Deputy Prime Minister Eduards Berklavs. He sought to Latvianise the party and establish greater Latvian control over local industries through the use of local raw materials. Officially, this was justified by the desire to contribute more efficiently to the All-Union economy. Unofficially, the main aim was to check the heavy industrial development which was pulling Russian workers into the republic. The ploy was only crushed after interventions by Khrushchev himself. Eduards Berklavs has described how, after the Latvian government had tried to halt further Russian immigration, Russians in Latvia sent a letter to the Kremlin denouncing the rebirth of 'bourgeois nationalism'. The reaction led to the dismissal of numerous party officials at every level. Mr Berklavs himself was sent to mainland Russia as a film-distribution official – a very much milder destiny, of course, than would have been the case under Stalin.[21]

Mr Berklavs (now a leader of the radical National Independence Party) is today widely honoured in Latvia for his attempts to protect his country against Russification; the crushing of his movement, however, placed Latvia in an even worse position than before. Immigration continued, and the Party was effectively broken as an instrument for defending Latvian interests. Many Latvians attribute the caution of Latvian moves to independence, and the poor quality of much of the Latvian establishment in our own time, to the lingering effects of the purge of 1959–60. The cultural reaction which occurred during those years also retarded Latvian attempts to recover from the cultural effects of Stalinism.

Industrial expansion under Soviet rule in the Baltic States, as under the Tsars and the first republics, consisted above all of light industry, consumer goods and food-processing, although Latvia also has some steel-making capacity. Shipbuilding and ship-repair are important in Riga and Tallinn. Here, and in Liepāja, are large trawling fleets, manned almost entirely by Russians, since Moscow did not trust the Balts to go to sea for fear of defection.[22]

Soviet industrial revolution in the Baltic, together with the flight from the land resulting from collectivisation and rural despair, produced the highest rate of urbanisation that the region had ever known. By 1980, 70 per cent of Estonians and Latvians, and 62 per cent of Lithuanians, lived in towns. Forty years earlier, only about a quarter of Lithuanians, and a third of the other Balts, did so. The influx led to severe housing shortages and increased bitterness between Balts and Russian immigrants. These shortages, and the high proportion of working women in the Baltic, contributed to keeping native birth rates among the lowest in Europe, as they had been since the 1890s, although every Balt was aware of the need to produce babies for the sake of national survival. As elsewhere in the Soviet Union, the level of abortion was appallingly high; it caused particular cultural trauma among traditionalists in Catholic Lithuania. Today it is declining as contraceptives become more freely available from the West.

The endemic grey depression of Soviet life also had its effects. One Latvian girl told a friend: 'You know, I never in my life really ever expected to be happy'. Reflecting this mood was the very high rate of alcoholism, among the highest in the world. Anyone who has visited the Baltic will know of sad middle-aged people, whose families excuse their drinking by pointing to the hopelessness and the endless petty humiliations of Soviet rule, as well as to the lack of sanctions against drinking in an economy where jobs were guaranteed in any case. One old Polish woman in Lithuania once told me that she still reveres Gorbachov, no matter what, because 'he tried to stop my old man from drinking' – a reference to the anti-alcohol campaign of Gorbachov's first year in power. Suicide rates were also high, Lithuania having the highest in Europe after Hungary.[23]

However, for what it was worth, relatively high food production, mass demand in the Soviet Union for the products of their industries, together with their more prosperous and hard-working traditions, helped to give the Baltic States the highest quality of life in the Soviet Union; they were indeed known as 'the Soviet West'. Living standards rose steadily during the 1960s and early 1970s, before tailing off and beginning to decline in the later years of Brezhnev, and going into free fall under Gorbachov and his successors. In the analysis of the Soviet revolution, there is plenty of room for application of the 'J-curve theory', whereby revolutions tend to occur when steadily rising economic expectations find themselves frustrated. As elsewhere in the Union, the later Brezhnev period in the Baltic Republics was era of stagnation, in which faceless bureaucrats played an endless game of musical chairs. The population at large was not subjected to repression, and a considerable amount of cultural freedom was allowed, within strict limits. Those courageous people who overstepped the limits were of course often hit very hard (though the savagery of Latin-American and other regimes was lacking). But most people simply got on with their own lives.

By the 1980s, Communist Party membership in Estonia and Lithuania was made up chiefly of people from the native populations. In Latvia, a majority was still Russian. The role of Estonians and Latvians from Russia had naturally declined with the years – most of the suitable cadres had been brought back from Russia after the reconquest in 1944. However, some of these and their descendants were to play a leading role in opposition to the independence movements of Latvia and Estonia, and gave a spurious impression that this opposition was not wholly Russian but had some 'indigenous' roots.

In all three republics (as elsewhere throughout the Union Republics), the post of second secretary of the Party was effectively reserved for Russians. Unseating these figures became one of the first tasks of the national movements and the national Communists. Similarly, throughout the republics, the deputy commander of the KGB was also a Russian, keeping check on his 'native' boss. Russians were also of course entrenched in positions throughout the Party, though not sufficiently to prevent all three parties from swinging towards support for independence in the late 1980s.[24] Ironically, one state institution in which 'natives' had always been allowed to predominate, even under Stalin, was that of the 'Supreme Councils', or parliaments, precisely because their functions were almost entirely symbolic. As the independence movements gathered pace, however, the parliaments became of key legal significance.

In the last years of Soviet rule, the predominance of 'natives' was secured not simply by selection but also by gerrymandering: thus Russian-dominated urban constituencies in Tallinn often had considerably more voters than 'native'-dominated rural ones. Such manipulation is a small example of the kind of discreet localised nationalist activity which occured even within the Soviet system.

The Soviet Establishment: Past, Present and Future?

As elsewhere in the former Communist bloc, the future of the former Communist establishments is central to the politics of the Baltic States. The term 'de-Sovietisation', adopted by the Right in all three states, refers mainly to a desire to purge members of the old establishments from the leading roles they continue to hold in the states and economies of the region – except, of course, where they have themselves become Right-wing leaders ('decolonisation' tends to refer to the desire to remove the Soviet Army and the Russian populations of Latvia and Estonia).

Landsbergis and others have spoken of the need for a 'Nuremberg Trial of Bolshevism'. Few Balts would have any objection to putting on trial those chiefly responsible for the repression of Stalin's time, if any were still alive; and there is massive support in Latvia for the trial of Alfrēds Rubiks, the hardline Communist leader charged with planning the Soviet military intervention in the Baltic in January 1991 and implicated in the August coup. What makes many people deeply uneasy however is when it seems, as in Lithuania, that talk of a 'Nuremberg Trial' is simply a Right-wing political campaign against the ex-Communist section of the political opposition, part of which is still widely popular and respected for its role in achieving independence. (The role of denunciations in Lithuania is discussed in Chapter 8.) The overall intention of replacing the former establishment reaches into every corner of economic and agrarian reform and especially, of course, the issue of privatisation.

The Right-wing throughout the Baltic, and especially in Lithuania, condemns the former establishment not just for past collaboration with Soviet rule, but with present involvement and potential future treachery, should Russia again try to take over the Baltic States. The Right sometimes quotes the views of the French scholar Françoise Thom, who alleges the existence of a 'second echelon' of communist leaders which has manipulated the course of events in the Soviet Union in recent years so as to take power itself.[25]

As the Lithuanian Foreign Minister, Algirdas Saudargas, has warned, 'even if these people do not wish to be traitors, Moscow has plenty of information to blackmail them into collaboration'. This is doubtless true, but Moscow has information on most politicians. A close ally of Mr Saudargas was the leader of the Right-wing Independence Party in Lithuania, Dr Virgilijus Čepaitis, who was largely responsible for the practice of denouncing political opponents as KGB agents. Dr Čepaitis himself, however, later proved to have been a KGB informer for many years. Yet none of its extensive net of agents did the KGB any good in the end when it came to controlling the Soviet Revolution. There is no reason to believe that a reduced and battered KGB will be more effective in the future.

As to the 'second echelon', an identifiable stratum of this description certainly exists in the Baltic States and throughout the former Soviet Union, but the suggestion that it constitutes an organised united political force aiming at the restoration of the Soviet Union reflects a mixture of paranoia – understandable in view of past experience – and ambition, whether conscious or unconscious: underlying much of current politics in the Baltic, as in the rest of the former Soviet Union, is a struggle by new social groups to displace the old establishment in order to occupy its jobs.

The leading feature today of the former Commmunist establishment is political and above all economic opportunism. Indeed, it was the leading feature of the vast majority of Communist Party recruits from the 1960s. In the words of Jānis Āboltiņš, a Komsomol official and state manager who later became economics minister in the pro-independence government of 1990–91, 'I was asked to become a full-time Komsomol leader. . . . After a few days hesitation I agreed. I wanted to get a flat in Riga.'[26] From the beginning Āboltiņš appears to have felt little but contempt for the entire Communist system he served – a contempt which he now extends to the more radical Latvian nationalists. Whether this makes him more attractive is doubtful. What is obvious is that he was not someone who was ever going to defend Soviet rule if the going got rough; the nationalists for their part suspect with reason that he could also not be relied on to serve the cause of independence to the bitter end, or to remain loyal in the event of a Soviet repression. While such former Communist officials are gradually being edged out of state offices, their takeover of the emerging private sector is proceeding at full swing. It occurs largely through the phenomenon of 'spontaneous privatisation', the taking over of state companies by their managers as their own property, a practice which is advancing rapidly in all three republics, and in Latvia seems to be almost out of control. There have been frequent reports in the press but, as of October 1992, not a single prosecution.

A typical tactic is to rent or sell part of the enterprise you manage to a private company controlled either by yourself or by close associates. This, it may be argued, at least allows in principle for the continuation of production under private ownership. More destructive is the virtual theft which takes place when managers sell their produce to private companies (often, again, controlled by themselves) for Baltic state prices, which in turn sell it to the West and pocket the huge difference. This has been especially prevalent in firms controlling 'coloured metals'.

In Estonia, four 'families' (including connections and clients of various kinds) are often said to dominate much of the state's private capital, especially in terms of banking, real estate and hotel development. Three are led by members of the old establishment. Bruno Saul was the hardline Communist Prime Minister of Estonia until he was replaced in 1988. He is now a director of the Tartu Commercial Bank and an owner or part-owner of several companies. Olari Taal was manager of a major state construction enterprise until 1991. He then became Industry Minister in the government of Edgar Savisaar, and Economics Minister in the government of Tiit Vähi (also a former state manager in the very lucrative field of transport). Uno Veering, leader of another wealthy and powerful family, was another Communist manager, and Deputy Premier under Vähi. The fourth family mentioned, that of Toomas and Lembit Sööts, is led by a returned Canadian businessman and his brother. Much of the wealth of such families is founded in their having had an early opportunity to buy up prime pieces of real estate for sums in roubles which, although a fortune to Soviet inhabitants, were derisory by Western standards. As Tallinn land prices move upwards, buyers can make astronomical profits on their investments.

The successor parties which have emerged from the pro-independence wings of the Commmunist parties have to an extent been providing cover for this process, but so indeed have establishment members in the national movements. It leads to some splendidly ironic situations. Thus, in Lithuania, it has been the former Communists, the Lithuanian Democratic Labour Party of Brazauskas that argued for speedy privatisation, large-scale private investment and, in general, a version of 'management's right to manage'. It is of course because the managements themselves, and many of the 'new rich' from the former black market belong to or are close to the old political establishment. Even new entrepreneurs who emerged after 1988 are in many cases from the Komsomol, which was given special rights to start co-operative business in the final years of Communist rule, precisely because Komsomol leaders were in a position to anticipate the future and wanted to get into business.

The Lithuanian Right, however, motivated by a desire to eliminate the former establishment but also by a populist and anti-capitalist tradition, has introduced a strongly egalitarian programme, with shares being distributed to the whole population, and shops being sold to their workers, not to entrepreneurs. So in Western economic terms, Left is often Right and Right is Left, a feature Western, and particularly American visitors, find difficult to comprehend.

In all three republics, other than Soviet loyalist figures who sank with Soviet rule, members of the old establishment and managerial classes are spread across several different parties. In some cases they have even adopted extreme Right-wing positions.

While many local Communist officials are being replaced through local elections, it might be assumed that, as in Eastern Europe, industrial managers would retain their posts. However, this class too risks being buried, along with Baltic industry, a collapse which would itself have partly nationalist roots. In the Baltic States, arguments for the replacement of the managerial élite are national as well as practical and moral. Practically, it is urged that such men simply cannot adapt to a free market economy, and must be replaced. Morally, it is said the 'collaborationist' managerial class does not deserve to profit from privatisation, nor increase its wealth.

Neither of these points is proven. Very few people in the Baltic have practical experience of Western business, and the old managers are often no worse than anyone else at adapting. More to the point, Western business lessons may not in any case be appropriate to the situation in Baltic industry for some time to come. As to the art of survival in a post-Communist economy, the old managers are often geniuses (see Chapter 9).

Morally, the manager of a factory cannot simply be equated with a KGB officer or Communist Party boss, or his position deemed intrinsically more reprehensible than that of a manager anywhere else in the world. To this, however, Latvians and Estonians respond that managers helped to bring Russian workers into their republics; for this reason many would be happy enough if much of industry were wholly to disappear. From their point of view, 'the worse, the better'.

Industrial managers in the Baltic States during the last years of Soviet rule divide into Soviet loyalists, adherents of independence and a larger group which simply kept its collective head down and balanced the conflicting demands of Moscow and the local government. The first group was made up primarily of Russian managers of the great 'All-Union' factories of Latvia and Estonia, controlled from Moscow and supplied with Russian workforces: the factories were organised as Soviet-loyalist island fortresses. In Lithuania, where Russian workers are fewer and most of the All-Union managers were Lithuanian, this phenomenon is less marked. In Estonia, during 1989, Estonian managers, mainly of republican enterprises, joined in a 'League of Work Collectives' to support independence. They were led by Ülo Nugis (later speaker of parliament and a leader of the Right-wing Republican Coalition Party) who, as director of the 'Estoplast' firm, had gained some renown within Estonia for his long struggle to remove his factory from 'All-Union' control. The League claimed to be 'the largest political party in Estonia', with 400,000 members; with blithe seigneurial arrogance, like Soviet loyalist managers, they had simply enrolled their entire workforces under their own political banner.

The attempt did not last long, and the managers soon began to seek protection for their interests through a variety of political forces, even as Estonian workers joined different Estonian parties. For the managers, as for the former Communist establishment in general, the story today is one of political fragmentation. In Latvia during 1992, the government of Ivars Godmanis was often described as being in the hands of the former Soviet establishment; but was opposed by the former Communists, who had now swung to a radical nationalist position.

The Dissidents

In the Soviet Baltic Republics dissent never really went away, even during the depths of Soviet rule. As we have seen, a few gallant partisans rejected the amnesty offered after Stalin's death and continued hiding in the forests, occasionally attacking the police, in some cases well into the 1960s. A proportion of the peaceful dissent of the early 1960s took an open and 'loyalist' form, confining itself to protests by academics and local citizens about the establishment of new industries. The ostensible ground for such protests was often fear of ecological damage, but the real reason was often fear of new Russian settlement.

Spontaneous outbreaks of popular anger also revealed that the people at large had not forgotten their lost independence or their hatred of Soviet rule. The first major Lithuanian demonstration took place in 1956. Sports victories and rock concerts precipitated several of these outbreaks, if only because they had provided legal reasons for large numbers of young people to assemble in the first place. Victories of East European or local teams against Soviet or Russian ones led to mass demonstrations against the occupiers. The largest Baltic demonstration before Gorbachov took place however in Kaunas, in Lithuania, in May 1972, after a student, Romas Kalanta, burnt himself to death in protest against Soviet rule. Thousands of youths rioted for several days; some 500 were arrested.

Eight years later, in October 1980, Estonia saw both widespread student protests and the first major strike under Soviet rule, at a Tartu repair factory. The slogans were economic, and reflected a general downturn in the economy, but the workers were also clearly influenced by a prevailing atmosphere of political anger. At no stage in the seemingly unchanging, strictly controlled years of Soviet rule could the Soviets in fact be completely confident of the security of their rule in the Baltic.

Organised political dissent was very much the work of the intelligentsia, except in Lithuania where Catholicism provided both a mass impulse and a number of martyrs. Christianity was also an inspiration to some Estonian and Latvian dissidents. For much of the 1970s, the 'Chronicle of the Lithuanian Catholic Church', initiated in 1972 and regularly smuggled to the West, was the heart of Lithuanian resistance. Later it was joined by the 'Catholic Committee for the Defence of Believers' Rights', and the Helsinki Group, the survivors of which were to give birth to the extreme nationalist Lithuanian Liberty League in 1988. Several of the Chronicle's distributors were arrested and imprisoned. The speech of one of them, Nijolė Sadūnaitė, at her trial in June 1975, deserves to be included in any anthology of Catholic resistance:

> The Chronicle of the Lithuanian Catholic Church, like a mirror, reflects the acts that atheists perpetrate against believers. Evil is not pleased by its own foul image, it hates its own reflection. The mirror however does not lose its value because of this. . . .
>
> And you rejoice in your triumph? What remains after your victory? Moral ruin, millions of unborn foetuses, defiled values, weak debased people overcome by fear and with no passion for life. This is the fruit of your labours. Jesus Christ was correct when he said, 'By your fruits shall ye know them'. Your crimes are propelling you onto the garbage heap of history at an ever-increasing speed.

Sadūnaitė's book, *A Radiance in the Gulag*, also gives the flavour of the naïve, incantatory quality of Lithuanian popular Catholicism:

> Going against Goliath in God's name, we shall always be the victor! Trusting in God, let us do everything that we must; without his permission, not even a hair from our heads will fall. God is our refuge and our strength![27]

After the victory of Brazauskas in the first round of the October 1992 elections, Sadūnaitė told a meeting outside parliament that 'God and the Virgin have turned their faces from Lithuania', and that Communist rule would usher in a wave of abortions.

The events of 1968 in Czechoslovakia were a major stimulus to dissent in all three republics, and the 1960s and 1970s saw a series of political trials. In October 1980, forty leading Estonian intellectuals sent an open letter to *Pravda* denouncing Russification and Russian settlements in Estonia. The letter was of course not published. Presumably because they did not openly challenge Communist rule, and because they included some of the most famous names in Soviet Estonian culture, the authors of the protest were not officially punished, though they were penalised in various informal ways.[28]

A joint document by dissidents of all three republics first appeared in 1969. In 1974, seventeen Latvian communists, including Eduards Berklavs, signed a protest against Russification. Several more protests were composed during the 1970s, leading to arrests and long prison sentences. The most important Baltic documents of the struggle for independence appeared in 1979 and 1980. The appeal of 23 August 1979, on the anniversary of the Molotov-Ribbentrop Pact, was signed by forty-five Balts, of whom thirty-six were Lithuanian. It denounced the pact and its consequences, and appealed to the United Nations to denounce the illegal Soviet occupation of the Baltic States. Similar appeals appeared in December 1979 and January 1980.

Two names, those of the Estonian dissidents Mart Niklus and Jüri Kukk – a chemistry lecturer at Tartu University – were on both documents. Kükk was arrested shortly afterwards and died in prison in Russia, as a result of brutal force-feeding during a hunger strike in 1981. By the 1980s, however, dissent in all three Baltic States could almost be said to have achieved the status of 'movements', although few signs of these appeared on the surface of national life, and many Balts lived with only the haziest knowledge of their existence.

To anyone knowledgeable about the contemporary Baltic, one thing about the appeals of 1979–80 is immediately noticeable: of all the names on them, few play a role in politics today and none has yet become a major national leader. This is in sharp contrast to the situation in the Caucasus, where leading nationalist dissidents like Zviad Gamsakhurdia and Abulfaz Elchibey have consistently played leading and even dominant political roles. Dissidents have been most honoured in Lithuania, though even there not to the extent one might have expected. One obvious reason is that the main political leaders in all three republics were not themselves dissidents, so may well feel embarrassment when confronted with the heroism of others. This feature does not, however, damage the leaders in the eyes of the mass of the people, for the equally obvious reason that the mass of the people were not dissidents either. In any case many Balts dislike nonconformists of any kind. In the words of Mihkel Tarm, writing of Estonian attitudes to the dissidents: 'The Estonians are different from the Lithuanians, who revere martyrs. Estonians feel that if you landed in prison, you must have been a bit crazy. You obviously just weren't smart enough to manoeuvre properly in the face of the system'. An Estonian deputy from the Centre-Right *Isamaa* ('Fatherland') alliance in September 1992 fiercely attacked the ex-dissident leadership of the more radical National Independence Party (ERSP), saying that,

> Unlike these people, most Estonian conservatives are not exhibitionists, and are not trying to be tragic heroes. We do not think that the best way of approaching a wall is to run against it with your head. In the ERSP there are many mentally unbalanced people. This party never had any brains, it only borrowed them from the emigration in America. . . .
>
> It is true that they were willing to risk anything in the struggle against the Soviets; but for the sake of Estonia, I would not ask my country to take such risks . . . Ironically enough, although they are so anti-Communist, their thinking is quite Bolshevik. They are obsessed with conspiracies, and see spies everywhere. They ask 'Are you a real patriot? If so, why aren't you in our party? Are you with us or against us?'

All three states, in creating traditions, have concentrated mainly on heroes and symbols from the first period of (often authoritarian) statehood in the 1920s and 1930s. One aspect of extreme-Right movements in the Baltic today could be seen as an attempt by old dissident movements to gain the prestige and power they feel they have deserved, and to exclude forever the Communist establishment which persecuted them. It is easy enough to understand their rage. Alfonsas Svarinskas, for example, is a Lithuanian priest and dissident. In 1992 he was a radical nationalist member of parliament. One of the prosecutors at his trial was Egidijus Bičkauskas. Bičkauskas in 1990 became Lithuanian ambassador to Moscow, and a more powerful and better-paid figure than Svarinskas, let alone all the other dissidents like Sadūnaitė. There is only one problem with the seemingly entirely moral and justified demand that people like Bičkauskas be displaced to make way for the former dissidents: Bičkauskas has proved an efficient diplomat who has done much to keep Lithuanian relations with Russia from deteriorating too sharply, and for most of 1992 appeared in public opinion polls as Lithuania's most popular public figure. Svarinskas is a Lithuanian Torquemada-in-waiting, a vehement clerical nationalist extremist who has called, amongst other things, for the mass execution of former Communists, on the pattern of the execution of Nazi collaborators in France 1944.

Some dissidents in the Baltic have thus to a great extent excluded themselves from the political mainstream. In some cases they were simply worn out by their sufferings in Soviet prisons and camps. In others, like Sadūnaitė, they were simple, brave people not fitted for leadership. Some are too honourable for political life which, in the Baltic, is increasingly dirty. Others like Mart Niklus, who do have political ambitions, have excluded themselves by their extremism and even personal neuroticism, whether by their calls for mass revolution in the dangerous years of the struggle for independence, or by their attitudes to Russian immigrants and former Communists, or both.

This of course is one of the saddest features of the dissident heritage: that of the tiny minority that found the courage to protest against Soviet rule, so many found it only in nationalism, and often of a basically chauvinist and backward-looking kind. This is however not always the case. Some of the dissidents who are most bitter in their denunciations of the former Communist establishment appear genuine in their lack of bitterness against Russians as a people. It may well be, as several former dissents maintain, because they co-operated with Russians in the dissident movement and shared the sufferings of Russians in the camps. Lagle Parek, for example, now Chairwoman of the Estonian National Independence Party, speaks with understandable affection and admiration of Irina Ratushinskaya, with whom she was imprisoned. Former dissidents like Parek stress that their opposition is only to the presence of the Russian 'immigrant' or 'colonist' population in Estonia.[29] Parek herself admitted, on the other hand, that former dissidents in Estonia have done almost nothing since the achievement of independence to maintain relations with Russian former dissidents or the Russian democratic movement. She attributed this to 'lack of time', owing to the demands of the consolidation of independence. Since one of the key issues in this consolidation is relations with Russia and Russians, the excuse is, however, not a very strong one.

One interesting case is the Lithuanian radical nationalist, and Leader of the Liberty League, Antanas Terleckas. He, in fact, is anti-Russian as well as anti-Communist but remarkably for a Lithuanian nationalist, produced in 1989 one of the strongest and most moving denunciations of Lithuanian anti-semitism and of the Lithuanian role in the Holocaust; nor does he seem particularly worried by 'the Polish menace'.[30]

The forces behind the Estonian and Latvian Congress movements (see Chapter 8) also came from the dissident tradition, and have been successful in shifting the political debate and consensus in a radical nationalist and 'restitutionist' direction – in the sense of a return to the forms of the pre-1940 republics. So far, however, they have failed to draw much political advantage from this for themselves. One reason is precisely their obstinate legitimism, which repels many fellow members of their sober and pragmatic nations. Another could simply be that dissidents, by their very nature, are often not very good at practical politics.

Some dissidents, not surprisingly, are bitter at the lack of honour shown them and their exclusion from power in the countries they helped to liberate. Their bitterness is of course greatly increased by the fact of their former KGB persecutors not merely unpunished by the courts and drawing state pensions but, in many cases, having gone very successfully into private business on the strength of hidden funds and old underworld connections.* What makes it worse is that conspicuous new opportunities to spend money means that the wealth of the former Communist establishment is becoming more and more visible.

On 23 August 1991, immediately after the failed counter-revolution in Moscow, I stood outside the KGB headquarters in Vilnius with an old Catholic dissident, Viktoras Petkus, who had served a total of twenty-five years in Siberia for his patriotism. Three times he was released, and three times he resumed his patriotic activity, and was again arrested and sentenced. Over our heads drifted smoke from the burning archives as the KGB, before pulling out, destroyed its history, (this time, unlike June 1941, the stock being cleared was only paper, not humans). In Petkus's words,

> My happiness today should be greater. But you see, there are people in this crowd who have been imprisoned in the cellars of this building. I myself was taken to Siberia from here. They say that an official from Moscow has arrived today to negotiate with the Lithuanian government over the level of pensions KGB staff should receive, proportionate to their income. Today, they are getting salaries of 700 roubles a month, and my pension is 150 roubles. It is as if they had done that much more than me for Lithuania.[31]

How much of a political role former dissidents will play in the future is not clear. What is certain is that their moral prestige is very considerable and may grow as the mainstream political forces are seen to make a corrupt mess of things. The dissidents' exclusion from wealth and power, and their resentment at the continued growing wealth of the old communist élites, could also make them rallying points for popular discontent. For, with economic change, the number of excluded and dispossessed Balts could well become legion.

---

* For example, the former KGB commander in Tartu, who is now running both an import-export business and a personal and business security service. Former KGB men are involved in such businesses all across the Baltic (and the former Union is general), often using their links with both the bureaucracy and with the underworld to good purpose.

5

Imagined Nations: Cycles of Cultural Rebirth

I was born singing, I grew up singing,
I lived my life singing.
My soul will go singing
Into the garden of God's sons.
        from a traditional Latvian
    folksong, or *daina*, translated by
                Pauls Raudseps

The opening of the Third Congress of the Sajūdis movement in the Sports Palace, Vilnius, on 14 December 1991 was truly dramatic. An unfamiliar figure stepped up to the microphone and, in a gesture from the Victorian stage, set one foot forward, placed a hand to his breast and extended the other towards the audience. After holding the pose for a second, he began to declaim: 'Today we have come back to our Lithuania, our conscience, our blood; My God, my God, how have we come back to our dear Lithuania. . . . Never did we forget this sacred fire when we were sacrificing our lives for it. Through all the years of the empire of hell we never faltered. . . .'[1] My interpreter fell silent, her mouth half open, and foreign journalists boggled.

The melodrama, however, was intentional and indeed professional, for the speaker, as we later discovered, was no politician but Kestūtis Genys, an actor from the Kaunas Drama Theatre. Sajūdis, the ruling party in Lithuania, had chosen to open its national congress with a poetic monologue, performed with maximum effect. Indeed not simply the opening, but the whole introductory section of the Congress was basically national-religious theatre. We rose for the national anthem, and to honour the dead of January 1991, and then again to hear a beautiful memorial lament. Throughout the first morning of the Congress, a choir in national dress stood at the back of the platform. In between the speeches, they advanced and delivered patriotic anthems.* All rose

---

* When it comes to patriotic music, the apotheosis is surely attained in a Lithuanian record of the country's national anthem, presented by the Lithuanian government

for these, and for the prayers which also interrupted the speeches. The audience again rose for Dr Landsbergis's entry into the hall, for his ascension of the platform, for his presentation with a ceremonial sash and state medal for courage (acknowledging his leadership in January 1991), again at the end of his speech, and when he left the hall. In all, there were at least nineteen standing ovations that morning. The whole business was irresistibly reminiscent not only of the rituals of past Communist Party Congresses, but of the rhythms of the Catholic mass, which has had a deep effect on Lithuanian culture.

Folklore and Nationalism

The ceremonies of the Latvian Popular Front have echoes of such ritualism, as did those of the radical nationalist Latvian and Estonian Congresses. These however do not approach the intensity of Lithuanian nationalist ritual, which Estonians indeed find perfectly ridiculous.

In the reborn Lithuania, supreme national rituals are closely associated with the Church, which now plays a part in all major national events and commemorations. In Latvia and Estonia, the supreme national occasion is by contrast, a secular one (though sometimes with neo-pagan overtones): the great national song festivals. The political importance of song in the Baltic States has been noted many times. In the one hundred-and-fifty-year-old process of the creation of national-cultural symbols, the 'invention' of Baltic tradition, they are probably the most powerful symbols of all. Baltic national revolutions, and especially that in Estonia, have been dubbed 'the singing revolutions', a description akin to that applied to Baltic national movements before 1917 which are said to have 'sung their way to freedom'. In Estonia, at least, the use of song as a sort of weapon is of immense antiquity; both Estonian and Finnish folklore record traditions of 'singing matches', a kind of peaceful single combat between rivals.[2]

The first Estonian and Latvian national song festivals, in 1869 and 1873 respectively, were political as well as cultural events of the first importance, the culmination of a decades-long process of national-cultural development influenced by contemporary German nationalist folk festivals. To understand why, one must remember that, until the

to foreign guests. The first band consists of the Lithuanian national anthem, performed by choir and orchestra; the second band, of the same anthem sung by a different choir, and more slowly; the third band, the same anthem played by the orchestra alone; and the last band, the national anthem played and sung by all three, *fortissimo*. On each band all three verses are sung, so that by the end the listener has heard the melody repeated twelve times, and the words, nine times.

early nineteenth century, peasant folk-songs and legends were, to all intents and purposes, the essence of Latvian and Estonian culture. Literature in these languages consisted otherwise solely of religious tracts, prayers, hymns and translations, even though literacy was already well advanced and, in Estonia by the end of the century, perhaps at a higher level than in Britain. There was of course also a folk-tradition in the visual arts, but whereas this was rather limited, Baltic folk-songs were and remain unparalleled in Europe for their richness and beauty. Their influence runs like a thread through all subsequent cultural developments and schools of Estonian and Latvian literature from the mid-nineteenth century. Hence great reverence is paid in Latvia to the memory of Krišjānis Barons (1835–1923) who assembled and codified the *dainas*, or Latvian folksongs, 217,996 items in the published edition, and some 1.5 million in all. With a song for every living Latvian, it is said to be the world's largest collection of oral folklore. In Lithuania and Estonia, men like Jonas Basanavičius, Friedrich Reinhold Kreuzwald and Jakob Hurt were engaged in similar tasks.[3]

Nor was focus on folklore for the want of any other medium. Singing had always been immensely important for the Baltic peoples, and undoubtedly played a major role in their ancient pagan religions and magical practices.[4] The earliest written records of traditional Estonian songs were in the form of evidence in seventeenth-century witch-trials. For this reason, Christian pastors devoted much energy to stamping out these 'satanic songs' and replacing them with German Christian hymns. Today, every village has its choir, which often sings to professional standard and children are strongly encouraged to participate. In the words of the Latvian poet, Imants Ziedonis:

> My child, we are a nation of eaters, but put your spoon down in your bowl while a song is being sung. Don't look at that man eating, don't learn from him. He has eaten all his songs. He can't tell the difference between songs and lettuce.[5]

Localised festivals of folk song and dance take place regularly at every level of society, and are major social and public events. They find their apotheosis of course in the great national song festivals, which take place every few years. When they began, under Russian imperial rule in the nineteenth century, they symbolised not only the unity and aspirations but the very existence of the Baltic nations, which the Baltic Germans in particular were disposed to deny. Before 1917, each national festival was seen as a further step in the consolidation and mobilisation of the spirit of Baltic nations. Under Russian, as later under Soviet, rule the festivals were also the only legal opportunity for large numbers of people to gather and show their national allegiance, albeit in a veiled way. In recent years,

6   General view of the Latvian National Song Festival, Riga, July 1990.

of course, they were also vital symbols of the struggle for independence against Soviet rule. It was at the 'Baltika' festival of 1988 that the three national flags were first raised together under Soviet rule.

In recent years the presence at the festivals of groups of Baltic exiles has also symbolised at an international level the unity of the Baltic nations, overcoming the Soviet forces which drove them into exile and separated them from their families and homeland. It also celebrates the way that these communities, or some of them, have preserved their national cultures in exile.

With independence now achieved, the festivals will presumably once again play the role they possessed under the first Baltic republics, when they symbolised the survival of a higher, unbreakable national unity and purpose in the face of all political conflicts and disputes. As such, of course, they proved useful symbols for the authoritarian regimes which eventually took power in the three states. It is interesting to note that although today the song festivals are always performed by choirs in traditional peasant dress, which bestows an air of immemorial antiquity, in fact this only became the practice in Estonia after the 1934 coup of Konstantin Päts. Before that, people turned up in their 'best' clothes. The rules as to what constituted the correct costume for each region were laid down by experts from the Estonian National Museum; a typical episode in the 'invention of tradition'.

The national festivals are indeed vastly impressive occasions. The choirs number in the thousands and the participants, in the cases of Latvia and Estonia, make up a very large proportion of the ethnic Latvian and Estonian populations. The sound of hundreds of thousands of voices symbolise national harmony in every sense, like Rousseau's 'General Will' set to music.[6]

The stress on the connection between folklore and national identity in Baltic thought stems naturally from Baltic history, but it was also a central element in the philosophy of the first great European thinker (possibly indeed the only one) to take a close interest in the Balts and their traditions. Johann Gottfried Herder was a pastor and teacher in Riga between 1764 and 1769 and developed a keen interest in Latvian and Estonian folklore, examples of which he included in his collection. *Stimmen der Voelker in Lieder* ('Voices of the Peoples in Song' – a significant title). Herder was strongly influenced by this folklore, and by the manner in which it had kept some form of Baltic identity alive even in the absence of a 'higher' culture. Largely on the basis of his Baltic experience, Herder enunciated the theory that every nation had its own special and incommunicable national spirit and culture, the highest expression of which was their folksong and poetry. These he called 'the imprints of a nation's soul'. For nations which had been suppressed by other nations, politically or culturally (as he saw his own Germany having been colonised by French culture) the only route to the recovery of a national cultural and hence political identity was through the rediscovery of folklore.[7]

Herder's thought had a great influence on local German scholars who, after him, began to collect Baltic folklore and, through them, on emerging Baltic scholars and nationalists. To this day, Herder exerts a vast influence on Baltic philosophy. His stress on national individuality, and denunciations of internationalism and cosmopolitanism, have become even more popular as a result of opposition to the grim Soviet version of 'internationalism' which threatened to destroy Baltic culture. In the case of the Baltic cultures which have emerged since the mid-nineteenth century, the vision of Herder has been to some extent fulfilled, particularly in terms of poetry (in Latvia and Lithuania, the dominant literary form) which has been vastly influenced by folklore and folk-song. An Estonian emigré poet, writing in 1973, considered that ' . . . the Baltic writer rebels against, or falls back on and interacts with, his folklore heritage, just as contemporary English authors, whether knowingly or not, draw on a literary tradition which goes all the way back to Chaucer in an unbroken line'.[8]

This rural and folkloric imagery is what gives much of Baltic literature its beauty, power and distinctiveness in the context of European culture today. A Latvian emigré scholar, Vaira Vīķis-Freibergs, adopting a concept from Marshall McLuhan, has said that the *dainas* have an essential 'coolness' of style, reflected in 'a strong reserve and reticence towards the direct expression of deep emotions', which has been passed on to Latvian literature. She contrasts this with Russian folk-style and culture, which she says are at the extreme 'hot' end of the scale.[9]

Natural and animal imagery, often taken originally from folksong, is very common in Baltic literature, and especially poetry, to this day and, for that matter, in Baltic languages and popular idioms in general. This has often been linked to a sort of 'neo-pagan', animistic, holistic belief in the divinity of all living things. Many Balts are fascinated by questions relating to shamanism and the idea of a world in which the spirits of men and animals interact. In Estonia it is to be found strongly represented in the poems of Jaan Kaplinski, for example. Kaplinski's own holistic philosophy is formulated in Neo-Buddhist terms, but in his approach to nature he undoubtedly owes much to this specifically Baltic tradition, as does the strong ecological consciousness of so many Baltic writers. A typical, though unusually beautiful and powerful, example of such an approach in Lithuania is the poet Sigitas Geda, of whom a critic has written that he 'talked in a friendly way to a grasshopper, whom he held to be of the gods' and that 'Geda draws no clear-cut boundaries between people, animals and nature – they all seem extensions of each other in a landscape where "The brown reeds smell of the forefathers' bodies" and "Icebergs, stones, birds and humans have walked across Lithuania"'.[10]

Animal images, and birds in particular, can get in almost anywhere in Lithuania. Soon after the Lithuanian declaration of independence, the philosopher Arvydas Šliogeris told me that, 'the Lithuanians see independence as a big green bird with a red beak. Of course they will feel disappointed, because such a bird has not in fact landed on the Lithuanian parliament'. By the bird, he later explained, he meant to symbolise 'anything miraculous and wonderful'. During a discussion on economic reform with the Lithuanian government, a Lithuanian-American academic suddenly exclaimed: 'Take a good look at this powerful bird, free enterprise; do you want to shoot it, or will you follow where it leads?'

The presence of neo-pagan elements and motifs in contemporary Baltic culture has strong organic roots in Baltic peasant cultures as these continued and evolved from the pre-Christian period, though of course they became thoroughly mixed with Christian elements. In this sense, while these modern pagan elements are obviously very different from the original paganism, most are also quite distinct from the neo-paganisms of modern Western Europe, so often either profoundly foolish or deeply sinister.[11]

However, in the course of the past century, there have also been strong attempts by Baltic nationalist elements (and, between 1920 and 1940, the national states) to reshape these traditions to their own purposes. Thus the authoritarian Latvian regime of President Ulmanis made quite extensive use of neo-pagan, 'ethnic-religious' motifs during the 1930s. A neo-pagan religious group, the *Dievturi* (*Dievs* means 'God' in Latvian), was formed, closely linked with Latvian fascist groups to the Right of Ulmanis. *Dievturiba* has now been revived. Its membership is extremely small, though it enjoys considerable prestige on the far Right of politics. Even Latvians who disapprove of its ideology accord it a certain respect because of the unusual purity and beauty of its rendering of Latvian folk-songs, and the memory of the repeated imprisonment of its members under Soviet rule. There are also neo-pagan groups in Lithuania, where however the dominance of Catholicism in national imagery means that their direct political impact has been even more limited.[12] The relationship between the neo-pagan and Catholic strands of modern Lithuanian culture is intensely complicated.

Several of the nineteenth-century Lithuanian national poets and writers, like Maironis and Baranauskas, were Catholic priests. However, later in the century there also emerged a strong streak of liberal nationalism which blamed Catholic conservatism for Lithuanian backwardness, supineness, Polonisation and reliance on outside authority.

In the context of a Baltic 'time-lag' in terms of the adoption of Western ideas, so strongly re-inforced by Soviet rule, it is interesting to note that liberal positivist thought gained the ascendancy in Lithuania only in the 1890s – at the precise moment when, in Western Europe, thinkers were beginning to abandon it in favour of other approaches and ideologies, often with romantic roots. This may help account for the relatively shallow roots struck by positivism within Lithuanian culture.

From the 1880s, liberal writers like Kudirka explicitly recalled Lithuania's great medieval pagan past in opposition to the negative features of contemporary Catholic Lithuania. Since the Catholic element could not be omitted in any full conception of Lithuanian national identity, it is significant that, for example, the words of the Lithuanian national anthem, written by Kudirka, are a rather uneasy mixture of Catholic and neo-pagan imagery.

The official culture of Smetona's authoritarian regime was largely derived from this liberal tradition – an apparent paradox paralleled, for example, in Italy where the tradition of nineteenth-century activist anti-clerical liberal nationalism passed in the twentieth into Mussolini's fascism. Smetona's relations with the Church were also frequently strained, though because of its power, the need to consolidate Lithuania's young national culture, and the lack of real radicalism in Smetona's party, the rift never went as deep as in Italy.

Images of an imagined pagan past are widespread in Latvian and Lithuanian political rhetoric today, and pictures of that past are used to support one or other national and ideological orientation. Thus in the nineteenth century, authors made their pagan heroes argue for democracy as well as for independence. Soviet writers, and many Baltic patriots as well, portrayed ancient Baltic society as strongly egalitarian (this of course being the common currency of most imagined 'golden ages' worldwide). Today, the idea that ancient Baltic society was matricentral has been used both by proto-feminists, and by politicians arguing that the ancient Balts were a peaceful, unaggressive people, vulnerable to aggressive nomadic proto-communist Slavs. The implication is that this is also true of the Balts today. Often, especially in Lithuanian rhetoric, this pacific image co-exists uneasily with images of glorious Lithuanian victory and conquest.[13]

One aspect of the neo-pagan and historical revival which has become completely generalised and internalised is that of first names. Until the end of the nineteenth century, Lithuanians and Latvians used either local versions of general Christian names, like Jānis or Jonas, or bore traditional peasant names, possibly derived initially from pagan roots but with no clear connection with the tradition (as, for example, the names of the peasants in Donelaitis). The 'rediscovery' of national history in Lithuania, and the 'recreation' of national myth in Latvia meant a tremendous vogue among the intelligentsia for historical and mythological names, a vogue which is now common in Latvian society. Today, Vytautas, Mindaugas, and Kestūtis (all medieval grand dukes) are among the most common Lithuanian names; a century and a half ago they were largely unknown (though Vytautas survived in Slavonic as 'Witold'). Supporters of Landsbergis sometimes make play in their propaganda of the identification of his name with that of Vytautas the Great. The giving of such names was a quiet protest against Soviet rule when the regime was encouraging the use of 'Vladimir', or weird revolutionary hybrids. One Lithuanian friend reported that her younger brother had been named Mindaugas, 'as a very small way of showing that we were still attached to Lithuania and the Lithuanian tradition'. On 6 July 1992, the anniversary of Mindaugas's coronation (the 739th anniversary in fact, the choice of which shows a certain impatience on the part of the Lithuanian government) was celebrated with great pseudo-medieval ceremonies in Kaunas. According to a Swedish observer, 'whether this will become a regular national holiday depends on which side wins the next elections'. The sweeping victory of the former Communists therefore means that the anniversary will almost certainly not be institutionalised. The Lithuanian Right wing loves such ceremonies, while the Left and Centre have sometimes deliberately associated themselves with pop concerts as a way of showing their 'youthfulness' and 'modernity'.

In Estonia, such historical re-enactments have little resonance, a sign of Estonia's greater closeness to the modern West. There, use of folklore in party politics is restricted to the more extreme Right. Even the Centre-Right 'Fatherland' (*Isamaa*) alliance in the elections of September 1992 made much greater use of pop and rock concerts. The Isamaa Prime Minister, Mart Laar, explained that this was partly for cultural reasons, and partly because so many pop and rock singers were Isamaa supporters. In Estonia, folklore already plays a national role much closer to that of Scandinavia. For while even the limited Estonian stress on folklore is unusual by Anglo-Saxon standards, in the Scandinavian and other democracies, displays of folklore are used to bolster both national and local identities. As these identities come under threat from modern mass culture, the official use of folklore in many areas has perhaps become even more marked.

The Creation of Language

Alongside the political creation of the Baltic nations, the codification of their folklore, and the first indigenous literary creativity came the forging of the modern Baltic languages out of numerous peasant dialects. German linguists assisted the process by developing a keen interest in the roots of the Indo-European language group, of which Lithuanian is one of the most antique examples.

In Lithuania and Estonia, the process of linguistic harmonisation and standardisation was more or less complete by 1914, and in Latvia by the 1920s. The process was greatly intensified under the independent republics, through school systems and official media, and was finally completed under Soviet rule. The creation of the standard languages brought fierce polemics in the press and struggles between linguists championing different dialects.[14] In Estonia, the result was a conclusive victory for North Estonian over South Estonian, which had hitherto been virtually a separate language, but today, under intensive state pressure, has almost entirely faded. A form of it is still spoken by some of the Setu people in Estonia and the Pskov region of Russian, and the poet Jaan Kaplinski has used it in some of his work. The 'unification' of Latvian has not proceeded as far, in that the Latgalian language is still recognisably distinct from 'standard' Latvian.[15]

In Latvia and Estonia, the movement for 'purification' of the language was most often directed against German words, and in Lithuania against Polish words and orthography. Today, of course, the stress is on removing Russian borrowings, though fears have also been expressed that the Baltic languages may be swamped by a wave of Americanisms. Articles on the subject have appeared in the Right-wing press in all three republics, and Lithuanian television has a weekly programme devoted to encouraging people to speak correct Lithuanian. At the Third Sajūdis Congress the radical nationalist, Antanas Terleckas, in the middle of someone else's speech, suddenly grabbed the microphone and roared at the unfortunate speaker, 'Why do you use this filthy Soviet term "organ", when you could use the proper Lithuanian word "institution" (*institucija*)!'

The hereditary prestige of Vytautas Landsbergis for the Lithuanian intelligentsia stems in part from a family connection with the creation of the modern Lithuanian language. His maternal great-grandfather, Professor Jonas Jablonskis, was chiefly responsible for drawing up and codifying Lithuanian grammar and vocabulary in the later nineteenth century. At the same time, Dr Landsbergis's paternal grandfather was in a sense putting Jablonskis's work into practice by writing the first plays to appear in Lithuanian, as well as developing Lithuanian journalism.[16]

The activity of the Landsbergis family can indeed be said to span almost the whole history of Lithuanian culture from its creation in the mid-nineteenth century to the present. Landsbergis's father was a distinguished architect under the first republic, who also fought for Lithuanian independence in 1918–20 and who served in the Lithuanian administration under the German occupation of 1941. At the time of writing, he was still alive and was regularly hailed at Sajūdis gatherings as the 'Patriarch of National Independence'. Landsbergis himself is the most distinguished critic and analyst of Lithuania's national artist and composer, M. K. Čiurlionis, and by keeping knowledge of his work alive under a Soviet system hostile to it, helped defend Lithuanian culture; however, his suggestions that this constituted a form of active resistance are exaggerated.[17]

Myth as History and History as Myth

In developing their national languages and literatures, the Balts were not only concerned to provide themselves with the tools of modern cultural nationhood. They had also to prove to the world that they possessed a full cultural identity, and to overcome the sense of inferiority produced by many centuries of foreign rule during which any educated Balt automatically became a German or a Pole. They had to throw back in his teeth the words of the Baltic German pastor who declared in the mid-nineteenth century that,

> Those who know our 'nationals' have long since lost all hope for the Latvian people. It is a stillborn nation. The Latvians have no national past and no history, they cannot have a future. The only character traits

which distinguish them are their totally backward and crippled language
... and their blinding hatred for the Germans.[18]

In both the ancient classical and the Herderian traditions of the
nineteenth-century, the highest form of folk creation was the epic. This in
turn, in the classification of the German writer Wilhelm Jordan, could
only be produced by an 'epic people' which was, at the same time, a
Kulturvolk. The enterprise was pushed forward by the creation of *Ossian*.[19]
A vital impetus for the Balts was given by the publication in Finland
between 1835 and 1849 of the *Kalevala*, compiled by Elias Lönnrot from
fragments of ancient Karelian folk-poems. In its basic material, the
Kalevala is a good deal more authentic as a folk-epic than *Ossian*, but
stands nonetheless in the Ossian tradition.[20] The result of these
influences in the Baltic provinces was the publication in 1861 of the
Estonian epic poem *Kalevipoeg* ('The Son of Kalev'), by Friedrich
Kreuzwald and in 1888 (in Latvian) of *Lāčplēsis* ('The Bear-Tearer') by
Andrējs Pumpurs. *Lāčplēsis* followed unsuccessful attempts by other
Latvian authors to create such an epic.

Both the giant Kalevipoeg and Lāčplēsis were central figures in
ancient Estonian and Latvian prose folk-tales; the reworking of the
material into patriotic verse epics was therefore an 'organic' development
in Baltic culture. It however required a transformation which went
considerably beyond that of Lonnrot with his *Kalevala* material, because
an epic poetic tradition simply did not exist in Estonian and Latvian
folklore. It must also be said that neither Kalevipoeg nor Lāčplēsis were
aggressive heroes as heroes go, and are portrayed as defending their
nations, not leading them into conquest. The transformation of the
stories into legends also involved the modification of archaic peasant
tastes by aspiring Victorian ones: thus Kreuzwald left out several aspects
of the Kalevipoeg tradition in Estonian folklore, one of which had Christ
catching Kalevipoeg by the testicles and throwing him into a marsh as
punishment for his sexual licence – an episode which also presumably
symbolised the victory of Christianity over the old gods.*

The impulse to create an Estonian epic came from Kreuzwald's friend,
Friedrich Robert Faehlmann (1798–1850), who first proposed 'building a
national epic' around the figure of Kalevipoeg. Faehlmann himself had
already published (in German) a series of 'Estonian' myths based on
Finnish legendary characters (with classical Greek trappings) which
became Estonian cultural symbols. In the words of an Estonian critic,
'Such universal acceptance of a largely fictional creation must be a rare
occurrence in the history of literature.[21] More major epics were explicit in

---

* Lithuanian editors in the past also changed some of the scatological terminology in
  Donelaitis' *The Seasons*.

119

7   Lāčplēsis, the 'Bear-Tearer'. His original name was Lāčausis, 'Bear's Ears'.

their intention to serve as national inspirations and rallying-cries, and both end with invocations to their nations suggesting that the heroes will return to lead them and restore their past glory.[22] The impact of each on their nations was tremendous, equivalent to that of the song festivals, the assemblers of folklore and the creators of the standard languages.

In the Estonian case, the importance of *Kalevipoeg* has faded over the years, possibly because of Estonian access to the more 'authentic' and artistically superior Kalevala, and because of the more modern, Western tone of Estonian culture in general. The writer Jaan Puhvel argues that although bits of *Kalevipoeg* 'have been brandished as a theatrical prop', it has mainly served as a roadblock. But in Latvia, Pumpurs's work has been a source of inspiration for successive generations of writers and artists to the present day. As such it also helped to perpetuate the influence of Romanticism in Latvian literature long after it had vanished elsewhere in Europe.[23] In the plainly Herderian words of a contemporary Lithuanian writer,

> As the nation enters history, the word of the poet must acquire the properties of a narrative discourse, must grow to become a myth that could in some ways function like those of epic Greek antiquity, when they gave the people a soul, an identity liberated by time. . . . The present situation of the Baltic States requires a new approach to the myth of nationhood, one that would cut through the bourgeois sentimentalism of a small country and the reveries of the romantic era to reach back to the roots which were there at the dawn of history and before.[24]

Thus the authors of the national epics, and in Lithuania, the recreators of Lithuanian history and folklore, did indeed 'invent a tradition' which stretched back into an imaginary past and influenced a real national future.[25] This is deliberately symbolised in the episode in *Lāčplēsis* in which the hero overcomes monsters which guard the scrolls containing the ancient wisdom of the Latvians in a castle sunk beneath the lake.[26]

The epics therefore served three national needs. They were, in the view of the intelligentsia, true 'folk-epics', emerging from genuine, ancient folk-traditions and 'mirroring the nation's soul'; they were proof that the Baltic languages could produce great modern writers; and they gave a history, and a sense of history, to peoples who had possessed neither. Both Kreuzwald and Pumpurs re-worked their material so that the enemies of their heroes became the Teutonic Knights. Real historical characters and events from the late twelfth and early thirteenth centuries, like the Livonian chieftain Kaupo and his visit to Rome, were inserted into the Lāčplēsis story. The pagan demi-gods of folklore were also extracted from pagan legend and inserted into an actual national past, at the same time as, in *Lāčplēsis*, Latvian paganism was endowed with a partly real, partly imaginary 'Olympus' of classical-type gods.[27]

Looking to the Latvian future, Pumpurs made Lāčplēsis argue for a Latvian democratic tradition. The Communists, for their part, portrayed the Lāčplēsis of *Fire and Night*, a play on the theme by the Latvian poet Jānis Rainis, as a symbol of the shackled, sometimes misled force of the proletariat, and the play itself as a staging of the materialist view of history. In this interpretation, Laimdota, the hero's rather colourless beloved, stood for an 'anaemic, backward-looking romantic nationalism', while the spirited witch Spīdola stood for 'progress'. It seems this was indeed Rainis's intention to an extent; the play was completed in 1911, when he was still a strong social democrat.

These epics became rallying cries for successive generations of Balts, whenever the nation and its culture seemed in danger of destruction by foreign oppressors; and they provided an imaginative link between modern Balts and their ancestors of the 'golden age', before conquest by the Germans. According to the Latvian-American critic, Valda Melngaile, 'for many Latvian poets, song stands for history'.[28] In the first Latvian Republic, the 'Order of Lāčplēsis' was the premier state decoration for courage and service, and it is now being revived in the second republic. A Latvian-Russian friend told me that she had grown up in Riga feeling 'surrounded by Lāčplēsis'. Apart from the sculpture on the Freedom Monument and frequent performances of Rainis's play at school and university, there is in Riga a Lāčplēsis Street and a Lāčplēsis Cinema. Many hairdressers and boutiques are named 'Laimdota'. Spīdola, the witch, is a favourite name for Latvian ships and boats; 'Kangars', the traitor in the epic, has become a generic term for the treacherous. The beginnings of the national movement in 1988 were accompanied by the rock-opera *Lāčplēsis*, by Māra Zālīte, in which the hero's unusual ears symbolise his willingness to hear the call of his people. (Lithuanians for their part are renaming whole blocks of Soviet-named streets after their ancient gods.) In the verse of the Latvian contemporary poet, Māris Čaklais:

> Pumpurs is a voice
> sewing up the space:
> 'There is a long, long way
> to be danced.
> You will require a voice
> clear and bright.
> There is a far, far future
> to be sung.'[29]

The attempt to answer all these national and cultural needs simultaneously involved the Balts, however, in a set of contradictory beliefs about the epics which, for a long time, they dared not analyse for fear of breaking their spell. Thus the very people who spoke of the epics as stemming directly from the folk-tradition also praised the authors not as 'compilers' but as original creative geniuses. Moreover while the folk-tales themselves are always referred to as ancient manifestations of pagan religious culture, the heroes have also been portrayed as historical figures.

So far as the presentation of Lāčplēsis in the Latvian visual arts is concerned, this landed the Latvians not on the horns of a dilemma but rather on the ears of one. According to legend, Lāčplēsis was the child of a male human and a female bear, which suggested relations deeply embarrassing to a Victorian like Pumpurs. This aspect was hence underplayed in his epic, so most Latvians mistakenly believe that Lāčplēsis was merely the bear's foster son. In any event, his mother left him with an unavoidable feature – the ears of a bear: his original name indeed was 'Lāčausis', or 'Bear-Ear'.[30] This is where 'myth as history' posed a problem. A Latvian mythical demi-god with bear's ears would have presented no particular difficulty; there have been far stranger figures, mythologically speaking. But for the leader of the thirteenth-century Latvian national resistance movement to be depicted in art with bear's ears was obviously unthinkable – the Germans, Russians and Estonians would have laughed for the rest of historical time.

The way in which Latvian artists overcame this difficulty provides one of the more curious episodes in the history of national iconography. The approach has been basically twofold: to conceal, and to transfigure. Thus on the Freedom Monument in Riga the sculpture of Lāčplēsis is given long hair, so that it is impossible to see his ears. Other artists, feeling that the ears have to be represented somehow, have detached them from his head and stuck them onto his helmet, like furry ear-muffs on a Russian hat. Even then however, knowing that spectators might still look under the helmet, they had to cover the ear-spaces with long hair. Despite the unequivocal attachment of Lāčplēsis to his ears in both Pumpurs' and Rainis' epic accounts I have yet to find a single Latvian artistic representation, out of dozens investigated, which presents them in their proper location.[31]

What makes the artists' dilemma especially painful however was summed up by a Latvian guide, to whom I pointed out this anomaly. She looked at me coldly: 'The ears are to be understood as a sign of moral authority', she said, 'Of course they were not physical ears'. While she was wrong about the physicality, it is quite correct that in both the ancient myths and the modern narratives, the ears gave their owner not merely authority but also physical strength. They were the equivalent of Samson's hair, and the 'Black Knight' only succeeds in fighting Lāčplēsis to a draw at the end of the epic by lopping them off.[32] So by taking away his ears, what the Latvian artists have done is *symbolically castrate their own national hero!*

8   The Latvian mythical hero, Lāčplēsis, of the eponymous epic by Pumpurs, fighting the Black
Knight. Note the bear's ears on Lāčplēsis' helmet.

Cultural Politics in the Reborn States

In today's reborn Baltic States, the connection between culture and politics is particularly explicit in the case of Lithuania. There Dr Landsbergis represents a form of 'cultural politics' not simply through his ancestry and image for the Lithuanian intelligentsia but also through his own central political motivation.[33]

The response of leading cultural figures within the Baltics to the political scene after independence has of course been varied. The overwhelming majority supported the struggle for independence, some playing a leading public role. Of these, a few, like the Lithuanian poet Sigitas Geda, have withdrawn from public life, disgusted with the corruption and infighting. Others, like his fellow poet Kazys Saja or the Estonian poet Paul-Erik Rummo, became parliamentary deputies on the Right. Others again, like the Estonian Jaan Kaplinski and the Lithuanian exile Tomas Venclova, have become strong critics of what they see as the narrow and chauvinist nationalism of some sections of their countries. Jānis Peters, the former Secretary of the Latvian Writers Union who played a key part in founding the Popular Front, as of early 1993, still occupied a key post as Latvian ambassador to Moscow. A few, like the Estonian poet and novelist Jaan Kross, have succeeded in remaining public figures admired by all for their integrity and impartiality. Kross, Rummo and Kaplinski were all elected as deputies in 1992, leading an observer to comment that whatever its other faults, the Estonian parliament was probably the only one in the world to contain three potential Nobel prizewinners.

While Baltic poets may with time become unpolitical however, very few can become apolitical. Since the beginnings of modern Baltic culture it has been the duty of Baltic artists to provide an example in terms of symbols and ideology. In the words of a post-1944 Baltic emigré writer, 'The task of Latvian literature in exile is to create symbols for the experience of the Latvian at this time, symbols which would include answers for the future: how the Latvian nation shall survive in the shadow of death and how it shall indeed achieve a future'.[34]

Baltic exile literature, and especially verse, was overwhelmingly coloured by nostalgia for the lost homeland, by themes of yearning and separation, and by the search for eternal symbols which would transcend the miserable and possibly hopeless circumstances of the present. But this was also true for the Soviet Baltic authors – indeed even more poignantly so – because they were often 'internal emigrés', spiritual exiles within their own countries and, because in conditions of censorship, their search for national symbols had to be a hidden endeavour. Censorship, as always, encouraged allegory; and allegory in turn pointed to the use of either folklore or history, the natural, traditional source of nationalist imagery. Meanwhile, not merely were most artists seeking in some way to express the national spirit and resist Soviet culture, but they were impelled by the sheer dreariness, the moral and physical squalor of Soviet life, to seek refuge in questions of private existence and in folklore and nature. This tendency was also a reaction against the brutal shock of collectivisation, which not only ruined agriculture, but ruined the traditional rural society which was the basis of the national tradition itself. There was a tremendous impetus therefore to save what could be saved, and use or at least record it before it disappeared. The words of the Lithuanian exile critic, Rimvydas Šilbajoris, link the nineteenth-century search for national myths with the twentieth century search for national cultural regeneration:

> The Lithuanians, a people with possibly the greatest stories to tell from medieval times, never could find even the basic outlines of the myth that their nation must have been, judging by its historical deeds. The alternative chosen by some Lithuanian poets was to turn inward, towards the human mystery of their own selves, as if to some spacious world from which a mythological perception of existence may rise like some sort of 'memory inside the blood' to nourish and shape the poet's imagination, so that a given moment in the course of history would also become suffused with this mythological presence and transform itself into poetry. . . .[35]

As a result, after Stalin's death, and Khrushchev's 'thaw' in the 1950s, there was a tangible literary move, especially in Lithuania and Latvia, towards folkloric themes and imagery. It was accompanied by a great, if covert, internal philosophical reaction against positivism as exemplified in its most grim, coarse, and ultimately discredited form by Soviet Marxism-Leninism. Today this is reflected not only in straightforward uses of traditional forms and motifs, but in sophisticated post-modern reworkings of them.

The anti-modernist tendency, present in any case in the Baltic peasant and folkloric-romantic tradition, was considerably strengthened by the fact that everything ugly in modern society could now be seen not as the consequence of general economic and social trends, but as yet another evil consequence of alien rule. The effect was that, in much of the Soviet Baltic literature that Balts really loved and admired, the countryside, and rural values, tended to receive an overwhelmingly positive shade, and the towns an overwhelmingly negative one. One Lithuanian author is said by Dr Šilbajoris to 'describe the moral depravity of his urban characters as if it were the very essence of their souls'.[36] Numerous works bathed the 'lost paradise' of rural childhood in a golden glow. Even in relatively unromantic Estonia, the urban novels and short stories of Arvo Valton, Mati Unt and others are dominated by themes of coldness, alienation and falsity. In the 1920s and 30s, the greatest classic in the tradition of the

Estonian realist novel, the series 'Truth and Justice' by Anton Hansen Tammsaare, was indeed dominated in its first and last volumes by a grim, unrelenting struggle with a harsh and unyielding land. Nonetheless, it is only when the protagonist, Indrek Paar, returns to the land and the struggle from the falsity and even insanity of his urban life that he 'finds himself' again, and discovers a purpose to existence.[37]

This celebration of traditional values certainly helped prevent Soviet rule from achieving legitimacy. However, this rejectionist aspect of Baltic and other Soviet national cultures was disguised and indeed warped by another factor of great contemporary importance, which I term (after the semi-official national culture of the German Empire before 1914) the 'Wilhelmine' nature of Soviet official culture. This was characterised *inter alia* by a slavish adulation of power, industry, 'Progress' in its most brutal and domineering form, but simultaneously by an endless harping on the value of conservative, rural, homely, familial, traditional, folkloric and religious values, all presented in a general glow of kitsch and nauseating roseate sentimentality, much of it by authors who were themselves already thoroughly urbanised.

The 'Wilhelmine' sensibility came in reaction to modernisation, but was also of course directly sponsored in the name of social order by a threatened authoritarian state. If you omit the religious element, this is a pretty fair picture of much of officially generated Soviet culture in the last decades of the Union. In Russia itself the nationalist aspects could be more or less open, and even in the other republics a certain amount was allowed. The numbingly boring uses by the Soviet state of sanitised and 'safe' national folk-cultures are all too familiar to visitors to the former Union, and fitted in as perfectly with Soviet rituals as they do with the new national ones. Thus too, the high official status of Soviet authors who celebrated rural and traditional values (of the most ossified kind) was not compromised by the fact that much of what they were writing could as well have come from the Baltic emigrés in America. Similarly, the very popular Soviet Lithuanian author, Justinas Marcinkevičius, opened his play *Mažvydas* (1977) with a Lithuanian pastor teaching children to spell their first word, 'Lithuania':

> As you say this word, upon your lips,
> You'll feel the taste of blood and honey,
> You'll hear the Oriole call before the rain,
> You'll catch the smell of hay. . . .

and so on. This stomach-turning stuff is not, it must be said, characteristic of Marcinkevičius's work as a whole, let alone of Baltic poetry at its best. On the contrary, one of the great values of folkloric imagery in Baltic literature is precisely that it avoids triteness and kitsch, providing instead motifs of universal lyricism and power. Nonetheless, these lines are fairly representative of both at their worst, and certainly of the kind of poetry which is now being written by amateur bards for political and patriotic occasions. As a patriotic Latvian McGonnigal in the radical nationalist paper *Pilsonis* had it, presumably referring to the Russians in Latvia:

> While white souls are trying to fly
> High in the sky,
> Black souls are dragging them down and trying to doom them to
>   extinction.
> Wolves are invading our sacred places,
> And our gardens where seeds of the Latvian tricolour are
>   growing. . . . [38]

However, the field of culture also symbolises and embodies the most positive sides of Baltic nationalism: its capacity to inspire and move; its intense love for old, precious and unique traditions; and its basically peaceful and unaggressive character. Today, Baltic writers and artists are addressing the question of how the national concerns of Baltic culture should be expressed in this new age. In this context, they face two main problems. The first is the danger of remaining patriotic bards, expressing 'national values' and articulating the 'national spirit', though now with the support of the dominant political forces.[39] Those who do are likely to lose touch with the transformation of their societies and find themselves perpetuating a tradition which is 'Soviet in form and national in content'. This is now probably the dominant cultural form in all the former republics of the Soviet Union, as nationalism is the dominant political form. This is not only because nationalism is the only force which can replace communism in the structure of state, society, culture and academia. It is also because, following the 'Wilhelmine' argument, some aspects of Soviet and patriotic culture had a good deal in common, making the transition between them an easy one.

Similarity between the Soviet and the nationalist style is even more marked in the area of public monuments. It is amusing to note how intellectuals of the various republics, though contemptuous of the ugly, brutalist style of Soviet monuments, are full of praise for Soviet monuments to their own national heroes, even when constructed in exactly the same style. The most famous surviving national monument from the period of the first republics in the Baltic is the Freedom Monument in Riga, constructed in the 1930s. This is not of course Soviet in style, but it is certainly disturbingly brutalist, showing all too clearly the influence of the prevailing official styles of contemporary Germany and Italy. The elaborate statuary is however more reminiscent of pre-1914 Germany, suggesting (as so often) a certain lag in the transmission of Western cultural influences to the Baltic. Today, Latvian newly-weds often go to the Freedom Monument to lay flowers, as those in Soviet Russia used to go to the Tomb of the Unknown Soldier.[40]

The second danger of course is that Baltic culture will simply open itself to Western mass culture, as so many Balts themselves are doing, and vanish into the Western sea. The danger seems particularly acute because of the poverty of the Baltic States, as well as their small size. The specific features of Baltic culture described in this chapter are indeed already becoming less followed by the newest generation of Baltic creative artists, while most young people in general are thoroughly attached to Western popular forms.

After so many years of guarding their national cultures against destruction, this prospect is naturally viewed with particular horror by many Baltic intellectuals. The entire cultural, economic and political transition is for many highly disturbing in personal terms, even given the exaggerated hope and subsequent disillusion common to all revolutionary processes. The explanation has something to do with emerging from the 'internal emigration', identified in this chapter, which was in its way a comforting place to live, as well as being relatively secure economically and socially for most writers and artists.

Max Weber spoke of the 'disenchantment of the world' through modernisation. This is what threatens Baltic culture, now that the possibility has gone of blaming Soviet rule for everything bad and ugly. Jaan Kaplinski personifies this dilemma in some ways. On one hand, he has strongly denounced the narrow and chauvinist aspects of contemporary Estonian culture, and the hatred of the Russians:

> The Citizens Committees [an Estonian radical nationalist force] represent a new religion and know what a true Estonian is. Anyone who doesn't agree is a heretic and not a true Estonian ... [for example] if someone says that the Russian language could be a second state language in Estonia, he is not a true Estonian. There is an opinion here that 'an Estonian is always closer to another Estonian', but for me, Boris Yeltsin for example is much more sympathetic than some of our Super-Estonian politicians. ... Because Estonians are a small nation, they tend to put pressure on their compatriots, so that every Estonian should 'think as an Estonian' and think like the majority. But I have my own convictions and will never give them up, whatever the majority may say.[41]

On the other hand, Kaplinski loves the rural and folklore tradition (albeit transfigured in his verse by universal values and influences from widely different cultures) and so dislikes urban life that he can hardly bear to live even in the small university town of Tartu. He has denounced the influence of mass Western culture as 'Barbification', after the popular doll:

Barbie is a model introducing us to the brave new world that we are entering. Regrettably, this brave new world is totalitarian, it has no place for a different life, for different people. . . . I'm deeply worried by the fact that practically no new children's books have been printed in Estonia in the last couple of years, and that instead, children are fed with the so-called Barbie-culture. The continuation of this trend is a serious threat to Estonian culture and the Estonian identity. Barbie-ism is potentially even more deadly than Bolshevism because we do not see it as a danger. No normal person wants to be engulfed by a swamp and fights desperately for survival, but . . . is it more pleasant to suffocate in rose petals than mud?[42]

It is difficult not to sympathise with Kaplinski, when Western mass culture is indeed so crass and Western 'higher' culture often so vacuous. The effect of the former is encapsulated in the availability on cable TV in the Baltic of bland West German soft-core pornography, now achieving the miracle, beyond the power even of the Soviet State, of making sex boring. Similarly, at a street exhibition of modern Western art in Riga during the summer of 1991, the upended metal grills, the monster cardboard cut-out of one of the artists, and the rest of the shallow, narcissistic masquerade – as ritual and empty in its way as anything produced by Soviet culture – made one yearn for Baltic folkloric symbols, which, if not completely true, at least have meaning and beauty.

The issue is expressed in another form in William Wilson's book, *Folklore and Nationalism in Finland*. After tracing what he clearly sees as a generally unhealthy Finnish obsession with national folklore for the past century-and-a-half, the author ends with an optimistic picture of Finnish students turning from this to the study of contemporary popular culture, for example, 'narrative formulas in comic strips'. I cannot really share his enthusiasm. There are hundreds of thousands of comic strips, and hundreds of academic theses about them; but there is only one *Kalevala*. Similarly, while Lithuanian nationalist intellectuals are often mad, they are at least uniquely mad, or madly unique. The highest ambition of many Estonians, by contrast, is merely to become a sub-species of slightly spoiled Swede. A deeper question is whether the heroic Finnish resistance of 1940 and 1944, to which Wilson gives due credit, would have been possible without the kind of pride in Finnish national culture so assiduously fostered by the nationalist folklorists and cultural figures of whom he so disapproves. This is a key problem in the Baltic States, and one to which no conclusive answer can ever be given.

6

Lost Atlantises: The Half-Forgotten Nationalities of the Baltic

'Shraib un farshraib.'
('Write and record.')
> The dying words of Simon Dubnow,
> Jewish historian and thinker,
> killed in a raid on the Riga Ghetto, 1942

An Area of Mixed Settlement

In a passage of his memoir, 'Native Realm', from which the title of this chapter is taken, Czeslaw Milosz writes that, 'a country or a state should endure longer than an individual. At least this seems to be in keeping with the order of things. Today, however, one is constantly running across survivors of various Atlantises. . . .' For more than four decades, it seemed that the independent Baltic states and cultures themselves were such, doomed irretrievably to be submerged within the Soviet Union, and remembered only by dwindling groups of Baltic emigrés, forever separated from their homelands by the Iron Curtain.

Thanks to the decay of the Soviet Empire, the work of Mikhail Gorbachov, and their own heroic efforts, the Baltic States have been rescued from this ocean, barnacle-encrusted but still recognisable. Until the middle years of this century, however, the region also included three other famous cultures: those of the Baltic Germans, of the Poles of the Eastern Marches, and of the Litvaks, or Jews of Lithuania. Except possibly in the case of the Poles, these have sunk, or are sinking for ever. This being so, is it worth discussing them? The answer is yes, for several reasons. The first is that most of the books called 'A History of Lithuania', or 'A History of Poland', are nothing of the kind. They are histories respectively of the Lithuanians and the Poles. The other nationalities living within the states in question are treated only in passing, if at all. This book however is explicitly intended to complicate the picture.

A second reason is that these were themselves, in their time, great cultures, and contributed significantly to the history and culture of the Baltic States as a whole. As a matter of piety, they should be remembered not only by their own nationality. The Polish culture of the eastern borderlands has produced some of the greatest examples of the very literature of exile which, after the emigrations of 1944, became part of the Balts' own culture, and indeed a *leitmotiv* of twentieth-century literature in general.

The Jewish culture of historic Lithuania was among the most fertile intellectual subsoils the world has known, and produced an almost endless list of thinkers and artists, one of the last of whom was Sir Isaiah Berlin, born in Riga before the First World War. The final survivors of Jewish society are still alive in the Baltic, and included such distinguished figures as the novelist Grigory Kanovitch. Given the present rate of emigration however, they will soon all be gone. It is only right to celebrate them once more before they disappear.

Thirdly, these lost societies are sometimes not as deeply submerged as, during the Cold War, we had thought. We have had ample recent experience of how jagged remnants of concealed difficulties can gash the hulls of proud-sailing national barques. This has been true of the issue of Baltic participation in the Holocaust, and of the Polish minority in Lithuania and its historical claims, which before the Soviet counter-revolution of August 1991 looked set to become the most dangerous weapon in the Kremlin's arsenal against Lithuania.

Finally, the central issue in the history of minorities living within the majority Baltic communities is still very much alive. It is that of how to regulate the relationship of nations, each with their own language, culture and, above all, set of national loyalties and priorities. The West too is facing these questions, given the presence of immigrant communities, but has not yet begun to solve them. In Eastern Europe this century, the failure to resolve this issue has led and is leading to repeated catastrophes.

In the West, the existence of the problem during the Gulf War was highlighted by the position of the Muslim minorities in relation to the War. In terms of cultural autonomy, an intriguing recent case is the attempt by Muslim activists in Britain to establish a 'Muslim Parliament' representing the interests and regulating the religious and educational affairs of all Muslims within the British state. There are historical precedents such an institution would have affinities with the Council of the Four Lands and the Council of the Land of Lithuania, which from the sixteenth to the eighteenth centuries, a period often subsequently remembered as a qualified sort of Golden Age of Polish Jewry, governed the internal affairs of the Jewish communities in the Polish-Lithuanian Commonwealth. The tradition of these Councils was also in some ways revived within the officially institutionalised Jewish cultural autonomy which existed in Lithuania between 1919 and 1926.

There are of course very deep differences between the psychology and likely behaviour of small immigrant minorities in Western Europe, with their distant roots, and those of East Europe: very large, long-settled communities with cultural centres in the very land occupied by the majority communities, and bordering on large states inhabited by their ethnic compatriots. This distinction seems self-evident, but is apparently not so. Dr Landsbergis, asked in 1990 about the possibility of refounding the Polish University of Vilnius, as it had existed for 350 years, responded simply: 'And in Britain, do you have a university for Urdu speakers?' The West should not take the attitude that the problem of the minorities within the region cannot possibly have any connection with its own varied difficulties. An American journalist was irritated when a Latvian reacted to his question about the status of the Russians in Latvia by saying aggressively 'and what about the Blacks in Los Angeles?' When Balts take this stance with regard to Northern Ireland, I myself reply that it is precisely experience of the problems of Ireland which make me sensitive to the dangers of ethnic conflict elsewhere.

The Baltic Germans

The traditions of the Baltic Germans ultimately derived from those of medieval crusaders, and were in consequence sometimes admirable, but rarely aimiable. In time, the orginal belief in a mission to bring Christianity to the Baltic was supplanted by a feeling that the Baltic Germans had a mission to bring Western civilisation to the East.

In their argument against the rising tide of Baltic nationalism during the nineteenth and early twentieth centuries, the Baltic Germans used the classic language of colonial settlement, that their ancestors had 'developed the wilderness' and 'brought peace to the warring tribes' – to whom of course generations of Baltic German writers denied the slightest right to reject the 'peace' or 'civilisation' on offer.[1] The feeling of innate superiority over all their neighbours increased the element of self-righteousness which in turn was linked to their religious identity. From the time of the Reformation, the Baltic Germans were strong Lutheran Protestants, in contrast to their Catholic and Orthodox neighbours.

Oddly enough, perhaps the greatest single Baltic German hero was a determined opponent of the Reformation, Wolther von Plettenberg, Grand Master of the Teutonic Knights until his death in 1535. Plettenberg is famous chiefly for his skill and determination in warding off the growing attacks of the Russians. However, the grim obstinacy with which he maintained his allegiance to the lost cause of Rome also appealed to later generations of Baltic Germans and reinforced their self-image.

The final generations of Baltic German noblemen in imperial Russia saw themselves in a sense as honest mercenaries, faithful unto death to the Tsar, but above national loyalties. The Cathedral in Tallinn is full of their effigies, dressed in the uniforms of half-a-dozen different states, and killed in as many royal services between the Middle Ages and the battle of Tsushima. Their attitude was couched in terms of their aristocratic traditions, but increasingly derived from their national dilemma. A small people, hopelessly outnumbered in their own territory, and bitterly unpopular with the local majority, they had little choice but to stress their loyalty to the Russian Emperors, even when those emperors were turning more towards Russian nationalism and breaking the promises made by Peter the Great to the Baltic German nobility. Most continued until 1914 hoping that their identity and rights could be protected within the Empire. In the words of Julius von Eckardt, 'We wanted to be a part of the edifice of a transformed Russia, albeit a uniquely carved building block'.[2] This was also the position of the native Balts before 1917 (see Chapter 3), and for a similar reason: they feared that, outside Russia, they would promptly be swallowed by Germany. By 1914 some Baltic Germans, alienated by the increasing Russian nationalism of St Petersburg and fearful of an alliance between the Russians and the Balts, did in fact place all their hopes on a German conquest. When Germany failed, they lost everything.

In this sense, the position of the Baltic Germans has analogies with that of small peoples like the Ossetes and the Abkhaz under Soviet rule. They have been branded as supporters or dupes of Muscovite Communism, but given their situation, they had little choice but to rely on Moscow for support.

In the Russian Empire of the eighteenth and early nineteenth centuries, the Baltic Germans did indeed play a 'civilising' role, above all in the fields of state administration and law. They provided many Russian officers, and some of the Empire's most distinguished admirals and explorers (two of whom are buried in the Cathedral in Tallinn). They were favoured by successive Tsars, leading to the famous and bitter request of General Yermolov (an ethnic Russian), to Alexander I, 'to be promoted to the rank of German'. Tolstoy's portrayal of the execrable Berg in *War and Peace* is a good example of the mingled mockery and loathing felt by many Russians for the Baltic Germans, although it also of course often concealed rueful admiration for their qualities.

While in Russia the Baltic Germans had a reputation of dour philistinism, in Germany they were sometimes regarded as mercurial, manic-depressive, almost Slavonic: 'himmelhoch jauchzend, zum Tode betruebt' (rejoicing to heaven, depressed to death). Similarly, while in

Russia they were regarded as tremendously efficient and hard working, in Germany their reputation was rather that of a luxurious and idle aristocracy. The lesser barons were also regarded as boorish and provincial – even called a *Spiessadel*, and as more used to dealing with horses than people. A perennial (though no doubt apocryphal) anecdote is told of the baron who put his wife out of her misery with his revolver when she broke her ankle.

From the later eighteenth century, German scholars of the enlightenment who visited the Baltic provinces also accused the barons of cruel and oppressive treatment of their Latvian and Estonian serfs. The first major name in this tradition was Garlieb Merkel, who wrote at the end of the eighteenth century that for the landlords, the idea that the Latvian peasants were their equal was equivalent to the biblical story of Balaam's ass being able to talk: 'they didn't deny it, but they didn't believe it'. He recorded a Latvian peasant saying in connexion with the right of appeal against the landlord to the courts: 'For every number of complaints, ten times the number of whippings.'[3]

Baltic Germans liked to point out that their rule was milder and more enlightened than that of the Russian landlords, which was doubtless true but hardly a great compliment. The reputation for harshness attached above all to the nobility of Livonia and in particular the Latvian areas. In the Estonian territories, whether because of Swedish rule or because the Germans liked and trusted the Estonians, relations between landlord and peasant were smoother.

However great their attachment to the land where their ancestors had lived for almost seven-hundred years, honest Baltic German observers in the twentieth century admitted that their role and identity had always been a colonial one.[4] Their attitude to the indigenous Balts also reflected this very precisely. For centuries, severe restrictions were placed on the entry of non-Germans (*Undeutsche*) into the urban professions. Within the German community itself, strict divisions existed between the nobility, the wealthy urban citizenry and the petty bourgeoisie.[5]

The exclusion was of course far from watertight. Apart from the families of tribal chieftains who retained their lands by dint of swearing allegiance to the Teutonic Knights, a large number of native Balts did succeed, over time, in joining the guilds, the professions and especially the Church. The seventeenth-century chronicler Balthasar Russow was apparently one such. But he wrote in German, and most rose out of the peasantry or the urban poor at the price of Germanisation. In the words of the historian Heinz von zur Muehlen, those Estonians who wished to rise in the world 'had to jump, not bridge, the national gap'.[6] The Baltic peasantry, for their part, always regarded the German landowners not simply as oppressors but also as interlopers, even after adopting their religion and to a degree their culture. Their feelings are encapsulated in innumerable traditional folk-sayings and proverbs, which long predated the rise of Latvian and Estonian nationalism in the later nineteenth century. The Estonian words for German (*Saks*) and landlord – or 'better class of person' – are closely related.

The Germans reacted to the rise of these national movements with great bewilderment. They had become used to regarding the Balts simply as peasants speaking peasant dialects, in the same way as the Bavarians or the Frisians spoke Germanic peasant dialects. 'To be both Latvian and educated is an impossibility', one nineteenth-century German spokesman declared roundly. Baltic Germans in the *Lettisch-Literaerische Gesellschaft* (or 'Latvian Friends', as it was known) who played a leading part in establishing the study of Latvian folklore, recoiled in horror and deliberate incomprehension (like the biblical 'hardening of the heart') when the Latvians began to develop a national spirit, and denied utterly that they were capable of a literary language. Until the Revolution, Baltic German spokesmen treated the national movements as identical with the revolutionary socialist ones. It was of course partly a ploy to prevent any alliance between the Russian government and these movements, but it also reflected the Baltic German dilemma; as soon as they admitted that the Latvians and Estonians were nations, rather than rebellious peasants stirred up by agitators, their whole historical and intellectual position would collapse.

The ease with which the Germans were able to spurn the national movements stemmed from their profound ignorance of the feelings of the peoples they ruled – once again, a feature characteristic of colonialism, but rather surprising in rulers who had inhabited the region for hundreds of years. The barrier between the communities was termed by the twentieth-century Baltic German author, Siegried von Vegesack, a 'glass wall', through which the different nations could see each other, but not meet or touch.[7] In literature, even Baltic German authors who felt relatively sympathetic towards the Latvians and Estonians were generally able to portray them and their culture only in terms of fairly crude caricatures – when they did not ignore their existence altogether – as in much of Baltic German writing before the revolution of 1905.

The atrocities committed in 1905 by Latvian rebels against German landowners and pastors (which were of course amply repaid by the Germans when the imperial army restored order) had an effect on the Germans comparable to that of the Indian Mutiny upon the British. A hitherto sentimental image of loyal and simple peasants was replaced by a hostile one, and the way opened to mutual atrocities, on a much larger scale, during the revolution and civil war in Latvia after 1917.

Liberal German voices were left stranded. Honourable conservatives saw no option but to go down fighting.[8] They too, after all, had deep roots in the country. In the words of a Baltic German newspaper:

The Baltic German is no longer the same as the Reich German. . . . Over the centuries, the Baltic air and soil, as well as Baltic history, have made him what he is. The same factors have shaped the Latvian national character.[9]

These words could be echoed today by Baltic Russians, Poles or Jews. Unfortunately the same German newspaper showed very little understanding of, or care for, the feelings of the Latvian nationality sharing the same soil. Only time and exile have given the Baltic Germans more understanding of the other Baltic peoples – if only because, after the Second World War, they were joined in exile by large parts of the Latvian and Estonian intelligentsias. An exchange between a German frontier guard and a Baltic German woman refugee on the quay at Rostock in 1919 is emblematic of the experience of all the Baltic peoples:

'What nationality are you, please?'
'I'm a Balt.'
'Now look, *gnaedige Frau*, you can't be a Balt. There is no such nationality. You have to be either German or Russian.'
'But I'm a Balt! A Balt!'[10]

A Baltic German authoress (albeit of mixed origins) condemned her own tradition up to that fateful year in words put into the mouth of a half-German, half-Latvian character, addressing a Baltic German:

Your guilt is not the one which the propagandists scream about. Such cruelties have taken place all over the world. . . . Your guilt was and is a different, more subtle one. It is that of having separated yourselves. You did not live with us, representatives of other races, as if on the same Earth, in a common homeland. That is not a sin of commission, but it is the guilt . . . for which you must inevitably disappear.[11]

A family anecdote also corroborates this spirit. An uncle of mine was a small boy in Livonia during the German occupation of the First World War. He remembers still the shock and outrage of Baltic German families seeing German soldiers walking arm in arm with Latvian girls.

The incomprehension and lack of interest shown towards Latvians and Estonians by the Baltic Germans was not however simply a function of their ruling status. To a greater or lesser degree, people throughout the region have this attitude to each other, and Latvian and Estonian literature is no less full of caricatures of the Germans. *The Emperor's Madman*, by the Estonian poet and novelist Jaan Kross, is a portrait of a revolutionary Baltic nobleman imprisoned on the orders of Alexander I. The work is certainly more sophisticated and intellectually interesting than most Baltic German literature, but its portrait of the Baltic German society in which much of the action takes place is quite unconvincing.

The 'glass wall' seems then to be a function of nationality – and to some extent of class – rather than solely of colonialism.

In 1939–40, after the Molotov-Ribbentrop Pact had handed the Baltic States to Stalin, but before he had actually annexed them, the entire Baltic German community was evacuated on Hitler's orders. Most of their property was abandoned. Hitler's plans for German colonisation of the Baltic had nothing to do with the Germans who had actually long lived there. Instead, they were given lands confiscated from the Poles and from which they fled before the advance of the Soviet army in 1944–45.

Today the Baltic German community, living all over the world, though principally in Germany, is difficult to define. It is shrinking fast, and will probably continue to do so, while to some extent held together by family tradition (or snobbery) and by continued intermarriage among the Baltic German nobility. This plays as distinguished a role in the Federal German Foreign Service as it did in that of the Russian Empire. In exile, Baltic German intellectuals have forged close links with Latvian and Estonian emigrés, and the *Journal of Baltic Studies*, for example, has always carried numerous articles on Baltic German themes, written by leading Baltic German scholars and historians. So in a sense, at the academic level at least, the old conflict has been overcome.[12]

Latvian and Estonian writing about the Germans has become in general much more positive, recognising for example the contribution of the nobility to the improvement of Baltic agriculture far beyond that of Russia. This is not simply because the Germans are no longer a threat, nor a consequence of nostalgia or of clinging to the past. Until 1945, Estonia and Latvia were in a sense poised midway between German and Russian culture. In Latvia especially, a rejection of the German tradition was one factor propelling sections of the intelligentsia towards Russian culture and, through that, towards a sympathy for Communism.

After decades of Soviet rule and Russification, rejection of the East is for the moment almost universal. The massive swing towards Western models naturally brings with it a reappraisal of the role of the Baltic Germans who were, after all, for centuries the chief representatives of Western culture in the region; and this is strengthened by a natural reaction against Soviet propaganda in the Baltic, which played so endlessly upon German wickedness and the German menace. Today it is even possible to find Latvian and Estonian intellectuals expressing the feeling that German conquest in the thirteenth century may at least have preserved the region from conversion to Orthodoxy and early Russification, and helped it to become part of Europe – a sentiment which would have caused outrage between 1920 and 1940. 'And so the whirligig of Time brings in all his revenges.'

The Jerusalem of Lithuania

The Jews, with 7.6 per cent of the population, were the largest national minority in the first Lithuanian republic. Until the coup of 1926 they enjoyed full cultural autonomy, with a minister for Jewish affairs. Thereafter, although subjected to certain pressures and restrictions and a constant barrage of anti-semitic propaganda from the Right-wing press, their position remained good compared to that in Poland and other East European countries.

Indeed, Lithuanian behaviour towards the Jews had always been less violent than that of most peoples in the region. In June 1941, however, Lithuanians turned on the Jews and massacred thousands in a campaign which, though inspired by the Germans, proceeded largely independently of direct German involvement. The massacre has of course cast a deep shadow over Jewish-Lithuanian relations, and also over Western perceptions of Lithuanian nationalism in general. It would be wrong to speak of an indelible stain on the Lithuanian nation, because collective responsibility cannot be attributed to Lithuanians, as to Jews or anyone else. What is true however is that Lithuania's refusal to acknowledge and discuss the full import of the tragedy continues to cast a stain over, or rather to blur, large parts of Lithuanian historiography and culture. It contributes to the survival of primitive chauvinist ideas, and to Lithuania's cultural isolation from the West.

Though these features are true also to an extent of Latvia and Estonia, this section concentrates on the Lithuanian Jews, because they greatly outnumbered those of the other Baltic states, and because Vilna was the historic centre of Yiddish culture. Moreover the historical connection between nationalism and anti-semitism was stronger in Lithuania than in Latvia and Estonia, where the anti-semitic atrocities of 1941–44 were more the responsibility of the Germans (though with local assistance) and, even where spontaneous, were less the result of deep-seated prejudice and more purely a reaction against Soviet rule.

The traditional Lithuanian belief is that 1940–41 saw a clash of two nations, in which first the Jews, with Soviet help, betrayed and attacked the Lithuanians, and then the Lithuanians, with German asssistance, wreaked their revenge on the Jews. This view is generally held both by Lithuanians abroad, irrespective of political allegiance, and by most of the population within Lithuania. It was summarised by a Catholic priest, Father Algis Baniulis, Rector of the Seminary in Kaunas, whose views seem typical of much of the Lithuanian clergy, and which contain just enough accuracy to compound its pernicious tone:

> There has been no official statement by the Church in Lithuania on the genocide of the Jews; but speaking as a Lithuanian, I have read in books that the Jewish people were among the first to spread Communism, and in

1940 they took part in the genocide of Lithuanians, so it was a natural reaction that in 1941–42 we took part in the genocide of the Jews. When citizens help in the betrayal and conquest of your country, revenge is natural. It was not a confrontation between Catholics and Jews, but between two nations.[13]

The surviving Jewish populations in Lithuania and Latvia were, not surprisingly, therefore, deeply distrustful of the rise of the national independence movements in the late 1980s. In Estonia, there had been no problem for years, until Jews began to request official recognition of Estonian involvement in the Holocaust, the elimination of the small pre-war Jewish community (something the Estonians had hitherto totally ignored), and the role of the Estonian SS in the destruction of the Warsaw Ghetto. There was immediately a furious reaction which led to considerable alienation between the two communities. The Estonian parliament officially 'regretted' the involvement of individual Estonians in the Holocaust, but no real historical examination of events followed.

In all three Baltic republics, Jews were among the leaders of pro-Soviet opinion before 1991. In all but one case their primary motivation was the fact that their families had been murdered by Latvians or Lithuanians in 1941, and that it was not being adequately acknowledged by the new national forces. Even Irena Veisaitė (Weiss), a fervent supporter of Lithuanian independence, described with tears in her eyes her feelings at the first Congress of the Sajudis national movement:

> They were going on and on about Lithuanian victims and sufferings, and I suddenly thought, what the hell am I doing here? My mother was a victim, my whole family, my three-year-old cousin, and they have no place here, not even a mention. But then I thought, it is the first time that Lithuanians can talk about their sufferings, about the truth. We must understand their happiness and share it ... but to this day, there have been only a very few statements from the intelligentsia, and a few official gestures concerning the Lithuanian role in the Holocaust.[14]

In view of the widespread alienation of the Jewish community from the independence process, it is striking that the role of public spokesmen for the Jewish position has been adopted by strong supporters of the independence movements. Examples are Hagi Shein, in Estonia, who after the victory of the Centre-Right forces in the September 1992 elections, became head of Estonian Television – itself a sign of Estonian tolerance; Mawrek Wulfson in Latvia, and Emmanuelis Zingeris (Singer) in Lithuania. Even Jewish opponents of independence presented themselves as defenders of national equality and Soviet law, rather than as Jewish spokespeople. It was true of Isak Livshinas in Lithuania, and Tatiana Zhdanoka and Irina Litvinovna in Latvia. Yevgeny Kogan in

Estonia represents perhaps a different case: it is not clear that being half-Jewish played any part in his attitudes, which are more those of the son of a Soviet naval officer.

The general Baltic view has been that the division between Jews for and against independence reflected those who had lived in the Baltic before 1940, and often spoke Baltic languages, and those who had come under Soviet rule and spoke Russian. In fact this is only partially the case. Jews from pre-1940 families are just as likely to hate the Balts, for having murdered their families, while more recent immigrants – at least among the intelligentsia – may easily be anti-Soviet, pro-democratic, and therefore (at least until independence was achieved) pro-Balt.

Jewish spokesmen in Latvia and Lithuania were very useful to the national movements. It is striking that, after becoming deputies, both Mawrek Wulfson and Emmanuelis Zingeris (Singer) were made chairmen of the Foreign Relations Committees of their respective parliaments – where they could use their foreign contacts, and impress foreigners with the multi-ethnic nature of the national movements and governments. It is equally striking that both were forced to resign, in autumn 1991, within a few weeks of each other, after independence had been achieved and they had begun to raise questions of Baltic involvement in the Holocaust. In the meantime, however, their participation had done a good deal to diminish anti-semitism in the two republics.

Jewish history in Lithuania dates from the fourteenth century. Jews were invited to settle in the area by the Grand Duke Gediminas (Gedymin). Others may have been incorporated as a result of the expansion of the Grand Duchy south and eastwards, and may originally have been descended from the legendary Khazars. Also of Eastern origin are the Karaites, a small heretical Turkic-speaking Jewish sect, who seem originally to have come to Vilnius as mercenary soldiers in the service of the Grand Dukes. These believe in the Old Testament, but not the Talmud.

From an early period, however, the dominant culture of the Jews in Lithuania has been that of the Ashkenazy, migrating eastwards through Poland from Germany. At one stage, historic Lithuania contained over a quarter of all Ashkenazy Jews. Long after the disappearance of the Grand Duchy during the third partition of Poland, Jews referred to the whole of its former area, including what is now Byelorussia, as *Lita*, and a *Litvak* was any Jew from this area. At the Versailles Peace Conference of 1919, a Lithuanian representative, asked about his territorial demands, is supposed to have joked that what he would really have liked was everything the Jews called Lithuania.

The earliest records of the Jewish Council of Lithuania date from 1533.

Official permission to build the first synagogue in Vilna was given in 1573, though legend has it that the first prayer-house was established in 1440. Thereafter the Jewish population grew steadily, swollen in the mid-seventeenth century by refugees from the uprising of Bogdan Chmelniecki in the Ukraine, which massacred Poles and Jews alike. Lithuania by contrast was a haven of peace, with no severe pogrom by Lithuanians before 1941.

Litvaks, among other Jews, gained the reputation of a cool temperament and a dry, rational and authoritarian attitude to life. These are also characteristics associated with the importance of Lithuania and especially Vilna as a centre of Orthodox (*Mitnagdim*) rabbinic resistance to the messianic movement of the Hasidim in the eighteenth century. The leading figure in this resistance was the Vilna *Gaon* (Genius), Rabbi Elijah ben Solomon Zalman (1720–1797), whose Vilna prayer house in Jews' Street was a place of pilgrimage until wrecked by the Nazis and finally demolished by the Soviets.[15] His was only one of dozens of such prayer-rooms, tucked into the courtyards and back-alleys of the Old City, separate from the synagogues. The Great Synagogue itself had the dimensions of a cathedral; its builders had circumvented Christian restrictions on the height of synagogues by placing its floor well below ground-level. In the words of a later Jewish poet, looking at the Jewish city within a city destroyed by the Nazis: 'You are a psalter spelled in clay and iron/A prayer in every stone, in every wall a melody'.[16]

Vilna became a great centre not only of Jewish worship and Talmudic study, but also of furious dispute between Hasidim and Orthodox. In 1784, the Gaon declared the Hasidim heretical; upon his death, the Hasidim of Vilna held a celebration which led to a riot. By the twentieth century, hostility between Hasidim and Orthodox had diminished in the face of the common threat of secularism and assimilation. A new three-way cultural-political struggle developed between Zionists aiming at departure for Israel and other forces, most notably the famous Bund (a Jewish Socialist Labour group, founded in Vilna in the 1890s), which aimed at securing the rights and culture of the Jews throughout the East European states.

The conflict sometimes led to violence, particularly after the rise in the 1920s and 1930s of Vladimir Jabotinsky's extreme Zionist Revisionist movement, with its paramilitary wing. The particular bitterness of the dispute resulted from its being also a cultural and linguistic struggle, the Zionists promoting a secular Hebrew education while the Bund supported Yiddish, the language actually spoken at home by more than ninety per cent of the region's Jews. Conservatives and Hasidim also favoured a Hebrew educational system, but of a religious kind. All the groups cut across each other, of course, to some extent. The last echoes of their struggles can be seen in the remains of the Baltic Jewish communities today, as they debate whether to stay or to emigrate – and almost always choose the latter.

In autumn 1991 a representative of the Simon Wiesenthal Foundation in Israel visited Vilna, intent on bringing the Lithuanian state to book for its rehabilitation of war-criminals. Few Baltic Jews appeared to oppose the basic aim, though some were extremely unhappy about the hectoring tone and coarse approach, which alienated even sympathetic Lithuanians. 'You see', said one, 'Zuroff doesn't care if in ten years there are any Jews left in Vilna or not. He thinks that we should all move to Israel in any case. But some of us feel at home here, and would like to stay here – if we can.'

As a city of religion and of Zionism, Vilna, despite its prestige, was only one centre among several; but as the capital of the Yiddish language, it reigned supreme. By the 1930s, it was home to the famous YIVO, the Yiddish Institute of Learning (reconstituted in 1940 in New York), and the Strashun Library, the greatest collection of Yiddish books and publications in the world, both dynamited by the Nazis and then bulldozed by the Soviets. Vilna's supremacy, and Yiddish high culture itself, were both of short duration. Yiddish emerged as a literary language only in the later nineteenth century, in the face of immense obstacles, and survived only a few decades before being destroyed by the Holocaust, possibly forever.[17]

Although, as we have noted, Lithuania had seen very little anti-Jewish violence, a fundamental element of fear and hostility had certainly existed on both sides. For a flavour of this, a modern visitor to Lithuania can go to the Devils' Museum in Kaunas, where a Lithuanian artist has collected hundreds of traditional renderings of the Devil, mostly from churches, to form a fascinating folkloric exhibition. All but a handful of the representations are quite obviously meant to be Jews. Many are anti-semitic caricatures, others are neither anti-semitic nor caricatures, but rather good portraits of real people, some indeed portrayed as kind and sympathetic. What is perfectly obvious however is that when a Lithuanian traditional artist wanted a model for the Devil, he selected a Jew – even when he may have thought of the Devil not specifically as a Jew, but possibly even as a German!

It should be noted however that the Devil was a more ambiguous figure in Lithuanian folk-tradition than in the West. He is separated from pagan spirits, like the *Kaukai* and *Aitvarai*, who were morally neutral, and could bring both good and evil, by only a few centuries. Sometimes the Devil was portrayed in Lithuanian folklore as a clown, sometimes as a rather stupid fellow who thinks he is clever but can be manipulated by a wily farmer. But what these spirits clearly were was *foreign*, alien to the world of men. In Czeslaw Milosz's *Issa Valley* (a lightly fictionalised

Nevezis Valley, at Kedainiai) the Devil was called 'The Little German'.[18] For the Lithuanian peasants, Jews remained aliens, despite the centuries they had lived side by side. A friend from the Lithuanian countryside admitted that,

> My grandmother always used to tell us stories of how the Jews would trap Christian children, to sacrifice them and use their blood. And yet my grandmother isn't against the Jews. She would always tell us how well she got on with local Jews, and how hard-working and useful they were; and she thought the murder of the Jews by Lithuanians was a terrible crime.

For her, Jews clearly remained an alien, mysterious and therefore frightening people. And yet she accepted them as a natural part of the landscape (along with other elves and demons, perhaps), and regarded their murder simply as a crime, without indulging in the hedgings and self-justifications of the Lithuanian nationalist intelligentsia and clergy.

I have felt 'on my own skin', as the Russians say, the particular mixture of freezing indifference and ingrained mistrust with which many Lithuanians react to a stranger in their midst. A Lithuanian emigré scholar has written of Lithuanian literature that, 'Rarely since the eighteenth century have foreigners been inserted into prose strictly for local colour or exoticism; seldom is their alienism emphasised with a positive connotation . . .'.[19]

Quite apart from Christian demonology, the entire mode of thought and behaviour of Jews and Lithuanians is very different. Jewish irony, for example, is utterly alien to the Lithuanian tradition. It works on Lithuanian nationalists and their soupy certainties like garlic on vampires. Associated with this is the element of detachment in the Jewish position. The phenomenon of the linked Weiss-Strom-Kagan families, which include Soviet Russian officials, American and Lithuanian academics, and even a British peer, evokes automatic distrust among Lithuanian nationalists. The assumption is that such people must, wherever they live, be potential traitors. The concept of honest service to a host country not one's own is incomprehensible to them.

As for the Catholic Church in Lithuania, it had little doubt about either devils or Jews. Catholic priests made up a very large proportion of the first and second generation of Lithuanian writers before 1914, and their work played an important role in taking anti-semitism from peasant consciousness into the literary culture of Lithuanian nationalism. A certain element of anti-semitism was also present in the works of secular, liberal writers, as these sought reasons for Lithuania's backwardness, and came into professional conflict with Jews who then occupied the greater proportion of the urban positions.

This last element developed after the creation of the Lithuanian state in 1918. Lithuanians began to find themselves, in their 'own country', greatly outnumbered in the educated professions. Moreover, by virtue of the weakness of Lithuanian education, they were incapable of competing on equal terms with the Jews, Poles or Germans. The result was a dual state policy, of vastly expanding education (partly irrespective of quality), encouraging Lithuanian migration to the towns, and pushing Lithuanians into professional jobs.[20] The result, by the middle 1930s, was a virtual social revolution, with the creation of a Lithuanian urban middle class, and a graduate workforce, where none had existed before. In 1897, only 11.5 per cent of the population of towns was Lithuanian. By the 1930s, this had risen to more than 50 per cent. This led however to a typically 'Third-World' phenomenon: thousands of semi-educated young people and aspiring petty-bourgeois dependent upon an economy too weak to provide the jobs to which they aspired.[21]

The result, as so often, was to accentuate chauvinist hostility to the most visible and economically successful national minority. Leaving aside Voldemaras's clandestine 'Iron Wolves', the most anti-semitic groups in Lithuanian society before the last War were the Lithuanian Businessmen's Association, which urged a boycott of Jewish businesses, and the various Lithuanian student corps, which demanded that Jews sit on separate benches in the lecture-halls, be subjected to a stricter *numerus clausus*, or even be excluded from the university altogether. Across the border in Vilna, Polish groups were making exactly the same demands.

During the first years of the Lithuanian republic, there had been several Jewish officers in the army, and a number of senior Jewish officials. Apart from the Minister for Jewish affairs, for several years the Deputy Foreign Minister was also Jewish. Hebrew street signs were permitted in Jewish areas. But after the 1926 coup, the atmosphere changed, and almost all the officials were dismissed or frozen out. With parliament suspended, Jewish representatives could no longer influence events through participating in coalitions.

Despite this, however, Smetona himself has a generally positive reputation among educated Jews in Lithuania today. They remember that he himself always avoided anti-semitic rhetoric and policies, and that he had Jewish friends. The tradition is echoed in the allegiance of Emmanuelis Zingeris and other Jews to Landsbergis, whom they distinguish from his more chauvinist supporters. They also remember that although Landsbergis' father was a member of the short-lived Lithuanian provisional government under German rule in 1941, he and his wife sheltered Jewish friends from the Nazis, at great personal risk.

It is important to remember that before the massacres of 1941 occurred, Smetona's regime had been destroyed by the Soviets, Smetona himself had fled to America, and Lithuanian resistance to Soviet rule had come largely under the control of Smetona's extreme Right-wing opponents, based in Berlin, and themselves under Nazi orders. It is therefore quite wrong – as some Jewish authors do, and all Soviet propagandists have done – to draw a connection between Smetona's regime and the wartime killings.

At the same time, Lithuanian culture in the 1920s and 1930s cannot be entirely absolved of moral responsibility. Under Soviet rule, some Jews assuredly gave the Lithuanians good reason to hate them; but if a large part of the Lithuanian population was prepared to see the entire Jewish community as responsible for Soviet atrocities, and to connive in their murder or decline to protect them, this was substantially because of the prolonged and assiduous negative stereotyping of Jews in Lithuania as a whole.

In the 1920s, Jewish organisations supported Lithuania's claim to Vilna; more than three hundred Jews volunteered for the Lithuanian army to fight the Poles, and were publicly thanked by Smetona. On the other hand, Jews certainly felt towards Lithuanians the same distrust they experienced, with good reason, towards the other gentile peoples of Eastern Europe. As a Yiddish saying has it, 'a chicken that crows and a Lithuanian who speaks Yiddish, their heads should be cut off' – an expression reflecting the rarity of the phenomenon, but also a strong hostility and sense of the risk presented by a non-Jew speaking the Jewish language. Added of course to mutual cultural suspicion was the old antagonism between sharp-witted townspeople and dim-witted farmers – or crooked townspeople and honest farmers, depending on the point of view.

Until 1917, the Jews – as everyone else, but perhaps more so – had had no real sense of Lithuania as a nation. As can well be imagined of a people with a 3,600-year literary history facing one whose first real literary work appeared only in the later eighteenth century, they seem to have found it difficult to take Lithuania's historical and cultural pretensions very seriously, insofar as they took any notice of them at all. This is well reflected in post-Holocaust Jewish writing about the Jews of Lithuania. In Nancy and Stuart Schoenbaum's *Lithuanian Jewish Communities*, pre-Christian Lithuania, viewed by nationalists as a golden age, is treated with grotesque (and inaccurate) brevity:

> Farming was conducted in forest clearings. The tribes were fierce and raided other groups in the area. The people were pagan, believing in demons and monsters and practicing human sacrifice.[22]

So far as the Jewish intelligentsia was concerned, Lithuanian language and culture had few attractions, compared to those of Germany, Poland and especially Russia. Not merely was knowledge of these languages the passport to a wider world, but their literary cultures were sufficiently broad and varied to admit foreign writers who loved their new tongue –

just as English culture has done. Lithuanian literature by contrast was confined to a choice between a nationalist-Catholic-didactic tradition and a secular-positivist-nationalist-didactic one, both based on peasant folklore and with few major modern achievements to their credit. Asked why he wrote in Lithuanian, Mark Zingeris replied that the destruction of the Jewish languages in the region had left him no choice, and that, 'I find it a disaster to be a writer in Lithuanian; but when I am in this abyss and there is nothing to get me out except my wife's hair, the only thing that saves me is the beauty of the language itself. Even so, I have to try to write in a Lithuanian of my own; the Mother-Goose language of the Lithuanian literary tradition is not part of my skin.'[23]

In contrast, Jewish assimilation into Russian culture before 1917 was helped not only by that culture's far greater breadth and depth, but also by the alienation of much of Russia's intelligentsia from the Tsarist state, which caused it to oppose the anti-semitism of the Tsars as a matter of honour. The nineteenth-century Lithuanian and Polish intelligentsias, on the other hand, not having states of their own, were more likely to idealise their own language and culture in national-religious terms, and exclude all other ethnic groups.

Love of the Russian literary language was one of the strongest impulses drawing Jewish intellectuals towards Russia; it overcame great gulfs of caste and nationality. Lev Mandelstamm described how, as a poor but educated Jewish boy in a small Lithuanian garrison town under the Russian Empire, 'Through Captain Melyantev of the artillery, I learned something of literary theory, while Lt. Colonel Engelhardt encouraged my studies and lent me the latest works of Russian literature. . . .'[24]

Later, for Jewish poets like Osip Mandelstam and Joseph Brodsky, the Russian language, and its classical culture, became the focus of a passionate loyalty, divorced from most of the attributes of what is usually thought of as patriotism, but faithful unto death – literally so in the case of Mandelstam. This was a linguistic patriotism, open to all nationalities, similar to the modern German concept of a 'constitutional patriotism', attached to democratic institutions and divorced from a former, discredited nationalism.

Given the isolated and frustrated position of the secular Jewish intelligentsia of Poland and Lithuania during the 1920s and 1930s, such an attraction to Russian culture ran hand-in-hand with revolutionary feeling. Czeslaw Milosz describes how, earlier, in Poland under the Russian Empire,

> the old image of the Jews as enemies of Christ was replaced by a new one: young men in high-necked Russian shirts, rallying to a foreign civilisation. The Socialist movement, which was becoming stronger and stronger, split into two currents: anti-Russian (independence for those countries seized

by the empire) and pro-Russian (one revolutionary state formed by all the lands of the monarchy). Russian-speaking Jews were the mainstay of the second current, only to become, in revolutionary Russia, fomenters of all kinds of heresy.[25]

So difficult had become the Jewish position in Poland and the Baltic by 1939 that, for many secular Jews, including even the Left-wing of the Zionist movement, the Soviet Union appeared to offer an escape not only from personal frustration and restrictions, but also from the national dilemma of the Jewish people. Their only real chance of national cultural autonomy would be in a supranational, benign (supposedly), and secular empire. A certain traditional Messianism, mingling easily with revolutionary socialism, may also have played a part. There is indeed an extent to which the role in which the early Marx cast the proletariat – as the universally oppressed class whose liberation therefore signifies that of all mankind – is really much more applicable to the Jews of Eastern Europe before 1939. Viewed on a purely theoretical plane, liberation from their own oppressors formed an integral part of a revolution freeing all the peoples of the region from the capitalist connection and national hatred. Communism under Stalin (or indeed at any other time) did not, unfortunately, quite work like that. Nor did the other nationalities in the region see things quite that way.

The result was a situation in which the vast majority of educated Jews in the region leaned to the Left (repeatedly in interviews with survivors of the pre-War communities, I have heard phrases like, 'My father was a capitalist who hated capitalism'.). By 1940, of course, there was a further overwhelming reason for Jews to welcome even conquest by Stalin's Russia: the fear of Nazi Germany. Apart from fear of outright Nazi conquest, there was also a suspicion that a Nazi-backed putsch might bring to power a Lithuanian fascist government. In the words of Aaron Garon,

> This was the key difference. If the Jews met Soviet troops with flowers, it was above all because they thought that they would protect them from Hitler. . . . In 1941, 7,000 Jewish people were deported to Siberia by Stalin along with the Lithuanians; but even they later thanked God for it, because it saved most of their lives.[26]

Most, though not all, Lithuanians, by contrast, feared Moscow more than they did the Germans.[27] With two peoples, living in the same land but obeying the dictates of opposed national priorities, ignorant of each other's culture, indifferent to each other's interests, and in an atmosphere in which anti-semitism was fed by Nazi propaganda as well as by indigenous prejudice, the stage was set for catastrophe.

When Soviet troops invaded Lithuania in June 1940, they were welcomed
by large parts of the Jewish population. In the words of Irena Veisaitė, a
Jewish Lithuanian from a wealthy and educated family with close links to
the Lithuanian establishment and intelligentsia:

> We saw the tanks come in. My mother came home and sat with her head
> in her hands. She said, 'what are the Jews in Slobodka doing? Lithuania is
> losing its independence, and they are greeting the Soviet troops with
> flowers'. But I was in a very Left-wing school, and we had been taught to
> admire the Soviet Union. We really thought that it was not anti-
> Lithuanian, that the Soviets would also liberate Lithuanians from
> Smetona's regime.[28]

It has been estimated that, in the 1930s, more than half the tiny
Lithuanian Communist Party was made up of Jews. Following the
occupation, these naturally came to occupy senior positions, while
thousands of others were recruited into the new state structures. As in
Eastern Poland after the Soviet occupation, many Jews appear to have
flaunted their new equality, causing gentile anger which even fear of the
NKVD – the Soviet security police – could not altogether suppress.
According to Harry (Herschel) Gordon, then a Jewish boy in Kovno:

> The Jewish people felt very free. This was not too bad. No impoliteness
> was allowed; this was true for the Russians, Jews and Lithuanians. No-
> one could call us names or insult us because if they did they would be sent
> to jail for six months. Every Jew held his head high. If he met a
> Lithuanian on the sidewalk, the Lithuanian would step off the curb to let
> him by. Before the Russians came, it had been just the reverse. The anti-
> semites' eyes were popping out of their heads from the pressure of having
> to keep their mouths shut! . . . There is a Jewish saying: 'If we are on a
> horse today, then the Lithuanians are ten feet under'. We would enjoy it
> while it lasted. What would happen later we didn't want to know. We
> lived for the day. But the anti-Semites knew what they were talking about;
> what they would show us we would remember for generations to come.[29]

This sudden reversal of roles, a previously subject population lording it
over its ethnic neighbours, is virtually a staple in modern East European
history and literature. The Jews however were desperately *visible*. In the
words of Aaron Garon,

> In Lithuania as elsewhere, Jews had been almost entirely excluded from
> the administration. So when the Soviets gave the chance to join the state
> power, naturally many Jews joined; and the response of the Lithuanians,
> who had never seen any Jew in a state office, was that 'they're all Jews!'[30]

The Communists in fact relied on three groups for support: Jewish
sympathisers; a small number of Left-wing, anti-Smetona Lithuanian

intellectuals, like Justas Paleckis; and some Lithuanian workers and poor peasants. A slogan of the Lithuanians who rebelled against Soviet rule in June 1941 was 'Down with the government of Beggars and Jews'. However, from the nationalist point of view, then as now, it was obviously more convenient to forget Lithuanian collaboration with Soviet power and remember only that of the Jews. Jews were also prominent in the NKVD, whose activity in Lithuania reached its height on 14 June 1941, with the deportation of thousands of Lithuanian citizens to Siberia. When the Germans invaded only eight days later, hundreds of those still held in Lithuanian prisons were shot before the NKVD retreated, their bodies found by the Lithuanian rebels. Three out of the five members of the Lithuanian commission responsible were Jews. Aleksandras Štromas (Strom), a Lithuanian Jew whose father was killed by the Lithuanian rebels, recalled that,

> A very nice, timid and well-educated Lithuanian lady once confessed to me that, although very much ashamed of the feeling, she was unable to suppress her hatred of Jews, however much she tried. This hatred, she told me, originated in the spring of 1941 when an NKVD squad, consisting of three Jewish men and one woman, came to arrest her parents, whom she never saw again. The head of this squad was a Jew whom the family had considered a friend.[31]

With remarkable honesty and objectivity, Štromas continued:

> As a Jew ... I must admit our own true faults, such as a certain insensitivity to the grave problems facing our gentile compatriots; the self-centredness that only too often urged some of us to seek our particular goals without giving much consideration to how the achievement of these goals would affect the interests of others; the frivolousness which led quite a number of us to assume that what is good for the Jews must be even better for the gentiles. Too many of us, led by such considerations, were more than ready to engage in all kinds of subversive and revolutionary activities threatening the integrity and even survival of our host countries.

Just as most Lithuanians have avoided any real accounting for what happened in 1941, so very few Jews have felt capable of a thoroughly honest examination of Jewish attitudes to the Lithuanians or other East European nations before 1939; and indeed Štromas has been severely criticised for his statements.

What many Lithuanians missed then, and continue to miss now, is not simply that the NKVD contained Lithuanians as well as Jews, but that its victims also included Jews, in fact proportionately almost twice as many Jews as Lithuanians. Lithuanian capitalists, political leaders and religious figures were all deported, among them some seven-thousand Jews in all. Jewish Communist activists, workers and informers had themselves turned on their Jewish managers or their old Jewish political opponents. Among the Zionists deported from Lithuania to Siberia was Menachem Begin, a member of the Jabotinsky party. Soviet deportations were therefore in no sense a 'Lithuanian genocide'. Apart from anything else, although conditions were often atrocious, most of those deported survived.[32]

By the time of the June deportations, leaders of the Lithuanian resistance in Germany had already given the orders which were to lead to the massacres that followed barely a week later. The directives of the Lithuanian Activists Front (LAF) for the Liberation of Lithuania, issued in Berlin on 24 March 1941, contained the following passage:

> For the ideological maturity of the Lithuanian nation, it is necessary to fortify anti-Communist and anti-Jewish actions, and to spread the belief that German-Russian war will break out, the Red Army will be expelled, and Lithuania will be independent again. It is very important at the same time to get rid of the Jews. We therefore need to create such a bad atmosphere for Jews in the country that no Jew can ever again think that in the new Lithuania he would have even minimal rights or any possibility of existence. Our purpose is to make all Jews leave Lithuania together with the Russians. The more who leave Lithuania on this occasion, the easier it will be to get rid of them totally. The hospitality extended to the Jews by Vytautas the Great is cancelled forever because of their constant betrayal of the Lithuanian nation.

According to the Lithuanian exile historian, Saulius Sužiedelis, who first published this section of the directive in a Lithuanian magazine in May 1992, the LAF leadership at that time incorporated almost every Lithuanian group which sought independence. The section had previously been excluded from the versions of the instructions published in Lithuanian emigré works. As Sužiedelis says, it is not known what concrete measures the LAF envisaged. Their general moral responsibility for what followed can however hardly be denied. The German authorities and intelligence services were certainly doing their best to push resistance groups in the Soviet Union towards anti-semitism, but there is no doubt that it was the ideology of the Lithuanian Right, as well as the effects of the Soviet occupation, which ensured that German influence fell on fertile ground.[33]

The extent to which anti-semitism had taken over even moderate Catholic Lithuanians is clear from the words of Jonas Matulionis, finance minister within the short-lived Lithuanian Provisional Government during the first weeks of German occupation. Explaining to a Jewish representative why he could do nothing to stop the killings and why therefore the Jews should move into the ghetto, he said:

The Lithuanians are divided on the Jewish question. There are three main views: according to the most extreme, all the Jews in Lithuania must be exterminated; a more moderate view demands setting up a concentration camp where Jews will atone with blood and sweat for their crimes against the Lithuanian people. As for the third view? I am a practising Roman Catholic; I – and other believers like me – believe that man cannot take the life of another human being . . . but during the period of Soviet rule I and my friends have realised that we do not have a common path with the Jews and never shall. In our view, you must be separated from us and the sooner the better. For that purpose, the Ghetto is essential. There you will be separated and no longer able to harm us. This is a Christian position.

The thought that Christianity might have had some responsibility for the position of the Jews during these years did not occur to Matulionis, either then, or (it would appear from his memoirs) during his Canadian exile. Nor has it to most Lithuanian Catholic priests today.[34]

Even if it is wrong to talk of national guilt, it should not – since guilt is the Church's business – be too much to say that the Lithuanian Catholic Church bears a weight of responsibility for the fate of the Jews which undermines its right to speak on any moral question. It might expiate its guilt through confessing it, but seems to have no intention of doing so, preferring to refer to the small minority of courageous priests and laymen who did indeed risk or lose their lives in helping Jews.

Upon the Nazis's invasion of the Soviet Union on 21 June 1941, LAF sections immediately attacked the retreating Soviet forces, seizing public buildings and strategic positions. Simultaneously, and before the arrival of the Germans, came attacks on the Jewish population of Kaunas. There can be no doubt that these attacks were conducted by Lithuanian partisan forces under orders from their officers. In the words of Woldemar Ginsburg,

To our surprise, the trouble came from gangs of well-organised, armed and uniformed Lithuanians who appeared from nowhere and started a campaign of terror against the Jews. In Kovno (Kaunas) alone, more than two thousand Jews were killed by the Lithuanians in the first week.[35]

According to Joseph (later Lord) Kagan, who escaped from the Kovno Ghetto,

The pogroms and the terror in the streets and the happenings up at the 9th Fort were strictly an issue between the local Lithuanian population and the Jews. . . . [36]

Later, after the Jewish populations had been herded into ghettos (to protect them from the Lithuanians, according to the Germans), the Nazi authorities employed partisan units and Lithuanian local authorities to begin the organised genocide of the Jews. Juozas Mielius, then a *Seniūnas*, or elected muncipal official, described what happened at the estate of Akmelu, near Žeimeilis. The Germans had given orders to the local Lithuanian municipality, headed by a former Lithuanian officer, Major Jesiunas, to round up local Jews. Wanting nothing to do with the killing, Mielius hid and watched:

> The executioners came in cars from Linkuva and other areas. They were in civilian dress, and all were Lithuanian. They were volunteers, who wanted revenge because their families had suffered under the Russians, or who had some grudge against the Jews. They also took some of the Senunai as guards. The Jews were naked when they were shot; first the young men, then the old people, women and children, several hundred in all. One Jewish barber succeeded in running away, because the killers were not very experienced. Afterwards, they distributed the clothes of the Jews. Finally, after all the Jews had been killed, a car containing Germans arrived, inspected the scene, and took the Jews' possessions. They behaved in a very matter-of-fact way. And after that the general distribution of Jewish property started . . . when the Russians came back, they searched Jesiunas' barn and found Jewish furniture there. . . . After the massacre, the Senunai were all invited to a party to celebrate.[37]

There were, however, exceptions to the support or indifference of the Lithuanian population towards the murder of their Jewish neighbours. Irena Veisaitė was herself saved by two families, both of Lithuanian army officers. One was that of General Kazimieras Ladiga, who had himself been deported and murdered by the Soviets in 1941, and whose family was devoutly Catholic as well as patriotically Lithuanian. The general's widow, whom Irena Veisaitė describes as her 'second mother' (her own mother had been murdered soon after the Nazi invasion), was herself deported by the Soviets in 1946. Her cousin, Aleksandras Štromas, was also saved by Lithuanian friends.

The priest Father Bronius Paukštys is commemorated at Yad Vashem. After the War, the Soviets sentenced him to ten years in Siberia. A number of Lithuanians who assisted Jews were denounced by their Lithuanian neighbours and executed by the Germans; there is no-one to remember them. Others still fear the attitude of their neighbours. In Mikulishke, a Polish village in Byelorussia, I met an old woman who showed me the photograph of a Jewish girl she had saved during the war. She had never even told her husband.

It must be said however that Baltic lack of awareness of the Holocaust owes a good deal to Soviet rule. In the aftermath of the war, the Soviets demolished even those damaged synagogues which could have been rebuilt, and removed a memorial to the tens of thousands of Jews killed at

Ponary (Paneriai). The monument erected in its place, as all other Soviet monuments in the Baltic, spoke of the victims only as 'Soviet citizens'. Later, as elsewhere in the Soviet Union, the nationalism of the local republican majority benefited from Soviet censorship in the suppression of uncomfortable aspects of the national past. Thus an English-language guide to Vilnius, published in Lithuania in 1987, contains not a single reference to the Jewish tradition in the city, and almost nothing about the Poles.[38]

A further group which should bear responsibility for Baltic ignorance is the Baltic emigration. One might excuse its collective silence or outright falsification of the issue by recognising it did not wish to give ammunition to the Soviet occupiers. These did indeed continually refer to alleged 'collaboration' between Baltic nationalists and Germans in their propaganda, both within the Soviet Union and in the West. There were however also certain groups of exiles, like the 'Santara-Šviesa' among Lithuanian liberal intellectuals in North America, who did examine Baltic involvement in the Holocaust – and were bitterly attacked for it by other emigrés.

Soviet manipulation of the memory of the Holocaust (partly via the KGB) increased as the Baltic national movements gathered strength in the late 1980s. It was probably the single most effective weapon within the Soviet propaganda armoury, precisely because it could always be guaranteed a resonance among the many in the West – not exclusively Jewish – who were all too ready to repeat simplistic charges. Another reason for the silence of the exile community however must be that some of its original leaders, as well as a good many ordinary members, had themselves been directly involved in the massacres.

The bulk of emigrés therefore condoned both the omission of any serious public discussion of the question, and the production even now of potted histories of the Baltic States in which the role of the national minorities is either dismissed or ignored altogether. The picture is now, however, being improved by the work of historians like Dr Sužiėdelis, and a considerable number – though far from a majority – of younger Baltic emigré intellectuals do indeed reveal an honest and even agonised approach to the question.

The elimination of the memory of the Jewish presence in Lithuania itself also of course deeply affected the remaining Jewish communities. Today the decaying houses on Jews' Street and Gaon Street still recall the poverty and intimacy of Jewish life in Eastern Europe, so familiar from Jewish literature. The area is likely soon to be transformed altogether, as it contains what was once Vilna's only good restaurant, the *Stikliai*, around which are emerging a nest of tourist boutiques selling 'antiques' and folkloric souvenirs. One synagogue remained open in Vilna (as in Kovno), though most professional Jews avoided it for fear of damaging their careers. Only with Gorbachov's ascendency could a Jewish musical and dance ensemble be established. Under Soviet rule, whereas modified forms of minority folkores were tolerated, that of the Jews was suppressed, except during the relative thaw between 1956 and 1963. Recently, Jewish traditional performances in Tallinn, for example, have seemed more like Western pantomime than authentic cultural events.[39] I myself obtained a greater sense of the spirit of Lithuanian Jewish culture one evening in the Draugystė Hotel in Vilna, when a family party asked for a Jewish dance, and all danced together in a strange mood of gaiety, intimacy and sadness, defying the harsh lights and mass-produced surroundings of the Soviet-style restaurant. They were leaving that week for Israel.

By 1970, only 61 per cent of Jews in Lithuania claimed Yiddish as their mother tongue; the great majority spoke Russian at home. Almost three quarters of all Jews in Latvia and Lithuania were in fact post-war immigrants from Russia. During the 1970s, however, consciousness of Jewishness increased along with the possibility of emigration and continued alienation from the indigenous Baltic populations. The alienation was in part the result of continued memories of Lithuania's role in the Holocaust, in part traditional anti-semitism, and in part, as Jeffrey Ross has indicated, the consequence of Soviet Russians using the Jews 'as a sort of lightning rod to deflect national sentiment away from themselves'. Ross has called the Jewish position in the Baltic one of 'structural marginality'.[40]

Writing in 1988, Zvi Segal said that because of the Holocaust and the role that Baltic nationalists had played in it, 'the rift between the Baltic and Jewish peoples remains unbridgeable, even today'.[41] The community in Lithuania has been reduced to barely 5000 people. The end of Soviet rule has brought an influx of money to Lithuania to restore Jewish monuments and support the remaining community, but as the writer Grigory Kanovitch observes, 'if things go on as they are, there will soon be more Jewish organisations in Lithuania than there are Jews'.

The Balts argue that as nations they had no part in Nazi crimes because they did not have their own governments or armed forces, and were themselves subjected to Nazi oppression. This is indeed true. Nazi requisitions and labour conscription provoked resistance, which was met with atrocity. In Eastern Lithuania, reprisals for activities by Soviet partisans (mainly Byelorussians and Jews) sometimes fell on the Lithuanian population, as in Pirčiupis where 119 people were burnt to death by the Germans, or in the Latvian village of Audriņi. Baltic leaders who resisted Nazi demands or plotted the restoration of independent government were deported to the Stutthof concentration camp; in Latvia and Lithuania, a considerable number of nationalist officers in the German forces were shot and their units dispersed.

A further Baltic argument is that, just as it was not Jews as a group, but only Jewish individuals, who sided with Soviet rule in 1940–41, so only certain Balts took part in the Holocaust. In the case of Latvia and Estonia this is to a considerable extent true. All three Baltic governments and parliaments have officially regretted any such involvement. However, all have found themselves in a dilemma over how to rehabilitate those of their compatriots who fought for the Germans in order to defend the Baltic States in the 1940s, without seeming to give rehabilitation to war criminals – an almost insoluble problem, especially after so many years. Thus in March 1993 the Latvian National Guard and other official groups called for an official commemoration of the Latvian SS Legion, saying that most of its men had been patriots fighting to defend Latvia. They were right – but so are those who accuse the Legion of dreadful atrocities.

During autumn 1991, the issue provoked two international scandals; in Lithuania, what seems to have been a blanket rehabilitation generated a series of articles in *The New York Times,* and the visit of the Wiesenthal Society representative.[42] The Lithuanian government responded that it was refusing rehabilitation to those against whom war crimes had been proven, but since it refused to publish their names, little credence could be attached to this. The official response of the Lithuanian Procuracy to the charge that it was rehabilitating war criminals was issued on 7 September 1991. It claimed that war criminals were being screened out, and that the Soviet judgements were in many cases not fair or just. After the 1992 elections, Brazauskas as acting President admitted that there had been cases of wrongful rehabilitation.

The Latvian government has allocated state pensions to Latvian soldiers of the German SS and police battalions, while proposing to withhold them from Soviet veterans. However, it has also signed an agreement on extradition for war crimes with the US and Australia. In November 1992, a major scandal erupted when the American magazine *Life* published an article by Edward Barnes entitled 'Soon They Will Come for Us', alleging massive contemporary Latvian anti-semitism and the threat of pogroms. The article was bitterly criticised as a grotesque exaggeration, based on a few selected sources, not only by Latvians but also by mainstream Jewish leaders in Latvia. The latter complained that, although they had been interviewed by the journalist concerned, none of their remarks had been quoted. In general, the vengeful attitude displayed towards the Balts by many members of the Jewish diaspora is wholly understandable; and it can hardly be criticised by the Balts, since they and their diaspora often display a similar hatred towards the Russians, with considerably less justification. Nonetheless it must be said that neither approach does much for justice or historical clarity.

In Estonia, the autumn of 1991 saw the establishment of a veterans' association uniting soldiers from wartime units. Protests from the Jewish community stimulated supportive comment in Sweden, where a threat – later denied by the Prime Minister – was made to cut off aid. This in turn provoked an increase in anti-semitism, with acts of vandalism and threats to Jewish leaders. Estonians tend to blame all on Soviet provocateurs, and deny that 'anti-semitism has never existed in Estonia'. It has certainly been less conspicuous than elsewhere in Eastern Europe, if only because the number of Jews has been so few (around 5,000 before 1941). But, according to a French eyewitness account, Soviet occupation in 1940 led to a similar rise in anti-semitism as in Lithuania: and much Estonian talk that 'the fake revolution of 1940 had been fomented by the Jews, all the key posts were in the hands of the Jews, all the commissars of the Red Army were Jews', and so on.[43]

In contrast to these battles over the past, establishing monuments to the former Jewish inhabitants would seem an uncontroversial route to reconciliation. This is indeed beginning; in Lithuania, 23 September, the anniversary of the liquidation of the Vilna Ghetto, has been formally named the 'Day of the Genocide', with the Lithuanian flag displayed with black ribbons on official buildings. On that day in 1992, in a moving ceremony in the Lithuanian parliament, Landsbergis presented medals to Lithuanians who had helped Jews to escape, or to their families (including one to his own father), and speeches were delivered by Irena Veisaitė and other survivors.

However, the commemoration of the historic Jewish presence in the Baltic, and its destruction, involves the contemporary Balts in a dilemma which goes beyond questions of guilt. In some ways it runs against the national spirit, or at least that aspect of it reflected by the nationalist Right. For most Lithuanians Vilnius was always and exclusively Vilnius, never Vilna or Wilno. The construction of Jewish monuments in Vilnius would remind people of a different truth – and could have implications for the whole Lithuanian view of its national past, concentrated at present on mono-ethnic images and traditions.

The other pivotal problem is that the killers of 1941 were not simply a handful of local 'rabble', as many have said. They were identical to a large part of the forces that carried out the 1941 rebellion against Soviet rule – in other respects a genuinely heroic enterprise. A serious examination of the role of those forces and their commanders would merely mean that part of the national myth would not be tarnished, it would slide into a moral abyss.

Examining the spiritual background to the venomous anti-semitism of the Lithuanian (and to a lesser extent Latvian) resistances in 1941 would also involve an examination of Lithuanian official culture and ideology in the 1920s and 1930s, a time that the Lithuanian Right wishes to glorify.

9 The Ninth Fort and Monument to the Dead, near Kaunas, Lithuania. This was the scene of the murder of eighty-thousand Jews and thousands of Soviet prisoners of war during the Second World War. It was also used as a prison and place of execution by Stalin's secret police.

This in turn would raise fundamental questions about the relationship between the Lithuanian state and Lithuanian ethnicity. Landsbergis exemplifies the problem. He is in many ways a man of genuinely broad civilisation. However, in relation to the position of the ethnic minorities he sought, while in power, two morally incompatible things. On one hand, he wished to deny them real cultural autonomy (such as existed for the Jews between 1920 and 1926, and could be resurrected for Poles and Russians today), on the grounds that their cultural rights are guaranteed within the general frame of Lithuanian citizenship. On the other, Landsbergis's policy stance indicated an official national culture so permeated with Lithuanian religious and ethnic influences that no member of an ethnic minority could feel fully at home within it. It remains to be seen whether his fall will produce a more open atmosphere.

The Frontier of Poland

The dispute over the status of the Polish minority in Lithuania is hopefully over. It reappeared during the period in which Landsbergis and the radical wing of Sajudis dominated Lithuanian politics and sought to exploit anti-Polish feeling to consolidate their power. However, it could surface again and is, in any case, worth studying as an encapsulation of the historically-derived ethnic problems threatening so many parts of Eastern Europe.

If the 'Polish menace' to Lithuania is today almost entirely the product of paranoia, the Lithuanians of Wilno (Vilnius) live with a powerful reminder of a time when it was a very present danger. In Rossa (Rasu) cemetery, beside the grave of his mother, lies the heart of Marshal Jozef Pilsudski, the founder of Polish independence after 1918, and for whom the recreation of the Polish-Lithuanian Commonwealth was a lifelong dream. Pilsudski was responsible for the annexation of Wilno by Poland in 1922, and his choice of resting place for his heart reflects his political inclinations as well as his local ancestry as a Polish-Lithuanian nobleman. In the words of one of the characters of Tadeusz Konwicki, a Polish-Lithuanian writer, '. . . you see, a human being can live anywhere, but to die, he must return to his own earth . . .'.[44]

Pilsudski's grave is never without its wreaths, and on Polish national days is decorated with red and white flags, as are the graves of Polish soldiers killed in battle against the Bolsheviks and the Lithuanians between 1918 and 1921. Some of the tributes are left by Polish tourists, for whom Pilsudski's tomb is a place of pilgrimage. Most, however, come from local Poles, of which there are some 280,000 in Lithuania, or 7.6 per cent of the population.

Before the last war, Poles made up between 15 and 18 per cent of the population of what is now Lithuania. After the Soviet reconquest of 1944, however, cattle trucks transported thousands both east and west: east to Siberia, and west to the new Communist Poland, within its completely new borders. The destruction of an entire human landscape has been chronicled by many Polish-Lithuanian writers who felt themselves thereafter in permanent exile, even within Poland. Konwicki wrote that in his homeland there remained, 'the same river, the Wilenka, the same meadows, the same trees and the same varied forests, like different races, but not a single human being from those among whom I grew up through ten years of my life . . .'.[45]

Konwicki's hometown, Kolonia Wilenska, in and around which several of his novels are set, is now 'New Vilnia', an industrial suburb of Vilnius. It bears little resemblance to its former condition, though as so often in the Baltic, nature and a certain rustic simplicity have softened the hand of Soviet industrialisation; apple trees lean over factory walls, and pastel-coloured wooden houses line the railway-tracks. Almost half the population of New Vilnia is made up of Polish workers, though few would know their town was once the home of a distinguished Polish novelist. After 1945, deportation and emigration virtually eliminated the Polish intelligentsia in Lithuania. According to the Polish-Lithuanian deputy, Czeslaw Okinczyc, 'in the whole of the Polish population of Lithuania there are fewer than a hundred intellectuals, if by that you mean people from a Polish intellectual tradition, not people who simply received a higher education under Soviet rule'.[46]

With the intelligentsia went the clergy, the nobility, the bourgeoisie, and the more enterprising peasants. The 'noble villages', where every small farmer had a coat of arms, were swept away. Today the social world of pre-1939 Polish Lithuania survives only in memory and in literature.[47]

Metropolitan Polish disdain for Lithuanian Poles is partly a question of language. Poles in Warsaw often refer to the horrible mistakes of spelling and grammar in *Kurier Wilenski*, the main Polish-Lithuanian newspaper. They blame the isolation and Russification of the Lithuanian Poles, but the real reasons are more profound. What the majority of Lithuanian Poles actually speak at home could be a form of Byelorussian, or Polish, or neither of the two but a different language altogether, sometimes called *Gwara Wilenska*; this is simply one among the range of Slavonic dialects extending between Russia and Poland and, in the Polish-Lithuanian Commonwealth, termed 'Ruthene'. The legal language of Grand Ducal Lithuania was a variant of 'Ruthene'.

Today, official Ukrainian, codified from the mid-nineteenth century, is gradually uniting the various dialects of the Ukraine. Official Byelorussian is beginning, belatedly, to do the same in Belarus – although there are intriguing stories of attempts by a local linguist to create yet another Slavonic 'linguistic nation' in the Pripyat Marshes of southern Belarus. As for the rural Lithuanian Poles, what they call themselves is the *Tutejszy*, which means simply 'the locals', or 'the people from here', which used to be what peasants almost everywhere replied when asked their nationality. Many Byelorussians also call themselves this. (*Tutejszy* is one of those curious words which can be used to describe oneself, but which represents an insult if used, for example, by a Lithuanian.)

In the past, one sort of *Tutejszy* could be distinguished from another not by language but by religion; a Catholic was almost automatically a Pole, while under the Russian Empire, an Orthodox was legally a Russian. The Uniates fell in between, and were consequently persecuted universally, while Poles and Russians denied that the Byelorussians existed at all.

Soviet migration and restrictions on religion have greatly complicated the national picture. Today, when asked his nationality, a citizen of New Vilnia may scratch his head: 'I am a Pole registered as a Byelorussian', or, 'Well, my father was a Pole, and my mother said she was a Russian, though she came from Byelorussia, and my father's mother came from the Ukraine. . . .' It often comes with the complaint that, 'until recently, no-one ever asked me this question. Nobody cared what nationality you were.' In the meantime, Russification has affected all the local Slavic populations, so that even 'Polish' families in the Lithuanian countryside will often name their child 'Ivan', rather than 'Jan' (though his grandmother may still call him Jan). Those who have served in the Soviet army also swear in Russian.

The *Tutejszy* are a sad and impoverished people, especially since collectivisation and Sovietisation have destroyed much of their formerly rich folklore. But they retain a sort of localist bloody-mindedness which should surely move the heart of any Englishman. A good deal of the *Tutejszy* opposition to Lithuanian independence was prompted not by the memory of past Polish rule nor even by specific contemporary grievances. It came out of a simple anger that for the ninth time this century the *Tutejszy* and their lands were being shifted from one sovereignty to another without themselves being consulted. This was compounded with anti-intellectual feeling directed against Polish-Lithuanian supporters of independence, and a general resentment against Poles from Poland 'coming here and looking down their noses at us, then giving us advice'. In characteristic border style, a Lithuanian Pole once declared: 'The people in Poland do not know what it is to be Polish. We are the true Poles, because we are fighting here for our Polishness.' Ironically, the speaker was pro-Soviet.

Such sentiments emerged strongly during a visit to a *Tutejszy* farming community in Soleczniki (Šalčininkai) district. Soleczniki has the highest proportion of forest land in Lithuania, and the farmers seem still to be operating in forest clearings. Only a few miles from Wilno, it feels like a different world. The *Tutejszy* are among the poorest farmers in Lithuania, and the house of the Baranowski family is bleak and decrepit, with a concrete floor, peeling walls and bare light-bulbs, at once harsh and dim. Across the border in Byelorussia, the floor would probably have been of beaten earth, and the walls papered with sheets of newspaper and magazines. In a corner, where an Orthodox family would keep its icon, there is invariably a picture of St Anthony. Pictures of the Pope, oddly enough, are rare and tend to be confined to the better-off. Perhaps only those who can afford to visit Poland can buy them, or the Lithuanian Catholic Church is uninterested in dispensing images of a Polish Pope. It could be that St Anthony, whose worship is common to both *Tutejszy* and Lithuanians and has deep pagan roots (like that of St John in Latvia), is the true god of the *Tutejszy* and quietly takes precedence over Christ and the Vicar of His Church. In the past the exact religious status of people of the area was as undefined as their language or nationality.

As I sat on a hard chair in the Baranowskis' parlour and sipped a glass of milk – all they had to offer – three generations of the family gathered, hard-faced, weary-looking farmers in working clothes. I enquired whether, given the choice, they would prefer to be in Lithuania or Belarus. 'We don't give a damn for either of them,' the father replied; 'we

161

want to be ourselves, and if it were possible, we'd like to rule ourselves separately from anyone else. We have always been here, and we have always been Poles.'

Lithuanians often point out that Poles in Lithuania have far more Polish schools and churches than those in Belarus, and reproach those who preferred in the past to send their children to Russian schools. This overlooks the point that, linguistically, the Poles are far closer to the Russians and Byelorussians than they are to the Lithuanians; and also that, without a Polish university in Lithuania or the easy possibility of going to work or study in Poland, a Polish education in Lithuania hardly provides a future.

'Why should I send my kids to a Polish-language school?' Mrs Baranowski asked; 'so they can be collective farmers like us? If they are to have a future, they have to learn in Russian or Lithuanian, and for us, it is easier to learn in Russian.' Soviet authorities played of course on this factor when promoting their Russification programme. In 1992, more than two-thirds of Polish-Lithuanian children were still attending Russian-language schools, though the number was dropping.

For this reason too, Poles desire their own university in Wilno. Lithuanians such as Landsbergis argue that the local Polish community could not support such an institution, and they may be right. But the concept of a Polish university in Wilno has great resonance for metropolitan Polish intellectuals, who recall that Wilno University, now Lithuanianised, was the Alma Mater of Mickiewicz, Milosz and many other great Polish figures. In the long run, therefore, a Polish university in Wilno could expect to receive both financial support and teachers from Poland; but the prospect remains anathema to Lithuanian nationalists.

The Russification of the Lithuanian Poles, and their frequent pro-Soviet behaviour, has increased the distain for them felt by metropolitan Poles. The words of Dr Adam Rotfeld are typical:

> The Poles in Lithuania today are a pretty disagreeable lot. I think the Lithuanians are correct in their behaviour towards them, and I think that most Polish intellectuals also understand the Lithuanian position. The Poles in Lithuania did in fact look to Moscow for protection. . . . For Poland today, the question of the old borderlands is really a cultural, not a political question. There are political parties which would like to exploit it, but they are small.[48]

Czeslaw Milosz has done much to shape this attitude to the borderlands. In a speech on 28 May 1992 (delivered partly in Lithuanian), accepting an honorary degree from Kaunas University, he declared: 'I have always believed in Lithuania's claim to Vilnius. I wanted my beloved city to be more than a Polish province. It gives me great pleasure that it is now one of Europe's capitals'. For many years

Milosz played a leading role in reminding the West of the illegal Soviet occupation of the Baltic States. His basic understanding of the word 'Lithuania', however, like that of the Jews, is very different from the mono-ethnic vision of many Lithuanian nationalists. Milosz has been called 'the last citizen of the Grand Duchy of Lithuania'. His dream is close to that of his friend, Tomas Venclova, the leading contemporary Lithuanian poet, who has said that Vilnius could become the Strasbourg of Eastern Europe, a place of the mingling of many cultures and of pan-European loyalty.[49]

Both writers owe something to the tradition of the *krajewscy* (the 'Borderers') in the early part of this century. These were mainly Polish-speaking intellectuals from the Eastern marches who sought to prevent the division of historic Lithuania along ethnic lines. The greatest poetic influence on Milosz was Adam Mickiewicz, whose epic *Pan Tadeusz* begins with the famous invocation,

> O Lithuania, my fatherland,
> Thou art like health; what praise thou shouldst command
> Only that man finds who has lost thee quite.
> Today I see, and praise, thy beauty bright
> In all its splendour, for I yearn for thee.[50]

The understanding of 'Lithuania' with which Milosz grew up was close to that of Mickiewicz and Pilsudski, both of whom came from similar backgrounds in the Polish-Lithuanian gentry. Among contemporary Polish intellectuals the cultural engagement with the borderlands question derives in part from the political tradition of Pilsudski. The Marshal hoped to revive the old Commonwealth with the ancient borders and ethnic diversity in which he gloried. Pilsudski was far from a narrow Polish chauvinist, and no anti-semite. At the same time he had no very coherent idea of how ethnic minorities might be accommodated within the new Polish state; under his rule, persecution of Ukrainian, Byelorussian and to a lesser extent Jewish culture continued. His dream was smashed by the Second World War, the Jews wiped out and Poland's borders shifted forcibly westwards. A fear for the western borders with Germany is today the chief reason why Poles eschew claim to territory in the East.

Polish moderation towards Lithuania is not however simply a matter of pragmatism. Poland today is essentially the mono-ethnic dream of Pilsudski's nationalist opponent, Roman Dmowski, if hardly as he would have wished it. Many Polish intellectuals find this narrow Poland rather boring. However, their nostalgia for the borderlands is now largely stripped of Pilsudski's imperialism, of Dmowski's chauvinism, and unstained by the brutal necessities of police rule over unruly and alien peasant populations. It has transcended its past, and turned into something which might serve as an inspiration to the relations between other European cultures and their former colonial territories. For it incorporates deep knowledge and feeling, but with fewer illusions, and less of the sentimentalism and self-flattery that characterise much of Western thinking, Left and Right, about the former empires.

The contemporary Polish literature of the borderlands suggests a way through the whole human dilemma of the contrast between national cultures that are deeply felt but chauvinist, and universal cultures that lack all feeling and texture. The works of writers like Milosz are intensely specific, rooted in particular landscapes and local traditions. But at the same time they transcend these landscapes to root themselves in a common humanity which in turn is all the stronger because it embodies direct personal experience of inhumanity and national hatred. So far had Polish liberal intellectuals moved by 1990 from the idea of recovering the lands to the east that, initially, Lithuanian hostility towards Poland was often met with sheer bewilderment.

For most Lithuanians however, the old Polish-Lithuanian Commonwealth has overwhelmingly negative connotations. This should not, however, rule out an appeal to past emotional ties; leaders of former British colonies, for example, often refer to such ties (albeit in a formulaic way) in their relations with the British government.

One of the elements of the best Polish literature of the borderlands was always a somewhat satirical view of Poland and the Polish national character. Another, pre-eminently in Mickiewicz's work, is the stress on national reconciliation and co-existence; the great musical celebration of Polish history which concludes the work is played by a Jew. Czeslaw Milosz has compared the conflicting attitudes which characterised the Polish-Lithuanian gentry this century with that of the Scottish educated classes, linked by language and political allegiance to England but firmly attached, at the same time, to their own distinctive national tradition.[51] But Sir Walter Scott could romanticise the Highlanders precisely because their political hopes had been cut to ribbons at Cullodden, half a century earlier. If Rob Roy MacGregor had turned up in Edinburgh as a nationalist journalist demanding independence for Scotland and Gaelic as the official language, Sir Walter would have had some hard choices to make. The curious feature of Polish-Lithuanian culture before 1939 was its simultaneous romanticisation of Lithuanian medieval greatness, rather in the manner of Scott, and basic contempt for contemporary Lithuanians, reminiscent of Lowland Scottish distaste for the 'bare-arsed highlanders'.

For educated Poles before the Second World War, Lithuania was not a nation but an assemblage of peasants, speaking a peculiar dialect. Examples abound of wounding Polish contempt for the new Lithuanian intelligentsia and its claims. The boorish behaviour of some Lithuanians towards their Polish sympathisers today should be seen as a continuing response to this attitude.

Before 1939, Polish Catholics in mixed communities often did their best to stop Lithuanian, the 'peasant dialect', from being used in church. Scuffles occasionally occur now at the Gate of the Dawn chapel in Vilnius, a place of pilgrimage revered by both nations, when Lithuanian worshippers delay the Lithuanian-language mass in order to postpone the Polish-language one which follows. Polish worshippers then push in brusquely, elbowing Lithuanians out of the way. Both sides speak of crudeness by 'young toughs', but my own observation suggests the worst offenders, on both sides, are little old ladies. The fact that the medieval Church was a major source of 'Polonisation' has not been forgotten. The memory underlies Lithuanian clerical opposition to the importation of Polish priests into Lithuanian-Polish parishes, and resistance to anything that might hinder Lithuanianisation.

The manner in which the past weighs on contemporary Lithuanian Catholicism was demonstrated by Archbishop Julionas Steponavičius of Vilnius, whom I interviewed in February 1990, and who died the following year. Like Cardinal František Tomašek in Prague, Steponavičius was one of those ancient Catholic prelates who, having survived so many changes and yet remained consistent, appeared to embody in their own person the character of the Church as the Rock of Ages. For his defence of Christianity and the rights of the Church under Khrushchev, the archbishop was exiled from his diocese in 1960 to live in a small village in northern Lithuania, returning only in 1989.

Like Tomasek, and like the bulk of Catholic priests that preceded him, Steponavičius came from peasant stock, a solid figure with a reddish, craggy face and large, farmer's hands. Both his virtues and his vices were different sides of the same stubborn tradition. As a Lithuanian priest in Poland prior to 1939, he suffered the restrictions, contempt and suspicion of Polish authorities within and beyond the Church. During the war itself, along with other Lithuanians, his life was threatened by the activities of the Polish resistance, the Home Army.[52] The Home Army's struggle against the Germans and their Lithuanian auxiliaries not infrequently extended to attacks on Lithuanian civilians. On the Lithuanian side, the infamous 'police battalions' spread terror in the Polish population and across the border in Byelorussia. If today many ordinary Byelorussians retain anti-Lithuanian attitudes, it is above all the result of these massacres, the memory of which was constantly fuelled by Communist propaganda, especially after the rise of the Lithuanian independence movement.

Archbishop Steponavičius himself appeared not to have transcended the experiences of wartime, nor to have made much attempt to do so. Questioned about the possibility of a Polish mass in Vilnius Cathedral, he replied simply that the Cathedral was the centre of Lithuanian spiritual life, a national symbol, and the Poles had enough masses in other churches. It was at least an honest response, in contrast to that of other priests and politicians, each of whom has passed the decision to the other.

The new Archbishop of Wilno, Audrys Bačkis, appointed from the Lithuanian emigration (he was a Papal Nuncio), is reportedly trying to moderate clerical nationalism within his diocese, and indeed to encourage the Christian Democrat Party away from limited nationalism and towards a more open and European vision. John Paul II visited Lithuania in autumn 1993 and, in that connection, steps were taken to avoid any appearance of tension between the Polish Pope and Lithuanian Catholicism.

Underlying many Lithuanian attitudes is a widespread belief that the local Poles are not Poles at all, but Polonised Lithuanians. Many 'Polish' noble families were indeed by origin Lithuanian, and to judge by the names of villages, even in recent centuries Lithuanian settlement extended deep into Belarus. However, the way that this suggestion was raised in Lithuanian newspapers as the national movement got under way in 1988 was grossly insensitive and counter-productive; because in the words of Janusz Oblaczynski, a moderate leader of the Polish Union in Lithuania, 'it suggests that what was "Polonised" can and should be de-Polonised. This is basically a Stalinist approach. If a people are a problem for you, then no people, no problem.'[53]

Several Lithuanian leaders, and many Lithuanian intellectuals, have conceded that this approach was a mistake. But the Lithuanian section of the main English-language reference guide to the three Baltic States, created by the official encyclopaedia boards and published in 1991, openly declares not merely that the Poles are Polonised Lithuanians, but that they were Polonised as recently as 'the nineteenth and twentieth centuries', an assertion which is absurd as well as provocative.[54] According to Tomas Venclova, hostility to Poland existed even in the Lithuanian dissident movement of the late 1970s and early 1980s, which in consequence made little attempt to make contact with or draw strength from the Solidarity movement.[55] As Czeslaw Okinczyc admitted, however, the Poles also erred: 'In autumn 1988, representatives of Sajūdis attended a Polish meeting, and Polish representatives immediately began to drag up every Polish grievance not just from the present but also from history. Of course, no good came of it. The Sajudis people went away, and there weren't any serious discussions between Sajūdis and the Poles until a year later, after the Polish Union had been founded.'[56]

That year, meanwhile, saw the declaration of Lithuanian as the republic's official language, without, initially, any guaranteed status for minority languages. On the Polish side, declarations of limited autonomy by Polish local councils were promptly cancelled by the Lithuanian Supreme Council. Lithuanian fears grew following articles in the Soviet press pointing out that the reversal of the Molotov-Ribbentrop Pact should logically involve the return of Wilno to Poland. Meanwhile the Polish Union, led by local Polish intellectuals, was emerging as the main agency of constructive dialogue between Poles and Lithuanians. In the elections of February 1990, the Union sponsored pro-independence Polish candidates against the anti-independence platform of the Soviet loyalist wing of the Communist Party. Typically, however, the Union found itself having to compete with Sajudis, which put up a non-Polish-speaking Lithuanian for the overwhelmingly Polish constituency of Soleczniki, thereby splitting the pro-independence vote and ensuring defeat at the hands of the Communist candidate, Leon Jankeliewicz.

Ten Polish deputies were returned to the Supreme Council in the elections, of whom six were members of the Soviet loyalist wing of the Lithuanian Communist Party, the remainder independents backed by the Polish Union, Sajudis, or the pro-independence Communists. The Soviet Communist deputies abstained in the independence vote of 11 March 1990. The others voted in favour. The following ten months saw a process of consolidation among the Polish deputies. In January 1991, under pressure of Soviet military intervention, they formed a single Polish Faction, which declared its support for Lithuanian independence and strongly denounced Moscow's policy. In the words of a Polish deputy, 'the violence on January 13th made it clear even to the Communist deputies that they simply couldn't sit on the fence any longer. They had to come out publicly either for or against independence.'

The move was the result also of considerable pressure from Warsaw. Preceding months had seen visits to Wilno by delegations from the Polish parliament and Senate, all registering unofficial support for Lithuania's independence struggle; the Polish government had expressed its sympathy soon after the declaration of independence. In the face of Lithuanian suspicion, however, the delegations found themselves in a difficult position. Visits to meet and speak with ordinary people in Polish areas such as Soleczniki were impossible, for fear of their being misconstrued by the Lithuanian government as 'encouraging Polish separation'. Professor Bronislaw Geremek, leading a delegation in April 1990, said that Poland was anxious not to seem to encourage the Polish minority in Lithuania to act against Lithuanian interests.[57] The attitude extended to the Polish press, which rarely asked searching questions about local Polish issues at Lithuanian press conferences. Some Polish Right-wing parties, in particular the Christian Populists (ZCHN), have tried to exploit the alleged oppression of the Lithuanian Poles to advance their cause, but in the Polish elections of 1992, the issue played only a small part.[58]

Lithuanian ministers and government supporters, however, denounced Poland for 'cowardice' in not pre-empting the rest of the world and immediately recognising Lithuanian independence! Lithuanian parliamentary delegations to Poland pointedly omitted Lithuanian-Polish representatives, further limiting constructive influence from Solidarity and the Warsaw government. Polish television, however, provided Lithuanian Poles with access to Polish sentiment. In May 1990, the Lithuanian government transferred one of the Central Soviet channels, broadcasting in Russian, to Polish television. In 1991–92, the Landsbergis administration severely restricted Polish broadcasts – except for 'Dynasty', as rebroadcast in Polish, which had become very popular with Lithuanians.

In the ten-month period between the declaration of independence and Soviet military intervention, relations between the Lithuanian government and the Polish community stagnated. On one hand, the rump Soviet Communist Party in Lithuania was active on collective farms and in the factories of New Vilnia, influencing ordinary Poles against independence. On the other, the Lithuanian government, under increasing influence from the radical nationalists, failed to make any significant gesture towards the Polish minority.

Apart from the symbolic question of a Polish mass in Wilno Cathedral, Polish demands revolved and still revolve around four main issues: the availability of higher education in the Polish language; an official status for the language; a guarantee of administrative divisions in which Poles will form a solid majority; and a privatisation and restitution process which will return land in Polish areas to former Polish owners, resisting the process of 'Lithuanianisation'. None of these involve separation from Lithuania.

The issues are interrelated, because if the borders of the Vilnius municipality are extended to incorporate much of the surrounding Polish countryside, then not merely will the Poles lose their majority in the area, but municipal rules for the return of property will apply, restricting each farmer to a paltry 0.2 hectares. The Lithuanian government has also refused to recognise sale of land documents from the period of Polish rule between 1918 and 1939. And, of course, former Polish (or Jewish) residents of Lithuania who are now citizens of other states cannot apply for the restitution of their land, although in the case of Lithuanian emigrés, dual citizenship, though strictly illegal, can usually be arranged.

Pressured by the crisis of January 1991, the Lithuanian parliament made a major concession over the question of language, passing an amendment to the state language law permitting the use of minority languages in areas in which the relevant minorities constituted a substantial proportion of the population. In practice, however, the amendment works only where the minority is in fact a local majority. Thus in Wilno and Klaipeda, while Russians represent over a quarter and over a third of the population respectively, this has not prevented the banishing of Russian from street signs, official name-plaques, and many official documents.

Many Lithuanian nationalists make little secret of their desire to divide the existing Polish districts so as to give each district a Lithuanian majority and ensure Lithuanian as the sole official language. A Sajudis leader and deputy chairman of the Wilno City Council confirmed that intention in April 1991, and Right-wing deputies admit it openly.

The Poles for their part have been demanding a single territorial division embracing all the Polish-majority areas: the whole of Wilno and Soleczniki Districts, together with parts of Troki (Trakai) and Pobrade. On 29 January 1991, in response to the Polish Faction's declaration of support for independence, the Lithuanian parliament instructed the government to draft a programme to meet Polish concerns over administrative divisions and higher education. It did not happen; neither did parliament enforce it. This apparently minor act of betrayal in the depressing history of inter-ethnic promises could have had severe consequences both for Lithuania and for the stability of the region.

At the end of May 1991, when it became apparent the Lithuanian government would do nothing, Polish local authorities, with strong covert Soviet support, moved to create their own autonomous area with its own assembly, flag, police force and army. It was to be within Lithuania, though its inhabitants were to have the right of dual citizenship with Poland or the Soviet Union.

Two-and-a-half months later, of course, the failed Soviet counter-revolution led to the Kremlin's acceptance of Lithuanian independence and the abandonment of its anti-Lithuanian strategy; but had the Soviet Union persisted for another year or so, the Lithuanian government might have encountered Polish regional institutions which were a good deal harder to dismantle, and a conflict such as that in Transdniestria might have occurred.

The Polish-Soviet hardliners had a potential armed force to hand. This was OMON, or the 'Black Berets', the special police unit which had defected from the Lithuanian Interior Ministry during the January military intervention and was subsequently responsible for a series of violent occupations of buildings and attacks on Lithuanian frontier posts. OMON was led by a local Pole, Major Boleslaw Makutinowicz, staffed by Poles and Russians, and had considerable support within the local minority communities.

Memories of previous Polish armed organisations surfaced at a congress of Polish municipal deputies held in the village of Mosciszki (Moštiškes) and at which the Autonomous Region was declared: a richly-bemedalled veteran of the Home Army loudly recalled Lithuanian wartime atrocities. The Polish parliamentary deputies held aloof and condemned the gathering. Landsbergis attended, in an attempt to persuade delegates not to proceed with the declaration. He began his speech in Lithuanian but delegates, knowing he is fluent in Polish, demanded that he change.

The congress exposed the worst features of both sides: the arrogant and boorish treatment by local Poles of the head of the state to which they belonged; and the arrogance and pettiness of Landsbergis, failing to take advantage of an opportunity to gain Polish sympathy. His speech, eventually delivered in Polish, patronised and criticised Poles for allowing themselves to be exploited by Moscow, but failed to address a single one of their concrete concerns or demands.

Two aspects of the Mosciszki village congress made one doubt the viability of an autonomous Polish region. The first was the sheer poverty of the village itself, and the second the limited education and horizons of the delegates, predominantly village officials and collective farm managers.[59] At the time, the Communist authorities were still in control, making intermittent threats of a possible Byelorussian claim to Lithuanian territory. The likelihood has now receded, with Lithuania and Belarus, in November 1991, signing an agreement to guarantee each other's frontiers. There are, however, still occasional mutterings by Byelorussian nationalists about a possible claim to Wilno, a threat used by Lithuanian nationalists in their perennial effort to keep national paranoia on the simmer.

Immediately after the failed Moscow coup and the concession of Lithuanian independence, the Lithuanian parliament, on the leadership's initiative, suspended the district councils of Wilno and Soleczniki indefinitely, alleging anti-constitutional and conspiratorial activity.[60] The suspension followed an unofficial request by the Polish government for no further change in the position of the Lithuanian Poles, and prompted a serious deterioration in Polish-Lithuanian relations. Although the Polish government soon retracted its demand that the councils be restored before full diplomatic relations could be re-established, relations between the two countries remain disturbed.

A joint – but modest – declaration was signed guaranteeing the rights of the Polish minority in Lithuania (and of the small Lithuanian minority in the Suwalki area of Poland), and in November 1992 elections were finally held. Despite the preceding anxiety and recrimination, the local Polish electorate showed very little interest and turnout was low.

During a visit to Wilno in January 1992 the Polish Prime Minister, Krzysztof Skubiszewski, had carefully avoided raising issues that might offend the Lithuanians. Even so, in a particularly coarse gesture, the Lithuanian Right refused to stand or to applaud his speech to parliament. They had demanded an official Polish apology for General Zeligowski's seizure of Wilno in 1920! Indeed some aspects of Lithuanian nationalist policy seem unbelievably petty. Thus, adhering to the letter of the language amendment, Lithuanians currently permit the use in official documentation of Polish spelling of towns and districts, but insist on Lithuanian names. Hence one finds neither Soleczniki nor Šalčininkai, but *Szalczininkai*. According to an appropriately embarrassed Halina Kobeckaite, chief of the Lithuanian department for ethnic relations, the major progress of the months before May 1992 was agreement that the Polish letters 'ł' and 'z' may be used in official Polish appellations within Lithuania.[61]

Polish diplomats have pointed to the contrast between Lithuanian attitudes and those of the Ukrainians and Byelorussians, both of whom have been far more forthcoming in permitting the establishment of full cultural links between Poland and the local Polish minorities. The minorities in those two republics are indeed less compact than that of Lithuania, and may seem to present less of a threat. On the other hand, however, relations between Ukrainians and Poles have historically been even more bitter and violent than those between Poles and Lithuanians.

It is not clear to what extent the Lithuanian Right genuinely believes in a Polish threat to take back Wilno, or whether its purpose is to provoke Lithuanian fears in a purely cynical and opportunistic way. My own sense, from discussions with Right-wing Lithuanian deputies, is that they do believe Wilno to be a target. They are obsessed with the fear of the evil, alien 'Somebody', described in Chapter 1.

However, the Lithuanian Right also seems to be manipulating the 'Polish menace' for personal and party advancement, and perhaps also to 'rally the Lithuanian nation'. A similar obsessive concentration on the Wilno issue in the 1920s and 1930s was inspired by much the same purpose: to give a new and insecure nation a focus for national feeling, and to draw a strict line between Lithuanian and Polish culture.[62] Under Smetona's dictatorship, Lithuanian newspapers often concentrated on the Wilno issue to the complete exclusion of any domestic political coverage, and for obvious reasons.

Dislike of Poles and fear of Polish conquest remains largely absent among ordinary Lithuanians, and appears to be principally an obsession of the nationalist intelligentsia. In the northern area, the Polish presence was always limited in any case. Even in the south, the issue seemed to play no part in the 1992 elections. So does a Polish threat to Lithuania exist? For the foreseeable future, the answer must be no. When asked to comment on the issue for Polish radio, President Lech Walesa replied that, 'we might as well talk about a piece of land on the moon'. And

Polish representatives repeatedly emphasise that Poland recognises the existing frontiers.[63]

Poland has its own difficulties, and Poles are well aware that to re-open their claims to the east would lead to an immediate call from the German Right for the return of the Polish Western territories to Germany. In these circumstances it is difficult to imagine a fresh Polish advance eastwards.

As Landsbergis's power waned and vanished in late 1992, relations between the two countries improved. The Lithuanian government of Aleksandras Abisala (a nationalist, but also an intelligent realist) made a genuine attempt at compromise, for which it was attacked by radical Lithuanian nationalists. On his visit to Poland in September 1992, Abisala signed a series of agreements which considerably reduced the tension. His most significant practical success was agreement on the creation of a second border crossing-point, to add to the single and inadequate one at Lazdijai. The endless queues on the border, exacerbated by corruption and national ill-will, did severe harm not only to the Lithuanian economy, but to the entire land-link between the Baltic States and western Europe. Polish entrepreneurs could, if allowed, play a major part in developing the Baltic.

At the official opening in Wilno of the Polish radio station, *Znad Willi*, Kazimieras Motieka, a centrist deputy chairman of parliament, said that 'politicians have been dwelling on historical problems for their own opportunistic ends ... we must now forget this and try to go forward together'. The victory of Algirdas Brazauskas and the former Communists in the elections of October 1992 also seemed to point towards calm, although the possibility remains that the Right will seek to exploit the Polish issue to weaken a Brazauskas-backed government.

It also seems unlikely that Russia would again help the Poles of Lithuania, unless the Lithuanians were to blockade or even annexe the Russian enclave of Kaliningrad (Koenigsberg). In general, Russia seems far more interested in the huge Russian minorities of Latvia and Estonia. The Soviet Russian alliance with the Lithuanian Poles was always an unnatural one. Interviewing a crowd of Russian fascists on a St Petersburg street in January 1992, I queried their rowdy claims to Wilno. 'What about the Poles?', I asked. 'What Poles?' was their reply.

It has always been my belief that three-quarters of the Polish-Lithuanian 'problem' could be solved by a handful of symbolic gestures on the Lithuanian side, gestures which, after autumn 1992, have indeed begun to be made. But the unnecessary awakening of the dispute with Poland, whether for nationalist or opportunist motives, remains one of the most depressing aspects of Landsbergis's period in office. It remains a central tragedy of East European history that men like Landsbergis, so addicted to their own national symbolism, seem incapable of the slightest comprehension of the national symbols of any other country. For them, everybody else is always 'Somebody'.[64]

7

The Baltic Russians

The body of this people is like a fat cocoon,
Inside which sleeps a caterpillar soul,
While shaping its breast for flight
Unfolding its wings, flexing and adorning –
But when the sun of freedom shall rise,
What kind of insect will fly out of that shroud?

Adam Mickiewicz
(translated by Czeslaw Milosz)

The concern expressed in this chapter for the status of the Baltic Russians, and of Russians outside Russia in general, comes not from affection for them, or from a sense that the circumstance of their location is in any way justified. It comes from a strong belief that they are dangerous.

A Latvian, reading an early draft of this book, observed that while it attacked Baltic 'racism' towards the Russians, it was itself guilty of racist comments about the Baltic Russians. The point, however, is not that I regard Baltic attitudes to the Russians as especially pernicious in comparison with those of Western nations; they are often perfectly understandable and justified. The point is that they remain dangerous. In practice, strong pressure on the Russians to leave will endanger the peace of the region and of Europe.

There is also one exception to the general moral justification for Baltic behaviour: the position of Russian and Russian-Jewish intellectuals and businessmen in Riga is rather different, for several reasons. First, because the Russian community in Riga (even if not in its present dimensions) is of historic standing; secondly, because it broadly supported Latvian independence; thirdly, because it is essential to Latvian prosperity; and fourthly, because Riga has always been a multinational city, neither purely Latvian nor purely anything else. Seen in the long historical term, the attempt to turn Riga into a city with a purely Latvian face and identity is at odds with its traditions.

In my discussions with Balts over the question of guaranteed rights for the Russian minority, the argument has usually been at cross purposes.

174

They have argued in terms of international law, historical justice, and specific Baltic interests. I have replied on the basis of pragmatism, practical risks, and the interests of Europe and of the former Soviet region as a whole. In the light of experience of ethnic conflict elsewhere, I am concerned about the appalling consequences which could result, throughout the former Soviet Union, from attempts to dismantle the demographic legacy of Soviet rule. This concern may be exaggerated. Since living in the Baltic, my instinct both as a journalist and a historian has told me that, to go by the past, Baltic policies towards the Baltic Russians will, sooner or later, lead to an explosion. It may well be, however, that, for reasons set out in this chapter, these 'ancestral voices prophesying war' are mistaken in the case of the Baltic States.

It is in any case bitterly unfair that the Balts should be asked to modify their behaviour for fear of its effect on chauvinist nationalism in Russia, or the ethnic harmony of Kazakhstan. But history, like geography, is often unfair, and I argue that if Russia does swing in the direction of fascism, the result in part of the position of Russians living outside Russia, then the Balts themselves may suffer acutely. A Scandinavian diplomat explained his country's policy:

> We hope for peace and ethnic harmony in this region, which would itself make it more likely that the Baltic States can carry out economic reforms and move towards Western Europe; but I don't see this desire as directed against the Balts – after all, this is also very much in their own interests.

Although to the Balts it may well seem unfair, I do not regard it as immoral that Western Balts should talk in terms of the general interests of Europe, or of the former Soviet peoples. Moreover, while the Balts have a strong case in international law for regarding most of the Russians as illegal immigrants, a moral argument can also be made for the rights of the Russians, and has been made, by Helsinki Watch amongst others.

A Question of Identity

A common charge against the Russian-speaking minorities in the Baltic is that they have no real national identity: they are pure examples of *Homo Sovieticus*. An aspect of this has been the Baltic Russian attachment to the symbols of Communism. Thus in the Russian-populated Estonian town of Narva, the statue of Lenin once stood, not because of positive enthusiasm even among former Communist authorities, but purely as a visible sign of opposition to the 'nationalist' government in Tallinn. A Russian factory worker in Tallinn, asked in spring 1991 about a huge painting of Lenin on the wall of his plant, shrugged his shoulders sadly:

I know that today it does not look as if Lenin achieved very much, and that even in Russia he is charged with crimes; but you see, we need some sort of national symbol. In England too, you have national symbols, don't you? Like Churchill, for example?[1]

The loss of national culture is of course not a problem for the Baltic Russians alone. It has been suggested, by Paul Goble among others, that under Stalin a kind of implicit contract was created, by which the Russian nation as a whole agreed to surrender its national culture to that of the Soviet Union, in return for a supposedly trans-national Union guaranteeing Russian pre-eminence in what was in effect a continuation of the Russian empire. It meant that both national and traditional imperial symbols were destroyed or devalued by association with Soviet propaganda, and are therefore more difficult to recover than the symbols of the Balts or the Georgians.[2] It is also important to note that despite the view of many Balts, such an 'implicit contract' does not denote collective guilt for the crimes of Stalin or his successors: the Russians were never consulted, in free elections, as to their support for Communism. Traditional Russian culture, and the Russian educated classes, bore the full brunt of Communism. Russians do not view themselves as beneficiaries of the Soviet system, but as its chief victims. Russian workers in the Baltic, too, are incapable of comprehending why the Balts should view them as privileged exploiters, since their income and living standards are on average lower than those of the Balts themselves.

A formal Russian apology for Soviet crimes therefore appears inappropriate, and will certainly not be forthcoming. What can be asked, of course, is that Russians, and Russian intellectuals in particular, should be more aware of the relationship between Russian nationalism and Soviet imperialism, and show some commitment to a conclusive break with the past.

Russian self-confidence today is undermined by the traditional Russian tendency to bitter and even hysterical self-criticism, mixed with quasi-messianic beliefs that Russia was destined to save the world, a combination familiar in Third World countries exposed to First World modernisation, precisely the fate of Russia since Peter the Great. Communism fed on the second conviction, and Communism's fall is leading to a striking revival of the first. It is very common in Russia today to hear the expression, 'in the civilised world', implying that Russia is not civilised and perhaps never will be. Such abject despair is worrying, both because it can lead to paralysis of the will and because it suggests that in due course, as a reaction, there may be a reversion to the messianic variant, signalled, perhaps, by the rise of Vladimir Zhirinovsky.

The humiliation of grinding poverty and a dispossession of ideals would be dangerous enough on its own: an opinion poll, for example, has suggested that a majority of Muscovite girls would like to become hard currency prostitutes. The effects of this on the Russian male psyche, and the possible implications for politics, can be imagined.

A common analysis of support for fascism has been in terms of *declasse* social groups, or those threatened with social upheaval. In the context of the replacement of a Communist society with an impoverished, Third World version of a free market, this fate threatens the entire population. Even the minority who stand to do well from the new order are being shaken out of long established patterns; for most, the effect is not dissimilar to the strains placed on the German petty bourgeoisie between 1918 and 1933. For the moment, however, the Baltic Russians' self-image as an imperial people has been greatly undermined. Unlike most imperial peoples, the Russians have generally been poorer (and often, it must be said, dirtier and more drunken) than many of the peoples over whom they were ruling. Most Russian immigrants to the Baltic came from the working class or the peasantry, whereas the local populations comprised a substantial middle class and intelligentsia, damaged but not destroyed by Stalinism. The discrediting of Communism led many Baltic Russians, especially younger ones, to look towards the West. This in turn led to support for independence, and hopes of a move towards Western standards. In the words of Nikolai Slinsky, a Russian technician at the 'Communard' plant in Vilnius, shortly after the Lithuanian Declaration of Independence,

> I have been abroad several times, and seen how people live there. I would like Vilnius to be like the towns I saw in Finland. And as long as Lithuania is democratic, like the West, there will be no problem for Russians here.[3]

An opinion poll in Latvia in December 1991 showed that while, as expected, more local Russians than Latvians favoured a connection with the former Soviet Union (though only 33.2 per cent of Russians to 23.4 per cent of Latvians), the proportion of those favouring an orientation to the West and to Japan was extremely close: 36.9 per cent Russians to 39.2 per cent Latvians.[4] Economic hopes have so far been disappointed, resulting in a great wave of disillusionment among Balts as well as Russians. Any resulting Baltic Russian reaction against independence has however been diminished by the fact that, across the border, Russia itself is even worse off.

On the other hand, the fear of Russian workers (and of many Balts), that if the Baltic Republics left the Union, Russian raw material and oil supplies would decrease, damaging the Baltic economies, has proved entirely accurate. Its impact has, however, been deadened, because the decline has come in the context of a general collapse in the Soviet trading system, harming all the former republics alike.

In the Baltic Republics, therefore, it was difficult indeed for Russians to see themselves – as did British and French colonists in their empires – as bearers of civilisation and prosperity. The Baltic Russians became increasingly aware of the failure of the Soviet system, and of their association with it. In the words of Goethe, 'to be hated hurts no-one; it is contempt that drags men down'.

A large proportion of Baltic Russians have been prepared to acknowledge that the Balts have a superior civic culture, are cleaner, more orderly, and harder-working. They may qualify this by saying that Russian life is 'friendlier', or 'more humane', but this is the *exact* reverse of the usual coloniser: colonised self-images. In marriages between Balts and Russians, the tendency has been for Russians to become Baltified rather than vice versa, a check on the 'Russification' of the region; in Latvia in 1990, 36 per cent of marriages were across nationalities (including marriages between Russians and Ukrainians and so on). Growing ethnic tension, however, may account for the increase in divorce within inter-ethnic marriages, from 37 per cent in 1987 to 40 per cent in 1990. Marriages between Estonians and non-Estonians have been much rarer.[5]

Of pre-eminent importance in avoiding the development of strong Baltic Russian resistance to independence *au pied noir*, has been the peaceful strategy of all three Baltic national movements, and the natural restraint of the Baltic populations in the face of every provocation to violence. This feature has been central to the prestige of the Baltic movements, not only in the West but also in Russia, and among Baltic Russian intellectuals. These claim it has also influenced the character and behaviour of the Russians in the region. In words that have been echoed by many Baltic Russians, Boris Yulegin, Deputy Mayor of Tallinn, said that:

> The Russians who have lived here all their lives have changed a lot. They have taken on something of the Estonian coolness, restraint and habit of hard work – whether they like it or not! They do not feel at home when they go to Russia. The Russians who come here also sometimes do not understand our character, and ask us, 'Why don't you protest? Why don't you go on the streets?'[6]

In view of the size of the Baltic populations, the local Russian response to calls for rallies, strikes, and political resistance before the summer of 1992 was pitifully small, and even the response to referenda and elections was deeply divided.

Despite this, it is still useful to analyse the position of Russia as a whole, and of the Baltic Russians in particular, within the context of the European experience of decolonisation. It is important to remember that just as many of the uncertain features of contemporary Baltic ideology result from the 'time-lag' of Soviet isolation, so Russian attitudes and dilemmas are sometimes reminiscent of those of Western Europeans a couple of generations ago. In the autumn of 1992 Russia stood in a position not wholly dissimilar from that of France in the mid-1950s, between the end of the war in Indo-China and the full intensification of the war in Algeria.

Losses suffered during the Second World War and in Indo-China destroyed the will of the French people to hold on to their colonial empire, just as Britain's exhaustion after 1945 made it impossible to think of holding on to India.

Even before de Gaulle, the French had begun an orderly, negotiated withdrawal from most of their colonies and protectorates. Except Algeria; but Algeria was not presented to the French people as a conventional imperial, colonial conflict: after Dien Bien Phu, such a war would have been bitterly unpopular. Instead, it was fought precisely on the grounds that *ici, c'est la France,* that the presence of one million Frenchmen (or, like the 'Russians' in the other former Soviet republics, a mixture of nationalities but predominantly French-speaking) made Algeria part of the soil of France itself.

It was through this argument that the alliance of *Pieds Noirs* and embittered military veterans of Indo-China cajoled the French nation into an extended, bitter struggle. It was backed by the assumption that since Frenchmen could not possibly live under Muslim majority rule, the only alternative was 'the suitcase or the coffin' – emigration or death. After several years of savage warfare, of course, it became a self-fulfilling prophecy.

Today, defeat in Afghanistan, economic collapse, the total discrediting of Communism, national revolt (albeit mainly peaceful) and the end of the Communist Party – the iron frame of the Soviet empire – have led to the disintegration of the Soviet Union and of much of the old Russian empire. Sheer exhaustion, as much as anything else, saw the Russian people accept, at least before 1993, the loss of empire with extraordinary equanimity (when compared to Britain and France), despite the fact that some of the abandoned territories had been part of Russia for longer than the entire national history of the United States of America.

After the First World War, Russia was also in a state of exhaustion, but the empire was rebuilt by Lenin with the help, in part, of 'national Bolsheviks', Russian Imperialists like General Brusilov (and even Marshal Tukhachevsky) who saw Communism as the only means to unite Russia and reconquer the lost territories. (That, however, was in the context of an age of European empires. The world cultural atmosphere today is of course different.)

Sections of the former Communist and radical nationalist press continue to demand that the Baltic States should remain within a sphere of influence amounting in effect to imperial control. Thus a *Pravda* article in June 1992 argued that,

> Withdrawal of Russia from the Baltic States would mean not just closing our window on the West, which has already been done, but also boarding it up, which is going on at present. Russia simply cannot exist without the Baltic ports. . . . Therefore Estonian politicians will have to consider the renewal and development of links with Russia . . . [and] the Russian nation, which once saved the Estonians from Nazi genocide, has no choice but to re-open its European window. How this might be done is another question. . . .[7]

The article's strongest language is, however, reserved for the question of rights for Russian residents of Estonia. Liberal Moscow papers like *Izvestia, Moscow News* and *Nezavisimaya Gazeta* also often express the hope that the Balts will retain close economic links with Russia, but they do not use the neo-imperialist language of *Pravda*. All, however, are becoming increasingly concerned about the treatment of Russians living in the Baltic.

Even among those who oppose independence for the Balts and others, there is little real enthusiasm for force. Most of the supporters of Vladimir Zhirinovsky, for example, tend to retreat when confronted with the reality of war on a massive scale.[8] The hope in much of Russian government is to retain the Baltic States within a sphere of influence. But were it not for the existence of substantial Russian minorities, it is doubtful even this effort would be made, given Russian weakness.[9] An opinion poll published in *Izvestia* in January 1993 suggested that while a majority of Russians wanted their country to regain its status as a great power, only some four per cent thought it should be through military force and aggressive foreign policy; the great majority sought it through a strong economy.

The protection of the minorities is a theme which both the old Soviet and new Russian imperialists have a strong interest in exploiting. But the situation in Moldavia, Ossetia or the Baltic States is not being presented by Russian television as a struggle for empire;[10] nor is it seen as such by most Russians. For them, the duty of the Russian government to protect the position of Russians (and pro-Russian minorities) in neighbouring states is seen not as an imperial but as a *national* duty.

Some Russian intellectuals (Professor Yuri Afanassyev is a leading example) feel differently, regarding most of these populations as legacies of imperialism. The dissident Russian poet, Boris Chichabin, has written,

> We are all answerable to God. During the stagnation years I used to visit the Baltic States and often encountered the unfriendliness of the local

population. I always felt like crying out: 'Friends, your attitude is misplaced! I am different!' But the words stuck in my mouth, because I too am to blame for the occupation and enslavement of the Baltic States.

But to expect the majority of the Russian people to be decisively influenced by feelings of post-colonial guilt would be to require more of them than the peoples of the other former Soviet republics and indeed of the former Western imperial nations as well.

The issue of responsibility for the former imperial territories is of course a heaven-sent weapon for all those in opposition in Russia to use against whichever government is in power – the tactics of Ruslan Khasboulatov against Yeltsin being a flagrant example – and a way of distracting public attention from failures at home. In the words of a Russian diplomat, 'the Russian politicians are trying to solve the problems of Russians in Riga because they don't know how to solve the problems of Russians in Moscow'.

To retain mass support, Russian liberals cannot be seen to be too soft on the question of Russian rights. With some twenty-five million Russians living outside national borders, there are of course also practical reasons for any Russian government to ensure that they are secure, and do not return to burden an impoverished Russia and worsen the attitude of Russia's population to its own internal ethnic minorities.[11]

The Baltic Russians through History

Some sort of Russian presence has existed in the lands that are now Estonia and Latvia since the Dark Ages, though numerically small. After expulsion by German crusaders of the Russian princes that had dominated parts of the region, the Russian population in the Middle Ages consisted of small groups of merchants from Novgorod and Pskov, together with a number of Slavic (or Slavicised Balt) communities in what is now Eastern Latvia. This is excepting the enormous Slavic Orthodox community which came under Lithuanian rule between the thirteenth and fifteenth centuries, but was later incorporated into what are now Russia, Byelorussia and the Ukraine.

From the sixteenth century, the small Russian communities in the ethnic Baltic heartlands were joined by Russian political refugees and religious dissidents fleeing persecution by Ivan the Terrible and his descendants. The largest group was made up of 'Old Believers', the Russian Orthodox who refused to accept liturgical reforms introduced by the seventeenth century Tsars, culminating in those of Peter the Great, still remembered by these communities as Antichrist. A few Old Believer villages survive in Latgale, on the northern shores of Lake Peipus

(Peipsi), and in Lithuania. They were subjected to Soviet persecution and, partly as a consequence, tended to support Baltic independence.[12]

After the conquest of Livonia and Estonia by Peter the Great, the population was gradually expanded by increasing numbers of Russian officials, soldiers, and merchants. Most were transients, but some put down roots and remained. At the same time, branches of the Baltic German nobility intermarried with Russian noble families. Until the later nineteenth century the number of Russians in the Baltic provinces was never large. At this point the Russian government, in pursuit of its Russification policy, attempted to settle Russian peasants on the land. This archaic colonial idea failed but, unplanned by the imperial government, the workings of imperial capitalism (as in Malaya, the West Indies, Fiji and so on) were drawing tens of thousands of impoverished Russian peasants to new factories and docks springing up on the Baltic coast. According to an American scholar, 'Riga became in these decades one of the most ethnically, linguistically and religiously diverse of the major cities of Europe'. According to a census in 1913, Riga was 39.8 per cent Latvian (an increase from 23.6 per cent in 1867), 20 per cent Russian, 13.9 per cent German, 9.5 per cent Polish, 7 per cent Jewish and 6.9 per cent Lithuanian.[13]

Since both Russian workers and Balts saw the local German élites and the imperial government as their common enemies, there was little tension between them. In 1915, the Russian retreat and the consequent evacuation of the factories and their workforces led to a drastic reduction in the size of the Russian population. The resulting labour shortage, especially on the farms of independent Latvia, was compensated by Polish and Lithuanian migrant labour. The pejorative image of the Lithuanian as a dirty, shiftless, landless labourer lingers in Latvia to this day.

After the Bolshevik revolution and the achievement of Baltic independence, the pattern of the Old Believers was repeated, with Russian refugees seeking refuge in the Baltic States. Some were explicitly religious, as in the case of the Mikniškes Orthodox community in South-Eastern Lithuania. The educated sections of this new Russian emigration were a heterogeneous mixture, including both former White officers and their families, and (in Latvia) large numbers of Russian-speaking Jews. Between the wars Riga was the largest Russian emigré centre after Paris.

Russian immigrants complained of Baltic 'coldness' towards them, of anti-Russian rhetoric from the press and politicians, and of state discrimination (especially in education), but most were very grateful to have found in the Baltic States a refuge from Communist savagery. The nostalgic, mournful verses about their lost homeland anticipated those of Baltic exiles when their homes too were ravaged by the Communists.

On the 'Day of Russian Culture' held in Narva, Estonia (which then had a Russian minority of some 30 per cent, but now has a majority of 94 per cent) on 18–19 June 1938, the Archpriest Alexander Sakharov thanked the Estonian government for allowing the Russians to live 'in peace and prosperity'. According to the Russian emigré scholar Temira Pachmuss, all the speakers, including the Estonian ministers, spoke in Russian. The Festival of Russian Song, also in Narva, attracted thousands of singers from all over Estonia.[14]

As in Eastern Europe and Manchuria after 1944–45, Stalin's determination to wipe out the Russian opposition forces in exile meant that the Russian communities in the Baltic suffered early, and particularly badly, after the conquest of 1940. Of those prominent Russian intellectuals who failed to escape to the West or to Finland, the great majority were executed or died in camps. The Russian community in Tallinn in particular has never recovered from the loss, which eliminated a group which might later have built bridges between the Russian and Balt communities.

Soviet partisan activity among Russian workers in the Baltic occurred during the German occupation, and was ruthlessly suppressed. The scars it left were exploited by Soviet loyalists in recent years, but with limited success.[15] The Russian population in the Baltic after the war was overwhelmingly new and had no direct acquaintance with past atrocities – or, indeed, of life in a free society.

New Russian settlement began almost immediately the fighting ceased in 1945, beginning with officials and demobilised soldiers given jobs in the region. These in many cases moved straight into flats abandoned by the refugees who had fled to the West, or belonging to Balts deported to Siberia. Baltic claims for the return of their property are a factor causing tension in the region now.

Within only a few years the influx made up for the colossal losses of the war years, and was responsible for an absolute rise in the population of both Latvia and Estonia. The Estonian population had fallen from 1.13 million in 1939 to some 850,000 in 1945; by 1955 the population had risen again to 1.15 million, chiefly through the arrival of some 230,000 non-Estonian immigrants. By 1959, ethnic Russians, 8.2 per cent of the pre-war population, amounted to 20 per cent of the total.[16]

In Latvia the population was swollen by 535,000 non-Latvian immigrants, rising from around 1.4 million at the war's end to 2 million by 1955. The Soviet pretext was that these workers were necessary to develop the economy and compensate for wartime losses. Lithuania, with its higher birthrate and bigger reserve of rural labour, had more grounds to resist the influx, and only some 160,000 non-Lithuanians arrived during the post-war years.

Thereafter immigration continued more slowly. In Latvia and Estonia, it diminished steeply in the 1970s as Russia's own birthrate and labour pool fell sharply. In Lithuania, where industrial expansion persisted after the native labour pool had been exhausted and the death of Snieckus had removed a covert defender of national interests, immigration increased sharply. In 1965–69, the figure was only 29,000, but by 1980–85, it had grown to 59,000. Lithuania's larger native population however meant this still left the Russian minority at less than ten per cent of the total. In Estonia, by contrast, the native proportion of the population fell from 88.2 per cent in 1938 to 74.6 per cent in 1959, and is only around 61 per cent today. In Latvia, the figure fell from 75.5 per cent before the War to 62 per cent in 1959, and some 52 per cent today. By 1990, according to the Latvian census, the process had ceased, and a net emigration had begun: 3,989 more people left Riga than arrived that year. By 1992, emigration by Russian speakers was more than 20,000.

The clear intention of the Soviet government was to dilute the Baltic populations and bolster pro-Soviet loyalties. The attraction, however, as it had been before 1914, was principally the higher living standards of the Baltic States ('the Soviet West'), which sucked in workers, especially those young and unmarried, from all over the Union. As an incentive, many (though by no means all) were offered flats on the grounds of being needed 'specialists', while Balts frequently spent years in the housing queue. As one Latvian put it:

> The Russians take the apartments in a house, and leave us the attic and the cellar. Then they say that we are discriminating against them because they have nowhere to hang their washing or store their wood!

In the principal cities the population change was even more to the Balts' disadvantage. Even in 1940, Riga had been only 63 per cent Latvian, the balance made up of Russians, Germans, Jews and some Western merchants. The Latvian percentage rose sharply as a result of the deportation, evacuation or murder of many of the minorities, but fell steeply again after 1945. Today Latvians make up only 36.5 per cent of Riga's population. They are also in a minority in each of Latvia's six main towns, ranging from 49 per cent in Jelgava to only 13 per cent in the eastern city of Daugavpils. In Tallinn, Estonians had formed 85.6 per cent of the population in 1940, but today represent only around 49 per cent. But whereas in Latvia, Russians live in towns across the country, in Estonia they are concentrated in Tallinn and the north-east. Other Estonian towns, like Tartu, Parnu and Kuresaare (formerly Kingisepp) have solid Estonian majorities. In Vilnius the trend was entirely the other way. Lithuanians, a small minority before the war, are today in a majority, although some 45 per cent of the city's population remains Polish, Russian or Byelorussian.

In Latvia and Estonia, the great majority of the present 'immigrant' population entered the republics before 1970, or was born to parents who had done so. The residence requirement for citizenship, on which much Western attention has been focused, is therefore largely irrelevant for the purpose of excluding the bulk of the Russians. The really important factor is the language test, quotas (in Latvia), and, in terms of the Russian political élites, the proposed Latvian requirement excluding military veterans, past-Communists and opponents of Latvian independence.

Ethnic Russians make up the large majority of the non-Balt populations. In Latvia they represent 34 per cent of the population, with Byelorussians 4.5 per cent, and Ukrainians 3.5 per cent. These latter groups tend to be classed generically but loosely as 'Russian-speakers', and this is probably fair. As a result of being made to study in Russian schools and work in Russian-speaking workplaces, and of intermarriage, most have lost any close connection with their original nationality. Russia has offered citizenship to all those who declare themselves to be Russian.

The Baltic governments have tried to drive wedges between non-Balt communities by means of regional cultural societies and other tactics, but this has been undermined by the lack of education among the communities concerned, as well as by the tendency of the Baltic populations to regard all non-Balts as 'Russians' and to treat them accordingly. This of course tends to solidify non-Balts within a sort of quasi-Russian, quasi-Soviet identity, and has led to some strange identifications. In Riga, I listened for months to my Latvian landlady abusing the 'noisy, dirty Russians' next door – before discovering they were in fact Georgians.

In February 1990, soon after the bloody Soviet suppression of the Baku revolt, I met an Azeri foreman in a Lithuanian factory whose allegiance to the Soviet Union seemed indistinguishable from that of his Russian mates – because, he claimed, he was afraid of the 'Lithuanian fascists'. Despite this, the mixture of nationalities among the workforces of Russian-speaking factories in Latvia has been one factor working against collective political action.

The very real threat, under Soviet rule, of being reduced to a minority within their own homeland and eventually swamped altogether has left deep scars upon the Latvian and Estonian psyches. Everyone agrees that further immigration must cease. Russian immigrants of any description would have attracted hostility from the Balts (or any other indigenous nation in the same position, those in the West most emphatically included), given their huge numbers and association with foreign conquest, political tyranny, debasement of culture and public manners, and economic decline. It has been precisely the proletarian nature of the Russian immigration that has contributed to the resistance to it, especially among Estonians, so very different in temperament and culture. I have seen Estonians, normally so very calm, twitching and shaking with repressed physical hatred as they speak of the 'Asiatic, Mongolian barbarians' who have settled among them, and of their foul habits.

This kind of gut racial hatred is less of a problem in more easy-going (and Slavicised) Latvia. There too, however, one can very often hear mothers chastising their children that 'you're behaving like a Russian . . . you're eating like a Russian'. This cultural difference threatens to become even more marked if the Balts take advantage of economic change to rise into a new middle class, while Russian workers decline relatively or even absolutely in prosperity.

Latvians blame the dirt and decay of Riga and the other cities upon their Russian majorities – and they are often right. There is indeed about some of the Russian workers in the Baltic an air of the 'Dark People', the sullen, suspicious, unknowable, potentially terrible peasants of the Russian tradition. This in turn evokes Pushkin's words about the revolts of those same peasants, 'senseless and merciless'. More often, however, I have found the people perfectly friendly, but ignorant, as much bewildered as angry. Their deception by the Communists, their lack of knowledge of history, and their social isolation from the Balts has meant that they simply, for a long time, had no idea what the Baltic national movements were all about, or why local people disliked them.

Only a small proportion of Russian-speakers in the Baltic have learned to speak Baltic languages adequately. Until recently a majority did not speak them at all: according to a 1988 poll in Estonia, only 38 per cent could speak even minimal Estonian, though the picture has doubtless improved since then. This, and the general Russian indifference to local culture, has been a major source of Baltic anger. As a bitter joke has it:

> 'In the Soviet Union, if you know four languages, what are you?'
> 'A Zionist.'
> 'And if you know two languages?'
> 'A Nationalist.'
> 'And if you know one language?' [i.e. Russian]
> 'An Internationalist!'[17]

Today, this failure constitutes a major threat to the position of the Baltic Russians, as all three republics demand knowledge of the language as a qualification for continuing to hold many state jobs, not merely as doctors, teachers, and officials, but even as waiters.

Living amidst Russians, working in Russian-majority factories, watching Russian television and with all necessary documents translated into Russian, most simply had no reason to learn the local languages. Nor did the generally very inadequate level of Estonian and Latvian teaching in Russian schools encourage learning. In a newspaper interview in 1990, a half-Russian, half-Latvian woman explained why she had never learned Latvian:

> You see, Latvian didn't seem to us like a real language. The good books and films were all in Russian. In our house in Riga the most notable resident was a Russian colonel. . . . I have to admit that there was a period in my life [at school] when I was ashamed of my half-Latvian roots. . . . We made fun of Latvians, skipped our Latvian language classes, and sent our teacher out of the classroom crying. To be Russian was more glamorous, more glorious, more true-to-life . . . Latvia didn't even exist in Russian schools here.[18]

Knowledge of Latvian among Russians is higher than that of Estonian, partly because the communities in Latvia are closer, but mainly because Latvian, like Russian, is an Indo-European language, whereas Estonian is a Finno-Ugric tongue of exceptional complexity. Even so, in 1989, only 23 per cent of non-Latvians could speak Latvian with any degree of fluency.

Today, a willingness to learn certainly exists, and Russian bookstores are full of 'teach yourself Latvian' manuals. Much depends on factors such as class, education, and location: Russians in cities with a high proportion of Balts are much more likely to learn than those living in towns such as Daugavpils. But most depends on individual motivation. Some ordinary workers seem to be making honest efforts to learn; some officials and businessmen are still arrogantly refusing to do so, believing themselves to be indispensable.

The image of the Baltic Russians as made up overwhelmingly of proletarians is true for Lithuania and for Tallinn. In north-east Estonia (where about half the Russian-speakers of Estonia are concentrated), the huge Russian majority has produced a Russian educated-class of teachers, doctors, and managers and scientists at factories and power stations. In Latvia, the picture is different. Riga, as the capital of the Soviet Baltic, attracted a higher proportion of educated Russians, just as it had under the Russian Empire. According to a 1989 census, 13.4 per cent of non-Latvians in the republic had received a higher education, compared with only 11.5 per cent of Latvians. It is quite true that Russians make up the majority (62 per cent) of the industrial workforce, but together with Russian Jews they also dominate the managerial class, the technological establishment (58 per cent of scientific jobs and 51 per cent of information and computer services), and – of great significance for the future – the great majority of positions within the new, private business sector.[19]

Other than this, whether the existence of a Russian-speaking educated class proves a boon or a curse for Latvia depends very much on who succeeds in Latvian politics and what their intentions are towards the

Russians. If, eventually, a compromise is sought with the Russians, then this middle class will provide valuable intermediaries. Whereas, hitherto, the general breakdown in communication between even moderate Russian politicians and intellectuals and the Latvian nationalist forces is worrying, the determination of the business class to maintain good contact with the government and to show support for the new state is one positive feature.

So long as the Latvian government remains friendly to business, some sort of basic ethnic co-existence is probably assured. The real danger would follow any future national populist government with a programme targeted against 'foreign speculators', Russian professionals ignorant of the language, and unemployed industrial workers. In this eventuality, Russian resistance in Latvia would be more formidable than in Estonia, not simply because they are more numerous, but because they would be better and more articulately led.

The Last Stand of the Soviet Union

The Communist Party, among all its other functions, was the institution designed to bind together the élites of the different Soviet nationalities under Russian hegemonic leadership, bridging national differences and suppressing rivalries in the name of 'Internationalism'. After mid-1988, however, the Baltic Communist Parties began to unravel in the face of the newly-formed Popular Fronts, until finally, between December 1989 and May 1990, all three parties, and the press that supported them, split along essentially ethnic lines.[20]

The three Popular Fronts all developed Russian language newspapers, edited by pro-independence Russian intellectuals. While the local television stations broadcast Russian programmes, most local Russians preferred to watch the central Russian station, if only because of its superior quality. This preference explains why the rise of Boris Yeltsin, as reported by Russian television, was of great importance in influencing opinion among the Baltic Russians.

As reformist (and covertly pro-independence) interests gained control of the three parties, local Russian Communists and hardliners in Moscow joined to create Soviet loyalist movements, under Communist and retired military leadership, and looking directly to Moscow for support. In Estonia the movement was called 'The International Movement of Workers in the Estonian SSR'; in Latvia, it was known as the 'International Front', and in Lithuania as 'Unity' (*Yedinstvo*). The 'Intermovement' in Estonia held its founding Congress on 14 March 1989, accompanied by a demonstration numbering an estimated thirty to forty thousand. Oddly, although the three movements had precisely similar objectives, there was relatively little co-operation between them, and leaders in Latvia, for example, were often surprisingly ignorant of developments in the other two republics – probably because they all looked first to Moscow for help and instruction.

What the forces opposing Baltic independence had principally in common was their 'reactionary' position; as Soviet 'loyalists', they all favoured the survival of the Soviet Union in some form or another. Beyond this, they varied from mainstream Communist and military hardliners to the leaders of the 'Equal Rights' Faction in Latvia, (Sergejs Dīmanis and Tatjana Zhdanoka, for example) who in Russia would probably have been supporters of Boris Yeltsin. These claim to have sought initially to join the Popular Fronts, but to have been repelled by their 'chauvinist atmosphere'.

The key problem for the loyalist moderates was that their absolute opposition to Baltic independence left them with no choice but to ally with the hardliners. This in turn led them into justifying a whole series of shameful actions (beginning with the annexations of 1940), which discredited them utterly in the eyes not only of Balts but of most Western observers as well. Most have now been swept away, along with the Soviet Union, except where they created a solid local base of support, like Vladimir Chuikin, the charismatic former Communist mayor of the Russian-majority town of Narva, in north-east Estonia. Chuikin, unlike many of the hardliners in Lithuania and Estonia, but like the parliamentary leaders of the pro-Soviet opposition in Latvia, was a 'new man', or relatively so, who owed his rise to Gorbachov's accession to power.

The leadership of the pro-Soviet wings of the Baltic Communist Parties contained not simply Russians, but a good many native Balts, as well as Balts brought up in Russia, who could or would not make the transition of Brazauskas, Gorbunovs and Rüütel to a support for independence. This was in some cases because their past made it impossible for them to portray themselves as nationalists; in others, they seem to have remained loyal to the hand that raised them; in all cases, there seem to have persisted some sort of belief in Soviet ideology. During the Soviet referendum of 17 March 1991, which he helped organise, Algirdas Kondruška, a Lithuanian Professor of Marxism-Leninism, explained why he had remained a loyal Soviet Communist:

> Yes, my wife asks me that: 'why are you still a Communist when everyone is asking for independence?' Even the former Director of the Party School is now writing in the papers that I am a traitor. But you see, the Soviet Union helped me to study at Moscow University, and I am grateful. . . . It is true that there I learned to have much in common with Russians, but my first motive is professional. I have always taught in the Party School,

10 Demonstrators at a meeting of Interfront, a Soviet loyalist organisation, in Riga, January 1991.

> and to change my views overnight is impossible for me. It is a question of honour; I must go on with the Party to the very end.[21]

Kondruška, however, spoiled this not unsympathetic picture by adding, with the grotesque exaggeration – sometimes hysterical, sometimes deliberate – characteristic of Soviet loyalists, 'of course, if the Soviet Army were not here we would all be hanging from trees'.

In this category were also serving and retired officers and managers of Moscow-controlled, 'All-Union' factories in the Baltic. Some were of long service in the Baltic, and some, like Colonel Igor Lopatin in Latvia and Vladimir Yarovoi, manager of the Dvigatel plant in Tallinn, seem to have been deliberately inserted by Moscow, after the launch of the national movements, to help shore up Soviet loyalism.

Behind such men stood the senior hardliners of the KGB, Interior Ministry and Military Command in Moscow who were ultimately to attempt the counter-revolution of August 1991. Associated with them were some (though not all) of the local military commanders in the Baltic, men like the regional commander, Colonel General Fyodr Kuzmin, and the Vilnius garrison chief, Major General Uskhopchik. The relationship of other local commanders (such as Admiral Belov in Estonia) to the hardliners was more ambiguous; what exactly went on within the military during those months may never be known.

Many left for Russia in the aftermath of the August coup. Rubiks in Latvia and Valery Ivanov, a Soviet loyalist leader in Lithuania, were arrested; but a number of hardline retired officers remain, especially in Latvia, such as Colonel Gennady Romashov, a leader of the 'Russian Society of Latvia', formed after the achievement of independence. The more formidable Colonel Viktors Alksnis, an ethnic Latvian brought up in Russia (see Chapter 3), remains a figure on the imperialist Right in Moscow. Two of the hardline Interfront leaders in Estonia, Yevgeny Kogan and Mikhail Lysenko, have also become active in reactionary politics within Russia.[22]

Unlike Alksnis, most members of this category revealed themselves to be incapable of responding imaginatively to changing political circumstances; they were rigid intellectual products of Soviet education and Soviet establishment. Others, especially in Lithuania, were simply deeply stupid or incompetent, the scrag-end of the Communist Party.[23]

The attempt by hardline Soviet loyalists to 'manipulate' the Russian-speaking populations of the Baltic into opposition to independence provides an interesting case-study for which there are historical precedents. In pre-1914 Germany, it has been argued, much of German nationalism was the product of deliberate manipulation by landed élites, and the imperial government they controlled, to defend their own political interests. In pre-independence India, similarly, Muslim separatist politics has been seen as the product of manipulation by the British and by endangered Muslim feudal élites, rather than of a genuine mass fear of Hindu rule.

Such claims need to be examined closely; in their crudest form they represent no more than the standard line that unrest arises not out of genuine grievance but is the work of 'outside agitators'. Thus the denial of spontaneity to pre-1947 Muslim politics excuses the Indian Congress of failing to do more for Muslims. In the Baltic too, charges that local Russian fears were externally fomented relieved the nationalist movements of the obligation to reassure the Russian population.

Manipulation through misinformation by the Soviet state media, the local pro-Soviet press and local Russian officials was of course blatant and continuous.[24] It was accompanied by instances of deliberate provocation to provide an excuse for intervention. In the context of the 'historiography' of manipulation, however, the striking point is that very little was achieved. Only a small minority of local Russian-speakers were persuaded actively to oppose independence. In South Ossetia and Moldavia, by contrast, Communist attempts to stimulate rebellion among local minorities were strikingly successful.

What this indicates is the obvious but often forgotten point that while manipulation can play a part in sparking conflicts, it can only do so if the appropriate historical, social and cultural climate already exists. Where it does, as in Ossetia for example, it becomes extremely difficult in practice to distinguish between manipulation and the real fears of the Ossetes, derived from history and Georgian behaviour.

What is clear, however, is that thanks to local conditions and Baltic qualities, such a climate did not exist in the Baltic during the years between 1988 and 1993. A section of the Russian-speaking population was indeed worried by symbolic actions such as the restoration of the old national flags, and by the anti-Russian (as opposed to anti-Soviet) tone of some Baltic newspaper articles, bits of which were assiduously reprinted by Soviet loyalists as part of their propaganda. A key factor in generating support for the Interfronts was the passage by the Baltic Supreme Councils in 1988–89 of laws establishing the official status of the Baltic languages and requiring a residence qualification (if only a short one: two years in Estonia) for those wishing to stand for elected office.

The residence clause affected only migrant workers and equally migrant Soviet officers. But the language law, with its requirement that a whole range of state officials, medical workers and even waiters should learn the local language or lose their jobs, affected a large part of the Russian-speaking population.

The Baltic Russians have complained that the period provided for the learning of the languages was too short, and that Baltic language teaching in Russian schools was in any case highly deficient, and remains so, especially in Russian-majority towns like Narva. The excuse given is lack of money and the unwillingness of Estonian teachers to work in Russian schools and Russian-majority areas. In 1992, both Latvia and Estonia extended by a further two years the time limit for Russians in towns, like Narva and Daugavpils, with overwhelmingly Russian populations and, consequently, particular learning difficulties.[25] Russians, however, suspect that the Balts do not wish them to succeed, in order to exclude them permanently from public life and avoid a 'dilution' of Baltic language and culture. In general, the appeal to Russian workers' prejudices against the 'bourgeois intellectual' Baltic leaderships was one of the most effective weapons in the Kremlin's armoury, not simply for cultural reasons but because it was backed up by a very real (and justified) fear of economic reform and unemployment.

Associated with the Intermovements was the plan to mobilise Russian-speaking workers of the 'All-Union' factories, and indeed the factories themselves, in the struggle against independence. In all three republics, Communist officials, especially from the 'official' trades unions, were active on the shop floor, rousing the workers. In Estonia and Latvia, the attempt went further, with the creation of the 'United Council of Work Collectives' (OSTK). The movements were linked by the factory directors, Yarovoi and Shepelevitch. A further Interfront leader in

Estonia was Yevgeny Kogan, whose extremist speeches even caused friction with the rest of the Soviet loyalist organisation. A later recruit was the thuggish Mikhail Lysenko, a former policeman who had been dismissed on charges of corruption.

In the first instance the OSTK was directed against Estonian attempts to remove factories from the control of Moscow. Later the trend was to establish the factories as Soviet-Russian fortress islands in the Estonian Sea. Thus the 'Integral Commission', a formal association of factories and OSTK, was established in July 1990 with powers akin to those of a fully operational local government, uniting social services, insurance schemes and housing projects as well as representing the interests of the factories and their workforces in dealings with both Moscow and the Estonian government.

In August 1989, the OSTK and Intermovement called a general strike, ostensibly in protest against the electoral residence requirement. More a lockout than a strike, since it was supported by the Soviet managers and the workers continued to be paid, it was supported by only something between 18,000 and 30,000 workers, or 5–8 per cent of the workforce. It did, however, succeed in disrupting public transport and supplies within Estonia.[26]

Throughout the next two years, governments and observers in the Baltic expected a repetition of the strike on a much larger scale, possibly involving violence. However those strikes which were organised during May 1990 and on subsequent occasions were in fact miserable damp squibs. They affected only All-Union factories, and then not all of them. Public transport workers, though overwhelmingly Russian, refused to join the action.[27]

Aside from the pervading Baltic air of calm, there were two main reasons for the failure. The first was the simple threat of unemployment. Russians working for Estonian state enterprises in particular had good reason to fear retaliatory dismissal. The second reason involves the paradox of managers and official trades unions calling a strike at all – a paradox of which the workers were quite aware. During the Tallinn strike of May 1991, I asked a Russian worker what he thought of Yarovoi and the other leaders of the Soviet loyalist forces. 'Those Communist bastards!' he said. 'Do you think I don't know they've been stealing from us all these years? Of course I know it, and I know about their cars and their dachas and their mistresses. But what other leaders do we have here in Estonia?'

Thus the Soviet Communist Party's support among Russians in the Baltic was weakened by exactly those factors which were weakening it in Russia itself. Only a few leaders, like Chuikin in Narva, were able to distance themselves from the Communist past. Chuikin was rewarded by a high anti-independence vote in the referendum of 3 March 1991, whereas Daugavpils in Latvia, with an old-style, hardline Communist municipal council and a majority Russian population, produced – most surprisingly – a pro-independence vote, albeit by a small majority and on a low turnout.

The Baltic elections of February–March 1990 led to Soviet loyalist forces winning most of the seats in Russian-speaking areas. In Latvia, however, the Popular Front gained many Russian votes in the first round of voting on 18 March. By the second round in April, the storm of hostile Soviet propaganda which followed the Lithuanian declaration of independence had alarmed the Russian-speaking population, and the PF vote dropped sharply. The final results were: Popular Front candidates: 139 (including 6 Russian speakers, 2 Poles and 2 Jews); 'Equal Rights' candidates (backed by the Soviet Communist Party and/or Interfront): 62 (including 8 ethnic Latvians).[28]

Even allowing for a certain element of gerrymandering, and for the greater apathy of the Russian-speaking population (it is to be presumed, on the basis of the turnout figures in Daugavpils and other solidly Russian towns, that the majority of those not turning up to vote were Russian-speakers) this would still suggest a large minority of Russians voting for the Latvian PF, with smaller – though still substantial – minorities doing so in Lithuania and Estonia. Thus in the port town of Liepāja, with a 67 per cent Russian majority, the PF won 5 out of 9 seats, and in Riga, with a 63 per cent Russian-speaking population, it won 31 out of 69. On the other hand, it did not win a single seat in the overwhelmingly Russian eastern city of Daugavpils.

In Latvia, Soviet loyalist deputies grouped behind the 'Equal Rights' Faction of the parliament. Most had also been sponsored by Interfront and the pro-Soviet wing of the Latvian Communist Party. In Estonia, the Soviet loyalist deputies were formally divided between Interfront and the Communists, although they shared the same platform. In Lithuania, the Soviet loyalists (two Russians and six Poles), sat as members of the Soviet Communist Party until, during the military intervention of January 1991, the Poles joined the united Polish Faction, declaring its support for independence.

The parliamentary strategy of Soviet loyalists in the face of declarations of legal independence in all three republics was the same. Comprehending that they would in any case be defeated, they abstained, attempting to deny the legitimacy of the process. During the fifteen months before the August coup, while consistently opposing further moves towards independence, the loyalist blocs began to divide into more, and less, intransigent groups. In both Latvia and Estonia, the latter began to support the government in several areas of economic policy.

Further moves towards reconciliation in Estonia, however, were interrupted by the passage of a new Estonian citizenship law, defining most Russians as 'immigrants', and a new constitution leading to elections in September 1992. In both Estonia and Latvia, the Soviet loyalist forces were eliminated from parliament as a result of the disenfranchisement of the bulk of the Russian population in the elections of 1992 and 1993.

Alongside the Soviet loyalist parliamentary campaign went resistance by local authorities in Communist-dominated minority areas. In all three republics such councils declared that they would not follow laws passed by the new national parliaments which were in violation of the Soviet constitution.

After the seizure of the Lithuanian Procuracy by Soviet troops in April 1990 and the establishment of an alternative 'Procuracy of the Lithuanian SSR', attempts were made in several areas to detach the police (largely Russian and Polish) from the control of the Lithuanian Interior Ministry, and create islands of Soviet authority. Due in part to the small size and scattered nature of the Russian community in Lithuania, however, and in part to an effective mixture of bribes, diplomacy, and personal appeals by the Lithuanian Interior Minister, veteran Police General Marijonas Misiukonis, these attempts were frustrated. Defections were limited to some 150 in all, including those who had joined OMON in January 1991.

In Latvia, Soviet loyalist influence led to two near-mutinies – in May 1990 and January 1991 – among the overwhelmingly Russian police force of Riga when it rejected the Latvian Supreme Council's choice of Interior Minister, shouted down the Latvian leadership and loudly applauded hardline Soviet representatives. Several police districts declared they would ignore the orders of the Latvian Procuracy, but follow those of the Soviet Procuracy which had broken away from the Latvian institution. In ordinary police work, however, effective co-operation was in fact maintained.[29]

Now, after independence, considerable tension remains between these police forces and the new police battalion and Home Guard, recruited from Latvian volunteers alone and established by the Latvian government during the independence struggle; it is feared that, in the event of ethnic conflict, these units would be among the chief protagonists on either side (see Chapter 9).

In Estonia, a determined effort was made in summer 1990 to create alternative representative and administrative structures, based on Russian-dominated local councils and big factories. In the north-eastern town of Kohtla-Järve, a congress of Soviet loyalist deputies voted on 26 May to set up a two-tier 'Inter-regional Council' with authority over local government and industry. If it had worked, the Council might have posed a serious threat to Estonian stability. But failure seemed likely from the start: the opening meeting could not even achieve a quorum,

11 Arnolds Klausens, the Latvian Communist leader and (*behind*) Alfrēds Rubiks, at a Soviet loyalist meeting at the Second World War Victory Monument in Riga, October 1990.

while deputies known to oppose the scheme were barred entry by Soviet paratroopers guarding the event. Several months later the whole scheme collapsed, and Soviet strategy in Estonia reverted to the 'Integral Commission' already described. It marked a retreat from an attempt at representative authority to the 'fortresses' of the All-Union factories.

In Lithuania, meanwhile, the four months following the declaration of independence on 11 March 1990 had seen both a partial economic blockade by the Kremlin, and the occupation of buildings belonging to the Communist Party (purportedly to prevent their being unilaterally held by its pro-independence wing) and to the DOSAAF Soviet reserve military training organisation. The occupations were carried out mainly by Soviet Interior Ministry (MVD) troops, which exercised considerable restraint and appeared anxious to avoid harm to civilians.

Strikingly enough, there was during this period not a single instance of mass violence by the pro-Soviet Russian and Polish populations of Lithuania because, for all their efforts, the Soviet side simply could not rally sufficient local Soviet loyalists to provide the necessary cover. The only pro-Soviet demonstration involving more than 5,000 people was immediately after the declaration of independence; then there were approximately 30,000 demonstrators. Most demonstrations were not merely small, but also attended largely by the elderly. The sight of badly dressed, misshapen Russian women shrieking hysterically at these meetings was one with which every observer became familiar. It is not the stuff of which successful counter-revolutions are made. Demonstrations in Riga and Tallinn were equally small, despite the hundreds of thousands of Russians in those cities.

In fact, since the launch of the national movements, there have been only three demonstrations which showed any sign of turning seriously nasty. The first two occurred in Tallinn and Riga on 15 May 1990, eleven days after the Latvian parliament's declaration of legal independence.

I myself witnessed the demonstration outside the parliament building in Riga, attended largely by cadets from the Soviet Aviation Academy and soldiers in civilian dress. These were demanding a meeting with the government and the revocation of the declaration of *de jure* independence. The cadets clearly enjoyed pushing and shoving as they tried to break through the Latvian crowd and the police line guarding the building; but it was far from (as the Latvian government reported) 'an organised attempt by paratroopers to storm the parliament'. If it had been, the building would have been stormed, or the Latvian police would have had to open fire to prevent it.

The Tallinn demonstration was led by Mikhail Lysenko, and was rather more serious. Some of the ethnic Russian police guarding the parliament seem to have pulled back and allowed the demonstrators into the courtyard. But even they seemed bewildered about what to do next, and left quietly enough when masses of Estonians turned up in response to a government appeal over the radio.[30]

The third instance of mass violence, one with much more serious implications, was the Soviet loyalist demonstration in Vilnius in January 1991, which briefly broke into the parliament. Although the declared pretext was a protest against newly announced price rises, the incident was clearly part of a co-ordinated plan to destabilise Lithuania.

The irony of the 15 May demonstration in Riga was, in retrospect, that the military demonstrators were driven back by the Latvian OMON, or 'Black Berets', later to gain an infamous reputation. OMON, whose initials in Russian stand for the Special Purpose Militia Units, was set up throughout the Soviet Union during the summer of 1988 as riot squads in case of public disturbance.[31] The different OMON groups were placed under the command of the Republican interior ministries. In autumn 1990, however, as hardliners gained the ascendancy in the Soviet government, OMON in Latvia was placed under the Soviet Interior Ministry. Almost all the ethnic Latvians in the force soon quit. By autumn 1990 the Latvian OMON was in the forefront of Soviet pressure on the republic, and in January 1991 the Lithuanian OMON followed suit.

Soviet hardliners meanwhile, presumably by means of the KGB, had been escalating tension in the Baltic through a series of small and harmless bombings in the region, incidents which were then blamed on 'the Baltic nationalists', a lie so transparent that few Soviet loyalists even believed it. Immediately after the failed Moscow coup, there was a more serious bomb attack on the headquarters of the Estonian Home Guard in Tallinn, in which one man was seriously wounded. There has been no continuation of this strategy so far.

In Vilnius, military seizures during the period leading to the attacks on the television station and tower on 13 January 1991 were accompanied by the defection of the Lithuanian OMON, under its commander, Boleslaw Makutinowicz, to the Soviet side. Over the following months, Makutinowicz was joined by several dozen more local Russian and Polish police. If the Soviet plan to create a Communist-ruled Polish Autonomous Region in Lithuania had succeeded, Makutinowicz would presumably have been its Commander-in-Chief, its 'Napoleon of Soleczniki'.[32]

On 20 January 1991, after a series of attacks on other targets, the Latvian OMON stormed the Latvian Interior Ministry, killing two policemen. Two Latvian cameramen and a bystander were killed in the indiscriminate OMON firing that followed. While the exact motive for the attack is unclear, it is safe to assume that orders came from above. Various Soviet explanations, ranging from the rape by Latvian nationalists of an OMON officer's wife to OMON's being fired upon from the Interior Ministry were thin and contradictory. There have also been suggestions, on the Latvian side, that a 'third force' may have been involved, firing on OMON to provoke the attack, but that seems unlikely. According to the survivors of the Latvian camera crew, the shots that killed their colleagues clearly came from OMON.[33]

Mlynik and the Latvian OMON are also held by the Lithuanian Procurator's office to have been responsible for the cold-blooded murder of Lithuanian police and border guards at Medininkai on 30 July 1991.[34] The incident followed several months of OMON attacks on Baltic border posts in an attempt to destroy an obvious symbol of Baltic independence. Medininkai, however, was on a quite different scale. The earlier attacks had involved beatings and humiliations, but no-one had been killed. The Medininkai killings gave reason to fear that the hardline Soviet campaign of 'provocation' was moving on to a new level. Barely a fortnight later, however, the failure of the August counter-revolution ruined their schemes. The thought, however, that those responsible may still be present in the Baltic, waiting for an opportunity to restart the campaign, is obviously of deep concern to many Balts.

The failure of even moderate Soviet deputies in Latvia and Estonia to condemn the January killings (in contrast to the Polish Communist deputies in Lithuania) drove a deeper wedge between them and the national majorities; and so far as the Russian-speaking populations in general were concerned, Soviet violence seems indeed to have encouraged support for independence, or at least generated disgust at Soviet Communist rule. Soon afterwards, referenda on independence were held in all three Baltic governments. Whereas the great majority of Russians and Poles in Lithuania voted against the plan, in Estonia and still more in Latvia a very large minority of Russian-speakers voted in favour. As a Ukrainian woman engineer in Riga said:

> I am completely opposed to what happened in Vilnius and Riga in January, and I am going to vote for independence. I think that our lives will be better. The Soviet Union is backward and cannot join Europe. . . . Yes, I am a little worried about my status in a future Latvia, and I may be making a mistake to vote 'yes' . . . but I know that in democratic countries people are not divided into first and second class citizens. Besides, if we all had better living conditions, we would understand each other better.

Another Ukrainian, a worker, said she would vote against independence:

> No, I don't like what they did in January, but I think that Latvia should remain in the Soviet Union. Latvia cannot live without Soviet raw materials, and how are we going to buy them in the West? Or is the West going to give them to us for free? . . . Many different people live here and after the war we rebuilt Latvia together. My husband has been a factory

worker here for 30 years. My son is a sailor based here – he works in a crew with many nationalities. There are Latvians in the crew, but they are the minority, so naturally they must take account of the feelings of the others. . . . All these problems are caused by politicians and journalists, in the past all nationalities used to get on together and there were none of these problems.[35]

Both the Lithuanian and Latvian governments claimed that a majority of Russians had voted in favour of independence. This was also widely reported in the West, but an analysis of the results shows that the real figure in Latvia was between a quarter and a third of Russians voting. There is, on the other hand, good reason to believe opinion polls which throughout 1991 showed Chairman Anatolijs Gorbunovs, Prime Minister Ivars Godmanis, and Foreign Minister Jānis Jurkāns to be the three most popular political figures among Russians as well as Latvians far outstripping the Soviet loyalist leaders.

The failure of the Moscow counter-revolution led to a general collapse in the Soviet position throughout the Baltic, and to commensurate Soviet as well as international support for Baltic independence. The effect on the local Soviet loyalist forces was shattering: the loss of overt support from Moscow and the Soviet armed forces; the destruction of much of their structural base, the banning of the Communist Parties and allied organisations, the confiscation of their property, and the nationalisation of the 'All-Union' factories. For months afterwards, nothing was heard of these forces; and with the exception of north-east Estonia, their prestige has never recovered. Indeed, it is precisely because the Russian communities were so tied to the Communist and Soviet loyalist banner that, in Lithuania and Latvia at least, they now find themselves so divided and leaderless. At the same time the attitude of the Baltic nationalist parties to the Russians has hardened, and the debate over the rights of the Russian community has entered its most critical phase (see Chapter 8).

Apart from the remnants of the 'Equal Rights' group, Latvia contains several other Russian political formations, all at odds with one another. The largest is the 'Democratic Initiative' group, made up chiefly of former Soviet loyalists trying to reconstitute themselves as loyal would-be Latvian citizens. On the Right is the 'Russian Society of Latvia', headed by Colonel Romashov and other former hardliners, increasingly presenting themselves as traditional Russian nationalists. This body includes a good many military veterans. To the Right even of this, and a considerable embarrassment to most of the Russian representatives, are the Cossack Circle, which expresses open sympathy with the Cossacks fighting in Moldova. And finally, on the outer fringe, is the anti-semitic

Monarchist Club, the 'Russian Historical Society', and assorted crazies.[36]

Even in north-east Estonia, I sensed the mood of demoralisation and cowardice gripping the Communists when I travelled to Narva to interview the mayor, Vladimir Chuikin. At the last minute Chuikin evaded me, providing instead via one of his stooges a post-dated document 'proving' that he had been on leave during the coup, and giving a series of embarrassed excuses for the Narva Council's previous defiance of the Estonian constitution, destruction of Estonian border posts and creation of a pro-Soviet para-military force, the 'Workers' Detachments'. However, in October 1992, Chuikin and the former communists won convincing victories in local elections called by the Estonian government in an effort to unseat them.

This would obviously have been the moment for the Balts to appeal to moderation, and permanently split the Russian-speaking leadership. Indeed the Estonian Prime Minister, Edgar Savisaar, helped create a new force, the Russian Democratic Movement, with precisely that end in mind. The problem however was that the general swing of Estonian politics towards more radical nationalism did not permit Savisaar and his allies to make the concessions needed for an alliance with these groups.

The threat of north-east Estonia to secede from the republic seems now to have gone into abeyance. Vladimir Chuikin has become something of an expert at brinkmanship, threatening the Estonian government, yet never going too far. His hesitation may be based on fear of the consequences of secession, continued hope of Western aid for Narva, or doubt that a referendum on the subject would in fact gain the necessary support. In my own visits to Narva up to the summer of 1992, I found the overwhelming majority of local Russians opposed to secession, including those very critical of Estonian behaviour. 'After all, this is Estonian land', one elderly woman told me.

Defending the Legacy of Peter: The Soviet and Russian Military Presence

Although the Soviet military was deeply involved in the campaign to keep the Baltic republics within the Union, military action was in the end rather slight – principally because the Balts presented no legitimate excuse for an escalation. The killings of January and August 1991 were perpetrated by OMON or by only one military branch, the paratroopers.

The lack of common purpose among the military was especially evident during the August counter-revolution. Despite the fact that the Soviet officer corps in the Baltic was probably the most hardline and imperialist of the entire Union, by the second day of the coup it became clear that the plotters in Moscow had not taken even a fraction of the Baltic senior officers into their confidence. Military coups succeed in general when a substantial section of the officer corps is involved, and every regional commander has been carefully briefed on what to do, which buildings to occupy, and whom to arrest. In the Baltic, few garrison commanders were party to the plot, even if they sympathised with its goals: while they made formal declarations of states of emergency, they did nothing whatever to implement them during the three days the coup lasted.[37]

The military intervention of January 1991 also suggested a conspiracy in which too few people had been consulted, too few were fully committed, and too many were afraid of being left holding the buck. The picture that emerges from a report by the Democratic Officers' Movement, 'Shield', based largely on monitored radio exchanges, is one of considerable confusion, with junior officers requesting clear orders, and their superiors not giving them. Such orders as were given by radio were in some cases to open fire, in others to show restraint. (As for the Soviet procuracy report alleging that Lithuanians had attacked the soldiers, this was one of the most disgraceful single episodes of Gorbachov's presidency.) 'Shield' alleged that orders must have come directly from Gorbachov, but their only evidence was that according to the Soviet command structure, this was the procedure. As the attempted coup made apparent, however, the Soviet command structure had already begun to disintegrate.[38]

Paradoxically enough, the lack of cohesion may not necessarily prove, in the longer term, a positive factor. The greatest danger for Russia, the region, and even the Balts themselves could prove the disintegration of central command, and warlordism by Russian local commanders. There are already ample signs in Moldova of 'prancing proconsuls', dreaming of making a political name by 'defending' local Russians, and of returning in triumph to Moscow.

By late 1992, Russia had reached agreement with Lithuania on a military withdrawal by August 1993. Yeltsin, in September 1992, declared that no agreement can be made with Latvia and Estonia while they discriminate against local Russians, but Russian officials have indicated that they mean in any case to withdraw by the end of 1994. Indeed Yeltsin's suspension of withdrawal was described by Major-General Ziauddin Abdurrahmanov, the air-defence commander in Estonia, as 'incomprehensible', since it had already proceeded too far to be stopped. He observed that the bulk of the remaining military personnel were officers' families for whom no housing could be found in Russia.

Withdrawal from Estonia is in fact proceeding fast, and by September 1992, as I discovered during an unscheduled visit, much of the naval base at Paldiski had already been cleared. Western diplomats estimated that fewer than 15,000 Russian troops remained in the republic. As one officer admitted, after the introduction of the Estonian currency the army could simply no longer afford to feed itself.

The military in Latvia may present a tougher problem. Liepāja is one of the most important bases on the Baltic, and the nearby Skrunda space-radar station is both an expensive and important part of Russia's anti-ballistic missile defences – or so the Russians insist. If the Latvians were amenable, however, it should be possible to arrange joint control during a phased withdrawal period, but they have opposed it.

Russia favours a policy of gradual withdrawal in part because of the acute accommodation crisis within Russia itself. The line is supported by the 'Officers' Association' which has threatened to disobey the order to withdraw if the social needs of officers and their families are not guaranteed.[39] Since the grotesque promotion structure of the Soviet armed forces resulted in 22,000 of the 56,000 troops in Latvia being officers and NCOs, a considerable rump of disaffected soldiers may remain even if the conscripts disappear altogether.[40]

In recent years, the Soviet officer corps has had a special attitude to the Baltic for two reasons (apart from the fact of so many officers having settled there): firstly, the Balts were rightly seen as the cutting edge of the disintegration of the Soviet Union. Among some officers, this has led to a particular hatred of the Balts, which could pose a threat in future.

Secondly, Latvia and Estonia (or rather, the former state of Livonia) was the continuous object of Russian strategic ambitions since the fifteenth century. Older officers still see them as strategically vital. At the start of 1994, the armed forces and Russian government were still determined to keep the Skrunda radar station for at least 10 years. For the navy, the Baltic States cover by far the greater part of the former Soviet Baltic coastline, and include three naval bases, at Paldiski (Estonia), Liepāja (formerly Libau, Latvia) and Klaipeda (formerly Memel, Lithuania).

However, the naval bases are being abandoned. Many younger naval officers with whom I have spoken have attached no strategic significance to these bases, and say that their emotional significance is also much less than that of Sevastopol. A Lieutenant Commander (Captain Third Rank) in St Petersburg told me that,

> If we simply give Sevastopol and the Black Sea Fleet to the Ukraine, Russia ceases to be a Black Sea and Mediteranean power, and we lose much of our influence; but in the Baltic, even if we lose Paldiski and Liepāja, we still have St Petersburg and Kaliningrad. . . . Besides, the whole concept of the need for Baltic bases is outdated. They don't really defend Russia, and even if they did, it would be against NATO. Does anyone seriously still think we are going to go to war with NATO, or NATO with us?[41]

The specific naval identity within the former Soviet (and now Russian) armed forces is of some interest in view of the likely future role of the military in Russia's government. Throughout the Soviet period, the navy maintained the strongest traditions of the old Russian imperial service. Its officers tended to be better educated than those in the army, and more likely to hold covertly anti-Soviet views. This led, in the early 1980s, to the formation of a dissident group within the Baltic fleet, eliminated by the KGB, and is the spirit which may have contributed to the attempted defection of a Soviet frigate to Sweden. The navy indeed was the first Soviet service to fly the 'Andreyevsky flag'.

While the symbolic transition from Soviet to Russian allegiance is easier for the navy than for the army, the fall of the Soviet Union has in reality been even more painful for the navy, for two reasons. The first is the threatened loss of historic bases at Sevastopol and, to a lesser extent, in the Baltic. The second is the pervasive loss of a sense of purpose. There are good reasons to fear that the Russian army will have a function in the future; the navy's strategic forces by contrast look completely pointless. Paradoxically, but not unnaturally, the navy, despite its past liberalism, may therefore be the most chauvinist and belligerent of the services in the years to come.

The naval command's desire to keep Liepāja was also fuelled by the astonishing degree of 'spontaneous privatisation' now occurring within the Baltic fleet – the diversion of naval equipment and facilities for the private profit of individual officers or of the officer corps as a whole. The Latvians, seeking the return of the port of Liepāja, handed by Moscow to the fleet in 1965, have been blandly referred to as a shadowy 'private corporation' called 'Russo-Balt-West', apparently directed by the fleet command in Kaliningrad. The navy claims simply to have 'rented' the port to the 'corporation' – an act worthy of Captain Kidd. Profits are being used 'for the social needs of the servicemen'. In Tallinn, a 'private company' called 'Fonon', using naval vehicles leased by three logistics officers to themselves, is prospering. On 27 July 1992, a clash occurred when Estonian troops attempted to recover a military building which had been sold to Fonon, and were driven out by Russian marines.[42]

In December 1991 I spoke with two young naval lieutenants in St Petersburg, identified only as Alexander and Oleg. Both were leaving the service shortly. Alexander explained that,

> The best professionals are leaving the fleet, and the ones who are staying are the older officers and those who are not so bright. This is not good for Russia or the world in general, [because] the former Zampolits (political officers), though the more intelligent and modern officers laugh at them, do have a certain influence, and they are encouraging the spread of extreme, even fascistic ideas.

They differed on the issue of the Baltic bases. Oleg declared that,

> We must keep those bases, because if the Baltic States separate completely, we would be almost cut off from the Baltic Sea. We would lose everything that Russia has gained since the time of Peter the Great.

Western pressure to leave would, he added, be 'interference in our internal affairs', and would encounter a furious response from the officer corps. With a grin, Alexander observed, 'This is the imperial point of view. I don't think that these bases are important'; but he added that:

> The duty of the armed forces will be to defend Russians wherever they live ... the proposal to disenfranchise Russians living in the Baltic is particularly bad and dangerous. ... The Balts should remember that at the moment, Russians are still looking for a national identity. If, due to attacks on Russians by other nationalities, this identity turns out to be an extreme Great Russian one, then the Balts could be wiped from the face of the earth.

Since the collapse of the Soviet Union, and its reversal of the approach of the final Gorbachov years, Yeltsin's government has been more friendly towards Lithuania than towards the other two Baltic States. Lithuania seems sometimes to respond, as in the case of the agreement on withdrawal between Yeltsin and Landsbergis in January 1992. The difference in the Russian approach seems based on both contemporary and historical factors. The principal reason for Russian hostility towards Latvia and Estonia today is their treatment of Russian minorities; in Lithuania there are far fewer and they have received full access to citizenship. Historically Russia was more interested in access to the Baltic through the former Livonia, while the ethnic Lithuanian lands were not incorporated into Russia until the end of the eighteenth century. Today, the main Soviet strategic interest in Lithuania is as a corridor to the Kaliningrad (Koenigsberg) enclave.[43]

More important in the long run than the strategic and historical dreams of the older officers is the fact that, under Soviet rule, the Baltic States, and especially Latvia, have been a favourite retirement spot for officers, often given jobs within the local administration – especially in the housing departments, which facilitated the settlement of yet more officers. Retired military personnel became part of the backbone of the Soviet loyalist movement in Latvia. Naturally it provoked furious resentment among the Latvians: in the Latvian citizenship law Soviet veterans are explicitly excluded from citizenship. The Latvian radical nationalists advocate the denial of residence permits to officers and calls for their expulsion; a good deal of administrative harrassment is allegedly already occurring in respect of the allocation of accommodation and of residence permits to Russians returning to Latvia from military service in Russia.

This in turn angers not only the veterans but Russians in general, because in Liepāja, for example, veterans and their families are said to constitute almost a sixth of the population. General Fyodr Melnichuk has said that in its negotiations on withdrawal, the army insisted on citizenship for veterans: 'for us it is a matter of honour and duty to look after the interests of former soldiers'. The demand was echoed by the Chairman of the Officers' Association, Colonel Vladimir Kandalovsky.[44] If the military adheres to this condition for withdrawal, they could be there forever. By October 1992, Yeltsin was including the rights of veterans among the conditions demanded from the Balts for military withdrawal.

The great fear of the Balts is that military activity is continuing in the form of the covert provision of arms to former Soviet hardliners in the region, in preparation for a revolt along the lines of that in Transdniestria. While there is no proof, it is plausible enough; General Melnichuk admitted to me that theft and illegal sales of arms are occurring, although limited to thirty-six cases during the previous year, and those the work of criminals. A Russian manager in Narva reported in June 1992 that he was concerned about the quantity of guns available in the town. These were in the hands of security guards and private individuals, but could in a crisis be put to political use.

This fear lay at the core of the campaign of the Baltic governments to remove Russian armed forces from their territory. It gained considerable Western support which, in turn, seems to have edged Moscow towards withdrawal. By early summer 1992, the Balts appeared to have successfully blocked attempts to bring in large numbers of new conscripts, an important element in the rapid diminution of the military presence. Succeeding months saw a series of incidents in both Lithuania and Estonia in which nationalist forces tried to stop 'unlicensed' movement within the republics and, in Estonia, to seize military buildings by force. Both sides however exercised restraint, with the Balts firing at the tyres of vehicles and the Russians into the air. General Melnichuk observed (whether sincere or not):

> We have experience of this process in Germany and Hungary; we know that the withdrawal of the troops is unavoidable. But during this withdrawal period, we must have an internationally recognised status of forces agreement to avoid the possibility of clashes. . . . We have officers here who are veterans of Afghanistan. How do you think they feel when some eighteen-year-old Lithuanian kid sticks a loaded pistol in their face and tells them to stop when they leave the base to go shopping? There is a real danger of our officers' patience breaking, though we believe that we

12 Soviet veterans of the Second World War at a commemorative meeting near the junction of the Russian, Byelorussian and Latvian borders, July 1990.

have persuaded them that they are now in a foreign country and that it is their duty to keep calm.[45]

By autumn 1992, it seemed as if such talk was already bluff, just as the Russian government was deliberately exaggerating the numbers of Russian troops in the Baltic, presumably for bargaining purposes. On the ground, in Estonia and Lithuania at least, the whole military position was crumbling. Morale was very low, with officers embittered by low pay and the atrocious living conditions of their families, anxious either to leave (if accommodation were available in Russia) or to resign from the army altogether and seek work in the Baltic – if permitted to do so.

In September 1992, led by some Estonian Greens, I entered the Soviet military base at Paldiski by driving through a large hole in the fence. While the whole peninsular was technically off-limits, it was obvious that the navy had neither the men nor the will to guard it. (They were, however, still guarding the two nuclear reactors, shut off but not yet dismantled.) This is land from which Estonian farmers were expelled when the navy took over, now covered with thick, uncut young forests.

Surreal monuments to military wastefulness occur at random, like a field covered with large mooring buoys, inspected by grazing cows.

The former submarine harbour was guarded by a middle-aged Russian woman in jeans. She turned us away – so we found another gap. The submarine facilities had been abandoned and wrecked. Several of the large repair sheds had been burnt, and around them lay piles of smashed equipment and pools of diesel. Rain beat through holes in the roof and windows, soaking the shreds of military documents scattered over the floor and washing down Communist slogans painted on the walls.

Amidst the desolation, a single building was operating – a small power station serving the town. It appeared to be manned by three Russian grandmothers in black dresses, like the final chorus of a tragedy. Snaking through the land were curious thin trenches, where pipes and communication cables had been ripped up to be sold for scrap. Civilian fishermen lined the harbour wall. 'Some are fishing for fish, and some for copper,' declared our guide.

Not all the ruination however was the product of withdrawal; much of it, like a half-finished pier of crumbling concrete blocks, had obviously been there for years, a symbol of the long decay of the Soviet armed forces, so curiously unobserved by Western military intelligence.

It took an hour for a marine patrol to find us. Its composition was representative of the closing days of the Soviet military in the Baltic: two Commanders (Captains Second Rank), one Lieutenant Commander, two Lieutenants – and seven privates. They took us to the school for submarine officers which, though closed for several months, still housed the office of the admiral commanding the base, a spot of light approached down endless dark and abandoned corridors.

Rear Admiral Alexander Olkhovikov was a pioneer of the Soviet nuclear submarine forces, and a former student at Paldiski. His mood during our interrogation – for having 'violated military property' – was curious. On one hand, he was clearly powerless, the interview having a purely ritual character of which he was fully aware. At the same time, he was clearly suffused with an almost ungovernable rage. His subordinate officers by contrast seemed merely depressed and resigned, complaining about their living standards, their pay, and above all their uncertain future: 'We are all living on our suitcases, waiting for withdrawal, but we don't know where to'. I asked one about the picture of Lenin still hanging above the Admiral's desk. 'It's a work of art,' he replied sardonically.

Standing in front of a crumbling marble plaque honouring the school's prizewinning students – which would be taken to Petersburg in the final withdrawal – an elderly commander with a grey moustache told me he had spent his entire life in the navy, and now probably faced early retirement. He was going to have to survive on a pension, 'or rather, a joke,' as he said. The only home for him, his wife and their fourteen-year-old son would be the tiny flat of his mother, in Kazan in the Tartar Autonomous Republic; 'but they have separatists there too, don't they?'

Kaliningrad and the Kaliningrad Question

The future of the 21,000 square kilometre Kaliningrad enclave (or rather exclave) is beginning to worry Western chancelleries. A fantasy writer might indeed think of using its fate as the origin of the Third World War; enough countries have claims to the former East Prussia, although most seem happier to preserve *the status quo* than risk the enclave going to their rivals.

Marion Countess Doenhoff, the former Editor of *Die Zeit* and member of an old East Prussian landowning family, has suggested a Russian-Polish-German condominium, though her colleagues reportedly rejected the idea as too dangerously redolent of German expansionism, and very difficult to administer. This would indeed be so, given the ethnic composition of the 960,000-strong population. It is drawn from all over the former Soviet Union, but is completely Russified. The entire German population fled or was massacred during the Soviet advance of 1944–45.

During my first visit, in 1991, the Chairman of the Executive Committee was called Anatoly Yusuf, and had a Tartar father and a Russian mother. A Russian intellectual with German historic interests said disdainfully that 'here, you find the pure form of Soviet Man – a mixture of people from different areas, with no cultures of their own. They even speak pure Soviet Russian'. Ida Zhurba, formerly head of the cultural section of the regional administration, told me that the first task in the region was to establish some kind of Russian culture. She pointed out that, until 1988, there was not a single Russian Orthodox Church in the whole region, and theatre and music were conspicuously underdeveloped.

I asked Alexander Khmurchik, a former seaman turned jovial *apparachik*, and editor of *Kaliningradskaya Pravda*, whether there was a strong local loyalty in the population. He replied,

> There are very nice girls here. They dress better than in the rest of Russia, because the seamen bring them back Western clothes. But a local patriotism? If there is such a thing, it is concentrated on the desire to gain local prosperity by making this a Free Trade Zone.

Ida Zhurba remarked,

> What is special about us? The rain! And that there is always fish to eat. Also, that we are a very naval town, strongly marked by the military. But beyond that, I wouldn't say that ordinary people here feel especially like 'Kaliningraders'.

Things have moved on since then, and rather artificial attempts are in progress to 'rediscover' a local identity by exploring the pre-1945 history of the area. Various shops and publications have appeared using the name 'Koenigsberg'. Some local intellectuals call themselves 'neo-Prussians' and stress their distance from Russia. For the name of the city, some have suggested Kantgrad, after its most famous son, though it is hard to believe that he would have approved. The monument to Kant, on the wall of the ruined Cathedral, together with that to Schiller, are the only two German monuments left standing in the centre of the city.

The name Kaliningrad, after the vile Soviet President under Stalin, Mikhail Kalinin, is indeed a severe embarrassment. The Russian city of Kalinin has reverted to its ancient name of Tver. Changing Kaliningrad back to Koenigsberg however is hardly possible. It would almost imply a German claim, and besides, as Yusuf said,

> Koenigsberg was completely destroyed. For better or worse, this is a new city, with a new population. . . . If it were proved that Kalinin was a criminal, we might be forced to change the name, but then we should find a neutral one, like Pribaltiisk ['City on the Baltic'].

One ingenious proposal has been to go back to the name Koenigsberg (the King's fortress) but in a Russian form: Korolgrad, just as the Lithuanians call it Karaliauskas, and the Poles, Krolewiec. The military presence, already strong, grew greatly after 1990 as a result of Soviet-Russian military withdrawal, first from Eastern Germany and Poland, then from the Baltic States. This led to severe housing problems, as well as fears in Poland and especially Lithuania about the presence of such massive forces on their borders. These forces, however, appeared in 1993 to be in full decay.

The military presence also does not necessarily make Kaliningrad politically conservative. Alexander Ostakhov, editor of the reformist *Prospekt Mira*, said that the naval officers on the local council are often more liberal than the former Communist officials, 'because they have travelled and seen the West', and because of their high technical education. Many officers, especially from the fleet, have moved successfully into private business. The Kaliningrad area as a whole voted strongly for Boris Yeltsin in the presidential elections of June 1991, and reformist candidates looked set to do relatively well in the parliamentary elections of December 1993.

The Russian military, and Russian nationalists in general are, however, certainly determined to retain Kaliningrad as their last military base on the southern Baltic, and as Russia's last prize from the Second World War (apart from the Kuriles, of course). As Yusuf put it, 'we are holding Russia's Western gate'. Unless therefore Russia were to disintegrate completely – and this does not seem likely – Kaliningrad will not be up for grabs. Both Russian and local leaders have stressed repeatedly that it is inalienable Russian territory.

Germany, from which East Prussia was taken in 1945 and its German population driven out, renounced territorial claims in the East as part of the treaty on German reunification in 1990. For a long time to come, therefore, the German state cannot hope to recover the territory, and will have no interest in doing so. Quite apart from the question of what to do with the Russian inhabitants, a move by Germany over Kaliningrad would raise suspicions of German expansionism all over Eastern Europe. In particular it would cause the deepest alarm in Poland.

For that very reason, Poland itself could hardly make a claim, for fear of raising the spectre of German claims to its own previously German lands. Agitation in Poland for the annexation of the territory has been restricted to the extreme Right, although centrist politicians and even government officials have spoken of the possibility of its future becoming moot.

Lithuanians would dearly like to claim the territory, which they call 'Lesser Lithuania'. It used to have a largely Lithuanian-speaking population (see Chapter 6, n. 26), and still contains between 18,000 and 30,000 Lithuanians; but Vilnius fears both the Germans and the Poles, and certainly does not wish to put itself in the position of Estonia and Latvia by annexing another 960,000 ethnic Russians. The destabilising factor in this scenario may therefore be not so much international as internal: on the one hand, the uncertain future of Russian democracy and government, raising fears of dictatorship and disintegration; on the other, the economic state of the territory itself.

Although by 1993 Kaliningrad's economy was beginning to undergo a slow and painful transformation, its people were still dependent to a dangerous extent on military bases and a crumbling military industrial complex precariously supplied from Russia, and now in full decline. Although the local fishing and cellulose industries remain dynamic, and there were some 75,000 German tourists in 1992, it is not clear that they can fill this gap. As Ostakhov declared, with a touch of pride, in June 1991,

> There is much talk of converting the military industries, but at present we are still trying to find out what they are actually making . . . . Conversion will also certainly mean fewer jobs, and less work for our highly-trained engineers. After all, these were not cheap handicraft industries for tourists – we have a factory here which makes engines for ballistic missiles.

The local authorities, whose leaders seem intelligent and active, are trying to create a 'free trade zone', but are facing huge obstacles, quite apart from the long delay in ratification by Moscow which was imposed by the political struggle. St Petersburg, Belarus and indeed the Baltic States themselves are all drawing up inept plans of this kind ('too many bridges and not enough traffic', as a Riga banker told me). Despite the proposed incentives in terms of tariffs and taxes, the isolated position of Kaliningrad and the political turmoil in Russia has so far discouraged large-scale Western investment.

Moreover, because Kaliningrad was a closed military area, the first Western ship since 1945 docked in the port only in June 1991, so until then local people lacked even those limited direct contacts with Western traders common to other Soviet ports. Mr Yusuf told me in June 1990 that the local council had never even been informed by the Defence Ministry how much freight was passing through their territory. The main road across Lithuania to Belarus and Russia is very attractive, still lined with trees dating back to Prussian days – and has been neither widened nor repaired since then. The old German Autobahn to Berlin had however, by the end of 1993, been largely restored with German help.

After 1991, small-scale private trade grew enormously, above all with Poland. By the end of 1993, 615 joint ventures had been founded, most of them with Polish and German firms and connected with small-scale import-export enterprise. Large numbers of local people had entered the trade, soaking up the unemployed not only from the factories but also from the armed forces. Very slowly the appearance of the city began to change, and by December 1993 the main avenue featured both an excellent pizza restaurant and a seedy sex shop. On the other hand it was still called Leninsky Prospekt: as with the city itself, reverting street names to their German originals, or finding new ones, had so far proved politically and emotionally too difficult.

The idea has been raised of resettling in Kaliningrad the 'Volga Germans', deported to Central Asia by Stalin during the Second World War. It has been supported by some right-wing German groups, but not by the German government. Fearful of the growing nationalism of the Central Asian populations, the two or so million Germans remaining in Kazakhastan and elsewhere are leaving in increasing numbers, and by the end of 1993 some seven thousand had settled in Kaliningrad. They have been tolerated by the local population partly because most are now far more Russian than German in culture – few speak German, and most have intermarried with other nationalities. Some local Russians speak far better German than the Russian-Germans, having learned it through business, study in Germany or by acting as tourist guides. None fears German re-annexation.

Having sold their property in Central Asia for a pittance, most of the Russian-Germans in Kaliningrad are dreadfully poor, generating pity rather than fear. Local people hope that they may draw German aid to the region, but so far this has proved illusory, precisely because Bonn has been extremely anxious not to raise Russian fears. A few private German aid workers have taken an interest in the enclave. Representatives of the German neo-Nazi groups have also unobtrusively scouted out the enclave, but they are very much on the fringe of German politics.

Whether sufficient Soviet Germans would move to make the enclave into a German territory, and whether the local Russian population would tolerate it, however, seems extremely doubtful. With the idea of recreating their old territory on the Volga effectively still-born in the face of local Russian resistance, most Germans leaving Kazakhastan head straight for the flesh-pots of Germany.

Tourism from Germany is increasing, but is hindered by the very assiduity with which the new Soviet rulers flattened the remains of the city after 1945. The new concrete city centre presents an appearance which is bleak and ugly even by Soviet standards, in tragic contrast to the beauties of Koenigsberg befor Hitler's War.

Germans who lived in Koenigsberg before 1945 sometimes burst into tears at the sight of it now, from shock rather than from nostalgia. They wander the streets, pursued by child-beggars, their eyes fixed on remembered buildings that no-one else can see, their minds full of the appalling sufferings of their flight from East Prussia in 1945, which even other Germans have long forgotten. For the Russians the tourists symbolise the isolation and alienation of exile in a particularly painful form. A more cheerful sight are the fine beaches and small spa towns along the coast. These were not so badly damaged in the War, and like the surviving suburbs of Koenigsberg, retain a German bourgeois charm, with their quaint neo-Gothic villas.

One potential danger stems from the fact that local agriculture cannot sustain the local population. Much of the rural population looks diseased, drunken, elderly and hopeless. Until the end of 1993, imports from Poland and the West had stabilised the food situation. If supplies to the enclave were to break down altogether, the West may have to bear the responsibility, which in turn might one day awaken German ambitions, unlikely though this seems today. One hope for the region, on the other hand, might be that Western and especially German and Scandinavian aid will flow to Kaliningrad precisely to prevent the area becoming a source of destabilisation.*

---

* *The New York Review of Books* of 13 May 1993 contains an article by Amos Elon on Kaliningrad entitled 'The Nowhere City'; it contains an evocative description but, in my view, exaggerates the geopolitical instability of the enclave's future, and the possibility of a German claim. The most thorough German discussion of the enclave is *Koenigsberg morgen: Luxemburg an der Ostsee*, by Wilfried Boehm and Ansgar Graw (Blau Aktuelle Reihe, 1993). It concedes that the area will have to stay under Russian sovereignty, but suggests sponsorship by the Council of Europe and other Western organisations.

8

The Independence Movements and their Successors, 1987–92

'We shall endure. All overlords will go.
Away the stranger, who has seized your land.
Time has decided, time has decreed it so.'
            – Imants Auziņš

A Confusion of Terms

In the looking-glass world of post-Communist politics, few parties or institutions are quite what they seem, and few politicians say quite what they mean. This is not always intentional; one of the most difficult though fascinating aspects of writing about the Soviet region results from the almost complete lack of conceptual landmarks. Nothing quite like these events has ever occurred before, so there are no analytical models to fall back upon, and few of the usual terms and descriptions really fit. Until new models and descriptions are developed, however, we have to continue using the old ones. The problem is that local politicians and journalists, wishing to imitate the West – or simply for want of anything better – use these false models to describe themselves and then play them back to us, thus confirming naive Western observers in their own misconceptions. The result is a real mirror-game, a copulation of illusions.

Thus the 'conservative' (his own description) Latvian politician, Valdis Šteins, published in a Riga-based English-language newspaper in July 1992 a portrait of the Latvian political spectrum based on a comparison with that of the European Parliament. He described the range of parties, from communists through socialists, liberals, conservatives and so on, concluding that 'we can see . . . that the political spectrum in Latvia is very wide, and that it corresponds to the situation in other European countries. . . .'[1]

Few Western observers, without a detailed knowledge of the region, would distrust this apparently factual, objective and soberly-written account. Yet it gives a completely (though quite possibly unconsciously) false picture of the real state of Latvian party politics in the summer of 1992. In the first place, Šteins creates this neat picture by virtue of leaving out all the Russian deputies, thereby ignoring the central national tension in Latvian politics as a whole. By doing so he is also able to categorise most of the Latvian nationalist parties as 'Centre-Right', whereas in terms of their attitudes to the Russians, most can only be called 'Extreme-Right' or 'radical nationalist'. Moreover the Latvian 'parties' are by-and-large no such thing, but simply groups of individuals gathered around particular leaders, slogans or interests. Up to the time of writing, they have no party organisation, no structure, no registered membership, no policy-making bodies, and most emphatically no party discipline. The 'parties' in the country and 'factions' of the same name within the parliaments are usually only tenuously connected, and sometimes completely at odds. In the opaque primeval soup of Baltic politics, these political amoebas split, form new transient unions, and split again.

Some of the formations which have arisen in all three republics over the past two years have barely had the lifespan of mayflies. (The 'conservative' Šteins, for example, began as a social democrat.) They have also been as numerous as mayflies. There are, in Latvia today, four 'political parties' each of which claims exclusive representation of the interests of farmers. Interest-group politics of the most crass kind is mitigated only by the divisions in the respective interest groups.

One could perhaps speak of two fundamental interest groups: those who belonged to the former Communist establishment (or who believe they stand to lose from certain kinds of reform), and the 'new men'. Parliamentary debates on privatisation have certainly provided ample examples of the way ex-Communist deputies from widely differing parties have tended to pull together to defend establishment interests. But as we have seen in Chapter 4, this does not mean at all that the former establishment opposes reform as such, let alone that it necessarily represents a 'Left-wing' position in the Western sense. The 'Secure Home' Party in Estonia, founded by former Communist state managers and officials, describes itself as 'Right-wing', and so, in most respects, it is. It just wants privatisation to be as far as possible to its own supporters' advantage.

An analysis of contemporary politics in terms of standard Western 'Left–Right' ideological pattern makes little sense in the Baltic. In the West, national questions of course play a part, but the real distinguishing and opposing policies are in the area of economic and social policy. Within the Baltic, no clear comparable Left–Right division is visible. There, and in much of the former Communist world, the great defining features are attitudes to history, nationality and (particularly in Lithuania), culture.

Apart from questions of personal history – such as membership of the Communist Party (or the KGB) on one side, or the dissident movement on the other – ideological division focuses on attitudes to the pre-1940 republics. The commitment of most within the 'Right' to the restoration of private agriculture is as much connected with this view, as with a desire for efficiency. Indeed some are committed to restoring to each family precisely the land that belonged to it before 1940, irrespective of the effect on current farming practice (see Chapter 9). The most accurate description of this mindset would be 'radical restitutionist'.

Congress movements in Latvia and Estonia were founded on the explicit premise that the forms of the 'First Republics', in particular in relation to citizenship, had remained unbroken by Soviet rule and should be restored as before and in their entirety. For their part, most of the leaders of the Popular Fronts, while they stressed the legal continuity of independence, also tended to believe that the new states should be based on 'existing realities', particularly as regards the position of the new Russian populations in the region. The gradual shift on this issue of large sections of the Popular Front towards a position closer to that of the Congress was a central political theme between 1990 and 1992.

In Lithuania, attitudes towards the dictatorship of Smetona and its legacy of authoritarian nationalism represent a major demarcation. It is connected to the essentially cultural question of whether Lithuania should move closer to the West or, as the more nationalist tradition would have it, seek a uniquely Lithuanian way of its own.[2] For the Lithuanian 'Right', nationalist attitudes are linked to their obsession with the history of Lithuanian-Polish relations, a factor which is of much less concern to the Centre or 'Left'.

In Latvia and Estonia, the Right's desire to restore the pre-1940 republics and their citizenships is closely linked to the desire to exclude – or even expel – the Russian-speakers who moved into the republics under Soviet rule, or at least make them undergo a rigorous naturalisation procedure, whereas proponents of the 'Second Republic' have taken a more compromising stand. The best means of describing the political scene in Latvia and Estonia is through a grid, rather than a spectrum, the centre point of which represents moderation in policy:

(for Estonia):

Left	*First Republic*
	Est. Citizen
	Nat. Ind. Party
Moderates	
	Fatherland

Popular Front	
	Secure Home
Est. Communist Party	
Russian Dem. Movement	
Second Republic	*Right*

Thus in Estonia, the Fatherland (*Isamaa*) block, with its commitment both to the First Republic and to free market economics, stands squarely on the horizontal line on the right of the grid, and fairly close to the centre. Edgar Savisaar's Popular Front stands in the same position on the Left side. Marju Lauristin's Social Democrats began with Savisaar but subsequently moved to occupy a position close to the vertical line within the top, 'First Republic-Left' half of the grid, but also close to the Centre.

The 'Secure Home' (*Kindel Kodu*) alliance stands in a curious position. In terms of its current policies, it supports both the First Republic and free-market policies (as it ought, given so many of its members have become capitalist proprietors). Because of the Communist background of its members, however, it is identified by all the other parties as behind a 'New Republic'. *Kindel Kodu* also opposes restitution of pre-1940 property and wants to preserve collective farms as co-operatives under their existing management. Placing a party like this within any spectrum would be problematic.

The extreme nationalist 'Estonian Citizen' group of Colonel Juri Toomepuu stood, in 1992, somewhere beyond the fringe and in the top right-hand corner. Given its members' propensity for populism, the group might in future move sharply to the Left on economic policy, even

217

though it will always remain within the 'First Republic' section. This is true of all the parties now called 'Right-Wing'; in the Baltic. Their commitment to the 'First Republic' is unshakeable, so great in fact that by comparison it completely dwarfs economic policy. Their commitment to the economic policy of the Right-hand corner is modest, and relatively liable to be drowned within a 'First Republic' tradition of anti-capitalist populism.

For an extreme example of a 'Left-wing' (or rather populist-opportunist) party now strongly committed to a 'First Republic' position, one has the former Latvian Communist Party, now called the Democratic Labour Party. This would be well out along the vertical line of the top half of the grid. Its leader, Juris Bojārs, illustrates the wonderful opportunities for populism and the changing of position within a system in which clear economic policies seem not to be required.

Bojārs is an ex-KGB Major and 'international lawyer' who emerged from the Popular Front. By switching to a strongly nationalistic position, he has ingratiated himself with the now-dominant nationalist element without losing his ability to appeal to the workers with Left-wing attacks on the government's free-market reform. Whether this will succeed in propelling him into a future Latvian government seems doubtful, however, for he is widely mistrusted, and may be barred from standing for parliament because of his KGB past. In both Latvia and Estonia, though not in Lithuania, the phenomenon of former Communists trying to engineer a comeback through an appeal to nationalism has been manifest.

Analysing the political scene is made still more difficult by the fact that the mass of the population is so extremely indifferent to it. In these circumstances public opinion polls, and even elections, tend to give a false picture. When, in July 1992, I conducted my own limited 'vox pop' survey on thirty individuals in Riga, not a single one expressed support for any particular political party or indeed any political leader. Even general political views seemed unfocused and not very strongly held.

Moreover, this was the case not simply after the achievement of independence but, to a surprising degree, during the independence struggle. It indicates that although the vast bulk of the indigenous populations was deeply committed to independence, cynicism about and detachment from the independence movements themselves was far greater than the rallies and demonstrations suggested.

This was demonstrated too by the huge vote for the former Communists, and against Landsbergis and his rump Sajūdis, in the Lithuanian elections of October 1992. To a far greater degree than most observers realised – and this is no doubt true of many revolutions – nationalist struggle in the former Soviet Union has been largely a function of small groups of activists, working upon much vaguer feelings held by the population as a whole.

Under Landsbergis, between 1990 and 1992, nationalist activists attempted to stamp Lithuania with their own neo-traditionalist vision, a product partly of genuine religious and cultural values, and partly of a paranoid fear of Poland, Russia, of internal traitors, and indeed of the cultural influence of the West. The story of these years is the story of the failure of this vision, though it would be unwise to predict that it has failed forever.

Lithuania, like many Communist countries, was profoundly changed by Communist rule, far more so than Landsbergis realised. One crucial difference was that peasant conservatism, largely (though by no means entirely) attached, during the First Republic, to clerical nationalism, tended this time to be aligned with the former Communists, so long as these had taken a stand against Moscow.

The nationalists also suffered from the fact that decades of Communist Party rule had discredited the very term 'party'. Many politicians attempt to dissociate themselves from allegiance to a particular party, presenting themselves as somehow standing above party politics, and ironically enough the most successful practitioners of this approach – Rüütel and Gorbunovs in the Baltic, and Edvard Shevardnadze in Georgia, all emerged from the womb of the Party of Parties.

The Rise of the National Movements, 1987–90

No-one, Balt or non-Balt, who witnessed the great pro-independence demonstrations of 1988–91 will forget them or the tremendous emotional impact they had: the songs, the tears, the sense of relief as people were able to say in public things which for fifty years they had been scared even to whisper in private; 'For ye shall know the truth, and the truth will make you free'.[3]

The speed of the independence process was due partly to the sheer size of the nationalist demonstrations and their cumulative effect in undermining the will of the Communist rulers. Most striking of all was the 'Baltic Way' of 23 August 1989, when two million Balts (two-fifths of the entire native population of the region) formed a continuous 370 mile human chain from Vilnius through Riga to Tallinn to demand independence. Between the first demand, in April 1988, for an Estonian Popular Front, to the Lithuanian declaration of independence on 11 March 1990 was a period of only twenty-three months. During the final months, in the autumn of 1989, the East European revolutions provided an added impetus; prior to that the Baltic independence process had been mainly self-generating, and had itself stimulated similar movements elsewhere in the Soviet empire.

To many Western observers (and indeed to Gorbachov himself), the

Baltic independence movements appeared to spring from nowhere. They were, however, preceded and accompanied by pro-independence groups stemming from the Baltic dissident movements, which took, and still take, a more radical line than the 'Popular Fronts' and their successors.

The first autonomous political action in the Baltic States during Gorbachov's presidency came from the tradition of ecological protest which had long had a partially tolerated place in the Soviet (and especially Russian) scene, and which was therefore difficult to suppress. In all three republics, however, national concerns were either close to the surface or completely open. In Estonia, opposition to state plans for phosphate mining was motivated by a genuine fear of further wastelands like the oil-shale mining areas of north-east Estonia, but also because the plan involved bringing in thousands of Russian workers. There was opposition to similar industrial development in Latvia and Lithuania, and in all three republics the Communist leadership itself gradually usurped such popular demands in an effort to regain popularity.

In Lithuania, plans by Moscow to expand the republic's ecologically-dangerous chemicals industry was one factor leading to the formation of Sajūdis in June 1988. The core of ecological protest, however, involved the building of a fourth reactor at the Ignalina nuclear power plant, already the biggest in the Western Soviet Union, opposition to which swelled of course following the disaster at Chernobyl in April 1986. Baltic servicemen were among the soldiers and workers, often completely unprotected, used in the Chernobyl clean-up operation. Subsequent rumours played a major part in stimulating Baltic anger, as did the appalling treatment often meted out to Baltic (and other) soldiers in the Soviet army.

Several leading contemporary Baltic politicians cut their political teeth in the ecological protests during the first three years of Gorbachov's rule. The term 'Green' is however one of those Western words which needs to be treated with caution when applied to the Baltic States. In all three countries, the Green parties stand on the nationalist Right, and their current main activity is agitation for the removal of the Russian armed forces. The connection of the Greens with the Right is partly to do with the fact that both stemmed originally from the nationalist dissident cause. It has also deep cultural roots in the centrality of nature to Baltic national culture, extending in the case of some nationalists to something like a 'blood and soil' ideology identifying the Baltic nations with the land.

In Estonia, another very important proto-political force was the National Heritage Society, ostensibly devoted to the restoration of artistic monuments. In April 1988, the society was the first to fly the old national flag, and in January 1989 it issued the first call for the creation of a Congress. The Estonian Christian Democrat parties stem largely from this body.

One of the curious features of the struggle for independence in the Baltic has been that while the three republics have usually moved at different speeds, they have not moved in the same order. The question of who was really 'first' has been a focus of many jealous national claims. Between 11 March 1990 and the achievement of real independence in August 1991, Lithuania led the confrontation with the Kremlin. But from 1988 to 1989, Estonia was the leader, by several months, on the road to independence.

In 1987–88, however, Latvia, supposedly the most cautious of the three, was definitely the pathbreaker in patriotic demonstrations and revelations. The first step was taken by the 'Helsinki-86' group, founded in Liepāja by a mixture of long-standing dissidents and new recruits. It called a demonstration at the Freedom Monument in Riga on 14 June 1987 to mark the anniversary of the Stalinist deportations of 1941. Such 'calendar demonstrations', marking vital anniversaries of the first independence struggle or the 1940s, were to become regular occurrences over the next three years.[4] The Helsinki-86 group was harassed and scrutinised by the KGB, and there was good reason to think that, as in all previous instances, fear would discourage all but a handful from attending, and the demonstration would be quickly dispersed by the police. Instead Gorbachov's own impact made it a success: the Latvians had gained in self-confidence, and the police had lost it. Moreover, this first demonstration, ostensibly against a Stalinist crime rather than Soviet rule as such, was calculated to confuse the Soviet authorities: Gorbachov and the central press had for some time been engaged in denunciations of Stalin.

For days after the 14 June demonstration, protestors returned to the monument to lay flowers – a practice which would itself have guaranteed arrest a few years before. It was followed by demonstrations on 23 August, the anniversary of the Molotov-Ribbentrop Pact, and 18 November, the anniversary of Latvia's first declaration of independence. This last occasion proved too much for the authorities, and police attacked the demonstrators, injuring several of them. Some Helsinki-86 members were also expelled to the West. It did not, however, stop demonstrations spreading to the other two republics. The 23 August 1987 demonstration in Tallinn was attended by some two thousand people and addressed mainly by former political prisoners. A year later, crowds numbering hundreds of thousands were common in all three states.

An early sign of Estonia's lead in economic reform was the 'four-man' proposal of economic autonomy made on 26 September 1987. Its signatories were all soon to play leading roles, most notably Edgar Savisaar as Prime Minister and Siim Kallas former leader of the official Communist Trades Unions and, from 1991, chairman of the State Bank.

As protest mounted, the Communist Party in the Baltic began to fragment. History, or rather historiography, was the major unraveller. The Baltic experience demonstrates the central dilemma of Gorbachov's entire effort, a dilemma he appears still not to understand. Glasnost was inevitably going to bring a new honesty about the past; but since the entire Communist claim to legitimacy and to positive achievements was based on lies, this honesty would sooner or later bring down the whole system.

The key role in undermining the Communist will to power was the Soviet Union's manifest economic failure in comparison with the West, and a keen awareness among younger Communist officials that they would have better lives under a capitalist economy. However, the discrediting of the Communist past was also a crucial, if secondary, factor.

From this point of view the Soviet Empire was in a worse position than the old Russian or other European empires, which based their claim to legitimacy on a simple right of conquest. Soviet rule was based on lies, and when these were exposed, that rule collapsed. Similarly, when autocratic control was removed, Soviet 'democratic' institutions proved surprisingly capable of expressing the people's will, and in the Baltic and elsewhere, this will was directed at the destruction of the Soviet Union.

In the Baltic the revelation of the full extent of the deportations and executions of the 1940s played a part in undermining Soviet rule, but the key factor was of course the publication of the truth about the Molotov-Ribbentrop Pact and the way the Balts came to be annexed in 1940. The main Estonian radical nationalist party, the National Independence Party, emerged out of a body calling itself 'The Group for the Disclosure of the Molotov-Ribbentrop Pact'. When the Supreme Soviet in Moscow admitted, as it did in summer 1989, to the existence of the secret protocols of the Pact and to their illegitimacy, it had in effect admitted the illegitimacy of Soviet rule; any subsequent Soviet political activity in the region could now be only a rearguard action or an attempt at the reimposition of military rule, without any democratic or legal justification.

While the dissidents organised demonstrations and appeals to the West, revelations about the past emerged from the previously docile, Communist-controlled institutes of history and Writers' Unions, as their younger or more patriotic members contested the power of the Party hacks, and forced them out of office. On 1–2 June 1988, an 'extended plenum' of the Latvian Writers' Union heard the Party veteran, Mavriks Vulfsons, reveal that no revolution had taken place in Latvia in 1940, and there had been no popular movement for Soviet rule. Vulfsons pointed out that he had himself at the time been a Party activist in Riga: 'I was there; I know'. Though he was fiercely attacked by Communist hardliners, public discussion of historical questions now became unstoppable. At this stage, the old national flags, still technically illegal, were being openly carried during demonstrations. Protests were, however, still heavily scrutinised by the police, and sometimes attacked. The Party, although fast losing control over the creative unions, the universities and much of the press, was still in charge both of the 'forces of order' and of most of its own membership, especially in Latvia and Estonia where the membership was largely Russian.

Appeals for help to Yegor Ligachov and other key Moscow conservatives came from the Baltic Communist leaderships. These heralded a counter-attack against Gorbachov's reforms on 13 March 1988, while he was in Yugoslavia, with the publication of the famous 'letter of Nina Andreyevna' in the paper *Sovietskaya Rossiya*, denouncing indiscipline, ideological confusion and attacks on the Soviet past. Gorbachov defeated this move, but it had important consequences in the Baltic. The toleration, or even perhaps active encouragement, extended to the Popular Fronts and Sajūdis by the reformist sections of the Moscow leadership and the KGB in 1988 resulted from their being viewed as allies against the hardliners within the Communist Party.

This was made explicit during the visit of Gorbachov's leading liberal Lieutenant, Alexander Yakovlev, to the Baltic in August 1988. Yakovlev's meetings with Popular Front leaders led to the dismissal of the hardline Latvian and Lithuanian Party leaders over the next months, in advance of the founding congresses of the Popular Front and Sajūdis in the autumn of 1988. Yakovlev's visit led to a drastic reduction in state pressure against the national movements, such that Sajūdis members were to distinguish between the periods 'before' and 'after' Yakovlev.

Yakovlev himself later described his discussions with Baltic nationalists in terms which emphasise the collapse of self-confidence and will to rule among the more intelligent and liberal Communist leaders:

> I had to admit to them that we had an empire, that there really was a centre which dictated to the republics. I had to agree with them. Anything else would have been blasphemy. So I supported them, and I still think I was right.[5]

The question of whether or how far the KGB may have contributed to the formation of the Popular Fronts in 1988 cannot be answered until its archives are opened – if they have survived. Certain KGB elements may well at the time have thought they were simultaneously strengthening Gorbachov against the Party conservatives, and moderate Baltic reformers against the ex-dissident nationalist radicals. It has since been established that there were certainly several KGB informers, and possible agents, among the original founders of Sajūdis in Lithuania. Speculation on this theme, however, has been influenced by post-Soviet Paranoia, Baltic emigré attitudes to 'former Communists', and by the propaganda needs of Right-wing forces opposed to the Fronts and their successors, as well as by better-based arguments.

For their part, Soviet loyalists have always argued that the CIA was behind the national movements, via agents from the Baltic emigrations. There can be no question that the CIA did have close links with the emigrés, and some have been rumoured to be agents. There is however no evidence that they played a key role and, in any case, the policy of the Bush administration after 1989 was to retard Baltic independence, not encourage it. If any sections of the CIA were pursuing a different course, then like the KGB, they are unlikely to advertise the fact to historians.[6]

On 23 August 1987, only a few hundred people had dared attend a meeting in Lithuania. The meeting was organised by dissidents and former political prisoners, mainly members of the Catholic group which had, over the previous twelve years, published the *Chronicle of the Catholic Church in Lithuania*: Antanas Terleckas, Viktoras Petkus, Vytautas Bogusis, Nijole Sadūnaite and others. None of the future leaders of Sajūdis were present. In May the following year, the dissidents announced the existence of the 'Lithuanian Liberty League' (*Lietuvos Laisves Lyga*, or LLL), saying that it had existed secretly since 1978. They too were subjected to police harassment, though at the same time Gorbachov, under pressure from the West, was ordering the release of Baltic political prisoners – like Lagle Parek in Estonia, released in 1988 after serving five years of a seven-year sentence. These promptly returned to the Baltic to swell the ranks of the nationalist parties.

On 14 November 1987, the Lithuanian Artists' Union threw out its entire leadership. Petras Griškevičius, the First Secretary of the Lithuanian Party since 1973, was present at the meeting and died of a heart attack that night. He was succeeded by Ringaudas Songaila, a more circumspect but still entirely loyal Communist. Songaila's leadership, however, lasted a bare eleven months. On 20 October 1988, he was replaced by a reformist Party Secretary, Algirdas Brazauskas. The appointment was largely the result of the growing strength of Sajūdis, formed in Vilnius on 3 June 1988.

Sajūdis formation had every appearance of spontaneity, and if there was a KGB hand, it was not blatant. The context, however, was that of the Nineteenth Soviet Communist Party Congress, which Gorbachov had called as a spur to reform. In each Baltic republic, institutions and groups were invited to submit nominations of delegates. The previous day, at a congress of the 'Creative Unions' in Riga, Viktors Avotiņš had also proposed the creation of a Latvian Popular Front.

In Lithuania, the Academy of Sciences formed a commission under its Secretary, Professor Eduardas Vilkas, to propose changes to the Lithuanian constitution. At this point a Popular Front had already been formed in Estonia, and Estonian representatives came to encourage the Lithuanians to follow suit.[7] On 3 June, a public meeting was held under Vilkas's chairmanship in the hall of the Academy in Vilnius. What happened next can be interpreted more or less according to taste. Vilkas appeared rapidly to lose control of the meeting, as demands were made for the formation of a new political body. Representatives of the Liberty League claim not merely that the whole affair was planned by the KGB, but that even Vilkas's resistance was part of the plan, in order to contribute to the credibility of the process. Vilkas himself has said that, with the President of the Academy absent, he was anxious only to find an 'alibi' which would prevent the authorities from throwing blame on to his shoulders.

The result of the meeting was the formation of an 'Initiative Group' of thirty-six which, in turn, produced the 'Movement (Sajūdis) for Lithuania's Restructuring'. According to a Western participant, Dr Alfred Erich Senn, ten of the names had been decided in advance, the rest appearing to emerge spontaneously. It is amusing, in retrospect, but also very difficult, to imagine some of these people as having once worked closely together. The three most easily identifiable elements in the group, which for the next two years was to provide the leadership of Sajūdis, were intellectuals from the arts and humanities, intellectuals from technical and scientific fields, and junior members of the Communist establishment. The elements overlapped of course, and membership did not necessarily determine subsequent political behaviour, although certain trends are visible.

The intelligentsia drawn from the humanities included a professor of musicology, Vytautas Landsbergis, not at this stage notably different from his colleagues; two young philosophers, Dr Arvydas Juozaitis (also an Olympic champion swimmer), later to become a leading liberal and bitter opponent of Landsbergis, and Vytautas Radžvilas, leader of the Liberal Party; Vytautas Petkevičius, another philosopher and advocate of a Soviet confederation, who later left the leadership after Sajūdis swung in a more radical direction (and he himself was shown to have been a Soviet auxiliary in the partisan war of the 1940s), only to return to parliament in 1992 as a deputy for the Labour Party of Algirdas Brazauskas; Dr Virgilijus Čepaitis, who was to become a radical nationalist leader and Landsbergis's right-hand man before he too was ruined politically by revelations that he had been a KGB informer; and the poet Sigitas Geda.

The technical and scientific intelligentsia was numerically under-represented by the physicist Zigmas Vaišvila; Arturas Skučas, an architect and later a radical and Commander of Landsbergis's bodyguard; and Kazimieras Antanavičius, a non-Communist economist and later leader of the Social Democrat Party. Among the junior members of the Communist establishment were Kazimiera Prunskiene, an economist (from July 1989 Deputy Prime Minister for Economic Reform in the Communist government, and from March 1990 to 1991, Sajūdis Prime Minister); Romualdas Ozolas, a lawyer and advisor to the Central Committee (later Deputy Prime Minister under Prunskiene); another 'lawyer', Kazimieras Motieka (later Deputy Chairman of Parliament and rival to Landsbergis); and Professor Bronius Kuzmickas, yet another philosopher (later a Landsbergisite and another Deputy Chairman). In all, 17 of the 36 founders of the Initiative Group were Communist Party members. This does not necessarily mean that they were part of the 'nomenclatura' of privileged senior Communists, though they could be called part of the wider Soviet 'establishment'.

A plethora of philosophers is one of the striking features of the group. Another is that the overwhelming majority of members were from Vilnius. A former bulldozer-driver, Kazimeras Uoka was the only worker present.

The fate of Sajūdis over the next three years was to be its gradual takeover and radicalisation by representatives from Kaunas who were often also members of the technical or scientific intelligentsia: men like Audrius Butkevičius, a doctor and later Defence Minister, Algirdas Saudargas, a physicist and later Foreign Minister, and Aleksandras Abišala, a former Komsomol official and engineer, and later Prime Minister. An important marker was the appointment of Virgilijus Čepaitis (a radical, though not from Kaunas) as the head of the Sajūdis Committee for the selection of candidates for the February 1990 elections – an appointment which had obvious consequences for their political colouring.

The typical profile of the Right-wingers and radical nationalists who later entered parliament or occupied one of innumerable government offices was that of a technically trained white-collar worker from Kaunas or the provinces: they were engineers, small managers, schoolteachers, lawyers, agronomists and the like. The difference between them and the Vilnius intelligentsia mirrored the old cultural tension, noted in Chapter 3, between relatively pluralist Vilnius and the more ethnically pure Kaunas. It also reflected a certain class difference, as far as this term can be used in post-Communist society. The 'Kaunas Faction', as it was later known, represented the 'intellectual petty bourgeoisie': hating Communism, but without access to Western culture, they had steeped themselves in the traditional culture of Lithuania in 1939, or whatever of it had survived. They were passionately ambitious to drive the existing establishment and bureaucracy from their places.

At the start, of course, none of this was apparent. The Liberty League, and some Lithuanian emigrés, accused Sajūdis of being a Communist front organisation, set up by the KGB, and continued to do so at intervals right up to the declaration of Lithuanian independence. By the Sajūdis Congress of 22–24 October 1988, however, the rise of the Kaunas faction and of pro-independence feeling within Sajūdis was very apparent. On 24 October, Rolandas Paulauskas, a popular composer from Kaunas, made the first public call for complete independence. Brazauskas continued trying to buy both time and popularity, announcing during the Congress, for example, the return of the cathedral to the Catholic Church: since the 1950s it had been an art gallery. In Moscow, however, not only hardliners but also men like Alexander Yakovlev now began to speak sharply against the movements he had encouraged only a few months earlier.

In November 1988, Brazauskas and Lionginus Šepetys, the Speaker of the Supreme Council, under intense pressure from Moscow, blocked a sovereignty declaration similar to that already passed by Estonia. Such a declaration was not to be passed until 18 May 1989, seven months later; Latvia followed on 28 July. It was accompanied by a law on economic self-management, accepted by the USSR Supreme Soviet on 27 July 1989, but thereafter resisted by the Soviet government.

November 1988 represented a failure of nerve from which Brazauskas's prestige among Lithuanian patriots has never fully recovered. It contributed to the crushing Sajūdis victory in the elections to the Congress of People's Deputies in Moscow in March 1989 (36 out of 42 seats) and to the support of even moderate Sajūdis deputies in March 1990 for a motion to replace Brazauskas by Landsbergis as Chairman of the Supreme Council. This step separated Lithuania from Latvia and Estonia, where the Communist Chairmen were retained as a symbol of compromise.

One reason for this was the greater speed with which pro-independence ideas progressed within the Estonian Communist Party. Five out of seven members of the executive committee of the Popular Front, founded in April 1988, were Party members; two were even prominent: Edgar Savisaar as former head of the State Planning Commission (Gosplan), and Marju Lauristin as a mildly dissident journalist, but above all as the daughter of one of the founders of Soviet Estonia, Johannes Lauristin, killed by the Germans in 1941. The leading role of such figures is a reminder that the Popular Fronts were essentially founded by the liberal wing of the Communist establishments.

In June 1988, Karl Vaino, First Secretary of the Estonian Communist Party, was sacked by Moscow on the advice of his own Ideology Secretary, Indrek Toome.[8] Vaino had provoked furious protests from Moscow when he tried to nominate (rather than elect) delegates to the nineteenth Soviet Party Congress – an action rejected by Gorbachov as he fought his own battle with the Moscow hardliners. Vaino was replaced by Vaino Väljas, formerly Soviet ambassador to Nicaragua. Väljas was to move closer to the Popular Front position on most issues, including that of republican sovereignty: not until autumn 1989 did the Popular Front make full independence its official platform, even though radical groups within the Front had long been demanding it.

Väljas and Toome (who from 1989–90 was Prime Minister and leader of negotiations with Moscow) threw the weight of the Party behind a plan for Estonian economic sovereignty, the acronym for which, IME, means 'miracle' in Estonian. The Communist chairman of the Supreme Council, Arnold Rüütel, was also labouring to build personal bridges to the Popular Front, an effort which later helped ensure his survival in office long after many of his colleagues.

Väljas criticised the Popular Front for not itself constructing more effective links with the increasingly restive Russian minority in the republic. At the same time he himself moved to increase the proportion of Estonians within the Party and the Supreme Council (to about two-thirds of the total), vital in securing the passage of the legal steps on the road to independence.

The struggle of the Communist and Reform Communist elements to survive as parties in the Baltic lasted four years, and in Lithuania is continuing with renewed force. On 16 November 1988, the Estonian Party appeared to take on a new lease of life when the Supreme Council voted a declaration of sovereignty, giving Estonian laws precedence over Soviet ones and itself the right to veto the jurisdiction of All-Union legislation in Estonia. Although the action was declared unconstitutional by the Praesidium of the Supreme Council in Moscow, the Estonian Communists refused to back down, going on to pass laws which affirmed Estonian as the only official language, and restricted the voting rights of recent immigrants.

In Latvia events moved more cautiously, primarily because there, more than half the Party members were Russians. Thus while the Lithuanian and Estonian Parties were, by majority vote, to separate from the Soviet Communist Party in December 1989 and March 1990 respectively, the Latvian Party split down the middle. In April 1990, a majority remained loyal to Moscow and elected as its First Secretary the hardline former Mayor of Riga, Alfrēds Rubiks. Rubiks replaced the lacklustre Jānis Vagris, appointed in October 1988 by Gorbachov in an effort to keep the Latvian Party together. Vagris's predecessor had been Boris Pugo, the former KGB official appointed Soviet Interior Minister by Gorbachov in the autumn of 1990 who then betrayed him during the attempted coup of August 1991.

The Latvian Popular Front, founded – like Sajūdis – in June 1988, was always the victim of a tug-of-war between the Communist and ex-

Communist moderates and the more radical nationalists. On 31 May 1989, with the moderate leadership absent at the Congress of People's Deputies in Moscow, the radicals engineered a declaration by the Popular Front Board that it was necessary to discuss the question of complete independence.

The National Independence Movement bridged the gap between the dissident forces and the Popular Front (and later between the 'Latvian Congress', their 'alternative parliament', and the Supreme Council) just as Gorbunovs in turn sought to mediate between the Popular Front, the different wings of the Communist Party, the Russian minority, and the Kremlin, and with some success.[9]

This then was the situation in which the three republics entered 1990, preparing for the Supreme Council elections that spring. Under pressure from the Popular Fronts – in turn pressured by more radical forces – all three Supreme Councils had passed declarations of sovereignty, new language laws, assertions of control over national resources and industry and, above all, refutations of the legitimacy of the Soviet annexations in 1940 – stopping short, however, of full declarations of independence.

The Communist leaders had committed themselves in principle to the restoration of independence, but couched in vague terms. The Popular Fronts and Sajūdis were actively demanding independence, but they too were vague about the stages through which it might be achieved. During these years the words 'independence', and still more 'sovereignty', acquired a whole spectrum of meaning unknown in the West.

Indeed between the Kremlin, the national movements and the local Communist Parties there was a virtual conspiracy that 'independence' did not really *mean* independence, that 'sovereignty' meant something less than the full right to self-determination, and that both could somehow be accommodated within the Soviet system. It was a convenient self-deception, since no-one wanted a stand-up fight, but it had a thoroughly bewildering effect on the local Russian population: it was not unusual at this time to hear exchanges like this:

> 'Are you in favour of independence?'
> 'Yes, of course. Every country should be independent.'
> 'So you are in favour of leaving the Soviet Union?'
> 'No, no! I am for independence *within* the Soviet Union.'

By the end of 1989, Communist rule, the iron frame holding the Empire together, had been thoroughly undermined, both within the Baltic and by events in Eastern Europe. Gorbachov's dramatic visit to Vilnius in January 1990, in an attempt to prevent the Lithuanian Communist Party from proceeding with its decision to separate from the Soviet Communist Party, was merely another example of his failure to comprehend what was happening to the Soviet Union. At that stage simply keeping the

13   A protest meeting in Riga, Latvia, to demand the withdrawal of the Soviet army from the Baltic States, 17 June 1990. The main banner reads, 'End the Occupation', the small placard in the centre calls for a 'Nuremberg Trial' for Communists, while the one on the extreme left is a parody of the famous Soviet Second World War propaganda poster 'The Motherland Calls You'. It reads 'The Motherland Calls You – Home'. In the background is the Freedom Monument (see Chapter 5).

Communist Party united was irrelevant in terms of preventing further moves towards independence. Gorbachov would have needed to cancel the Supreme Council elections due the following month and impose central rule by military means. Such action would seem to have gone against his own instincts, as well as his need for Western support. When, a year later, he did authorise the military to attempt such a solution in the Baltic, it was both half-hearted and already far too late.

'Be Realistic: Ask the Impossible': The Declarations of Independence, 1990

By the Lithuanian elections of February 1990, Landsbergis had been chairman of the Sajūdis Council for fifteen months. He was elected in November 1988, in a contest with Romualdas Ozolas and Arvydas Juozaitis. Ozolas and Prunskiene had received more votes in the contest for membership of the Executive Committee, but Landsbergis was elected chairman for six months. Later he was able to beat off challengers and make his position permanent, partly through superior tactical skill and toughness, but above all as a compromise candidate uniting the different elements in the movement: the Vilnius liberal intellectuals who had founded it; the Kaunas nationalists who had penetrated it; and the reform Communists who continued to build a bridge between it and its main rival, the Communist Party.

Neither Juozaitis, the archetypal liberal intellectual, nor Ozolas, the liberal Communist, would have been acceptable to the 'Kaunas Faction'; yet neither then nor later was this faction able simply to take over Sajūdis as a whole; when the Right finally did so with Landsbergis' encouragement, the result was to split the movement and reduce it to a rump. Even then, the Kaunasite core itself split, and much of it turned against Landsbergis.

In his initial role as consensual leader, Landsbergis was helped both by his apparently mild and diplomatic character and by his ancestry and background, which spanned the high Vilnius intelligentsia and the Kaunas nationalist tradition. Right up to 11 March 1990, however Landsbergis remained only a first among equals. During the elections he had made less impression on the Lithuanian public than had Brazauskas, or the feisty Kazimiera Prunskiene who, as Deputy Prime Minister, had gained popularity through tough negotiation with the Kremlin over economic autonomy.

The general public preference for Brazauskas over Landsbergis reflects a general pattern in the former Soviet republics: while the Communist Party itself had become highly unpopular, ordinary people continued, in many cases, to prefer individual Communist leaders over the leaders of the opposition. In Lithuania, even as his party shrank, Brazauskas remained consistently ahead of Landsbergis in most opinion polls, except for the year or so following the events of January 1991.[10] It reflects partly the instinctive conservatism of those, especially older voters, raised under Soviet rule, and partly simple anti-intellectualism. There is even an element of racism (assiduously stoked by Soviet misinformation) which accused Landsbergis, wrongly, of being a German or a 'half-Jew'.[11]

Landsbergis has always had a grander image of himself than has Brazauskas who, when leader of the Communist Party, used to walk in public without guards – unlike the old Party leaders in Moscow, but very much in the Gorbachov spirit. Landsbergis, however, was soon so surrounded by hulking bodyguards that even when he did appear, few could see him. Other Sajūdis leaders imitated him until their retinues began to take on a rather menacing appearance.

There is a good deal of simple dislike for Landsbergis's style and character among ordinary Lithuanians. In the words of a farmer's wife,

> Landsbergis speaks in such a complicated way, as if he's talking down to us. And I also don't think he's honest. He doesn't say what he really means and wants, even when we all know it. All this moderation and reasonableness is just a big pretence.

A combination of slyness and sanctimoniousness has also been particularly infuriating to former colleagues of Landsbergis, many of whom feel betrayed by him. Indeed Landsbergis puts one in mind of Disraeli's remark about Gladstone, that he did not mind Gladstone's keeping the Ace of Trumps up his sleeve, if only he would not claim that it was the Lord God that put it there. The view of a student, in contrast, was that,

> One of the reasons I like Landsbergis is that he speaks so beautifully. It's not just that he is always so rational, but he uses the Lithuanian language beautifully, and he knows Lithuanian literature and culture so well. He always makes me feel better. . . .

The physical appearance of Landsbergis and Brazauskas also affected attitudes: to see them together is to be reminded of some fairy-tale about a mole and a bull. Brazauskas is a populist figure, enormous, red-faced and loud-voiced, very like something from a cattle-fair. Landsbergis by contrast is short, plump and balding, with a little academic beard. In the old days, 'before Landsbergis became Landsbergis' (as someone put it), his preference for a crumpled brown-corduroy jacket made the resemblance to a mole positively uncanny. His habitual tone of voice is nasal and low, and often halting – perhaps an affectation intended to give the impression of hesitancy, modesty and moderation. He has a tendency towards academic jokes and sarcastic remarks, after which he titters gently to himself. But of the two men it is probably Landsbergis who has the stronger nerves. Although not a naturally brave man (according to an old associate) he has, through a sheer effort of will and patriotism, made himself extremely courageous: in standing up to Moscow, especially in January 1991, he showed the most steely determination. Brazauskas, on the other hand, has on occasion seemed badly rattled. He has persistently over-estimated the threat from Moscow, doubtless very often for political reasons, to boost his own value as a mediator. In the words of a Lithuanian-American journalist,

> Brazauskas is not a traitor. He is genuinely loyal to Lithuania. His problem is that he is a defeatist. From the beginning of the independence struggle, he has always been saying, 'We can't do that, it's too dangerous; we can't do this, it's too difficult'. If we had all thought that way, we would never have achieved anything.

One example came on the first day of the attempted Soviet counter-revolution of August 1991. Brazauskas evidently expected the coup to succeed, and told me that democracy in the Soviet Union and Lithuania would be put back by a decade. Landsbergis sometimes underestimated short-term threats, but his long-term view of the Soviet Union's decline proved much more accurate. The British journalist Edward Lucas has summed up this nice combination of extremism and judgement as 'barking up the right tree'.

It may seem curious, in view of the undoubted support of the vast majority of Lithuanians for the idea of independence, but the 11 March 1990 declaration of *de facto* independence came very much as a surprise, and an unwelcome one at that. In the elections of February 1990, Sajūdis stood on a platform of complete independence, and won on it; but the general expectation was that independence would come in stages, beginning with a declaration *de jure*, the course that Latvia and Estonia in fact pursued. In practice the independence process as it actually occurred was a response to objective factors, but also to the determination of the radical nationalist minority in Sajūdis, who succeeded in galvanising the more cautious majority. Speaking on 3 February 1990 to the movement's pre-election conference in the Sports Palace in Vilnius (the slightly incongruous setting for so many national celebrations and funerals over the following two years), Landsbergis set out the possible courses of action. He began with a long disquisition on Lithuanian resistance against Communism, and on the damage wrought by Communism on the Lithuanian spirit, and denounced 'toadyism and [a] spirit of subservience and compromise', evidently to discredit the Brazauskas Communists whom he warned might reform and 'continue their negative activities'. He declared clearly that 'we are an illegally annexed country, the sovereignty of which must be fully re-established', then stated that there could be two paths towards this goal, both of which would begin with the election of a new Supreme Council and the appointment of a delegation for negotiations with Moscow:

> The first . . . is the model of decolonisation; an agreement on moving step-by-step, re-establishing equal state relations [with the Soviet Union] without causing an upheaval on either side, preparing and establishing economic, military, and transit agreements, and co-ordinating the final handover of power to the legal Lithuanian government. . . . The other way would be to regain sovereignty ourselves, expressed by unilateral political action. This would be done prior to any negotiations, and in the face of sharp political confrontation. . . . It would involve the formal re-establishment of independence and [an assertion of] the continuity of the Lithuanian Republic. Independence from the jurisdiction of the Soviet Union could be proclaimed, but it would have various possible

233

consequences. We would become dependent on circumstances and on our society's capacity for resistance, which has not yet been tested, on a [national] unity which seems real and yet unreal, and on civic consciousness. We would have to foresee the risk of chaos, yet without knowing the views of foreign countries or the extent of their support. . . .[12]

Though couched in Landsbergis's usual circuitous style, this is clearly advocacy of the first (later Estonian and Latvian) variant, and an argument against the Kaunas radicals who, in internal discussions, were pressing for an immediate declaration of full independence. Most voters with whom I spoke expected a continuation by stages of the legal declarations (on sovereignty and the illegality of the annexations, for example) of the previous eighteen months.

During the February 1990 election campaign, I visited the rural constituency of Jurbarkas, accompanying the Sajūdis candidate, Laima Andrikienė, an agronomist who had studied at Manchester University. Her opponent was one Zairys, head of the local council and a long-standing Communist boss, who revealed his unreconstructed nature by refusing to see me. The voters seemed thoroughly sick of his rule and that of the 'apparat' in general, and showed it by giving Andrikienė, and the idea of independence, a large majority. But election meetings were small and not especially enthusiastic; questions were not about paths to independence, but about food prices, taxes, and the provision of machinery. At one meeting a plump, elderly woman in a fake fur coat – like a turnip-eating herbivore swallowed whole by a rather mangy leopard – hammered away at the problem of collective farm debt, and the responsibility of the state. The contrast between this woman and the other collective farmers, with their Soviet clothes and dirt ingrained into the very skin of their faces on the one side, and the candidate in her smart English overcoat on the other, was acute.

Seeming to respond to the public mood, Andrikienė spent very little time on flights of nationalist rhetoric, and concentrated on arguing that independence was necessary for economic renewal; she presented herself as the kind of Westernised technocrat who could help in this process. What were not presented were the plans for the rapid decollectivisation of agriculture by parliamentary decree, and for the return of land to pre-1940 owners. Had these been revealed, it is probable the Sajūdis vote in the Lithuanian countryside would have been drastically reduced. Decollectivisation was a central factor in the crushing Sajūdis defeat two years later when, in the October 1992 election, Andrikienė lost Jurbarkas and retained her seat only through being second on the Sajūdis proportional vote list.

The 1990 elections, held on 24 February (with run-offs between 4 and 10

March), produced 99 Sajūdis deputies, 25 pro-independence Communists, 7 Communists loyal to Moscow, and 5 independents. The result, however, was not quite so clear cut, because 12 of the 'Sajūdis deputies' were also Communist Party members. A gentleman's agreement meant that leading pro-independence Communists and leading Sajūdis representatives did not run against each other – something the Communists later had cause to regret: it cost them the possibility of defeating several leading Sajūdis Right-wingers, none of whom was especially popular.[13]

In the days preceding the first meeting of the new Supreme Council on 11 March, the Sajūdis assembly (Seimas) and Deputies' Caucus met to discuss strategy. At the Seimas on the 8 March, the dominant mood appeared initially to be one of caution: the Liberty League leader, Antanas Terleckas, in a characteristic intervention, accused the deputies of having not blood but water in their veins. Terleckas, at this stage, was opposed to Landsbergis' becoming chairman of the Supreme Council.[14] Landsbergis himself first asked that the declaration question not even be discussed, warning that he might need to hold international consultations. In the words of a radical deputy, Landsbergis, at this stage, 'obviously could not make up his mind. It was impossible to say how he was going to act. He kept calling America, trying to get advice.' The calls were made to Stasys Lozoraitis, Ambassador to the US of the pre-1940 Lithuanian republic and, in 1993, rival to Brazauskas for the office of president. Lozoraitis advised Landsbergis to declare immediate *de facto* independence. He reported, over optimistically, that ex-president Reagan had been urging Lithuania's case with Bush, his successor.

When, on 8 March, Ozolas led a Sajūdis delegation to meet the US Ambassador in Moscow, they were told there was no possibility of immediate recognition; but as Ozolas later admitted, they simply refused to believe it, apparently thinking that a declaration would force America to respond. Andrikienė and other radical deputies clearly also believed that recognition was imminent. When I tried to suggest otherwise, they refused to accept it, declaring that the West, having never recognised Soviet annexation, was morally bound to recognise independence.

The Seimas concluded by authorising the deputies to declare independence, but without stating what form the declaration should take. A Sajūdis spokesman announced on television that independence would be declared, further compromising the deputies. An additional question was the nature of the constitution an independent Lithuania should adopt: some radicals, backed by Algimantas Gureckas, leader of the emigré 'Lithuanian World Community', urged a return to the 1938 constitution, with amendments, but this was rejected on Landsbergis's advice.

Even as the Seimas was taking place in the hall of the Trades Union headquarters, adjacent to the Supreme Council, the deputies were gathering in a lecture room downstairs. It was much too small for the ninety or so members, and in the resulting confusion I was able to slip in, and sit among them.

The deputies' decision can be interpreted at three levels. First, and fundamental to everything, was that every Sajūdis deputy was committed to independence: it was only a question of when; but in the words of Professor Vilkas, by then himself a Sajūdis deputy,

> To have voted against an immediate declaration would have been seen as voting against the declaration itself, not against the date, and no-one wanted to be recorded as against the declaration.[15]

During the debates in the caucus I had the clear impression that a majority of deputies were very concerned and hesitant about an immediate declaration of full independence. Indeed several voiced their disquiet, but when it came to the final vote on the evening of 10 March, only three opposed the motion (though others, like Vilkas, absented themselves from the later stages of the discussion). The following day, although all the Brazauskas Communists would have opposed an early declaration given the power, they too voted in favour when the declaration came before the Supreme Council.[16]

The failure of moderate Sajūdis deputies to oppose the vote was not simply a selfish fear of the effect it might have on their later careers; it was also because they could not bear to appear before history, and possibly before their own consciences, as having taken such a stand. At the time I was reminded of Kamenev and Zinoviev, the only two members of the Bolshevik central committee to vote against the October 1917 coup, a fact used against them in every subsequent party struggle. As in all revolutions, once the principle of independence had triumphed in Lithuania, then as long as the independence struggle lasted, whoever could articulate that position most boldly would have the moral edge. This was the cultural hegemony of nationalism with a vengeance.

The deputies' decision was also influenced by certain specific arguments and developments. Chief among these was the argument that Lithuania had to act quickly to secure its legal position before the new Congress of People's Deputies convened in Moscow, gave Gorbachov new presidential powers, and approved a planned 'law on secession', establishing a ten-year qualification period for a republic to leave the Soviet Union. This danger was repeatedly mentioned in speeches. Vilkas, Professor Kazimieras Antanavičius and Egidijus Bičkauskas (later envoy to Moscow) however argued that it was irrelevant, that Lithuania's legal right to independence would be unaffected by the Moscow Congress, and that to declare independence during the session would give hardline Soviet deputies the chance to pass punitive resolutions against Lithuania, making it difficult for Gorbachov to take a moderate line, even if he wished. Bičkauskas asked:

> Why should we give a card to the hardliners? I don't understand this hysterical hurry. Moscow is sure not to introduce any authoritarian regime at this stage, but ... this Congress in Moscow is a 'black Congress'. If we do something rash now, Gorbachov may be forced by the reactionaries to act against us, despite his own wishes. ... Instead, we should work quietly and have the four basic documents ready to hand.

Vaišvila countered that,

> Going on and on negotiating with Moscow on the present basis is not going to get us any further. Do any of you really believe that it will be possible to force Moscow to recognise the illegality of the Molotov-Ribbentrop Pact? [Declaring independence now] may seem drastic and illogical, but it is the only thing that will move things forward.

The third element in the decision was, of course, personal interest. According to former Sajūdis deputies (but now in opposition to Landsbergis, and hence perhaps unreliable as a source), negotiations went on throughout the week between Landsbergis, Prunskienė and Kaunas Faction leaders, the latter promising to support Landsbergis as chairman of the Supreme Council and Prunskienė as prime minister in return for their support for an immediate declaration. Prunskienė's surprising advocacy of immediate independence may well have owed a good deal to this offer (though the other prime ministerial candidates were Vilkas and Antanavičius, scarcely more welcome to the Right, which lacked any convincing candidates of its own). It may also have helped Landsbergis to make up his mind. Other figures angled for other minorities and positions. In Latvia and Estonia, the national movements were to take control of the government (in Estonia, under Edgar Savisaar, a reform Communist figure comparable to Prunskienė), leaving the chairmanship, for the sake of compromise, in the hands of Communist leaders. In other republics the national movements took the chair while allowing Communists to continue running the government.

In Lithuania, the national movement took control of both the chairmanship and the government. The deputies expected that Ozolas would be one of the deputy chairmen, but during the caucus discussions he attempted to put forward his candidacy against Landsbergis for the chairmanship. The following day, Landsbergis made sure Ozalas was excluded (the vote for Landsbergis against Brazauskas was 91 to 38). Vaišvila (by Prunskienė's account) begged her for the deputy premiership, but she slapped him down: 'Oh, stop jumping about, Zigmas!' Vaišvila was to have more than ample revenge over the following nine months as a Rightist critic of Prunskienė's government, and on her fall indeed became deputy premier.

One deputy to Landsbergis, Česlovas Stankevičius, came from the Kaunas Faction; the other two, Bronius Kuzmickas and Kazimieras Motieka, were from Vilnius, but Right of Centre. With Brazauskas and Ozolas as deputy premiers, the stage was set for the confrontation between the Praesidium of the Supreme Council – led by Landsbergis and supported (at this stage) by most deputies – on one side, and Prunskienė's government on the other.

When the Supreme Council declared *de facto* independence, and the deputies rose to sing the national anthem on the evening of 11 March, a crowd gathered outside in the freezing rain and surged forward to tear down the Soviet insignia over the door. But it was a very small crowd – between three and six hundred – in strange contrast to the huge gatherings earlier in the struggle.

For the following week or so, the prevailing mood in Vilnius was one of doubt and uncertainty. In the words of a student, Edita Urmonaitė:

> The mood among my friends was not very cheerful. We were surprised by how fast it had happened, at night and without any public discussion; and then there had been so many declarations. Many people didn't take in the significance of this one at first. When an American-Lithuanian student came and told us how she had burst into tears of joy when the declaration was made, we all looked at her as if she was mad.

The replacement of Brazauskas by Landsbergis as chairman of the Supreme Council undoubtedly added to the mood of insecurity. The great majority of ordinary Lithuanians I interviewed in the succeeding weeks said they would have preferred Brazauskas as chairman, largely because of his governmental experience and good personal relations with Gorbachov. The Soviet leader apparently harboured a deep personal loathing for Landsbergis. The need to keep open lines of communication to Moscow was a major reason for the inclusion of Brazauskas and other Communist officials in the government. In the words of Algimantas Cekuolis, a Communist journalist, founder of Sajūdis and strong supporter of independence, in February 1990:

> The Lithuanian Communist Party today has only one purpose – to maintain ties with Moscow, so as to be on the safe side until Moscow agrees to normal interstate relations. If Moscow refuses to negotiate, then there is no point in keeping the LCP.

Cekuolis and many others – such as the Ideology Secretary, Justas Paleckis – left the LCP (or the Lithuanian Democratic Labour Party as it was later renamed) in the conviction that it had no future. The result was that by the elections of 1992 it had only seven deputies in the Supreme Council. Bitter faces were to be seen among the defectors when that number multiplied tenfold after the elections.

In March 1990, the Lithuanian Communist Party collected tens of thousands of signatures for a petition asking for Brazauskas's re-election. This made no impression on the Sajūdis deputies, but increased the hostility of the Right to the independent Communists, whom they now accused of 'splitting the nation' just as pressure from Moscow was beginning.

Within days of the 11 March declaration of independence, demands came from the Congress of People's Deputies and from Gorbachov for its cancellation. Direct pressure followed through the seizure by Soviet paratroops of Lithuanian deserters from the Soviet army, housed in a psychiatric clinic near Vilnius under the 'protection' of the Red Cross flag. Lithuanian and other Baltic soldiers continued to desert in large numbers but, after this, had the sense to hide quietly with relatives and friends. The Soviet military captured some, but the great majority escaped. The Spring draft was a total failure in the Baltic, as in the Caucasus and much of the Western Ukraine. The High Command made periodic threats, but these became increasingly ritualistic as the entire local conscription machinery either collapsed or was taken over by local Baltic authorities as they set out to create their own armed forces.[17]

After the initial capture of deserters, the seizure began, initially by Soviet Interior Ministry troops, then in some cases by paratroops, of buildings in Vilnius owned by the Communist Party but now under the control of the majority Brazauskas party. The buildings were however of no governmental significance, and in several cases the independent LCP had agreed to pass them to academic institutions. Their seizure therefore served no useful purpose, and the unobtrusive military presence in them did not impinge on the life of the city, in whose heart they remained like lumps of cold, dark, invisible matter.

It is difficult to know whether Gorbachov's strategy was a further case of barking up the Communist tree, thinking the Party still identical with the State; or whether he was attempting to make the Soviet Communist Party the protector of 'extra-territorial rights' for Soviet citizens in an independent Lithuania; or whether he was simply completely baffled about what course to take.

The measures, however, only increased the determination and morale of ordinary Lithuanians. Those who, immediately after the declaration, had been critical of Landsbergis and Sajūdis, became increasingly supportive, and popular demonstrations returned to their pre-independence dimensions. The West also became alarmed, and opinion grew in support of Lithuania. By late spring, however, it had become clear that a continued oil blockade (the only sanction which really worked) would play havoc with the Lithuanian harvest and lead to severe food shortages. The blockade was, however, partly undermined by the Soviet military: individual soldiers sold military petrol on the black market, and on at least one occasion, an entire Soviet unit, with its transport, joined the harvest in return for a share of the crop (a throwback to the last decades of the Empire!)

The fuel shortage, and strong advice from Western leaders during her trips abroad, convinced Kazimiera Prunskienė to seek a compromise with Moscow through a 'moratorium' on the implementation of the declaration of independence, if not the declaration itself. Much of the Lithuanian Right continues to allege that Prunskiene's move resulted from orders from Moscow, or that she was blackmailed because of her alleged earlier connections with the KGB. But past KGB informers included the main leader of the Right, Virgilijus Čepaitis and (apparently) several other prominent deputies. There is no evidence that it led any of them to work against Lithuania in this period.

Prunskienė's advocacy of a moratorium marked the beginning of the split between her government and Landsbergis' parliamentary majority. The split was far from clear cut, because majorities in parliament were continually shifting, while the government itself included such leading radicals as Foreign Minister Algirdas Saudargas. Tension, however, resulted not simply from Prunskiene's 'compromising' policies, but also from uncertainties about the rights and powers of government and parliament respectively. Similar tensions have emerged elsewhere in the former Soviet Union The split was long hidden from the public, in part to avoid direct confrontation, but also because Landsbergis finally, and with great reluctance, came round to the moratorium idea, even though he continued to throw responsibility for it on to Prunskiene.[18]

Despite its complicated and even murky genesis, the declaration of Lithuanian independence became a national talisman, if more for the politicians than for the mass of the population. Even moderate Sajūdis deputies declared that 'we were not elected in February so as to suspend independence', or 'the people would not understand us if we were to do this': the declaration had become a Golden Calf, a god which they had made and to which they were now wholeheartedly devoted. This was true of course above all for Landsbergis, whose entire personality seems to have become bound up with the declaration.

The moratorium was accepted by the Supreme Council on 23 June, and Soviet oil shipments to the Lithuanian oil refinery at Mažeikiai were resumed immediately. The harvest was safe, and mass unemployment had been avoided, if temporarily. But the moratorium was approved only with the proviso that it should follow full interstate negotiations between Lithuania and Moscow. The Praesidium and Parliament demonstrated their lack of confidence in Prunskienė by ordering that they, not the government, should form the negotiating commission. Since they also demanded that Moscow should agree to the Lithuanian agenda – in effect recognise the independence process – the talks never happened, nor did the moratorium. By mid-autumn in any case, Gorbachov had lost whatever interest he had in negotiation.

Prunskienė continues to insist that a great chance was lost by failing to open negotiations at a time when Moscow may have been conciliatory, but this is very questionable. The experience of Latvia and Estonia suggests that the Soviet government would have tried to stall serious negotiations indefinitely. The Balts in any case could have done nothing to prevent the ascendancy of the Soviet conservatives in autumn 1990, or the military intervention that followed, short of freezing the entire independence process in an attempt to help Gorbachov stabilise his position. This was the hope of many Baltic moderates, but formed no part of the radicals' agenda. These argued that the Soviet Union was bound to collapse anyway, and that the Baltic should simply stake an absolute legal position and wait for developments elsewhere to destroy the power of the Kremlin. In this the radicals were entirely correct, and their analysis sharper than that of many moderates and Western analysts. By contrast the policy of Prunskiene, by the winter of 1991, was manifestly bankrupt: in her position, a Western prime minister would have been forced to resign. It was the manner and timing of the move to bring her down, not the move itself, which left deep scars in Lithuanian political life.

The Lithuanian declaration of independence placed the Latvians and Estonians in a difficult position. Honour suggested similar declarations of full independence: it will be many years before the Lithuanians forgive their Baltic neighbours for their failure to issue these. Prudence, the plans already made, and above all the presence of the large Russian minorities, dictated a more gradual approach. As it was, the Lithuanian declaration and Moscow's response to it, resulted in a drastic reduction in local Russian support for the Latvian Popular Front, demonstrated by a declining vote between the first and second rounds of the election.

It had been feared that neither in Latvia nor Estonia would the Popular Front gain the necessary two-thirds majority to enact constitutional changes under their own (Soviet) statutes. In this eventuality, the plan of the radicals, and indeed the moderates, was for the Estonian and Latvian Congresses to declare independence. This would obviously have had grave consequences, undermining the legitimacy of the independence process among local Russians, democrats in Russia, and Western governments.

In fact, thanks to Russian support (put by Dainis Īvāns at 30 per cent of the Russian vote in Latvia) and Russian apathy, the elections in both Latvia and Estonia led to two-thirds majorities for the Popular Fronts and associated pro-independence candidates. In Latvia, 68.2 per cent voted for the Popular Front and only 21.5 per cent for opponents of independence, with 10.3 per cent for 'neutrals' (most of whose representatives voted for independence).

The new Estonian Supreme Council adopted the most cautious of the three declarations – so much so that many Estonians have forgotten it was made. It simply cancelled the Soviet annexation, and declared that Estonia was in a period of transition to full independence. Much more important was the formation of a Popular Front government by Edgar Savisaar, with a cabinet made up largely of pro-independence former Communists. In the words of Professor Endel Lippmaa, chief Estonian negotiator with Moscow, in April 1990:

> We have in fact done what Lithuania did, but by a long series of such small steps that it was difficult for Moscow to tell when exactly we got really nasty. What Lithuania did was take a big step, as if Moscow didn't exist.[19]

The limited nature of the Estonian declaration was in part the work of the national radicals. Loyal to the Congress, and denying in principle the legitimacy of the Supreme Council, they wished to preserve the 'sacred' symbols of the pre-1940 republic for a 'real' declaration of independence. On the eve of the new session of the Estonian Supreme Council, the council of the Estonian Congress passed a resolution declaring that in the 'transition period' Estonia could not be a real state, but supporting it in any case. Trivimi Velliste explained that,

> We don't want to legitimise anything phoney as a cover for continued Soviet rule. We cannot declare independence twice, and there is no point in following the Lithuanians and declaring full *de facto* independence now when we have even less chance than the Lithuanians of actually controlling the country.

In a shrewdly prophetic comment, he added that,

> We don't want to devalue the concept of independence. What will people feel and say the next morning if independence has been declared and nothing has changed? The achievement of real independence could last a year, more or less. The crucial thing is political developments in Russia. We don't know when or how the collapse of Communist rule in Russia will come, but it is already obvious that it is bound to happen.[20]

A fortnight later, the Estonian Supreme Council upgraded its initial declaration to match that of the Latvians; in the name of Baltic solidarity, the Estonian Congress did not protest. On 29 April, the Kremlin had made a final attempt to head off the Latvian declaration: Soviet representatives in Moscow persuaded a Latvian negotiating delegation comprising representatives of both the Communist government and the Popular Front to agree to talks on joining a Soviet confederation. Gorbachov also offered Latvia the status of the Grand Duchy of Finland under the Tsars – full internal autonomy excluding defence and foreign affairs.[21] Both offers were rejected by the Latvian Popular Front. While its leaders did not rule out a future confederation, they declared that negotiations would need to follow the achievement of real independence. Over the next fifteen months, negotiations on practical steps towards independence took place at regular intervals. There is little point, however, in detailing them, since most were mere formalities, the two parties setting out their positions again and again; the Soviet government had no interest in making significant concessions.

On 4 May the Latvian Supreme Council, in a law on 'The Renewal of the Independence of the Republic of Latvia', declared null and void the Soviet annexation, restored (but, as in Lithuania, immediately suspended) the constitution of 1922, and established a transition period leading to *de facto* independence, to be concluded by the convening of a Latvian parliament. Since by late 1992 this parliament had still not been convened, many Right-wing Latvians argue that the transition period was not terminated by the declaration of independence that accompanied the attempted Moscow coup on 21 August 1991, but is in fact still in force.

As in Lithuania and Estonia, the Latvian Supreme Council followed its main declaration with a subsidiary pronouncement on Latvia's accession to the human rights conventions of the UN and the CSCE, and with an appeal to the governments of the world to,

> support the endeavours of the people of Latvia to achieve the complete renewal of the independence of Latvia and to give the new government full moral, diplomatic and possibly material assistance. In particular, we ask you to use all your international authority to persuade the government of the USSR to begin negotiations on an equal basis. . . . The Baltic question is an international issue. If Europe is to be reunified the Baltic question must be resolved.

Following the declaration, the leaders adjourned to the Daugava embankment, where – in sharp contrast to Lithuania – a huge crowd, tens of thousands strong, gathered to celebrate. Leaving the meeting, Popular Front Chairman Dainis Īvāns, then the most popular figure among Latvians, was bombarded with greetings and almost buried in flowers.

The declaration was accompanied by the election of a fresh Praesidium and government by the new majority. The Praesidium was headed as before by Anatolijs Gorbunovs, chosen for his popularity and ability to negotiate with the Kremlin, but above all because of the need to reassure the local Russian population. Gorbunovs was joined as vice-chairmen by Īvāns (who stepped down from his PF post) and by Andrejs Krastiņš, leader of the radical National Independence Party. The new government was headed by Popular Front vice-chairman Ivars Godmanis, a physicist who had newly joined the Party from the Centrist forces in the Front.

Many Balts remain bitterly disappointed by the absence of Western diplomatic recognition in 1990–91, and by the subsequent failure to put economic pressure on the Russian government to withdraw its troops from the Baltic states. Landsbergis repeatedly warned of the threat of 'another Munich' and, according to Prunskienė, 'suspicion that . . . the Western states would betray Lithuania ran like a red thread through his policies and statements'.

Western concern with the fate of the Balts, and pressure on the Soviet government, was, however, unquestionably a key factor in deterring serious military action – against the Lithuanians in particular – in 1990, and in frustrating the plans of the Russian hardliners in January 1991. If the West had stood back, Gorbachov could not have crushed the Baltic nationalist movements, but the struggle for independence would have been much more difficult.

The 'Bloody Events': January to August 1991

Matters between the Baltic States and the Kremlin were therefore at an impasse when, in the autumn of 1990, Gorbachov swung towards the Soviet hardliners, rejecting the Shatalin economic reform plan and appointing Valentin Pavlov as Prime Minister and Boris Pugo as Interior Minister. How far he approved the detail of their actions in the Baltic States remains unknowable. As suggested in Chapter 7, one reason why both the January 1991 military intervention in the Baltic and the August counter-revolution failed was precisely that so few Soviet leaders were willing to take full responsibility.

In September 1990 a series of minor bomb attacks hit Soviet and military targets in Latvia. There seems little doubt these were in fact the work of Soviet hardliners, *provokatsii*, to create an excuse for military intervention and presidential rule from Moscow. From December, the Soviet High Command issued statements insisting that conscription would be implemented in the Baltic, using force if necessary.

At this point Edgar Savisaar's Estonian government demonstrated its skill in maintaining good relations with the Soviet generals while conceding few essential points. Regular meetings with local commanders diminished the risk of clashes, while a meeting of Savisaar with Marshal Yazov on 9 January resulted in an agreement to check the dispatch of troops to Estonia pending a joint commission to discuss the fate of Estonians unwilling to serve in the Soviet army. The commission of course got nowhere, but throughout Savisaar's government Estonia suffered much less from Soviet military action than the other two republics.

The price of the January compromise, however, appears to have been the temporary disbanding of Estonia's 'alternative service force', made up of those refusing to accept Soviet conscription. Its members were told by the Chairman of the Commission for Alternative Service to take 'a kind of vacation . . . I advise them to spend it with their friends, relatives or in the forest'.

The Soviet campaign was aimed primarily against Latvia, for several fairly obvious reasons. Latvia of course contained by far the largest number of local Russians; its police was basically loyal to Moscow; both Boris Pugo and the most powerful Communist remaining in the Baltic, Alfrēds Rubiks, were ethnic Latvians; and there was a wide choice of local figures available to staff the 'National Salvation Committees' set up by hardliners in each republic to take power if necessary and give Soviet plans some semblance of 'legitimacy'. The campaign was timed to coincide with the Gulf War, during which Western attention would supposedly be distracted.

If in the first week of January Moscow switched its attention to Lithuania, it was almost certainly the fault of the Lithuanian political establishment which chose this inapposite moment to bring its internal conflicts to the boil. This is an episode from which few emerge untainted – except the Lithuanian people, who behaved with a courage and discipline worthy of a better leadership.

By the end of December 1990, relations between Prunskienė and the parliamentary majority had reached their lowest point. Throughout the year they had been exacerbated not only by parliamentary disapproval of Prunskiene's allegedly compromising attitude towards Moscow, but by anger at the slow pace of economic reform, at delays on privatisation, and at rumours of governmental corruption. After the moratorium debate, the Liberty League had begun to accuse Prunskienė and other Centrist and ex-Communist ministers of being 'agents of Moscow', and by the autumn, even the official parliamentary newspaper, *Lietuvos Aidas* (the 'Lithuanian Echo', modelled on the Soviet 'State News', but claiming to be the linear successor of the *Lietuvos Aidas*, the state newspaper of Smetona's regime) had joined in the accusations, encouraged by the radical nationalists and, covertly, by Landsbergis.

Prunskiene herself was furious at continual parliamentary meddling in what she regarded as her area of responsibility. Matters were made worse by the fact that the Sajūdis bloc was breaking apart: even elementary party discipline was absent and the government could never be sure of a majority on any issue. Landsbergis at this stage was increasingly aligned with the radicals and under the close influence of Virgilijus Čepaitis, its most prominent leader, although as chairman he still exercised a certain moderating influence.

On 30 December the Supreme Council passed a resolution forbidding the government to raise the price of food. This was both technically provocative and, in view of rising inflation and the worsening state budget deficit, economically nonsensical, and was denounced as such by both Prunskiene and Professor Antanavičius, the Social Democrat leader. Under the circumstances, however, the action made good political sense, since price rises were bound to be used by Soviet hardliners to stir up unrest among local Polish and Russian workers, which in turn might provide the Kremlin and the army with a pretext to intervene.

The possibility of military intervention was already acute, with greatly increased troop movements, the occupation of fresh buildings, and the introduction of paratroop units from the division based in Pskov. General Kuzmin, the Commander-in-Chief in the Baltic, announced that the units had been brought in to enforce conscription. On 2 January, paratroopers seized the Press House in Riga, injuring several people. The local Soviet Communist leadership threatened to sack the staff if they did not end their protest strike and agree to print Communist publications. Disregarding the Supreme Council's order (which was of doubtful constitutional validity, or would have been if there had been a real constitution to refer to) and a threatened strike by both Communist and Sajūdis-backed trades unions, the Lithuanian government raised food prices by an average of 320 per cent on 7 January. The official explanation was that the state was spending seven million roubles a day on food subsidies. The action was immediately denounced by radical nationalist deputies, and, the same evening, by Landsbergis, on television, who warned that crisis might lead to serious disturbances which would be exploited by Moscow.

The following morning a crowd of 5–7,000 local Russian and Polish workers (possibly augmented by Soviet soldiers in plain clothes), organised by the local Soviet Communists and the pro-Soviet 'Yedinstvo' movement, assembled outside the Supreme Council, demanding its resignation and that of the government. Also outside and demanding the dismissal of Prunskienė were demonstrators from the Liberty League and the radical-wing of Sajūdis. Around 30 pro-Soviet demonstrators broke through the lines of the parliamentary guards and smashed their way through the main door and into the lobby. The guards then drove them back using fire-hoses.

The incident betrayed a lack of organisation on both sides. A genuine Soviet *provokatsia* would have required more men. On the Lithuanian side, guards loyal to Landsbergis and recruited from radical nationalist volunteers, who had replaced the police protecting the parliament on the grounds that they were insufficiently reliable, proved to have no training in crowd control. Immediately after the riot, the Supreme Council voted to suspend the price rises. Prunskienė travelled to Moscow for talks with Gorbachov, attended also by the Lithuanian envoy to Moscow, Bičkauskas. Gorbachov gave no assurances on the questions of military intervention or presidential rule.

The Lithuanian Right continues to allege that around this time Prunskienė had received instructions to resign and provoke a political crisis. She of course denies this but, in her autobiography, glides over the details of the meeting with Gorbachov. While Prunskienė's collaboration in a Soviet takeover was highly unlikely, there was certainly a sense on the Left that in view of the behaviour of Landsbergis and his supporters, the radicals should be forced to assume power and take responsibility for any subsequent disasters.

In this sense at least, Prunskienė may not have been averse to provoking a crisis. Both she and the former Lithuanian Communist Party of Brazauskas (now the Lithuanian Democratic Labour Party) had stressed the need for compromise with Moscow, and criticised the parliamentary radicals for a policy 'based on ambition, and not on serious political and economic calculation'. It would have been surprising if Gorbachov had not considered the advantages of dealing with Prunskienė rather than the impossible Landsbergis.

On her return to Lithuania, and on learning the news of the Supreme Council's revocation of the price rises, Prunskienė announced her government's resignation. This may indeed have seemed an inevitable consequence of political defeat, but as Laima Andrikiene observed, 'Parliament had defeated Prunskienė again and again on other issues, including very important ones, and she never offered to resign. So why do it on this occasion? It is obvious that she wanted to provoke a crisis'.

In her autobiography Prunskienė herself hints that the Right-wing campaign against her was itself planned by the KGB.

Prunskienė's resignation was accepted by a majority of 50, and on 10 January, after lengthy discussions, Dr Albertas Šimenas, a mathematician and economist, was proposed by Landsbergis as her successor. The appointment indicated Landsbergis's wish to continue reconciling the different parliamentary factions, as Šimenas belonged to the Centre faction. It also, however, revealed his determination to have a prime minister who could not possibly challenge him, for Šimenas was a nonentity, with no governmental experience, whose very name was unknown to most Lithuanians. Prunskienė promptly denounced the new

14 Soviet paratroopers, and a Soviet tank (15) outside the occupied press headquarters in Vilnius during the Soviet military intervention of January 1991.

government, saying it would not last three months. In fact, it was to last fewer than three days.

Šimenas proved to have very weak nerves. On the critical night of the 12–13 January, he disappeared and could not be traced. On his return the following afternoon, he attempted to resume the prime ministership, but it had already been given by the Supreme Council (once again on Landsbergis' initiative) to a Right-wing economist, Gediminas Vagnorius. Šimenas vanished to a nursing home for several months. He claimed later that on 12 January he had taken his family to a safe place in the countryside, and been unable to contact the government to let them know. Suspicion continues among opponents of the Right that the whole business was a plot to bring a Right-winger to power; that Šimenas was advised to hide (from possible capture by Soviet troops) by the radical nationalists in control of the Lithuanian security services, who then omitted to inform parliament; or in the words of a Lithuanian journalist, 'Vaišvila whispered something in Šimenas's ear that frightened him so much he ran away and hid in the forest'.

Following the resignation of Prunskienė, the military intervention in Lithuania gathered pace, and more paratroops were flown into the country. Fresh pro-Soviet demonstrations took place, and in Latvia a strike was organised among local Russian workers, though the response was poor. Military helicopters flew over the principal Baltic cities, dropping pamphlets encouraging people to demonstrate against the governments. On 11 January, paratroopers stormed the Press House in Vilnius, firing in the air. Four people were injured. Lithuanian Defence Department buildings in several cities were also occupied. Landsbergis tried to contact Gorbachov, but the Soviet president refused to speak with him.

Concrete and barbed-wire barricades were erected around the Lithuanian Parliament, and remained there until Brazauskas came to power almost two years later. A retired Lithuanian emigré Colonel from the US army advised on building the defences. The Lithuanian guards told me that to counter the threat of a helicopter landing paratroops on the roof, they had unscrewed the beams supporting it.

On the 12 January, the Lithuanian police force was split by the defection of Major Boleslaw Makutinowicz and part of the Lithuanian OMON. Thanks largely to the conciliatory policies and personal prestige of the Lithuanian Interior Minister, General Misiukonis, the defectors were limited to 32 (all local Russians and Poles), though several dozen more joined them over succeeding weeks. Roadblocks were set up on the outskirts of town, although the Soviet soldiers did not seem to know for whom or what they were looking. Following appeals from Landsbergis, crowds gathered to protect the Supreme Council, the television and radio station and the TV tower.

At 11pm that night, the National Salvation Committee announced that it was taking power. An hour later, paratroops with armoured vehicles left the main military base in Vilnius and made their way to the TV station and tower. Others approached the Supreme Council but did not attack. The troops at the TV tower began by firing blanks, then shot into a crowd which attempted to block their progress, the same occurring at the TV station. Thirteen Lithuanians were killed in all, and several hundred injured by bullets or by troops lashing out with their rifle butts. A woman, Loreta Asanavičiūte, was killed when she lay down in front of an armoured personnel carrier. One KGB officer was killed, and another lost a leg. The Soviet army subsequently alleged that Lithuanian guards had opened fire on the troops, but Western correspondents on the scene saw no evidence of this, and the probability is that these two men were shot accidentally by their own side, during scenes of the wildest confusion.

At the Supreme Council, a huge crowd waited, convinced that their turn was next. In the words of a student who was present,

> From the 11th, when the Press House was occupied, my friends and I went to the parliament or the TV centre every night, and slept a bit during the day. Before the killings, people were still cheerful, and there was singing and dancing, though the weather was miserable – it kept sleeting. On the 11th, there was even a big rock concert outside the parliament. We expected to be attacked on the 12th, but nothing happened. Then at about midnight on the 12th–13th, the radio announced that tanks were moving towards Karoliniskis, and soon afterwards, we could hear shooting. Over the radio, the announcer said that she could hear Russian voices in the building, and then her voice was cut off. That was very frightening. We all thought that they would come next to the parliament. I was afraid, and so were others, but in general the mood was more angry. That was so even when people came from the TV tower and told us what had happened; some of my friends came, and their faces were quite changed, stony. It took months for some of them to get over it. Landsbergis broadcast over the loudspeakers, asking us to move to the side, so as not to be caught in the crossfire when the parliament was attacked. He said something like, 'we need live witnesses, not more victims'; but we didn't move. . . . All sorts of rumours ran through the crowd, and it would surge in one direction or another – that was dangerous, because the square was completely packed. There was a fear of spies. I saw people catch one man – they were screaming that he was a provocateur, and they were going to throw him into the river, but they let him go. . . . A Catholic priest, Grigas, was going through the crowd, leading prayers and talking to people, and I remember admiring him because he was so calm, but also being irritated, feeling that he was using the occasion to make his own religious propaganda. . . .

16   The night of 13 January 1991 in Vilnius: part of the civilian crown defending the television station tries to save a woman who has thrown herself in front of an armoured personnel carrier. Fourteen Lithuanians were killed by Soviet troops that night.

A week later, the scene was repeated in Riga, as during the OMON attack on the Interior Ministry, crowds waited at the Supreme Council in case that too was attacked. Behind their barricades in Vilnius, the Lithuanian parliamentary guards, armed with shotguns and hunting rifles, were preparing to make a last stand. Often seen as a sinister collection, there was at least no doubting the courage of the guards on this occasion. If the building had been stormed and they had resisted, there would without doubt have been a massacre. One of them told me later that,

> The intention is not to win, because we all know that this is impossible; the intention is to die, but by doing so to make sure that Moscow can't tell any lies as they did in 1940. To make sure that the whole world knows that Lithuania was prepared to fight for her freedom.

Over the following days, the guards were joined by a dozen Ukrainian volunteers, dressed in turquoise and gold uniforms, an incongruous sight within a parliament building which had taken on the shabby, chaotic look of a revolutionary headquarters. Inside the parliament, sixty or so deputies (around two-fifths of the total and not a very impressive figure) were trying to cope with what looked like an imminent Soviet assault at the same time as a government crisis caused by the disappearance of Šimenas. The Foreign Minister, Algirdas Saudargas, then abroad, was designated head of a 'government in exile' if military rule were imposed at home.

In a move which has been used against her ever since, Prunskiene then made a determined effort to regain the post of prime minister, appealing to her former colleagues to help her resume control without reference to parliament. The Supreme Council however elected Vagnorius as 'provisional' premier. Prunskiene continues to insist the procedure was unconstitutional, because the appointment could only be temporary, and there was no quorum.

Over the following weeks, Prunskiene travelled abroad, repeating the charges, even accusing Landsbergis of fascism. Her popularity within Lithuania, hitherto very high in almost every opinion poll, has never recovered from an act of supreme political selfishness at a time of national danger. Landsbergis, at the same time, achieved an unwonted popularity which was to last for the greater part of the year. As Prunskiene herself admits, he showed on the night of 13 January some of the characteristics of a true leader. In his speech broadcast to the nation that night, his tone was quite different from normal; clear, hard, incisive sentences replaced the mumbling academicism as he promised to resist to the end and called on the nation not to bow to tyranny. As he himself told me afterwards, he had at that time 'no plans for personal survival'.

As described in Chapter 7, the succeeding days and weeks, though tense and sometimes violent, were essentially a prolonged anti-climax. Even the bloody attack by OMON on the Interior Ministry in Riga a week later was more like the lashing of a reptile's severed tail than part of a co-ordinated plan for the reconquest of the Baltic States. A similar pointless lashing characterised the long series of OMON attacks on Baltic border posts which stretched from the winter until the Soviet counter-revolution of August 1991, and which reached a bloody climax at the Lithuanian border post of Medininkai on 31 July, when seven border guards were killed, allegedly by the Riga OMON. Until August 1991, and then only half-heartedly, the Soviet army was not again involved in major action against the Baltic States.

The internal political conflict in Lithuania appears completely to have misled the Soviet hardliners, probably including Gorbachov, about the temper of the Lithuanian people. They clearly thought an assault would not meet serious popular resistance. The dead outside the television tower cured them of this illusion. To have stormed the parliament would have meant dozens or even hundreds more dead, and it seems that for this the Soviet leadership lacked the courage, or possibly in some cases even the ruthlessness, in the face of a storm of protest that was building both in Russia and in the West.[22]

The failure to push the attack on the Baltic States through to a bloody conclusion may well have constituted the failure of Mikhail Gorbachov to support to the end a policy which he had initially approved. The resulting resentment among hardliners in the Baltic was very clear during succeeding months, and contributed to the decision in August to get rid of the Soviet president. On the other hand, the humiliating failure of nerve in January may well have undermined the resolve of officers to support the counter-revolution in August. If so, the dead of 13 January deserve recognition not only from Balts but from tens of millions of people across the former Soviet Union. Praise is also due to customs officers and border guards who for months stocially endured beatings and humiliation from OMON without being able to resist.

The events of January 1991 also have a more long-lasting consequence. Despite the sleazier aspects of Lithuanian politics at the time, the episode has provided Latvians and Lithuanians with their own modern martyrs, a feeling that they have fought and suffered for their independence. The solidarity and the courage of the peaceful, unarmed crowds outside the parliaments in Riga and Vilnius, convinced that they were about to be attacked, but standing their ground, is indeed one of the most moving political images of modern times, not only for Balts but for Europe. It furnishes a fine instance of 'the power of the powerless' of which Vaclav Havel has written.

In the classic style of successful movements of passive resistance, their only defences were world opinion, and the confusion, internal division, weakness and guilty consciences of their opponents. The manner in which the Balts won their struggle should be a factor in diminishing militarism in the Baltic, and counter the ambitions of Lithuanian nationalists who seek to exploit the memories of January 1991 for their own ends.

Eight months later, in Cathedral Square near the parliament in Riga, it seemed that the scene in Vilnius on the night of 13 January was to be repeated. Five Latvians had already been killed by OMON as they attempted to occupy government buildings. Towards noon on the 21 August, OMON armoured personnel carriers approached parliament from across the square, driving the crowds back with batons and tear gas. Then, apparently on the verge of the final assault, unaccountably they turned and retreated. Word had come from Moscow. The coup against Gorbachov was collapsing, and the Baltic States were independent.

The Fragmentation of Politics and the Difficulty of Government: Lithuania

After the August coup attempt, the Soviet Communist Party was banned in all three Baltic states, though some of its members continued to play a prominent role in local Russian politics within Latvia and Estonia. There, pro-independence wings of the Party had already disintegrated or been reduced to a rump.[23] Former Communists fanned out across the political spectrum. Communist Party buildings, from which Soviet troops now withdrew, were taken by the states, in some cases leading to unseemly squabbles between new would-be owners.

Given their personal popularity, Arnold Rüütel in Estonia and Anatolijs Gorbunovs in Latvia could probably have continued leading small but fairly successful post-Communist parties. Instead they chose to mobilise their popularity by severing links with the Party and becoming 'national figures', ostensibly above party politics. If like them, Brazauskas had been retained as chairman of the Lithuanian Supreme Council on 11 March 1990, he too might have followed this path, and the Lithuanian Communist Party disintegrated completely. If Landsbergis, for his part, had imitated the 'apolitical' approach and remained a symbolic figure, he might have avoided later defeat. In their different circumstances, Brazauskas, Rüütel and Gorbunovs escaped responsibility for government during the period 1990–92, whereas Landsbergis saddled himself with it and with the unpopularity it brought.

The unity of the national movements, however, did not long survive that of the Communists. Indeed in Lithuania the Communists, renamed the

Democratic Labour Party, were to keep their core intact, while Sajūdis declined. In Estonia the Popular Front appeared, by the end of 1992, to have been replaced by a relatively stable new party system, and in Latvia, before the elections of June 1993, a similar process seemed at last to be beginning.

In both Lithuania and Estonia, attempts were made to turn the national movements from broad umbrella coalitions into disciplined parties. The attempts failed, both for ideological reasons and because they were associated with the personal ambitions of the leaders, Landsbergis and Savisaar. Thus a determined effort to transform Sajūdis into a membership party came at its second Congress in April 1990. The plan was orchestrated by Čepaitis, with Landsbergis playing a strong supporting role behind the scenes. Čepaitis, as secretary and chief organiser of Sajūdis, had already made himself widely unpopular through his ruthless manipulation of candidacies and committee memberships, and an attempt to make him Chairman, replacing Landsbergis, was greeted with a storm of derision.

The attempt alienated many non-Rightists, and over the ensuing year the movement withered. Before the March elections, the Sajūdis offices on Cathedral Square had been the centre of Lithuania's political life: now the focus had moved to the Supreme Council. Connected with this was the increasing concentration of national symbolism, and to a lesser extent power, around the person of Landsbergis himself. He came to be addressed by his own supporters (and by much of the Western press) as 'President', although, unlike Yeltsin, he had not been elected to such a position. Like Gorbunovs and Rüütel, Landsbergis' official title, until the elections of 1992, remained 'Chairman of the Praesidium of the Supreme Council'. The attempts to transform himself into a fully executive president defined much of Lithuanian politics in 1991–92.[24]

During this period Brazauskas and his party came under increasing attack from Sajūdis. There were frequent accusations in the government press that he was an agent of Moscow, and the planned 'desovietisation' law appeared designed to drive him out of politics altogether. Brazauskas himself sometimes seemed to give way to moods of depression and even despair. Either deliberately or for this reason he refrained from any overt counter-attack. Instead, he pushed forward figures like Prunskiene and Juozaitis who, in the months before the August 1991 coup attempt, founded the 'Forum for Lithuania's Future', an attempt to generate opposition to Landsbergis. The Forum attracted the violent hostility of the radicals, and its meetings were attacked with stones and petrol-bombs.[25]

Opposition to Landsbergis personally, however, continued to grow. This was in part a matter of style rather than of concrete policies, of which in any case Landsbergis had few. Along with the presentation of Landsbergis in presidential guise went the increasing ritualisation of official politics, evoking a past which naturally tended to worry Lithuanian and foreign liberals. I myself became aware of this at the funeral of the seven men killed at the Medininkai border post on 30 July 1991, a moment which can be said to symbolise the end of Sajūdis as a broad national movement, and the beginning of the end of Landsbergis' fleeting popular status as national leader after January 1991.

Like the funerals of those killed in January, the Medininkai funerals were laden with Catholic and national imagery: irrespective of belief, the bodies were laid out in the Sports Palace at Vilnius with crucifixes clasped in their hands. This time however, a clear effort was made to secure the maximum propaganda value of the event for Landsbergis and the government in power, in which parts of the Church co-operated fully. Other former leaders of Sajūdis were excluded from any prominent role at the funerals, and real national solidarity took second place to the rhetoric of national unity in the service of the government. The sight of members of the Lithuanian government, largely made up of ex-Communists and ex-Komsomol officials, genuflecting and crossing themselves at the wrong junctures, however, provided moments of comedy, especially as they kept glancing round to see if anyone else knew better.

The apogee of religious and national symbolism in Lithuania was reached in December 1991 at the Third Congress of Sajūdis (see Chapter 5). The movement then, or what was left of it, could hardly have been more different from its beginnings a mere three years before. The Chairman, Juozas Tumelis, (Landsbergis was by now honorary Chairman) declared that,

> Sajūdis will always be needed, as it was by the television tower and the parliament on January 13th . . . the experience of our neighbours shows that a multiparty system can be worse than dangerous. . . . We need the Lithuanian Sajūdis [Movement] because there is still a Party [ie the Brazauskas party] which preserves the old structures and wants to regain power . . . and because Lithuania is still threatened by enemies. . . .

Landsbergis ascended the stage flanked by two uniformed paramilitary volunteer officers, who saluted as he was draped in the ceremonial sash of Chairmanship. The speech provides a useful example of his style and ideology:

> Attempts to work for Lithuania but against Sajūdis are ridiculous. Sajūdis has stood for the old, pure, honest Lithuania, not a dependent colony . . . Sajūdis is the expression of the spiritual rebirth of the whole nation and of

the nation's hope and will . . . [but] all the inherited devils want this rebirth to be aborted, so that we will return to the old Soviet distortions . . . Sajūdis must carry out such changes that people will trust us and love one another. . . . Rebirth will be achieved when men sing as they work.

Throughout the entire speech there was nothing concrete or specific about any aspect of state policy, apart from ecological protection ('nature is crying as it is murdered'). Towards the end, Landsbergis declared that 'To speak concretely, we have to know what seeds we will sow in our native soil, so that in future we will not be faced with an unexpected crop . . . Sajūdis should encourage the people themselves to resist robbers and terrorists'. He declined to outline a Sajūdis programme, but indicated that, 'Stressing certain priorities will be similar to a programme. These should be honest work; family; native land.'

A French colleague noted that this was Marshal Petain's programme: 'Travaille; Famille; Patrie', which Landsbergis may have absorbed during a recent visit to France. On the other hand, however, it is quite possible these 'priorities' emerged instinctively as the normal stuff of Right-wing populism.

Throughout the Congress, the Liberty League leader Terleckas roamed the hall, orchestrating support for radical declarations such as the exclusion from parliament and state positions not simply of former Communists but of Liberals and Social Democrats (the final, moderated, declaration referred only to former senior Communists with responsibility for the KGB). In his own speech there were seven references to 'sabotage', nine to 'theft', and fourteen to various forms of 'treason'.

Even as the Congress endorsed a Landsbergis presidency, there were signs that the effect of his public prominence was beginning to be the reverse of what was intended, even among the Right. A Lithuanian army officer grumbled,

On Monday, you turn on the television – Landsbergis.
On Tuesday, you turn on the radio – Landsbergis.
On Wednesday, you open the newspaper – Landsbergis.
On Thursday, you're afraid to open a tin of fish!

Landsbergis' declining influence resulted also from the political failure of the critical three months following the August coup and the achievement of independence. Had he seized then, with his prestige high, the chance to push for a new constitution, he may have succeeded. But he failed to do so, in part through his perennial unwillingness to get to grips with the details of politics, constitutions or administration. Even one of his own parliamentary supporters, criticising plans to create a French-style system of local 'prefects' (directly responsible to the President), considered that 'This would simply be a recipe for spreading across the whole country the chaos which already exists in Landsbergis' own office'.

Given the failure of parliamentary government in the 1920s, Landsbergis had solid objective arguments for an executive presidency, and most Lithuanians probably favoured it. But it was above all the association of the presidency with Landsbergis's own personality that discredited it. Landsbergis' loss of control stemmed partly from the fact that, following international recognition in August 1991, he began a seemingly endless series of foreign trips, some of them necessary (to the United Nations, for example, on the occasion of Lithuania's accession), but others frivolous.

The great majority of politicians who had emerged from Sajūdis were opposed, or at best lukewarm, towards the idea of a presidency. Their own power had emerged out of a parliamentary system: remembering that very recently Landsbergis had been barely first among equals, the deputies were unlikely to favour his elevation so far above their heads. Such feelings applied on the Right as well as the Left, and particularly among the hardline Kaunas nationalists who had never taken Landsbergis to their hearts. Early in 1992 these formed the 'National Progress Faction' which came to oppose both Vagnorius and Landsbergis, as well as the demands for an executive presidency.

In 1990 the difference between Landsbergis and the Kaunasite extreme nationalists seemed to lie both in his greater moderation and in his much broader cultural horizons. It is for this reason that a number of enlightened and liberal members of the intelligentsia both in Lithuania and the Lithuanian emigration continue to insist that Landsbergis' shift to an intolerant Rightist position came not through his own ideology but from the power and determination of the Right – that in a sense Landsbergis played the role of a Smetona, deflecting Right-wing radicalism and keeping the country together.

There may initially have been some truth in this but, by the time of the 1992 elections, Landsbergis was in some ways more extreme than most of the Kaunasites themselves. A much more important factor in Landsbergis' shift to radical positions has been ambition, or rather a specific ambition that only the Right could fulfil, because it belongs in principle to the culture of the Right: to become the 'Father of the Nation' on the pattern of Smetona, not simply a president, but a national image to which future generations would refer. The ambition has been fed both by Landsbergis' complete self-identification with Lithuanian culture and by his vast personal vanity. Its effect was to increase the opposition to him among his erstwhile peers, such that he was forced to rely increasingly upon the rump of Sajūdis and on former enemies within the Liberty League, which in turn alienated more of his former supporters. By September 1992, a commentator on Radio Free Europe Lithuanian

Service described Sajūdis as 'a machine for making enemies'. This vicious circle was reflected in Landsbergis' rhetoric. The more hysterical it became, the more supporters he lost in the Centre; and the more supporters he lost, the more hysterical his language as he tried to gain more votes on the Right.

From autumn 1990, Landsbergis had allowed *Lietuvos Aidas*, under his authority as chairman of the Supreme Council, to make slanderous attacks upon opponents of the government, accusing them of treachery and of links with the KGB. The hysteria intensified alongside Landsbergis' campaign for the presidency, and reached a climax in the late spring of 1992. On the initiative of a signature campaign organised by Sajūdis, a referendum on the presidential question was held. By now, however, the National Progress Faction stood in opposition to Sajūdis. The loss also of several Centrist deputies resulted in the loss of Sajūdis control over the Supreme Council.

On 17 May, Sajūdis held a rally outside parliament, attended despite driving rain by several thousand people. Landsbergis made a speech of unprecedented bitterness, declaring that a victory for the parliamentary majority would bring a return to the Russian empire, and that the Left was following the 'scenario of 1940', encouraged by the Russian troops on Lithuania's soil:

> This is not a political struggle, it is a moral struggle, between truth and lies, love and hatred. Our singing revolution was a cry of hope. Should it now surrender to lying traitors and counter-revolutionaries?

Terleckas too was present, and made a speech which highlighted the dangers of forming an alliance with this maverick. While he supported Landsbergis' presidential aspirations, he launched a savage attack on Vagnorius (who was standing beside him) on the grounds of corruption and insufficient patriotism. When the crowd booed, Terleckas roared,

> Yesterday you were cheering Prunskiene. Today you're cheering Vagnorius. Who will you be shouting for tomorrow? Stupid crowd!

It was a speech worthy of Coriolanus, but under the circumstances, not a great help to Landsbergis. The most disquieting aspect of the meeting, and of Sajūdis speeches at this time in general, was the repeated statement that parliament had betrayed the nation, that the deputies no longer represented the people, and that Sajūdis itself now represented 'the nation's will'.

The referendum on 23 May bore out Sajūdis fears. Only 57.5 per cent of a bewildered and disgruntled electorate turned up to vote. This meant that although 69.4 per cent of these approved a presidency, and only 25.6 per cent opposed it, the result was well short of the 51 per cent of all eligible voters required under Lithuanian law. Five per cent cast invalid ballots, in some cases as a means of showing approval of a presidency in principle, but dislike of Landsbergis' candidacy and the methods used to push through the presidential scheme. This defeat effectively put an end to Landsbergis' campaign, though in the days that followed he launched a fierce counter-attack, alleging the opposition was carrying out a 'creeping coup' instigated by Moscow.

In the course of the summer, attempts were made in parliament to remove the government of Vagnorius. These were greatly helped by the fact that several ministers, including Vaišvila (Deputy Premier) and Audrius Butkevičius (Minister of Defence) themselves belonged to the National Progress Faction – which was in opposition to the government! A farcical situation developed, with Vaišvila publicly charging his own Prime Minister with corruption and incompetence, while the Prime Minister (because of his lack of constitutional power) remained unable to sack him without the approval of a parliament in which he no longer had a majority.

In these circumstances the obvious thing for Vagnorius to do was resign, but he clung desperately to power, evidently believing that the parliamentary majority, deeply divided as it was, would not force his resignation because it would be unable to agree on a replacement. So confident was he that on 28 May he even offered his resignation to Landsbergis.

When the parliamentary majority accepted the offer, Vagnorius attempted to avoid his fate by simply refusing to turn up to parliament. This farce went on for weeks, reducing the government to a state of paralysis, until on 22 July the Prime Minister was finally removed after Landsbergis apparently decided his position was untenable. Vagnorius was replaced with Alexandras Abišala – a leading Right-winger and able administrator – in a caretaker role until fresh elections could be held on 25 October. Abišala used his period in office to end the feud with Poland which Landsbergis and Vagnorius had been so assiduously stoking over the previous year (see Chapter 6).

These political developments took place amidst a continuous shower of mud, by now being flung by both sides. In October 1991, when after more than a year of being abused by Čepaitis as agents of Moscow, the Left hit back with KGB documents proving that Čepaitis himself had volunteered to act as a KGB informer in the 1980s. Čepaitis was stripped of his parliamentary mandate, and has now vanished from politics. By a nice irony, according to opinion polls he and Prunskiene are now the two most unpopular politicians in Lithuania.

The affair, however, opened the floodgates of charge and counter-charges of KGB involvement. Sajūdis members of the commission investigating the KGB openly gave documents to *Lietuvos Aidas* to use against their opponents, and members of the parliamentary majority

17 Professor Vytautas Landsbergis at a rally of the Sajūdis movement in Vilnius, 11 March 1992.

gave them to their newspapers in the same way. Soon almost no-one in politics lacked the smear of collaboration with the Communist Party or the KGB, except, it must be said, Landsbergis himself.

Even the defence of imprisonment by the Soviets was disallowed: both Aloyzas Sakalas, the Social Democrat leader, and even Terleckas himself, were accused of informing on their fellow prisoners. As the Left and the National Progress Party members of the KGB commission counter-attacked with documents of their own, Landsbergis lost two of his remaining major supporters, vice-chairmen Bronius Kuzmickas and Česlovas Stankevičius.

Accusations of KGB involvement also surfaced in Estonia during the 1992 election campaign, but to a much lesser extent than in Lithuania. In Estonia, novelist Jaan Kross, a universally respected figure, was appointed to head the commission for investigation into the KGB. He declared his commission would ensure strict control was kept over the archives, so as to prevent them being used in political battles, and that their conclusions would finally be handed over to parliament. Concerning exposed ordinary KGB officers and informers, he added,

> I myself would simply distance myself from them. That is a matter of personal choice; and of course if such people stand for election, the Estonian people can vote against them. All the same I would not forbid anyone to stand; that would be undemocratic.

All three states did in fact adopt laws barring former KGB agents from standing for parliament and high office. Though understandable, this obviously leaves great room for abuse, not least by the KGB itself. As Professor Rein Taagepera remarked during the Estonian 1992 elections,

> I am struck by how many people, especially the anti-communist radicals, believe implicitly that everything a KGB file says must be true! If I were in the KGB, I would have spent the past three years fabricating files to discredit the Baltic leaders. I would have done this either to serve the interests of Moscow or for blackmail to make money for myself.

This is indeed taking place, probably on a large scale. For several thousand roubles, a Lithuanian journalist bought, in 1991, his KGB file from the KGB officer who had interrogated him, and learned the name of the colleague who had denounced him.

Moreover, the faith that everyone named as an informer in the KGB archives really was an informer ignores the way that the KGB really worked. Figures as different as the former KGB Commander in Lithuania, General Marcinkus, and the Latvian radical leader Andrejs Krastiņš have pointed out that not merely did junior officers win praise and promotion for recruiting 'significant sources of information', they were even given financial bonuses. They obviously therefore had a strong interest in exaggerating both the number and the importance of their contacts, in circumstances where their superior officers could not really check whether they were telling the truth or not.

As well as the problem of identifying KGB informers has been the moral question of why petty informers (some of them forced to inform by threats or blackmail) should be exposed and punished when some former top Communists in the Baltic now occupied leading national positions. This issue surfaced during a debate in the Latvian Supreme Council in March 1993 on a bill barring not only informers but also KGB officers from parliament. This move was aimed specifically at Juris Bojārs, leader of the former pro-independence Communists (now renamed the Latvian Democratic Labour Party). Bojārs had so far avoided the rules against the KGB for the curious reason that he had never made any secret about having been no mere informer, but a ranking KGB Major. In the debate, a deputy sympathetic to his party attempted to counter-attack by demanding that senior Communist officials and teachers of Marxism-Leninism should also be banned – a blow at Chairman Anatolijs Gorbunovs and Popular Front leader Uldis Augstkalns, both now on the nationalist side of politics. In a debate which swung between bitterness and comedy, another deputy, Jānis Krumins, then proposed that all barbers should be barred from holding public office, on the grounds that they failed in their patriotic duty by not cutting the throats of occupants who came to them for a shave.

Apart from political strife and national paranoia fuelled by such 'revelations', the other really dangerous element in Lithuania was the lack of any real sense of the need to respect democratic and parliamentary rules. One major reason for the prolonged nature of the crisis in 1992 was that Sajūdis deputies, finding themselves in a minority, decided to paralyse parliament by denying it the quorum to pass legislation. First they boycotted individual votes, and then, in July, quit the hall of parliament itself to hold separate meetings in the Praesidium hall upstairs, under Landsbergis' chairmanship. The Left and Centre groups could not plausibly complain, however, for it was they who, as the parliamentary minority in spring 1991, began the practice of walking-out rather than face defeat, undermining the legitimacy of the parliamentary process as a whole.

This goes to the heart of one of the major weaknesses of 'liberal' groups in much of the former Soviet Union, that while they claim to be defending democracy and parliamentarianism against the threat of authoritarian nationalism, they themselves have very little idea how democracy works.

It contributes to the generally shallow and inchoate nature of their programmes and ideologies.

The Lithuanian crisis also highlighted the difficulty of basing politics and stable government on so many different groups and individuals, much of whose behaviour is purely opportunist. The anti-Sajūdis alliance in 1992 ranged from former Communists all the way to the most extreme nationalists. Many politicians based their actions as much on personal animosity as on any ideological or policy stance. This was true of the hostility of Vaišvila to Vagnorius, and of Vagnorius to the head of the State Bank, Vilius Baldišis. In part this is simply a function of Soviet manners: people exercise power in the crudest way, are incapable of tact or diplomacy, and hurl insults as a matter of course. It would not matter so much within an effective governmental framework; but the crisis also demonstrated that the adapted Soviet constitution had wholly broken down, encouraging irresponsibility in both government and parliament.

On the eve of the elections of October 1992, the popularity of both parliament and its deputies had sunk drastically: the view expressed in opinion polls was that the old deputies must not be re-elected. A sitting deputy, asked why he did not campaign more actively in his constituency, replied, 'Are you mad? My only chance of being re-elected is if they don't realise I was in the last parliament'.

As Chapter 9 reveals, however, the internal political conflicts of 1990–92 did not in the end prevent the passage of a considerable amount of reformist legislation. Moreover, even as the government crisis was proceeding, different factions in parliament were able to reach compromises on a date for elections, the form of the voting system and, most important of all, the draft of a constitution.

The new constitution provides for a government responsible to parliament, but with stronger presidential powers than those in Estonia, or indeed originally envisaged by the Lithuanian parliament. The president has the right to propose to parliament candidates for a range of offices, without having to ask the advice of the prime minister: these include the commanders of the army and security service, the State Controller and chairman of the State Bank, as well as senior judges. The constitution provides that the president can only appoint or dismiss ministers on the recommendation of the prime minister, but since parliament also has the right to dismiss individual ministers, there would seem to be plenty of room for complicated and destructive three-way battles.

The main criticisms of the constitution by Lithuanian liberals and some foreign observers have been directed, however, not at its governmental provisions but at the collectivist tone of parts of its first four chapters – on the individual, society, the economy and the state – which propound the primacy of nation and family over the individual.

The voting system was modelled in part on that of Germany, combining 71 individual candidacies in individual constituencies (in Lithuania, held to favour the Right) with 70 from party lists (held to favour the Left and Centre). The proposed legislature was fundamentally parliamentary, but without the excessive powers which had done so much damage in the previous two years. Overall, the adoption of this compromise constitution reflects once again the Lithuanian national tradition of moderation and pragmatism, which contrasts so starkly with the romantic, dramatic rhetoric and fierce political conflict common to Lithuanians.

In view of the developments sketched above, the defeat of Landsbergis and Sajūdis in the October 1992 election came as no surprise to most Lithuanians. What did cause surprise was the scale of the victory for the Democratic Labour Party (LDDP), Brazauskas's reformed Communists. The opinion polls had predicted the support for the pro-Landsbergis parties accurately, but underestimated the vote for Brazauskas by around 50 per cent. The reason, almost certainly, is that a sizeable majority of voters had decided to vote LDDP, but were afraid, with Landsbergis still in power, to say so to strange pollsters – an object lesson in the difficulty of carrying out such polls in former Communist countries.[26]

The steep decline in living standards was undoubtedly the largest single factor in ensuring Sajūdis's defeat. In the village of Vilunai, in Kaišadorys, I encountered no-one with anything good to say for the outgoing parliament. 'All the politicians are lying. They have stolen everything from us, like devils', an old man said. In this particular constituency, the former Sajūdis Prime Minister, Gediminas Vagnorius, was standing against Brazauskas. A local farmer told me that,

> Yesterday, Sajūdis agitators came to each house, telling us to vote for Vagnorius. They told us, 'If you want to live as you used to under the Communists, vote for Brazauskas, but if you want to live in a new Lithuania, vote for Vagnorius'. But we replied, 'What has Vagnorius done for us? We lived much better before'. So we are all going to vote for Brazauskas. Vagnorius made many nice promises, but in his government he quarrelled with the ministers and they quarrelled with each other. Nothing but accusations and insults, as if they had nothing better to do, as if the people didn't have problems. . . . The priests have been going round encouraging people to vote for Vagnorius, but in this part of Lithuania they don't have so much influence.

Some months earlier, a Russian politician had told me that, 'if Leonid Brezhnev could run for President of Russia today on the basis of a comparison between living standards in his day and those under Boris Yeltsin, he would win by an overwhelming majority'. Living standards in Lithuania (as in the other Baltic States) had deteriorated sharply in the months preceding the election, as the government tried to prepare for winter by economising on fuel. By October, most households were limited to two days of hot water per week, and some had none at all. Heating was switched on only in mid-October, two weeks later than usual, and restricted to 13 degrees centigrade.

The fact that the outgoing parliament was the one that had declared Lithuanian independence had no resonance at all with ordinary people – and indeed, Sajūdis could hardly profit from this reputation since it was by now accusing most of the deputies who had voted for independence of treachery. In general the hostility of voters to the existing parliament worked against Sajūdis. However, since it, like the LDDP, had recruited large numbers of new candidates to replace the many defectors from its ranks, it suffered less than the smaller parties set up by those defectors. The Social Democrats, Liberals, Centrists, Moderates, and National Progress Party were all critically dependent upon a small number of well-known names. Speaking to a Sajūdis election meeting in the rural town of Smalininkai near Jurbarkas, Laima Andrikiene declared that,

> Ninety-eight Sajūdis deputies were elected in 1990, but only 42 still support Sajūdis. That is why we haven't been able to change anything. . . . Somebody has perverted these deputies. The KGB General Eišmantas said that 'we will destroy the parliament from within'. The deputies have been blackmailed and bribed with cars and other things . . . Why is life getting worse? Is it because of the reforms or because somebody is deliberately carrying out sabotage? Look at the prices in August and today: it is because the new government of Abišala, backed by the Left, has given no subsidies. . . . In the village shop, I was told that there would be no more bread until next week. This is deliberate sabotage, to make Sajūdis unpopular in the elections. . . . The shortage of petrol has also been done deliberately. . . .

But this did not wash with most voters; nor did the Sajūdis election poster, declaring that 'the deputies, like the whole country, are divided into two groups: Communists and non-Communists. The Communists have re-baptised themselves with many names: LDDP, Liberals, Social Democrats, Centrists, Moderates.' Most voters I interviewed remembered perfectly well that many of those denounced as crypto-Communists were old associates of Landsbergis.

Particularly in the small world of the villages, few people understood society could not be divided into good Communists and bad anti-Communists, that there were many shades of grey; for eighteen months, people had been complaining about ex-Communists now turned into very public Sajūdis supporters. I was told the story of a teacher criticised by her colleagues for not signing the petition to make Landsbergis President:

'Ah, now we see that you are still a Communist!'

'But you were all Party members too!'

'Yes, but we've shown that we've changed, because we now support Landsbergis.'

In a speech in Vilūnai, Brazauskas tied his arguments very closely to the condition of the farmers:

These elections have to renew the government, not to overthrow it. . . . In the past, we had to struggle against Gorbachov. Now we are free, acknowledged by the world, and we have to look at our internal situation. We can't just say, 'Hurrah, we're independent, now we can die. . . . The Lithuanian people today are suffering, not living. Here in the countryside, the collective farms have been ruined, with everything that goes with them. They no longer have the money to support old people. Instead of building on what has been achieved over the past decades, they want to flatten everything. Before, collective farms were imposed on Lithuania by force. Now, the Lithuanian government is itself trying to decollectivise by force, without consulting the farmers. The farmers have been deceived. Fertilisers, petrol, equipment is too expensive. Land is given only to former owners, who can't farm it. These gentlemen from the government go through the country saying, 'look, how green', but that's because there are now weeds everywhere. . . . We cannot buy fuel for world prices because we don't get world prices for our goods, so we have to deal with Moscow, but all the ministers who knew how to deal with Moscow have been sacked. . . .

On election night, Brazauskas added that 'I have thirty years experience with the Moscow bureaucracy. I know how things work there. I won't get lost in those Moscow corridors.'

These words, with their implication that Brazauskas, on the basis of his old Communist contacts with Yeltsin, would be able to get cheap Russian oil for Lithuania, had some impact on the voters, but the boast is likely to come back to haunt him. From 1992, Moscow's policy on oil sales was governed by commercial advantage, and Lithuania has very few strings to pull.

Brazauskas's approach in the elections, as in the previous two years, was generally sober and down to earth. He avoided personal attacks on Landsbergis and other Sajūdis leaders, which seems to have increased his prestige just as Landsbergis was forfeiting it by the nature of his campaign. The word most frequently used by voters who opposed Landsbergis was 'divisive'. In particular, he was felt to have failed in his duty as chairman of parliament, which was seen as being to reconcile the different parties and keep the peace. In post-Communist societies, unused to rough public debate, great stress is often laid on the need for harmony and unity. By speaking of this while quite obviously practising the opposite, Landsbergis did himself great damage.

In comparison with 1990, election meetings in 1992 were generally smaller and attended mainly by supporters of the party concerned. Far fewer turned up simply out of interest, partly because the campaigns of most of the parties were turgid in the extreme.[27] Party political broadcasts on television lasted an hour, and were almost unwatchable. Though planned to include prepared speeches followed by questions from the studio audience, the politicians, in good Soviet style, regularly used up all the time available.

The difference between the party programmes lay generally in the differing levels of nationalism, rather than profound differences of economic philosophy. With regard to Sajūdis and the LDDP, one Lithuanian observer remarked that 'our problem is, both the opposition and the governing party here are socialist'. This is not true in the field of agriculture, where the difference in approach was very marked. In other areas of the economy, the LDDP, like Sajūdis, committed itself to a free market, while emphasising the need for mass participation in privatisation and the social protection of the poor. Only the Liberal Party ran on a strictly free-market platform, and it was trounced at the polls.

In sharp contrast to Latvia and Estonia, the nationality issue played relatively little part in the thinking of ordinary Lithuanian voters, who did not regard the small Russian and Polish minorities as a great threat. This is without doubt the biggest difference between Lithuania and the other two states, and the key reason why Lithuania swung back to the 'Left' while they drifted steadily to the 'Right'.

The results of the Lithuanian parliamentary elections were:

LDDP	44.4%	(73 seats)
Sajūdis	20.9%	(30 seats)
Christian Democrats	12.4%	(18 seats)
Social Democrats	6.0%	(8 seats)
Nationalists		(4 seats)
Polish Union		(4 seats)
Centre		(2 seats)
Independents		(2 seats)

The turnout in the first round was 72 per cent, in the second only 60 per cent. Three extra seats were later allotted to the LDDP after it appealed against some flagrantly biased decisions on the part of the Election Commission.[28]

LDDP victories were spread across the country, although they were most numerous in rural areas and the south-east, with large Russian and Polish minorities who consistently preferred Brazauskas. The LDDP was as shocked as anyone by the results: it had not expected anything like a triumph on this scale, and had put up only 71 candididates for the 141 seats. When I interviewed Brazauskas four days before the election, he told me that,

> We are not setting our hopes on the government. We will suggest only one or two of us for ministerial jobs, in the field of agriculture and material resources. We will suggest a member of another party as chairman of parliament, one of us as deputy chairman. It will only cause unrest in the streets if a former Communist takes the top position. This top figure ought to bring the people of Lithuania together. To prove our loyalty to Lithuania, we need time and practical action, not just speeches. We need to wait until the Right gets over its disease of neo-Bolshevism, its habit of accusing all opponents of being traitors and enemies of the people.

On the evening of the first round, as the extent of the victory became clear, there was fear as well as jubilation in the LDDP headquarters, and the Party continued to stress its desire for consensus. There was, above all, fear of the Right's reaction: of violent demonstrations or even a coup by nationalist paramilitaries – though in the end most of Landsbergis' bodyguard was retired without trouble, retreating into the shadowy world of 'security firms' and 'sports clubs' from which it had come.

Although Landsbergis surrendered power with very bad grace, continuing to make hints about Moscow's influence and the threat to Lithuania's independence, he promised 'constructive opposition'. It was obvious he would not countenance a coup, even though one of his supporters, Kazimieras Uoka, the aggressive young Comptroller of State Finances, threatened mass demonstrations if Sajūdis failed to get more than 50 seats in the second round of voting. Western diplomats also warned privately that for the sake of Lithuania's international position, the changeover of power must be allowed to proceed smoothly. Brazauskas continued to try to distance himself and the LDDP from direct responsibility for the government. The smaller Centrist parties (which had in any case been almost wiped out) refused a coalition, but as his first Prime Minister Brazauskas chose the existing Deputy Premier, Bronislovas Lubys. A member of the Liberal Party, Lubys represented Brazauskas's desire for compromise, but as former manager of the huge Azotas chemicals plant in Jonava, he was also at the heart of the old Communist establishment now back in power. Most of the new ministers were from this background, though on the whole from the State, rather than the Party side of the former regime. In March 1993, Lubys was replaced with a more compliant figure, Adolfas Slezevičius.

Brazauskas now, not surprisingly, opted to become chairman, and to stand as president in the February 1993 elections. To avoid further humiliation Landsbergis dropped out, and in the end the only challenger to Brazauskas was Stasys Lozoraitis, the Ambassador to Washington and former Ambassador to the Holy See. For decades of Soviet rule Lozoraitis had been the chief representative of the legally continuing independent Lithuanian state. He had in effect inherited the role from his father, a Lithuanian diplomat and foreign minister.

Lozoraitis is a courteous, distinguished figure, his manners and style deeply marked by the years he spent in Rome (his wife is Italian). During the election campaign he was at pains to stress the need for consensus, and offered if elected to appoint Brazauskas Prime Minister. He made only one serious slip, when he spoke of the possibility of Lithuania's 'recovering' Kaliningrad, a statement denounced by Brazauskas as unnecessary provocation of Russia. Lozoraitis was backed by almost all the parties outside the LDDP, for the Centrists had become alarmed by Brazauskas's new dominance.

Lozoraitis's popularity among ordinary Lithuanians suffered from the fact that since his youth (he was born in 1924) he had spent relatively little time in Lithuania. He might have hoped to profit from the 'cargo cult', the general admiration for Westerners throughout Eastern Europe, but was attacked from within the emigration by Kažys Bobelis, former leader of the hardline nationalist emigré 'Committee for the Liberation of Lithuania' (VLIK) and son of the Commandant of Kaunas under the Nazis.

This unpleasant and even sinister figure was elected to parliament in October 1992 with the support of the neo-fascist 'Young Lithuania' group. Subsequently, however, he backed Brazauskas – seemingly out of pure opportunism – and was appointed by him as chairman of the Foreign Relations Committee.

On 14 February 1993, Brazauskas was elected President, with 60 per cent of the vote to Lozoraitis's 38 per cent. Coupled with his party's absolute majority in parliament, this gives Brazauskas a dominance unique among leaders of former Communist states in Europe. As the LDDP attempts to find deputies with whom to make a coalition show, even it does not regard its position as an undiluted blessing. The LDDP must now take full responsibility for economic policy and economic hardship.

In the first months of Brazauskas's rule there was no sign of a reversal of privatisation, except in relation to agriculture. The massive move of the state managerial class (Brazauskas's strong supporters) into private business meant they had a vested interest in privatisation – their kind of privatisation. There were, moreover, signs that the new government might be more favourable to business than Sajūdis, especially in terms of tax concessions and tariff reductions. More worrying is the growth of unhealthily close links between ex-Communist business and ex-Communist bureaucracy and government, or 'crony capitalism'.

18 Algirdas Brazauskas, President of Lithuania from February 1993.

One major concern, however, was that Brazauskas's populist election promises might trap the government into breaking Lithuania's agreement with the IMF. Brazauskas gave out contradictory signals, saying the agreement 'cannot be broken', but also referring to it as a 'burden'. The IMF was uneasy, both by this and by simultaneous promises to raise wages, agricultural prices and industrial subsidies and to lower food prices, bringing with them the danger of hyper-inflation.

By the time of the 1993 presidential election, Vytautas Landsbergis was, for the moment at least, no longer a figure of central political importance. During the campaign even the partisan *Lietuvos Aidas* advised Landsbergis' supporters not to get too close to Lozoraitis for fear of losing him votes among Centrists. The eclipse of Landsbergis astonished many Western observers; but what Landsbergis shared with his arch-enemy Mikhail Gorbachov was precisely the contrast between their popularity and prestige in the West and their lack of it at home: much Western reporting had given a thoroughly misleading picture of the political realities in their countries.

The selection of Landsbergis as 'The Representative Lithuanian Hero' by the Western media reflects their need to present 'foreign' cultures in ways that are immediately comprehensible in Western terms, with 'democratic' and/or 'progressive' forces opposing the forces of darkness. This kind of naive liberal positivism continues to blight Western reporting of much of the world; Left and Right-wing newspapers are equally guilty.

As with Benazir Bhutto, Cory Aquino and similar figures, the approach reveals a deep need for heroes, even (or especially) on the part of Western liberals who have relentlessly banished heroism from their own culture. In this respect, these well-meaning people are reminiscent of Professor Immanuel Rath in *The Blue Angel*, who from a loveless existence fell for a most unsuitable female, and was made a clown of when she revealed herself as she really was.

This is not to deny Landsbergis his share of either heroism or historical importance. His physical and moral courage were amply demonstrated after March 1990 and particularly in January 1991 when he really did emerge as a national leader. On the world stage, he was a mixed blessing for Lithuania, helping give his countrymen a reputation for reckless bravado. But the most curious and even tragic aspect of Landsbergis is that he so greatly misjudged the temper of his own people. He was not mistaken about their valour or steadfastness in time of danger, but failed altogether to appreciate their dour underlying pragmatism, or the degree to which they had been changed by Soviet rule and modernisation in general.

In the aftermath of the 1992 election, Landsbergis' whole attempt to recreate a backward-looking, religiously-coloured nationalism seems a mere piece of baroque theatre, brilliant but brief. It is, however, too early to say if it is gone for ever, or whether a long period of grinding national poverty and political turmoil might resurrect it, as a national blanket against the intolerable cold of the modern age.

There were beautiful sides to Landsbergis' nationalism, but others which were profoundly ugly. The greatest charge against him is perhaps that unlike the national leaders with whom he would like to be compared – Churchill and de Gaulle – he left the nation more divided than when he became its leader, and Lithuanian democracy badly scarred. There is, moreover, no sign that he has learnt from his mistakes: up to March 1993 his central tactic remained that of suggesting that Brazauskas and his government are working for Moscow. His wider historical importance lies in the push he and Sajūdis gave to the disintegrating Soviet Union, and in the resistance he and many ordinary Lithuanians offered the Soviet backlash in January 1991. In neither case was Landsbergis' or Lithuania's contribution decisive: Soviet decline was prescribed by wider factors. But without him, and the Lithuanians, the course of events might have been quite considerably different.

It is for this contribution that Balts will always remember Landsbergis with a certain gratitude, however great their criticism. As to whether the disintegration of the Soviet Union – as opposed to the end of Communism – was a good thing for the Soviet peoples or humanity as a whole, this question will be decided by history.

Ethnic Estonian Politics, 1990–92

According to the schema in the introduction to this chapter, Estonian and Latvian politics in 1990–92 represented a protracted duel between the proponents of the First and Second Republics, ending in victory for the former.[29] The formal protagonists in this struggle were on one hand the Supreme Councils (in Russia, *Soviets*), the 'parliaments' of the Soviet Baltic republics which, after the spring elections of 1990, were dominated by pro-independence Popular Fronts; and on the other, the Congresses, set up by radical nationalist groups and elected only by pre-1940 citizens and their descendants.

In the course of 1989 and early 1990, the radicals carried out voluntary registration of the potential Congress electorates. Elections were held in the winter of 1990 and the Congresses met in March and May in Estonia and Latvia respectively. In each republic, an absolute majority of ethnic Latvians and Estonians (almost 700,000 of the latter) voted in the

Congress elections. A very few pre-1940 Russians participated or were elected as observers.

The Congresses called the Supreme Soviets 'institutions of foreign occupation', and denied their legitimacy, at least in constitutional questions and 'matters of key national importance', such as citizenship for the Russians. Supporters of the Supreme Councils denounced the Congresses as revolutionary forces which would bring disorder and Soviet intervention.

Membership of these two bodies, however, overlapped. In Estonia, while the National Independence Party, led by former dissidents, refused any part in the Supreme Council, several more moderate nationalist parties, like the Christian Democrats, while they identified with the Congress principles, came under the Popular Front umbrella and entered the Supreme Councils in the 1990 elections. Around 40 Congress members also sat in the Supreme Council.

In Latvia, the 'Citizens Committees' (which organised the Congress elections), remained aloof from the Supreme Council, but the National Independence Movement (LNNK) was initially in alliance with the Popular Front and entered the Supreme Council where its leader, Andrejs Krastiņš, became deputy chairman. On the other side, even many Centrist supporters of the Popular Fronts and the Supreme Councils nonetheless welcomed the creation of the Congresses, and participated in elections to them, out of fear that because of the Russian populations, the Supreme Councils might not achieve a two-thirds majority in favour of independence; or that Moscow would impose central rule and pack these bodies with Soviet stooges.

In this case, it was felt, it was essential that the nations should have some legitimate elected body to fall back on. In Lithuania, the preponderance of ethnic Lithuanians in the population meant that there was no need for an institution like the Congresses. In 1990, the governments of both Edgar Savisaar and Ivars Godmanis sought compromises with the Congresses. Savisaar addressed the first session of the Congress in Tallinn, though he broke an agreement to share power with it. His government, formed when the Supreme Council met in April 1990, however, contained no representatives of the radical nationalists, being formed above all from men who like himself had been senior members of the former Soviet establishment.

Three of Savisaar's ministers were still Communist Party members when the government was formed. Savisaar himself, like Social Democrat leader Marju Lauristin, had resigned from the Party a short while before. Lauristin, who for a long time was Savisaar's close ally, was professor of journalism at Tartu University and had signed mildly dissident statements during Brezhnev's rule (see Chapter 4). She was also the daughter of the first prime minister of Soviet Estonia, Johannes

275

Lauristin, and step-sister of Jaak Allik, previously Communist Ideology Secretary. That she ended up as an ally of the Congress says something for both their and her own flexibility.

From 1990–91, the Congresses appeared to be losing the struggle with the Supreme Councils. Balts who were content with them as a fall-back were alarmed at their radicalism and the possibility of conflict with Moscow, and their support waned. Their endless criticism of the Popular Front governments came to seem divisive and negative at a time when the nations were in danger. They were also deeply divided internally, not least in their attitude to co-operation with the Supreme Councils. An Estonian emigré analyst, Riina Kionka, wrote in January 1991 that by the third Estonian Congress session the previous October, 'most observers pronounced the Congress more-or-less dead as a politically influential movement'.

Congress denunciation of the Supreme Councils as 'occupation bodies' was undermined when the Supreme Council in Lithuania proclaimed independence. The Supreme Councils in Latvia and Estonia declared *de jure* independence in 1990, and *de facto* independence in August 1991. It was the Supreme Council that the Estonian people rallied to defend when attacked by Soviet loyalist demonstrators on 15 May 1990. Thereafter support for the Congresses among ethnic Estonians and Latvians never rose above 25 per cent.

Ultimately, however, a large number of former Popular Front deputies in both Latvia and Estonia came to accept the Congress position on restitution of the First Republics and especially on the refusal of automatic citizenship to Russian 'immigrants'. There are various secondary reasons for this, including the intellectual and financial influence of large parts of the Baltic emigrations in the West, many of whom took a hardline restitutionist and anti-Russian position. There are also two central reasons. First, the restitutionists had at least a clear image of what they sought, backed by the golden glow which time and Soviet rule had cast over the First Republics. Their opponents spoke of liberalism, democracy and a modern society, but their own understanding of these terms was often too deficient for them to argue effectively for them.

Even more important, however, was the Russian question. The restitutionists, in arguing openly for strict limits on Russian citizenship and more covertly for encouraging or even driving them to leave, tapped an almost universal vein of anti-Russian feeling within the Baltic populations. In contrast, the moderate Popular Fronts' politicians who argued in favour of granting citizenship automatically to the Russians (the 'Zero Option'), did so, with rare exceptions, not out of commitment to a multicultural liberal democracy, or to civic values, but simply out of fear: fear of local Russian revolt or at least obstruction of the independence process, invasion by Moscow, or diplomatic isolation from a critical West.

When none of these things happened not merely did the moderates lose their public arguments, but much of their internal support for Russian rights vanished, and their public position shifted rapidly. Thus the swing of Marju Lauristin to an anti-Russian position after the achievement of independence in August 1991 can be explained partly by political 'necessity'. Her long negotiations, as head of the Citizenship Commission, to construct a more generous citizenship law, were finally ended by a wrecking motion on 16 October 1991, after which she told me that,

> I now support going back to the naturalisation law of 1938. We have no other choice, given the deep conflicts that exist over this issue. We have to go back to the only law that is there, that has legitimacy.

Thereafter, however, Lauristin's remarks about Russians and Russia took on a new, more hostile tinge, perhaps the result of her own long-suppressed feelings of hostility, or perhaps a more complicated process of justifying to herself her change of position.

Only a very few Balts, like the Estonian poet Jaan Kaplinksi, the Latvian Foreign Minister Jānis Jurkāns, or the Latvian emigré Nils Muižnieks, continued supporting Russian rights because they felt that it was right to do so, or because they disliked the idea of a narrow, stuffy, ethnic-based state; and their arguments cut increasingly less ice with the bulk of their compatriots.

Savisaar has also been a consistent advocate of compromise with the Russians, though his enemies have claimed this is only because of a calculation that when or if large numbers of Russians do in fact become citizens, they will vote for him out of gratitude. His supporters say that his position is based on an enlightened assessment of the need for ethnic harmony.

What his friends argue is difficult to say, because he has so few. Even by post-Soviet standards, Edgar Savisaar is an abrasive figure whose political problems have been partly due to his having alienated so many former allies. He was known as 'Piggy' by some Estonian officials, and not only because of his weight. Savisaar's crude manners are a feature of all too many post-Soviet politicians, and led to much unnecessary strife. His arrogance and abnormal sensitivity to criticism are also doubtless due to his origins, as the illegitimate son of a woman whom his enemies allege was Russian.

Although almost 70 per cent of the deputies elected to the Estonian Supreme Council in March 1990 belonged to the Popular Front, and continued to do so until after the achievement of independence in August

1991, it would be more accurate to say that the parliament was divided into four loose groups, only one of them wholly outside the Front. This group was made up of Soviet loyalists, and was overwhelmingly Russian, just as the others were overwhelmingly Estonian; it has been discussed earlier and can be discounted here because it played almost no part in the political disputes of the Estonians themselves. Savisaar's attempts to build bridges with moderate members of this group were frustrated by opposition from other Estonian politicians and the hardline attitudes of the Soviet loyalists themselves.

Of the three Estonian groups in parliament, the largest was the 'core' Popular Front, made up of the sort of people who had created the original party in 1988: junior Communist Party members and reformist but non-dissident intellectuals. In 1992, after numerous defections, this group transformed itself into a Front party under Savisaar's leadership, was defeated in the election, and went into opposition.

The second group was made up of the forty or so radical nationalist deputies who also sat in the Congress. In 1992 these were to form the *Isamaa* (Fatherland) moderate nationalist alliance, and the focus of the government of Mart Laar. They also were mainly intellectuals, though generally younger and more dynamic than the 'core' Popular Frontists, with fewer connections to the old Communist system. Unlike the more radical National Independence Party, however, their leaders were not ex-dissidents.

The third group consisted of senior Communists who had held power before the March 1990 elections, led by former Prime Minister Indrek Toome. At the end of 1989, with the Party already clearly doomed, they formed the *Vaba Eesti* (Free Estonia) group; most left the Communist Party, which by now had split between Russians and an Estonian rump under Enn-Arno Sillari. The rump diminished steadily, and failed to win any seats in the October 1992 election. Free Estonia continued to play a prominent role, and after many twists and turns, eventually gave birth to the *Kindel Kodu* (Secure Home) party, which came second in the 1992 elections.

Leading members of Secure Home tended to have been very much more senior in the State (and sometimes the Party) apparatus than the Popular Frontists. They harboured considerable resentment against Savisaar for having excluded them from power, even though there were in fact several leading former Communists in his cabinet. Arnold Rüütel, chairman of the Supreme Council before and after the 1990 election, was close to this group, though by keeping his associations discreet this silver fox of the Baltic political scene preserved a wholly unearned reputation for being 'above politics'. His anodyne phraseology expertly serviced the Estonian need for calm and reassurance, and concealed his lack of intelligence.

Rüütel, like Gorbunovs and even Brazauskas (in his Minotaurean fashion) is a handsome man in the Soviet understanding of the word. His manner is pleasant and unassuming, and he was described as 'hopelessly likeable' by one journalist who strongly disapproved of him and his retinue of sleazy ex-apparachiks. Meanwhile, Rüütel covered himself with the nationalists by moving steadily to a hardline position on the question of Russian citizenship – although, in contrast to his counterpart Anatolijs Gorbunovs in Latvia, this probably also corresponded to his own deeper feelings. Other Free Estonia figures, such as Toome, also moved towards an increasingly nationalist position.

Although Rüütel was involved in autumn 1990 in the first concerted attack on Savisaar's government – by an unholy alliance of the Free Estonia group and the Congress supporters – he never showed his hand, throughout the period of Savisaar's government, in the attempts to undermine the Premier. The first attack took the curious form of an accusation that the government, and specifically the Foreign Minister (and later President) Lennart Meri, had betrayed Estonian interests in collusion with the Bush administration by failing to secure a guarantee of Baltic legal independence in the 'Two plus Four' agreement on German Unity. It turned into a general attack on Savisaar, with the Congress supporters and Free Estonia jointly demanding his resignation and the formation of a government of national unity.

Leader of the attack on Meri was another minister, Professor Endel Lippmaa. A former senior member of the Soviet scientific establishment, Professor Lippmaa was closest to Free Estonia (later to Secure Home) and to Rüütel, although he posed as an independent. He showed no loyalty to the Savisaar government, although he remained in it until July 1991 as Minister without Portfolio for relations with Moscow.[30]

Though, before August 1991, Savisaar was repeatedly attacked by Lippmaa and others for his conciliatory policy towards Moscow, there is no evidence this lost him popularity with the cautious and pragmatic Estonians. On the contrary, he gained through being seen to have averted in Estonia the sort of Soviet attack which occurred in the other Baltic States in January 1991.

Throughout this period Savisaar held regular meetings with Soviet commanders in Estonia, to resolve any local sources of strife. In this way he also secured tacit Soviet agreement to a large part of the Estonian economic reform programme. The reforms failed to halt a steep decline in the Estonian economy, but provided a much better base for Western investment than elsewhere in the Baltic. This did not of course stop ordinary Estonians grumbling; while the educated classes were growing critical of Savisaar's dictatorial style. Much of the opposition was directed at his attempts to turn the Popular Front from a broad umbrella movement into a disciplined party – just as Landsbergis and Čepaitis

279

19   Anatolijs Gorbunovs, Arnold Rüütel and Vytautas Landsbergis, 12 May 1990.

sought to do in Lithuania, albeit from a very different political standpoint. Savisaar, however, could not count on the support of many politicians who were otherwise still his allies: Marju Lauristin, for example, had no intention of seeing her own power and the Social Democratic Party vanish into a Popular Front party under Savisaar's dictatorial leadership.

Like Landsbergis, Savisaar could not decide what he most wanted. On one hand, for the Popular Front to become *his* party, it would inevitably have to become much smaller and relinquish its claim to represent the whole nation. On the other, Savisaar wanted to preserve the Front as *the* national movement, and continue denouncing political parties in general as 'little groups which splinter society and bicker amongst themselves'.[31]

The critical damage to Savisaar's popularity and prestige came in June–July 1991, and was above all the work of Lippmaa. Unlike the obscure 'Two plus Four' controversy, which bewildered most Estonians, Lippmaa's second attack orchestrated a national consensus – on the issue of Russian rights and Estonian territorial integrity.

In early summer 1991, it seemed as if Soviet attempts to separate Russian-speaking north-eastern Estonia were moving towards a critical point (see Chapter 7). Savisaar decided to try to divide the Russians, and win over the moderate elements, by offering the status of a free-trade zone to the town of Narva. This was very much less than the full autonomy the hardline Soviet loyalists had demanded, but it provoked a furious response among Estonian nationalists, who accused Savisaar of preparing to surrender Estonian territory. The campaign was led by Lippmaa who – finally – resigned in protest, and engineered the rejection of the proposal during its second reading in the Supreme Council. In the course of the debate, Lippmaa, speaking of Savisaar, asked how a man with a Russian mother could defend Estonian interests. Shortly afterwards, the failure of the August counter-revolution rendered Savisaar's offer obsolete.

The achievement of independence, without bloodshed, boosted Savisaar's popularity. His power, however, never really recovered from the defeat of his Narva policy, and there were increasing calls from all sides for a government of national unity. Allies such as Lauristin distanced themselves and, in the autumn, Savisaar was strongly attacked for refusing to implement a voucher scheme for mass participation in privatisation which had been agreed by parliament. His position was further damaged by his covert attempts to help create a moderate Russian political force in Estonia, the Russian Democratic Movement, formed soon after the coup. If most Estonians had been prepared to compromise with the Russians over citizenship and language questions, this moderate movement might have developed into a valuable group of *interlocuteurs valables*. As it was, it was soon forced into opposition and by the following year had formed an alliance with the old hardline Communists forming together the 'Estonian Assembly of Russian Speakers'. As the Estonian position hardened, even Savisaar's Minister for Ethnic Relations, Dr Artur Kuznetsov, was dismissed and forced into opposition. There was then no Russian on the Estonian side of politics for whom local Russians felt any trust. When the new Centre-Right government of Mart Laar took power a year later, no non-Estonians were included, and the Ministry for Ethnic Relations was abolished, although in other ways this government has sought good relations with the local Russians.

After the Moscow coup, loyalist Russian town councils in the north-east were dismissed, and fresh elections called for 20 October. The Communists were returned to power in Narva and Sillamae, while in Kohtla-Jarve a democratic alliance of Estonians and Russians was returned, splitting the anti-Estonian position in the region. Since then, the threat of a secession of the North East appears to have receded, and local demonstrations in favour of autonomy have received very little support. In general, local Russian groups in Estonia now stressed their loyalty to Estonia and tried to distance themselves from their pro-Soviet pasts. The Russian Assembly stressed that it was not trying to become an alternative power-structure along the lines of previous Soviet attempts.

In September, a compromise between the Supreme Council and the Congress, which Savisaar had long resisted, was formalised with the creation of a Constitutional Assembly made up equally of representatives of both bodies. Given the numbers of radical nationalists in the Supreme Council, this inevitably led to a new constitution drawn up on the basis of that of 1922. Seven of the thirty representatives elected by the Supreme Council were Russians, but they were hopelessly outnumbered and had little influence.

The new constitution provided for a parliamentary government with a largely symbolic presidency. Parliament was to be elected by a complicated voting system, half proportional representation and half constituency. The failings of the 1922 constitution, which had helped destroy democracy during the 1920s and 1930s were to be avoided by strengthening the power of the prime minister and by creating a four per cent hurdle for parties wishing to enter parliament – though this was undermined by allowing members of parties which failed to secure this minimum support to get in by winning their constituencies.

The new voting rules encouraged the formation of a number of large electoral blocks, which contested the election in September 1992. Thus Lauristin and the Social Democrats, together with various other former Centrist Popular Front leaders (like Ignar Fjuk, who had split with Savisaar), came together to form the Moderate Alliance; the Christian Democrats and various other Rightist groups formed the Fatherland block, and parties representing the former Communist establishment made up the curiously named 'Safe Homes' movement – an attempt to play on Estonian fears of rising rates of crime. By the end of 1992, these blocks had cohered fairly well, and the Estonian political scene was more disciplined than in the great majority of post-Communist countries.

On 6 November, in a separate decision on the advice of the Constitutional Assembly, the Supreme Council decided to revert to the Citizenship Law of 1938, restoring citizenship automatically to pre-1940 citizens and their descendants (this was ultimately extended to emigrés as well), and stripping the existing Russian 'immigrant' population of its existing citizenship and forcing it through a rigorous naturalisation process. This was another defeat for Savisaar, a long-time proponent of the 'Zero Option' on citizenship.

The death-blow for Savisaar as Prime Minister came in January 1992, ostensibly the result of a severe energy crisis provoked by cuts in fuel supplies from Russia. Heating of homes and food supplies had plummeted at the coldest time of year. Emergency plans were drawn up to evacuate hundreds of thousands from Tallinn to the countryside, though in the event the evacuation was staved off by Western aid. Savisaar was accused of failing to prepare for the cuts by seeking supplies on the free market.

By this point, however, a majority of Estonian deputies were opposed to Savisaar, and the measure succeeded only with the support of the Russian and Soviet loyalist deputies, including three Soviet officers. These deputies actually outnumbered Savisaar's Estonian supporters. When the realisation dawned on Estonians that their government was dependent upon Russian votes, the anger was such that many of Savisaar's remaining supporters abandoned him, the attempt to form a commission to draw up the emergency powers was defeated, and Savisaar himself resigned. He devoted the following months to transforming what was left of the Popular Front into a party of the Centre-Left under his strict control, and to consolidating its role as the chief Left-wing, or rather populist critic of the effects of free market reform on ordinary people.

Given the suffering imposed by that reform, Savisaar is bound to play an important future political role as a spokesman for its victims. On the other hand, under the parliamentary constitution, Estonian governments for the foreseeable future will be coalitions, and since Savisaar had made himself so unpopular, the other parties are unlikely to enter a coalition with the Popular Front so long as he was leader of it.

To succeed Savisaar, a caretaker government was appointed to hold office until the introduction of the constitution and new elections. The new Prime Minister was the former Transport Minister, Tiit Vähi, a colourless former state manager from Southern Estonia who was close to Rüütel and the former Free Estonia (now Secure Home) group. The great triumph of his nine months in office was the successful introduction in June of the long-awaited Estonian currency, the Kroon (see Chapter 9). Otherwise, Vähi's government worked competently, although there were accusations that corruption and 'spontaneous privatisation' had flourished among his friends from the state managerial class. His controversial appointment of another member of that class, Ulo Uluots, as Defence Minister (over a force naturally largely composed of radical nationalists) led almost to a loss of state control over the Home Guard, which in the summer engaged in a series of clashes with the Russian army against the orders of the government.

On 28 June 1992, the constitution was adopted by an overwhelming majority – not surprisingly, given that all the main parties from both Supreme Council and Congress supported it. The Congress announced that it would dissolve itself as soon as the new parliament (*Riikikogu*) met after the election. A second proposal included in the referendum – to extend citizenship automatically to the five thousand or so non-citizens who had applied for it – was defeated by 53 per cent to 46 per cent. The introduction of a constitution by national consensus distinguishes Estonia from all other former Soviet republics but Lithuania, and is a further element in its international prestige – despite the exclusion of the great majority of its Russian population.

The emergence in May–June 1992 of opposition to the new constitution from a position even more radical than that of the National Independence Party and the Congress was, however, a surprise. Initially called 'Restitution', it emerged originally from the self-styled 'Government in Exile', an emigré group based in Sweden. Endel Lippmaa was among its leaders. 'Restitution' argued that the new constitution was illegal and redundant, since the constitution of 1938 remained in force. However, given that constitution incorporated an authoritarian presidency, and had been introduced during the dictatorship of Konstantin Päts, even the Congress found it unacceptable. Inconsistently enough, the 'Government in Exile' and the 'Estonian Citizen' also party to which it gave birth, rejected the 1938 Citizenship law as too liberal and called for it to be amended to restrict naturalisation still further.

Estonian Citizen was led by Jüri Toomepuu, a bald, whiskery, extremely volatile retired Lieutenant-Colonel of the US Army who, according to one of his own leading supporters, favours cut-outs of Rambo with his own head super-imposed upon them. In the election of 20 September, Toomepuu won twice as many personal votes as any other candidate, helping his party to an 8 per cent of the total vote and 8 seats in parliament. His supporters are bitterly anti-Russian, and have formed a 'Decolonisation Committee' to draw up plans to facilitate the Russian leaving. Not surprisingly in view of Toomepuu's past, they are also passionately interested in the armed forces.

The Royalist Party – an Estonian equivalent to Poland's 'Orange Alternative' – established as a sort of joke by a group of actors, television personalities and intellectuals, also polled 8 per cent of votes and the same number of seats. Some of the party's leaders are genuine monarchists who believe that a monarchy under a Swedish prince would help to restore Estonian traditional society and avoid vulgar competition for the top state post, but most simply want to liven the Estonian scene.

The Royalists, and the Estonian Citizen group, evidently benefitted from the protest votes of an electorate weakened by economic suffering and disaffected by the main political parties. I asked a Royalist voter if she really wanted a King: 'Oh no,' she replied, 'I'm a very moderate Royalist'. Few Royalist supporters had heard the widespread rumours that they were not a joke after all, but a group deliberately and secretly created by Savisaar to split the Right-wing vote.

The turn-out at the September 1992 election was 67 per cent, markedly lower than in the years of the independence struggle, but still high by some Western standards. Public attendance at election rallies had been minimal, and on polling day many voters did not know the difference between the parties: indeed many claimed the same platform. None – not even the Popular Front – advocated improved rights for the Russians:

with so few Russians in the electorate, there was no advantage in doing so. All the main parties now paid at least lip service to the free market and the restoration of the forms of the First Republic, while differing in emphasis. Even Secure Home claimed to be a 'Centre-Right' party, which as a party of former Communists turned private businessmen and 'proprietors of state industry, it indeed was. What characterised Fatherland and the National Independence Party in particular was 'desovietisation', the purging of the state and even of industry of the sort of people represented by Secure Home. Whether it would work was not clear.

The full results of the election to the 100-seat chamber were: Fatherland (*Isamaa*), 29 seats; Secure Home (*Kindel Kodu*), 17; Popular Front (Savisaar), 15; Moderates (Lauristin), 12; National Independence Party, 10; Estonian Citizen (*Eesti Kodanik*), 8; Royalists, 8; Greens, 1; and Entrepreneurs Party, 1. The Fatherland and Moderate alliances and the National Independence Party formed a coalition government, as they had indicated they would, under Fatherland leader Mart Laar, a cheerful and apparently able 32-year-old former historian. After two defections, from the Estonian Citizen and Secure Home groups, the government's majority rose to three, but remained precarious.

Fatherland had stood on a mixture of free-market economics, restitutionalism, and moderate nationalism, under the overall slogan 'cleaning house', represented by an election poster depicting a man with a broom.[322] The symbolism was widely taken as a reference to the unpopularity and corruption of the former Soviet rule, but Russians in the republic inevitably took it as a reference to them.

While the election results by no means represented an unequivocal endorsement of plans for the restitution of property or free market economics, Fatherland certainly presented a more modern image than its rivals. Secure Home did best among rural voters who supported the old Collective Farm leadership mainly out of anger at the worsening economic climate and at the manner in which decollectivisation had been implemented.

The membership of the new government was evenly balanced between its three constituent parties, and included several non-party experts and three Estonian emigrés. It had a strongly intellectual cast, and was seen by foreign observers as highly honest, potentially able, and relatively free from links with the Communist bureaucracy or the new 'business' circles. The most unexpected appointment was that of Lagle Parek as Interior Minister. The choice of a woman ex-political prisoner, without administrative experience, as head of an overwhelmingly male, and still largely Russian security force seemed provocative. Parek was also soon being accused of failure to get to grips with the job.

During the election campaign party differences were evident not simply in terms of ideology, but also in physical appearance. Secure Home's leadership, as might have been expected, consisted of solid-looking middle-aged men in business suits, very much on the old Soviet leadership pattern. The suits were now often of excellent Western design, but like the haircuts, very conservative. Fatherland's image was decidedly younger and more stylish. Its leaders wore up-to-date Western suits – but good ones, not the flashy variety favoured by most post-Soviet businessmen – and wore them with a certain air. Beards were much in evidence. The party's support among Estonian youth was greatly helped by the endorsement of the country's leading rock and pop bands.

The activists of the Popular Front and the Moderates, by contrast, looked like people who had just missed the bus: 1970s-style sideburns, clothes stylish a decade ago; indeed a very Soviet time-lag. Its supporters too tended to be about ten years older than those of the Fatherland, who were in general those whose adult lives had coincided with Gorbachov. The Popular Frontists, by contrast, were people whose formative years had been spent under Brezhnev, and who already had a place in society.

The former dissident leadership of the National Independence party evidently thinks the issue of clothes and image to be frivolous, although some of its leaders have a tweedy, musty respectability probably derived from pre-1940 family traditions. Its election poster portrayed a man in a top hat, like an advertisement for a Fred Astaire movie, meant to demonstrate a desire for a return to the pre-1940 status quo. The Royalists have appeared in public wearing everything from shamanistic headdresses to dustbin-liners.

In the first round of voting for the presidency, simultaneous with the parliamentary election, there were four candidates. By far the most popular was the existing chairman, Arnold Rüütel. So strongly was the intellectual tide now running against former leading Communists, however, that only Secure Home supported him. Throughout the campaign he was plagued by questions about his Communist past, and especially about his official links with the KGB. Fatherland fielded former Foreign Minister (then Ambassador to Finland) Lennart Meri; the Popular Front put up the leading Estonian-Canadian academic, Rein Taagepera, and the National Independence Party, Lagle Parek. The last three candidates declared they were standing against Arnold Rüütel rather than against each other. The Silver Fox was finally cornered: he could not win outright on the first, popular, ballot, and when the vote went to parliament, a majority of deputies were already pledged to reject him.

The popular vote for Rüütel was 41.8 per cent, as against 29.5 per cent for Meri, 23.3 per cent for Taagepera, and 4.2 per cent for Parek. To the considerable anger of ordinary Estonians, parliament blithely disregarded the near certainty that Rüütel would win a second-round popular vote, and selected Meri. Rüütel did not trouble to hide his chagrin, rejecting parliament's thanks for his services to Estonian independence with the words that they were like 'a waiter who has spilt wine over your coat and then clumsily tries to mop it up'.

The new President, Lennart Meri, is one of the most vivid and interesting characters in Baltic politics; but as a headline in the *Baltic Independent* had it, 'Charm and Ability Leave Questions Unanswered'. He is the nearest thing Estonia has to a 'cultural politician', like Landsbergis, and was chosen as a symbol of the substitution of Estonian for Soviet culture. Like Landsbergis, however, he had defended that culture from within the Soviet system, not outside it.

Like Landsbergis too, Meri's image stems partly from his family: his father was a senior diplomat during the First Republic, and as a youth Meri was deported with his father to Siberia. He made play with this pedigree during his campaign, though it rebounded on him when his father was accused of co-operating with the NKVD: how otherwise, it was asked, could he have been allowed to leave Siberia in 1945, just as tens of thousands of Estonians were heading in the opposite direction.

Meri's past, like that of many now attacking the old Communist establishment, was indeed not spotless. As a senior official of the Estonian-Soviet Writers' Union he collaborated with the Communist system in order to defend Estonian culture. In this role he was naturally compelled to make many speeches in praise of Marxism-Leninism, which his enemies now gleefully quote against him. This was also true of Landsbergis.

There was little wrong in this: it was the basic position of most of the intellectuals now supporting Meri's Fatherland government, as well as those behind the Moderates and the Popular Front, all of whom criticised the 'foolhardy courage' of the dissidents who later formed the National Independence Party. It was very probably the best policy for Estonia, let alone for Meri, though it sits uneasily with the favoured image of national resistance. As the *Baltic Independent* commented,

> Perhaps the biggest question mark over Meri's presidency is his association with Fatherland's election slogan, 'Cleaning House'. That someone who, as much as any other Estonian, showed how working inside the system could benefit his country, has now joined the anti-nomenclatura campaign in earnest, casts some doubt on his integrity and sincerity.[333]

As an adult Meri returned to Siberia to make films and write books with a certain nationalist agenda on the various Finno-Ugric tribes of the region, cousins to the Estonians. His most famous work is *Silver-Grey*, an imaginative reconstruction of Estonian prehistory. In appearance, Meri has the air of an inquisitive tortoise which has extended its head too far out of its shell and become stuck. In manner, and in breadth of culture, he is a European gentleman of the old school. His personal charm is very great, and his intellectual enthusiasm infectious. In a Baltic panorama in which former Communists and members of the new Right (often of course one and the same) often vie with each other in the [Soviet] crude and provincial narrowness of their attitudes, he represents an older and nobler past. Like Landsbergis, though, this sometimes leads him to patronise ordinary Estonians.

Meri is, however, not without his eccentricities. During my first interview with him – as Foreign Minister – in June 1991, he quickly overran the fifteen minute appointment allocated by his staff. An hour later, the Minister was cheerfully recounting the story of an expedition to Yakutia in which he ended up eating his own horse. He then whisked me off in his official car to an exhibition of Russian culture in Estonia under the First Republic, a subject in which he is conspicuously knowledgeable. His affection for Russian classical culture is deep.

Lennart Meri's charming but unpredictable behaviour often infuriates and exhausts his staff. His downfall as Foreign Minister came after he told a press conference in March 1992 that Estonia should act as a *cordon sanitaire* between the West and Russia, where 'massive hunger and cannibalism' was emerging.[34] The Estonian government was forced to distance itself from the statement, indicating it sought to act as a bridge, not a barrier. And Meri's plain talking is both splendid and dangerous. At the Helsinki summit of the CSCE in July 1992, Meri, though at that stage only the Estonian Ambassador to Finland, marched into a meeting of the Baltic leaders with George Bush and, addressing him as 'George', informed him his administration possessed neither a Russian nor a Baltic policy. In the words of an American diplomat, 'before that, Bush hardly remembered that the Balts existed. Now, thanks to Meri, he is furious with them'.

A few weeks after taking office, Meri was already embroiled in a dispute with the government over his attempts to run aspects of Estonian foreign policy. Under the constitution, the powers of the President are very strictly limited and do not include any role in government – but no-one who knows Meri ever thought that he would be able to keep within such limits.

As Estonia set out as a full-fledged state, the question of whether its politicians general would respect the rules and conventions of government was central to the country's future. At the beginning of 1993 there were two main problems facing the new coalition government. The first, that of the Russian minority, was a quiescent but continuing threat. The government's approach seemed a sensible mixture of firmness in principle and conciliation in practice. The National Independence Party, however, came under pressure from its radical supporters, and began to demand that non-citizens should even be barred from standing for local office. One of the permanent dangers of coalition government in Estonia is that policy towards the Russians may become more severe simply through the need to keep unstable coalitions together. The other is that majority government itself will prove impossible, leading to weak minority administrations.

The dangers are exacerbated by the fragility of the economy: for the foreseeable future much of the population is going to suffer great economic hardship. This, after only a few months in power, had contributed to a steep drop in the popularity of the coalition parties, and the government was coming under intense pressure from pensioners and workers to spend more on social welfare and subsidies. The sacking of officials in the name of 'desovietisation' led to accusations of party favouritism and incompetence in the appointments system.

Most worrying was the way in which the extreme nationalists of Estonian Citizen appeared to benefit from these problems. Their support grew sharply at the start of 1993, as nationalist voters became angry with the pragmatism of the Laar government. Estonian citizens also of course gained because of economic suffering. At the beginning of 1993, the signs for Estonia, however, looked generally bright. In comparison not simply with the other former Soviet republics, but with much of Eastern Europe as well, this former colony had already gone a long way towards creating the fabric of a prosperous, modern, independent and constitutional state.

Ethnic Latvian Politics, 1990–92

Latvia moved more slowly than the other Baltic States towards a new constitution and party political system, in part because of the larger Russian minority.

Their numerous representatives in the Supreme Council made it more difficult than in the other republics to create stable alliances of deputies behind particular reforms. A key cause of the delay in creating a new Latvian constitution was the fact that the Latvian deputies could not decide on the question of citizenship for the 'immigrants'.[35]

The power of Russian Soviet loyalist elements in Latvia was indicated, upon the declaration of *de jure* independence and the formation of the Godmanis government on 4 May 1990, by demonstrations of pro-Soviet forces, and Soviet officers, outside the parliament building, and a flood of threats from Rubiks and the Soviet Communist Party. In addition the (mainly Russian) Riga police refused to accept the new Interior Minister, insisting on the re-appointment of the previous minister, Šteinbriks, a hardline Soviet loyalist.[36] In the end a compromise was reached on a third figure, Aloizs Vaznis (a long-standing Interior Ministry official), but the dispute was a sign of the greater circumspection needed by the Latvian leadership on the road to independence.

During a violent demonstration and threatened strike by pro-Soviet forces on 15 May, the nerve of Anatolijs Gorbunovs appeared to crack. His suggested suspension of the 4 May declaration was, however, furiously rejected by most deputies. As one said, 'First we suspend *de facto* independence during a transition period, and then we are asked to suspend the suspension? Impossible!'

The Popular Front (PF) that assumed power in Latvia in May 1990 was not, however, dominated by the radicals, but as heterogenous as those of the other two Baltic states. It survived, both as a movement and as a parliamentary faction, longer than elsewhere, if for negative rather than positive reasons. The government of Ivars Godmanis also endured considerably longer than those in either Lithuania or Estonia, but once again partly for negative reasons: there was very little chance of any other faction being able to replace it. In 1991–92 however, the government and Popular Front appeared rather like a decomposing whale, preyed on by sluggish sharks until only the head – the government of Godmanis – remained.

The Latvian Supreme Council, as constituted on 4 May 1990, was made up as follows:

The Popular Front and associated deputies: Communist Party officials (some having already resigned from the Party), 7; local government officials, 13; industrial managers, 2; engineers and industrial scientists, 5; private businessmen, 1; academics and members of educated professions (including 7 doctors), 51; creative artists, 3; clergymen, 1; police officers, 0; lawyers, 3; journalists, 11; collective farm managers and agronomists, 35; workers, 5; profession not listed (but in some cases, former Communists), 7, making a total of 144 deputies.

The Equal Rights faction and associated deputies: Communist Party officials, 11; local government officials (these two categories are of course almost identical), 4; industrial managers and engineers, 14; private businessmen, 0; military representatives, 7; members of aviation institutes (closely associated with the military), 5; academics and members of educated professions, 6; creative artists, 0; clergymen, 0; police officers, 2; lawyers, 1; journalists, 1; agronomists, 1; workers, 1, making a total of 53 deputies.

This break-down by occupation reveals a number of interesting points, quite apart from the irony that the Soviet 'Equal Rights' faction, the self-styled 'defender of workers' interests', comprised only one worker deputy while the 'bourgeois nationalists' had five. The Equal Rights faction was much stronger than the Soviet loyalists in the Estonian Supreme Council, and until sixteen of its deputies were stripped of their mandates by the Latvian majority in summer 1992, for having supported the August 1991 coup, its co-operation was often essential in order to pass economic reforms. The pragmatic Equal Rights leader, Sergejs Dīmanis, co-operated willingly enough so long as ultimate Soviet authority was not affected. There was even talk of a long-term 'grand compromise' between the moderates of both sides, but any possibility of this was eliminated by the support given by Equal Rights leaders to the Soviet military intervention in January 1991, as well as by Latvian lack of interest.

The industrial lobby was overwhelmingly concentrated on the pro-Soviet and Russian side, for reasons analysed in Chapters 4 and 7. The Latvian side contained very few representatives of industry, and most of those were in fact academics occupying industrial positions. For equally obvious reasons, the pro-Soviet side contained only one representative of agriculture, whereas this was strongly represented on the Latvian side.

The most significant feature of the Latvian faction is not immediately apparent from the figures. It is that – to an even greater extent than in Lithuania or Estonia – the great majority of pro-independence deputies were either members of the Soviet establishment or people who had achieved at least a certain official status in society. This was even more true of the Godmanis government, where men such as former Komsomol leader Ziedonis Čevers remained in key positions up to 1993. The following three years brought continual pressure to replace these establishment figures with new and more radical ones. While Latvian politics swung in a radical direction, however, many of these people swung with it, and retained their leading role.

As in Estonia, Latvian opposition to the PF was led initially by the Latvian Congress, but while its policies were broadly well-liked, Congress itself remained generally unpopular. Unlike Estonia, where the Congress remained a broad forum for nationalist opposition to Savisaar – from radicals like Juri Estam to moderates like Mart Laar – the Latvian Congress came in 1991–92 to be dominated by extreme radical nationalists, such as Māris Grīnblats and Višvaldis Brinkmanis, whose statements threatened war with Russia and frightened the electorate. The radicals operated through 'Citizens' Committees' which organised elections to the Congress. Because of their irreconcilable opposition to the Supreme Council and the PF, they split in 1989–90 from the main radical nationalist group, the Latvian National Independence Movement (or LNNK) which had co-operated with the Popular Front and entered the Supreme Council alongside it in 1990.

The most senior Communist officials, like Prime Minister Bresis, did not of course stand for the PF, although after the Popular Front's electoral victory he attempted to persuade the Front to retain him as Prime Minister. Instead, they maintained Anatolijs Gorbunovs in the largely symbolic post of parliamentary chairman, to negotiate with Moscow, placate the local Russians, and calm the fears of older and more cautious Latvians. The three main tendencies within the PF were represented in the Praesidium of the Supreme Council elected in May 1990. Gorbunovs represented the Reform Communists; Dainis Īvāns represented the moderate nationalist intelligentsia, who before Gorbachov had tried to work for Latvia from within the system and without openly joining the dissidents; and Andrejs Krastiņš represented the radical LNNK, which at that time bridged the gap between the Popular Front and the Latvian Congress, as the Christian Democrats and others did in Estonia.

Gorbunovs was personally well suited to the task of creating a consensus. Critics have referred to his anodyne style, imagination and drive, though compared to the fire-raising characteristics of so many of his contemporaries, this in itself marked a real contribution to ethnic harmony. While Gorbunovs' long refusal to protect himself with bodyguards says something for his physical courage, questions have been asked about his moral stamina. On at least two occasions he succeeded in being out of the country when vital votes were taken, so as not to have to take a stand one way or the other: the first was during the formal split of the Communist Party in April 1990; the second during the vote on the citizenship resolution in November 1991.

In 1992, after long supporting the 'Zero Option' of citizenship for all residents of the republic, Gorbunovs, like Rüütel, moved to support a more restrictive citizenship. Finally, prior to the June 1993 elections, he moved conclusively to a nationalist and 'First Republic' position by joining the 'Latvian Way' electoral bloc.

Gorbunovs was born in 1942 to a poor peasant family in the Eastern province of Latgale. Selected by the party for his social background as well as his intelligence, he had a typical Communist career, rising through the ranks of the Komsomol and Party. Unlike Brazauskas and many of the former Communists who have clung to power, Gorbunovs' career lay within the party, not the State. Communist Secretary in the powerful Central (university) district of Riga, he first came to the public eye during the demonstrations of 1988, when a bewildered and frightened Communist leadership pushed him forward to address the crowd.

As Party secretary, and then Ideology Secretary, Gorbunovs, though not an intellectual himself, had forged close links with the moderate nationalist intelligentsia. A particularly strong influence was the poet Jānis Peters, Secretary of the Writers Union and later Latvian ambassador to Moscow, credited with pushing Gorbunovs towards high office. As in the case of Rüütel and his nationalist wife, the daughter of one of the founders of Soviet Estonia, this illustrates the closeness of personal links in the small Baltic elites. In all three states, the original Popular Fronts were founded by men like Peters, liberal intellectuals from the cultural elites (Communists Party members by necessity), and junior members of the Communist establishment, usually from the State rather than the Party. These also furnished the top ranks of the Latvian Front and its deputies. A typical view of a lesser activist was provided by a delegate to its Fourth Congress:

> I am staying in the Front because I think that it is still a real force that can work against the Communists and Moscow. The Congress has done nothing positive all this while, it has only slandered the PF, unfortunately with some success. The Congress is made up of people from the lower classes. Under Soviet rule, they couldn't get a good education or good jobs, some for honourable reasons because of their views, others because they were too stupid. . . .

An absolutely representative founding figure was Dainis Īvāns, (born in 1955), who in the last years of Brezhnev became a leading Latvian journalist, winning several Soviet prizes. In particular, he led the movement to expose environmental damage in Latvia. Following his resignation in November 1991, he vowed he would return to journalism.

As a journalist under Soviet rule – like Meri, the leading intellectual, or Landsbergis, the professor – Īvāns had regularly to make the obligatory bows to Marxism-Leninism and Soviet power, as the price of being allowed to continue working. As the radical nationalists turned against him in 1990–91, the old quotations were dug up and endlessly repeated – in particular, a glowing obituary of Leonid Brezhnev.

Dainis Īvāns combines a very Latvian romantic nationalism, and deep love of Latvian culture, with moderation in politics, and has not suffered from the intense, vindictive bitterness of many of the radicals. He quite obviously greatly dislikes the Russians and their presence in Latvia, and in his acceptance speech as Deputy Chairman declared emotionally that, 'Thank God, I was born a Latvian and wish to die a Latvian. I am not ashamed to say this, and I do not want my people to meet the same tragic fate that has befallen Russified Latvians, some of whom are in this hall.' He has, however, stood for compromise in the interests of internal peace and Latvia's future.

Īvāns also seemed genuinely uncorrupted by power, and throughout his term in office remained courteous and approachable. He sometimes appeared ill at ease – possibly mourning his distinctive bushy hairstyle and favourite dress, a scruffy pullover. Both were essential parts of his image, and his popularity among young people, but fell victim to the demands of office. The father of four children, Īvāns benefitted from a sense of patriotic self-sacrifice in the cause of boosting the national population. In November 1991, depressed by the endless attacks on him by erstwhile allies, Īvāns became one of the very few politicians to resign of his own free will. In Baltic terms, this is nothing less than astounding – most have continued to occupy their ministerial chairs long after the legs have been sawn from under them.

There could hardly be a greater difference in personality than between Īvāns and his colleague as vice chairman, Andrejs Krastiņš. This short, round, moustachioed individual (born in 1951) rather resembles a teddy-bear, but his character is Pooh Bear crossed with Robocop. Even a casual meeting with the man reveals a distinct glint of steel. On national issues he takes a hard line, while avoiding the outrageously provocative statements of the Congress.

For many years Krastiņš worked as a detective in the Latvian Interior Ministry (which has led to ritual accusations of having worked with the KGB), before leaving to become a lawyer in the early 1980s. It seems hardly a more honourable record than that of Īvāns, Peters and other Centrist intellectuals now so attacked by Krastiņš' party. The difference is that Soviet detectives were not required to make public statements praising Soviet rule. Their support for the system was of a more functional nature.

The motley trio of Gorbunovs, Īvāns and Krastiņš were required to maintain the parliamentary majority of the Popular Front and its allies, ensure the Equal Rights opposition did not cause parliamentary trouble, and smooth the way for reformist legislation. In the latter task especially, they largely failed, partly because of Russian and Soviet loyalist opposition, but more because of the fissiparousness disposition of the Latvian politicians. From the start, the Popular Front faction usually failed to agree on legislation: each proposal was repeatedly amended by individuals or small groups of deputies.

As in Lithuania and Estonia but even more so, legislative paralysis was worsened in Latvia by the inexperience of the deputies and weird hangovers from the Soviet system designed to confine real legislative power to the executive. Thus over controversial questions, the Supreme Council could establish the 'principles' on which a law was to be based, and then happily postpone the pain of passing the law itself for several months. Even when passed, laws often required further legislation detailing their implementation, and then resolutions actually ordering the state to apply them.

The entire system was a colossal inducement to continued legislative and individual irresponsibility. Not only the population at large, but even politicians themselves, are convinced of their right continually to criticise the government without suggesting an alternative. At the Latvian Popular Front Congress of November 1991 a dissident PF deputy, when asked whom he would support as prime minister and which policies he would endorse, burst out, 'But that's not for me to say! Godmanis is the government, he has the experts with him, it's for him to say what should be done. He should just do it better!'

For most of the period under study, therefore, Latvia presented a depressing picture, with the government seemingly paralysed, reforms moving at a slower pace than in the other two states, and radical nationalism inexorably gaining ground. Towards the end of 1992, however, supported by the IMF, the government finally moved towards a coherent economic strategy based on the creation of a stable currency, and this began to have an effect on the economy as a whole. The IMF plan was accepted in principle by all the main parties, and for the first time this provided a real element of policy consensus, on which Godmanis (and his possible successors) could build. Godmanis was also able to blackmail his opponents by threatening that if they did not fall into line, the IMF would cut off its loans.

Probably only an outside agency, and one with the prestige and the money of the IMF, would have been able to bring this coherence to Latvian policy-making. Up to mid-1992, this had seemed in a state of the deepest confusion. The government swung between *laissez-faire* in theory, and populism and Soviet-style authoritarian tactics in practice.

Such tactics were more or less compelled by the suffering and anger of the population under the lash of steep economic decline (see Chapter 9), but they increased the impression that the government did not really have an economic strategy and was simply reacting to events. During 1991, I noticed a strange tendency in Latvian officials to cackle like chickens when asked about state economic policy – the implication being that anyone who tried to understand it would infallibly go insane.

Looking at this political and administrative confusion, a Latvian-American journalist in 1991 described the government as 'not a representative of society, the parliament and the state, but simply as one force in society, pursuing its own interests, if necessary at the expense of all the others'. Such disappointment with Ivars Godmanis was very common in this period, though history is likely to pass a much kinder judgement. Unlike Savisaar and Prunskiene, Godmanis had no previous government experience. While they were accused of favouring the former Soviet establishment because they had been part of it themselves, Godmanis was accused of being helpless precisely because he had no previous governmental experience – an example of how as far as some radical critics are concerned, you just cannot win in post-Soviet politics.

A massive figure with a big beard and booming voice, Godmanis looks the embodiment of prophetic authority. A physicist by profession, he is a

20   Dr Ivars Godmanis, Deputy Chairman of the Latvian Popular Front and Prime Minister of Latvia from May 1990.

man of great personal intelligence and considerable openness and charm. However, throughout his period in office there was criticism of his tendency to snap decisions and to autocracy.

As in Estonia and Lithuania, the gradual disintegration of the Popular Front left Godmanis' government increasingly isolated, and this was made worse by the increasing shift of politics as a whole towards more hardline nationalist positions. Godmanis pursued a tactic of surrendering individual ministers and points in order to keep the rest of the cabinet together and retain parliamentary support for the government as a whole and for its basic policies. As far as economic policy was concerned, this tactic appears to have had considerable success. On policy towards the Russians, while Godmanis and his supporters blocked a fully hardline approach, they were still left with a set of policies which were very much tougher than anything which the Popular Front had envisaged only two years before.

Godmanis's government, formed in May 1990, was like those of Estonia and even to an extent Lithuania, overwhelmingly made up of existing state officials, albeit from that part of the establishment which had swung over to give support, or at least lip-service, to independence and reform. It was therefore too establishment-oriented and cautious for the Popular Front faction in the Supreme Council, which in turn was too cautious for the PF movement, which in turn was under attack for its moderation from the radical nationalists.

The background to the government's decline in popularity was a severe decline in living standards and the apparent paralysis of the reform process. Opinion polls (among both Latvians and Russians) showed that whereas in mid-1991 the government had a popularity rating of around 65 per cent, by the end of 1992 this had dropped to around 10 per cent, with 80 per cent expressing negative opinions. Nonetheless, crippled though they were by internal squabbles, the PF government, faction and the movement stuck together as long as the immediate Soviet threat remained. As soon as independence was achieved, in August 1991, they attacked each other and each also began to unravel internally. Within a week of the failure of the Soviet counter-revolution, the first major clash erupted when the PF movement put forward its own candidate as head of the National Guard in opposition to the one chosen by the Faction. In the end, a third, compromise figure had to be selected. The defeat of the counter-revolution and the collapse of the Soviet Union immediately destroyed the importance of the Equal Rights faction in the parliament, and the following year most were deprived of their mandates. The result of course was greatly to strengthen the hand of the deputies from the National Independence Movement (LNNK) and the radical wing of the PF. These were strengthened further by the drift to hardline nationalism of a certain number of previously moderate deputies.

One of the establishment ministers in the cabinet, the economics minister (and former senior Komsomol official) Jānis Āboltiņš, described in his diary (later published) for 14 November 1991 how Godmanis operated in the face of the new balance of power:

> Godmanis is about to reform the government. From the point of view of common sense, it's not the right time for such a move. But from Godmanis's point of view, it makes good sense. Tomorrow begins the Fourth Congress of the Popular Front. Godmanis can show them how actively he is fighting against the old bureaucracy. And after that, there will be the chance to do nothing in particular for the time being, because the new government will have 'just started to work. . .'.[37]

Āboltiņš himself was soon a victim of Godmanis' bowing to the Front's desire to sweep former Commonist officials out of office. One Latvian-American gave an unkind but accurate parody of Godmanis's response in parliament to one attempt to force a change in the cabinet:

> And if *one* minister is forced to resign by parliamentary pressure. . . .'

(in thunderous tones, the forefinger raised in Soviet fashion)
'Then the *whole* cabinet will immediately meet. . . .'
(with growing menace)
'And decide what to do next'.

The key difference that emerged between the faction majority and government on the one side and the movement on the other inevitably chiefly concerned not the bureaucracy but the restoration of the First Republic and the exclusion of the Russian 'immigrants'. The Popular Front had previously taken a publicly conciliatory line towards the Russians. Now the PF movement swung sharply in a nationalist direction, and at its Congress in November 1991, adopted a set of slogans basically indistinguishable from those of the radical nationalists.

Dainis Īvāns spoke bitterly of this change in an interview with *Moscow News* in November 1992:

> Since Independence, the people have been poisoned with a primitive idea: 'everything is permitted, we are the masters, any problems can be resolved if we forget the past 50 years, and for this there is only the need to re-establish the old state. . . .' The radicals cannot understand that Latvia was not in a coma all this time, that it has lived, even if a hard life, but lived. Three generations built, ploughed land, bore children and died. And must all this be obliterated, forgotten and taken away? Regrettably, this is the choice that the Latvian people are being offered. And not unsuccessfully, too. . . .

The verbal radicalism of PF leaders like its Chairman, Romualdas Ražukas (by origin an ethnic Lithuanian) was to some extent a deliberate maneouvre, worked out with Godmanis to defuse pressure from below and keep the movement and the faction together. This tactic worked: despite all the bitter attacks on the government, the bulk of the Popular Front, and of former PF deputies in parliament, continued to support of Godmanis whenever votes were actually taken to remove him. Nonetheless, pressure from the radicals was very strong, and can only be taken as reflecting a consensus in the politically active part of the Latvian population. This does not necessarily mean the Latvian nation as a whole, much of which I have always found to take a fairly relaxed view of the Russian presence. Unfortunately, these people also take a relaxed view of political engagement, in consequence of which their political influence is slight. In the words of the pro-independence Russian deputy Alexei Grigoriev, formerly editor of the PF's Russian-language newspaper, in July 1992:

> I do not think that the national radicals are basically more popular among

Latvians, but they are certainly better organised, while the centre is divided and weak. . . . Our [the moderates'] mistake from the beginning was not to have taken a stronger stand within the Popular Front. We should have announced a separate position at the Second Congress at the end of 1989. We refrained, for fear of splitting the movement. The result is that the extremists, better organised, more vocal and with facile, nationalist solutions, succeeded in taking over the Front and expropriating its name . . . a common pattern in post-totalitarian politics.

In his opening speech to the Popular Front Congress on 15 November 1991, Ražukas launched a blistering attack on the Supreme Council ('full of supporters of a foreign state!') and the faction, saying that the main reason the PF was needed was to fight the Zero Option. He accused the government of allowing 'ex-functionaries, including non-Latvians, to plunder Latvian resources. . . .' And this was the moderate candidate.

The PF now moved to adopt a slogan hitherto used only by the radicals: 'Deoccupation, Desovietisation, Decolonisation'. Deoccupation referred to the Soviet army, and desovietisation to purging the bureaucracy. Decolonisation referred to the Russian 'immigrant' population, now called 'colonists', and was a no-longer veiled threat to pressure them to leave. The PF also now stood squarely for a return to the pre-1940 republic and the 1922 constitution.

As a result of the Fourth Congress, the Popular Front faction split, with a third of its deputies leaving to found a new radical nationalist 'Constitution' (*Satversme*) Faction – though its strict adherence to the 1922 constitution did not prevent it from promptly arguing for double citizenship for Latvian emigrés (banned under the 1922 constitution) in an effort to attract emigré support and money. Another radical breakaway fraction, the Homeland (*Teversme*) followed. The remnant of the PF Faction was now reduced to 53 deputies, out of 132 elected on the Front's ticket in March 1990. More than half the deputies in parliament were now formally unaffiliated to any faction, though they belonged to a plethora of short-lived parties.

The withdrawal of both radicals and centrists from the PF meant that, at its Fifth Congress in November 1992, its remnants were now able to convert themselves into a membership party. Its new Chairman was Uldis Augštkalns, a former teacher of Marxist philosophy. The National Independence Movement also converted itself into a membership group excluding other parties.

In the summer and autumn of 1992, radicals in parliament combined with the former pro-independence Communist Party (now the Democratic Labour Party under former KGB Major Juris Bojārs) to try to topple Godmanis. He survived, but was forced to abandon Jurkāns and other ministers. By the end of 1992, it had become clear that the existing political configuration could not agree either on a new constitution or a naturalisation law, and that therefore Latvia, unlike Estonia and Lithuania, would have to hold elections without them. This suited the radicals, because a law re-establishing pre-1940 citizenship, and thereby excluding most of the Russians, had already been passed. As the run-up to the June 1993 elections began, the parties began to form large electoral blocs in order to overcome the 4 per cent hurdle for admission to parliament. Even more than in Estonia, this led to some strikingly unexpected developments. Considerable worry was caused by the apparent popularity of Bojārs' former Communists, who pursued a strident mixture of nationalism and economic populism, very familiar from the tactics of other former Communist Parties in eastern Europe. Opinion polls suggested that it had profited from its old organisation, contacts and wealth and its new nationalist approach to become the largest single party (in this cause Bojārs had even made use of anti-semitism). Its Left-wing populist attacks on the government brought support from an increasingly impoverished Latvian population. Unlike the radical nationalist forces, it also sought to profit from local Latvian resentment of the Latvian emigrés, and opposed measures to give them voting rights. However, the Party was badly damaged when Bojārs was barred from parliament as a former KGB officer.

The former moderate wing of the Popular Front gave birth to the Democratic Centre Movement, led by several of the original founders of the Front: Jānis Škapars, the editor of the literary journal *Literatūra un Maksla* (which, like Īvāns, had expressed criticism from within the Soviet system), Foreign Minister Jānis Jurkāns and others. It was encouraged by Dainis Īvāns. This group based its outline on the PF election programme of 1990, which (with good reason) it accused the new, radical leadership of the Front of having abandoned. However, before the Democratic Centre had even got underway, it split, in part along ethnic lines, with Jurkāns (an ethnic Pole, although this has never been stressed) and pro-independence Russians like Grigoriev and Vladlen Dozortsev separating or being excluded from the others. Jurkāns' strident international championship of equal rights for the Russians, seen as disloyalty to Latvia, had made him intolerable even to many moderate Latvians. When I interviewed one of the Latvian intellectuals in the other section of the Democratic Centre, I was depressed to find him denoucing Jurkāns as a 'tool of the Russian-Jewish businessmen'.

Jurkāns and his supporters set up a party charmingly entitled 'Harmony for Latvia – Economic Rebirth' (which was indeed heavily backed by local business money). This drew in many Latvian former Communist officials opposed to the chauvinism of Bojars and the opportunism of Gorbunovs (or for whatever reason unable to join them).

As a result of the elections, Harmony for Latvia emerged as the largest group among the anti-nationalist forces, with 13 deputies to the 7 of the Equal Rights Faction. These groups owed their success to the presence of a substantial proportion of Russian-speakers, descended from the pre-1940 minorities, among the Latvian electorate. According to official figures, Russians, Byelorussians and Ukrainians together constituted some 18 per cent of voters.

Undoubted victor in the elections, however, was an entirely new alliance, 'Latvia's Way', with 36 deputies. This was a bouillabaisse of both radicals and moderates from the PF, moderate Latvian emigrés under the leader of the World Federation of Free Latvians, Gunars Meierovics, and former leaders of the Communist establishment. What strengthened it above all was its acquisition of Anatolijs Gorbunovs, still the most popular Latvian politician.

A cynical view of Latvia's Way would be that its only glue was pure opportunism. However, its leaders were also held together by basic agreement on economic reform, along the lines already pioneered by Godmanis. After forming the core of the new government after the elections, the Latvia's Way bloc showed considerable determination in sticking to IMF recommendations and maintaining the strength of the Lat currency in the face of considerable social protest. Following the elections, Latvia's Way formed a coalition government with the Latvian Farmers' Union, which had won 12 seats. A Latvia's Way leader, Valdis Birkavs became Prime Minister, with Guntis Ulmanis, nephew of Kārlis Ulmanis and a Farmers' Union leader, as President. Together, the two parties still constituted a minority in the 100-seat parliament, but received informal support from the Democratic Centre Movement's five deputies.

The radical nationalist parties were barred from power, but still made a fairly strong showing. The National Independence Movement (LNNK) came second with 15 seats, while the Fatherland and Freedom Party and the Christian Democrats each won 6. The LNNK may have suffered from its unwise welcome to a sinister German extreme rightest politician, Joachim Siegerist, leader of the small German Conservative Union. Siegerist is, or claims to be, the son of a Baltic German who served with the Latvian SS Legion during the Second World War. He was, as a result, able to claim Latvian citizenship without speaking a word of Latvian. He gained admission to the LNNK by helping to finance their campaign, and attracted public attention with huge media advertisements. Siegerist gained considerable support from older Latvian voters, but alienated many others. The privately voiced disdain of Western diplomats meant that the LNNK came to see him as an increasing embarrassment.

The victory of Latvia's Way reassured both Western observers and many Russians within Latvia. The Russian business community in Latvia was relieved that the threat of a national-populist economic policy had greatly lessened. However, the citizenship law proposed in November 1993 by the coalition government was still tough enough to draw international criticism and worry many Russians, while not being nearly tough enough for the radical nationalist opposition. The continuing economic hardship of large numbers of both ethnic Latvians and ethnic Russians made a swing to radical nationalism an enduring threat, while the rise of Vladimir Zhirinovsky increased the risk that violent protest might be exported from Russia to Latvia.

The Baltic Independence Movements and the Baltic Russians

Viewed with hindsight, much of the Latvian and Estonian propaganda directed towards both the Baltic Russians and the West during the years 1988–91 has a rather ironic ring. One of the principal charges against Latvia and Estonia is that their national leaderships have broken their word on Russian rights. The question of the legal and moral justification for it is a separate issue, discussed in the Conclusion.

In March 1990, I wrote in *The Times* that,

> The Popular Front in Latvia emphasises that its struggle is for 'popular rule, economic prosperity and social justice' for *all* nationalities. . . . The Front's approach represents the triumph of enlightenment and common sense over the personal feelings of its leaders towards the Russian community, which are rarely amicable. . . .[38]

Jānis Jurkāns, then the International Relations chief of the Popular Front of Latvia, told me in February 1990 that,

> We are trying to persuade the local Russians that we are going to build a multi-ethnic democracy in Latvia, with equal rights for all; but they have been fed so many Soviet lies that it is difficult to persuade them. . . .[39]

The second Congress of the Popular Front, held two months previously, had stressed that the goal of the PF was independence, but also 'the guarantee of the equality of all people living in Latvia, irrespective of their social status, nationality, religious or party affiliation'.[40]

At this stage Popular Front leaders lost no opportunity to stress, at least to an international audience, that the Front was supported by many local Russians – 30 per cent of them, according to Ivars Godmanis, then the Popular Front's Prime Minister-designate. Shortly before assuming office in May, he stressed that 'independence can only be achieved if the different national groups go down the road together. . . . Sovereignty and independence are not questions of nationality. . . . Every ethnic group in Latvia is guaranteed equal rights'.[41]

The rhetoric of a trans-national, Latvian and Russian struggle for democracy was employed strongly in Latvia during the events of January and August 1991. The slogan of the 1863 Polish rebellion against the Tsar, 'For Our Freedom and Yours', was widely used and painted on barricades outside the parliament in Riga.

Godmanis's government went on favouring a policy of compromise with the local Russians up to the elections of 1993; but the ground was cut from under its feet by a general shift to a more hardline position. Thus by its Fourth Congress, in November 1991, the Latvian Popular Front was referring to the Russians that had entered the republic under Soviet rule as 'illegal immigrants', while the PF chairman, Romualdas Ražukas, stressed that 'The PF supports the concepts basic to the Citizens Congress' – the radical nationalist body with which much of the Popular Front had always been at odds.[42]

Jurkāns, by now Foreign Minister, found himself progressively isolated by his abrasive arguments on behalf of the Russians, and in October 1992 was abandoned by Prime Minister Godmanis and forced to resign.

One aspect of the shift in opinion was the increasing emphasis on the fact that a majority of Russians had opposed independence, which contrasts oddly with the public claims by Latvian leaders, in March 1991, that a majority of Russians had voted for independence in the Latvian referendum that month.[43] Most of the moderates and every leading member of a national minority had left the PF by its Fourth Congress; indeed not one Russian spoke at it. The Congress adopted a programme, widely at variance with those of its first three Congresses, which called for a return to the Constitution of 1922, and the restriction of citizenship to pre-1940 citizens and their descendants. According to this programme, the extension of citizenship to others should only be considered after the withdrawal of Soviet troops, and by a parliament elected by the pre-1940 electorate. The Popular Front in the country and the majority Popular Front deputies in parliament split on the issue.[44]

The shift to an anti-Russian position is partly due to a general hegemony of nationalist over liberal pluralist ideas, and emigré liberals have linked defence of Russian rights to defence of liberal democracy in general. Thus the Latvian emigré academic Nils Muižnieks, in an article for *Atmoda*, posed the question: 'Independent Latvia: Latvian or Democratic?'. Talk at later Latvian Popular Front Congresses, of the need for 'Latvian-thinking people', and of how 'specific groups of people' (in other words, Russians, Jews and former Communists) were 'plundering our national wealth' was deeply jarring for any emigré liberal, however patriotic.

At the conference of the Association for the Advancement of Baltic

Studies in Toronto in June 1992, Dr Toivo Miljan of Wilfred Laurier University warned of the possibility of the development of parallels with South Africa and said that Estonians 'must recognise the civic rights of those living amongst you [but] ... the Latvians, Lithuanians and Estonians weren't tolerant in the 1930s, so where are they supposed to get it from now?' This highlights the fact that extreme nationalist hostility to the Russians in Latvia and Estonia is not simply the result of the massive immigration under Soviet rule; it is also due to a direct and explicit revival, by some of today's radical nationalist groups, of the extreme nationalist ideas and stifling cultural atmosphere of the Baltic States of the 1930s. According to one Latvian liberal: 'the question isn't just the Russians. The question is whether there will still be oxygen to breathe in Riga.'

In February 1990, a Jewish friend in Tallinn (and a strong supporter of independence), Eugenie Loov, told me simply that:

> The greatest mistake of the leaders of our independence movement was not to make a substantial appeal to the Russians in Estonia at the very beginning. The reason they did not do this is because they hate them.[45]

In many cases this appears to have been true: Popular Front representatives in both Latvia and Estonia simply disguised their real feelings in order not to play into the hands of the Soviet government and loyalists. In other cases, the commitment to national compromise was real enough, but was not based on any real belief in multi-ethnic democracy, but on a fear of a mass Russian reaction. As this did not happen, Baltic leaders began a move to harder positions on national questions, trying to appeal to what appeared to be the national consensus of ethnic Latvians and Estonians.

This has been true of Latvian Supreme Council chairman Anatolijs Gorbunovs. Until the autumn of 1991, he was still publicly committed to the Zero Option, to grant citizenship to all Latvian residents irrespective of length of residence or knowledge of the language. Gorbunovs delivered some powerful speeches in support of national compromise, arguing in the immediate aftermath of independence that 'one half of a population cannot successfully build an independent state without the other'.[46] On 6 May 1990, two days after the Latvian declaration of sovereignty, he spoke in Russian on Latvian television, addressing the Russian-speaking inhabitants of Latvia and promising them that,

> All those who want to be citizens of Latvia can be. There is also a special note guaranteeing the rights of non-Latvian citizens in Latvia. It is not serious to talk about 'second class citizens'.

By summer 1992, however, Gorbunovs was advocating a referendum on citizenship restricted to pre-1940 citizens and their descendants alone.

The speed of the shift from an anti-Soviet to an anti-Russian position in 1991–92 is explicable partly in terms of Russian government policy and concern over military withdrawal, fuel supplies and the citizenship question. But in the view of former Estonian Prime Minister, Edgar Savisaar, and others, the Balts themselves played a role in the deterioration of relations. This was especially true of the decision by both the Estonian and Latvian Supreme Councils to demand the return of minor territories annexed by Stalin in 1945: in the case of Latvia, Pytalovo (Abrene); and of Estonia, Pechori (Petseri) and Ivangorod (Jaanilinn). The claim was in defiance of the spirit (if not the letter) of the Helsinki Conference and of the treaties signed between Latvia, Estonia and Boris Yeltsin in January 1991, when the Balts desperately needed Russian help. At the time, even radical nationalist deputies supported the signature of the treaties, which also spoke in vague terms of the peoples of both countries having the right to a 'free choice of citizenship'.

The disputed territories, though inhabited originally by Finnic and Latgalian peoples, even before their military conquest by Latvia and Estonia in 1920, had Russian majorities even then, and now have enormous ones. An Estonian nationalist once told me that 'In my view, the wishes of 1,200 hardworking Setus (an Estonian-related people living in Petseri and Southern Estonia) should count against the wishes of 26,000 good-for-nothing Russians any day', a view the Russian majority can hardly be expected to share. The more rational view, put forward by men like Velliste, was in favour of compromise settlement, but only in the context of a new international conference and Russian recognition of Estonia's legal rights. Even this, however, was foolishly legalistic, since there was nothing the Estonians could gain except an unnecessarily irritated Russia.

The Estonian emigré academic, Rein Taagepera, also criticised the Estonian Right, saying they behaved 'as if the earth swallowed up Russia when Estonia achieved independence'. His view was that, 'Estonian politicians should remember without fail that Russia has always been our great neighbour, and that we should treat it with greater respect than we are now doing'.[48]

Baltic politicians seemed, by 1992, to have almost completely forgotten the very substantial help given them by Boris Yeltsin during the military intervention of January 1991, when he appealed publicly to Russian soldiers not to obey orders to attack Baltic civilian targets or become 'pawns in the hands of dark reactionary forces'. At the time, the statement was given the widest possible publicity by the Baltic governments. Yeltsin himself, at considerable personal risk, visited Tallinn to sign the Estonian–Russian Treaty, and narrowly escaped kidnap by local Soviet loyalist forces. He, together with the Russian democrats who supported the Balts, have good reason to feel aggrieved not simply by the subsequent Latvian and Estonian position on Russian rights, but also by the barrage of anti-Russian propaganda, coming even from figures like Marju Lauristin, alleging that the Russian people are 'inherently imperialist'.

It was the habit in the Baltic, under Soviet rule, to blame every misfortune on the fact of that rule. The mentality is not easily shaken off and the fear is that, when the Russian army has gone, the resentment will simply be transferred to the local 'immigrant' populations. The characteristic is already manifest: some Balts have in any case long been accustomed to blaming local Russians for much of the crime, prostitution and disorder in their countries. Withdrawal of the army will of itself do little to improve ethnic relations. Already, most Balts falsely equate 'Russian' with 'Soviet', even though Latvians themselves, like Dzerzhinsky's two Chief Lieutenants, Jakovs Peters and Martins Lācis, provided some of the most ferocious exponents of Communist terror.[48]

'A return to the Latvia of 18 November 1918' (the date of the first declaration of independence) – the slogan of the Fourth Popular Front Congress and the Constitution Faction – was always a code for exclusion of Russian 'immigrants', even though it also had a wider emotional resonance. Moreover, in circumstances of complete legislative and indeed intellectual confusion, a return to pre-1940 forms came to seem not only the most legitimate but also the simplest solution. In the words of Mart Laar, leader of the Right-wing Estonian Christian Democratic Union and the Fatherland alliance, and from October 1992, Prime Minister,

> Our approach should be honest. If we say something, we should keep our word. Maybe what we needed to say to the Russians from the beginning would not have been pleasant, but it would have been the truth and on it we could have built an honest relationship; but until recently, we have not been honest with them.[49]

The radical nationalist Citizens' Congresses in Latvia and Estonia had indeed always said the same thing, with varying degrees of incisiveness. So far as those that had entered Estonia under Soviet rule were concerned, Trivimi Velliste said, at our first meeting in February 1990, that,

> The Russian colonist population here is effectively a military garrison in civilian clothes, and there can be no question of giving them citizenship until they have satisfied some important requirements. . . . If you give these people, who by international law are illegal immigrants, false hopes, you will only create confusion in their minds. It is much better to tell the truth: 'Who annexed Estonia in 1940? Stalin and Zhdanov. You will have

to understand the consequences of that.' Having told them that, we can build an honest and legal relationship, and those who do not want to accept it, can leave.[50]

This indeed has been the approach of the Centre-Right Estonian government which won power in the September 1992 election, and in which Velliste himself was Foreign Minister. In his view it is wrong to speak of the Russians in Estonia as a 'minority': 'Legally, the word 'minority' applies only to those Russians who were settled in Estonia before 1940. The rest are colonists.'

The language of the Latvian Congress has been more extreme, partly because of the difference in national style, partly because of the even more acute demographic situation. The Congress also refers to most of the Russians in Latvia as 'colonists', and increasingly argues that under the clauses of the Geneva Convention governing occupied countries, they have no right to be in Latvia at all and should depart with the Russian troops. In August 1992, the Committee of the Latvian Congress issued a warning 'to the colonists from the USSR in Latvia' [in its own translation]:

> You are living illegally on the Latvian territory.... That's why the Congress of Latvian Republic Citizens as an authorised representative of Latvian republic offers you to leave Latvian territory. You will be forced to leave sooner or later. Delaying your departure, you provoke the activities of those forces which are ready to solve the question of the decolonisation of Latvia by means of force, in which neither you nor we have any interests.[51]

The sentiment is widespread, even if some phrase it less harshly. In July 1992 the Latvian Supreme Council passed a law establishing stiff requirements for the issue of residence permits to those wishing to settle in the country. The 'Constitution' group and LNNK then announced that they understood this to apply also to those non-citizens already living in the republic – which would have meant the expulsion of hundreds of thousands of the population. The parliamentary majority rejected this interpretation, but the radicals continue to assert it, and if it came to power, would presumably make at least symbolic gestures to put it into effect. One of the Congress leaders, Višvaldis Lācis (also of the Latvian National Independence Movement, or LNNK), told me that,

> In my party, we want the Russians to leave, because otherwise, how will we be able to live in an independent Latvia where only 50 per cent of the population are Latvians? We would be subjected to a permanent biological war, and if their birthrate is higher, then we would be threatened with extinction.[52]

In 1989, public articulation of this view was confined to the Congresses, even if it was commonly said in private conversation. By May 1992, it was even proposed by Arnold Rüütel in a speech to participants at the Bergedorfer Gespraechskreis.[53] Politically speaking, the dangerous erosion of Russian *interlocuteurs valables* which has occurred in Estonia, and to a lesser extent in Latvia, since the achievement of independence has had as much to do with perceptions of the general mood and fears for the future as it has with concrete steps taken by the Baltic governments and parliaments. In the words of Katya Borschova, formerly a Latvian Russian journalist for the Popular Front Russian-language newspaper, in July 1992,

> We feel under constant pressure because of the continual barrage in the Latvian press and on television; the constant talk of 'colonists', 'aliens', 'fifth columns', 'illegal immigrants'; the constant stress on a Latvian Latvia, the exaltation of everything Latvian, the denigration of everything Russian. This is especially irritating when it comes from individuals who only a year ago were stressing that this was not a national struggle. It is having the effect that Russians who had been strongly committed to learning Latvian are now giving it up, simply because they can't stand to be bullied into learning. . . . All this is especially depressing for those who, like me, worked for independence and stood on the barricades in January and August. We feel betrayed and made fools of . . . Russians here are now saying to us, 'you see, Interfront was right after all in its warnings, and you, you deceived us'. . . . Among Russian intellectuals, the tendency now is to look down on the Latvians, 'little children pretending to be a nation – we have to understand their mistakes'; but yes, a certain mood of hatred for the Latvians is also growing, because of the pressure, even among Russians who are ashamed of this feeling.[54]

This exemplifies a central flaw in the Latvian and Estonian approach to the question of Russian citizenship. Strict procedures for acquiring citizenship are often justified in terms of the need for local Russians to 'prove' their loyalty and commitment. At the same time, however, these nations are increasingly expressing themselves and defining their national identities in ways that can only repel other nationalities. A realistic appeal to the loyalty of national minorities can only be made in terms of institutions and universal values – and it was indeed in these terms that appeals by the Baltic national movements both to local Russians and to the West were couched between 1988 and 1991. The present appeal to support purely ethnically based ideas of the state is, in contrast, illogical and bound to fail. Although in Estonia, at the beginning of 1993, most Russians were eligible to apply for citizenship, very few had done so.

A good deal of mutual resentment has resulted from the coarse style of the post-Soviet press on both sides. The patronising tone of much of the local Russian press has infuriated Latvians: indeed Katya Borschova's own paper, *Baltiskoe Vremya*, was guilty of this. The result was that the Popular Front dismissed the paper's editor and appointed a sycophant and opportunist more amenable to the Latvian interest.[55]

Under the new editor *Baltiskoe Vremya* collapsed. A subsequent attempt by the dissident journalists to set up a new Russian democratic paper then also failed, amidst feuding between the Russian journalists and a general collapse of will. This characteristic Russian divisiveness is true of Russian politics in Latvia in general, and is an explanation for the deep political apathy among the Russian-speaking population during the eighteen months after August 1991.

By summer 1992, the Russian Democratic Movement in Estonia, founded eleven months earlier, after the achievement of independence, had moved into close alliance with the Russian Trades Unions and the Russian-dominated municipalities of the north-east. This 'Co-ordinating Committee' was supported, openly or tacitly, by a considerable number of Russian intellectuals and managers who previously backed independence and opposed the actions of the local Communist municipalities. These were alienated by what they feel to be the anti-industrial policy of the Estonian government and by the threat to their jobs posed by the language and citizenship laws. One known to have been a supporter of independence is Valery Myachin, Director of the big 'Narova' furniture factory in Narva. In July 1991 he denounced the policies of the local Communist leadership before the Narva city council. By May 1992 he was deeply worried, both because the trade barriers between Estonia and Russia were likely to bankrupt his enterprise, and because of his own position:

> I have taken two courses in Estonian, and at one point even spoke it quite well; but here in Narva it is impossible to keep it up, because there is no-one to speak it with. And when I go to hold talks with the ministry in Tallinn, of course we speak Russian together – anything else would be impracticable. So it's very unlikely I'll be able to pass their language test. My children, yes, perhaps – anyway, they're young, they learn more easily. . . . Now I've been told privately by Estonian officials not to worry, that they know my worth and that my job is not at risk. But the point is that if in future things change, and someone comes along who wants my job, all they have to do is use the language test or the citizenship law to have me chucked out.[56]

This goes to the heart of the matter. The citizenship laws and language tests, or proposed ones, are not in themselves unreasonable by West European standards – though they may well seem so in the particular context of East European history in the twentieth century. They include, for example, the provision that non-citizens may vote in municipal elections – though the example of Latvia and Lithuania suggests that since the parliament retains the right to suspend such bodies more or less at will, the concession may be less meaningful than it seems.

The Lithuanian citizenship law is indeed extremely liberal, and has never been criticised. It grants citizenship to all permanent residents who registered before November 1991, and can do so without inhibition since the Lithuanian minorities are so much smaller than those of the other two republics. This brings out the essential falsity of the argument that the Estonian and Latvian approach is simply based on strict legality and the legal imperative of a return to the pre-1940 state order. No-one could have exceeded Landsbergis and the Sajūdis radicals in their nostalgia for the pre-1940 republic; but because this demographic aspect was lacking, they felt quite able to compromise even on such a key issue as citizenship.

The Estonian citizenship law, passed in November 1991, grants automatic citizenship to pre-1940 nationals and their descendants. Others have to satisfy a two-year residence qualification, pass a fairly severe language test which includes a test on Estonian history, and swear an oath of loyalty. The result in effect is that the vast majority of Russian-speakers were excluded from voting in the September 1992 election.

The draft naturalisation law finally put forward by the Latvian government in November 1993 was a good deal tougher than that passed in Estonia. It provided for a ten-year residential qualification, conversational knowledge of Latvian, and a 'legal income'. Former Soviet military servicemen from outside Latvia, and people who worked against Latvian independence through 'anti-constitutional methods', were excluded. The draft law's most worrying aspect was its provision for an annual quota, set by government and 'taking into consideration the demographic and economic situation in order to ensure the development of Latvia as a single-nation state'. It has been calculated that if some of the proposed quotas were adopted, it would take over five hundred years for all the Russians in Latvia to acquire citizenship, even if they passed all other requirements. However, the Latvian government submitted the draft law for scrutiny and approval by the Council of Europe, provoking Russian lobbying in opposition to it.

The US-based human rights body, Helsinki Watch, – which always strongly supported the Baltic right to independence – wrote to the Latvian Supreme Council deploring the draft law:

> The draft law effectively denies citizenship to people who until August 21st 1991 were considered citizens in Latvia and enjoyed the full rights and privileges that citizenship confers. ... Many of the draft law's proposals violate the spirit of CSCE documents, the Universal Declaration of

Human Rights and the International Convention on Civil and Political Rights. By joining the CSCE, Latvia committed itself to upholding the human rights standard set out in these documents. . . .

Particularly objectionable are [the specific exclusions]. . . . Such political and medical categories are vague, subject to wide and arbitrary interpretation. . . .

Helsinki Watch maintains that the 16 year residence requirement is excessive and unnecessarily interrupts the lives of people who (in good faith) settled in Latvia without ever expecting to be rendered a foreigner in an independent country. The language requirement is an extra hardship. If a test is set, then the law must provide for extra gratis language training.[57]

Even this law, however, was rejected by the Latvian Right as too mild. In any case, they denied the right of the 'Soviet' Supreme Council to decide this matter at all, declaring that the decision belonged to a future parliament elected by pre-1940 citizens and their descendants alone.

Given time, the emergence of a generation of Baltic Russians educated in the local languages, and the fast progress of spontaneous language-learning among their elders, would in the natural course of things lead to a majority of local Russians gaining citizenship. The expressed hope of moderate Balts is that, in the meantime, the Russians would have learned also to think of themselves as Balts and not as an imperial nation. But will the moderates remain in power? Will it be them administering the language tests? Or, in the words of Jānis Jurkāns, 'Are we going to go on raising the hurdles against getting citizenship higher and higher, using the excuse that international law says nothing on the subject, and secretly rejoicing that the Russians won't be able to make it?'[58]

Several few weeks after making this statement, Jurkāns was forced to resign under radical nationalist pressure. As he told me bitterly a few weeks earlier,

These idiots [the Latvian radical nationalists] attack Kozyrev [Russian Foreign Minister] as a 'Russian imperialist', and me for being 'soft on the Russians'. They haven't even noticed that Kozyrev is on the extreme liberal end of Yeltsin's government, and is under continual criticism from his own chauvinists and reactionaries for being 'soft on the Balts'.

At present, with ethnic relations within the Baltic relatively quiet, the chief danger lies in the probability of a future more nationalist government in Moscow and of a new and harsher Russian strategy. On the Baltic side, the danger also lies in the possibility of more radical nationalist governments taking power, and the risk that the language and citizenship laws may be used by them to exclude as many local Russians as possible.

In a reasoned exposition of the Latvian case on citizenship, Viesturs Karnups, the Latvian-Australian chief of the newly created and recruited Citizenship and Naturalisation Department, told me that,

> Latvians have nowhere else to go. There is no other Latvia. If this Latvia is not truly Latvia, then the Latvian culture, tradition and language will disappear from the face of the earth. So Latvians want to see a Latvian Latvia. They would wish a multicultural Latvia only in the sense of a multicultural Australia, in which other cultures and languages are free to develop to a limited extent, but state support for them is seen as a privilege, not a right.[59]

However, he continued that, 'The intention of this department is not to find excuses for excluding people, but to create opportunities for people to become citizens who fulfil the requirements, and who wish to integrate into Latvia.' He also let slip the phrase, 'my officials are known throughout the government for their enthusiasm and incorruptibility'.

This in a way sums up the moral ambiguity of nationalism: its power to inspire, and its power to harm. No-one doubts that Karnups's officals, amidst a post-Soviet civil service riddled with laziness and corruption, are indeed hard-working and honest. But where does their motivation come from? Their patriotism. And what is their patriotism telling them to do? Most local Russians believe that it is telling them to exclude Russians whenever possible.

A form of harassment to emerge during 1992 related to the refusal of residence permits to people rejoining their families after working abroad, and to ex-servicemen. Those who had worked briefly for the military in menial jobs were sometimes given residence registration dating only from the end of their employment, even if they had been born in Latvia. There is also evidence that the application of the language law is sometimes skewed even against Russians who speak good Latvian. It also gives radicals and busybodies plenty of opportunity for interference, bringing prosecutions against shops for displaying signs in Russian but not Latvian, and other minor misdemeanours. Public symbolism is being made exclusively Latvian: the Moscow District of Riga has been renamed 'Latgale', despite the fact that Moscow Suburb (*Moskauer Vorstadt*) is its historic name. All over central Riga, street signs in Russian have been removed. None of this amounts to 'human rights abuses', but it naturally causes resentment; Russian-speakers make up, after all, 63 per cent of Riga's population.

Apart from administrative harassment, the exclusion of 'immigrant' Russians from political power makes them vulnerable to two main dangers. The first is that future radical governments might use economic pressure to force them to leave. In the words of Višvaldis Brinkmanis of the Latvian Citizens Congress, asked how the Congress would persuade local Russians to return to an even more impoverished Russia:

> The big factories here will inevitably collapse, and it is out of the question that Latvia should pay unemployment benefit to their workers who come from among the colonists, so they will have no choice but to return to Russia.... As far as workers in the military industrial factories are concerned, they are simply part of the occupation army, and like that army, they should not receive legal permission to stay in Latvia.[60]

Some Russian-speakers are in fact leaving, if they are pensioners and can sell or exchange their flats, if they have jobs to go to in other republics, or if they still have close family elsewhere. According to Estonian government statistics, 17,000 Russian-speakers left Estonia during 1992; a similar number left Latvia. If the trend continues, it would greatly reduce the number of Russians in the Baltic. But as a Ukrainian worker at the 'Radiotehnika' plant in Riga put it,

> If we are to have no rights here, it would be better to leave; but how? The government is offering us 100,000 roubles compensation, but a flat in the Ukraine now costs more than ten times that. Even if we are allowed to sell our flats here, if only citizens are allowed to buy them then supply will be far greater than demand. ... Besides, where am I to go? I was born in Riga more than forty years ago, my children were born here. I have relatives in the Ukraine, but not close ones, and anyway, can they give me a job? Are there more jobs in the Ukraine than there are here?[61]

Marju Lauristin has claimed that when the Estonian government sent negotiating teams to talk with the Russians of the north-east, they had failed to present a concrete demand. But it was not so. The Russians had indeed put forward at least one very important demand, but the Estonians had refused it, despite their repeated promises to the West that full and equal social and economic rights for the Russians would be maintained, regardless of citizenship. As a Popular Front spokesman declared in July 1989: 'We consider unfair the participation in the fate of the region of all the inhabitants of the republic, [but] citizenship does not infringe on the social rights of other residents. The restriction only affects participation in the adoption of laws.'[62]

The Russians' demand was that the Estonian constitution should explictly rule out future discrimination between citizens and non-citizens in the fields of property ownership, choice of occupation, government (including local government) employment, social welfare, unemployment benefits, pensions and health care. Instead, clauses 28, 29, 31 and 32 of the Estonian constitution explicitly leave this possibility open, as in clause 28:

> Everyone shall have the right to health care. Estonian citizens shall be
> entitled to state assistance in the case of old age, inability to work, loss of
> provider, and need ... *unless otherwise determined by law* [my italics], this
> right shall exist equally for Estonian citizens, and citizens of foreign states
> and stateless persons who are present in Estonia.

Article 30 likewise states that:

> positions in state and local government shall be filled by Estonian citizens.
> In accordance with the law, such positions may in exceptional cases be
> filled by foreign citizens or stateless persons.

If strictly administered, this clause would destroy most of the benefits
coming to non-citizens. Will it be strictly administered? That depends on
future Estonian governments, which the Russians will have little say in
electing. The programme of the main Right-wing force in the new
Estonian government, the Fatherland alliance, does, however, guarantee
social and economic equality, and has been emphasised in conciliatory
moves by the new Prime Minister, Mart Laar, so that for the moment
such discrimination will probably not occur.

The second long-term danger, however, remains that exclusion from
political representation will leave the economic interests of Russian
workers and Russian businessmen largely unprotected. Latvian law
already explictly excludes non-citizens from owning real estate or setting
up joint-stock companies, though they can lease land and invest in
Latvia. Businessmen are vulnerable to (often justified) populist attacks
on 'foreign money-launderers'; workers, of course, to the whole free-
market transition. In other countries, including Poland and Russia,
economic reform and de-industrialisation have been retarded by an
awareness that the human, but especially the political costs, are too high
to bear. The Russians in the Baltic will have no such protection, and will
not be wrong to see their resulting misery as in part the result of their
political disenfranchisement.

In a post-Communist society in which patronage and influence over
the state are critical, the Russians, in spite of all guarantees, could find
themselves disadvantaged in a range of other fields as well, and most
notably in education. The Baltic universities increasingly operate only in
the Baltic languages, and quietly discriminate against Russian
applicants.

Višvaldis Lācis, the Latvian Congress leader, told the Popular Front
Russian newspaper that, 'Certainly we will not drive Russians out of
Latvia by force; but your status here will be that of the Turks in West
Germany. . . . You are not second class citizens here; you are nothing.'[63]

Some such economic, political and social status is in fact precisely what
awaits a great many Russians in the region. Economic and social

discrimination, more than the loss of citizenship, is what most Baltic Russians fear: Soviet citizenship was never a very meaningful concept in any case, and relatively few sought it. All, however, are worried by the threat of economic pressure. And both the fear and the reality of such pressure will be increased by their lack of political representation.

One of the more curious sub-genres to have emerged from the teeming womb of Soviet humour is that of the Pooh Bear and Piglet jokes – or rather *Vinni Pukh* and *Pyatachok*. As the following exchange makes clear, their characters have suffered as a result of life in the former Union:

> Pooh and Piglet are walking down a road;
> Piglet: 'Where are we going, Pooh?'
> Pooh: 'We're going to the forest to eat a pig.'
> Piglet (indignant): 'And if the pig doesn't agree?'
> Pooh (in official tones): 'The pig is not to be consulted!'

In the case of the Baltic States and the Russians, the roles are of course reversed; it is the three little piglets who are trying to take the bear to the forest – which may turn out to be not quite such a good joke after all.[64]

9

Building on Ruins:
The Recreation of the Baltic States

'My name is Ozymandias, King of Kings.
Look on my works, ye mighty, and despair!'
                        Percy Bysshe Shelley

The Baltic, Year Zero

In comparison with the countries of Eastern Europe, the Baltic States, as
constituent parts of the Soviet Union, were at a colossal disadvantage as
they set out to free themselves from Communism and reform their states
and economies. Whereas the East European satellites possessed at least
the formal attributes of independent statehood, however theoretical they
may have been, the Baltic States lacked their own currencies, armed
forces, border guards, diplomatic services, central or even local banks,
railways, airlines, and even tourist offices. The Balts had effectively been
insulated behind two iron curtains, since the Soviet frontier with Eastern
Europe had also been largely closed.

The Baltic economies were wholly integrated into that of the Soviet
Union, and overwhelmingly controlled from Moscow: the great
proportion of local revenue, including virtually all the hard currency,
vanished to Moscow. Even with goodwill on the Soviet side, the task of
separating Baltic institutions from centralised Soviet ones would have
been a hideously complicated process.

Where the Baltic Soviet republics did have their own institutions, these
were very often mere departments of 'All-Union' ministries in Moscow,
staffed from the centre. This was true of the Baltic 'Foreign Ministries',
and even of the police. Other areas, such as education or agriculture,
functioned under 'republican administration', but implementing policies
laid down from Moscow. Each institution had therefore to be constructed
largely from scratch, rapidly, and in conditions of political insecurity.

The four-year struggle for independence delayed effective economic reform, and the presence of the Russian minorities made that reform more hazardous. The Balts had also to effect reforms and build institutions amidst an economic decline without parallel in the peacetime history of Europe. Even the Great Depression of the 1930s did not see industrial production decline by more than 30 per cent over two successive years, real wages fall by some 45 per cent, or fuel prices rise by more than 10,000 per cent over the same period, while inflation climbed for a time to more than 1,000 per cent per annum and real unemployment soared.

Within this context, a close scrutiny of the Baltic record on reform inspires admiration, even if the results are still mixed. The Baltic republics may trail Poland, Hungary and Czechoslovakia in some fields, but they are generally far ahead of all the other former Soviet republics, and of much of the Balkans. The Baltic governments had, moreover, achieved by late 1993, their success without serious social or ethnic conflict.

Alongside economic crisis, the disintegration of Soviet ethics and rules of behaviour (such as they were) has also brought moral crisis. The moral earnestness of the national ideologies has often been accompanied by acute demoralisation in practice, as the socialist sins half-concealed under Soviet rule have emerged and been joined by those of primitive capitalism. Tallinn is today often referred to by its inhabitants as 'the Wild East'. Incongrous though that may appear on a first visit to its quiet Scandinavian-Gothic streets, a glance at its crime statistics or a few hours spent listening to gossip about state corruption will explain all, as will an evening spent in the bar or night-club of one of Tallinn's hotels, with their clientele of inebriated Caucasian 'Biznissmeni', local prostitutes on their arms.

And Tallinn remains a quiet place compared to Riga. The rouble restaurant at the Hotel Riga – the city's biggest – is so outrageously sleazy, its inhabitants so unselfconsciously proud of their money, their molls and their hideous clothes that it is one of the funniest – and saddest – places in the Baltic States. The contrast between the Balts' sober cultural self-image and the enormous, visible wealth of flashy non-Balt former black marketeers is clearly a source for future tension.

The Baltic governments are indeed faced with a dilemma. They have been much criticised, and often rightly, for maintaining restrictions on private business. Yet much of that business is in the hands of non-Balts, often of the most unscrupulous kind. Continuing state controls, however, tend only to spread the corruption still deeper within the state itself, and no effective anti-corruption laws, let alone institutions, yet exist.

Much of the former Soviet Union is deteriorating into a condition familiar from the Third World: a small number of the rich, mainly parasites on either the West or their own states; a struggling and embittered middle class relying largely on state and military employment; an impoverished proletariat, and a large underclass, surviving on casual labour, rag-picking, prostitution and theft. The whole edifice will be topped, perpetuated and partially controlled by huge, incompetent and deeply corrupt civil services.

The Baltic States are well on their way to avoiding this fate, and may be the only former Soviet republic to do so. This is thanks to their proximity to the West, their traditions and national pride. I have often criticised Baltic nationalism, but in the post-Communist world it is of irreplaceable importance in providing some sort of hedge against blatant corruption, and in mobilising a sense of service and sacrifice. It is especially true of Estonians, with their puritanical traditions. In the words of Foreign Minister Trivimi Velliste,

> [The danger of corruption becoming endemic in the state and society] . . . is probably the most serious point we could discuss today. It could be an even more critical danger than the ex-Soviet military here. But this is also possible to solve by means of evolution. That is, I believe in the ethical instincts of the majority of the people. Human beings have some deeply rooted ethical instinct, and this is how political decision-making is ultimately formulated. . . . This is however once again a question of the generations. The kids now entering school certainly won't be as corrupt as maybe their fathers were.[1]

This forecast lends authority to the repeated emphasis of Right-wing nationalists on the need for the 'moral regeneration of the nation'. On the one hand, this is all too often associated with chauvinist and anti-Russian views, and sometimes with anti-capitalist ones. On the other, it is certain that the members of the Estonian Right-wing government which took power in October 1992 are people as honest and dedicated as one would find anywhere in European politics; and their honesty is intimately connected with their Estonian nationalism. The connection between nationalism and honest effort is not as apparent in the other two republics. In Lithuania, there is often a very catholic gap between the rhetoric of high national ideals and the actual practice of government. In Latvia, the weakness of the state, together with the cosmopolitan nature of the port-city of Riga, ensures that wild, uncontrolled capitalism flourishes even more strongly than in the other two states.

Prime Minister Godmanis warned of the danger of a 'bananisation' of Latvia. The chief of the Popular Front's economic reform commission, Aivars Bernanš, sketched what this would mean:

> It is bad for a country if there is no authority and no law; but if there is authority without law, as here, then the people with authority can do what they like. We suffer from social inertia – the bad habits acquired in the

first stage of economic reform could persist for a long time. Then we would have to exert major force later in order to make the economy civilised.

For example, if international organisations give major aid to Latvia before a law on conflict of interest is passed, regulating the business activities of officials and deputies, then we will end up in the position of many African states: a total merging of the government and business, 'crony capitalism', and a monopolisation of the market by the mafia. In this case, as in the Third World, foreign aid would become a means only for improving the economic situation of the bureaucracy and its friends. That is why there is an article in the Popular Front programme that any financial aid should be strictly controlled and should go to helping the social infrastructure, health care and education, and not to developing state enterprises. . . .

Such proposals, however, have been little implemented: *The New York Times* once wrote that 'conflict of interest in the former Soviet Union is defined as an opportunity not to be missed'. They have also been regarded by Russian-dominated industry as a covert means of discriminating against industry and favouring the Latvian parts of the economy.*

Achieving Military Control

If a fundamental characteristic of the modern state is its monopoly of armed force, then the Baltic States still have a long way to go. At the start of 1993, Soviet troops remained in the Baltic and the Baltic governments' command over their own military was far from proven. Demonstrable progress had, however, been made since the struggle for independence began; then the three states barely even controlled their own police forces.

In contrast to the wars of 1918–20, the recent independence struggle was not a military undertaking; no-one suggested it would have been possible to defeat the Soviet forces in battle, even if weapons had been available. Until August 1991, OMON and the Soviet army repeatedly raided the headquarters of the Baltic volunteers, and Soviet propagandists warned the local Russian population that these 'fascist militias' would become their oppressors.

The new military forces therefore emerged very slowly, and remain

---

* The level of corruption existing in Estonia was emphasised in January 1993 when two leading harbour officials were arrested for diverting 5,000 tonnes of heating oil given by Sweden as humanitarian aid and selling it in the West. Sweden announced that it was temporarily suspending its aid.

very limited. Lithuania created a Defence Department in April 1990, but Estonia only did so two years later. As during the first period of independence, there is no significant co-operation between the armed forces, and it is by no means clear that one Baltic state would fight to help another.

The Baltic forces have been formed above all on the basis of volunteers from the national movements. Former Soviet officers who joined included the chiefs of staff of both the Latvian and Estonian armies, Colonel Dānis Turlajs and Colonel Ants Laaneots. Relatively few Balts had been allowed or wished to become officers in the Soviet army. Though it included 700 Latvian officers, many of these, like Viktor Alksnis, were Russified and absolutely loyal to Moscow. However, as elsewhere in the former Union, a certain number of Baltic Afghan veterans are among the 'elite troops' of each new national force.[2] Few other Balts have any recent fighting experience at all, with the exception of one or two emigrés from the US armed forces.[3]

Even the residual Soviet forces in the Baltic States remained in 1993 more powerful than anything those states themselves could put into the field. The Baltic armies are still only a few thousand strong and lack air cover, tanks or heavy artillery. The strategy of all three states, in the eventuality of invasion, would be to mount a brief formal resistance – to underline the national will to resist, unlike 1940 – and then to fight a guerrilla campaign.[4] It has sometimes been termed the 'CNN Defence', emphasising that the real defence of the Baltic States lies in Western public opinion.

There are widespread doubts in all three states – influenced by Soviet propaganda – as to whether there is any point in paying for a defence force at all if it could offer only formal resistance to a Russian attack. Even a Latvian defence official replied 'twelve minutes' when asked how long the Latvian forces could hold out.[5] Brazauskas and the opposition used the cost of the Lithuanian Defence Department as a point of criticism against Landsbergis and Sajūdis. After Brazauskas's own victory in October 1992 the Rightist but anti-Landsbergis Defence Minister, Audrius Butkevičius, agreed to stay on in government; by December he was already calling for the doubling of the defence budget, and seemed likely to obtain it, if only to avoid a repetition of the military discontent of the 1920s. All the armed forces are of course unhappy with their lack of support, and a Latvian borderguard once declared pathetically that the reason his force could not be equipped with dogs was that the dogs would die of starvation.[6]

The Estonian government planned a defence and border force of 5,000 men by 1993. In the long term they need one or two tank battalions, an armoured infantry battalion and two air squadrons, but know that for the foreseeable future they will not be able to afford the equipment. The Latvians project a force of 9,000 men, 3,000 of them volunteer regulars and the rest conscripts.[7] Under Landsbergis, the Lithuanian government, in keeping with the Lithuanian self-image, planned a very much larger force of 30,000 men (including the Home Guard) of which 16,000 have been recruited. They have however to rotate their weapons, and spend much of their time pointlessly guarding government buildings. Butkevičius has justified this size of army by declaring it would deter an attacker; but if the real plan is token resistance followed by guerrilla tactics then some confusion exists.[8]

The acquisition of weapons has been a major problem. The French have been forward (provocatively so, as far as Moscow is concerned) with military training and advisory missions to the Baltic States, but have stressed that 'supplies will be purely a commercial matter'. Germany, Sweden and Finland have granted non-offensive military aid in the form of trucks, uniforms and training equipment, and Finland gave Estonia an armed coastguard vessel. In Lithuania, Butkevicius worked a complicated deal on the international arms market which involved Lithuania in taking a cut of a large consignment of automatic weapons and rockets headed for the Caucasus, in return for allowing these to pass through the country. In Estonia, a scandal erupted in 1992 when in december 1991 Estonian border guards allowed a Russian businessman, Alexei Sagun (the Citroen dealer for Tallinn), to transport 21 Soviet armoured personnel carriers through Estonia on their way to an arms dealer in Germany. They were blocked and finally confiscated by the Estonian government in July 1992.[9]

It is still not clear whether the trans-shipment was illegal, or whether the Estonian government simply saw an opportunity to acquire armoured vehicles for nothing. The Estonians also confiscated 15,000 Makarov pistols en route through Tallinn to an arms dealer in Britain, and distributed them to the security services. Thousands of anti-tank rockets headed for Nagorno-Karabagh were also appropriated.[10]

The bulk of Estonia's stock of automatic weapons, to the end of 1993, consisted of Bulgarian and Romanian-made AK-47s and AK-74s (among the shoddiest examples of the species). Considerable quantities of arms have also been bought by Latvia and Estonia from intermediaries representing the old Soviet troops. Significantly, the open sale of Russian arms has only been authorised in the case of Lithuania, since Russia has no quarrel with Vilnius over its citizenship policies.

A further problem is simply recruitment. There is little enthusiasm for military service among the Baltic young, and all three states have found difficulty in attracting sufficient conscripts and preventing massive desertions. Conscientious objection is not acknowledged except on strictly religious grounds.

The horrible maltreatment of soldiers by their fellows in the Soviet army was one of the most disgusting aspects of the Soviet Union during the period of its decline. In 1990 alone, 18 conscripts from Latvia and 25 from Lithuania, including four ethnic Russians, died during military service. To judge by the accounts of two Estonian deserters in August 1992, ex-Soviet soldiers continue some of their brutal practices within this new army: the deserters, ironically, took refuge in Moscow!

Latvian forces have also been severely criticised for brutality and lack of discipline. Latvia introduced a fine of Rs50,000 for evasion of service, but even this did not prevent a particular soldier deserting his unit on four occasions, returning when it pleased him. Colonel Turlajs informed journalists in October 1992 that he had compiled a list of incidents of drunkenness on duty, 'but it would take half the day to read it'.[11]

A distinctive feature of the Baltic States, and especially of Latvia, is the way in which the new defence forces have become involved in the work of the police. This is due above all to the preponderance of ethnic Russians within the old Soviet police, or 'militia', in Latvia and Estonia. It is striking that in Lithuania, where ethnic Lithuanians always dominated the police, the defence forces have played a much lesser role.

Before police reforms in March 1991, the Latvian force was only one third Latvian: in Riga, 87 per cent of police were Russian-speaking. There was a similar proportion in Tallinn. In Vilnius itself, a majority of the police were Russian or Polish, but elsewhere the force was overwhelmingly Lithuanian.[12]

The Soviet militia were also poorly equipped, and did not as a rule carry pistols. Like the Tsarist empire before it, the Soviet Union was rather thinly policed by Western standards; in the spring of 1991, the Estonian police numbered only 2,500, compared to the 5,000 it said it needed.[13]

Political control by the KGB was of course a different matter. The KGB was also responsible for dealing with organised crime, and under Gorbachov sought to stress this function. The 'anti-mafia' sections of the local KGBs have in fact been largely retained by the new states, which are in no position to replace them.

In view of the police's ethnic composition, it is remarkable they gave so little trouble during the independence struggle – although this might still occur in north-east Estonia or in the Latvian cities. In Lithuania and Latvia, Soviet loyalist resistance was to some extent defused by the fact that the most hardline elements left the regular police to join OMON. Apart from this, the only overt political action occurred in Latvia, where several Russian-dominated police districts declared loyalty to the Soviet Procuracy in Latvia and not to the Latvian Republic.

During the critical period moreover, all three governments either left or placed old policemen in charge of the Interior Ministries so as to ensure the loyalty of their men. They also proceeded cautiously with the removal of policemen. By the strict letter of the law, no non-citizen can be a policeman, and police recruits have also to pass a strict language test. In November 1992, for example, a fifth of the police in Ventspils, Latvia, failed the test and faced dismissal. But in general, the language qualification for the police force has been only partially implemented. In Latvia, new policemen must be citizens, but existing non-native police officers have not yet been dismissed. Even the radical Estonian Interior Minister, former dissident Lagle Parek, handled the police in the north-east with diplomacy. Formal exemptions for a year or more were given to the forces in overwhelmingly Russian towns like Narva and Daugavpils, and in both Latvia and Estonia, the criminal investigation departments remained Russian-dominated, and even conducted their business in Russian, in view of the shortage of new detectives. Nonetheless, so far as the ordinary uniformed police are concerned, discreet pressure on Russians to leave, coupled with mass recruitment of native Balts, led to a striking change in the ethnic composition of the police force in Estonia, where by the end of 1992, 65 per cent of the Tallinn force was Estonian.

The new Baltic police have, however, inspired little confidence, being generally extremely young, often violent and sometimes wholly ill-trained. Meanwhile the old force, demoralised by poor pay, by the collapse of the Soviet Union, by the mistrust shown by the new governments, by ethnic prejudice and by insecurity over their future, has virtually collapsed.[14] In Gorbachov's Soviet Union, uniformed police were often to be seen working as private security guards for restaurants and firms in return for a pay-off for themselves and their superiors. Thus OMON in Latvia founded the 'Viking' security group, and then blamed some of its own illegal activities on its prodigal son! Many policemen have now left to work full-time in the private sector, or have moved into organised crime, with which many of course always had close links.

In October 1992, the Latvian Interior Minister Alois Vaznis forbade the police to carry automatic weapons, saying that there had been repeated cases of their misuse. The main reason for the decision was almost certainly to avoid armed clashes between the Russian-dominated police and the Latvian paramilitary groups which had taken over many of their functions. The tension between the forces is considerable, and violence has been threatened. Popular rumour has it that the struggle is for the control of protection rackets, but purely ethnic and political stresses play the major part.

Both the positive and negative aspects of the Baltic paramilitaries are exemplified by the Latvian National Guard, or *Zemessardze*, a territorial volunteer defence force subordinated to the Defence Ministry and increasingly involved in police work. The force is recruited mainly from young men from the countryside, and are often regarded by Latvian farmers as their only defence against urban gangs which terrorise isolated farms, stealing quantities of food and animals.[15] The National Guard is therefore a kind of Latvian Yeomanry, and like the English Yeomanry of the past, is not averse to cracking the heads of their class or ethnic enemies.

The National Guard now rarely co-operates with the police, whom they claim are in league with the gangs, tipping them off about ambushes and raids. The police force for its part loses no opportunity to denigrate the National Guard, calling it undisciplined, trigger-happy, ethnically prejudiced and corrupt.[16] Even the Latvian General Procurator, Janis Skrastins, classed the National Guard in May 1992 as a 'non-state force' and expressed worry about its political affiliations and reliability. The existence of this and other paramilitary forces, he said, 'reminds me of the Italy and Germany of the 1920s, when every political party had its military squads, which fought for the party's goals'.[17]

The 'trigger-happy' accusation seems alarmingly accurate, as dangerous incidents are increasingly reported.[18] In the first ten months of 1992, the National Guard was responsible for 54 shooting incidents, in which 7 people were killed and 31 wounded. After one such occurrence in October 1992 in the predominantly Russian town of Ventspils, the town council called for the removal of the Guardsmen, describing them as more dangerous than the criminals.[19]

In January 1992 I interviewed Juris Polievskis, Deputy Chief of Staff of the National Guard, at its Riga headquarters, a building in the Courland district of the city formerly occupied by the Soviet Commissariat, and full of barred doors and decades of stale cigarette smoke.[20]

Polievskis accused the customs officers in Daugavpils, locally recruited ethnic Russians, of corrupt connexions with smugglers, 'if only because they are paid so little', about which he was doubtless right. Between January and August 1991, customs officials at the newly established border posts often displayed stoic courage and dedication to duty in the face of recurrent attacks, beatings and humiliation by OMON, seeking to destroy this symbol of independence. Since then however, both the customs and the Latvian and Lithuanian border forces have earned a lamentable reputation for corruption and incompetence. During a strike by Latvian customs guards for higher pay in September 1992, officers from Ventspils themselves declared that,

> The material condition of the customs officers is miserable. Most of them think more about their garden allotments and potato fields than about their work. At least 10 per cent of the customs officers take bribes.

Even in Estonia, a quarter of the officers of the border guard were dismissed in the first nine months of 1992, and more than 100 conscripts deserted.[21]

In July 1992, the German government made an official protest about the behaviour of Lithuanian customs and border guards towards German citizens crossing the Polish frontier. Latvian border guards have twice killed one another in armed fights, though whether over the division of the spoils or out of drunken boredom is not clear.[22]

Meanwhile, smuggling is increasing rapidly throughout the Baltic. In autumn 1992 the most important single item of contraband was non-ferrous metals. The profits to be made from these in the West led to a situation in which no fragment of copper wire could feel safe at night. The most daring incident was the theft of the bronze plaque from the door of the Latvian Parliament. Less funny has been the theft of electricity cables, pieces of railway track, and public monuments, and the reported murder of several members of metal-smuggling groups in Estonia. Among the wilder rumours were that the men had been involved in plutonium smuggling from the former Union to the Arab world, and had been murdered either by their Arab partners or by Mossad as a warning to other would-be traders.[23]

Scandinavian police are also worried by the threat of a major heroin trade extending from Soviet Central Asia. In December 1992 the Latvian police, upon the advice of Interpol, arrested the managers of a Latvian pharmaceuticals company, Latbiopharm, and charged them with the manufacture the previous year of illegal narcotics worth 130 million Deutschmarks. In late summer 1992, authorities in Daugavpils smashed a local heroin-processing workshop supplied from Central Asia via a Russian military airport. Large-scale co-operation exists between organised crime and parts of the Russian armed forces – which have all the transport and weapons that any mafia could desire. Indeed, even as the Russian troops depart, they bequeath three major problems. The first is their arms dumps – leakage from which is being made worse by the very speed of the withdrawal. The second is unexploded munitions on firing ranges, and pollution in general. The third is the two nuclear training reactors at Paldiski – though these are likely to be dismantled with Scandinavian help.

Organised crime in the Baltic has the potential to make from drugs many times the profits of legitimate business, and thereby become a major power in the land. To judge from my meeting with the Narcotics Department of the Tallinn police, the Baltic authorities are as yet in no condition to prevent such a trade. The only comforting factor is that Baltic criminals are equally inexperienced.

There have also been incidents of the smuggling of illegal immigrants to Scandinavia, which could obviously multiply as Russian economic decline continues. At present most of the immigrants attempting to pass through the Baltic to the West originate from the Third World, having obtained visas for Russia, where they are 'adopted' by smugglers.[24] By early 1993, several boatloads of Kurds had been intercepted by Swedish coastguards in the Baltic Sea.

The regular police, the National Guard, the tiny armies, and the border guards are, however, not the only armed forces in existence. All three states now suffer from an excess in this respect which, while not as threatening as in other parts of the former Union, need to be carefully watched in view of the ethnic composition of the Baltic, and the shallow roots of democracy.

While the Latvian army and border guards report to to the Defence Ministry, the National Guard is responsible to the Latvian Supreme Council and its chairman Anatolijs Gorbunovs. Real control is exercised by their commander, Rightist deputy Girts Kristovskis. In November 1992 public controversy erupted when the Defence and Interior Ministers combined to accuse Kristovskis of establishing a second Latvian army outside the state. But in addition to these forces, there is yet a further security force responsible to the Supreme Council, or rather to a leading politician. This is the Security Service, formerly the Special Police Battalion.

The battalion was founded late in 1990 to counter the defection of OMON from the Latvian Interior Ministry and to provide security for parliament, and recruited entirely from ethnic Latvian volunteers. Initially, as a police force, it came under the control of the Interior Ministry. However during the counter-revolution of August 1991, the Interior Minister, Alois Vaznis, ordered the battalion to disarm and abandon its headquarters in order to avoid a clash with the Soviet forces. This humiliation caused intense bitterness, and contributed to Vaznis's removal a few months later.[25] The battalion was transferred to Supreme Council control, where it was under the effective command of the extreme nationalist deputy chairman (and former policeman), Andrejs Krastins. It was also involved in police work in Riga, causing friction with the regular police. In November 1991, at the Latvian Popular Front Congress, a lieutenant in the battalion (an immensely tall country youth with the hammer-and-sickle crest on his old uniform faintly silvered over) told me that,

> So far, we are the only new Latvian police. Why that is, you should ask the government. My friends were not career policemen. We come from the countryside, and volunteered to defend the parliament during the January events. We have practically no contacts with the old police, and the Interior Ministry looks on us as rivals . . . I think that most of the police, especially in Riga, have not changed their attitude. They will swear loyalty to Latvia to keep their jobs, but they will betray us in a crisis. They did that in August, when only our battalion was loyal, and the whole

Interior Ministry was treacherous or simply didn't know what to do, like Vaznis. . . . We have great difficulties finding Latvian recruits, and the old police even more so. Most Latvians do not want to be policemen. It is not a prestigious profession, and the pay is low. This is really one of the biggest problems for Latvia, but it seems no-one in the government has realised it.[26]

Outside of and opposed to the present state system were the *Aizsargi*, the paramilitary force of the radical nationalist Latvian Congress, which rejects the Supreme Council's authority and calls for a return to the Latvia of 1940. The *Aizsargi* have been accused of planning a coup, and to judge from their propaganda, would probably like to do so, but despite some emigré support, they lacked the weaponry of the 'state' forces. *Aizsargi* were repeatedly being accused of infiltrating the National Guard in order to get weapons.

All these separate forces had their own intelligence units, as did the Council of Ministers (in other words Prime Minister Ivars Godmanis), making a total of five, all doing the same work, quarrelling with each other, and accusing other units of being a threat to national security, penetrated by the KGB, the radical nationalists or whoever. One effect of the security forces was therefore to make many citizens feel even more insecure. By mid-1993 there was still no overall legislation defining their duties or supervising their activities.

In Estonia the forces were better integrated. The main question – other than the future of the Russian police in the north-east – concerns the volunteer Defence League, or *Kaitseliit*. In October 1992, a third of the force rejected the authority of the Defence Ministry, claiming to accept only the orders of the President. Its members were under the influence of the 'government in exile' and its 'Defence Minister', Colonel Toomepuu. On 9 October, several dissident soldiers beat up a senior officer in the headquarters in Tallinn.[27]

During the summer of 1992, the *Kaitseliit*, against government orders, provoked clashes with the Russian army by intercepting military columns and shooting out their tyres. Under pressure from alarmed Western diplomats, the government issued statements emphasising that the armed forces had to be subject to democratically elected authority. One *Kaitseliit* group near Narva assaulted four Russian civilians and was severely reprimanded by its own officers. Regular army units, and especially the elite Kuperjanov regiment, stationed in the town of Võru, have also gained a reputation for drunken violence. On 9 November 1992 a soldier of the regiment was shot dead in a fight with his superior officer, and several civilians were killed and wounded in drunken brawls. There have also been clashes between the army and police, each side firing shots in the air and trying to arrest the other.

The political divisions within the armed forces resulted partly from dissatisfaction with the government of Tiit Vähi, drawn from the former Communist establishment, and especially with his choice of Defence Minister, former Communist manager Ülo Uluots – not the ideal figure to command a young and enthusiastically nationalist force. The radical nationalist press exacerbated the position by deliberately undermining the authority of Uluots and Laaneots.[28] Under the Rightist government which gained power in October 1992, problems should diminish – unless ethnic conflict were to break out, which seems unlikely.

In Lithuania, the existence of paramilitary units reflected divisions within the Right rather than tension between Lithuanians and Russians. Under Butkevičius the Defence Ministry and Home Guard were nationalist, but covertly hostile to Landsbergis, whose own personal style was disliked by many of the young men in the force. Partly because of this, Landsbergis facilitated the strengthening of two other forces, the parliamentary guard – in fact a presidential bodyguard – under Arturas Skučas, and the *Šauliai*, a paramilitary volunteer force linked to the radical nationalist Liberty League. At the third Sajūdis Congress in December 1991, Landsbergis proposed turning the *Šauliai* into a state force, but was blocked by the Defence Ministry. After the October 1992 elections, the *Šauliai* threatened the stability of the Brazauskas-dominated government.

The presidential bodyguard remained a motley operation. Skučas himself appeared a narrow chauvinist whose influence was largely responsible for Landsbergis's increasing isolation, and his men came from highly suspect backgrounds. After the first round of voting in October 1992, Skučas was quoted in the press as saying that 'there are 20,000 armed men in Lithuania who will never swear loyalty to a Leftist government'. Subsequently, however, with advice from cooler heads, he indicated he had been misinterpreted, that there was no possibility of a 'Georgian variant' in Lithuania, and promised to help ease the transition.[29] Skučas and many of his men have now left to work for private security companies.

The rise of the new security forces has occurred within the context of an immense increase in the crime rate and the anxiety this has generated, augmented as ever by police secrecy and the inadequacy of the press. In autumn 1992, a Lithuanian-American friend, Daiva Venckus, witnessed the aftermath of a brutal mafia-style multiple killing in her neighbourhood. She was surprised to find no mention of the event in the local press or in statements from the Interior Ministry, which clearly wanted to suppress the news, and simply include it in the statistics at the end of the year.

These statistics are striking enough. In Latvia, the murder rate rose by about 20 per cent each year between 1989 and 1992. In 1990 and 1991 assault increased by 14 per cent and reported rape 13.4 per cent. Burglary rose by 23.8 per cent in 1991 and leapt by 58 per cent the following year. 'This is because,' as a policeman said, 'many people finally have something worth stealing.' Of those arrested, 60 per cent were minors. Overall the crime rate in 1992 rose by 49 per cent in Latvia and 31.5 per cent in Estonia, though that still leaves the rate well below US urban levels. By November 1992, the Latvian Interior Ministry was reportedly considering allowing ordinary citizens to carry guns.[30]

By far the most significant 'crime' in the Baltic States does not show up in the crime statistics, however, and is quite beyond the power of the police or even the state to control. This is the 'spontaneous' privatisation of state property by state managers, who are thereby converting themselves into a new class of proprietors. Organised crime is also deeply implicated in the process, which causes widespread resentment and undermines the efficacy of the economic reforms.

Industry and Energy

Compared to the great empires of history, the Soviet Union has left a visually disappointing legacy. The drab, grimly modernist offices of the fallen Communist Party, or the concrete memorials to the Great Patriotic War, hardly compare in grandeur with the remains of Timgad, of Persepolis or Fatehpur Sikri. Soviet military installations in the Baltic were disintegrating even while still occupied; a few generations more and the forests should have reclaimed them completely.

And yet this was, in its way, a distinct civilisation, aspects of which have penetrated the consciousness of many nations. The great Soviet industrial plants provide an example. Here, one has a real sense of hubris and nemesis, of a massive human effort diverted by tyranny into senseless and destructive avenues, ultimately collapsing under its own weight. The image of Soviet industrialisation traversed the world as a model of how a poor country under ruthless leadership could supposedly take a short cut to development and power.

Today, Russia is in a worse position than before Communism. Most of the great factories are regarded as economic and ecological nightmares, which actually reduce the value of the raw materials they use. An ecologist might suggest that this circular movement is characteristic of Western industrial society as a whole, but the circle is a few centuries wider. In *The Decline and Fall of the Roman Empire*, Gibbon evokes the image of eighth-century Rome, where barely a tenth of the former population survived in holes and corners of the enormous ruins, periodically fleeing for their lives from bandits or Saracen pirates. Today, the gigantic workshops of Soviet heavy industry are falling silent, and in small sections of them, fractions of their former workforce are struggling to turn out cheap consumer goods on bits of the old machinery.

Due above all to the cost of energy and the partial breach of trading links with the rest of the former Union, industrial decline in the Baltic was much steeper even than in Russia. In Lithuania, industrial output fell by more than 50 per cent during 1992, in Estonia by 40 per cent and in Latvia by a third. The bulk of the workforces, however, still clung to their jobs: productivity had sunk to absurdly low levels.[31]

This sense of the collapse of an entire world was vividly brought home to me during a visit in November 1991 to the Metal Works in Liepāja, one of the largest plants in Latvia. Under Soviet rule, the works employed almost 5,000 workers, some 15 per cent of the town's active population. The port of Liepāja (Libau) flourished before 1914 as the terminus of one of the main railway lines from the grain-lands of the Ukraine, but by the 1930s had been reduced almost to a ghost town by the decline of Soviet trade.[32] Moscow simply closed the port in 1964 and handed it to the Soviet navy, from which the Latvians are now trying to recover it. Almost 70 per cent of the city's population is now Russian-speaking, including many naval veterans. Some are employed in the fishing fleet, from which Latvians were generally barred as too liable to defect while in foreign ports. Few of the fish however seem to have landed in Liepāja. Like other Soviet cities, it suffers from the problem of phantom fish-shops – stinking of fish, but without any physical fish actually present.

In the huge steel mill one of the furnaces still periodically sent out blasts of noise and red light, but these did not reach the further corners of the enormous gloomy sheds; for the two other furnaces had already been shut down as sources of supply and markets elsewhere in the Soviet region dried up. In the shadows between the great machines, impoverished, semi-occupied Russian workers hung around, chatting and worrying about their future. 'At least it's a place to keep warm', one of them told me.

The mill no longer had a real economic role – no-one wanted or needed its products. It did, however, have an immensely important social function, which included feeding its workforce and their families by sending transport and construction units to the collective farms in return for produce, and running its clinic and kindergarten. As with so many large post-Soviet plants, the whole operation was a giant inverted pyramid, a massive factory with a large number of workers and their dependants balancing precariously upon the activities of a tiny proportion of the workforce. The social function of the plant was about to be transferred to the city council, which admitted it would probably be unable to keep them going. With the end of the big factories a whole social landscape is vanishing.

In the Eastern Latvian town of Daugavpils the pyramid image was even more striking. By the beginning of 1993, according to the mayor, Valdis Lauskis (appointed by the Latvian government after the previous Communist municipal government was dismissed), most factories had suspended their operations, the great majority of people were unemployed, three-quarters of the population no longer paid rent, electricity or heating bills, and town services relied on the taxes of the only major surviving factory, a chemical plant.

Many managers of big industrial plants are now involved in running businesses importing Western luxury goods, buying them with factory money and importing them under state license for sale to their workforces, but then selling them at a profit to whomsoever can afford to buy. Sometimes the workforce gets a share of the proceeds, sometimes it does not.

The abandoned state of Liepāja in the 1930s resulted from the first economic *volte face* the Balts were forced to perform this century, when the severance of links with revolutionary Russia meant that almost all trade had to be oriented to the West or cancelled. After 1945, Stalin ruthlessly reversed the process, to the extent that by 1989 less than 5 per cent of the direct exports of each republic went beyond the Soviet Union.

In the early 1990s, Estonia in particular attempted a third complete turn, away from Russia and the former Soviet Union and towards the West. This contradicts the idea often preached by Baltic politicians, that the region should become a 'Hong Kong' between the Soviet Union and the West. This idea was partly undermined by the hostility of the more radical nationalists: thus did Mrs Lagle Parek, Chairwoman of the Estonian National Independence Party and from October 1992 Interior Minister, describe one moral-cultural motivation in Estonia:

[In our party] we do not in fact want Estonia to become 'a new Hong Kong'. That way, we might become richer economically, but Estonians do not fit that role, because spiritually they are closer to the soil. As a people we have always aspired to education and culture, even amidst the greatest difficulties, so we deserve today something a bit better than the role of a Hong Kong. I hope that in the course of time . . . Estonia will be a country that creates values, and does not just mediate them; because true joy comes from making something, not just circulating or possessing it.

The 'Hong Kong' idea was also weakened by reality: the steep decline in trading links between all the former republics of the Soviet Union. It must be said, however, that Estonia has adapted better than the other two states. Estonian firms are successfully concentrating on trying to buy cheap in Russia and sell dear in Scandinavia, whereas in Latvia and Lithuania, the reverse is often the case.

By Western standards, all the former republics have often behaved outrageously towards each other, with a ruthlessness, lack of scruple and short-sightedness which could only have emerged from a mixture of nationalism and Soviet bureaucracy with the crudest and most simplistic autarkic ideas – and a tradition of putting them into effect by autocratic and unilateral means. These 'beggar-my-neighbour' policies have impoverished everyone, but Baltic industry has been among the worst affected. As a relatively minor example, Latvia thought nothing of passing, without consultation, a law abolishing all investments and property belonging to citizens of other republics (not only Russians, but also citizens of supposedly friendly republics like the Ukraine) acquired before November 1991. Similarly Russia, in winding up the Soviet Bank for Foreign Economic Relations (*Vnesheconombank*), ignored the fact that it owed Estonia the equivalent of eighty million US dollars. Today, trading in the region is like setting up shop in a den of quarrelsome bears.

In the words of Janis Kopits, Director of a Latvian Commodities Exchange,

> If this trend continues, we shall soon be covering our nakedness with fig-leaves. We have nothing with which to enter the Western market. Realistically, we will not be able to oust Taiwan, Hong Kong and Korea. ... We cannot afford to destroy the Eastern connections that we already have.[33]

In trying to break into Western markets, the Balts face far greater internal obstacles than they did in the 1920s. They also face more substantial barriers in the West, particularly the European Community. Aid and political support from the EC are highly useful, but its trade barriers, and particularly the Common Agricultural Policy, are a curse for the Balts as for the rest of Eastern Europe.

Despite this, Estonia is already exporting to the West, thanks partly to the cheapness of its labour (when combined with education, the Balts' greatest economic asset), and partly also to the massive smuggling of non-ferrous metals through its territory. This has made some Estonians rich, and helped to keep the entire economy afloat. By 1993 Latvia was beginning to follow suit.

Under Soviet rule, not merely were the Baltic economies integrated into the Soviet one, but the great majority of the major factories, as well as the basic infrastructure, was classified as 'All-Union', and under the direct control of Moscow. In Lithuania in 1989, 40 per cent of enterprises were 'All-Union', 40 per cent 'Union-Republican', with Moscow playing the dominant role, and only 10 per cent under the full control of Vilnius. In the words of a Swedish report, the collapse of the Soviet command economy, and especially the military-industrial sector, 'has left the enterprises like battalions in a defeated army, after the disappearance of the high command'.[34] During the period 1989 to 1991, managements were balanced between the Baltic governments and Moscow, obeying neither, an ideal opportunity for 'spontaneous privatisation'.

The Baltic nationalist movements are massively prejudiced against heavy industry. In Latvia and Estonia this is primarily a consequence of its Russian workforce. Even without this, however, the rural traditionalist ideology of large sections of the movement would have pushed it in this direction, while the autarkist nature of Soviet thought ensured little initial understanding of the need to export. Incessant warnings from managers that government policies were strangling exports to Russia were met with the response, 'but why should we sell our goods for useless roubles?' The point about the need to prevent an inflationary flow of roubles into the Baltic was sensible; but an awareness of the need to maintain trade links with Russia for the sake of energy imports came only very late, and still tends to be swamped by the focus on Western markets. It meant that, while Lithuanian embassies sprang up in Western capitals, only in December 1992, after the victory of Brazauskas, was an embassy set up in Belarus, one of its most important immediate neighbours.[35]

The rise in the cost of Russian oil and gas has been one of the main factors which so far has frustrated the Baltic belief that freedom from Moscow's economic diktat would bring automatic efficiency and prosperity. In February 1990, the cost of Soviet oil was still only 60 roubles a tonne – less than one US dollar even at the official commercial exchange rate, or ten cents at the 'tourist rate'. By December 1992, Moscow was demanding the international price of $110 per tonne, and sometimes indeed payment in hard currency. No economy could stand such an increase. The Soviet 'blockade' of Lithuania in April–June 1990 – to pressure the suspension of the declaration of independence – had provided a foretaste of what was to come. In 1991 the forecast Lithuanian trade balance with Russia was Rs538.9 million. By 1992, thanks to oil, it had plunged deep into the red. Balts have alleged that Russia's oil price rises have also been motivated by a desire to extract political concessions.[36]

In terms of oil and gas, the Balts should have had considerable leverage: much of Russia's oil exports to the West pass through the Latvian port of Ventspils; the Lithuanian oil refinery at Mažiekiai supplies Kaliningrad and Belarus with petrol; and the Estonian power stations at Narva supply St Petersburg with electricity.[37] Paradoxically, however, the Balts's ability to bargain was weakened by the decline in Russia's oil production. Had Russia continued exporting oil at full capacity, the Latvians would have possessed a critical supply of Russian hard currency; but with Russian production falling, Ventspils is no longer so important to Moscow.

The reduction in the oil supply contributed greatly to industrial decline, and brought great hardship to ordinary consumers. In Estonia, the fuel crisis bit in January 1992 and brought down the government of Edgar Savisaar. In summer 1992, it helped split the Lithuanian government and bring down Prime Minister Vagnorius. By the winter of 1992 all three republics were in the same parlous condition: hot water was cut off altogether or provided only at weekends; central heating was reduced to a bare minimum, if it operated at all. Schools and universities closed because it was too cold to teach. Deaths from hypothermia and cold-related diseases soared, especially among the elderly. So, cruelly enough, did deaths from fire as, with government encouragement, people turned to old-style wood-burning stoves (*burzhuikas*, in Russian) in apartments not built to take them. The Latvian government procured 10,000 axes and saws, and set the Defence forces to chopping down trees.[38] Finally, the energy shortage has forced Lithuania, against its will, into continued and indefinite use of the huge nuclear plant at Ignalina, a newer version of that at Chernobyl.

The vulnerability of the Baltic to world prices for oil and raw materials, of which it possesses almost none, was one of the main Soviet arguments against Baltic independence in 1989–91. Like so many Soviet arguments, it proved entirely accurate. The Balts have been forced to pay hard currency for oil and gas, because Russia will otherwise secure better prices from the West. Their reciprocal attempt to charge hard currency for food and manufactured goods exported to Russia has failed because they have no alternative market. Collapse however was averted by a mixture of Western aid and Russian private traders in petrol.[39] It can be argued that the rise in energy prices to world levels was inevitable anyway, and has had the salutary effect of forcing industries to be more efficient or shut down. This is indeed true, but the precipitate speed of this change has had a devastating effect.

The decline of the Baltic economies is, however, not simply the result of leaving the Soviet Union, but of the collapse of the Soviet Union itself, and of its economic legacy. A major factor is the degree of monopolisation within the Soviet manufacturing system. Single factories or groups of factories would be responsible for the entire production of a particular class of item, which would be passed in turn to another monopolistic firm. Thus the Banga group of factories in Kaunas, Lithuania, produced every single television tuner made in the Soviet Union, and the railway carriage factory in Riga produced a huge proportion of the Soviet Union's passenger carriages. These factories themselves were and still are dependent for components upon single factories elsewhere in the former Union.

It is impossible to seek alternative suppliers, for nowhere else in the world, with the partial exception of Eastern Europe, produces Soviet-style industrial goods. Moreover, from 1990, anticipating the trading collapse of the former Union, the COMECON countries began to demand hard currency for their goods.

The result is that a delay or breakdown anywhere along the line of industrial supply will bring every factory to a grinding halt; political chaos and local autarkic policies have multiplied such delays. Such policies are the poisonous fruit of the coincidence of Soviet and nationalist attitudes, and themselves contributed to the disintegration of the Soviet system. What neither Gorbachov nor most Western observers realised was that to decentralise the Soviet economy without creating a proper market was simply to create a large number of economic autocracies, not simply at the national level but at provincial and city level also. Supplies were always insecure, so that all factories in the Communist bloc had the habit of hoarding labour, raw materials and indeed their own production, to barter for essential supplies as the need arose.

The decline in the ability of the command economy to *command* increased the habit enormously. Everyone tried to export as little as possible and to suck in as much as possible: it was mercantilism gone mad. The rise of democracy only encouraged this behaviour, as politicians pandered to the fears and prejudices of the people by promising to stop *them* from taking *our* food and consumer goods.

A tragi-comic sense of this in operation came during a visit to the Lithuanian-Byelorussian border at Medininkai in spring 1991. The Lithuanian customs guards were busy confiscating 'goods that are relatively plentiful in Lithuania, but the Byelorussians lack: food, furniture, consumer goods, electronics'. In the corner of the customs shed were some strips of building material and a large heap of eggs whose owners had refused to pay the required tariff. Two miles down the road at the Byelorussian post, a similar policy was in operation. 'We have been told to restrict the export of goods which are available in Byelorussia but in short supply in Lithuania, so that our markets shouldn't be emptied – food, consumer goods and so on.' In the corner of the shed were some roofing-tiles and a small heap of tins of fish.

Industries could gain state licenses to export and import, but found themselves involved in a web of corruption extending from government offices in the capitals to customs officers on both sides of the border. So damaging could this become that Latvian leaders of the Daugavpils City Council admitted they sometimes smuggled raw materials and spare parts from Russia through the forests so as to get them to the city's plants on time: 'Our industries here are big and are often monopolies: at present they rely absolutely on Eastern supplies and markets. Our main task and duty is to avoid chaos and industrial decline in Daugavpils.'[40] They did not need to add that chaos in Daugavpils could take the form of a local Russian revolt against Latvian rule. The outgoing Lithuanian Economics

Minister, Albertas Šimenas, admitted in November 1992 that the Sajūdis government's tariff policies had been mistaken, especially when it came to taxing Lithuanian exports and imported raw materials.

The loss of Soviet markets has left much of Baltic industry, and even agriculture, in a desperate position. The mass of the Baltic populations may have been lulled by the knowledge that they constituted the most economically progressive part of the Soviet Union, though Baltic experts were always aware that Baltic products would meet resistance on the world market. It was always assumed that low production costs would compensate for low quality. But what became apparent was that, due to the rise in the cost of energy and fuel, goods manufactured in the Baltic were often more expensive than those produced in the Far East. The Radiotehnika factory in Riga, for example, previously one of the showpieces of Latvian industry, was being hopelessly undercut not only on the international market but even within the former Union by cheap radios from Taiwan.

The Baltic consumer industries also suffered from the classic post-Communist problems of image, design and packaging. Even when, as in the case of Radiotehnika, their products were probably no worse than those of their international competitors, consumers both in the West and in the former Union inevitably preferred something bearing a foreign brand-name and with an attractive package. A minor but deeply irritating example of this was the practice in Baltic restaurants – a mixture of snobbism and profiteering – of selling expensive Western beer and often atrocious Western wines rather than decent local beer or good, cheap Georgian wine. In a fulfilment of the prediction made by the poet Jaan Kaplinksi, Estonia's charming hand-made toys were being hopelessly out-gunned by Barbie and Ken. On the other hand, Baltic furniture industries by 1993 were beginning to do very well on the basis of cheap exports to Scandinavia and Germany.

The fate of most Baltic consumer industries reflects the increasing class divisions within former Soviet society. In the words of the director of Radiotehnika, Peteris Sliede, 'the rich can afford to buy Japanese radios, and the poor can't afford to buy anything':

> We have been working intensively to develop new production, change our designs; and now it is too late. Our sales have slumped so far that now we have no money to invest in changing our production. We have only succeeded in creating one joint venture, with Sweden. It is not very effective, but at least it keeps a few people in work. . . . How many? Fifty, out of 4,200 on our books.

By August 1992, and for the same reasons, Estonian enterprises had stockpiled 2.5 billion Kroon ($200M) worth of unsold consumer goods.[41]

Most of the old managements had no understanding of the

importance of packaging, design, or indeed accurate book-keeping; but when it came to coping with post-Soviet chaos they had one great advantage over Western businessmen: they were used to this jungle, and were long-standing experts in the complicated art of the barter-deals needed to acquire raw materials and spare parts. Anathema though it is to many Western advisors, this barter system is going to be necessary for years to come, as long as any kind of trading system in the rouble bloc survives. Indeed, the increasing chaos of currencies and 'provisional currencies', and the collapse of the rouble, make it more not less necessary.

Privatisation and Corruption

The way out of these Soviet Baltic dilemmas was supposed to be privatisation and the free market. In the first euphoric days of the national movements it was thought these would lead the Baltic to Western economic levels in a matter of years. The assumption among the Balts was always that their shorter period under Communism, and their stronger commercial traditions, would guarantee success as soon as Moscow's control was lifted.

As I have shown, however, the commercial traditions of the Balts were, before 1940, fairly weak; trade and industry in Latvia and Lithuania was at least often in the hands of the ethnic minorities, against whom the Baltic peasants and new intelligentsia felt considerable prejudice. Under Soviet rule, the private sector in the Baltic was crushed to a far greater extent even than Czechoslovakia or East Germany.

The Balts were certainly more amenable to capitalism than the Russians; even so, according to a Soviet poll in February 1990, only 30.1 per cent of Estonians, 21.9 per cent of Latvians and 14.8 per cent of Lithuanians viewed individual capitalist activity favourably. The All-Union average was 14.7 per cent.[42]

Under Communism, the Balts lived better because they worked more efficiently and conscientiously. However, the private traders and black marketeers who tested the limits of the system were generally not Balts, but Caucasians and Jews. They are now being joined by increasing numbers of Balts, but hostile stereotypes still persist. As an Estonian private farmer put it,

> The word 'businessman' in Estonian has always had a bad sound, especially among ordinary people. It has always suggested speculation, crookedness, foreigners coming here to steal things and disturb our peace. And businessmen today aren't making this picture any better. The problem is that at the moment, everyone is forced to use every means to

build up their capital; but later, they will have to think of the good name of their business.[43]

That the Baltic approach had its advantages can be seen in the contrast between Baku and Vilnius. In Baku, former Black Market chiefs and corrupt officials enjoy a luxury that no Balt has achieved. It is obvious, too, that the local Communist leadership spent hardly a rouble of Azerbaidjan's oil wealth on public services, infrastructure or architecture. Vilnius, by contrast, was well administered by the standards of most Soviet cities.

The result is that while the great majority of Balts are pro-capitalist in principle, they often find real live capitalists very hard to bear. The difference was perfectly expressed in an exchange in 1991 between Professor Richard Eberling, a visiting American free-marketeer (indeed almost a Libertarian), and a Lithuanian Right-wing deputy and poet. The professor had been talking in almost evangelical terms of the beauties of the unrestricted free market, how it would liberate Lithuanians and make them better people. The deputy was most impressed,

> 'Ah, Professor,' he said, 'if only we had more people like you, who could really teach us how good capitalism is, and inspire us to reform ourselves!'

At this, I felt compelled to suggest it might be helpful if the Lithuanian government spent more time encouraging capitalism and less controlling and occasionally persecuting the capitalists it had; these might be unattractive products of the black market, but were the only ones available. I named a controversial Lithuanian company called Interlita. The deputy was astonished:

> 'But Interlita are criminals!', he exclaimed, 'they are profiteers! All they thought about was making money! They didn't think of Lithuania at all!'

At this, it was the Professor's turn to look astonished. The Interlita case is in fact a good example of the psychological difficulties of adaptation to the free market. A joint venture between a Lithuanian company sprung from the old Komsomol and a shadowy German partner, it flourished in 1990 under the government of Prunskiene, when it was allowed to carry out certain currency dealings in order to subvert the Soviet blockade and import computers into Lithuania. In autumn that year, the accusation of corrupt links between Interlita and the government became a major weapon of the Sajūdis radicals against Prunskiene. Interlita's founders were undoubtedly a fishy lot: no-one would be surprised to learn that there were in fact corrupt links between Interlita and the government of Prunskiene. However, when after Prunskiene's fall, the new government of Vagnorius seized the company's assets, it offered no proof of any wrong-doing. By the time of the fall of the Sajūdis government in 1992, the case had still not come to court. The whole affair was worryingly reminiscent of similar cases in the Third World: the mixing of patronage, business and politics; arbitrary action by the state each time a new government came to power; the endless unsubstantiated accusations of corruption in public ultimately convincing the mass of the population that the entire political elite was complicit.

Radical nationalists often allege that the move into private business by former Communists and Komsomol officials is part of a general strategy to take over capitalism and the new states. In fact, personal advantage provides a quite sufficient explanation. The move has, however, certainly happened on a massive scale, and often in a corrupt form, involving the effective theft of state property. This, like other forms of economic crime, flourished in the gap left between the collapse of Soviet laws and the development of new free-market regulations. As Vytautas Leipus, the police chief of Vilnius, said in 1991,

> It is very difficult now to tell when something is an economic crime and when it isn't. What is illegal speculation? What is legal trade? Even when something is still illegal, we sometimes know that we're not supposed to enforce the law because it's out of date, and often we don't know what to do. The old law on speculation is still in force, but now the whole of government policy is to encourage people to break it![44]

Given the absurdity of many Soviet and post-Soviet laws, even respectable businessmen were forced to break them to survive. In the growing climate of violence and extortion, many needed links with organised crime for their own protection, thus allowing the 'mafia' a foot in the door. The result is that it is often very difficult in Baltic business to tell the sheep from the goats. The two species tend to copulate with each other until even they don't know which is which.

The legal framework is confused and deficient. Up to the spring of 1993, prosecutions for 'spontaneous privatisation' had been brought only in Estonia, although some managements have been disciplined by the other states. Aivars Bernanš recounted an example of spontaneous privatization by the old bureaucracy in Latvia:

> In the Autumn of 1990, three former leaders of the local Communist Party and the local council rented a meat-processing plant in the town of Tukums from the state. It has a monopoly in processing the meat from three districts. They rented it for a purely symbolic price – Rs93,000 – and then made more than Rs4 million in pure profit in 1991 alone. From September 1991 a government commission began to investigate this case, but the Ministry of Agriculture has so far been deaf to every suggestion that this contract should be broken.[45]

Fear of the Black Market taking over the privatisation process was increased by the knowledge that so much of it was in the hands of non-Balts, and especially 'citizens of Southern republics', as the euphemism went. Between 1990 and 1992 this was a major factor restricting privatisation. In some cases, auctions of commercial property were cancelled when it was discovered the 'buyers' were acting as front-men for Caucasian businessmen.

The second group towards which radical nationalists feel strong hostility are the 'former Communist' managements, now often functioning as the 'proprietors of state property'. The Lithuanian decision to privatise by means of investment cheques was intended partly to check the predisposition of managers to become owners of their firms. These managers lay great stress of course on having been in the direct service not of the Party but of the State, an important distinction but one which does not alter the fact that they were part of the old Soviet establishment and can exploit its networks. Whether this makes them morally more guilty than any other industrial manager is an open question.

As in Russia and the Ukraine, the threat to industry as a whole, and the desire for state subsidies, tends to create in the Baltic a natural community of interest between management and workforce, equally anxious to avoid closure and lay-offs. This should be set against the common image of managers as mere asset-strippers, piratically stealing from their factories before abandoning them. Spontaneous privatisation in the form of asset-stripping certainly took place on a massive scale in the Baltic. A common procedure was for managers and a select group of workers to form a private company within the larger state company, to acquire its assets or produce at low state prices, and then sell them for the market price, preferably in the West, and pocket the proceeds. The new Estonian government took tough measures against such practices in November 1992.

Not all spontaneous privatisation took this destructive form. Managers in Latvia and elsewhere were selling stock in their companies to suppliers and customers, described by an American student as 'basically a way of ensuring the observance of contracts, by giving contractors a self-interest and a stake in the survival of the firms that they are dealing with'.[46] In these circumstances, the huge 'debts' of companies were partly illusory. State enterprises, every one of them theoretically bankrupt by any Western standard, ensure each others' survival by providing unlimited credit.

The breaking of huge Soviet plants into smaller units headed by the dynamic sections of their existing management often made excellent economic sense. This was, for example, essentially the means by which Talleks, the first major firm to be privatised in Estonia, secured its future.

By the end of 1992, while the obstacles to 'immigrants' benefitting from privatisation remained in place, all three states had more or less abandoned the attempt to stop former managements benefitting from privatisation. In a sense, they were only accepting what they could not prevent.

A major obstacle also was the decision of all three states to return property to its former owners, where factories had been privately owned before 1940. As the Germans have found, distinguishing what existed previously from what was developed or destroyed under Communism is an almost impossible task. The Centre-Right government in Estonia came pledged to the absolute sanctity of restitution, or full compensation, though even this seemed likely to be modified in time. The Latvian government decided that after 1 January 1993, no further claims would be accepted.

The Lithuanian response to the privatisation dilemma took the form of an egalitarian scheme introduced in 1991 by which investment cheques were allocated to the whole population. The limit an individual could invest in any particular enterprise was Rs5,000 (then around $100), which meant it would require dozens of people even to buy a small shop. Larger enterprises were to be privatised only by the cheques or by the distribution of named shares to their workers.[47]

Under pressure from Western advice and 'life itself' (as Soviet-speak has it), this egalitarianism was progressively modified, and by the end of 1992 had practically disappeared. The need for hard currency and foreign investment ensured that money was given an increasingly important role. Most people used their investment cheques to purchase their apartments. Some families or groups with an entrepreneurial tradition pooled their entitlement to buy small businesses. Others, inevitably, were cheated by bogus companies or 'investment banks' promising high rates of return.

The privatisation of shops and small businesses in Lithuania proceeded fast and was in general well-conducted; by mid-1992, more than 1,000 enterprises with a buy-out value of Rs200,000 or less (1991 prices) had been sold for cash and investment cheques. This represented 80 per cent of the property available within that category, and 10 per cent of the total, excluding housing and agricultural land. By the end of 1992, however, privatisation in Lithuania, unlike Poland, had not, it must be said, led to any great improvement either in supplies or in service.[48] In Poland the burgeoning of private enterprise depended crucially on currency reform and on the creation of a strong convertible Zloty. In Estonia and Latvia, the Kroon and the Latvian Rouble/Lat had the same effect. Lithuania, in contrast, was still stuck with a feeble 'provisional currency', heavily influenced by the Russian rouble. With the introduction of the 'Litas, the situation in Lithuania also improved.

The privatisation of large enterprises in Lithuania progressed much more slowly. By mid-1992, the government claimed to have 'privatised' almost half the major establishments, though upon closer examination this often turned out to mean that the state still owned 51 per cent of the business concerned, that a single department had been privatised, or even that the 'privatisation' consisted merely of distributing a small proportion of shares to the workforce.

During 1992, as the attempt to sell major enterzrises to local residents faltered, the government made increasing efforts to attract foreign investors. It was announced that several categories of business would be sold only for hard currency (now of course much easier for local buyers to acquire). Western advice was sought: a British firm, McKenna, handled the legal aspects of privatisation, and a Scandinavian firm was given the extremely difficult task of valuing the properties concerned.[49]

The response initially was disappointing: by January 1993 only nine out of 114 enterprises listed for privatisation had been sold, for a total of $830,000, half of which was paid for a single hotel in Kretinga. In the words of one Lithuanian-American observer, 'Well, what would you like to give your worst enemy for Christmas? How about a Lithuanian heavy-industrial plant?' Most Baltic industry is simply not commercially viable, least of all in the economically disturbed circumstances which seem likely to persist for a considerable time to come.

Successful privatisation has largely been in the field of services, catering and hotels; though some consumer-goods factories in areas such as tobacco and shoemaking have also attracted interest. One enterprise that reportedly sold particularly well was a funeral home – the distress caused to bereaved relatives by rapacious state undertakers has become legendary.

Foreign investment in privatisation up to the end of 1992 was very slight in all three states. It was in any case regarded by radical nationalists as a threat rather than a support, and there was much talk of 'selling out national property to foreigners', and of the Baltic States becoming 'filials of Japan'. In the words of a Latvian Rightist deputy, Janis Lagzdins,

> Our Popular Frontist local authorities and ministries take great pleasure in privatising objects for hard currency, and if we don't set strict legal restrictions, then the property of Latvia will be sold out to all the transients of the world.[50]

To this, free market reformers and foreign advisors have replied wearily that the Balts would be very fortunate to persuade foreign capital to take any interest at all in clapped-out Soviet industries. Foreign capital has almost all gone to wholly new enterprises and developments. Rules prohibiting foreigners from purchasing full ownership of a state enterprise have now been dropped. In Latvia and Lithuania, foreign investment in the media, education, drugs, communications and armaments, and the extraction of raw materials are all banned, as is foreign ownership of land, though it can be leased for extended periods. These rules are not in themselves a major practical obstacle to investment in most of the economy, but as the IMF warned, they do not create a very welcoming atmosphere.

In Latvia and Estonia, privatisation was delayed by the crucial question of citizenship. While there was an understandable desire to restrict ownership of former state property to citizens, most knew that to delay privatisation until the citizenship issue had been settled would mean delaying it for years, and that to exclude local Russians from participation would provoke bitter criticism locally and in the West.

In Latvia a decision was taken to allocate investment cheques to resident non-citizens on the basis of years worked in the republic; full citizens, however, received a bonus of 20 extra investment cheques, equivalent to ten years' work or ten square metres of accommodation floor space – a substantial advantage. Soviet military service was not computed as years worked, and some military veterans got very little.

In Estonia, investment cheques were issued only to buy housing; enterprises were to be bought at auction, with strict scrutiny of business plans and preference given to the existing workforce and management. The first limited wave of privatisation collapsed at the end of 1991 amidst accusations that firms were being sold off on the cheap to their managements. In November 1992 the Supreme Court attempted to cancel even the two largest successful sales, on the grounds of legal irregularity, but it was overturned by the new government, which argued that to re-nationalise companies would undermine confidence in the whole process.

After a further long delay, Estonia became, in mid-1992, the only former Soviet republic to develop a single agency for privatisation, the Estonian Privatisation Company, modelled on and advised by Germany's Treuhand. This was to be the largest single privatisation scheme in Eastern Europe outside Germany – a daring move given that Estonia, to put it mildly, lacked the huge sums which have gone to preparing East German firms for private ownership. The scheme was criticised by Centrist representatives of the former establishment, like former Deputy Economics Minister Erik Terk, for being insufficiently regulated.[51]

This and the German link proved the downfall of its Director, Estonian emigré Andres Bergman, formerly a salesman in Germany. On 27 November 1992 Bergman was dismissed by the new Estonian government, accused of failing to control corruption but also of unfairly favouring German firms, and the programme was temporarily suspended for reorganisation. Restitution also played a part; the Estonian Justice

Ministry said that some of the enterprises were based on those confiscated by the Communists in the 1940s.[52]

This setback came only ten days after the agency had begun the process of selling 38 large enterprises. Far Eastern as well as European firms had indicated an interest, though sceptics observed the motivation was more to find an Estonian outlet for their own products than to institute production in the country.[53] Small-scale privatisation, however, was flourishing in Estonia by the end of 1992, greatly helped by the success of the new Estonian currency, the Kroon, introduced on 20 June 1992. The greater part of the country's shops and small enterprises had been sold by the end of that year, most in fact transferred to their existing workforces for heavily subsidised, largely token sums.[54]

As other countries have found, handing shops to their workforces does not automatically produce an improved work-ethic; but rapid and considerable improvement was visible in some cases. In November 1991 I visited the privatised 'Elegaanz' clothes and shoe shop in Viru Street, Tallinn, and spoke with its managers. The appearance of the shop, with its new white paint, cheerful lighting and attractive window display suggested a new spirit. The staff itself had purchased the shop from the state, after presenting a business plan. It was now better motivated and harder-working, and since people with money bought everything in sight to hoard for the future, sales were not a problem – whenever stock could be obtained. By the start of 1993, many streets in central Tallinn looked like Western high-streets.

Latvia's privatisation was slower and more chaotic. Although in a formal sense privatisation had not begun before 1992, in point of fact managers and work collectives had already privatised a very large part of the economy from within, with no legal regulation or legal guarantees. Most shops were already functioning as private companies.[55] In January 1991, Aivars Bernanš told me that,

> By the start of this year, there were about 250 private shops in Riga, of which 50 were privatised state shops; but up to now, there has been no legal basis for this privatisation, it was almost always a case of an administrative decision – only a 'sale' if you can call a mutual deal involving a bribe to an official a sale.

When it happened, Latvia's formal privatisation scheme was a mixture of investment cheques, roubles and hard currency. The procedure was slowed and complicated by a decision to carry out a 'decentralised' privatisation, allowing ministries and local authorities to sell off enterprises under their jurisdiction. This not only gave a field-day to bureaucratic corruption, but led to many local authorities actually reversing the process and running enterprises as their own property.[56] At the end of 1992, after the sacrificial dismissal of Economics Reform

Minister Arnis Kalniņš, it seemed that many of the Latvian restrictions would be thrown out as the state frantically sold off enterprises to raise hard currency to cover its growing deficit and to buy fuel. Given that few ordinary Latvians have money to spare, this seemed likely to ensure even more ownership in the hands of the existing managements.[57]

A major threat to the future of the Baltic States lies in the connections between its new entrepreneurial class and the leaders of organised crime, particularly in connection with the seizure of state property. An article in *Lietuvos Rytas* in September 1992 described how the privatisation of the four main food stores in the Lithuanian town of Šiauliai was cancelled after the process was taken over by local racketeers.[58] According to the paper, competitors in the auction and local officials had been threatened. In similar cases, those who persisted saw their new property burned or blown up. Autumn 1992 saw a spate of explosions, especially in Latvia, which were evidently the work of organised criminals fighting over property.

Very many new businesses have to pay protection money, and organised crime is often used by businessmen to warn rivals off their patches. In Lithuania, over the single weekend of 5–7 December 1992, two private foodstores in Vilnius, one of them recently privatised, were bombed, and one private and one state enterprise were destroyed by arson attacks in provincial towns. The Vilnius Police Commissioner called for new laws which would bring the instigators, as well as the bombers, to trial.[59]

Criminals in the Baltic, as in the rest of the former Union, tend to be known collectively as 'the mafia'. This is one of those Western terms which, enthusiastically adopted by post-Soviet vernacular, and played back to Western journalists, causes general confusion. According to the deputy police chief of Tallinn, Sergei Kozlov, there is in the strict sense no Mafia in the Baltic.[60]

In Russia, and especially in Moscow, closely knit Caucasian ethnic groups like the Chechens, with their clan links, hierarchies, and codes of silence, in many ways resemble the Sicilian Mafia. So far their activities in the Baltic have been limited, since they are so ethnically identifiable: a Chechen drugs-smuggling operation in Tallinn would be easy to spot, for example, so long as the police had not been completely corrupted.

Balts use the term 'mafia' to describe several different things. It is used most commonly as a general description of the underworld and the Black Market. Every little cigarette smuggler or filcher of copper wire whom you meet in a cheap restaurant today likes to drop heavy hints that he is in the 'mafia'. The second, and more accurate description, is of organised crime rings involved in large-scale smuggling, the massive theft of state property, and the administration of protection, extortion and prostitution networks. Their activities resemble those of the Sicilian Mafia, though their internal structures generally do not.

The third use of 'mafia' is as a negative representation of the old Soviet establishment in the Baltic, using their networks to dominate the administration, and most especially, to allocate themselves state property as part of 'spontaneous privatisation'. The word is also used simply as a nationalist catch-all for the unattractive side of the free market. In the words of Jānis Āboltiņš,

> In Latvia there is all this fear of the 'mafia' on the part of many deputies. But what is the Soviet mafia? In my view, they are just the people who are prepared to work and get ahead. They are like the first colonisers of America![61]

The comparison with seventeenth-century Puritans is striking, but somehow I cannot quite see them at home in a Soviet night-club. Although Āboltiņš is correct that dynamic private business in the former Union has inevitably emerged from the Black Market and cannot be blamed for this, it is impossible to regard the real organised criminal as anything other than a deeply sinister and dangerous force. The problem is the grey area between the genuinely hard man and the more or less legitimate businessman.

The risk is that, as in the United States or Italy, organised crime in the Baltic will use its cash and connections to buy large sections of the 'legitimate' economy. In the former Soviet Union, this will also involve building on existing alliances with the old and new bureaucracies. The criminals involved come not simply from the Baltic and the former Union, but also from the West. At least two leading Scandinavian criminals moved to Tallinn in 1991 to escape the attentions of their own police. Posing as legitimate businessmen, they were welcomed with open arms by the Estonian establishment.

In December 1992, the Lithuanian Procurator General, Artūras Paulauskas, warned the new government that sophisticated criminal groups had been created in Lithuania, with increasing connections in the West. He said they had backed several deputies in the recent elections, and penetrated most government institutions, and that the 'godfathers' of these groups 'do not even trouble to conceal their influence on important government decisions'. In an implicit attack on the Defence Ministry, Paulauskas said that its Black Market deals for arms had given the 'mafia' a handle on the state. He said in particular that organised crime within Russia, including the Chechen groups, were establishing joint ventures in Lithuania to launder money and, possibly, to smuggle drugs. He called for Western aid in setting up police groups to fight organised crime, saying that the existing security forces were wholly inadequate to the task.[62] The prospect of the Baltic States becoming a conduit for heroin smuggling from Soviet Central Asia is highly worrying to Western police, although up to 1993 the only large consignments intercepted were of hashish.

The Left-wing government which took power in Lithuania in December 1992 promised action and created special police units to fight organised crime. However, Prime Minister Bronislovas Lubys admitted that corruption was now widespread in the government. He pointedly told a gathering of Interior Ministry staff that several police commissioners, including one in Kaunas, had received cars as presents from tax dodgers. Many observers, however, felt that an LDDP-dominated government, with its links to the traditional bureaucracy, would be as unlikely as Sajūdis to fight corruption successfully. The threat of a criminalisation of the state and economy, such as has occurred in much of the Third World, is therefore a great menace facing not only Lithuania but all the states emerging from the former Soviet Union.

In the Scissors: Baltic Agriculture

The sharp decline of Baltic agriculture has been perhaps the greatest economic disappointment of all. National ideology as well as historical experience had suggested that this was an area promising great success. Ideology in all three republics laid stress on the Balts' peasant identities and virtues, and the interwar republics had very accomplished peasant agricultures which exported on a large scale to western Europe. Under Communist rule the Baltic republics were by far the most successful agricultural region of the Soviet Union and owed much of their relative prosperity to this fact. When freed from the command economy and collectivisation, it was widely thought that agriculture would help soak up urban unemployment. By December 1992, however, some Estonian politicians were arguing that Estonian agriculture was hopelessly unprofitable and should be abandoned altogether. They pointed to the general failure of Northern European agriculture to compete with that of the United States, except with the help of massive subsidies. Estonian Deputy Minister of Agriculture, Maido Pajo, told me that over the next decade employment in agriculture would have to be reduced by at least a third.[63]

The way events have turned out is also a reproach to all those 'experts' in Western offices who have never met a pig, let alone a post-Soviet pig, but have been perfectly prepared to make predictions and recommendations for Soviet agriculture on the basis of the experience of China. It is even possible that Mikhail Gorbachov, so much criticised for his failure to push through privatisation, actually understood more about Soviet agriculture than these Western critics.

Rapid agricultural decline without compensating improvements in other fields would be a social disaster for the Baltic States, if only because such a high proportion of the population lives off the land. In Lithuania in 1989, 32 per cent of the population lived in the countryside, and in Latvia 28 per cent. That year agriculture provided 29.6 per cent of Lithuania's national income, a quarter of Latvia's, and a similar proportion of Estonia's – and higher, if timber is included.[64] By Western European or North American standards, these are huge proportions. When one thinks of the political influence wielded by far smaller rural populations in the West, it is clear that the Baltic peasants are going to play a key political and social role.

If there were any prospect of making a profit, and they could face the backbreaking work, many in the cities, having been born in the countryside and retaining close relatives there, would not find it so very difficult to return. The mass urbanisation of most parts of the Baltic States occurred only during Soviet rule, and a widespread attachment to nature, and to ideals of rural society, remain central to Baltic culture. A large proportion of the urban population cultivates its own allotments, much more seriously than their equivalents in the West – though an increasing number of families have now relinquished their patches of land after they have been repeatedly raided by gangs, and their vegetables stolen.

These rural links also have practical effects. It is a rare Balt who does not have a farming relative who can give him a bag of potatoes, or sell or barter it at a family price. This factor is already contributing to a differentiation in living standards between Balts and most of the local Russian populations who, as relatively recent immigrants, do not have these links with the immediate countryside and have to depend on their shrinking wages or savings.

'Informal' supplies to relations and friends constituted the only aspect of agriculture which flourished during the period 1990–92, although by 1993, Latvian meat-farmers were beginning to profit from Polish traders buying up their beef for hard currency, in order to make huge profits by sales to the West, often in circumvention of EC rules. Agriculture in general is therefore still acting as a support mechanism for individual families, but not for society as a whole.

The steep decline in agricultural production highlights a central point about the nature of the Soviet collective farm which is of immense importance for Russia and other former Soviet republics today, even if the Baltic escape this trap through stabilising their currencies. The collectives were originally mechanisms intended not to increase production but to guarantee procurement. This is connected to a key truth about peasants, which the Tsarist and provisional governments learned in 1915–17, the government of Lenin in 1918–21, the government of Stalin in 1927–29, and many governments in Africa and the Third World in the 1970s and 1980s. This is that peasants will simply cease to produce for the market in circumstances in which the terms of trade are rigged against them or in which, due to this or to inflation, their products will not bring them real money or real goods. The urban worker has to continue working in these circumstances because he has to eat. The peasant does not. Instead of taking his grain to market he will feed it to his pigs, and eat the piglets himself.

The situation in Baltic agriculture in 1990–92 was a new form of the 'Scissors Crisis' which helped introduce collectivisation to the Soviet Union in 1929. For ideological reasons and to retain the support of the urban working classes, the Soviet government had fixed food prices so low as to make it unprofitable for the peasants to sell: the two arms of the scissors were drawing apart. The result, by 1928, was a food shortage in the towns. The only alternatives were to make a new compromise with the peasants, as Lenin did in 1921 with the New Economic Policy, or to deprive them of their own land and dragoon them into a system where they would be forced to supply the state, because they lived on their wages and these depended on their fulfilling their quotas. Stalin of course chose the latter. A vicious twist of the scissors was inflicted in 1992 because the Baltic peasants had become dependent upon mechanisation and therefore upon fuel. By 1993, however, the new private shops in the towns, paying high prices in real currency, were, it seems, beginning once again to persuade Latvian and Estonian peasants to sell. The shopkeepers are going directly to the farmers, cutting out the monopolistic middlemen.

In one way, Lithuanian agriculture was in a better position than the other two in this period, because it is more primitive – and therefore still uses more horses. However dairy and cattle husbandry also suffered because under Soviet centralised planning, the Baltic was made dependent upon supplies of artificial fodder from Russia and the Ukraine, and these have become vastly more expensive or have dried up altogether. In 1992, when an exceptionally severe drought and the collapse of the collective farms killed off most of the Baltic hay harvest, a catastrophe for Baltic animal husbandry was only averted through the donation of hundreds of thousands of tons of Western fodder. This underlines the importance of Western aid and of the small size of the Baltic States. If a drought and agricultural decline of this magnitude were to strike the whole of Russia and the Ukraine (inherently unlikely, of course), Western aid could not possibly cover the gap and real starvation might ensue.

During the first nine months of 1992, the number of farm animals in the Baltic decreased sharply. Milk production in Estonia fell by 22 per cent and meat production by a third. The result is that while food prices rose so far as to drive the urban populations towards impoverishment, it was still not enough to cover the even faster rise in the costs of agricultural production. Matters were made worse by a characteristic feature of many of the Gorbachov and post-Gorbachov reforms: the 'freeing' of key industries to become private monopolies which rig prices at will.

In the Baltic countryside during this period, a small number of food processing enterprises still dominated the scene (one central plant processed all of Estonia's powdered milk); they paid the farmers the lowest prices they could, and charged consumers the highest. As they privatised themselves, they often simply refused to honour their debts with their suppliers, or they genuinely went bankrupt because urban consumers would not or could not buy their products. By mid-1992, the Estonian state itself was heavily in debt to its farmers.[65]

By November 1992 debts owed to Latvian agricultural producers stood at 1.7 billion Latvian roubles, and Prime Minister Ivars Godmanis complained that there was no legislation to punish enterprises for failing to pay up. He requested the extension of the special government commission set up to ensure food supplies. The parliamentary debate was accompanied by populist attacks on price-rigging by 'non-Latvian' traders in Riga's central market, described as 'Latvia's national shame'. Racketeers in the markets do indeed rig the prices, but this is a small factor in comparison with the structural problems of Latvian agriculture.[66]

In a development which has depressing implications, by the end of 1992 the costs of production had risen so sharply that farmers in Latvia and Estonia were being undercut by cheaper dairy products entering the Baltic not only from the former Soviet Union but also from the West. In Estonia the problem was made worse by the preference for white over rye bread (possibly because it shows their Scandinavian superiority to the rye-eating Russians). The production of brown flour in Estonia is sufficient, but supplies of white flour from Russia have declined steeply, and in 1992 millions of dollars of Western aid was spent importing it instead of paying for imports of desperately needed animal fodder. One could observe that, as with the Estonian refusal to have larger families in order to ward off Russian immigration, this forms part of a persistent Estonian tendency to try to imitate Scandinavians, irrespective of their real location on the edge of the Eurasian continent.

Reacting against Western imports, Baltic farmers and their parliamentary representatives demanded higher protective tariffs (already running at an average of 15 per cent in Latvia and 60 US cents per kilo in the case of imported butter), which would do obvious damage to Baltic hopes of exporting to the West. A spokesman for Latvia's Agriculture Ministry declared that 'these measures are absolutely necessary on the Eastern border and still more on the West, or the Danes and Germans will kill us with their cheap margarine and butter'. [67] In Estonia, a farmer told me sourly that 'when the wild boar raid my vegetables, even they eat the Swedish potatoes and leave the Estonian ones'. The Laar government, however, resisted higher tariffs.

The problems of Baltic agriculture were greatly increased by the speed and nature of decollectivisation. A mixture of restitution and equal distribution of the collective land has naturally meant that the great majority of new farms have been too small to be commercially viable, even if all other economic conditions were right. Before 1940, the average size of a Latvian farm was some 10 hectares, whereas the average size of the new private farms is 17 hectares. A Latvian Agriculture Ministry official told me that farms will need to be about 70 hectares in order to survive in the free market, especially since productivity per man and per hectare in the Baltic is only a fraction of that in Scandinavia. As it is, the new owners are usually making no effort to produce on a large scale. They are carrying out improvements on the land, and buying and breeding new animals in the hope of better times.

One of the difficulties of establishing individual farms was the shortage of the proper equipment. In Estonia in 1991, there was only one tractor for every 15 collective farmers. The heavy Soviet-built tractors also damage the soil, use huge amounts of fuel, and are too big for smaller farms. The supply of lighter East German tractors has diminished both as a result of the collapse of East German industry and because farmers cannot afford to pay in Deutschmarks.

The more dynamic of the 'new' farmers I met in the Baltic are those descended from 'strong farmers' of the pre-1940 period, and have therefore received large parcels of good land. Most have also studied farming, and in several cases have attended agricultural training courses in Scandinavia, sometimes returning with ancient but still usable agricultural equipment; but such cases are relatively rare. The morale of Baltic peasants is much higher than that of their Russian equivalents, but many are much too old and tired to begin private farming. A further hindrance is that specialised work on collective farms has left people ill-equipped to tackle the all-round functions of private farming.

An extra problem has been created by the restitution of land to former owners. The miserable levels of compensation, made even worse by inflation, mean that every former owner, including pensioners in Chicago, want to get their actual land back. The nationalist parties, with their emphasis on a return to the conditions of 1920–40, have also insisted on restitution unqualified by considerations of efficiency.

The administration of the restitution has, however, been handed to local commissions which often operate on the basis of personal patronage or favour, or have tried to ensure that the people receiving the land can and are willing to farm it. The resulting struggles have meant large areas of land hanging in a legal void and going out of production. In other cases, the people taking the land proved completely unable to work it. To make matters worse, rules were introduced – to prevent speculation in land – in both Latvia and Lithuania forbidding new owners from selling or renting their land for a number of years. In the words of Mati Naruski, a private farmer on the restored land of his grandparents near Otepää, in Southern Estonia,

> Restitution has helped me personally, but it has also caused many problems. How many of those who get the land will actually use it? People are afraid to take money compensation instead of land, because it is too low and because of inflation. They would rather take the land. But many of those who take it are too old or do not want to farm, and others cannot begin because fuel is so expensive and food prices are so low. So they just sit on the land and wait to see what happens, perhaps meaning later to sell or rent it. But Estonians are not a people who like to rent land – they want their own farms. So the result will be that much land will be idle. I think that land should go to those who can use it.[68]

While the radical nationalists wanted simply to destroy the collective farms altogether, the consensus in 1990 was that the profitable and successful ones should be maintained in the medium term, albeit converted into joint-stock companies or genuine collectives. This was also the line taken by almost every candidate for a rural seat in the election of 1990. Some simply lied to the farmers about their real intentions. Others failed to take into account the fact that, as soon as it was known that the collectives were scheduled for ultimate destruction, and that the authority of the managers (and the Party) had vanished, the old Soviet tradition of pilfering would increase to such an extent that even successful farms would be destroyed from within.

Among the guilty parties were the managers themselves, securing their futures after their collectives disappeared. But another frequent picture in 1992 was the tattered carcass of a collective farm, still in existence but stripped of most of its land and economically dead, preyed upon by a ring of semi-private farms. Their owners continued to draw wages as collective farm workers, while actually doing no work for the collective, pilfering its equipment, and carrying out improvements on their own farms, but not producing on them. The result was a situation in which neither the collective nor the new farms were able to supply the market. In these circumstances, it would have made good sense to preserve the collective farms until economic conditions and the supply of fuel stabilised, while gradually transforming them into co-operatives. Instead, deafened by ideology and choirs of Western advisers, the Baltic governments placed themselves in a situation in which it seems that the only large-scale production of Baltic pork in future may be of the Gadarene variety.

Underlying the attack on the collectives was a political desire to smash the power base of the old Communist establishment in the countryside. The result, however, has been to annoy much of the peasantry, the effect of which was visible during the Estonian and still more the Lithuanian elections of autumn 1992, when most rural areas voted for parties based on the former Communists. The agrarian parties, based on the new private farmers, did badly. The influence of the old collective farm managers was undoubtedly a factor, and it is worth analysing this influence.

For obvious reasons, the restoration of the property relations which existed before 1940 has by no means been popular with many Baltic peasants whose families then owned little land. Young dynamic farmers from these backgrounds feel especially angry when they find their desire for more land blocked by the return of previous owners.

The anger about restitution may also derive in part from a much older Baltic tradition of mass peasant hostility to the bigger farmers. These were called in old Latvia and Estonia the 'grey barons' – the implication being that they were taking over some of the functions of the German barons, traditional oppressors of the peasantry.[69]

The other barons in the today's countryside are the 'red barons', the former collective farm managements. These are undoubtedly still very influential, and as in industry, many are now going into private agricultural business on the strength of the old networks as well as of their agricultural expertise. There has, however, been too much talk of 'ignorant peasants' being 'propagandised' and 'manipulated' by the old *apparat*. At least as important was the fact that, in the first place, many peasants saw a real community of interest with the managers in the face of the reforms, and second, that the managers were mostly from farming backgrounds themselves, in sharp contrast to the urban nationalist intellectuals responsible for those reforms in Lithuania (in Latvia, farming communities themselves were left alone to conduct the actual business of privatisation, which made for much less peasant hostility to the process). There was also a feeling among ordinary farmers, as one of them told me, that, 'after all, the managers did not invent the collective farm system. They were born into it, like the rest of us. Everyone worked where he could.' Collective farmers are also angry that the collectives are spoken of by nationalist politicians as 'criminal organisations'. A Lithuanian farmer demonstrating in 1991 outside the parliament told me that,

In 1949, the Communists committed a crime against us when they took our land and forced us into the collectives. But all the same, we now have

353

a share in the collectives and don't want to see them wrecked. After all, they were the best in the Soviet Union! They need to be turned into co-operatives. What the government is now doing is sacking popular managers who resist their policies, and using laws and taxes and prices to force us out of the collectives without consulting us, just as before the Communists forced us into them. No-one is asking our opinion.

There is an interesting parallel to be drawn here with the issue of the supposed 'manipulation' of peasant movements by noble landowners before the First World War, especially in Germany. There too, the traditional analysis has been that the peasants were effectively dupes of the nobles, who manipulated them, against their own best interests, by means of nationalistic slogans. More recent historiography has suggested that the peasants often saw the landowners as useful representatives in the higher reaches of government, that nationalism was intrinsic to the developing peasant culture, and that the peasants and nobles had common economic interests opposed to those of the urban consumers. Peasants do not need to be taught by barons, black or red, to dislike urban intellectuals.[70]

When in 1991 farmers demonstrated outside the Lithuanian parliament over prices and the way decollectivisation was being carried out, Landsbergis patronised them, refused to answer any of their points, and accused them of serving the interests of Moscow. They got their revenge in the elections the next year.

The victorious LDDP continued its old line of stressing the strong Lithuanian tradition of co-operative farming which existed before 1940. Their vice-chairman, Gediminas Kirkilas, said that 'there is no way back to the collective farms', but that private farmers would be encouraged to form co-operatives on the basis of the former collectives.[71] These would be completely independent of state control. He stressed the need to maintain the social functions of the collectives – clinics, kindergartens, and the support of the elderly. He said that urban inhabitants and emigrés who had been given back their land would be given the choice of either beginning to cultivate it immediately, returning it to the state for compensation, or selling it to an active farmer. These measures will certainly be popular in the Lithuanian countryside. Whether in post-Soviet economic conditions they will improve the performance of agriculture will doubtless take some time to become clear.

In the words of a Swedish report on the Baltic economies,

It is important to realise that the family farms introduced in the Baltic republics so far are of greater importance as a cultural and national manifestation than as a means for improving productivity. It will take some years yet before the private farms will make a real contribution to improving productivity. ....[72]

The national-cultural image of the free hard-working peasant farmer was indeed the key motivation of the agricultural reforms in the Baltic in 1990–92. The image is an attractive one in many ways, certainly when compared to the drunken, slovenly conditions prevailing on many collectives. In July 1992 I visited the farm near Otepää of Taavi Park, a short, sturdy man with a patriarchal beard. After collectivisation, he and his family had become industrial workers, but he maintained his connection with the land by spending his holidays living with rural cousins. In 1949, before his family was deported to Siberia, their farm covered 77 hectares, of which he had got 62 back. So far, however, he was farming only 16 of them, while clearing the forest and brush which had encroached on the rest. He kept six cows and six bullocks, but had had to give up his sheep because of a shortage of fodder. Among his equipment was a British tractor, of some long-forgotten make, which he had seen rusting in a shed while studying agriculture in Sweden the previous year.

Mr Park proudly showed me his family tree, which went back to the eighteenth century, and the deed by which his great-great-great-grandfather had, in 1865, bought the farm from Baron von Sivers. The house, which he was restoring, was built from wood by his great-grandfather who, aged eighty, was deported to Siberia by Stalin,

> but he immediately began to plant potatoes on the small plot of land he was given. The Russians were amazed! By the end of his time there, he had become quite a prosperous farmer. He was 96 when he died in Estonia, and he always told me to come back here to farm the land. . . . You know, there is an anecdote that the Politburo once debated how they could get rid of the Estonians. One of them said, 'we don't have to do anything. Just give them their land back and they'll work themselves to death. . . .'[73]

As Arnold Rüütel said, 'the restoration of private farming does not just mean re-organizing production but the restoration of traditional values in our lives'.

The New Currencies

No symbol of independence was more ardently desired in the period 1990–92 than the restoration of the pre-1940 Baltic currencies. It was believed that these would bring economic miracles, and politicians, like prophets, repeatedly promised the Appearance of the Kroon, the Litas and the Lat, and anathematised each other when it failed to materialise. The independent currencies, backed by Western aid, did indeed prove to be magnificent successes for the Baltic States.

When the Estonian Kroon (Crown), the first new currency in the former Soviet Union, was finally introduced in June 1992, it was an object of deep envy for the other two Baltic States. Its re-emergence was a source of great pride to Estonians and considerable prestige internationally.

It may be remembered that at the beginning of the national governments in 1990 their resources were so slight and their countries still so integrated into the Soviet Union that they could not even print their new currencies themselves, let alone distribute them; indeed they did not initially even possess enough hard currency to have them printed abroad. The shoddy, locally produced Latvian and Lithuanian 'temporary currencies' were relatively easy to forge and suffered accordingly.[74]

One of the reasons for the long delay in the introduction of the Lithuanian Litas was that the government of Vagnorius contracted with an unreliable company in America to have them made, and finally had to reprint several categories of notes. This contributed to bitter public friction between the chairman of the State Bank, Vilius Baldišis, and Prime Minister Vagnorius, which contributed to the fall of the latter in July 1992. Printing the notes abroad before August 1991 was complicated by the need for secrecy to prevent the Soviet customs seizing them at the border.[75]

In Estonia, similar trouble dragged on for more than a year between State Bank chairman Rein Otsason and Prime Minister Edgar Savisaar who, on coming to power, unwisely promised the introduction of the Kroon by the end of 1990.

There was, however, strong opposition to the introduction of the currencies, and it played a part in delaying them. The resistance came above all from leaders of industry and their defenders, terrified that independent currencies would cut them off from their markets and sources of supply elsewhere in the former Union. Most vocal of course were the Russian managers. In June 1992, shortly before the introduction of the Kroon, Valery Myachin, manager of the Narova furniture factory at Narva, told me that,

> If the Kroon really does become a hard currency, it could kill off most of Estonian production, because the quality of Western production is so much higher than ours. Anyway, the Kroon will collapse after a while because of the weakness of the economy, but by the time it does, industry here may have been destroyed. At present, 90 per cent of our trade is with the former Soviet Union. If we introduce the Kroon without full agreement on how to carry on payments, it will lead to a practical blockade. Things are difficult enough already, with debts not being paid, supplies drying up, and both sides demanding licenses for export.[76]

It was above all this fear, as well as the underdevelopment of their financial structures and their relative lack of hard currency reserves, that initially dissuaded the Lithuanians and Latvians from emulating the Estonians and establishing their own hard currencies, convertible against Western currencies but not against the Rouble. Instead, they introduced 'provisional currencies', the Latvian Rouble in Latvia, and the 'Talonas' or Coupon in Lithuania. Initially these circulated alongside the Rouble and at parity with it. On 24 September 1992, the cash Rouble ceased to be legal tender anywhere in the Baltic, though both the Talonas and the Latvian Rouble continued to be convertible against it.

Given the confusion prevailing in Latvian and Lithuanian financial structures, and the lack of agreement on accounting with Russia and the other republics, anything else would have threatened the continuation of trade. The introduction of some form of indigenous currency was, by spring 1992, more or less forced on the Balts by an acute shortage of Roubles. As inflation soared, the Russian government and State Bank in Moscow came under intense Western pressure to restrict the printing of money. The resulting cuts in the supply of cash were passed on to the other republics in the Rouble zone. Estonia needed 300 million Roubles a month but received only 180 million in January, 150 million in February and 100 million in March.

As inflation gathered pace, the shortage of cash began to cause severe hardship in Estonia and to a lesser extent in the other two Baltic States. Unpaid salaries rose to 300 million Roubles; pensioners queued for hours outside banks to collect their increasingly meager pensions, only to discover that the supply of notes had run out. There were stories of elderly ladies dying of cold, exhaustion and possibly despair.

The salaried middle classes became increasingly desperate. Resentment of 'profiteers', with their hard currency and their ability to buy goods at will, became increasingly sharp. In Estonia, rules were introduced that salaries above Rs3,000 had to be paid not in cash but into accounts, and with no system of cheques or credit cards, this effectively meant freezing them. In March 1992, with no Roubles left at all, the town of Tartu was forced to introduce its own Tartu money, printed on the back of old Soviet ration coupons stored in case of war.[77]

The IMF and World Bank were highly sceptical of the value of an early introduction of national currencies, and warned in particular against breaking links to markets in the East. Describing Latvia, the IMF reported in May 1992 that,

> The introduction of the new currency, the Lat, should be delayed. Little progress has been made in developing the central bank's ability to control monetary policy. The Bank of Latvia is not clearly separated from the commercial banks and does not have the means to regulate them once they are distinct bodies.[78]

The Estonians, under Prime Minister Tiit Vahi and the new State Bank chairman, Siim Kallas, hence showed considerable determination in pressing ahead with the Kroon, and were vindicated by its performance. The IMF finally gave public approval to the move, but did not initially back it financially.

After several false rumours, the attractively designed Kroon was introduced on 20 June 1992, during the long holiday for the Midsummer Festival, St John's Day. The Kroon was pegged to the Deutschmark at a rate of 8:1, within a band of 3 per cent, and was regulated and maintained by means of a Currency Board. The Estonians proved perspicacious in not choosing as a peg the neigbouring Finnmark, which plunged that autumn during the European exchange crisis. The Kroon went on sailing smoothly in the wake of the mighty Mark.

On the same day the Rouble was immediately banned from circulation and from exchange against the Kroon, and the police made several exemplary swoops against traders and Black-Market exchanges. Residents were given three days to exchange up to 1,500 Roubles at a rate of 1:10. Enterprise funds were also converted at this rate. Private cash and accounts above Rs1,500 were converted at 1:50. The impact was modified by the fact that most had already got rid of their Roubles in an anticipatory spending spree, changed them into hard currency, or simply seeing them swallowed up by inflation.[79]

The severe restrictiveness of this changeover (in sharp contrast for example to the changeover from Ostmarks to Deutschmarks in East Germany) proved its worth in the succeeding months, when in the face of pessimistic predictions the Kroon held steady against the Deutschmark and rose slightly against the Dollar. The initial exchange rate set by the government had clearly been exactly in accordance with the market estimation. The Kroon also rose sharply against the Rouble. Immediately after the Kroon's introduction, and on IMF insistence, the Estonian government raised sales and income tax sharply to reduce the budget deficit and support the Kroon.[80]

In August, the IMF praised the Kroon and released $120 million to support it and the Latvian Rouble. In November, they released another $41 million for the Kroon. These sums are small by international standards, but large in relation to tiny Estonia. Together with the gold reserves of pre-1940 Estonia, restored by Britain and the other Western powers to which they had been sent before the republic was seized by Stalin, they meant that Estonia, and later Latvia, had strong backing for their currencies. In proportion to their size, these sums were many times larger than the $1 billion stabilisation fund which was crucially important in making the Polish Zloty convertible in 1990. By December 1992, therefore, Bo Kragh, the Swedish deputy chairman of the Estonian State Bank could boast that the Kroon was the most stable currency in Eastern Europe and stood thirtieth among the currencies of the world.

This has been a major factor in attracting foreign investment to Estonia, and every Western study has put Estonia at the head of former Soviet republics in terms of economic reform.[81] It is also hoped that stable currencies will attract back tens of millions of dollars repeatedly sent to the West by Baltic businessmen.

The Kroon is a source of great pride to the Estonians, many of whom bought new wallets so as not to have to put their national currency in the same place as the former 'occupation roubles'. The abolition of the use of hard currency in special shops also had a major psychological effect, as ordinary citizens took Estonian money to buy previously segregated Western goods. The effect wore off quickly, however, as Estonians realised that the previous hard currency shops were simply luxury shops for the wealthy, with prices ordinary Estonians could not afford. By the end of 1992, Estonia had become a generally poor country with a small propertied elite. Inflation, however, had sunk steeply.

The Kroon's stability against Western currencies greatly aided trade with the West but, as expected, made trade with the rest of the former Soviet Union more difficult. At the time of its introduction, no accounting procedures between Russia and Estonia were in place. When they were subsequently developed, they were largely crippled by bureaucracy, mutual distrust and simple unwillingness on both sides to pay debts. The compensating inflow of goods from the West, at Western prices, naturally drove inflation up still further. The bulk of the population found itself receiving Soviet wages but paying Western prices – a most uncomfortable situation.

The Estonian government of Tiit Vähi, and after November, the new Right-of-Centre administration of Mart Laar, inevitably came under intense pressure from trades unionists, local Russian representatives, industrialists, agrarians and the Leftist parliamentary opposition to raise minimum wages, pensions and subsidies to industry and agriculture – action Estonia had officially promised the IMF it would not take.[82] The Popular Front and its parliamentary offshoot, the Centre Faction, led by Edgar Savisaar, were especially articulate in 'defending the underprivileged', and accused the government of being 'manifestly hostile to pensioners'.[83]

The Laar government in particular was well aware of the danger that larger state spending and a massive budget deficit (or an increased supply of Kroon) could undermine the new currency and tip the country back into hyperinflation. By the end of 1992 the deficit had reached almost 70 million Kroon ($5.5 million) and most Western aid was being spent on importing fuel or improving long-term energy efficiency. Laar bitterly denounced the previous Vähi government for agreeing, just before leaving office, to raise the minimum wage from 200 to 300 Kroon ($28). This was indeed almost certainly a partisan step designed to embarrass the Rightists and embroil them in a fight with the labour movements at the very beginning of their term of office. It was strongly denounced in private by representatives of the IMF, but the Laar government found it politically impossible to go back on Vähi's promise.[84]

The new government vowed not to increase subsidies to industry and to recover state-owned enterprises which failed to pay their debts. However, in the first days of his government Laar did in fact step in to support a major enterprise, and paradoxically with the encouragement of Western advisors. The recipient was the giant Kreenholm textile business in Narva, which in 1990 had employed more than 12,000 workers, almost all of them ethnic Russians, and in 1992 still employed 7,000, in a town in which real unemployment stood at 50 per cent. By this stage, even moderate Russians in Narva were howling that a further deterioration in the economic situation could lead to revolt, and diplomats were taking notice.

Kreenholm was one of the consumer factories which had been expected to do well in the free market. By autumn 1992, however, it had been crippled by the scarcity of raw cotton supplies from Central Asia, the price of energy, and the failure of other enterprises in Estonia and the former Soviet Union to pay their debts. By November these ran at Rs854 million ($2 million) from the former Union and 36 million Kroon ($2.9 million) from Estonia.

The Laar government therefore breached its own strict principle of letting bankrupt industries collapse by waiving interest on unpaid taxes owed by Kreenholm, which by then were running at 500,000 Kroon ($40,000) a day, and suspending the principal. The government said that the same forgiveness would be extended to other companies 'if they are worth saving'. Politically the move was clearly necessary, though it opened the way of course for endless pressure by special interest groups, especially in the Russian areas.[85] The government also discussed with industrialists their demand that the State Bank should increase the amount of circulating capital to cover the huge unpaid debts from the East – a prospect viewed by Western advizors with considerable alarm.[86]

The Baltic governments did virtually nothing to co-ordinate their monetary policies in the course of 1990–92. When Latvia introduced its Rouble as sole legal currency in July 1992, it gave as explanation the flood of Russian Roubles from Estonia into Latvia following the introduction of the Kroon.[87] In Lithuania the temporary currency introduced in 1992 alleviated the cash shortage, but did little to stabilise the general economic situation. In Latvia, State Bank chairman Einars Repše stuck with exemplary determination to the tight money policy dictated by the IMF, and was helped by the constitutional independence of his bank from political control, modelled on the status of the German Bundesbank. By early 1993, this had reduced inflation to less than 10 per cent a month and brought the Latvian Rouble to around 140 to the dollar, at a time when the Russian Rouble had already sunk to almost 700.

According to a Swedish economist, Anders Aslund, Latvia had pursued the most cautious fiscal policy of any former Soviet republic in this period: 'the Latvians seem to have accepted all the IMF demands that they could possibly fulfil in time'. By early 1993 this had brought down inflation and stabilised the Latvian Rouble. From March 1993 the state began the gradual introduction of the Lat. Unlike the Kroon, any quantity of Latvian Roubles (or foreign currency) could be exchanged for Lats. This strategy appears to be working as well as the Estonian scheme, and the Lat stands a good chance of success.[88]

The tight hold on the emission of money and credit by the Latvian Central bank under Repše was of course in sharp contrast to the situation in Russia, the Ukraine and Kazakhstan. The reasons for it were partly greater openness to Western advice, and relatively greater Western rewards for following that advice. Above all, however, they were political and ethnic. In these other republics, and indeed in Lithuania under Brazauskas, the industrial managers remained the single most politically influential class, as the industrial workers were the most numerous, and they have been able to extract massive and inflationary state credits for their industries.

In Latvia the exclusion of the Russians from a political role meant that the mainly Russian managers and workers had far fewer means of bringing influence to bear – least of all on Repše, whose own political roots are on the radical nationalist side of politics. However, it must also be noted that Repše up to the start of 1993, was able to resist higher credits for Latvian-dominated agriculture.

Lithuania and its temporary currency, the Talonas, also benefitted from pre-war gold reserves and Western aid.[89] In December 1992, the Talonas slumped sharply to 308 to the dollar, though still well above the Russian level. Analysts suggested this reflected the increasing 'dollarisation' of the Lithuanian economy and of trade links between the Baltic and the former Soviet republics, such that the Baltic temporary currencies were simply growing less important. Enterprise transactions between Lithuania and Russia were increasingly transacted via hard currency accounts in the West. Assuming that sufficient dollars (or other hard currency) are available, this could even help stabilise trade and the Baltic economies.

This is however hardly a long-term solution, or an encouraging sign for the future of the dreamed-of Litas. At the end of 1992, all the Baltic governments were coming under heavy pressure to break the conditions set by the IMF, and were looking to Western state aid as the only way out of the dilemma.[90]

Banking on Chaos

The weakness of the Baltic banking structures was a central reason given by the IMF in 1992 for recommending a delay in the introduction of local currencies. Two years earlier, the Baltic republics had had virtually no banks at all. The main banks in the region were simply branches of the various central banks in Russia, while small local banks (also of course state-owned) were compulsorily overseen from Moscow.

So until August 1991, banking in the Baltic States consisted largely of a struggle to wrest from Moscow the right to operate at all. The Soviet Foreign Economic Bank's veto over hard currency operations played havoc with Baltic attempts to develop financial links with the West, since Western banks were naturally unwilling to get involved in this legal minefield.

The Soviet State Bank also had complete control over payments for all inter-republican trade within the former Union, and used this to try to block the republics from establishing trading links which did not go through the ministries in Moscow. The baleful effects of this policy remain to this day in the failure of the republics to establish stable trading relationships. In the words of a Ukrainian broker in Riga in September 1992, explaining why Latvian-Ukrainian trade was decreasing,

> There are changes in Latvian legislation [in this field] every couple of months. The Commonwealth of Independent States is in any case not too eager to trade with the Baltic States, since it is much more difficult to get a licence for exporting goods to the Baltic than for trading with the West. Besides, there are no normal bank connections. You can transfer your money, but you cannot be sure where it will end up.[91]

Nonetheless, commercial banks did begin to establish themselves in the last years of Soviet rule, almost always set up by groups of state enterprises. A typical example was the Riga Commercial Bank, founded in July 1989 by 14 state enterprises. It had an initial capital of Rs10 million. It was the first Latvian commercial bank to begin hard currency dealings, and by the spring of 1991 had deposits of Rs50 million.[92] The Latvian State Bank was not established until July 1990, on the basis of the branches of the Soviet central banks in the republic – 'but it is impossible to make one lion out of a hundred cats', as a Latvian banker told me. Private banking had hardly begun. Two years later, anyone trying to draw money from a Baltic bank was still vividly reminded of the slowness, incompetence and sheer confusion of the Soviet tradition.

By Western standards, the minimum capital requirement of the commercial banks was absurdly small – five million Roubles, the equivalent of $42,000. They were weakened further by the tendency of the new State Banks, especially in Lithuania and Latvia, themselves to carry out commercial operations for profit. The Latvian Bank, after merging with various other state banks (the Agricultural bank, Construction Bank an so on) advanced 83 per cent of all commercial credits in the country. However, this picture of overwhelming state control was diminished by the fact that about half its own branches had practically escaped from its authority and were acting as commercial banks pure and simple. The Lithuanian State Bank in 1992 held 70 per cent of all private and commercial accounts in the country, and under Vilius Baldišis often appeared to suffer from an ideological hostility to private banking.

By far the strongest banks in the period 1990–92 were in Estonia. This was partly due to Finnish influence, and partly to the relatively conciliatory policy of the Savisaar government towards the Kremlin, which led to the granting of more Soviet licences and to an occasionally indulgent blind eye. It was therefore a severe blow to Estonians when on 17 November 1992 the government was forced simultaneously to take over and suspend the activities of Estonia's two biggest commercial banks (the Tartu Commercial Bank, previously praised as the most efficient in the Baltic, and the United Baltic Bank). It also stopped all withdrawals from the state-owned North Estonian Bank. Together these held more than 300 million Kroon, or half of all bank deposits in Estonia. The banks had simply run out of money to meet depositors' demands. The cause in part was the failure of the former Soviet bank for Foreign Economic Relations (*Vnesheconombank*) to honour its debt – of $40 million – to the Estonian banks. Estonia had no means of extracting these sums from Moscow.

The bank directors, however, were also bitterly criticised for mismanagement and possible corruption, as were the regulatory authorities for failure to step in earlier to defend depositors' interests. For weeks previously, withdrawals and transfers were taking up to a month to complete, in defiance of regulations that all transfers should be completed within 48 hours. Some depositors were simply refused when they tried to withdraw funds.[93]

In the West, such a banking failure would have had a shattering effect on the stock markets and probably the economy as a whole.[94] In Estonia, there barely was a stock market, and many people and enterprises still avoided the commercial banks. The 'Black Tuesday' crisis was, however, a vindication of every supposedly backward Estonian farmer who had preferred to turn his savings into hard currency and hide them under the floorboards. The crisis increased hostility to the former Soviet establishment in Estonia, because its members dominated the failed banks.

Controversial though the Estonian banks became, they were still less prominent and less debated – and certainly less powerful – than the dominant Latvian 'bank', Parex. By the autumn of 1992, Baltic newspapers were taking it as read that Parex, rather than the Latvian government, was chiefly responsible for determining the exchange rate of the Latvian Rouble, although this was possibly an exaggeration.

Parex is a creature from the Pleistocene age of capitalism – primitive but effective within its own environment. It illustrates both the opportunities and the dangers of banking and the entire move to the free market in Latvia, dangers not least for the bankers themselves. Parex was founded in Riga in 1988 by two young Russian Jews, with previous Komsomol connections, Viktor Krasovitsky and Valery Kargin, largely on the basis of investment by Jewish emigrants from Latvia who had done well in the West. Doubtless because of its Komsomol links, it was the first institution on the whole territory of the then USSR to receive permission to trade freely in hard currency.

Parex was then not a bank at all, but a giant money-changing office which flourished on the basis of the convertibility of the Latvian Rouble against the Russian Rouble and the strong trade links between Latvia and Poland, which led to a strong flow of hard currency back into Latvia in return for Soviet-made manufactured goods and some Latvian agricultural ones, as well as smuggled metals and so on.

Latvian regulation of money-changing was liberal – or more often non-existent – by Russian standards. One of Parex's directors told me with a grin, 'because we are a closed shareholder company not a bank, we are not obliged to publish our financial details – and this suits us very well!' When Parex was publicly criticised by Prime Minister Godmanis for speculation, Kargin told him that if his government had not developed a system of financial regulation and control, then that was his problem, not that of Parex.

By July 1992, Parex had an average turnover of 5–7 billion Roubles (about \$15–20 million) and several million dollars in hard currency each week – a Kingfish in the Latvian pond, and a very large business even by Moscow's standards. As Kargin told me with a certain arrogance, 'Latvian government hard currency reserves are not very significant compared to ours, and have no great influence on events'. Parex, he added, is also a 'state-supporting institution', and in 1992 froze its exchange rates for several weeks to help the Latvian Rouble. This he says will doubtless not stop future attempts to impose punitive taxes on Parex: 'our organisation is Jewish-supported, and it has always been the fate of Jews to pay off governments in order to live in peace!'

The premises of this Latvian 'giant' illustrated all the paradoxes of the economic 'transition period' in the Baltic States. Despite the company's wealth, it remained in a small set of offices in a crumbling nineteenth-century apartment block. In January 1992, so many people and so much equipment were crammed into the rooms that I had to conduct an interview with Kargin in the corridor, leaning against a coffee percolator. In the background machines for counting banknotes, over-stimulated by inflation, chattered hysterically to each other. Possibly because of this makeshift impression, possibly because of a certain distrust of Parex's nature, Western banks were very slow to establish links with it, something that caused Kargin evident resentment. By July 1992, Kargin himself had moved into a large office in the same building, stylishly decorated in a modernist black and white pattern. The image was, however, rather spoilt by a bulky Soviet radiator and a gaping hole in the window, waiting for an air-conditioner and meanwhile letting in the noise and dust of the street.

The short, plump, 31-year old Kargin would be a thoroughly yuppified figure, in his striped shirt and fashionable tie, were it not for his boyish enthusiasm, his sense of being a pioneer in a great adventure. The world in which he operates also makes the so-called Wall Street 'jungle' look like an English country garden, 'and if you want to stay alive in the jungle, you must live as the jungle does'. Parex's enemies inevitably allege that it has links with the 'mafia'. One way or another the operation has certainly attracted the interest of organised crime. A few days before our second meeting, Kargin's Mercedes ('the most expensive car in Latvia') was blown to pieces by a bomb in Jurmala – as a warning, it seems, not a direct assassination attempt, though Kargin naturally wouldn't tell me what the warning was about. In March, Parex's branch manager in Liepāja had been killed and his office looted.

Kargin likes to give Parex the air of a merchant principality: it mints its own small coins as advertisements. When I asked him about the policemen privately hired to guard his office, a practice banned by the government, he replied that 'it's quite true that this is now banned, but we are Parex, and we can usually get our own way'. Kargin and Krasovitsky however both come from families that settled in Riga before 1940, and so are automatically citizens. As Kargin himself said,

> Business here is controlled far more by Jews and Russians than by Latvians, and this angers the Latvians, although it is partly their own fault; Russians and Jews are being pushed out of state employment here, so they are going into business – it's like a child being forced to swim. A situation is developing where government structures are dominated by Latvians, the economy by non-Latvians, as in Malaysia, where I have been twice.

Krasovitsky added that 'Latvia has a government of poor Latvian people:

poor intellectual politicians and poor bureaucrats. Naturally they don't like business'. And Kargin stressed the insecurity of the whole situation: 'Here we have a saying: "temporary government, temporary parliament, temporary business"; everyone is waiting for the next train.'

The Church

The Church in Lithuania sustains great national prestige owing to its role in the dissident movement, as well as its overall identification with national culture. Several clerics, including the nationalist deputy Alfonsas Svarinskas, and later the Auxiliary Bishop of Kaunas, Sigitas Tamkevičius, were prominent dissidents who served long prison sentences for their activities in defence of church and nation.

The symbolism of Church and State, or even Throne and Altar, flourished briefly under Landsbergis in 1991–92. After his defeat in October 1992, he even proposed that a Catholic prelate should be elected as compromise president, 'to unite the nation'; it was politely declined by the Church. At a mass in Vilnius Cathedral to celebrate the Third Sajūdis Congress on 14 December, and to launch the presidential aspirations of Landsbergis – and timed to coincide with the birthday of the medieval King Mindaugas – the priest in his sermon declared that,

> We must pray for Sajūdis, for its complicated problems and its great future. We are glad that Sajūdis is the leader of our nation and that it will help the nation to find a bright future ... we will also remember Mindaugas, our only King. Mindaugas is dear to us because he unified the nation in complicated times. He understood the need for unity if we wish to be independent.

During the October–November 1992 election, many priests and at least one bishop campaigned publicly for Sajūdis, and even appeared in its television propaganda. After the LDDP victory in the first round of the election, a Sajūdis poster appeared reading, 'A Tear in God's Eye. Lithuania, where are you going?'

The tendency of the Lithuanian Catholic Church to favour an authoritarian-tinged nationalism stems from the intense conservatism of the Church in general, insulated, within the Soviet system, from the effects of the reforming Second Vatican Council. Now that there is a backlash against aspects of Vatican II in the Western Church and especially the Vatican, Lithuanian priests, rather than feeling they need to change, feel justified in their own conservatism, even on matters (such as anti-semitism, the identification of Church and nation, or even the absence of a role for the laity) of which the Pope himself would disapprove. In the words of a Lithuanian-American academic,

Under Soviet rule, only the stupidest people were allowed to become priests; the intelligent were deliberately filtered out. That is why we have all these neanderthals running the Church. Unlike in Poland, there can be no public dialogue between the Church and the liberal Catholic intelligentsia, and no major Catholic impact on new cultural developments, because the Church is simply not up to it.

In fact, even before the 1992 election, Landsbergis's attempt to gain mass support by identifying himself with the Church had failed, partly because the Church's own influence had been thoroughly undermined by Soviet rule, by secularisation and urbanisation, and perhaps also by the Lithuanian tradition of ritualistic rather than reflective Catholicism.

The plethora of programmes and religious images on Lithuanian television seems to have caused as much boredom and irritation as devotion, especially among the young. A striking feature throughout what used to be the Western Soviet Union is that religious observance has been undermined equally, or even especially, in the countryside, previously of course its heartland. The revival of religious symbolism in public is now primarily the work of urban intelligentsias. It results more from necessity than choice – the necessity of finding viable ethical guidance through the flattened moral desert left by Communism. In private, this is also felt by ordinary worshippers, and there has been a tremendous increase in religious 'rites of passage' – baptisms, marriages and funerals. It is, however, doubtful whether religion will in fact be able to take on a wider social and cultural role.[95]

In Latvia and Estonia, the governments, and still more of course the Right, are also careful to associate themselves with religion, but to a much more limited extent. Observance tends to cease with prayers before Congress meetings, and church services on national days. In Estonia, a small number of Lutheran clerics play a political role through the Christian Democratic Union, led by pastor Illar Hallaste. The non-Lutheran churches (in descending order of size, Baptist, Orthodox, Methodist, Adventist, Pentecostal and Catholic) tend to mistrust the influence of the Lutherans, and have established a Council of Estonian Churches as a counterbalance. In 1991 there were in Latvia 210 Lutheran communities, 186 Catholic, 90 Orthodox and 65 Old Believers.

In October 1992 the new Estonian parliamentary majority introduced Lutheran morning prayers before each session of parliament, but it was strongly opposed by the Centre and Left as a violation of the constitution and an attack on freedom of conscience. The dignity of the innovation was also undermined by the Royalists, who decided they would hold prayers according to the orginal Estonian pagan religion. After a brief consultation of works on Shamanism, they lit a sacred fire in one of the parliamentary wastepaper baskets and danced around it, emitting strange cries. This was of course mainly a joke, but, albeit to a lesser extent than other Balts, Estonians too hanker after their 'own' religion, and after a feeling of closeness to natural forces which Christianity cannot give them.

The Lutheran churches of Latvia and Estonia, having always been closely associated with the Baltic German rulers, started from a weaker position, and were weakened still further by the general decline in Protestant belief throughout Northern Europe and, after 1940, by the inevitable compromises under the Soviet regime. As in Russia, this has encouraged the mushrooming of evangelical churches and sects. Some have local roots, others have been founded and funded by American missionaries. In Estonia, the former Leningrad television channel has been turned over, for several afternoons a week, to dubbed American 'televangelist' programmes. The mystical element in the Baltic traditions also naturally inclines some people to various holistic Estonian religions. Hare Krishna is frequently in evidence, and the Moonies have been propagandising intensively.

The appearance of such groups is acutely worrying to the traditional churches, especially in Lithuania where, in 1992, the Catholic hierarchy prevailed upon the Sajūdis government to block a proposal for an American-backed ecumenical college in the town of Panevėžys. On this occasion the American backer was at least a respectable and charitable Mennonite businessman. However, the acting administrator of Vilnius archdiocese, Auxiliary Bishop Juozas Tunaitis, declared that, 'We have many strange sects here and don't want another one. It's time to consolidate the nation and not to split it. The example of Yugoslavia shows the danger of more than one religion.'

Peoples Divided

Pauls Raudseps, deputy editor of the Latvian paper *Diena*, once sketched what he saw as the likely general development of the three Baltic societies. He thought that, in Estonia, wild capitalism, extreme social differentiation and conspicuous consumption would ultimately be modified by the Estonian national ethic and style; in Lithuania, something similar would occur if only because of an underlying peasant hostility towards capitalism. Lithuania would therefore remain poorer and less developed than Latvia, but without such extremes of wealth and poverty. In Latvia, in his view, an atmosphere of *laissez-faire* encouraged by legal and political anarchy would accelerate the development of certain sectors, and would lead to an ostentatiously rich capitalist class, an impoverished underclass and considerable social and economic resentment.

By 1993, however, there were already much more positive aspects to the Baltic scene, especially in Estonia. Although private investment from the West had so far been very much less than the Balts had hoped, it remained proportionately far greater than in Russia and parts of Eastern Europe. In countries with smaller populations than some Western cities, even a small number of new factories can make a substantial impact. Thus in Latvia, Pirmaden, a new American shoe-making venture, absorbed much of the unemployment from the crumbling state electronics giant Elektrotehnika. In Estonia, Finnish business was heavily engaged in several fields. A Swedish-Swiss company, ABB, was investing $10 million in a new plant to produce insulated pipes for energy saving in Lithuania – though the fact that up to the end of 1992 this was the largest external investment in Lithuanian manufacturing was discouraging.

Scandinavian investment suffered from domestic economic difficulties, but Swedish and Finnish aid had already contributed greatly to improving telephone connections between the Baltic States and the West. The whole Estonian telephone network was rapidly being transformed.

A few Baltic-owned firms were also beginning to penetrate Western or Central European markets. This involved some surprising success stories, like the military-industrial Dvigatel plant in Tallinn, using its sophisticated equipment and skilled workforce to produce a variety of high-value technological products. At a less skilled level, the Lithuanian company Kendra began successfully exporting bathtubs to Poland. With the end of the political tensions between Vilnius and Warsaw and, one hopes, the end of the absurd blockages on the Polish-Lithuanian frontier and in the minds of Lithuanians, Poland could become a major Baltic trading partner, and the Zloty a more readily available hard currency.

Most encouragingly, the Balts were clearly beginning to capitalise on one of their great advantages, a labour force which is highly educated and extraordinarily cheap by Western standards. In each of the states Western computer firms invested in the assembly, programming and marketing of computers for the Soviet market, and in some cases have begun to sell to the West as well. In several cases, firms have grown out of co-operation between the old Academies of Sciences and new private businesses. A small number of recognisably European businessmen have appeared, well-educated and with a real understanding of the rules by which Western capitalism works. Most are very young, like the budding Estonian media magnate Hans Luik, a huge, piratical figure with a red beard, somehow appropriate to the new Estonia. In Latvia, a great success was Software House, run by Latvians though with Russian financial backing. Originally a computer firm, it came to control Latvia's main oil pipeline.

These developments may help check the loss of interest in education, and the discernible 'fast-buck' mentality which, since the 1970s has been a saddening characteristic of Baltic youth. This variety of sleaziness is harmful even for the free market: the tendency to 'bandit economics' common to so many post-Soviet businessmen, frequently alienates their Western partners.

Baltic schools do, however, exhibit commitment and enthusiasm. By 1993, the teaching of literacy, mathematics and scientific subjects was excellent, geography was at least better taught than in the USA, and above all there was a passionate interest in learning foreign languages.[96] The humanities, however, were finding great difficulty in climbing out of the Marxist-Leninist mire without falling straight into a nationalist one. Some of the new history text-books do not simply read as if they had been written in the 1930s – they *were* written in the 1930s! Difficulties may arise among Russian teachers and pupils required to use works which denigrate their nation.

Even though education in all three states is still wholly state-controlled, a division along class lines is already very apparent. Thus the director of a prestigious Russian-language Gymnasium in Riga, with a high proportion of Jewish pupils, reported that,

> We have no real problem with books, stationery or food because many of the parents of our pupils are well off, and they help the school. One has even given us several computers so that the children can learn early how to use them. But I know of course that other schools do not have such advantages.[97]

So far as the better-educated and well-motivated young people are concerned, the fall of Communism has led to an immeasurable lightening of their lives and widening of their horizons, especially of course in terms of ability to travel and study abroad. However, the arrival of MTV is not an unqualified step forward for civilisation. By far the most popular television programme in all three countries is a Mexican soap opera entitled 'The Rich Also Cry' – a comforting thought, presumably – which is atrociously dubbed into Russian and rebroadcast by Moscow TV. Indeed, it might even be termed a force for ethnic harmony within the Baltic, since the most nationalist Balts and the most resentful Russians are united in their love for the heroine, Marianna.

The press has become far livelier than under Soviet rule – it could hardly have been less – although there are still very few good papers, and quite a number of pornographic rags. As so often in the former Communist world, literary and cultural publications have actually lost readership because their *raison d'etre* as a focus for dissent has vanished, and people are in any case too busy playing politics or making money. The arts in general have suffered as a result.

Poverty, however, is the stark reality of life for many, especially the elderly. The signs are everywhere: the beggars outside churches, the ragged street-kids washing cars in Riga, or the increasingly ruthless attitude of Baltic hospitals, badly short of staff, fuel and medicines, to 'useless' elderly people. The *Baltic Observer* of 17 September 1992 carried an article describing how an elderly woman who had broken her arm in a fall had it set without an anaesthetic and was then dumped by hospital orderlies at a bus stop and told to make her own way home. No element of ethnic hostility was involved, but it is easy to see how, if relations deteriorate, incidents such as this might be given an ethnic colour and used to stir up hatred.

While public fear has focused on the 'mafia' and crimes of violence, more dangerous for the future fabric and morale of the Baltic States may be the almost universal habit of pilfering, fostered under Communism and entrenched by poverty. The practice is encouraged by the fact that even many educated people, let alone the masses, simply cannot understand why former criminals and criminal activities are now respectable, or the difference between making money from semi-legal commercial activities and stealing outright from the office, shop or factory where you work.[98]

The section of the population which is suffering the most is, perhaps inevitably, the one which is most politically apathetic. This has been lamented by those that regret the mass engagement of the independence struggle, but it is fortunate for the governments: only a politically anaesthetised population could accept what is being done to it without massive protest.

The physical appearance of the towns is changing rapidly, stimulated by Western investment. Tourism is booming, hotels and restaurants are opening, and well-dressed visitors speaking foreign languages are commonplace. In the streets of the main cities, attractive privately owned boutiques display an array of Western goods. Some of the fashions are now Baltic-made, as by Bruno Birmanis's fashion house in Riga, beginning now to achieve a European reputation.

On the other hand, the trams and buses that run past these shops to the grim concrete suburbs seem increasingly dirty, run-down, and infrequent, and the streets are rarely cleaned. Window-displays and street-lights are often blacked-out for lack of electricity, and walking at night is becoming increasingly dangerous, as well as eerie.

While for educated younger people the world has become brighter and more sophisticated, other sections of the population feel the coarser, colder side of the changes. Few people have time or resources for charity outside their own families, and even the Churches often seem more concerned to rebuild their monuments than to help the poor or the elderly. There are frequent complaints that the traditional morale and solidarity of the Baltic peoples – if it ever existed – are being lost to the harsh competitive ethic of primitive capitalism.

For several years at least, the sufferers from the free market may include a majority of the Baltic populations, especially the local Russians. The purchasing power of the average family dropped 44 per cent during the first months of 1992, and by the end of that year, most people were spending by far the greater part of their incomes on food. Consumption of meat and milk fell sharply, and that of bread and turnips rose. Total impoverishment has often only been avoided through the low – and virtually uncollectable – rents and electricity charges. Facing mass evasion of payment, the electricity authorities resorted to collective punishment by disconnecting entire apartment blocks.

In Latvia, the Save the Children Fund reported in mid-1992 that 87 per cent of the population was below the poverty line, though the statistic needs to be treated with reserve.[99] In all three Baltic States citizens have developed techniques of survival, including cultivating their own food and having several jobs. The colossal differential between the buying-power of Western and local currencies has led to those with a source of hard currency supporting many relatives; but while Latvians and Jews have relatives in the West, Russians do not.

By late 1992, all three governments were coming under intense pressure to support industries and social groups threatened by the changes, and there were signs of the kind of anti-IMF resentment well-known in the Third World. In Latvia, an Economics Ministry official, Dr Inna Steinbuka, argued that the demand-damping measures called for by the IMF were useless. The impoverishment of the population, in her view, itself brought a fall in demand, but within Latvia's monopolised market, closely linked with the former Soviet Union, this did not and could not have any effect in reducing inflation. Dr Steinbuka argued that to press ahead with strict money policy would lead to bankrupcies, massive unemployment, a catastrophic decline in GDP and state revenues, and finally a social explosion. Clearly representing the views of many in the Economics Ministry, she called for a gradualist policy to protect output.[100]

At the end of 1992, even the new Rightist government in Estonia was under intense pressure, while the Lithuanian government was busy promising higher prices to the farmers, lower prices to consumers, and a crusade against the food-processing plants, heavily flavoured with traditional prejudice against 'profiteering middlemen'. Prime Minister Bronislovas Lubys, in theory a liberal, was beginning to talk of the need for rationing, illustrating the natural tendency in all three Baltic states to revert to authoritarian thinking when things deteriorate seriously. Such action would however be an obvious option for any government facing a crisis of this scale.[101]

The only way out of this trap is through Western aid, which has indeed already been forthcoming in disproportionate amounts, and has helped stave off complete economic collapse. Much more however will be needed fully to stabilise the economic and political situation. This is in the West's interest, for, as argued in the Conclusion, a crisis in the Baltic could have a disproportionate impact on the West itself.

In one sense, however, the connection between the Balts and Russia does work to the Balts's advantage; for the Baltic States are in the position of the swift explorer, relative to the slow explorer and the lion. The story is well known:

> Two explorers in Africa are attacked by a lion. One of them turns to run. The other exclaims, 'What's the point? You can't outrun a lion!' 'I don't have to outrun the lion. I only have to outrun you.'

So long as through aid and their own efforts the Baltic States can remain visibly better off than Russia, and so long as the Russians in the Baltic are not excluded from this relative advantage, the danger of conflict will greatly diminish. For good or ill, this will also bolster the national morale of the Balts themselves by showing that, even if among the poor relations of the West, they are still superior to Somebody.

Conclusion: The West and the Baltic States

'The snows still fall like silent sifting sand,
Thrown up by gravediggers in some lost hour.
Old Europe, who shall stir a strengthless hand,
When imminent night draws down in mindlessness of power?'
Péteris Aigars (Herberts Termanis), Latvian poet of
  the First Republic: 'Elegy of the Snows', written in
  the late 1930s, translated by William K. Matthews

A keynote of Baltic national feeling since its rebirth in the 1980s has been the desire to 'return to Europe'. Balts feel also – and rightly – that the rest of Europe has a duty to help them do so. The problem is that the Europe many Baltic politicians seek to return to is not the Europe of today, but that of the 1920s and 1930s, when the Baltic was first independent.

Compared to life under Soviet rule, and indeed to much of Europe at the time, these really were idyllic years for the Balts; but they were not safe ones. Like the rest of Eastern Europe, the Balts were beneficiaries but also ultimately victims of the Versailles Peace Settlement, which was based on the *status quo* at the end of the First World War, when both Germany and Russia were prostrate. The central flaw of Versailles was that the situation in 1919 did not reflect the true underlying balance of power in Eastern Europe; and that in the long run, the settlement could only be maintained by a level of Western commitment which did not materialise until it was too late. This is the spectre which today haunts the Balts and the other former Soviet republics as they contemplate the threat of a renaissant Russian nationalism.

Given the Russian (as Baltic) manner for harking back to old models, it would be surprising if some Russian generals were not today studying the words of General Denikin, the White commander in the Russian Civil War, written after the White defeat and the partial restoration by the Bolsheviks of the Russian Empire:

The state link of Russia with her borderlands was ordained by history. . . .
This link would sooner or later be restored, either voluntarily or through

374

compulsion – economic war or an army offensive. And that would have been done by *any* Russia – Red, Pink, White or Black – which did not want to suffocate inside the limits of those artificial boundaries to which the World War and internal chaos had confined her.[1]

As argued in Chapter 7, imperialists in the strict sense are now relatively rare among ordinary Russians; but crude nationalists are legion, and large sections of the Russian population now lie outside Russia's present borders, some 2.3 million of them in the Baltic. This is what ties the old Soviet imperialists and the new nationalists together. This is the link which needs to be broken if disaster is to be avoided.

It is therefore of great importance that the West should think clearly about its interests and obligations towards the former Soviet Union. It must do so in relation to the Baltic States in particular, where it is already committed, emotionally and politically – to a far greater degree than in Kazakhstan, Moldova or even the Ukraine. But emotional commitment needs to be backed both by real support and good advice – or it can be positively dangerous.

There is much current debate about the 'frontiers of Europe', and where they lie: on the Oder? The Bug? Or, as both Gorbachov and Yeltsin would have it, at Vladivostok? The Balts are clear that the frontier should be seen as following their eastern borders with Russia, and that the Baltic States should be seen as bulwarks against an essentially non-European, 'Asiatic' Russia.[2]

When it comes to frontiers, however, there is a clear bottom line. One can talk about cultural frontiers or economic frontiers, but historically speaking there is only one good definition of a frontier: it is something a state or alliance of states is prepared to fight to defend. The West today is quite clear, not surprisingly, that it is not prepared to fight to defend the Baltic States, any more than it was between 1920 and 1940. Nor is the 'bulwark' image, with its military implications, an appropriate one. If there were an active Russian military threat to the West, the Balts could not halt it. They do not represent a bulwark: they are not even a fence. There is at present, however, no such threat to the West, nor will there be in the foreseeable future, given Russia's acute weakness and the lack of an ideological basis for such an offensive.

The possibility of Russian military aggression in the future is very real, but if it occurs it will be confined to the borders of the former Soviet Union, and justified by a rhetoric of 'restoring' order and 'protecting' Russian or allied minorities. To some extent, therefore, the degree of Western involvement will be a matter of Western choice – though only to some extent, because a major war in the Soviet region, or even the rise of an ultra-nationalist regime in Moscow, would have of course a disturbing effect on Europe as a whole.

The West is involved in the attempt to extract the Baltic States from Russia's sphere of influence, by putting pressure on Moscow to withdraw its troops and by aiding the Balts to strengthen their economies and escape dependence on those of Russia and the rest of the former Union. More intangibly, every official Western visitor, or indeed tourist, to the Baltic reinforces the attachment to Europe, holds out another incentive to the local Russians, and goes some way to discourage any Muscovite desire for reconquest.

Escaping from Russia's sphere is, however, in its way an even more difficult and delicate business than was the extraction of the Baltic States from the Soviet Union; for it goes against powerful strands of history and economics and, above all, because it could in some circumstances involve ethnic conflict between Balts and local Russians. It is nonetheless a praiseworthy enterprise. The Balts do have ancient links with Western and Central European culture, even if they have weakened under Soviet rule. The Balts moreover will never live happily within the Russian sphere. Leaving them there risks driving them to violence, and provoking the sort of regional crisis which it must be the duty of the West to avert. However the enterprise is only praiseworthy if the West embarks upon it fully aware of what it is doing, and ready to face any unpleasant or unforeseen results. An unwillingness to make such a deep, considered (and expensive) commitment may, paradoxically, be one reason why the West has not been firmer with the Balts on the question of Russian rights. To take a direct role in ordering the internal affairs of these states would imply taking on a measure of responsibility for their security – a responsibility which, for all their rhetoric, Western chancelleries are wholly unwilling to assume.[3]

In my view, real commitment should involve three aspects. The first is continued pressure on Russia fully to withdraw its troops – a withdrawal which does in fact seem to be proceeding rapidly. This would lessen tension, encourage local Russians to integrate into Baltic society, and hopefully inspire the Balts to look more kindly upon them. It would also of course reduce (though not altogether remove, given the porousness of the Baltic frontiers) the passage of weapons from hardliners in the Russian military to hardliners in the local Russian communities.

Secondly, the West must put pressure on the Baltic governments to guarantee the rights of the local Russian population, irrespective of citizenship, especially in the social and economic sphere. Western aid should be conditional upon the Latvians and Estonians honouring their repeated past promises. Apart from the dangers of locally generated conflict, nothing could be more damaging to Western prestige and influence not only in the Kremlin but throughout Russian society than for the West to take sides exclusively with the Balts in a case in which the overwhelming majority even of pro-Western Russians think that the complaints of the Baltic Russian minorities are justified.

Thirdly, the West should provide more substantial, and properly co-ordinated aid, with the deliberate aim not simply of helping the transition to a market economy, but of minimising unemployment and reducing food prices during that transition. This would do much to reduce the danger of socio-ethnic discontent among the Baltic Russian workers, especially since they would then see even more clearly that they were better off in the Baltic than in Russia.

The conditions imposed in 1992 in return for IMF aid were indeed necessary for the long-term stabilisation and reform of the Baltic economies. But in the short run their effect was to help drive parts of Baltic industry to the wall and increase the risk of socio-ethnic conflict and a political or even military crisis. The hiatus between the short and long runs should be bridged by increased Western aid. Compared to the huge sums being poured into the bottomless pit of Russia, let alone thrown away on frivolities in the West, there need not even be very much of it. By 1994 relatively small sums of Western aid had already had a major impact.

As opinion polls show, many Baltic Russians already look more to the West than to imperial protection from Moscow. They will not continue to do so however if they see themselves cut out of the benefits of the move towards the West. This is of course the nub so far as many Latvian and Estonian nationalists are concerned, because they want the Russians to leave, and know they will not do if they become prosperous where they are. In the words of Trivimi Velliste, 'We hope that a third or so will become Estonian citizens, a third may remain here with Russian citizenship, and a third at least will leave'.[4] Balts further to the Right of Velliste do not wish to extend citizenship to *any* of the 'illegal immigrants'.

While many Russians are in fact leaving the Baltic, it is difficult to imagine a process which would persuade as many as a third to return to an impoverished Russia without leaving the remaining two-thirds in a state of dangerous discontent, and the Baltic States in a condition of serious instability. Furthermore, however understandable the Latvian and Estonian desire to reduce the Russian population, the use of even subtle economic and administrative pressure to this end seems incompatible with the spirit of the CSCE, which in effect stresses that neither frontiers nor populations should be altered unilaterally, regardless of their provenance.

The West is not bound to support the radical Balts in this aim. A moral commitment to the restoration and maintenance of Baltic independence – as recognised originally by the League of Nations and now by the UN – certainly stands. This in turn implies support for the basic national character of the Baltic states. It does not, however, imply support for the exclusive political authority of the native ethnic communities in these

377

states, any more than recognition of Fiji or Malaysia amounts to support for programmes of 'Fiji for the Fijians' or 'Malaysia for the Malays'.

As the Swedish Prime Minister, Carl Bildt, pointed out to the Swedish parliament on 2 April 1992, Scandinavian and United Nations recognition was granted to the Baltic States as they existed in August 1991, with the borders and populations of the time, and not to the republics of 1939. It would be different if the Balts were, as they so often claim, threatened with extinction by the Russian presence; but they are not. So long as they can prevent further mass immigration their demographic position should remain stable or even improve, as it is indeed already doing. The greatest danger for the Balts, and especially the Latvians, lies in ethnic conflict.

Enlightened self-interest in the West would suggest assisting a reasonable (though not, admittedly, altogether just) balance, recognising the need for a secure predominance of Balts while guaranteeing the Russians a collective position which would not be vulnerable to amendment by any future radical Baltic governments. This should involve granting rights in the social, economic and educational spheres, and official status for the Russian language. Citizenship in itself is of lesser importance, and indeed is not the most pressing concern of many ordinary Russians; after all, the Soviet citizenship of which many Baltic Russians have now been deprived was not, itself, very meaningful.

Western diplomacy was very slow to get to grips with the dangers of the ethnic situation in the Baltic. When it finally began to do so, during the summer of 1992, it was only under pressure from increasingly bitter complaints from Moscow – complaints which, under Foreign Minister Andrei Kozyrev, were directed through the proper channels of the CSCE, UN and Council of Europe. (The CSCE response came under the so-called 'Moscow Mechanism', which allows one country to complain about another's application of CSCE principles.) The advent of civil war in Yugoslavia also began to drum into even the thickest skulls the need for preventive diplomacy.

As a result, and following a Swedish and British initiative, senior Western diplomats instituted periodic meetings in Stockholm, after August 1992, to discuss questions relating to the Baltic States. At the beginning of 1993 the CSCE, after two preliminary visits, dispatched a six-month mission to Estonia to examine the position of the 'immigrant' Russian population. This was the first occasion on which the CSCE had done anything of this kind and, as with all CSCE operations, the Estonian investigation was funded on a shoestring. It had, however, the very important effect of giving local Russian leaders a voice in the West, and of reassuring them they had not been forgotten.

Signs of interest of this kind, and visits by American diplomats to

Russian-majority areas, are also tremendously important because they suggest that if the local Russians keep quiet, Western aid will flow their way. This is indeed what American diplomats have been telling them. But promises must be followed by real money, or the incipient Western influence will disappear.

Western attitudes are slowly changing. A Western diplomat described to me a 'sea-change' in US State Department attitudes between August and October 1992. The attitude had been that this was not an important question for the US; that it was the Balts' own business. Thereafter the US became much more active, both through the CSCE and in steering its aid; thus cheap US cotton credits for the Kreenholm mill in Narva were deliberately intended to help avert a social crisis in this Russian-speaking area.

Western diplomacy in the region is still plagued by a number of problems. Apart from the informal Stockholm Working Group, which had no executive function, it remained largely unco-ordinated. Not even the beginnings of a general Western crisis-prevention plan were evident, and different Western diplomats told the Baltic governments different things.

In general, Western policy remains obstinately reactive, not proactive. In 1992 a diplomat informed me that the CSCE representatives had not visited Latvia, 'because Latvia has not passed its citizenship law yet, and the Russians haven't complained as much about Latvia yet'.

> At that stage Russian propaganda was directed more against Estonia, so the situation there seemed to be more acute. Diplomacy tends to be led by events; it is difficult to drum up support to deal with a problem that hasn't yet happened.

The UN dispatched a mission to Latvia, but found nothing legally wrong. This was in part perhaps because the UN, as a body representing nation-states, has never found it easy to discuss minority rights or external interference, except where the case is desperate – in other words, when it is too late. American diplomacy has also suffered from the familiar problem of domestic political pressure from the Baltic-American emigrations. In the course of 1992 a succession of US Senators – pre-pickled in Baltic propaganda and inadequately briefed – made flying visits to the Baltic. Most called for Russian military withdrawal without even mentioning Russian rights.[5]

A more fundamental problem is that contemporary Western diplomacy finds it difficult to deal with forms of oppression if they do not involve outright 'human rights abuses'. Three years ago, for example, one of the factors exacerbating the fears of the Serbian minority in Croatia was a Croat government decision to change a majority of the police chiefs in the Serbian areas. Given the power of the police in such societies, the Serbian reaction is understandable. It seems highly likely that few diplomats in the region bothered even to report this minor administrative alteration to their superiors. The consequences are appallingly clear.

Delegations visiting the Baltic States during 1992 certified – accurately – that no human rights abuses existed. But with 'human rights' as the bottom line, there is a tendency to underrate the dangerous potential of quieter and less conspicuous factors. There is a tendency also to miss the point which is, for the West, not whether the Baltic States do or do not match up to some abstract standard of human rights, but how a regional crisis can be averted. Diplomacy should certainly be inspired by morality, but its chief moral duty lies in the avoidance of evil consequences, not in the celebration of fine ideals.

Scandinavians, with their tendency to see everything in moral terms and their lack of experience of the problems of dismantling multinational empires, have been particularly at sea over the Baltic Russian issue. The British and French do have experience of decolonisation, but have not used it. The French, for example, have not cared to draw any very close comparison between their rather different attitudes towards settlers' rights in the Baltic States and in New Caledonia.

The Swedes in particular have also suffered from a guilty conscience, as one of the few Western states formally to have recognised the Soviet annexation of the Baltic States. They now evidently feel they have to compensate through unconditional support. However, if the central argument against automatic Russian rights in the Baltic is that their arrival under Soviet occupation was illegal according to international law, it may be asked why they should be expected to have had a better understanding of that law than past Swedish governments.

From a point of view of international law, the Estonian and Latvian argument, though strong, is not in any case beyond question. A strict reading of the Geneva Convention would seem to allow for mass deportation; but there is in fact no clause in international law that governs a situation – like that of the Baltic today – in which countries have been ruled by another state for two generations, and the situation recognised either *de facto* or *de jure* by the international community.

Western diplomats may argue that the different Western approach to Russian rights in the Baltic and in Kazakhstan, for example, is governed by the fact that both were independent between 1920 and 1940, but I suspect that cultural prejudice has more to do with it; and though it is entirely true that Estonian and Latvian policies towards the Russians have so far taken purely legal and non-violent forms, it still forms part of a pattern of exclusivist nationalism which risks tearing apart the entire fabric of Eastern Europe and of the former Soviet Union.

The Western press has also played a fundamentally dismal role. When, in 1990, I was one of the very few Western journalists to criticise some Baltic policies, I warned my Baltic friends that the uncritical support of the rest of the press could not be relied on; that for a hundred years and more, Western journalists had swung between two contradictory stereotypes of Eastern European nations, and would surely do so in their case. The first stereotype is of gallant little freedom-loving peoples, fighting against wicked empires for the sake of independence and liberal democracy. The second is horrid little anti-semitic peasants, trying to involve us in their vicious tribal squabbles. In relation to the Baltic States, much of the American press in particular has swung between these two poles with almost nothing in between. Where they have criticised the Balts (especially over anti-semitism), the criticisms have often been so extreme, biased, and badly supported that they have merely infuriated even reasonable Balts, and discredited Western advice in general.

In the course of 1992, there was a welcome shift in Western diplomatic thinking from pure emphasis on human rights to a stress on the economic position of the Russians. Even this, however, was inadequate, since it ignored the fact – set out in Chapter 8 – that in post-Communist societies, communities often need a share of political power to ensure a share of state patronage and economic advantage.

The give-away line among Western diplomats during 1991–92 was, 'but it is not our business how the Balts arrange their naturalisation process and so on'. This is also the line of many Balts themselves. And it would be fine if it were consistent; if, in the event of an ethnic crisis and resultant Russian intervention, offers of Western support would also be waved away by the Balts: 'No, thank you all the same – as we said, this is our business. . . .'

Instead, thanks to the moral and emotional commitment of the West, and the assiduous efforts of Baltic lobbyists, ethnic conflict in the Baltic States would almost certainly lead to a major crisis in relations between the West and Russia. This in turn could deal a death-blow to Westernisation and democratisation in Russia, and encourage the growth of an ultra-nationalism which would affect the lives of tens of millions in Russia, the Ukraine and Kazakhstan. Latvian and Estonian policies towards the Russian minorities have already had an appreciable effect in strengthening the hand of reactionaries in Moscow and weakening those of Yeltsin, Kozyrev and the Democrats. Was this well done? Is this a process that the West should be subsidising?

In any case, the 'not your business' line – if, after Yugoslavia, it needed any further criticism – was refuted more than eighty years ago when, during the Versailles Conference, Clemenceau urged Poland to sign the League of Nations 'Minorities Treaty':

Nothing, I venture to say, is more likely to disturb the peace of the world

than the treatment which might in certain circumstances be meted out to
the minorities. And therefore, if the Great Powers are to guarantee the
peace of the world in any sense, is it unjust that they should be satisfied
that the proper and necessary guarantees have been given?[6]

The responsibility of the West after the collapse of the Soviet empire is
fully comparable in scope to that facing the West after the defeat and
collapse of the German, Austrian and Russian empires during the First
World War. The West's difficulty in evolving a coherent strategy also
dates back to the central dilemma of Versailles: the conflict between
Wilsonian ideas of national self-determination and the linked
requirement for general stability and minority rights. Thus Brian
Beedham, in a postmortem on the West's failure in Yugoslavia, wrote
that immediately after the Croat and Slovene declarations of
independence, Western troops should have been stationed on the border
of Croatia to deter Serb aggression. But that since this would have left
unsolved the question of the Serb minority within Croatia,

> ... The protection given to Croatia would therefore have had to be
> accompanied by a promise that an agreement would be reached within,
> say, six months on how to protect the rights of Croatia's minorities. ...[7]

What Beedham does not say is what kind of agreement the West should
have insisted upon, given the probable failure of the parties concerned to
reach agreement on their own. His proposal involves casting the West in
a virtually imperial role – but without a clear imperial policy, or indeed
an imperial army. After the West's miserable failure in Yugoslavia, the
belief that it could intervene successfully to resolve conflicts in the former
Soviet Union once they have begun, or deter consequent aggression by a
future hardline Russian government, is naive; it can, however, play some
part in preventing such conflicts from breaking out.

In the case of the Russian minorities, it is inadequate to say, as does
Paul Goble, that because most of the Russians were not old minorities
but 'simply representatives of the imperial centre, dispatched to promote
Soviet power',

> ... The international community, including the United States, must
> make every effort to try to ensure that Russians in the new states enjoy
> equal rights as individuals, regardless of minority status. ...[8]

This comes dangerously close to the radical Baltic line that the Russians
as illegal immigrants are not a 'minority', and therefore must be treated
simply on a case-by-case basis. It is also out of touch with reality.
Clearly, where Russians constitute 94 per cent of a town's population, as
in Narva, or a huge proportion of a republic's population, they are going
to behave as a political unity and demand collective rights.

Finally, once again, this approach completely ignores the dangers of administrative harassment of, and discrimination against, a community without either legally guaranteed rights or some hold on political power. The case of Northern Ireland under Protestant rule between 1922 and 1969 is an example of this, and there are many others. Such harassment is of course unwritten and unspoken, but it can be extremely effective and lead ultimately to disaster. I believe that on balance such an explosion is unlikely in the Baltic States; but the danger is certainly there.

The sad thing is that by taking this line towards the local Russians, the Latvians and Estonians may in fact be diminishing, not increasing, their chances of reaching safety in the arms of the European Union. So long as there is some insulation against the Russian economy and Russian immigration, the fact of the Baltic States possessing large Russian minorities would not of itself prevent them joining the EU. Nor would a sensible Russian government object to this. What every Western diplomat accepts as out of the question is that the EU should admit states which risk conflict with their internal minorities and with Russia. Once within the European Union, co-existence should be possible. As long as Latvians and Estonians control their own television and radio, their own schools and universities and their own frontiers, they need not fear being overcome by the local Russians, especially if these Russians increasingly look to the same goals and values as they do, and if, as at present, many are actually leaving. One might hope to return to older traditions in which several distinct communities lived separate lives within the same frontier, with one community in a hegemonic position but others having a guaranteed place and rights, and the whole being supervised by a general European order.

Despite the economic crisis that seems set to continue wracking the Baltic States for a considerable time to come, and the threat of a general criminalisation of the economy and state, there are also encouraging signs of political stability. The Centre-Right governments in Estonia and Latvia are committed to Western values and free-market reform. The commitment to reform of Brazauskas's party in Lithuania is much more doubtful, but at least its victory means that a majority of Lithuanians have rejected chauvinist nationalism. In general, the anti-Western nationalist attitudes examined in parts of this book will probably decrease as new generations come to the fore – but only so long as ethnic tensions do not lead to the appalling primitivism seen in so many other places. It is the West's duty to help push and pull the Balts in the required direction.

No-one should reckon on the permanence of Western liberal capitalist values within circumstances in which they have become associated with economic misery for ordinary people, of every nationality; and even prosperity will not of itself bring safety or stability unless the Russians in the Baltic learn to live without empire, and the Balts learn to live with the Russians. Until that day comes, the Baltic States will remain – as they have been for the past eight centuries – a debatable territory.

Tallinn-Riga-Vilnius-Kaliningrad-Moscow,
February 1990–January 1994.

Notes

Abbreviations used in the notes

BI   *Baltic Independent*
BO   *Baltic Observer*
BNS   Baltic News Service
JBS   *Journal of Baltic Studies*
LDDP   Lithuanian Democratic Labour
          Party

Introduction

1   Friedrich Kreuzwald, *Estonian Fairy Tales*, (Tallinn, 1986), p. 206.
2   Czeslaw Milosz, *Native Realm* (London, 1987), p. 47
3   An interesting example of this time-lag effect on Baltic cultural attitudes, and the reaction of a liberal Westerner to it, is to be found in a report by Wilhelm Schmid in the *Sueddeutsche Zeitung*, 1 November 1992, on the creation of a Goethe Institut in Riga. He wrote that the Latvians 'hoped for support for their own "national identity", by linking it to the German culture from 40 years ago, before the links were broken, a culture which is still well remembered. . . . When it became clear that the Goethe Institut represents a very different Germany, the disappointment was enormous . . . In a civilised form one finds this in the hope for a rebuilding of links to the world of Thomas Mann, who in his *Observations of an Unpolitical Man* was in fact full of enthusiasm for the "nation".' The very fact that the writer puts the word 'nation' in inverted commas indicates the immense gulf between his thinking and that of his Baltic interlocutors, who would find such a distancing from the concept of nation absolutely incomprehensible.
4   Rimvydas Šilbajõris, 'Some Recent Baltic Poets, *Journal of Baltic Studies*, XX,3,89.

1   The Shape of the Land

1   A. H. Tammsaare's *Truth and Justice* has been translated into German and French, but not yet into English. An English edition of his *The Misadventures of the New Satan* was published in

the 1970s by the State Publishing House in Tallinn.

2 Eisentein's film 'Alexander Nevsky' contains a famous scene in which the weight of the knights' horses and armour breaks the ice of Lake Peipus, plunging them to their deaths.

3 Virza, quoted in Arnolds Spekke, *History of Latvia* (Stockholm, 1951) p. 24. Hills in the Baltic are however few and far between. The highest hill in Estonia is a slag-heap from the oil-shale mines, and I once walked to the top of Kruopine, at 293 metres the highest hill in Lithuania, without even realising it was there, until my Lithuanian companion proudly informed me what we were standing on.

4 Antanas Baranauskas, *The Grove of Anykščiai* (English translation, Vilnius, 1988).

5 Quoted in Valters Nollendorfs, *Journal of Baltic Studies* [hereafter *JBS*] V,2,1974, pp. 101–7).

6 Romuald Misiunas and Rein Taagepera, *The Baltic States 1940–1980: Years of Dependence*, (London 1983), pp. 91, 240. I am also indebted to the current Prime Minister of Estonia, Dr Mart Laar (formerly a historian of the resistance), for his information about the partisans in Estonia. For an account of this resistance, see below, Chapter 4.

7 *Lietuvos Rytas*, 14 August 1992.

8 Algirdas Julien Greimas, *Des Dieux et des Hommes* (Paris, 1985), pp. 193–224.

9 Latvian demographic statistics, pre-1914 in Spekke, *History of Latvia*, p. 316.

10 Armitstead was Mayor from 1901 to 1912, and gained a reputation for pragmatism and independence from national and ideological disputes. He was the grandson of a British railroad engineer and industrialist who settled in the Russian Empire. See Anders Henriksson, *The Tsar's Loyal Germans: The Riga German Community, Social Change and the Nationality Question, 1855–1905* (Boulder, 1983).

11 Interview with the author, 18 December 1991.

12 George Kennan, *Memoirs, 1925–1950* (Atlantic City, 1967), p. 29.

13 See three works by Latvian authors, Kārlis Skalbe (1879–1945) *Small Notes* [Mazās Piezīmes], Zenta Mauriņa (1897–1978) *Daring* [Uzdrīkstēšanās] and Uldis Ģermanis *For Knowledge* [Zināšanai] (Stockholm, 1986). All three are reflections on Latvian history and society which contain recurring definitions of the nature and characteristics of 'the Latvian'.

14 Interview, 29 June 1992.

15 Alexis Rannit, 'A Note on Estonian Humour', *JBS*,II, 3/4, 1972. I myself have often thought of the Estonians as a sort of mass supporting cast for one of the films of Ingmar Bergman. Like him, they do sometimes – Rannit's words notwithstanding – also have a very lively sense of the grotesque, which emerges in anecdotes and riddles, and contributes to their brilliant animated films and some fine absurdist plays and stories. One image in particular has stayed with me: Ott Sandrak, an Estonian scholar, asked.
'Why are mosquitoes a good thing?'
'I don't know.'
'Because they drink our blood.'
'And why is that a good thing?'
'Because then sparrows come and eat the mosquitoes. How would you feel if the sparrows came and drank your blood directly? Horrible!'

16 The street fights between Estonian and Russian youths are mentioned in Romuald J. Misiunas and Rein Taagepera, *Years of Dependence: The Baltic States, 1940–1988*.

17 *Tallinn City Paper*, 1, 3 August 1992.

18 *Tallinn City Paper*, 1, 3 1992, in its 'Tips and Explanations' for Western visitors: 'In line with their generally cool demeanour, Estonians do not tend to hug or hiss. If you try to hug

an Estonian, they are likely to drop dead from sheer embarrassment'. This is not true of the Latvians and Lithuanians.

19 Interview, 5 July 1991.

20 *For Crazies Only*, directed by Arvo Iho and starring Margarita Terekhova (Tallinn, 1990).

21 Vytautas Kavolis: 'Culture as Performance', in *Lituanus*, 3,1991. A concrete example of this peasant moderation is given in Milosz's *Issa Valley*, in the passage where an older peasant takes a young nationalist radical peasant to task for having thrown a grenade into a Polish landowner's home – a conversation the essence of which could perfectly easily be transferred to our own time. This can also be compared with the passage in the third volume of Tammsaare's *Truth and Justice*, in which Indrek quits the Revolution of 1905 in disgust after witnessing the sacking of a German landowner's house.

22 Kavolis 'Culture as Performance'. The Grand Ducal legacy also seems to have its effect on Lithuanian politicians; coupled with the Soviet tradition of the coarse expression of personal power, it can make them extraordinarily arrogant. Authority is a disease to which they are unusually susceptible. Their Estonian counterparts are also often arrogant, but this seems to stem from the common Estonian assumption of higher intelligence and virtue. With the Lithuanians, at least those who took power after March 1990, it comes from an overweening sense of the grandeur of their office and the nation they represent, though it is also swollen by the bumptiousness of newly arrived, insecure provincials in unfamiliar surroundings.

23 Algirdas Landsbergis, 'Folklore and Drama: an Encounter in Lithuania', in *Books Abroad*, August 1973.

24 *Baltic Independent*, 11–17 September 1992.

25 Mihkel Tarm in *Tallinn City Paper*, 1,3,1992.

26 Jānis Turbads (Valdis Zeps), *Mayor's Son Kurbads* quoted in Valters Nollendorfs. 'The Demythologization of Latvian Literature', *Books Abroad*, Autumn 1973.

27 Quoted in Valters Nollendorfs, 'Riga in the Lyric Poetry of the Postwar Latvian Generation', *JBS*, V,2,1974.

28 Pierre Louys (in Latvian, Pjērs Luiss), *Bilitis Dziesmas* (Riga, 1928 reissued 1990), translated by Jānis Sudrabkalns, illustrated by S. Vidbergs.

2 Surviving the Centuries

1 Tacitus, *Germania*.

2 In the course of 1992 there were Estonian moves to establish links with these peoples and even to encourage aspirations for independence from Russia.

3 The attitude of the Estonians to the Setus is mixed. On the one hand, they are appreciated as ethnic brothers, and because they are poorer and more 'backward' than the Estonians, their folk-culture is of particular interest to ethnographers seeking clues to Estonia's own past. Estonia has made a territorial claim to the Setu area now situated within Russia, on the basis of the fact that between 1920 and 1944 it formed part of Estonia. On the other, the Setus, when part of Estonia, were regarded with considerable disdain for their poverty and 'Russian ways', and it would seem that the main thrust of policy was not to celebrate but to 'Estonianise' them.

4 Efforts – with an obvious political motive – have been made by Soviet philologists to show that the Baltic and Slavic languages form one group. Apart from various political and religious loanwords from the Slav which appeared in the Baltic languages from the early Middle

Ages, certain older and basic connections are evident even to the non-expert, but in these cases it may well have been the Balts who influenced the Slavs, and not vice versa.

5   The use of the word 'Russian' for these medieval Slavic princes is disputed by Ukrainians, who point out accurately that the Muscovite 'Russia' which emerged after the thirteenth century was a very different state, and that they have as much right to claim to be the direct descendants of medieval Russia as have today's Russians. However, the 'Slavic Orthodox' tradition, religious and political, was in fact effectively seized and sustained by Muscovy. Baltic historiography too speaks of the medieval states as 'Russia'.

6   c.f. Spekke, op.cit., p. 113. He points out that this linguistic influence is not, however, reflected in place names, so Slavic settlement cannot have existed on a large scale.

7   In the nineteenth century, the crusaders were adopted by the German nationalist historian Treitschke as heroes of the Germanisation of the East, and in the twentieth century non-German historians used this to make them precursors of the Nazis.

8   The dispute between knights and the Church was largely about power and land, but also involved a vital question of principle. It initiated a debate in the field of human rights and international law which is of particular interest in the context of contemporary 'Columbus Debate' about the European impact on the native peoples of the Americas. This fourteenth and fifteenth century debate, like those in Spain after the conquest of the New World, concerned the natural rights of the heathens. From the first the Church attempted to protect those Balts who converted to Christianity, to limit the worst excesses of landgrabbing and enslavement, and to assure the Lithuanians that if they adopted Christianity they would be spared further attack. The knights for their part argued that the Balts' heathenism meant they did not possess automatic rights to property and freedom, even after their conversion to Christianity, and the Christians had the right to attack any remaining pagans in order to convert them, even if the pagans had not begun the war. Later, when Catholic Poland allied with pagan Lithuania against the knights, this debate grew in sophistication, with Polish representatives using quotations from Thomas Aquinas and other sources to argue that Christianity does not allow the waging of aggressive war against heathens and their conversion by force. In 1415, at the council of Constance, the Pope agreed with the Polish arguments and cancelled the Order's territorial claim on Lithuania. Many of the arguments first formulated in this debate were to be revived later in Spain, for example in the great debate between Sepulveda and Las Casas concerning the rights of the Amerindians. This tradition led to the famous papal declaration, 'All the Peoples of the Earth are Men', a theological basis for future Christian denunciations of racism and for parts of modern natural rights theories.

9   Interview, 27 December 1991.

10 In the twentieth century, the figure of Mindaugas has inspired a number of Lithuanian and Latvian plays dealing with the justification of doing evil for the sake of national unity and greatness. *Mindaugas*, written by Justinas Marcinkevičius under Soviet rule in 1969, can also be seen as an attempt by a semi-loyal Soviet Lithuanian writer to justify Party autocracy while at the same time subtly drawing attention to the question of how far the Party might be, consciously or unconsciously,

serving its own interests and power rather than those of the state. English translations of Marcinkevičius's *Mindaugas* and *Power* (Vara) by Mārtinš Zīverts are to be found in *Fire and Night: Five Baltic Plays*, ed. Alfreds Straumanis, (Prospect Heights, 1986).

11 See Vytautas Kavolis, 'The Devil's Invasion: Cultural Changes in Early Modern Lithuania', *Lituanus*, 35, winter 1989.

12 See Harry Dombkowski, *The Union of Lublin: Polish Federalism in the Golden Age* (Boulder, 1982), p. 8.

13 The most curious symbolic event in this marriage of the two nobilities was in 1413, when forty-seven Polish noble families each 'adopted' a Lithuanian opposite number, giving them coats of arms, which the Lithuanians had not previously carried.

14 For Finnish history in a Baltic context, see Bino Jubikkala and Kauko Pirinen, *A History of Finland* (London, 1961); D. G. Kirby, *Finland in the Twentieth Century* (London, 1979); Risto Alapuro, *State and Revolution in Finland* (Berkeley, 1988); William A. Wilson, *Folklore and Nationalism in Modern Finland* (Bloomington, Indiana, 1976); Edward Thaden, *Russia's Western Borderlands, 1710–1870* (Princeton, NJ, 1984); C. Leonard Lundin, 'Finland', in Thaden (ed.), *Russification in the Baltic Provinces and Finland, 1855–1914* (Princeton, NJ, 1981).

15 *Rigasche Rundschau*, quoted in Hendriksson, op,cit., p. 88. The door was never completely closed to the Balts – the very number of edicts by the Baltic town councils against masters taking on non-German apprentices show that this must have been fairly common. The most famous example of a sixteenth-century Balt rising in society (but becoming Germanised in the process) was the chronicler Balthasar Russow, apparently an Estonian by origin.

3 *Independence Won and Lost, 1918–40*

1 See Chapter 8 below for an analysis of the process leading to the Lithuanian declaration of independence of 11 March 1990.

2 For the interwar history of the Baltic States, see George von Rauch, *The Baltic States: The Years of Independence* (London, 1974); Tönu Parming, *The Collapse of Liberal Democracy in Estonia* (London, 1975); V. Stanley Vardys (ed.), *The Baltic States in Peace and War, 1917–1945* (Pennsylvania, 1978); Stanley W. Page, *The Formation of the Baltic States: A Study of the Effects of Great Power Politics on the Emergence of Lithuania, Latvia and Estonia* (Cambridge, MA., 1959); Jean-Baptiste Duroselle (ed.). *Les Frontieres Europeennes de l'URSS* (Paris, 1957); Leonas Sabaliunas, *Lithuania in Crisis: Nationalism to Communism, 1939–40* (Indiana, 1972); Alfred Erich Senn, *The Emergence of Modern Lithuania* (Morningside Heights, 1959); Toivo Raun, *Estonia and the Estonians*, op.cit.; John Hiden and Patrick Salmon, *The Baltic Nations and Europe: Estonia, Latvia and Lithuania in the Twentieth Century* (London, 1991); Heinze Gollwitzer (ed.), *Die Europaische Bauernparteien* (Stuttgart, 1977); Alberts Salts, *Die Politische Parteien Estlands* (Riga, 1926). See also Vincent McHale, 'The Party Systems of the Baltic States, *JBS*, XVII, 4, 86; V. Stanley Vardys, 'Democracy in the Baltic States, 1918–1934', *JBS* X, 4, 79; Alfred Erich (ed.), 'The Diary of Alfred Senn, 1921–22', *JBS*, IX, 2, 78; Zigurds Zīle, 'Minorities Policy in Latvia, 1918–40', *JBS*, XI, 1, 81. For memoirs of British participants in the Baltic wars of independence, see Herbert Grant-Watson, *An Account of a Mission to the Baltic States in 1919* (London, 1957) and H. de la Poer Gough, *Soldiering On* (London, 1954).

3 German policy in the occupied Baltic

was confused by the internal struggle in Germany between the High Command and its Pan-German allies on the one hand and the proponents of a compromise peace on the other. In Latvia and Estonia, the military planned to bring in large numbers of German settlers, land for this purpose being made available by the local German nobility. In Lithuania, the Germans wanted to join Lithuania in a personal monarchy with Prussia or Saxony, both Protestant states. A union with neighbouring Prussia would have been especially dangerous. The Lithuanian council (*Taryba*) stubbornly refused to accept this, and instead persuaded the Germans to allow a German Catholic prince, Wilhelm of Urach, to become King of a separate Lithuania under the name of Mindaugas II. The German defeat which followed brought this to nothing.

4 See Adolfs Silde, 'The Role of Russian-Latvians in the Sovietisation of Latvia', *JBS*, XVIII,2,87 and Andrew Ezergailis, *The Latvian Impact on the Bolshevik Revolution: The First Phase, September 1917–April 1918*, New York 1983.

5 The White Russian forces in the capture of Riga were commanded by my great uncle, Colonel Prince Anatol Pavlovitch Lieven (formerly of the Russian Imperial Guard), who was severely wounded in the course of the battle. After the war he served as military advisor to the Latvian government. For his part in the liberation of Latvia from the Bolsheviks, and because he refused to join the Germans, the Baltische Landeswehr or the White Russian adventurer Bermont-Avalov in attacks on the Latvian national government, he was accorded a Latvian state funeral on his death in 1937. He is buried on his former estate at Mežotne (Mesoten).

6 Joseph Buloff, *From the Old Marketplace*, translated by Joseph Singer (Cambridge, MA, 1991), p. 322. For a summary and analysis of the Polish-Lithuanian dispute up to 1940, see Arthur Erich Senn, *The Great Powers and the Vilna Question* (London, 1966).

7 For the evacuation and destruction of factories in Riga, see *The Times* 25 August 1915. Parts of the Riga library remained in Voronezh, the place of evacuation of many Balts, until finally returned by Boris Yeltsin!

8 The land reforms were historically and morally justified, but did of course involve confiscation of private property on a colossal scale and, for this reason, were strongly criticised by the American administration of the time as a 'Communistic' measure. This casts a somewhat ironic light on those Balts, especially from the emigration, who preach the sacredness of private property and the need to show the world a respect for legality when arguing for the return of all the property they owned before 1940, irrespective of the disruptive consequences for Baltic society and agriculture today. As in 1920, this demand today has political and national aspects, being intended partly to break the hold of the Communist managerial class – the so-called 'red barons' – on the countryside, and to build up the property of the native Balts *vis-à-vis* that of the ethnic minorities. Britain was also unhappy with the land reforms of 1920 for this reason, fearing that discontented German minorities in the Baltic States might give Germany an excuse once again to intervene in the region.

9 George Kennan, op.cit., p. 45, has a haunting description of a visit in 1932 to the once great port of Liepaja (Libau), by then deserted and crumbling after the disappearance of the Russian trade. This is a fate which today hangs over most of the industrial and port areas of the Baltic States.

10 An American teacher in Latvia, John Roche, wrote that 'my Latvian students, visiting Britain in the 1930s, were appalled at conditions in the port of Hull'. He quoted Ulmanis on the government's emphasis on agricultural production: 'if we can't export it, at least we can eat it'. (*JBS*, 6,1,75). An English traveller, Ronald Seth, commented on the simplicity, modesty, cleanliness and order of life in Estonia, and the lack of class distinctions in Estonian society. (Ronald Seth, *Baltic Corner: Travels in Estonia* (London, 1939). An American tourist, E. Alexander Powell, described Estonia as 'the cheapest and most interesting country in Europe.' *Undiscovered Europe* (Washington, 1932) Powell was especially struck by the modesty and unpretentiousness of Estonian politicians. Regrettably, this has also suffered from Soviet rule, Estonian ministers, like their Kremlin predecessors, habitually drive around Tallinn in screaming motorcades, scattering pedestrians and other traffic. The Speaker of the Supreme Council, Ülo Nugis, even has a police motorcade escort him in his summer cottage.

11 Vardys, op.cit.
12 Senn writes that 'many Lithuanians felt that the minority representatives should hold no places in their national governments' and that therefore, because of the large non-Lithuanian population of Vilnius, 'had Lithuania possessed Vilna in the 1920s, parliamentary democracy [in Lithuania] might not have survived even as long as it did'. Senn, op.cit. pp. 106, 236. See also Romuald Misiunas, 'Fascist Tendencies in Lithuania', *Slavonic and East European Review*, January 1970.
13 Leonas Sabaliunas, op.cit., pp. 25–40.
14 Vardys, op.cit.
15 Interview, 13 November 1991. Sabaliunas (op.cit., p. 27) quotes a

Lithuanian nationalist of the 1920s in words which I have heard echoed many times in the contemporary Baltic: 'In the speeches of the "great Western statesmen we once looked for lofty ideas and a true concern for the needs of mankind . . . Now we are almost sure that we will find there either the official and insincere statements about the "great principles" which no-one believes any more and which are never put into effect, or demagoguery, or a formal justification of some evil, or, finally, the betrayal of impotence.' This is the attitude which lies behind remarks such as that of the Lithuanian Foreign Minister, Algirdas Saudargas in 1991 (to a group of astonished Western diplomats) that Western democracy is a 'sham', and that true democracy stems from the heart of a nation.

16 Le Pen's lieutenant, Bernard Megret, has visited Lithuania at the invitation of the Tautininkai (Nationalist) Party, and a friend in the Latvian Congress asked me to pass on an invitation to him to visit Latvia.
17 Interview, 6 June 1991.
18 Interview, 1 June 1991
19 See Hain Rebas, 'Baltic Regionalism', *JBS*, XIX,2,1988. In his view, 'The Estonians, Latvians and Lithuanians have until recently despite minimal distances, lived more *next to* each other than *with* each other. For British and French policy, see Alfred Erich Senn, 'The Baltic Tangle', *JBS*, XV,4,84, and Merja-Luisa Hinkannen-Lievonen, *JBS*, XIV,4, 83. For the failure to co-ordinate Baltic diplomacy in the interwar years, see Rita Putiņš Peters, 'Problems of Baltic Diplomacy in the League of Nations', *JBS*, XIV,2,83. Baltic interwar diplomacy and the failure to achieve co-operation is also extensively discussed in 'The Baltic States in International Relations' (*Acta Baltica*, Stockholm University, 1988) and in the works listed in n. 2. above.

20 Bišers is quoted in Juris Dreifelds, 'Latvian National Rebirth', in *Problems of Communism*, July–August 1989, p. 87. He said that at the Congress of Peoples' Deputies the different national delegations advanced separate and different constitutional proposals, without prior joint planning.

21 See *The Baltic Independent*, 18–24 September, 1992.

22 This had the curious result that I myself, as a frequent traveller between the three republics, found myself on three occasions in 1990 the first apparent source of information between one government and another. For example in May 1990 the Estonians passed a law changing their constitutional position to bring it into line with that of the Latvians and create a more united stand against Moscow. At lunch the next day in Riga, I asked a senior Latvian minister for his reaction to this move. His reaction was surprise – he had not heard of it and a flood of anti-Estonian abuse, ending in the words, 'Those arrogant *****s! They never tell us anything!'.

4   *The Troglodyte International:*
The Soviet Impact on the Baltic

1 For Baltic population losses and changes this century, see Appendix 3.

2 Interview, 23 September 1992.

3 One major exception has been Dr Vytautas Kavolis. In his essay, 'On the Deformations of Intellectual Culture' in Rimvydas Šilbajōris (ed.), *Mind Against the Wall: Essays on Lithuanian Culture under Soviet Occupation* (Chicago 1983), he writes that 'it is extremely difficult to be critical of one's own stance when it is the only barrier against the abomination of false sacraments'. In particular, he points to the way that the Catholic dissidents and their press simply identified Lithuania with the Catholic Church, and secularism with Soviet rule.

4 For example the Latvian Lat, which had been worth ten roubles, was exchanged for one rouble.

5 In Estonia, the process of annexation and Sovietisation was controlled by Andrei Zhdanov, in Latvia, by Andrei Vyshinsky, and in Lithuania, by Vladimir Dekanozov.

6 Interviews 27 August 1992 and 1 May 1990.

7 See *The Baltic Independent*, 20 June 1991.

8 See Taagepera and Misiunas, op.cit., p. 76.

9 On the June 1941 rebellions, see the essay by Zenonas Ivinskis in V. Stanley Vardys (ed.) *Lithuania under the Soviets* (New York, 1965) and Seppo Myllyniemi, *Die Neuordnung der Baltischen Laender, 1941–44* (Helsinki, 1973) (Societas Historica Finlandiae).

10 Interview, 6 June 1991.

11 Some Latvian *emigrés*, landed by the Royal Navy to establish contacts with the partisans, were apparently betrayed by Kim Philby.

12 Interview, 20 March 1991.

13 Interview, 28 December 1991. See also V. Stanley Vardys, 'The Partisan Movement in Postwar Lithuania', *Slavic Review*, September 1963. Soviet loyalists for their part continue to this day to describe the partisans as 'bandits'. A portrayal of the war in Estonia from the Communist point of view is given by the novel *Raindrops*, by Paul Kuusberg, head of the Estonian SSR Writer's Union between 1976 and 1983. He describes how his hero, a local Communist official, dodges an ambush by the bandits, led by a local 'Kulak', who succeed, however, in killing his father.

14 An interview (on 29 December 1991) with a former Lithuanian partisan, Juozas Mielius, in Zeimelis village,

near Joniskis in northern Lithuania, brought out the intense complexity of those years in his part of the countryside. He became a partisan, but his wife's brother was with the *Stribai*. In his words, 'the *Stribai* were Lithuanian landless labourers, local Russians whose ancestors had been settled in Lithuania by the Tsars, or simply Lithuanians who wanted to avoid being conscripted into the Soviet army and sent to serve somewhere else'. In 1940, Mielius was denounced as anti-Soviet and nearly arrest. In 1941, he was a local Lithuanian volunteer, and an unwilling witness of Jewish massacres (see below, Chapter 6). In 1944, he hid escaping Russian soldiers from the Germans, and was harassed by his Lithuanian neighbours in consequence, and forced to move from his village ('by then, all the different sides suspected me'). He was subsequently denounced by a local Communist official with whom he had quarrelled over food requisitions, and had to move again. Like many others, he finally joined the Forest Brothers to escape call-up into the Soviet army. However, he criticised both the brutality of some Forest Brother actions and the idiocy of some unnecessary attacks by his group: 'They just wanted to show everybody that they had this machine-gun, this big machine-gun'. He was captured in 1948, and sent to prisons and camps in Siberia, from which he returned in 1956. Mielius is a fierce critic both of the Communists and of Lithuanian extreme nationalists who call for revenge for what happened in the 1940s; this independent view is linked to his anti-clericalism, which is common among the peasants in his part of Lithuania. In his words, 'I am a member of the Deportees Association [a group aligned with the radical nationalists] but I am not welcome there, because I believe neither in

devils nor in God. I am old now . . . and I am glad to be free of all the different ropes that people tie themselves up in. If you are afraid of God, and Devils, and Occupants, and Spies, what sort of freedom will you be able to give Lithuania?'.

15 Interview, 20 October 1992.

16 See Taagepera and Misiunas, op.cit., p. 133.

17 Raun, op.cit., p. 190., *The Power of Derision*, an interview with Arvo Valton, is published in *Pays Baltes*, a volume of the series 'Autrement' (Paris, 1991), pp. 118–123.

18 Dr Kelam sketched his life for me in an interview on 2 June 1992.

19 Taagepera and Misiunas, op.cit., pp. 261–2.

20 Interview, 25 May 1992.

21 Interview, 1 May 1990.

22 Baltic industrial production is listed in Appendix 4.

23 Figures quoted in BNS, 9 July 1992. In 1991, 1,141 Lithuanians committed suicide. The peak was in 1985, when 35 Lithuanians and 27 Estonians out of every 100,000 committed suicide. By contrast, the current rate in Sweden is only around 20.

24 For the structure of Soviet rule in the Baltic, see the essays in Dietrich André Loeber *et al.* (ed.), *Regional Identity under Soviet Rule: The Case of the Baltic States*, in particular the second section, *'Regionalism and Political Integration'*, containing essays by Rasma Kārkliņš, Egils Levits, Jan Ake Dellenbrandt and Sergei Zamascikov.

25 This illusion that all former Communists still somehow form part of a single unity is frighteningly widespread among Right-wing politicians in the West, notwithstanding all evidence to the contrary.

26 Jānis Āboltiņš, *Biju Biedrs, Tagad Kungs* ('Formerly Comrade, Now Mister'), (Riga, 1992), p. 10.

27 Nijole Sadunaite, *A Radiance in the Gulag*, translated by Fr. Casimir

Pugevicius, (Manassas, 1987), pp. 53–8, 128.

28 It is interesting to note that the signatories of this letter are today in totally different political positions. The poet Paul-Erik Rummo is a deputy on the Right. Marju Lauristin is leader of the Social Democrats in the Centre, but tending increasingly to an anti-Russian and even chauvinist position, Jaan Kaplinski, another poet, has become a maverick independent denouncing Estonian national intolerance but also the Americanisation of popular culture (see Chapter 5). In the September 1992 elections Kaplinski was elected to parliament for the Popular Front, now in effect a Left-wing party.

29 See Irina Ratushinskaya, *Grey is the Colour of Hope* (London, 1990), where Lagle Parek is mentioned. Interview with Parek, 3 August 1992.

30 Interview 16 September 1992. Terleckas' article appeared, interestingly, in the Russian rather than the Lithuanian edition of Atgimimas, 17 February 1989.

31 Petkus is one of the mainstays of the nationalist Christian Democrats.

5 Imagined Nations: Cycles of Cultural Rebirth

1 From my own record of the occasion, 14 December 1991.

2 A famous example is the magical singing match in the *Kalevala*, translated by Keith Bosley (Oxford, 1989), pp. 30–31.

3 See Jānis Arveds Trapāns 'Krisjānis Barons: His Life and Times' *Linguistics and Poetics of Latvian Folk Songs*, ed. Vaira Vīķis-Friebergs (Toronto, 1989).

4 c.f. George Kurman, 'Parallelism and Deep Structure in Estonian Folksong', *JBS* XX,3,89.

5 Quoted in Rimvydas Šilbajōris, 'Some Recent Latvian Poets', *JBS*,

XX,3,89. The musicality ingrained in Estonians was displayed during an election gathering of the Popular Front on 17 September 1992, at which the Canadian-Estonian presidential candidate, Rein Taagepera, burst into a perfectly delivered satirical song, to a folklore tune. He invited the participants to join in, which they did – also in perfect harmony.

6 Of course, for a natural rootless cosmopolitan like myself, the sight and sound of tens of thousands of blonde-haired maidens in folk-costume singing national songs in unison is somewhat disquieting – but then, rootless cosmopolitan prejudices are not inherently superior to anyone else's prejudices.

7 Johann Gottfried Herder, *Ideen Zür Philosophie der Geschichte der Menschheit* (Frankfurt, 1974).

8 Alexis Rannit, in *Books Abroad*, op. cit.

9 See *JBS*, VI,1,1975, and also Donatas Sauka, quoted in Helge D. Ringholm, 'Lithuanian Folk Song Poetics', in *Linguistics and Poetics of Latvian Folk Songs*, op.cit.

10 Rimvydas Šilbajōris, 'Existential Root Concepts of Lithuania in the Poetry of Sigitas Geda', a paper presented to the Conference of the Association for the Advancement of Baltic Studies, Toronto, 11–14 June 1992.

11 The transformation of the Lithuanian pagan heritage into a more 'modern' form began with the Renaissance. As mentioned in Chapter 1, medieval Christian chroniclers, looking for words to describe Lithuanian pagan spirits, naturally turned to classical antiquity and came up with names like 'dryad'. After the Lithuanian union with Poland, Lithuanian noble families, seeking to catch up with the Poniatowskis and dignify the paganism of their recent past, began to claim that their paganism was of classical origin and

that they themselves were descendants of the ancient Romans. I myself had an amusing taste of this in a conversation with a woman from the Rimsky-Korsakov family in St Petersburg. The Korsakovs were a Lithuanian family who accompanied a fifteenth century Lithuanian princess to Moscow to marry a Russian prince, and themselves became Russian nobles. They later successfully petitioned the Tsar to add 'Rimsky' to their name to denote their Roman origin. I enquired about this: 'Well,' Tatiana Vladimirovno said, 'family legend has it that we are descended from the god Jupiter, but this is not true of course.' I nodded sympathetically. Then she continued, 'But what does appear to be the case is that we are in fact descended from Pompey the Great!'

12 On 20 November 1991 I attended a service of the *Dievturība* Latvian pagan movement, and spoke to one of its leaders, Gunārs Freimanis. He told me that he had spent a total of twenty-two years in Soviet prisons for his membership of the movement, and that 'We are Latvian nationalists, and think that the Latvian state exists because the nation exists. God is for the nation, and in the revelation of God we can consolidate ourselves as a nation. . . . Christianity is the religion of the invaders. No Latvian writer has ever been a good Christian.' He added that 'We have always thought that Latvia should belong only to the Latvians'. Their supposedly 'authentic' Latvian religion, based on a trinity of gods, seems, however, to be mainly a nineteenth and twentieth-century construct. Despite their alarming ideology, and their links with a neo-fascist group, 'Imanta's Soul' (named after another Latvian pagan hero), I did not find the *Dievturi* as people very sinister. According to Mr Freimanis, there are fewer than three hundred of them in Latvia, although as the Latvian Right-wing press reveals, their spiritual influence extends very much further. Those I met were not young thugs, but a mixed crowd of all ages and conditions, not unlike British revivalists. The service itself was held in a room of the National History museum, and was very sober, without any of the neo-pagan nonsense found in the West. It was even moving, in part because of the extreme beauty and purity of the singing.

13 Arguments for matriarchal elements in pagan Baltic society have been made (not, in my view, very convincingly), in two serious and valuable works of scholarship by Lithuanian emigrés: Marija Gimbutas, *The Balts*, and Norbertas Velius, *The World Outlook of the Ancient Balts*. See also Aija Veldre Beldavs, in *JBS*, VIII,2,77. Beldavs quotes a Latvian woman writer from the earlier part of the century: 'Without exaggeration, we can say that our ancient household civilisation, moral, spiritual and material, has been created by Latvian woman . . . although the husband, the family head, rules outwardly, actually it is she, with the wisdom inherited from the goddess . . .'. Women were in fact responsible for transmitting the folkloric tradition. After conquest by the Germans, men's songs, of war and raiding, disappeared but women's songs remained; hence the image of a more peaceful, unaggressive cultural tradition than that of other countries is by no means wholly false, even if it does not apply to the Balts before the thirteenth century.

14 For a description of the process of linguistic standardisation before the First World War, see the essays by Raimo Raag, Daiba Metuzale-Kangere and Helge D. Ringholm 'The Baltic Countries, 1900–1914' in *Studia Baltica Stockholmensia*, 4, 1990, published by Stockholm University.

15 A legacy of this period in Latvia and Lithuania is the question of the spelling of foreign names. Estonians, as all other users of the Latin alphabet except for their Baltic neighbours, simply spell them as in the original. The Latvians and Lithuanians however were heavily influenced by the Russian approach, which has to render Western spellings phonetically into the cyrillic script. They therefore stick to their own phonetic spellings (often second-hand, copied from Russian spellings in the cyrillic script), as well as adding their own grammatical endings, even in the nominative; hence the famous English author Villem Meikpis Tekerai (Lithuanian) and Prime Minister Margareta Tečere (Latvian). Latvians add an 's' even when it is there already: hence 'sekss', and former US President Džordžs Bušs. A number of emigré Baltic scholars are campaigning against the tradition, which they see as a sign of continuing provincialism and isolation, but so far without success. Lithuanians in particular seem determined to stick to their tradition no matter what the resulting confusion. Thus the Lithuanian press rendered the visiting US Vice-President (Quayle) as Kveilas, which in Lithuanian resembles the word for 'stupid'.

16 Details about the Landsbergis family history were provided in an interview with Mrs Landsbergis in March 1990, during the early days of the new government.

17 See the interview with Professor Landsbergis published in *Valstiecu Laikrastas*, 16 May 1992.

18 Pastor Georg Brasche, quoted in Jānis Arveds Trapāns, *Krišjānis Barons: His Life and Times*, in Vīķe-Freibergs, op.cit., p. 21.

19 See Vaira Vīķe-Freibergs: 'Andrejs Pumpurs's Lāčplēsis ("Bearslayer"): Latvian National Epic or Romantic Literary Creation?', in *Studia Baltica Stockholmensia*, 2, 1985 ('National Movements in the Baltic Countries during the Nineteenth Century'), p.525.

20 The relationship between the *Kalevala* and the development of Finnish nationalism has been examined by William A. Wilson in *Folklore and Nationalism in Modern Finland* (Indiana, 1990), though I understand that he has modified somewhat his original view of an intimate connection between certain *Kalevala* interpretations and Finnish extreme nationalism.

21 See Endel Nirk, *Estonian Literature* (Tallinn, 1987), p. 55.

22 Before the writing of *Kalevipoeg*, Dr G. J. Schulz-Bertram was asked by the Estonian Learned Society, 'How can our society further most successfully the enlightenment and the spiritual renaissance of this people liberated from serfdom. He replied: 'I think, by two things: let us give the people the epic and the history, and everything is won.' (Quoted in Felix J. Oinas, 'The Finnish and Estonian Folk Epic', *JBS*, VII,1,76.)

23 Estonian literature has produced a parody of *Kalevipoeg* and of epics in general. *The Memoirs of Kalevipoeg* by Enn Vetemaa. In Latvian, myth and the mythologising of history, politics and contemporary events (especially in the Latvian emigré communities) have been satirically analysed in novels by the emigré authors Valdis Zeps and Dzintars Sodums – satires which are also, of course, in a backhanded way, a tribute to the power of the myths themselves. See Valters Nollendorfs, *The Demythologisation of Latvian Literature*, op.cit.

24 Judita Vaičiunaite, quoted in Šilbajōris, *JBS*, XX,3,89, op.cit. She also writes that 'The Nation then resides within the symbolic sequence of linkages between an ancient amber idol, the timeless sun, petrified pine sap, old grindstones, folkloric ornamental motifs of the sun, old bees wax,

honey, candles and the amber smell of apples ...', which appears to cover most of the available images.

25 The Lithuanians sometimes refer to *The Seasons* by Kristijonas Donelaitis (1714–1780) as their 'national epic'. This is certainly a remarkable work, since it was written virtually without precursors in the written Lithuanian language. However, it has nothing in common with the nineteenth century epics, and does not form part of the 'invention of tradition'. Compared with many later Lithuanian works, it is indeed striking for its complete omission of references to Lithuania's Grand Ducal and pagan past. Instead it concentrates on a lyrical but also highly realistic account of the lives and labours of the Lithuanian peasantry in Donelaitis's own corner of East Prussia. Its literary models are not romantic but strictly classical: Hesiod's *Works and Days* and Virgil's *Georgics*. *The Seasons* is certainly imbued with that semi-mystical love of nature characteristic of Lithuanian culture in general; but its explicit religious references are entirely Christian. From the point of view of the development of Lithuanian nationalism, it is significant both as a masterpiece to which later Lithuanian authors could look back with pride, and for its exaltation of Lithuanian peasant virtues against the sinfulness and nasty habits of their German overlords, and of foreigners in general. It prefigures later nationalist works in its call for Lithuanians to abandon such habits and return to the purer, more hard-working virtues of their ancestors. Donelaitis was a Protestant minister in an area of East Prussia inhabited by Lithuanians. In the course of the next century, thanks to deliberate policies of Germanisation, and depopulation due to plague, the area became overwhelmingly German. As a result in 1944–45 the population was cleared out and replaced by Russian settlers – a memory which causes understandable bitterness in many Lithuanians and has led to calls on the Right for the annexation of what is now the Kaliningrad region.

26 Andrejs Pumpurs, *Lāčplēsis, a Latvian National Epic* (Centenary English edition, Riga, Writers Union, 1988, pp. 54–67.

27 *Lāčplēsis*, op. cit. pp. 5–12.

28 Valda Melngaile, *The Sense of History in Recent Latvian Poetry', JBS*, VI,1,75.

29 Melngaile, op.cit.

30 Thus, *Lāčplēsis*, op. cit. page 152:
    'Lāčplēsis was born into the world
    by a she-bear in a deep forest,
    where his father, blessed by the gods,
    had lived a solitary life.
    Lāčplēsis inherited from his mother
    his bear ears and great strength.
    If someone were to cut off his ears in battle
    his great strength would immediately leave him!'
    And also see *Fire and Night*, op.cit., p. 126 ('A bear yourself,/With furry bear's ears . . .'), 37, 74, 88–9.

31 For Latvian artistic portrayals of Lāčplēsis. See the sculpture of him on the base of the Latvian Freedom Monument in Riga, designed by Kārlis Žāle. The edition of *Lāčplēsis* published in 1988 by the Riga Zinatne Publishers contains thirty-six renderings of scenes by eight different artists. The major 1947 edition is illustrated by Girts Vilks, probably the most famous Latvian illustrator of mythological themes. Lāčplēsis is portrayed by Voldemārs Valdmanis on the cover of the English edition of *Fire and Night*, which also contains photographs of theatrical performances of Rainis's play (pp. 2, 10 and 90). The 1953 Russian edition of *Fire and Night*, from the State Publishers in Riga,

also contains illustrations by Vald-manis.

32　See *Fire and Night*, op.cit. pp. 88–9' *Lāčplēsis*, op.cit. pp. 154–8. Of course, in the context of a post-Com-munist world in which Genghis Khan, Tamerlaine and Vlad Drac-ula have all become heroes of their respective nations, a bear might well seem one of the more humane avail-able candidates.

33　M. K. Čiurlionis, the subject of Dr Landsbergis's academic work, is a figure hard to place in any of the accepted categories of Western artis-tic tradition. Dr Andrea Botto has pointed out that, as a composer, Ciurlionis was closely linked to 'Western compositional outlines' (of a heavily neo-romantic variety), and has suggested that he shifted to painting precisely in order to develop a Lithuanian style and speak directly to the Lithuanian peasantry, at a time when 'peasant' and 'Lithua-nian' remained synonymous. Čiurlionis' symbolism, which some-times recalls that of William Blake, is drawn partly from Lithuanian folk-lore, partly from theosophy and other mystical trends and partly, it seems, from Ciurlionis's own troubled psyche. Several of his paint-ings are visual expressions of musical compositions. The Estonian poet Alexis Rannit has written that they are 'the projection of organised time into compositional space. . . . This unique and conscious structural elaboration is 'melted' into legend-ary or cosmic landscapes, imbued with a soft, innocent atmosphere.' In general, I have always felt that it is unfortunate that Ciurlionis was re-stricted to framed canvases for his work; a more appropriate setting, both artistically and nationally, for his particular genius would be in the form of giant murals.

34　Jānis Andrups, quoted in Valda Melngaile, op.cit.

35　Rimvydas Šilbajōris in *JBS*, op.cit.

36　Šilbajōris, referring the novelist Jonas Avyzius, in *JBS* XVI,2,85.

37　See for example Mati Unt's novel, *The Autumn Ball*, and Arvo Valton's short stories in the collections *Love in Mustamae* and *Eight Japanese Girls*.

38　*Pilsonis*, 21–27 July 1992.

39　See Vytautas Kavolis, 'On the Deformation of Intellectual Cul-ture', in Šilbajōris, *Mind Against the Wall: Essays on Lithuanian Culture Under Soviet Occupation* (Chicago, 1983) in which he analyses the lack of an independent and critical intellec-tual tradition within Lithuania: 'in general, the Lithuanian mind has been marked by an intellectual timidity, a lack of daring to tear one-self away from one's roots, a reluctance to think of oneself as being responsible for a re-assessment of the world's basic issues without the help of automated, obligatory code systems. . . . The dominant tendency has been catastrophically pedagog-ical'.

40　See K. Clark, *The Soviet Novel: History as Ritual* (Chicago, 1985).

41　*Literaturnaya Gazeta*, 20 November 1991.

42　*Baltic Independent*, 3, 19–26 June 1992.

6　*Lost Atlantises: The Half-Forgotten Nationalities of the Baltic*

1　Reading Baltic German authors about the 'wilderness' which the cru-saders conquered, I came across the intriguing German term *das Unland* for the first time. It suggests that, in a sense, not merely were the pagan in-habitants less than fully human, but the land was not really the land; it only became 'land' in the full sense when developed by the Christian Germans. See Alexis Freiherr von Engelhardt, *Die deutschen Ostseeprovin-zen Russlands* (Munich, 1916), p.3.

2　Julius von Eckardt, *Die baltischen Pro-vinzen Russlands* (Leipzig, 1868).

3   See Horst Adamek (ed), *Freimutiges aus den Schriften Garlieb Merkels* (East Berlin, 1959).

4   See Ernst von Mensenkampf, *Menschen und Schicksale aus dem alten Livland* (Riga, 1943), p.327.

5   Heinz von zur Muehlen, *Deutsch und Undeutsch im Mittelalterlichen und Fruehneuzeitlichen Reval* (Koeln, 1973). A fine expression of Baltic German noble attitudes is to be found in the memoirs of Camilla Baroness von Stackelberg, born 1895 in Livonia: 'It was natural for us to regard ourselves as Germans, and yet we remained unconditionally loyal to the Russian ruling family. At the same time, the Russians whom we knew in our province were regarded in general as corrupt officials, badly dressed, often depraved teachers, and simple soldiers. They were certainly in no way seen as fit for us to socialise with. . . . In Estonia, things were rather different. The closeness of Petersburg had its effect. One got to know good Petersburg society and its enchanting kindness, which attracted everyone. There was a saying – I forget by whom – that if the Tsar, instead of sending officials and second-rate regiments to the Baltic provinces, had sent one good regiment of Guards, Russification would have been successful.' Camilla von Stackelberg, *Verwehte Blatter: Erinnerungen aus dem alten Baltikum* (Berlin, 1992). It is interesting that the different attitudes of the Livonian and Estonian German nobles in the Baltic to the Russians were the reverse of those of their Baltic peasants. In the latter case, it was always the Latvians who felt closer to the Russians, and the Estonians who disdained them and kept them at a distance.

6   Muehlen, op.cit., p.405.

7   This was taken by Heinrich Bosse as the title for an article on Baltic German literature, 'Die Glaeserne Wand: Der Lettische Mensch in der Deutsch-Baltische Literatur', in *JBS*, XVII, 4, 1986. See also Friedrich Scholz, *Die Literaturen des Baltikums: Ihre Entstehung und Entwicklung* (Opladen, 1990).

8   An unpleasant but finely-written account of the war of the Landeswehr and the Freikorps is given by a member of the latter, Ernst von Salomon, in *Die Geaechteten* (Rowohlt, 1962). Salomon, like so many of the Freikorps and Baltic German exiles, was to join the proto-Nazi Right in Germany in the 1920s. Another propagandist account by participants is Cordt von Brandeis, *Baltikumer: Das Schicksal eines Freikorps* (Berlin, 1939), with a foreword by von der Goltz. A very different, fictional account of the last stages of the struggle is given in Marguerite Yourcenar's grim novella *Coup de Grace* (Paris, 1939, reprinted 1971), which was filmed by Volker Schloendorff.

9   Rigasche Rundschau, 1902. For the political dilemmas facing the Germans, see Anders Henriksson, *The Tsar's Loyal Germans: The Riga Germans, Social Change and the Nationality Question, 1855–1905* (Boulder, Co., 1983).

10 My own uncle, Lt.Col. Prince Leonid Lieven, was a child among the refugees who had just arrived from Riga, and overheard this exchange.

11 Mia Munier Wroblewskaya, *Wintersnot*, p.197, quoted in Bosse, op.cit. Idyllic portraits of life in small German communities in the Baltic, centred around the manor house and the parsonage, were a popular subspecies of German literature before 1914. In much the same way as Indians in certain British colonial romances, however, the native peasants were drawn strictly for local colour. For a much harsher Estonian view of manorial life, see the novel *Milkman of the Manor*, by Eduard Vilde, written in the 1890s.

12 The Baltic Jewish heritage by contrast, except in a very few cases, is

not reflected in this journal. The gulf has evidently proved too wide.

13 Interview, 18 May 1992. Antanas Terleckas, a leading Lithuanian Right-winger, once said that such statements could be made only by 'pitiful scoundrels who hold nothing sacred'.

14 Interview, 11 May 1992.

15 The 'Lithuanian' communities are among the sternest defenders of Orthodoxy in Israel today.

16 c.f. Lazar Ran, op.cit., p.xxi.

17 See the memoir of Lucy Dawidowicz, who worked at the YIVO from 1938–39, *From That Time and Place* (New York, 1987). Traditionally, literary culture had been over-whelmingly religious-based and therefore overwhelmingly in Hebrew. When the movement of en-lightenment (the *Maskilim*) arose, following from the work of Moses Mendelssohn (1729–1786) in Prus-sia, its exponents, concentrating on learning from the Western enlighten-ment and integrating into educated gentile society, naturally aimed at education in the languages of their host countries. They, no less than the traditional Rabbis, despised Yiddish as a 'Jargon', a mere hotch-potch of other languages, unfit for the edu-cated to speak. The first generation of Yiddish scholars and writers called themselves deprecatingly 'the Jargonists'. The move to establish Yiddish as a Jewish cultural lan-guage was not altogether different from movements in surrounding gentile society to raise Lithuanian, Ukrainian or later Byelorussian from the status of 'peasant dialects', and like them, was intimately linked to political ends, and inspired tremen-dous fervour in its proponents. In the words of Lucy Dawidowicz, 'for some of us . . . the YIVO had become a religion, a kind of surrogate Judaism'. She described the YIVO as the 'Ministry of Yiddish'. The hopes of the Yiddishists are summed up in the words of Nathan Birn-baum, who found in East European Jewry, '. . . all the characteristics of a living distinctive people, and it be-came clearer to me that we do not have to create anew a nation that already exists but it is essential that we nurture it. So I conceived *galut* (diaspora) nationalism. In Western Europe I championed East Euro-pean Jewry, stressing their vibrant peoplehood. Of Eastern European Jews, I demanded that they preserve what they had, and not dissipate it for futuristic visions.' This led Birn-baum, like Simon Dubnow, to champion the idea of 'national-cul-tural autonomy' within the states of Eastern Europe, with education in Yiddish as well as Hebrew. But of course, compared to the other 're-born' East European languages ('reborn' usually being a thoroughly false term, since in most cases they had had no previous literary incar-nation), Yiddish faced great difficulties. In the case of Lithuanian and the other gentile languages, nationalism and linguistic revival were inextricably mixed, and eventually, these languages found protection and encouragement in national states or quasi-states. The Jews could never found their own state in Eastern Europe, and among them, language and nationalism were to a great extent opposed, as the Zionists denounced '*galut-national-ism*' as a hopeless sham and declared that the Jews could find a true national identity only in Israel and in Hebrew. Relations with the world of the gentile states of course were cru-cial. The hopes of the autonomists were continually being rejected by the rulers of the states in which they found themselves. At the same time, even so ardent a Yiddishist as Lucy Dawidowicz came to believe during her year at the YIVO that to a great extent it was actually Polish anti-semitism which was keeping Yiddish

alive, because without it, Jews would tend simply to adopt the language of the majority, as in her native America. The Holocaust smashed the Yiddish-speaking communities of Eastern Europe beyond hope of recovery. The remnants were largely mopped up as a result of anti-semitic policies in the Soviet Union, assimilation in America, and the anti-Yiddish policies of the State of Israel, extending to a complete ban on education and publication in that language. Today, except in various research institutes, the only home and hope of Yiddish is among the Hasidim of the world – a singular irony, in view of the mutual contempt of the Hasidim and the secular Yiddishists of the past, although Hasidim also has an extensive, albeit deeply traditionalist literature in the form of its religious tales and proverbs. In Western Europe, the lack of a Jewish colloquial language was of course a key factor in assimilation. The contrast with Eastern Europe in the past was emphasised in a conversation between a Lithuanian friend and some French Jews. They criticised her sharply for describing the Jews of France as a 'nationality'. Her response was one of pure bewilderment: 'but the Jews in Lithuania call themselves a nationality!' The possession of their own everyday language, and quite different national culture and traditions (based on, but extending much further than 'religion') made this a natural position to take; and the approach of many Yiddishists, as well as Zionists, was based on this assumption.

18 Czeslaw Milosz, *The Issa Valley* (London, 1974), pp. 6–7: 'The Issa Valley has the distinction of being inhabited by an unusually large number of devils.... Those who have seen them say that the devil is rather short, about the size of a nine-year-old; that he wears a green frock

coat, a jabot, his hair in a pigtail, and tries to conceal his hoofs, which are an embarrassment to him, with high-heeled slippers. Such tales should be treated with a certain caution. It is possible that, knowing the superstitious awe in which the Germans are held – they being people of commerce, inventions and science – the devils seek to lend themselves an air of gravity by dressing up in the manner of Immanuel Kant of Koenigsberg. It's no coincidence that along the Issa another word for the Evil Spirit is the "Little German", implying that the devil is on the side of progress.' Milosz goes on to talk of the mixture of Christian devils with pre-Christian pagan spirits: 'Are the devils and those other creatures joined in a pact, or do they simply exist side by side, like the jay, the sparrow and the crow?'.

19 Violeta Kelertas, 'The National Image of the German in Recent Soviet Lithuanian Fiction', *JBS*, X, 4, 1979.

20 I am indebted to Dr Saulius Suziedelis for introducing me to this subject.

21 See Strazhas, op.cit., p.180, for Jewish-Lithuanian statistics, 1920–40.

22 Nancy and Stuart Schoenburg, *Lithuanian Jewish Communities* (New York, 1991), p.4. Only six pages, all of them biased and highly superficial, are devoted to the Lithuanian people amongst whom the Jews lived for 500 years.

23 Interview, 18 May 1992. The 'Mother Goose' remark, I realised later, is a reference to a work by Oskar Milosz, the first to introduce Lithuanian folklore to a French audience. Despite its dismissive tone, it is therefore a back-handed tribute to Zingeris' knowledge of the Lithuanian literary tradition. See Christopher Bamford (ed), *The Noble Traveller: The Life and Writings of O.V. de L. Milosz* (London, 1985).

24 Quoted in Lucy S. Dawidowicz (ed), *The Golden Tradition: Jewish Life and*

Thought in Eastern Europe (New York, 1967), p.157.

25 Milosz, *Native Realm*, p.93.

26 Interview, 11 May 1992.

27 The good behaviour of German troops in the First World War also persuaded many Jews in June 1941 that it would be safer to stay than to run the risks of joining the Soviet retreat.

28 Interview, 11 May 1992.

29 Harry Gordon, *The Holocaust in Lithuania* (Kentucky, 1992), p.16. For a national reversal of roles, see the impact of the Napoleonic invasion of Russia on Russia's subject Poles in *Pan Tadeusz* (New York, 1982), translated by Watson Kirkconnell, Part 1, p.311 ff.

30 Interview, 13 May 1992.

31 Dr Štromas' lecture was delivered at Assumption College on 10 April 1989 as the annual Rabbi Klein lecture, and was printed as part of this series.

32 Sylva Darel, *A Sparrow in the Snow* (New York, 1973), a memoir by a young Latvian-Jewish girl whose family was deported in June 1941, gives an account of this experience and their lives in Siberia.

33 The interview with Dr Sužiedelis (of Millersville University, Pennsylvania), from which this passage is taken was published in the Lithuanian journal *Akiraciai*, 10, 234, November 1991. For German attempts to influence the Voldemaras-led opposition to Smetona, and to spread anti-semitism in Lithuania, see the German documents quoted in Romuald Misiunas, 'Fascist Tendencies in Lithuania', *Slavic and East European Review*, January 1970, pp. 107–108.

34 Avraham Tory, *Surviving the Holocaust: The Kovno Ghetto Diary* (London, 1990), p.13 (diary entry for 8 July 1941). Jonas Matulionis's memoirs, *Neramios Dienos* ('Unquiet Days'), were published in Toronto in 1975. This statement does not appear. In the pages dealing with 1941, Matulionis skates as quickly as possible over what was happening to the Jews of Kaunas, and without giving any of the concrete details, which must have been perfectly well known to him. On page 18 he claims to have forgotten what order was given by the provisional government when a 'partisan commander' (his inverted commas) came to them and said that the Germans had ordered him to shoot Jews. The longest passage concerning the Jews describes a German demand for the transfer of confiscated Jewish bank accounts (p.26).

35 'Recollection of Prisoner No.82336', a privately published memoir by Woldemar Ginzburg, p.7. In an interview on 28 April 1990, Shmuel Kaplinksy, a former partisan who escaped from the Vilna Ghetto to fight in the forests, described his experiences. He retains a strong loyalty to the Soviet Union and its army which had rescued him and the remnants of his community from extinction.

36 'Knight of the Ghetto', a privately published memoir by Joseph (Lord) Kagan, p.10. See also 'Memoirs of Samuel Esterowicz' (in collaboration with Pearl Esterowicz Good). He writes extensively of autonomous Lithuanian involvement in the Holocaust, and of the anti-semitism of the Lithuanian authorities who took over in Vilna in October 1939. However, he also admits (p.225) that compared to Poland, there had been no really militant anti-semitism in pre-war Lithuania.

37 Interview, 29 December 1991. After the massacre by the Lithuanian 12th Auxiliary Service battalion in Slutzk, Byelorussia, on 27 October 1941, the town's German commandant wrote to his superiors condemning the unit's 'indescribable brutality' and begging, 'in future, keep this battalion away from me'. See the report in

The Times, 18 July 1992, of the unsuccessful libel case brought by
Antanas Gecas, a lieutenant in the
battalion, against Scottish Television.

38 Antanas Papsys, *Vilnius: A Guide*
(Moscow, 1981).

39 This Jewish ignorance of Judaism
has gone so far in Russia that in St
Petersburg, many ordinary non-
religious Jews are under the
impression that the US-based Luba-
vitcher Hasidim, who seem to be
taking over the main synagogue, are
simply normal Orthodox Jews – a
confusion which would not have
pleased the Gaon!

40 Jeffrey Ross, 'Interethnic Relations
and Jewish Marginality in the Soviet
Baltic', *JBS*, IX, 4, 1978.

41 Zvi Segal, 'Jewish Minorities in the
Baltic Republics in the Postwar
Years', in *Regional Identity Under Soviet
Rule*, op.cit. p.227.

42 The articles in *The New York Times*
appeared on 5, 8 and 10 September
1991.

43 Jean Cathala, *Sans Fleur, ni Fusil*
(Paris, 1981). In 1940, Cathala was a
teacher with the Alliance Française
in Tallinn. For an account by a
French teacher in Lithuania of the
Soviet occupation there, see Georges
Matore, *Mes Prisons en Lituanie*
(Boulogne, 1991). Concerning Lith-
uanian-Jewish relations, Matore's
account is interesting as that of a
neutral observer (who, however, sheltered Jewish friends from the Nazis
and was arrested by the Gestapo on
suspicion of doing so). On the pre-
war period, he remarks on the failure
of many Jews to learn Lithuanian: 'I
understood later that the Lithuanians were irritated by the contempt
shown by some Jews for the Lithuanian language, of which they were so
proud' (p.25). This was also criticised by Rosenblatt (Rozenblatas), a
Jewish lawyer with whom Matore
shared an NKVD prison cell, and
who was later forced by the Nazis to

accept a place in the administration
of the Vilna Ghetto (p.133). Matore
comments on the lack of anti-semitism in Lithuania before the war,
and says that 'the great majority of
Lithuanians' showed a 'lively sympathy' for the fate of the Jews –
something which does appear to
have been true of his own milieu at
Vilnius University, several of whom
helped Jews, but hardly more
generally (pp. 200, 214).

44 Tadeusz Konwicki, *A Modern Dream-
Book* (London, 1978). For a discussion of the role of the borderlands in
contemporary Polish literature, see
Daniel Beauvois (ed), *Les Confins de
l'Ancienne Pologne* (Lille, 1988). For
Polish-Lithuanian developments up
to 1991, see Stephen R. Burant,
'Polish-Lithuanian Relations: Past,
Present and Future', in *Problems of
Communism*, May–June 1991. These
themes are repeatedly touched on by
Czeslaw Milosz in Ewa Czarnecka
and Aleksandr Fiut (eds), *Conversa-
tions with Czeslaw Milosz* (London,
1987), pp. 3–58, 163–73, 193–200.

45 Beauvois, op.cit., p.253.

46 Interview, 24 March 1990.

47 This literature has from its very
beginning been overwhelmingly
dominated by the nobility. A Pole of
today, looking back at the 'Kresy',
the old borderlands, does so through
the eyes of noble writers, from Mickiewicz to Milosz, and their mainly
noble protagonists. I have sometimes wondered whether the lack of
sympathy shown by most of the
Polish intelligentsia for the predica-
ment of their compatriots in
Lithuania does not stem in part from
the painful contrast between the
reality of a population made up of
'Sons of Ham', uneducated and
rather Sovietised proletarians, and
the glorious world of Polish Lithuanian literature. If the Lithuanian
Poles of today were led by the descendants of Pan Tadeusz Soplica
and Pan Casimir Surkont, rather

than those of their peasants, the White Eagle might have flown a great deal more swiftly to their aid.

48 Interview, 30 May 1992.

49 See the discussion between Milosz and Venclova printed in *Odra*, 1, 1991.

50 *Pan Tadeusz*, op.cit. p.7.

51 *Native Realm*, pp.21–31.

52 Interview, 14 February 1990. Czeslaw Milosz has discussed the conflicting Lithuanian and Polish memories of the war between the Home Army and the Nazis' Lithuanian auxiliaries in an interview published in the *Pays Baltes* volume of the 'Autrement' series, ed. Yves Plasseraud (Paris, 1991), pp.178–88.

53 Interview, 15 February 1990.

54 *The Baltic States: a Reference Book*, published by the Estonian, Latvian and Lithuanian Encyclopaedia Publishers (Tallinn-Riga-Vilnius, 1991), p.176.

55 Interview, 13 June 1992.

56 Interview, 18 May 1992.

57 Interview, 27 March 1990. See also the interview with the Polish Ambassador to Lithuania in *Posicija*, 14 August 1992.

58 Interview, 13 August 1992. Okinczyc told me that '80 per cent of the symbolic war from the Polish side comes from ZCHN'. This of course marks a crucial difference from the Lithuanian side, where in 1990–92 it was the government itself, and the state newspaper, that were responsible for much of the anti-Polish propaganda.

59 Author's notes, 22 May 1991. Even so, I did not discount the risk of Polish rebellion altogether; I had recently returned from an even more decayed dump in South Ossetia, which had nonetheless succeeded in generating a vicious little civil war; and just across the border from Mosciszki is Belarus.

60 Wysocki's personal involvement in the actions against the border posts, had there been any doubt about it,

would appear certain from an interview that he gave to me on 3 April 1991. Wysocki had the manner of a truck driver in a bar, banging the table with his fist and shouting that a clause in the Lithuanian law provided for the execution of those who offended against the constitution, which is, of course, nonsense. The office opposite Wysocki's was occupied by his deputy, Leon Jakielewicz, a Communist Supreme Council deputy who was elected on a Soviet loyalist ticket, but who from January 1991, under pressure from his Polish colleagues, had publicly supported independence – and was mightily abused by Wysocki as a result. If Wysocki represented perhaps the most stupid side of Soviet loyalist politics, Jankielewicz exemplified the *apparachik* trying to keep his head above water in troubled times. He put me in mind not so much of a miserable little rat (as he was described to me by a Lithuanian nationalist), but a miserable little mouse, fallen into the workings of a historical clock and in imminent danger of being crushed. Some of his statements evoked sympathy, if not admiration. Thus, when I asked him why he did not go out and try to persuade his constituents of the need for independence, he replied, 'but they would throw things at me!'.

61 Kobeckaite's remarks were made at a seminar organised by the Information Office of the Lithuanian Parliament, 12 May 1992.

62 Joseph Rothschild, *East Central Europe between the Two World Wars* (Seattle and London), p.377.

63 Burant, op.cit., pp.83–4.

64 It is especially depressing to compare the sheer pettiness of Lithuanian official attitudes in 1990–92 with Lithuanian self-images such as that presented by Landsbergis in a taped address to Yale and Weber Universities in acknowledgement of honorary doctorates

awarded to him: 'Lithuania has defended a universal principle, an essential truth: the rights of all men and of all peoples. In a pragmatic world, concerned with state contacts and interests, she [Lithuania] represents the ideal of rights and liberties. One may say that Lithuania has contributed to the improvement of the world, but she has never been sufficiently supported by others. An idealist does what his ideal demands . . . the life of the soul is more precious than that of the body.' (*Lietuvos Aidas*, 15 August 1992).

7 The Baltic Russians

1 Author's notes, 25 February 1992.
2 Thus a Russian intellectual friend in St Petersburg, although she hated Communism and is deeply attached to Russian classical culture, is so distant from the Russian imperial tradition that in 1990 she did not even recognise the pre-1917 Russian military ensign, the Andreyevsky flag – and this although her father had been a Soviet naval officer. Such a failure to recognise a key pre-Soviet national symbol would have been out of the question for any oppositionist intellectual in the other republics of the Western Soviet Union, with the exception of Byelorussia.
3 Interview, 16 March 1992.
4 Opinion poll carried out by the Latvian Social Research Centre, December 1991.
5 Latvian census, 1990, published by the Latvian Statistical Department.
6 Interview, 21 October 1991.
7 From an article by Nikolai Volynsky, *Pravda*, 4 June 1992.
8 My own very sketchy opinion polls in St Petersburg suggest that in that city, as of summer 1992, less than 5 per cent of the population was attached to the whole gamut of neo-

imperialist ideas, though of course a very much larger proportion resented other nationalities and their treatment of Russians, and tended to put concern for a strong Russia above belief in democracy.
9 A Russian position paper acquired and published by Estonian politicians in June 1992 describes such 'nearby countries' as 'ours', and calls for Estonia to participate in a 'joint army' (c.f. *Baltic Independent*, 12–18 June 1992). The Foreign Affairs Committee of the Russian Parliament declared in October 1992 that 'Russian foreign policy must be based on a doctrine that proclaims the entire geographical space of the former Union a sphere of vital interests. . . . Russia must secure the role of political and military guarantor of stability on all the territory of the former USSR'. (c.f. *The Economist*, 14 November 1992). In March 1993, Yeltsin called for the UN to accord Russia a peacekeeping role throughout the former Union. This marked a major shift in the discretion of moderate Russian conservatives like Civic Union and Yergeny Ambartsumov, who have long advocated such a 'Monroe Doctrine' for Russia. According to a Western diplomatic source, Russian Foreign Ministry internal papers 'harp a great deal' on the need for access to the Baltic ports. In his view, part of the problem is that – like other European empires in the past – 'the Russians still think that to have access to a place you have to control it militarily'. One problem is, however, that many of the policies of the other successor states of the Soviet Union have an unfortunate way of confirming that belief.
10 The Russian military support for Ossetia is a case which may have certain parallels with the particular support of the British military before 1922 for the Ulster Protestants, who provided so much of the British

officer corps. According to the commander of the North Ossete Republican Guard, (himself a retired Soviet Major-General and Afghan veteran), Ossetes have, in proportion to their population, also provided a higher number of Soviet generals, and a higher number of soldiers decorated for courage than any other nationality in the Union, Russians included. Ever since the eighteenth century, they were Russian auxiliaries in the wars against Muslim peoples. They therefore have a certain built-in ability to gain sympathy in the officer corps.

11   c.f. Roman Szporluk, 'Dilemmas of Russian Nationalism', in *Problems of Communism*, July–August 1989, pp. 15–35: 'It would seem imperative for the liberal and democratic Russian intelligentsia to make sure that the spec. national or nationalist Russian concerns and issues are not left to extremists of the Pamyat kind.' In terms of practical political appeal, these concerns and issues include the fate of the Russian minorities 'abroad'.

12   I have only met one descendant of an Old Believer family who was a Communist Party official (Mikhail Alexeyev, secretary at the big Vilma factory in Vilnius), and he was soon sacked, apparently for being too moderate. One of the hardline Comunist leaders in Latvia, Anatoly Alexeyev – no relation – is descended from an old merchant family in Riga.

13   c.f. Stephen D. Corrsin, 'The Changing Composition of the City of Riga, 1867–1913', *JBS*, XIII,1,87. See also Wilfried Schlau, 'An Assessment of Demographic Development in the Baltic States', in Dietrich Andre Loeber *et al.* (eds), *Regional Identity under Soviet Rule: the Case of the Baltic States* (University of Kiel, 1990). Gert von Pistohlkors includes figures for Baltic demography 1913–40 in his 'Estland, Lettland und Litauen, 1920–1940', published in the series *Handbuch der europaische Wirtschafts- und Sozialgeschichte.*

14   c.f.Temira Pachmuss, *Russian Literature in the Baltic Between the World Wars* (Slavica Publishers, 1988), pp. 13–57. It is striking to note that despite the enormous expansion of the Russian community in Estonia through immigration under Soviet rule, Communist policy of avoiding 'unnecessary' provocation of the Balts meant that no such grand celebration has occurred in recent decades.

15   On 23 June 1991, during an attempted Interfront strike in Tallinn, I interviewed an elderly lady in the trawler repair yard, whose parents were arrested during the War by Latvian auxiliary police and subsequently executed; she was quite clearly being used by the Communist officials to stir up the other workers. Communists were also spreading stories that 'ten thousand machine-guns have been bought by the Estonian volunteers' and 'The Tallinn City Council is planning to bulldoze a Russian cemetery'.

16   Figures, based on the Soviet census, in Jan Ake Dellenbrant, *JBS*, XVIII, 3, 87. Extensive material on Baltic demography under Soviet rule is also to be found in Misiunas and Taagepera, op.cit., and Toivo Raun, op.cit..

17   An even more bitter Estonian anecdote (which might even be true) concerns a conversation between two Russian women in a shop queue in Tallinn. One asks the other, 'Tell me, when did the Estonians emerge here? Was it before or after the Revolution?'

18   *Atmoda*, 12, 28 February 1991.

19   Figures are from the Latvian SSR Statistical Committee's report for 1989.

20   This analysis is based on my work in the Baltic States, 1990–92, and various interviews with most of the figures mentioned.

21   Interview, 17 March 1992.

22 A very similar character to Viktors Alksnis is Colonel Kasparavičius, the military intelligence officer appointed to run the Soviet propaganda station established after the seizure of the Lithuanian television facilities in January 1991. He is a highly intelligent man, but one whose brain, nationality, and even personality, have become completely subsumed in his identity as an officer and loyalty to the army and the imperial power.

23 To describe Juozas Jarmolavičius (the Ideology Secretary of the Soviet Communist Party in Lithuania, 1990–91) as bull-headed has an unusual accuracy: his eyes are practically hidden by thick overhanging protuberances not of fat but of solid bone – a truly pithecanthropoid sight. After a year of silence, Jarmolavicius emerged in Moscow in October 1992, publishing in *Pravda* a viciously anti-Baltic and anti-American article. A press conference given by the 'Night Party' (as the rump pro-Soviet Lithuanian Party was dubbed because it was created rapidly one night after the majority of the Lithuanian Party had split from the Soviet one) before the Soviet referendum of March 1991 was a sort of preview of the pitiful performance of Yanayev and his co-plotters in front of the Moscow television cameras during the coup. Jarmolavicius and the other participants sweated, stumbled, and contradicted themselves and each other, while the hopelessly inadequate English interpreter (obviously the best they could find) begged them pathetically not to speak so fast. (Author's notes, 16 March 1991.)

24 One good reason for present Baltic mistrust of Russian television is that it uses so many of the same people who in the past were responsible for Soviet misinformation about the Baltic States; for example Sergei Medvedev, now a presenter of the main *Novosti* news programme, who after the Lithuanian declaration of independence provided a series of extremely slanted reports for *Novosti's* predecessor, the then *Vremya* programme. However, Russian television in 1990–91 helped the Balts. I wrote in the spring of 1990, after the declaration of Lithuanian independence, that the struggle in Leningrad to wrest the local television station from Communist control might mark the first sign of really useful help to the Balts from democrats in Russia, simply because so many Baltic Russians watch that station.

25 On 27 August 1991, Dainis Īvāns, the Latvian Vice-Chairman and former Popular Front leader, said that, 'The official language is Latvian and all official bodies must be able to use Latvian, [but] in effect, we may return to the principles of independent Latvia, where to function properly you needed to know three languages.... Local authorities in areas with Russian majorities will be able to deal with the language question in ways appropriate to these areas'. Before the declaration of Latvian sovereignty in May 1990, Īvāns criticised the Latvian language law as giving too short a time for learning.

26 c.f. Steve Crawshaw, *Goodbye to the USSR* (London, 1992), p. 45; Walter C. Clemens, *Baltic Independence and Russian Empire* (London, 1991), p. 156; Thomas H. Ilves, 'The Intermovement in Estonia', in Jānis Arveds Trapāns (ed), *Toward Independence: the Baltic Popular Movements* (Westview Press, 1991).

27 c.f. Clemens, op.cit.,p.165. Reporting only to their ministries in Moscow, these factories were insulated from local government influence. In the cases of military industrial plants, the Baltic governments did not even know

exactly what was being produced there. In May 1990, I asked Vladimir Yarovoi what his 'Dvigatel' produced, 'if that isn't a secret'. 'Pick-up trucks', he replied. 'Just pick-up trucks?' 'Pick-up trucks and ... er ... twine. You know, twine – for doing up parcels with.' Later, as everyone had suspected, it turned out to be producing parts for Soviet atomic reactors.

28 Figures published by the Baltic election commissions.

29 Author's notes, 28 January 1991.

30 Author's notes, 15 May 1990. That evening, I rang up a colleague then in Tallinn, Anna Pukas from *The Daily Mail*. I was furious that I had missed the 'attempted coup'. She just laughed, and said that she had been about to say the same to me, because nothing very serious had happened in Tallinn either. She added that Lysenko had seemed the one intent on stirring up the crowd, while Yarovoi looked as if he was alarmed by what was happening, and was trying to hold them back.

31 The fact that no such properly trained, properly equipped anti-riot force had existed before (the MVD troops were not really trained for the purpose) is a sign of just how unprepared the Soviet state was to face such unrest, simply because it had so little experience of it. Faced with serious trouble, the old-fashioned solution had always been to call in the army. Indeed, if the Soviet Union had possessed a large force of gendarmerie with tear gas and water cannon, it seems likely that on 13 January 1991 the television tower and station in Vilnius could have been stormed without loss of life. The use of brutalised, often drunken paratroopers equipped only with loaded automatic weapons and souped up with propaganda about the 'Lithuanian fascists' was almost bound to lead to killings, even if it was not the deliberate plan of the men who gave the orders.

32 This rather curious figure, whose thin, educated-looking face was totally out of keeping with his job, had indeed once wanted to be an actor. There was about Makutinowicz's involvement something of the air of a small actor trying to play a big melodramatic role, as could be seen only too clearly in the odious film made about him and his men in January 1991 by the hardline Soviet (now Russian neo-fascist) television star, Alexander Nevzorov, who over the next few months was to become the chief OMON propagandist. Nevzorov was subsequently the author of a piece of Latvian OMON propaganda concerning an alleged Latvian ambush of himself and the OMON commander, Czeslaw Mlynik (the second time, incidentally, that Nevzorov had miraculously survived an assassination attempt to which there were no independent witnesses. A sign of the sheer lack of imagination on the part of the Soviet hardliners is that not content with this, in April 1991 they alleged yet *another* assassination attempt on Mlynik – once again, without witnesses).

Mlynik, like Makutinowicz, is a Baltic Pole, but otherwise a very different character. Small and thickset, with a small head, a moustache and an expression of cheerful brutality, he is anyone's idea of a military police corporal. He and some of his men were reputed subsequently to be fighting in Trans-Dniestria. (Both the Lithuanian and Latvian OMON were withdrawn from the republics in the aftermath of the August coup, in which they played a leading part, and Russia thereafter resisted demands for their extradition to the Baltic States. Mlynik's deputy, Sergejs Parfyonov, was imprisoned in Riga.) OMON was thus an early example of the kind of semi-autonomous paramilitary groups which are becoming increasingly common across the former Union.

33 The stories which have gown up around this supposed 'Third Force' are a fascinating example of the power of rumour in post-totalitarian societies. These rumours have been fuelled by the slowness of the Latvian procuracy in publishing a report on the events, but are completely un-supported by hard evidence. No-one has seen any of the 'Third Force' personally; they have always talked to someone else who did. Serious, knowledgeable people have told me that 'OMON cannot have done it, because the people killed were more than two hundred yards away, and a bullet cannot travel that far'. Many allege that the cameramen killed were shot from behind, though their colleagues who were with them have never said anything of the sort. What is truly astonishing though is that according to one Latvian teacher, a considerable number of ordinary Latvians, including students, are ap-parently prepared to believe that not a Soviet, but a Latvian nationalist third force set out to provoke OMON in order to generate killings to rally national and international support. This was also true of some educated (and certainly not pro-Soviet) Lithuanians after the killings of the Lithuanian borderguards at Medininkai the following August. I myself, on the basis of personal knowledge of the Lithuanian and Latvian leaderships, do not believe this for a moment, and nor does any other Western observer of my acquaintance – but it is a striking example of the deep sediment of cyn-icism and detachment bequeathed by Soviet rule, and lying under the apparently united surface of Baltic support for the national movements.

34 Report of the Lithuanian Procuracy, May 1992.

35 Interviews with author, 1 March 1991.

36 I attended the second Conference of the Russian Society of Latvia (ROL) in Riga on 19 December 1991, with-out being very impressed. Many of the speakers complained of lack of interest, commitment and contribu-tions from the Russian community. Their approach, however, seemed sober and practical, in sharp contrast to the extremist language of some of their founders (like Colonel Romashov) before the August Counter-revolution, the effects of which were still to be seen in their hesitant and moderate approach. In August 1992 I visited the branch of the Society in Daugavpils. Positions had hardened, but this group of mainly elderly men was still not very formidable; in fact, I suspected it was rather more of a club, and that as soon as I left a bottle of vodka and a pack of cards would appear. More-over, although ordinary Russians in the town had heard of the Society, they knew very little about it, pre-ferring simply to grumble about their living standards. An intriguing sign of current Russian hesitation be-tween traditional Russian national-ism (which is increasingly the ideology of the Society), and looking Westwards, is the name, the *Duna-burg News*, given to the Society-backed paper in Daugavpils. I asked why they had taken the old German name of the town, instead of the Russian name of 'Dvinsk'. The editor explained they did not want to choose a name that would divide the different nationalities, and that Dvinsk had been its name for only 150 years under Russian imperial rule. From the back, a voice mut-tered, 'Besides, the way things are, no harm in being nice to the Ger-mans, is there?

37 For example, the Soviet garrison commander in Marijampole, Lith-uania (a paratroop officer, indeed), announced on the first day of the coup that he was taking over control of the local government – and pro-ceeded to do absolutely nothing.

Even Colonel Chernykh in Klaipeda, (now charged with participation in the coup by the Lithuanian Procuracy) though he undoubtedly passed on the orders and threats of the new regime, did nothing practical to seize control of the town.

38 The Shield Report was presented to the Lithuanian parliament by Captain (retd.) Alexander Yevstigneyev and his colleagues on 12 February 1991.

39 c.f. the statement by the Officers' Association, 17 December 1991.

40 I was shown the CFE figures at the Symposium of the North Atlantic assembly in Vilnius, 16 December 1991. The recommendations of the Symposium were that Russia should begin withdrawal immediately, and cease sending further conscripts, but that the Balts should accept a status of forces agreement for the withdrawal period.

41 Author's notes, St Petersburg, December 1991.

42 c.f. the report from Tallinn by the AFP correspondent, Stephane Bentura, on 9 August 1992.

43 For a picture of the Kaliningrad Enclave, see this chapter below.

44 Interview, 3 August 1992.

45 Interview, 16 May 1992.

46 See the report of the 'Baltic Security Council', sponsored by the RFE/RL Research Institute and held in Schloss Leopoldskron, Salzburg, 5–7 October 1992. See also *Die Zeit*, November 1991, and the article by Ruth Kibelka in the *Baltic Independent*, 9 October 1992, and that by Matthias Luefkens on 10 April 1992; for the end of East Prussia in 1945, see Countess Doenhoff, *Namen die Keiner Mehr Nennt*.

8   *The Independence Movements and their Successors, 1987–92*

1 *The Baltic Observer*, 2–8 July 1992.

2 Expression was given to this idea of a 'Third Way' in a press conference of the National Progress faction on 21 August 1992.

3 This section is based on my interviews with participants, on information provided by the Radio Liberty/Radio Free Europe bulletins, and on research papers about the Baltic; from the reports of the BBC monitoring service, Caversham; from documents included in the collection *Restoration of the Independence of the Republic of Estonia: Selection of Legal Acts, 1988–91*, and in Latvian and Lithuanian official publications; from the newspapers *Gimtasas Krastas* and *Tiesa* (Lithuania), *Rahva Hääl*, *Homeland* (English), *Sovietskaya Estonia* (Estonia) and *Atmoda* (Latvia), as well as Western press reports, especially from *The Times* and *Financial Times*; and from the books: Claire Thomson, *The Singing Revolution* (London, 1991); Walter C. Clemens, *Baltic Independence and Russian Empire* (London, 1991); Marianna Butenschoen, *Estland, Lettland, Litauen* (Berlin, 1992); Jānis Arveds Trapāns (ed) *Towards Independence: The Baltic Popular Movements* (Boulder, 1991), and Alfred Erich Senn, *Lithuania Awakening* (Los Angeles, 1990). See also the essays on the Baltic States in the now sadly defunct *Problems of Communism*, 1988–90.

4 The term 'calendar demonstrations', was taken from the religious struggles of the sixteenth century in Riga, when every major religious festival would be marked by mass Protestant demonstrations against the still dominant Catholic hierarchy and ritual.

5 Yakovlev was speaking on the BBC television series, 'The Second Russian Revolution', programme 5: 'Breaking Ranks'.

6 The then KGB commander in Lithuania, Major-General Marcinkus, has described this idea as a joke. 'Accepting it, one would have to believe that the KGB had an interest

in ruining the USSR'. However, General Marcinkus himself withdrew from the KGB in protest at the killings in January 1991, showing that by then, at least, the KGB itself was not immune to national feeling, and that many of its members were already hedging their bets.

7 Interview with Professor Vilkas, 23 August 1992. The founding meeting of Sajūdis is also described in Senn, op.cit. pp. 58–60. Dr Senn was himself present at the meeting. See also Kazimiera Prunskiene, *Ein Leben fur Litauen* (Ullstein, 1992), pp. 39–40.

8 In all three republics, the Ideology Secretaries, supposedly the mainstays of Marxist-Leninist purity, ended up in the forefront of the reformist sections of the Party – presumably because, by the nature of their function, they needed to be more intelligent and aware than the bulk of their colleagues. The last Ideology Secretary of the Estonian Party, Mikk Tittmaa, later became a visiting Professor in the United States.

9 c.f. John Lloyd's article in the *Financial Times*, 8 May 1989.

10 For example, even as Sajūdis was winning a smashing electoral victory over the Communists in Spring 1989, opinion polls carried out by the Academy of Sciences showed that Brazauskas was the most popular politician, with 84 points, while Landsbergis polled only 70. Sajudis however had 68 points to the Communist Party's 22 (*Komjaunimos Tiesa*, 16 June 1989). For a somewhat anodyne version of his life and political career, see Brazauskas' autobiography, *Lithuanian Divorce*, published in Vilnius in 1992. He takes great delight in quoting statements by Landsbergis during the period 1988–89 praising him and offering support. The photographs have evidently been selected to make Landsbergis, beside Brazauskas and Prunskiene, appear small and insignificant. This is fair enough,

however, since when Landsbergis was in power, photographs in official publications were carefully selected to omit Brazauskas and any other of Landsbergis' opponents.

11 The family may in fact be of German origin; as to the Jewish charge, it is simply a staple Lithuanian insult, much as it is among many Russians. It is made privately even by people on the Left and Centre of Lithuanian politics. See the interview with Landsbergis in *Valstieču Laikrastis*, 16 May 1992.

12 The speech is in Sajūdis records.

13 For the Lithuanian election results, see *The Lithuanian Review*, 2 March 1990.

14 This account is based on my own notes, subsequent interviews with leading participants, and an account by Rūta Grineviciiute in the newspaper *Lietuvos Rytas*, on the second anniversary of the independence declaration. For a detailed picture of day-by-day developments in Lithuania and the other republics, see *The Times*, February–June 1990, and the issue of 3 April 1990 for a picture of the divisions within Lithuania. Longer accounts by myself are to be found in *The Tablet* (17 February 1990) and *Encounter* (May and October 1990). For a portrayal of the actual declaration of independence, see *The Times*, 12 March 1990.

15 Interview, 23 August 1992.

16 The declaration was followed over the next few days by a series of laws on taking control of military installations, nationalisation of Soviet property in the republic and so on. Many of these, however, could only be implemented after the collapse of Soviet control following the August coup. The formation of the government is described in Prunskiene, op.cit., pp. 84–96. She was unable to appoint Justas Paleckis, a reformist Communist and son of the first Communist Chairman in Soviet Lithuania, as her Foreign Minister,

despite (or rather because of) his Soviet diplomatic experience. Instead she was forced to accept Algirdas Saudargas from the Kaunas Faction. Prunskiene did, however, get her own way in re-appointing General Marijonas Misiukonis as her Interior Minister. A less happy re-appointment was that of Romualdas Sikorskis as Finance Minister. During the debate on the formation of the government, Andrikiene (who had been Prunskiene's assistant and was furious at not having been given a government place) jumped up and angrily pointed out that as a junior official in the 1940s, Sikorskis had been responsible for seizing the property of some of those who, like Andrikiene's parents, were being deported to Siberia. Prunskiene defended him as an expert and one whose knowledge of dealing with Moscow would be indispensable in negotiations.

17 In late March I interviewed two Lithuanian deserters from an infantry unit on the Iranian border who had made their way back across the Soviet Union with the help of the Azeri Popular Front. Looking for them and the other deserters was an exceptionally unhappy Lithuanian Major in the Soviet army, who described his dilemma in words that I heard echoed in 1990–91 by officers from several Soviet nationalities: 'I have been ordered to come here, and as an officer I must obey orders. The Soviet army has been my whole life, and besides I am not a young man any more. I am not against Lithuania, and I certainly don't want to fight anyone . . . I just want to serve quietly to retirement and collect my pension.' One of the first acts of the new Lithuanian Supreme Council had been to declare conscription into the Soviet Army illegal on Lithuanian soil. This was necessitated both by the declaration of independence and by the passionate hostility to

military service caused by the terrible conditions in the Soviet Army. The Supreme Council's encouragement of serving Lithuanians to desert, when it was in no position to protect them, has been widely criticised. In the case of the concentration of some 40 deserters at the clinic, it has even been suggested that the intention was to make martyrs of them. It was certainly most unwise. Their pathetic faith in the Lithuanian Red Cross proved of course no defence, and on 27 March the clinic was raided. Twenty-eight of the youths were sent to a unit stationed at Anadyr, in north-east Siberia.

18 The interminable wrangling over the moratorium proposal was recorded in my own notes and in Prunskiene, op.cit., pp.126–142.

19 Interview, 15 April 1990.

20 Interview, 3 May 1990.

21 This account of the process leading to the Latvian declaration is taken from my own notes. See also *The Times*, 5 May 1990.

22 This section is mainly based on my own notes and eyewitness accounts. For the Shield report on the military intervention, see *BNS*, 14 February 1991.

23 This section is again based on my own notes and interviews; on the bulletins of the Sakala Centre; on the research reports of RFE/RL; on official publications by the Information Office (later Office of Public Affairs) of the Lithuanian parliament; on the semi-official government publication *Eastern Express*; and on various newspapers, above all *Lietuvos Aidas* (Lithuanian Echo), *Lietuvos Rytas* (Lithuanian Morning), *Respublika* and *Tiesa*.

24 Landsbergis' new unofficial (but very visible) status was manifested, early in the Sajūdis government, by the creation of what were called 'parliamentary guards', but which have in fact formed a Presidential bodyguard which seeks to turn itself into a

Praetorian Guard. It was organised by Arturas Skučas, a Kaunas radical and Sajūdis founder who in contrast to many of the Kaunasites has attached himself unconditionally to Landsbergis. With the help of a $1 million grant from the Vagnorius government, and various dealings on the international arms market, he was able to equip them with Uzi submachine guns and American-made rocket-launchers. The original force was recruited from a nationalist sports club in Kaunas. These 'sports clubs' have an unsavoury reputation in the former Soviet Union, and opponents of Landsbergis have made all kinds of allegations about this one in particular. While some of the bodyguards are both educated and apparently reasonable people, said to despise the extremism and paranoia of Skučas, others have a strikingly thuggish appearance. As time went on, more and more ministers surrounded themselves with such bodyguards, more it seemed as a sign of importance than from fear of attack, and they remained to the end of the Sajūdis government.

25 The Future Forum, though Brazauskas-backed, was a disparate group held together by passionate loathing for Landsbergis and the Kaunasites, and such mass support as it achieved was powered largely by growing economic discontent. Its programme stressed opposition to the 'threat of a Landsbergis dictatorship', the need for pro-Western economic reform without nationalist constraints, and above all the need for reasonable negotiations with Moscow, which at the time of the Forum's foundation appeared hopelessly stalled. Much of the Right-wing violence suffered by the Forum stemmed from Terleckas' Liberty League, then moving closer to Landsbergis and Sajūdis (which, only two years previously, Terleckas had been denouncing as a Communist front organisation). Landsbergis

denounced the violence in general terms, but did nothing to try to stop it. In any case, the Forum did not last long, vanishing without trace after the achievement of independence in August 1991.

26 Opinion polls had widely given Sajūdis and the pro-Landsbergis Christian Democratic Party jointly between 25 and 30% of the vote: they actually received a total of 33.7% of the proportionate list votes (20.9% Sajūdis and Christian Democrats 12.4%). The polls had also, however, been agreed in giving the LDDP 20–25%, whereas they received almost twice that (44.4%, and even more if the votes for individual candididates are included).

27 A worrying exception to the boredom of the campaign was the campaign of Kazys Bobelis. My own interview with Bobelis suggested he was either completely unaware of or completely unconcerned about the darker sides of Lithuanian nationalism, despite the fact that his father, as Lithuanian commandant of Kaunas in the first weeks of German occupation in 1941, had had much opportunity to see this at work. Bobelis' total refusal to accept any Lithuanian responsibility for the Holocaust, though typical, is likely to discredit him and his country; it clashed with Brazauskas's apparent willingness to accept that wrongful rehabilitation of war-criminals had taken place. Bobelis also appeared to have no grasp whatsoever of economics, Western or Eastern. This makes it rather ironic that Bobelis' victory in Mariampole was due to the same factors which produced the phenomena of Colonel Juri Toomepuu in Estonia and Stan Tyminski in Poland: the prestige of being an 'American millionaire', and the belief that such a man might bring the magical secrets of Western economic success. It was due also however to Bobelis' American style

413

of campaigning. In a platform discussion with other candidates, he spoke in a loud, confident voice, making a series of clear, simple points. When he spoke of the need for moderation, he thumped his hand on the table. The contrast between this performance and the embarrassingly inadequate nature of his responses in a personal interview was a striking testimony to the power of technique over content.

28 One attempt was made by Sajūdis to use extra-democratic means to reduce the LDDP's seats, when the Central Election Commission, apparently under Sajūdis orders, declared that it would cancel the mandates of people shown to have worked with the KGB. The CEC was forced to reverse its decision after strong criticism from Western observers and a judgement by the Supreme Court. However, it reversed three LDDP victories on narrow recounts, and questioned several more, leading to protests and appeals from the LDDP. My suspicions of the CEC may be exaggerated; Western observers noticed only minor and technical infringments. My confidence was not, however, increased by the sight of the CEC Chairman, Vaclovas Litvinas, flattering Landsbergis at press conferences; and still less by a conversation I had with the election commissioner in Marijampole, who had been dismissing complaints by Social Democratic representatives in an extremely crude and authoritarian manner. I asked him how long he had been with the election commission. 'Since Stalin's day!' he replied proudly.

29 The best English-language source for Estonian politics in this period is *The Estonian Independent* (later *The Baltic Independent*). *Estonia Magazine* (formerly *The Tallinn City Paper*) has longer articles and excellent portrayals of the mood and social atmosphere in Estonia in 1992–93.

The essays by Riina Kionka in the RFE/RL bulletins are also highly useful. Apart from my own notes, I have consulted official sources, the Sakala Centre and the newspapers *Eesti Ekspress, Rahva Hääl, Päehvaleht* and *Eesti Elu* (Estonian Life) and, from September 1990, the Baltic News Service (BNS). The Pollo organization is the leading source for surveys of public opinion.

30 Professor Lippmaa first made his name as a leader of environmental protests, then as a deputy to the Supreme Soviet in Moscow, and one of the toughest and most skilled Estonian negotiators with the Soviet government – a feature he shares with the Latvian Juris Bojars, also a Soviet establishment figure turned populist nationalist. The fact that he was often popularly referred to as 'the most intelligent man in Estonia' casts doubt, however, on the Estonians' famed rationality. Lippmaa's extreme Russophobia may be attributed in part to the fact that his family was killed in Tartu by a Soviet bomb in 1944. He certainly succeeded in keeping those feelings concealed during his work for Soviet science. From this work he has retained a strange obsession with the Soviet and Russian submarine threat to the West, which he mentioned in each interview with me. With a thin face, icy blue eyes, precise Estonian accent, and general air of high intelligence mixed with an appearance of tightly-suppressed neuroticism, Lippmaa suggests something between a mad scientist and a Protestant bishop as imagined by Ingmar Bergman. He is a pleasure to interview, since he is a source of excellent (and extremely incautious) quotes. He is also capable, at least verbally, of extreme ruthlessness. During an interview in February 1990, I pointed out to him that it was not unreasonable for the West to fear the collapse of the Soviet Union, in

view of the fearful loss of life which had attended the end of the colonial empires in India and elsewhere. He replied, 'So what? Half a million people were an insignificant part of the Indian population.'

31 See Riina Kionka, 'Identity Crisis in the Estonian Popular Front', *RFE/RL Report on the USSR*, 3, 19, 10 May 1991.

32 The name *Isamaa* translates literally as 'Fatherland'. It was chosen for that reason, and it worked. In September 1992 two voters told me that 'I am voting for "Fatherland" because I am for the Fatherland'. Realising, however, that the name would have an unhappy resonance for an English audience, the leaders of the block then tried to insist that the Western press call them by the name 'Pro Patria', an absurdity to which an unfortunate number of correspondents subscribed.

33 *Baltic Independent*, 25 September 1992.

34 *Baltic Independent*, 10 April 1992; *Novoye Vremya*, March 1992.

35 The sketch of Latvian politics in this chapter is based on my own notes and interviews, on the newspapers *Atmoda, Diena, Neatkarīgā ciņa, Sovietsky Molodyosh*, and *Baltiskoe Vremya*, and on the research bulletins of RFE/RL and the Baltic News Service (BNS), as well as on official documents published by the Latvian Statistical Department and the Press Office of the Latvian Parliament. The Sociology Department of Riga University has carried out some useful public opinion polls.

36 One senior Riga policeman, Colonel Pavel Shapovalov, had actually been elected to the Supreme Council on the pro-Soviet ticket, together with Lt.Col. Martian Bekasov, Deputy Chief of police in Režekne. Both are of course Russian.

37 From the entry for 14 November 1991 in his published diary; see Jānis Āboltiņš, *Biju Biedrs, Tagad Kungs*

('Formerly Comrade, Now Mister')(Riga, 1992), pp.43, 176. It is easy to see how this book would infuriate more dedicated patriots. Thus Āboltiņš' honesty includes his diary entry for 23 August 1987 (the first big national demonstration) at which time he was a Communist official: 'There was a meeting at the Freedom Monument today, obviously inspired by foreigners. There were some arrests. Those who organised the demonstration were certainly not present themselves. A pity – such incidents might give the excuse to go back to the old [pre-Gorbachov] order.'

38 *The Times*, 21 May 1990. Fourteen months later, I wrote a much more accurate article on the future of the Russians in *The Times* of 18 June 1991.

39 Interview, 28 February 1990.

40 Programme of Popular Front of Latvia Second Congress, December 1989.

41 At the Popular Front Caucus, 2 May 1992 (from author's notes).

42 Resolutions and Working Programme of the Latvian Popular Front Fourth Congress, 15–17 November 1991.

43 For example, the speech by (of all people) the Latvian Jewish leader Mawrik Wulfson (Vulfsons) to a German-sponsored conference in Tallinn (the Bergedorfer Gespraechskreis) in May 1992. He implied that the vast majority of local Russians were disloyal, by stating that a year before, only 28 per cent had voted for Latvian independence and 72 per cent against. (See *Records of the 96th Bergedorfer Gespraechskreis*, 30–31 May 1992.) There is no concrete basis for Dr Wulfson's precise claim of a Russian vote for independence of only 28 per cent on 3 March, any more than there was for the Latvian government's claim that a majority of Russians had voted in favour, because votes were not listed according to nationality. On the

assumption that a majority of those not voting at all were Russians, I myself reached an estimate of somewhere between 27 and 39 per cent of Russians who supported independence. Dr Wulfson's guess is therefore at the bottom of the possible range.

44 Author's notes, November 1991.

45 Interview, 7 February 1990.

46 Speech by Gorbunovs, 25 August 1991.

47 c.f. *BNS* 2 and 3 August 1992 (for statements by Taagepera and Savisaar). I have myself noticed a worrying trend in the Baltic Foreign ministries since August 1991, especially among the many returned Baltic emigrés, not to take an interest in internal developments or public opinion in Russia, nor to bother to read Russian newspapers. Instead, the overwhelming emphasis has been on developing links with the West. I have the impression that Russia was written off as the 'natural enemy' from the start.

By raising territorial claims, the Estonians have laid themselves open to a possibly devastating counterattack. In the Estonian-Russian Treaty of 1991, they achieved a considerable success when Russia expressly ruled out territorial claims against Estonia, thereby excluding any claim to Narva on the basis of contemporary demography. Now, Estonians have re-opened this issue, and given Moscow the chance to propose reciprocal referenda in Petseri (which the Estonians would lose) and Narva (which could cost the Estonians their north-east). Even Estonian radical politicians do not seriously expect to recover Petseri; they hope to use it as a bargaining chip to extract various concessions. What they completely failed to realise was that the Russians would simply refuse to negotiate on this matter at all, but that raising it would lead to anti-Estonian feelings

even among former supporters of Baltic independence, especially among the Democratic bloc in St Petersburg.

48 Thus a Latvian-American doctor, Aivars Slucis, wrote that, 'I feel about treating Russians in Latvia the same way that a Jewish doctor would feel about treating Nazis. . . . Those who tortured in the Lubyanka Prison did not speak a "Soviet" language, they spoke Russian and were Russians. . . .' (See the article by the *Observer* correspondent, Mark Frankland, in the *Moscow Times*, 9 February 1993.) Frankland points out that the original Cheka was led by a Pole and its twenty senior officers contained a majority of non-Russians, including three Latvians.

49 Interview, 23 June 1992.

50 Interview, 4 February 1990.

51 Dated 2 July 1992, and reprinted in the Sakala Centre *Monthly Survey of Baltic and Post Soviet Politics*, Tallinn, July–August 1992.

52 Interview, 23 February 1990.

53 *Bergedorfer Gespraechskreis*, 30 May 1992.

54 Interview, 23 July 1992.

55 I attended the meeting at Baltiskoe Vremya on 23 December 1991 where the new editor, Tatyana Chiladze, tried to win over the staff. Her behaviour was very much that of the classical Bolshevik Commissar, albeit without threats of violence. Chiladze's article had appeared in the Russian language *Atmoda*, in November 1991.

56 Interview, 2 June 1992.

57 The memorandum from Helsinki Watch was dated 4 November 1991 and addressed to Anatolijs Gorbunovs. Its argument that Russians holding citizenship prior to August 1991 should not be excluded is a central reason for the insistence of the radical nationalists of Latvia and Estonia (and now the political classes in general) on the basic validity of the pre-1940 order and

therefore the complete illegality of everything that happened under Soviet rule. Helsinki Watch also championed those that entered Latvia 'in good faith' under Soviet rule; its point challenges the moral subtext of the Latvian and Estonian approach. Previously, Popular Front and government spokesmen repeatedly stressed that no personal moral guilt attached to those ordinary Russians that settled in the republics. Moderate Balts still stress this today, but often contradict themselves and thus expose their basic thinking. In an interview with the Estonian novelist Jaan Kross on 10 July 1992, he began by saying that 'I accept that most of the Russians here are personally guiltless', but continued, 'those who say that we must simply accept the Russian population here as citizens are like someone saying that I must accept a bandit who has come into my house'.

58 Interview, 3 August 1992. See also the quote from Jurkāns in the *Herald Tribune*, 2 August 1992.
59 Interview, 4 August 1992.
60 Interview, 18 December 1991.
61 Interview, 3 August 1992.
62 Quoted in George Ginsburgs' article, *JBS*, XXI, 1, 1990.
63 Interview with Lācis in *Atmoda*, 8 October 1991. A similar remark was made by Tunne Kelam at the Estonian Congress on 25 May 1990.
64 I am indebted to Valery Kargin, Director of Parex, for this anecdote. (In Russian criminal slang, a *vinni-pukhochka* is an under-age prostitute.)

9 Building on Ruins: The Recreation of the Baltic States

1 *Estonia Magazine*, autumn 1992.
2 *Diena*, 30 April 1992.
3 See the article by Latvian Defence Minister Talavs Jundzis in *Neatkariga Cina*, 22 August 1992, thanking Latvian World War II veterans in America and Australia for their support.
4 c.f. the interview with Velliste in *Estonia Magazine*, op cit.
5 *BI*, 6 November 1992.
6 *Diena*, 12 September 1992.
7 *BO*, 10 September 1992, *Diena*, 30 April 1992, *BI*, 6 November 1992.
8 Interview, 13 August 1992.
9 *BI*, 28 August 1992.
10 *BI*, 10 April 1992 and 30 October 1992.
11 For the Estonian deserters, see *BNS*, 10 August 1992. For conditions in the Lithuanian army, see *Respublika*, 3 December 1992. For the Latvian forces, see *Neatkariga Cina*, 22 October 1992 and *Diena*, 1 October 1992.
12 *Atmoda*, 31 March 1991.
13 *Estonian Independent*, 14 March 1991.
14 Interview, 7 August 1991, and *BI*, 13 December 1991.
15 *BNS*, 16 October 1992.
16 c.f. the response of the National Guard commander, Girts Kristovskis, in *Diena*, 6 March 1992.
17 *Diena*, 9 May 1992.
18 *Lauku Avize*, 24 January 1992 and *Diena*, 21 December 1991.
19 For a description of the Ventspils incident and the reaction to it, see *Diena*, 3 November 1992 and *BNS*, 8 November 1992. For other incidents, see *Diena*, 16 and 20 October 1992. For a personal account of a raid by the new Estonian police, see *BI*, 3 April 1992.
20 Interview, 16 January 1992. See also *Neatkariga Cina*, 4 August 1992.
21 c.f. *Mazoji Lietuva*, 29 September 1992 for an account of 'mafia' control on the Lithuanian-Polish border. For Latvia, see *Neatkariga Cina*, 2 October 1992, *BNS*, 15 October 1992. For conflicting Latvian border guard and customs points of view, see the interviews with Ivars Redisons and Aivars Gulbis in *BO*, 24 September 1992.
22 See *Diena*, 1 August 1992 and *BO*, 24 September 1992.

23 For the murders of the metal traders and the rumours surrounding them, see *BI*, 11 December 1992. During the autumn and winter of 1992 Germany saw a series of arrests of members of gangs involved in smuggling atomic material out of the former Soviet Union, one at least with a Baltic link. See *BNS*, 9 December 1992, for Lithuanian-Ukrainian co-operation against atomic smuggling. For the theft of monuments, see *Neatkariga Cina*, 4 December 1992. For the drugs trade, *BNS*, 7 August 1992 and *BI*, 24 December 1992.

24 *BI*, 28 August 1992 and 30 October 1992.

25 *BO*, 23 July 1992.

26 Interview, 15 November 1991.

27 *BI*, 16 October 1992. For a report of an attack by drunken Estonian Home guards on the living quarters of Russian officers, see *Paevaleht*, 12 October 1992. The men were arrested by the Estonian police.

28 c.f. the articles on the subject in *Estonian Life*, the English-language supplement to *Eesti Elu*, edited by the radical emigré Juri Estam.

29 *Lietuvos Rytas*, 18 November 1992 and *BNS*, 19 November 1992.

30 *Atmoda*, 12 November 1991, *Diena*, 14 August and 12 December 1992.

31 *BI*, 20 November 1992.

32 Kennan, op.cit. p.45.

33 Quoted in *BO*, 3 September 1992.

34 c.f. the *Economic Survey of the Baltic Republics*, commissioned by the Swedish Foreign Minister, drawn up by a team led by Professor Brian van Arkadie, and published in June 1991, p.293.

35 Interviews, 11 April 1991 and 26 August 1991. Horrible examples of this attitude are recorded in the memoirs of former Latvian Economics Minister Jānis Āboltiņš.

36 c.f. Philip Hanson, 'The End of the Rouble Zone?', in *RFE/RL Research Institute Report*, 1, 30, 24 July 1992.

37 Despite repeated statements, the Baltic governments failed as usual to co-ordinate their energy policies or to carry out joint development of terminals and other facilities, as ministers admitted after a meeting in Riga in October 1992 (see *BNS*, 7 November 1992).

38 *BO*, 28 May 1992.

39 *Economic Survey*, p.294.

40 Interview, 3 August 1992.

41 Interview, 23 July 1992; *BO*, 30 July 1992.

42 USSR State Committee for Statistics, quoted in John Tedstrom, 'Baltic Independence: the Economic Dimension', *RFE/RL Research Institute Report on the USSR*, 3, 6, 8 February 1991.

43 Interview, 14 July 1992.

44 Interview, 7 August 1991.

45 Interview, 15 January 1991

46 Paper presented by Greg Rathnell to the conference of the Association for the Advancement of Baltic Studies, Toronto, 1 June 1992.

47 Interview with Antanas Kaminskas, head of the Lithuanian Privatisation Department, 9 September 1991.

48 *BO*, 4 June 1992 and 23 July 1992.

49 *BI*, 28 August 1991 and *Lietuvos Rytas*, 30 August 1992.

50 *BO*, 25 June 1992.

51 *BI*, 10 July 1992 and 28 August 1992.

52 Bergman was indeed a rather dubious character, whom his own aunt denounced, in a letter to an Estonian newspaper, as an Amway pyramid seller, lacking even secondary education, who had left Germany to escape prosecution for debt. (*Eesti Ekspress*, 25 September 1992.)

53 *BNS*, 20, 21 and 27 November 1992.

54 *BNS*, 11 December 1992.

55 *Diena*, 16 August 1991 and *BO*, 25 June 1992.

56 *BO*, 20 August and 27 November 1992.

57 *Diena* and *Neatkariba Cina*, both 22 October 1992.

58 *Lietuvos Rytas*, 29 September 1992.

59 *BNS*, 7 December 1992.

60 Interview, 24 July 1991.
61 Interview, 16 April 1991.
62 *BNS*, 14 December 1992.
63 *BI*, 27 November 1992 and interview, 10 July 1992.
64 See the figures published in the *Baltic Handbook*, 1991.
65 See the article by Dzintars Zaluksnis in *BO*, 30 July 1992, and the report on peasant protests against the closure of the Voru Dairy in southern Estonia, *BI*, 18 December 1992.
66 *BNS*, 11 November 1992.
67 *BI*, 27 November 1992 and 8 January 1993; *BNS*, 3 December 1992.
68 Interview, 14 July 1992.
69 c.f. Stanley Page, 'Lenin and Peasant Bolshevism in Latvia, 1903–15', *JBS*, III, 2, 1972.
70 I gained a sense of the impression made on many Lithuanian farmers by the Sajūdis government when I interviewed one Grakauskas, head of the parliamentary agriculture commission, responsible for the reforms. In his cheap striped suit, he was the very pattern of a petty lawyer risen through politics. He had never been a farmer. I asked him about the question of new tractors and agricultural machinery, which every farmer I had interviewed had told me was a major problem. He replied that, 'There is no shortage of equipment in Lithuania; agriculture here is managing perfectly well with the equipment that it has. It is only a question of taking it away from the Communist managements and distributing it properly.... Anyway, why are you asking me these questions? Don't you know that Lithuania is now a free market, so the import of agricultural equipment is no longer the business of the state?' The arrogant smirk with which he delivered this shameless line was very Soviet. What it said was, 'I know I'm lying and I know you know I'm lying, and I don't care; because I represent the State, and I'll tell you whatever I like.' My assistant, herself a farmer's daughter, left the interview fizzing with fury. 'Grakauskas?' her mother said, 'this onion knows more about farming than he does'. Interview, 11 December 1991.
71 *BNS*, 20 November 1992 and interview, 28 July 1991.
72 *Economic Survey*, p.329.
73 Interview, 15 July 1992.
74 *BI*, 2 October 1992 and *Lietuvos Rytas*, 18 November 1992.
75 *Lietuvos Rytas*, 20 November 1992.
76 *Interview*, 3 June 1992.
77 *BI*, 27 March and 3 April 1992.
78 As reported in *BI*, 15 May 1992.
79 *Paevaleht*, 20 June 1992 and *Rahva Hääl*, 23 June 1992.
80 *BI*, 26 June and 3 July 1992, and *BO*, 9 July 1992. Confusion in the tax system, accompanied by sharp, arbitrary rises, was one factor hindering economic growth in this period. See *BO*, 27 August 1992.
81 c.f. *Postimees*, 17 November 1992.
82 *BI*, 21 and 28 August 1992.
83 *BNS*, 3 December 1992.
84 *BI*, 18 December 1992.
85 *BI*, 20 November 1992.
86 *BNS*, 3 December 1992
87 *BI*, 10 July 1992.
88 See Anders Aslund, Latvia: A Successful Currency Reform', *Ostekonomisk Rapport*, 10, 4, 24 September 1992.
89 *BI*, 14 August and 16 October 1992.
90 See the analysis by Edward Lucas in *BI*, 18 December 1992.
91 Quoted in *BO*, 3 September 1992.
92 Interview with Ivars Vitols, vice-president of the Riga Commercial Bank, 16 April 1991.
93 *Paevaleht*, 18 November 1992; *BI*, 20 November and 11 December 1992.
94 *BI*, 4 December 1992.
95 For an analysis of the position of religion in the Ukraine, see George Urban, 'The Awakening', *The National Interest*, 27, Spring 1992. See also the essays in the RFE/RL Research Institute's *Report on the USSR*, 3, 21, 24 May 1991.
96 For the Baltic education systems, see

the series by Pilar Wolfsteller in *BI*, September–October 1992.

97 Interview, 28 October 1992.

98 *BO*, 5 January 1992

99 For social welfare and the decline of living standards, see *BO*, 16 and 23 July, and 1 August 1992.

100 The article by Dr Steinbuka appeared in *BI*, 6 November 1992.

101 *BNS*, 1 December 1992.

Conclusion: The West and the Baltic States

1 Quoted in Evan Mawdsley, *The Russian Civil War* (London, 1987), p.283.

2 These views were put forward by Dr Wulfson and Dr Lauristin at the Bergedorfer Gespraechskreis, and have also been expressed by a vast range of Baltic spokesmen, in public and in private.

3 The limits of Western commitment were perfectly (and with unintentional humour) summed up in a remark by Swedish Premier Carl Bildt in Stockholm in February 1993. He said that if Russia were to invade the Baltic States, 'No-one should think that Sweden would remain neutral and would not *raise its voice* against such a move' (author's italics).

4 Interview, 6 July 1992.

5 *BNS*, 18 November 1992. American diplomacy towards the Baltic has been bedevilled by the unwise practice of appointing emigré diplomats to serve in their countries of origin. There have been several such appointments in the Baltic as elsewhere in the former Soviet Union. I make no charge against the professional honour of these diplomats – indeed I have observed them attempting to be fair about the local Russians – but in view of their background, and of Baltic history this century, full objectivity must be beyond them, and would not be believed by the minorities in any case. A single middle-ranking emigré within each embassy would be useful: more is asking for trouble. A Polish deputy in Lithuania recounted a meeting with an American-Lithuanian diplomat. Asked, in Lithuanian, for his views on Lithuania after the declaration of independence, and not realising the nationality of his interlocutor, the 'American' allegedly replied, 'Well, the best thing is, now we [i.e. the Lithuanians] can tell those goddamned Poles where to get off'. This problem of complete identification with the Balts extends to some European embassies as well. A worried Western diplomat, visiting Riga from Russia in the summer of 1992, told me that, 'The Western diplomats here generally don't speak Russian and have never worked in Russia. They socialise entirely with Latvians and Latvian Americans, have Latvian girlfriends, and often seem to be competing to see who can be the biggest Latvian nationalist. They have no idea of how things are viewed in Russia, or the danger that Latvia might be in.'

6 Clemenceau to Paderewski, 24 June 1919, quoted in Zigurds Zile, 'Minoritities Policy in Latvia, 1918–40', *JBS*, XI, 1, 1980.

7 *Herald Tribune*, 27 July 1992.

8 Indeed, an Ulster Unionist Professor with whom in June 1992 I discussed the situation in the Baltic said, 'I don't understand the Balts. Surely what they ought to do is publicly guarantee the Russians full citizenship and civil rights and then get what they want by using the administration against them.' A Latvian friend to whom I repeated this, commented, 'Well we're not fools. We know that very well.'

Appendix 1
Historical Chronology, 3500 BC–1985 AD

Third Millennium BC: Finno-Ugric peoples, ancestors of the Estonians, settle on present territory of Estonia.

Second Millennium BC: Proto-Baltic peoples, ancestors of the Latvians, Lithuanians and Prussians, move to the Baltic coast.

First-Second centuries AD: Tacitus and other Roman writers describe 'Aesti' as living on Baltic, trading in amber etc.

1009 AD: Lithuania first mentioned in Christian chronicles.

12th–13th centuries: German and Scadinavian crusaders invade Baltic region.

1202–37: 'Brothers of the Militia of Christ' (Knights of the Sword) charged with conquering and converting the Balts. Their place then taken by the Teutonic Knights.

1204: Germans found Riga.

1217: Estonians crushed at battle of Fellin (Viljandi).

1219: Danes invade Northern Estonia and found Tallinn (Reval).

1242: The Prince of Moscow, Alexander Nevsky, defeats Teutonic Knights on the ice of Lake Peipus and frustrates their attempts to advance inland.

1236: Lithuanians defeat Knights of the Sword at Šaule.

1263: Death of King Mindaugas, who unified Lithuanians and founded monarchy.

1316–41: Reign of Lithuanian Grand Duke Gediminas (Gedymin), who conquers huge Slav territories to the East.

1343: 'St. George's Day Rebellion' in Estonia against German and

Danish rule, finally crushed only in 1345. As a result, Danish King sells Reval (Tallinn) and surrounding area to Teutonic Knights in 1346.

1385: Union of Kreva (Krewo). Lithuanian Grand Duke Jogaila (Jagiello) marries Polish princess Jadwige, adopts Christianity. Through Polish Catholic Church, Lithuanian nobility rapidly Polonised.

1392–1430: Reign of Grand Duke Vytautas the Great. His lands stretch almost to Moscow and cover most of the present Ukraine.

14th century: First Jews settle in area of present Baltic States.

1410: crushing defeat of the Teutonic Knights by Lithuanians and Poles at Tannenberg (Zalgiris, Gruenwald).

1525: First book in Estonian language.

1558: Armies of Ivan the Terrible invade and devastate Baltic provinces. War with Russia continues until 1583 when Russians finally defeated by Swedes. Population falls by more than a half.

1561: Sweden takes Estland (the north of present-day Estonia) and Poland takes Livonia (southern Estonia and northern Latvia). The Teutonic Order is wound up. Its last Grand Master, Gotthart Kettler, becomes Duke of Courland.

1569: Union of Lublin completes incorporation of Lithuania into Polish-dominated Commonwealth.

1629: Sweden takes Livonia from Poland.

1632: Foundation of Dorpat (Tartu) University in Estonia by the Swedes.

1710: Peter the Great conquers the Baltic provinces from the Swedes.

1721: Conquest formalised by the Treaty of Nystad, in which the Russian Monarchy guaranteed the privileges and local authority of the Baltic German nobility. They become backbone of Russian civil service.

1714–80: Life of Kristijonas Donelaitis, author of *The Seasons*, the first great work of Lithuanian literature.

1720–97: Life of the Vilna Gaon (Genius), leading Jewish Orthodox thinker and opponent of the Hasidic mystical movement then sweeping Jewish communities of Eastern Europe.

1739: Publication of first Estonian Bible.

1764–69: Johann Gottfried Herder a pastor in Riga. The folk-cultures of the Baltic have a major influence on his thought, which in turn helps give rise to the ideology of modern European nationalism. He encourages Baltic German scholars to begin taking a scientific interest in Baltic folklore.

1795: Third Partition of Poland. The whole of present-day Lithuania, except Memel (Klaipeda), falls into Russian hands.

1798–1855: Life of great Polish-Lithuanian poet Adam Mickiewicz.

1812: Napoleon's armies under Marshal MacDonald besiege Riga.

1816–19: Baltic German nobility in most of present-day Estonia and Latvia abolish serfdom, but without granting land to the peasants.

1830 and 1863: Polish-Lithuanian revolts against Russian rule.

1835–1923: Life of Krisjanis Barons, the great Latvian folklorist and nationalist, whose codification of the Latvian Dainas (folksongs) lays much of the basis for modern Latvian culture. His life spans entire period of first Latvian cultural and political movements up to the creation of the first Republic.

1849 and 1856: New reforms in Latvian and Estonian provinces distribute land to the peasantry, making renting and buying easier.

1861: Publication of the *Kalevipoeg*, the Estonian national epic, by Friedrich Kreuzwald.

1869 and 1873: First Estonian and Latvian national song festivals mark a major step in 'national awakening'.

1870: First railway in the Baltic provinces.

1884: Estonian Students' Society consecrates blue-black-white tricolour, later Estonian national flag.

1885: Beginning of intense Russification under Tsar Alexander III.

1888: Publication of *Lāčplēsis*, Latvian national epic by Andrejs Pumpurs.

1905: Revolution, accompanying that in Russia. In the Baltic, it was aimed principally at German landowners and Russian police, hundreds of whom were killed. Thousands of Balts perished in the repression which followed.

1909: Birth of [Sir] Isaiah Berlin, later British philosopher, in Riga.

1911: Birth of Nobel Prize-winning Polish-Lithuanian author, Czeslaw Milosz.

1914–15: First World War. German armies overrun half of Latvian provinces. Many Russians and part of Latvian population evacuated to Russia.

1915–16: Russian Imperial Army forms Latvian Rifle Regiments, later the core of both the Latvian national army and the Red Army.

1917: First and Second Russian Revolutions. Baltic national assemblies demand first autonomy, then independence from Russia. After 'October Revolution', Bolsheviks take over power in several areas of the Baltic. Germans capture Riga.

16 February 1918: Lithuanian independence proclaimed.

24 February 1918: Estonian independence proclaimed.

18 November 1918: After German withdrawal, and before Bolshevik conquest, Latvian National Council proclaims independence.

February–November 1918: Germans occupy the remainder of the Baltic provinces.

November 1918–January 1919: Bolsheviks invade Baltic provinces, capture Riga.

January–March 1919: Estonians under General Johannes Laidoner counter-attack, drive out Bolsheviks from Estonia.

22 May 1919: German, White Russian and Latvian forces recapture Riga.

June–July 1919: Estonian and Latvian forces defeat German forces. Battle of Wenden (Cesis). In subsequent offensives against the Bolsheviks they penetrate Russian territory.

1919–21: Poles, Lithuanians and Bolsheviks struggle for the Vilnius (Vilna, Wilno) region, which eventually falls to Poland. Polish-Lithuanian relations broken off until 1936. In 1923 Lithuania seizes Klaipeda (Memel) from Germany.

1920–21: Baltic States sign peace treaties with Soviet Russia, in which Moscow recognises their independence.

1920: Major land reforms in Latvia and Estonia strip Baltic German nobles of their land, distribute it to peasants. Milder reform directed against Polish landowners in Lithuania.

1922: Introduction of democratic constitutions in all three Baltic States.

1922: Baltic States admitted to League of Nations.

1 December 1924: Attempted Communist coup in Tallinn is put down by Estonian army.

1928: Estonia introduces a stable national currency, the Kroon.

1929: Beginning of world economic depression.

1934: Konstantin Päts in Estonia, and Karlis Ulmanis in Latvia, dissolve parliaments and political parties and impose quasi-authoritarian regimes.

1934: Co-operation Treaty between the three Baltic States. Practical co-operation however remained limited.

1939: Germany seizes Klaipeda back from Lithuania.

23 August 1939: Molotov-Ribbentrop Pact provides for Soviet domination of Latvia and Estonia. Lithuania added to Soviet sphere in a later agreement.

28 September–10 October 1939: The Soviet Union forces the Baltic States to sign defence co-operation agreements under which Soviet troops stationed on their soil. Moscow gives Vilnius, conquered from Poland, to Lithuania.

1939–40: Hitler orders evacuation of Baltic German community from Baltic States.

17 June 1940: Soviet Union invades Baltic States, forces governments to resign, holds rigged 'elections'.

3–6 August 1940: Baltic States annexed to Soviet Union. Repression begins immediately. Major confiscations of property.

14 June 1941: Tens of thousands of Balts arrested and deported to Siberia.

22 June 1941: German army attacks Soviet Union. Many Baltic prisoners who cannot be evacuated are executed by the NKVD. In Kaunas and elsewhere, Lithuanian resistance forces attack Soviet army. The uprising is accompanied by atrocities against the local Jewish population, accused of collaborating with the Communists. The revolt against the Soviet Army spreads to Latvia and Estonia. Short-lived Lithuanian national government, soon dissolved by the Germans.

28 August 1941: Germans capture Tallinn. Complete withdrawal of Soviet forces from Baltic States. Germans recruit local auxiliary police and SS units, which play leading part in Holocaust of the Jews. Jewish population herded into ghettoes or massacred. In July 1944, Jewish resistance in remnant of Vilna (Vilnius) Ghetto launches revolt and Ghetto destroyed.

1944: With Soviet army once again threatening Baltic States, tens of thousands of Balts join German forces to defend their homes.

August 1944–May 1945: Soviet army reconquers Baltic States, destroys attempt to refound national governments. Hundreds of thousands of Balts flee with Germans or across Baltic to Sweden. Their places taken by Russian-speaking immigrants and demobilised military personnel. Thereafter Russian-speaking element in population rises rapidly, until by late 1980s it stands at 38 per cent in Estonia and some 45 per cent in Latvia. Lithuanian Communist leader Antanas Sniečkus succeeds in partially resisting this.

1944–54: Partisan war against Soviet rule by the 'Forest Brothers'. Tens of thousands killed on both sides.

1947: Start of collectivisation of agriculture. Traditional Baltic rural society crippled.

March 1949: Biggest wave of deportations. More than 100,000 Balts sent to Siberia and Central Asia.

1953: Death of Stalin. In 1956–57, beginning of Khrushchev's 'Thaw'. Recovery of Baltic culture and literature.

1959: Attempt by part of Latvian Communist Party, led by Eduards Berklavs, to resist further Russification and Russian immigration is crushed by Khrushchev in a purge which reduces party to complete subservience for three decades.

1965: Brezhnev ends limited economic autonomy for the republics, reimposes strict centralism.

1968: Invasion of Czechoslovakia leads to increased repression in Baltic and increased dissident activity, which continues steadily over next decade.

1972: First publication of the Catholic dissident newsletter, *The Chronicle of the Catholic Church in Lithuania*, detailing Soviet repression in the republic. Several of those responsible are subsequently arrested and jailed.

1970s: 'Era of Stagnation'. Living standards, having risen slowly but steadily in 1960s, level off and then begin to decline. Steep decline of belief in Communism, even in ranks of Party.

1982: Death of Leonid Brezhnev. Andropov begins attempts at reform from above.

1985: Appointment of Mikhail Gorbachov as Secretary-General of the Soviet Communist Party. Introduction of 'Glasnost' and 'Perestroika'. Beginning of the end of the Soviet Union.

Appendix 2
Contemporary Chronology, 1985–1992

March 1985: Gorbachov is elected General Secretary of the Soviet Communist Party by the Politburo.

April 1986: Chernobyl disaster gives massive impetus to ecological protest in the Baltic States, and helps make that protest respectable in Soviet terms.

14 June 1987: On anniversary of Stalin's deportations of 1941, Latvian dissidents hold meeting at Freedom Monument in Riga. Several arrested.

23 August 1987: On anniversary of Molotov-Ribbentrop Pact, dissident groups hold meetings in Tallinn and Vilnius. Beginning of the period of 'calendar demonstrations'.

26 September 1987: 'Four-Man' proposal for Estonian economic autonomy. Gives rise to the pioneering 'IME' plan.

14 November 1987: Lithuanian Artists' Union dismisses the whole of its old-guard leadership. Death of First Secretary Petras Griškevičius. He is replaced by Ringaudas Songaila.

13 March 1988: 'Letter of Nina Andreyevna' initiates attempted conservative counter-attack in Moscow. Gorbachov responds by turning further to the people, appealing to them against the old guard.

April 1988: Foundation of the Estonian Popular Front, the first in the Soviet Union.

1–2 June 1988: At extended plenum of Latvian Writers Union, secret protocol of Molotov-Ribbentrop Pact publicly revealed and denounced. Mavriks Vulfsons declares that there was no pro-Soviet revolution in Latvia in 1940.

3 June 1988: Foundation of Sajūdis in Lithuania.

June 1988: Estonian First Secretary Karl Vaino replaced with the more liberal Vaino Valjas.

23 August 1988: Hundreds of thousands attend rallies to denounce the Molotov-Ribbentrop Pact.

19 October 1988: Replacement of Lithuanian First Secretary Songaila with Algirdas Brazauskas, formerly a state economics official. Brazauskas makes various conciliatory gestures, including the return of Vilnius Cathedral to the Church. However, he blocks passage of sovereignty declaration.

22–24 October 1988: First Congress of Sajūdis. Vytautas Landsbergis elected Chairman.

16 November 1988: Estonian Supreme Council passes declaration of sovereignty.

18 January 1989: Estonian Supreme Council passes law making Estonian state language, requiring its knowledge by the holders of various categories of job. Local Russians claim discrimination.

14 March 1989: Foundation of the Soviet loyalist movement 'Interfront' in Estonia. Soon afterwards, similar movements are founded in Latvia and Lithuania.

18 May 1989: Lithuanian Supreme Council passes declaration of sovereignty.

31 May 1989: Latvian Popular Front calls for complete independence.

27 July 1989: Supreme Soviet in Moscow accepts Baltic economic self-management, as proposed by Estonia.

28 July 1989: Latvian Supreme Council passes sovereignty declaration.

August 1989: Soviet loyalists carry out general strike in Estonia against independence movements and discrimination against local Russians.

23 August 1989: 'Baltic Way'. Some two million people form human chain from Vilnius to Tallinn to call for independence.

August 1989: Supreme Soviet in Moscow accepts existence of secret protocol to Molotov-Ribbentrop Pact, providing for Soviet domination of the Baltic States.

12 November 1989: Estonian Supreme Council declares Soviet annexation illegal.

19–20 December 1989: Lithuanian Communist Party splits from Soviet Party.

2 February 1990: Assembly of Estonian national and local deputies declares Estonian legal independence unbroken by Soviet occupation.

11 March 1990: Lithuanian Supreme Council declares full independence. Vytautas Landsbergis elected Chairman (head of state).

18 March 1990: Latvian and Estonian Supreme Council elections lead to two-thirds majorities for independence. When Estonian Supreme Council meets in April, Edgar Savisaar, former deputy head of the State Planning Commission, elected Prime Minister.

17 March 1990: Kazimiera Prunskienė elected Prime Minister of Lithuania.

27 March 1990: Soviet army seizes Lithuanian deserters near Vilnius. Over the next weeks, several former Communist Party buildings in Vilnius are seized by the army.

18 April 1990: Moscow shuts off shipments of oil to Lithuania.

26 April 1990: Francois Mitterrand and Helmut Kohl appeal to Landsebergis to suspend declaration of independence for the sake of compromise with Moscow.

4 May 1990: Latvian Supreme Council meets, declares Latvian *de jure* independence, and a transition period to full independence. Ivars Godmanis, a scientist and Popular Front leader, becomes Prime Minister.

12 May 1990: Three Baltic Leaders renew Baltic Co-Operation Treaty of 1934, establish Baltic Council, apply for membership of CSCE.

15 May 1990: Soviet loyalists stage violent demonstrations outside the Latvian and Estonian parliaments.

26 May 1990: Soviet loyalists attempt to set up an 'Interregional Council', a form of alternative government, in Estonia. When this fails for lack of support, they create the 'Integral Commission', based on the Moscow-run, Russian-staffed factories.

13 June 1990: Estonian Supreme Council passes law providing for full return of rights to private property.

29 June 1990: Lithuanian Supreme Council accepts in principle a moratorium on the declaration of independence. Soviet economic blockade ends. Fruitless talks with Moscow begin.

Autumn 1990: With Baltic-Soviet talks stalled, hidden forces, presumably Soviet hardliners, begin bombing campaign aimed at stirring up local Russians and discrediting Baltic national movements. In Latvia, OMON, a special police force, defects from the Latvian Interior Ministry to side with Moscow, followed in January 1991 by OMON in Lithuania.

December 1990: Announcement in the three republics of the formation of 'National Salvation Committees' to restore Soviet rule. Their membership is kept secret, but they are assumed to include the local hardline Communist and military leadership.

6 January 1991: Kazimiera Prunskienė announces steep price rises. When these are refused by parliament, she resigns. She is replaced briefly by Albertas Šimėnas. When he briefly goes missing without an explanation, he is replaced by Gediminas Vagnorius, a radical nationalist.

11 January 1991: Soviet paratroopers seize the press centre in Vilnius.

12 January 1991: Estonia and Russia sign treaty recognising each others' sovereignty and guaranteeing free choice of citizenship.

13 January 1991: Soviet troops seize the television centre and tower in Vilnius. Fifteen people shot to death or crushed by tanks.

20 January 1991: OMON Soviet special police storm Interior Ministry in Riga. Six killed. In succeeding months, OMON launches repeated attacks on Baltic border posts, beating the guards and burning the buildings.

9 February 1991: Referendum in Lithuania produces overwhelming majority for independence.

3 March 1991: Referenda in Latvia and Estonia also produce large majorities for independence, including many local Russians.

18 March 1991: Soviet referendum on continuing the Union is boycotted by most of the Baltic populations.

31 July 1991: Seven Lithuanian border guards at the post of Medininkai are killed, it is believed by the Riga OMON.

19–21 August 1991: Attempted counter-revolution in the Soviet Union. OMON kills six in various incidents in Riga.

20 August 1991: Latvian and Estonian Supreme Councils declare full independence. In following weeks, all three Baltic States receive international diplomatic recognition, are admitted to the UN and the CSCE. OMON is withdrawn from the Baltic. Statues of Lenin all over the Baltic are dismantled.

6 September 1991: Soviet State Council recognises Baltic independence.

20 October 1991: Local elections in north-east Estonia lead to return of Soviet loyalist majorities in two out of three towns.

6 November 1991: Estonian Supreme Council renews 1938 citizenship law, thereby stripping citizenship from immigrants who arrived under Soviet rule.

15–17 November 1992: Fourth Congress of the Latvian Popular Front sees a sharp swing to radical nationalist positions. Shortly afterwards, the PF faction in the Supreme Council splits, with radicals forming the Satversme (Constitution) faction.

23 November 1991: Swedish Foreign Aid Minister denounces Estonia over the holding of a meeting of Estonian war veterans, including those from the SS.

27 November 1991: Latvian Supreme Council passes law restoring citizenship to all those who held it before 1940 and their descendants. Decision on how to naturalise 'immigrants' under Soviet rule postponed.

28 November 1991: Russian Supreme Soviet adopts law granting automatic Russian citizenship to anyone living outside Russia's borders who applies for it.

14–15 December 1991: Third Congress of Sajūdis launches Landsbergis's bid for executive presidency.

13 January 1992: Prime Minister Savisaar demands right to declare

economic state of emergency in Estonia following sharp reduction in fuel supplies and major power and food cuts. On 23 January, following blocking of this by parliament, Savisaar resigns. He is replaced by Tiit Vähi.

22 January 1992: Latvian Supreme Council claims Abrene, part of pre-1940 Latvia annexed by Russia in 1945.

20 May 1992: Latvia joins IMF; receives loan of $85 million.

23 May 1992: Landsbergis defeated in referendum on creating an executive presidency in Lithuania. Landsbergis accuses the parliamentary majority of a 'creeping coup' against him and Prime Minister Vagnorius.

9 June 1992: Latvian Supreme Council passes law setting strict conditions for new residents in Latvia. The radical nationalist deputies announce that they consider these conditions apply also to existing non-citizen residents.

20 June 1992: Introduction of the Estonian Kroon (Crown), first independent convertible currency in the former Soviet Union.

28 June 1992: Estonians in referendum pass by huge majority the proposed parliamentary constitution. A second proposal, slightly to extend the franchise to non-citizens, is defeated.

4 July 1992: Prime Minister Vagnorius forced to resign by Lithuanian Supreme Council. He is replaced by Aleksandras Abišala, an independent Right-winger.

15–17 July 1992: Russian Supreme Soviet discusses position of ethnic Russians in the Baltic States; orders Russian government to prepare sanctions against Estonia for violating the Estonian-Russian Treaty of 12 January 1991.

15 September 1992: Latvian Supreme Council demands that Russian troops withdraw completely by the end of 1993. Russia insists that the end of 1994 is the earliest possible date.

17 September 1992: Several Latvian political parties combine to demand the resignation of the government of Ivars Godmanis.

20 September 1992: Estonian parliamentary election results in small majority for a Centre-Right coalition made up of the National Independence Party, Fatherland, and Moderate alliances. Arnold Rüütel gets largest number of popular votes in first round of Presidential elections. When parliament meets in October, Dr Mart Laar of Fatherland becomes coalition Prime Minister and Dr Lennart Meri is elected President by the deputies.

25 October 1992: Lithuanian parliamentary elections result in smashing victory for Algirdas Brazauskas and his former Communists (now the Lithuanian Democratic Labour Party). When parliament meets in November, Brazauskas is elected chairman to replace Landsbergis, pending presidential elections in February. Bronislovas Lubys, a Liberal and former Deputy Premier, becomes Prime Minister.

28 October 1992: After intense parliamentary criticism of his allegedly 'pro-Russian' stance, Latvian Foreign Minister Janis Jurkans is forced to resign – a sign of the continuing swing to radical nationalist positions in Latvian politics.

14 February 1993: Brazauskas elected Lithuanian President, beating the Rightist candidate, Stasys Lozoraitis.

Appendix 3

Baltic Demography and Geography

Lithuania:

Area: 65,200 square kilometres, bordering on Belarus, Latvia, Kaliningrad (Russia) and Poland.
Population (1989): 3.67 million (68% urban)
Largest towns in Lithuania:

Vilnius	592,500 inhabitants	(ca.55% Lithuanian)
Kaunas	430,000 "	(ca.80% Lithuanian)
Klaipeda	206,000 "	(ca.68% Lithuanian)
Siauliai	148,000 "	(ca.95% Lithuanian)

Ethnic composition of Lithuanian population by percentage (living in the territory presently covered by the Republic of Lithuania):

Year: (by official census)	1923	1959	1970	1989
Lithuanians	69.2	79.3	80.0	79.6
Poles	15.3	8.5	7.7	7.0
Russians	2.5	8.5	8.6	9.4
Jews	8.3	.9	.8	.3
Others (mainly Byelorussian)	4.4	2.8	2.8	3.7

Latvia:

Area: 64,600 square kilometres, bordering on Lithuania, Estonia, Belarus and Russia.
Population (1989): 2.68 million
Capital: Riga, 916,500 (1990), or 34% of the total population.

Ethnic composition of Latvian population by percentage:

	1897	1920	1939	1959	1979	1989
Latvians	68.3	74.4	75.5	62.0	53.7	52
Russians	12	10.2	10.6	26.6	32.8	34
Germans	6.2	3.8	3.2	0.1	0.1	0.1
Jews			4.8	1.8	1.1	0.9
Poles			2.5	2.9	2.5	2.3
Ukrainians/ Byelorussians			1.4	4.3	7.2	8.0
Lithuanians			1.2	1.5	1.5	1.3

It can be seen that the common Latvian lumping together of all the 'non-Latvians' as 'Russian-speakers' is not entirely accurate, since the historic Lithuanian and Polish communities speak their own languages and can also generally be counted on politically to support the Latvians against the Russians, as can a certain number of the Jews. The total of Russian-speakers (including the Ukrainians, Byelorussians, and various other Soviet nationalities) as of 1989 was therefore around 44% of the population, not 48% as usually presented, which is of course still bad enough from the Latvian point of view.

Population of Riga in 1913, by percentage (total population 481,950):

Latvians:	39.8	(in 1867, 23.6%)
Germans:	13.9	(" 42.9%)
Russians:	20.0	(" 25.1%)
Jews:	7.0	
Poles:	9.5	
Lithuanians:	6.9	
Others:	2.9	

Of these populations, the Germans were evacuated in 1939–40, the Jews and some of the then Russian population largely massacred in 1941–44, many of the Poles left after 1945, and the Lithuanians have very often assimilated into the Latvian population, especially its Catholic section. (Figures from Stephen D. Corsin, 'The Changing Composition of the City of Riga, 1867–1913', *JBS*, XIII, 1, 1982.) Today, Riga is approximately 36.5% Latvian, and more than 60% 'Russian-speaking', a term which includes several other nationalities, but with Russians in the majority.

Today, all seven of Latvia's main towns have Russian-speaking majorities, ranging from 87% in the eastern city of Daugavpils to 53% in Jurmala.

Estonia:

Area: 45,215 square kilometres, bordering on Latvia and Russia. The sea coasts face towards Finland and Sweden.
Population (1989): 1.57 million.

Population of Estonia (before 1918, province of Estonia), by percentage:

	1897	1934	1959	1970	1989
Estonians:	88.8	88.2	74.6	68.2	61.5
Germans and Swedes:	5.4	2.2	0	0	0
Russians:	5.1	8.2	20.1	24.7	30.3
Ukrainians and Byelorussians:			3.0	3.7	4.9

The capital, Tallinn, always had a higher proportion of Russians and other nationalities than the rest of Estonia. Today, it is just over 50% Russian-speaking. Of the other main towns, Narva is 94% Russian, and Kohtla-Jarve 65%, but Tartu and Pärnu have large Estonian majorities.

Appendix 4

The Soviet Baltic Economies on the Eve of the National Revolutions (1989–90)

(The figures are rounded off and so do not total 100 per cent. They are also based on Soviet statistics and are therefore inherently unreliable. It is doubtful that, even in 1989, the number of Lithuanian workers in construction was equal to those in agriculture, even allowing that in these figures, all the collective farm construction and transport units have been separated from the agricultural sector.)

Employment by percentage of the workforce, 1988:

	Estonia	Latvia	Lithuania
Industry (including food and timber industries)	32	41	34
Agriculture	12	12	13
Construction	10	10	13
Transport	8	7	6
Trade, catering	9	10	5
Education, culture etc.	12	11	12
Health care, sports	6	7	7
Other (including management and officials)	11	5	5

Share of production, 1989–90 (in %):

	Estonia	Latvia	Lithuania
Industry	44	60	56
Agriculture	25	20	23
Construction	11	7	10
Transport	6	5	4
Trade and other	13	7	7

(It is striking to note that according to Estonian official statistics, agriculture's share of Estonian net material production actually rose from 16.4% to 25.1% between 1980 and 1990.)

Industrial Production and Employment by sector, 1989:

Percentage of industrial production (number of employees x 1000 in brackets):

	Estonia	Latvia	Lithuania
Metalworking/ Machine building	14.4 (58.2)	29.2 (147.2)	25.7 (193.2)
Light industry	26.4 (43.3)	20.5 (70.0)	20.8 (61.7)
Food industry	23.9 (28.2)	25.4 (43.1)	26.1 (66.0)
Timber, paper	9.1 (28.0)	5.7 (33.8)	5.3 (41.4)
Chemicals	9.2 (16.2)	7.6 (23.2)	3.8 (18.2)
Power	6.0 (7.2)	1.4 (6.9)	4.6 (16.2)
Other (construction etc.)	11.0 (40.2)	4.2 (18.0)	13.7 (76.8)

(The most noticeable thing about these figures is the importance of heavy industry on one hand and food and wood industries on the other, emphasising the key dependence on the Soviet military-industrial complex and on the countryside.

Appendix 5

Biographical Guide to Political Figures, 1988–92

Lithuania:

Abišala, Aleksandras: Born 1955 in Russia to a family of Lithuanian deportees. A scientist and member of the radical nationalist Kaunas Faction. Speaker of Parliament, 1990–91, when he helped push through several necessary laws, but gained a reputation for arrogance which diminished his influence among deputies. 1991–92, Minister for negotiations with Moscow. From July to November 1992, Prime Minister, during which time the Lithuanian constitution was finalised and the dispute between Lithuania and Poland ended by his visit to Warsaw in September 1992.

Antanavičius, Kazimieras: Born 1937. Non-Communist economist. Founder-member of Sajūdis. 1990–92, Chairman of the Supreme Council Economic Committee. 1990–91, leader of the Social Democrat Party.

Brazauskas, Algirdas: Born 1932, into a family of officials and farmers under the First Republic. Joined the Communist Party and rose as an economic manager. From 1966 to 1977, Deputy Chairman of the State Planning Committee, thereafter a Central Committee Secretary for economic affairs. From 1988 to 1990, First Secretary of the LCP; from 1989 to 1990, Chairman of the Supreme Council. In December 1989, led the Lithuanian Party to become the first to break with the Soviet Communist Party. In March 1990, voted out as Chairman of Parliament by the new Sajūdis parliamentary majority, and replaced by Landsbergis. However, Brazauskas retained great popularity among Lithuanians, who saw him as both an efficient head of government and as a man who had struggled for Lithuanian independence against Moscow during his time as party leader. From 1990, leader of the renamed Lithuanian Democratic Labour Party (LDDP), in opposition to the Sajūdis-dominated government. In October 1992, the LDDP was victorious in parliamentary elections, and in February 1993 Brazauskas was elected President.

Burokevičius, Mykolas: Born 1927. Professor of Communist history; member of the Poliburo of the Lithuanian Communist Party, and from December 1989 to August 1991, leader of that section of it which remained loyal to the Soviet Party. Fled to Russia and is being sought by the Lithuanian legal authorities for involvement in the Soviet military intervention of January 1991 and the August counter-revolution.

Čepaitis, Virgilijus: Born 1937. Translator from English and Russian. Founder member of Sajūdis. A leading Sajūdis radical, from 1990 to 1991 seen as Landsbergis's 'grey eminence'. As Secretary of Sajūdis in 1989–90, was able to adavance the position of radicals within the movement and get many of them into parliament. In 1990–91, encouraged the movement to denounce the Leftist and Centrist parties, and most of the press, as agents of Moscow. At the end of 1991, was disgraced and stripped of his deputy's mandate when it was revealed that he had himself been an informer for the KGB.

Juozaitis, Arvydas: Born 1956. Philosopher and Olympic swimmer. A key founder of Sajūdis and liberal rival to Landsbergis for the leadership, 1988. After his defeat, became an embittered enemy of Landsbergis and withdrew from active politics.

Landsbergis, Vytautas: Born 1932, into a Lithuanian intellectual family involved in the Lithuanian national movement from its nineteenth century beginnings. By profession a Professor of Musicology. Elected Chairman of Sajūdis in November 1988. March 1990, elected Chairman of the Supreme Council and *de facto* head of state. Came to be seen by many in the West as the chief symbol of the Lithuanian struggle for independence, but except for brief periods, failed to consolidate this image among his own people. In October 1992, heavily defeated by the former Communists in parliamentary elections, and went into opposition.

Lubys, Bronislovas: Born 1938. State industrial manager, of the huge Azotas chemical plant in Jonava, 1985–92. However, from 1990 a leading member of the Liberal Party. From July 1992, Deputy Prime Minister; from November 1992 to March 1993, following Brazauskas's election victory, Prime Minister. In the early months of his government, under the lash of a sharply deteriorating economic situation, he appeared to swing back towards ideas of state control.

Lozoraitis, Stasys: Born 1924. A leader of the Lithuanian emigration in the United States. As Ambassador to the Vatican and then the United States, the chief remaining official and legal representative of the First Lithuanian republic during the period of Soviet rule, who helped to make sure that Western powers continued to refuse *de jure* recognition to the Soviet annexation of the Baltic States. From 1991, Ambassador of the new Lithuanian republic to the United States. Played an important role in discussions leading to the Lithuanian declaration of independence in 1990. In February 1993, unsuccessful candidate for President, against Brazauskas.

Prunskienė, Kazimiera: Born 1943. An agronomist and economist, raised by Brazauskas to the last Lithuanian Communist government. A founder member of Sajūdis. 1989–90, Deputy Prime Minister for Economic Reform. From March 1990 to January 1991 Prime Minister, before being toppled by the nationalists for being allegedly too close to Moscow. Thereafter lost popularity rapidly because of her attacks on Landsbergis from abroad, which were seen as dividing the country at a critical time. In 1991–92, a leader of the opposition Forum for Lithuania's Future. In 1992, stripped of her deputy's mandate for alleged collaboration with the KGB. Is closely involved with international womens' organisations, particularly those based in Germany.

Sladkevičius, Vincentas (Cardinal): Born 1920. From 1989, Archbishop of Kaunas and Primate of the Lithuanian Catholic Church. Strongly backed the Lithuanian independence movement, but was seen by many liberals both as a force for conservatism within the Church and as having allowed the priesthood to become too closely involved in supporting nationalist parties and in particular Landsbergis.

Sakalas, Aloyzas: Born 1931. Sentenced to prison under Stalin for patriotic activities. Physicist. Founder member of Sajūdis, and from 1992, leader of the Social Democratic Party.

Saudargas, Algirdas: Born 1948. Biophysicist and leading radical nationalist. 1990–92, Foreign Minister, during which period he frequently surprised Western diplomats with his forthright views on the deficiencies of Western democracy, Western treachery, cowardice and so on, as well as by his generally simian appearance and behaviour. His capabilities are better displayed in domestic politics.

Uoka, Kazimieras: Born 1951, into a working-class family. One of the very few nationalist leaders from the industrial working class, being by profession a bulldozer driver. A leading Sajūdis radical, and from 1990–92 Comptroller of State Finances, during which time he was frequently accused of abusing his office to denounce rivals of Landsbergis. Winner of the International George Meany Prize.

Vagnorius, Gediminas: Born 1957. An economist who joined the radical wing of the Sajūdis movement and was made Prime Minister by them in January 1991, after the fall of Prunskienė and temporary disappearance of Albertas Šimenas. The great achievement of his premiership was the pushing through of an effective programme of privatisation. However, aspects of this were damaging to agriculture, and Vagnorius came to be blamed for steeply falling living standards and for the rumours of corruption which surrounded the government. He also alienated colleagues by what was seen as his arrogance, and the population at large by the all too evident pleasure he took in his job, which led one disgruntled journalist to compare him to a pouter-pigeon. In July 1992, he was forced to resign by a parliamentary vote of no confidence.

Latvia:

Bojārs, Juris: Born 1938. Ethnic Latvian. Expert in International Law and Major, KGB (retd.). Founder member of the Popular Front. As the only Latvian Supreme Council deputy with any knowledge of comparative law, an important figure in drafting legislation. From 1992, leader of the Latvian Democratic Labour Party, successor party to the pro-independence wing of the Latvian Communist Party. In contrast to Brazauskas in Lithuania, took an increasingly nationalist line, siding with radical nationalist parties against the government of Godmanis. In March 1993, was barred from standing for parliament because of his KGB past.

Dīmanis, Sergejs: Born 1951. Ethnic Latvian; by training an economist. Leader of the Soviet loyalist 'Equal Rights Faction' in the Latvian Supreme Council from 1990 to 1992, when he was stripped of his mandate for supporting the Soviet counter-revolution of August 1991. Represented a more moderate position than the Communist hardliners, but never publicly broke with them.

Dinevics, Jānis: Born 1948. Ethnic Latvian. Lecturer in power engineering. Founder member of Popular Front. Centrist and strong supporter of Godmanis. From 1991, Deputy Prime Minister, in which capacity he struggled, with increasing lack of success, to keep the PF faction together behind the government.

Dozortsev, Vladilen: Russian-Jewish. Born 1939, and moved to Riga as a child. As his first name suggests, from a strongly Communist family, but with a father sentenced to the camps under Stalin. Liberal writer, from 1988 editor of the Russian literary magazine *Daugava*. A leader of the pro-independence section of the Russian community, but from 1991 progressively disillusioned with the Popular Front and its attitude to the Russians.

Godmanis, Ivars: Born 1951. Ethnic Latvian. Physicist. Founder member of the Popular Front and Deputy Chairman, 1988–90. From May 1990, Prime Minister. By 1993, his popularity had sunk badly, in part because of his policy of giving citizenship to the Russians, but mainly because of increasing economic misery. At first, was seen as failing to develop a real strategy for economic reform. By 1993, however, had achieved significant success, especially in creating a stable Latvian currency. By then, he had lost most of his original Communist ministers to pressure from the radical nationalists.

Gorbunovs, Anatolijs: Born 1942, into a Latvian farming family from Latgale. Engineer turned Communist Party official. From 1980 to 1985, Communist Party Secretary of the Central (Lenin) District of Riga, in which capacity he made contact with the reformist intelligentsia. 1985–88, Secretary of the Central Committee; From 1988, chairman of the Supreme Council and head of state. Was kept in that post by the Popular Front after its electoral victory in 1990 as a gesture of compromise towards the Communists and Russians. Retained strong popularity with Latvians as well as Russians, despite (at least until 1992) standing for a generous policy on the question of citizenship for the Russian 'immigrants'. In 1993, joined a new Centrist-nationalist force; the 'Latvian Way'.

Īvāns, Dainis: Born 1955. Ethnic Latvian; a prize-winning journalist in the last years of Soviet rule, concentrating especially on environmental issues. Chairman of the Latvian Popular Front, 1988–1990. First deputy chairman of the Supreme Council, May 1990–November 1991, when he resigned after severe criticism from radical nationalists over his moderate stance on the question of Russian rights, and in disgust at political infighting and corruption. Later a force behind the Centrist Democratic Centre group.

Jurkāns, Jānis (Jan Jurkan): Born 1946. Ethnic Pole. Philologist. Leader of the Popular Front foreign relations section, 1988–90; Foreign Minister, 1990–92. Increasingly attacked, and finally forced out by the radical nationalists for his advocacy of automatic citizenship for Russian 'immigrants'.

Krastiņš, Andrējs: Born 1951. Ethnic Latvian; by training a police detective, then a lawyer. Leader of the radical nationalist National Independence Movement. From 1990, Deputy Chairman of the Supreme Council. Played a leading part in building up the Latvian security services.

Kuzmin, Fyodr, (Colonel-General): Russian; Commander of the Baltic Military District, 1989–1991. Closely involved in the various attempts at military repression in the region. Member of the National Salvation Committee, 1991.

Ražukas, Romualdas: Born 1955. Ethnic Lithuanian. Neurosurgeon.

Chairman of the Latvian Popular Front, 1990–1992, during which time it swung to a steadily more hardline nationalist position. However, Ražukas was a compromise candidate for Chairman, and was often suspected of secretly carrying out the wishes of Prime Minister Godmanis by preventing the Front from becoming too radical.

Repše, Einārs: Born 1962. Ethnic Latvian. A scientist, and member of the Latvian Congress as well as the Supreme Council. On the pragmatic wing of the radical nationalist side of politics. From 1991, Chairman of the State Bank, in which post, on IMF urging, he sought successfully to maintain a strict monetary policy in the face of intense pressure from society and finally the Godmanis government. Architect of the restored Lat, the independent Latvian currency 1924–40 and from 1993.

Rubiks, Alfrēds: Born 1935. Ethnic Latvian, from an old Communist family. Communist Party official. Mayor of Riga, 1984–90, during which he gained a reputation for efficiency, but alienated conservationists, and ultimately the Latvian population as a whole, with plans for a Metro system which would have damaged the old city. First Secretary of the Latvian Communist Party, 1990–1991. As a hardline Communist, and leader of the National Salvation Committee, 1991, gained a reputation for ruthlessness. Was arrested and sentenced after the failure of the August 1991 counter-revolution.

Škapārs, Jānis: Ethnic Latvian. In the 1980s, Editor of the official intellectual magazine *Literatura un Makslas*, which tested the limits of censorship by publishing criticised authors. Together with Peters, at the heart of the liberal wing of the Communist intellectual establishment, and from 1990 a deputy. A founder of the Popular Front, but progressively alienated by its increasing radicalism. In 1992, helped found the Democratic Centre, but split with Jurkāns and Russian Centrists over the national question.

Vulfsons, Mavriks (Mawrek Wulfson): Born 1918. Jewish. Communist activist before 1940, then a Soviet army officer. Under Soviet rule a leading journalist, with a brief to utter limited criticism of abuses; then a Professor at the Academy of Sciences. In 1988, played a leading part in beginning to expose the truth about the Molotov-Ribbentrop Pact, by which the Baltic States were handed to Stalin. From 1990 to 1991, chairman of the Supreme Council Foreign Relations Commission, before being forced out for criticism of past Latvian anti-semitism. 1991–92, advisor to Jānis Jurkāns, and shared in his fall.

Zhdanoka, Tatiana: Born 1953. From a Riga Jewish family murdered by Latvian Nazi auxiliaries in 1941. By training a mathematician. A leading Soviet loyalist deputy. Like her close ally, Dīmanis, she claimed initially to have wanted to join the Popular Front, but to have been put off by its 'Latvian chauvinism'.

Estonia:

Chuikin, Vladimir: Born 1949. Russian. Mayor of Narva. Communist Party official. Strong opponent of Estonian independence. Re-elected, October 1991. Although Chuikin, as a member of the old establishment, is unpopular with many Russians in Narva, the line taken by Estonia on the citizenship question has consolidated the local population behind him. He is now taking a generally conciliatory line.

Kallas, Siim: Born 1948. State official under Soviet rule. Minister of Finance, 1975–79. One of the first proponents, with Edgar Savisaar, of Estonian economic autonomy. From 1991, Chairman of the State Bank.

Kelam, Tunne: Born 1936. Historian. Joined dissident movement in the late 1960s and was dismissed from his position. From 1988, a leader of the Estonian National Independence Party, and of the Estonian Congress.

Kogan, Yevgeni: Born 1954, son of a Russian-Jewish Soviet naval officer. Maritime engineer. Bitter opponent of Estonian independence. In 1991, following failure of counter-revolution, left for Moscow where joined the extreme conservative forces. Candidate for Mayor of Moscow, 1993.

Laar, Mart: Born 1960. Historian of the Estonian resistance to Soviet rule. A founder of the Estonian Heritage Society and the Christian Democrat Party. From 1992, a leader of the *Isamaa* (Fatherland) Centre-Right alliance. From October 1992, Prime Minister.

Lauristin, Marju: Born 1940, daughter of first Prime Minister of Soviet Estonia. By profession a journalist and sociologist. In the 1970s to 1980s on fringes of dissident movement. Founder member of Popular Front. From April 1990, Deputy Chairwoman of Supreme Council. From October 1992, Minister for Social Welfare. Leader of the Social Democrat Party, and from 1992, of the Moderate Alliance.

Lippmaa, Endel: Born 1930. Nuclear physicist. Deputy to the USSR Supreme Soviet and leading Estonian negotiator with the Kremlin, 1989–90. Maverick politician, basically attached to the former Communist establishment but frequently adopting extreme nationalist positions. In 1992, an opponent of the new Estonian constitution from a strict legitimist standpoint.

Meri, Lennart: Born 1929, son of an Estonian diplomat. By profession a writer, anthropologist and film-maker. Expert in Finno-Ugric studies. Secretary of the Soviet Estonian Writers' Union. 1990–92, Foreign Minister, then Ambassador to Finland. October 1992, President of Estonia. A charming and deeply cultured man, but impulsive.

Nugis, Ülo: Born 1944. State industrial manager, of the 'Eestoplast' firm. In 1986–89, struggled to free it from the control of Moscow. From 1990, Speaker of the Supreme Council, a position to which he was re-elected in 1992, after successfully making the transition from the Communist establishment to the new nationalist Right. An effective Speaker, but the third most personally unpleasant Estonian politician, after Savisaar and Lippmaa.

Otsason, Rein: Born 1931, Economist. 1988–89, Chairman of state Planning Committee. 1989–90, Deputy Prime Minister. 1990–91, Chairman of State Bank. Became involved in furious public disputes with Savisaar over the introduction of the new Estonian currency, and in 1991 left to become a private banker.

Parek, Lagle: Born 1941. From 1949–54, deported with her parents to Siberia. Leading dissident. 1983–87, imprisoned in Novosibirsk. Chairwoman of the National Independence Party. From October 1992, Interior Minister.

Rüütel, Arnold: Born 1928. Agronomist. Deputy Prime Minister, 1979–83. Chairman of Supreme Council, 1983–1992. Retained great popularity with Estonian people, in part by swinging to an ever more nationalist position on the question of citizenship for the Russian 'immigrants'. Won a plurality of votes in the September 1992 Presidential elections, but was then voted out by the new Right-wing parliamentary majority on the grounds of his past in the Soviet establishment, and replaced by Meri.

Savisaar, Edgar: Born 1950. Under Soviet rule, Chairman, Estonian State Planning Committee, then Deputy Prime Minister. Founder member of Popular Front. April 1990–January 1992, Prime Minister. Widely respected for his intelligence and determination, and as much disliked for his abrasive character. Criticised by the Right for his Communist past, for his cautious policy towards Moscow and for his advocacy of citizenship for the Russian 'immigrants'. Eventually forced out as a consequence of the collapse of fuel supplies in the winter of 1992. Turned what was left of the Popular Front into a Centre-Left party loyal to him personally. Defeated in the 1992 elections, and in opposition to the Laar government.

Toome, Indrek: Born 1943. Communist official. First Secretary of Estonian Komsomol, 1972–78, Deputy Prime Minister, 1984–87, Prime Minister, 1988–90. Thereafter, a leader of the 'Free Estonia' group of former leading Communists, before leaving politics for private banking.

Toomepuu, Juri: US Colonel (retd.) Extreme nationalist Estonian emigré, Defence Minister in the 'Estonian government-in-exile', and from 1992 leader of the *Eesti Kodanik* (Estonian Citizen) Party, which opposed the Estonian constitution of 1992. Received by far the largest number of personal votes in the September 1992 election.

Vähi, Tiit: Born 1947. State manager. From 1972–89, Director of the Valga Motor Depot. 1989–92, Minister of Transport. January–October

1992, Prime Minister. The great successes of his period in office were the introduction of the Kroon and the new constitution, but he was accused of being much too close to all his old colleagues in the former Communist economic establishment. A leading figure behind the *Kindel Kodu* (Secure Home) alliance.

Velliste, Trivimi: Born 1947. Philologist. From 1987, Chairman of the Estonian Heritage Society. From 1990, Deputy Chairman of the Congress of Estonia, and later a founder of the Christian Democrat Party and a leader of the Fatherland Alliance. 1992, Deputy Foreign Minister. From October 1992, Foreign Minister.

Yarovoi, Vladimir: Russian. State industrialist. Director of the Dvigatel (Engine) Factory in Tallinn from 1988. A founder of Interfront and strong opponent of Estonian independence, against which he helped organize several strikes. In 1990–91, attempted to set up parallel Soviet loyalist structures of government. Left Estonia for Russia following the failure of the 1991 counter-revolution.

Index